THE VIEW ACROSS THE RIVER

iso liwela umfula ugcwele – the eye crosses the full river
(though the foot cannot do so) = desire outstrips possibility

[Zulu Proverbs, in J.W. Colenso, *Zulu–English Dictionary*.
Fourth edition, 1905, edited and revised by H.E. Colenso]

RECONSIDERATIONS IN
SOUTHERN AFRICAN HISTORY

THE VIEW
ACROSS
THE RIVER

Harriette Colenso
and the Zulu Struggle
against Imperialism

JEFF GUY

University Press of Virginia • Charlottesville

Published in 2001 in Southern Africa by David Philip Publishers (Pty) Ltd, 208 Werdmuller Centre, Newry Street, Claremont, 7708, South Africa

Published in 2002 in North America by the University Press of Virginia, P.O. Box 400318, Charlottesville, Virginia 22904-4318, USA

Published in 2002 in the United Kingdom and Europe by James Currey Publishers, 73 Botley Road, Oxford OX2 0BS, UK

ISBN 0-86486-373-X (David Philip paper)
ISBN 0-8139-2133-3 (University Press of Virginia paper)
ISBN 0-85255-791-4 (James Currey paper)

British Library Cataloguing in Publication Data

Guy, Jeff
  The view across the river : Harriette Colenso and the Zulu struggle against imperialism
  1. Colenso, Harriette 2. Zulu War, 1879 3. Zulu (African people) – Biography
  4. Colonies – Africa 5. Government, Resistance to – South Africa – Zululand
  – History 6. Zululand (South Africa) – History
  I. Title
  968.4'045'092

U.S. Library of Congress Cataloging-in-Publication Data is available from the Library of Congress

Cover design by Toby Newsome based on a concept by Lesley Lewis, Inkspots, Durban

Printed and bound by CTP Printers, Cape Town

*To the memory of two friends who should be here to celebrate,
and confront, life in a new South Africa:*

*Brendan Hughes (1938–1985)
Colleen Taylor (1943–1995)*

CONTENTS

V A SORT OF PARADISE

VI THE QUEST

VII BREAKING DOWN

MAPS

PREFACE

In 1979 I published a book called *The Destruction of the Zulu Kingdom*. Unlike conventional accounts, which associate the end of the kingdom with the defeat of its army by the British in 1879, it argued that the defeat of Zulu power was a much longer, less obvious, and more bloody process in which those forces which opposed Zulu autonomy, but were unable to subvert it by direct military confrontation, exploited divisions and raised surrogate forces within the kingdom to complete the process.

The present book extends this history. It examines how, once the kingdom's political hierarchy had been destroyed, it was possible for the invaders to turn their attention to its productive capacity and material wealth, diverting it to serve interests beyond Zululand's borders. But this process did not go unchallenged and it is the continued resistance to imperial conquest which directs and controls the structure of the story told here. It concentrates on the women and men who led this resistance, the wife and daughters of the Bishop of Natal especially – and one in particular, Harriette Emily Colenso.

This book then is in part a biography, and one which does not engage with those who see domination and distortion as necessarily inherent in biographical narrative. From the approach adopted here, the problem for the biographer is the more obvious one: that of balancing and integrating the individual with the context. And the context is a difficult and complicated one to recreate. Firstly, we are dealing with a largely archaic historiography. With a few notable exceptions, the history of the Zulu kingdom remains in essence a colonial history, methodologically backward, dominated by racial and gender stereotypes and distorted by the attraction which the 1879 British invasion of the Zulu kingdom has for both historians and readers of history. This has had the effect of concentrating attention on a few months of violence in 1879, which are then presented in such a way that the significance of the war for the history of KwaZulu-Natal is obscured. One of the consequences of this distorted historiography is that the historian who seeks new perspectives cannot build on what has gone before but has to spend much time and labour in putting down foundations. Instead of assisting in the creation of historical background, much of the secondary literature is a hindrance. And, despite the achievements of women's studies, it remains very difficult for historians of women in Empire, particularly at a more popular level, to avoid stereotyping and trivialising their subjects as, for example, the devoted female missionary, the friend of the natives, the dedicated crusader for justice, or the intrepid lady traveller in the tropics. It is a major objective of this book to demonstrate by means of historical reconstruction that Harriette Colenso was, in her interaction with those around her in Africa and in Europe, knowledgeable and informed, practical and sensible, and in possession of genuine insight into African and imperial affairs. Obvious enough perhaps but – given the continued existence of stereotypes of race and gender – such qualities have to be demonstrated not just asserted.

Equally the mistakes she made and her failures were the consequence not primarily because she was a woman, but because she was a woman working in the age of imperialism: also an obvious fact, but one which has meant that, while I never lose sight of the central figure, I have had to move away from the woman herself, to spend some time on events in which she did not participate directly, but which did affect her. But, as the events of the book proceed, so the narrative threads draw together until, in the end, the major actors in this history meet to consider the richness of their past and the poverty of their future – on the island of St Helena, 5000 kilometres from Zululand where it all began.

Despite the limitations of the historiography of KwaZulu-Natal there have, of course, been historians who have had the capacity to innovate and show the way forward – and the most significant of these, I believe, is Shula Marks. Her contribution to the history of KwaZulu-Natal remains unchallenged and has been an inspiration to many historians of South Africa and beyond. I have been fortunate enough to have known her since I began this project and I am indebted to her for friendship and assistance. And it was she who, in 1963, published an article entitled 'Harriette Colenso and the Zulus, 1874–1913'.[1]

In amongst other projects and commitments this book was researched and written over three decades in four different countries. The debts one accumulates over such a long period are many. Joe, Heli, and Naimi have had to pay much, have done so willingly, and for this I will always be grateful. William Beinart, John Morrison, Motlatsi Thabane, Troth Wells and John Wright have remained indispensable friends, as has Jeff Rudin, who has always listened and often disagreed. Terry Ranger, first at Manchester and then Oxford, has given generous support and advice over the years. In the late 1980s and early 1990s I was a member of the History Department of what was then the University of Trondheim. It would have been understandable if students and colleagues considered my teaching and research projects somewhat remote from their interests and academic objectives – but this was not so. It is impossible to list all those who enabled me to sustain my commitment to this project and in so many ways helped to make my professional life in Norway such a positive experience – but I must mention Hanna Mellemsether, who is continuing to work on the important subject of the influence of Norwegians on South African history, Eva Helena Østbye for friendship and guidance in a strange land, Graham Dyson for his spirit and generosity, and Håkon Witt Anderson, Anne Kristine Børresen, Hans Otto Frøland, Brynjulv Gjerdåkker, Steinar Imsen, Jarle Simensen, Gudmund Stang, Inger Lise Stieng, Henninge Torp, for friendship and help, often beyond what could justifiably have been expected of them. In South Africa I have been encouraged and helped in completing this project by Shirley Brooks. I have been assisted in researching and writing this book by financial support from the University Research Fund, the Centre for Scientific Development, and the award of an Oppenheimer Visiting Fellowship, which enabled me to spend a semester researching from Oxford. But none of this would have been possible if my colleagues in the History Department of the University of Natal had not assumed added administrative and teaching responsibilities during my absence. For this I must thank Keith Breckenridge, Catherine Burns, Yonah Seleti and Sandi Thomson, and also for the energy, drive, ability and enthusiasm with which they have advanced the study of history in South Africa.

Jeff Guy
Durban

ABBREVIATIONS

APS   Aborigines' Protection Society
BPP   British Parliamentary Papers
CO   Colonial Office
CSC   Court of Special Commissioners
HEC   Harriette Emily Colenso
KC   Killie Campbell. The Campbell Collections, University of Natal, Durban
NA   Natal Archives (now the Pietermaritzburg Archives Repository)
      GH   Natal Government House
      SNA   Secretary for Native Affairs
      ZA   Zululand Archives
      ZGH   Zululand Government House
PRO   Public Record Office, Kew, London
RH   Rhodes House, Oxford
      AS   Anti Slavery Papers
SNA   Secretary for Native Affairs

I

WARRING
HOUSES

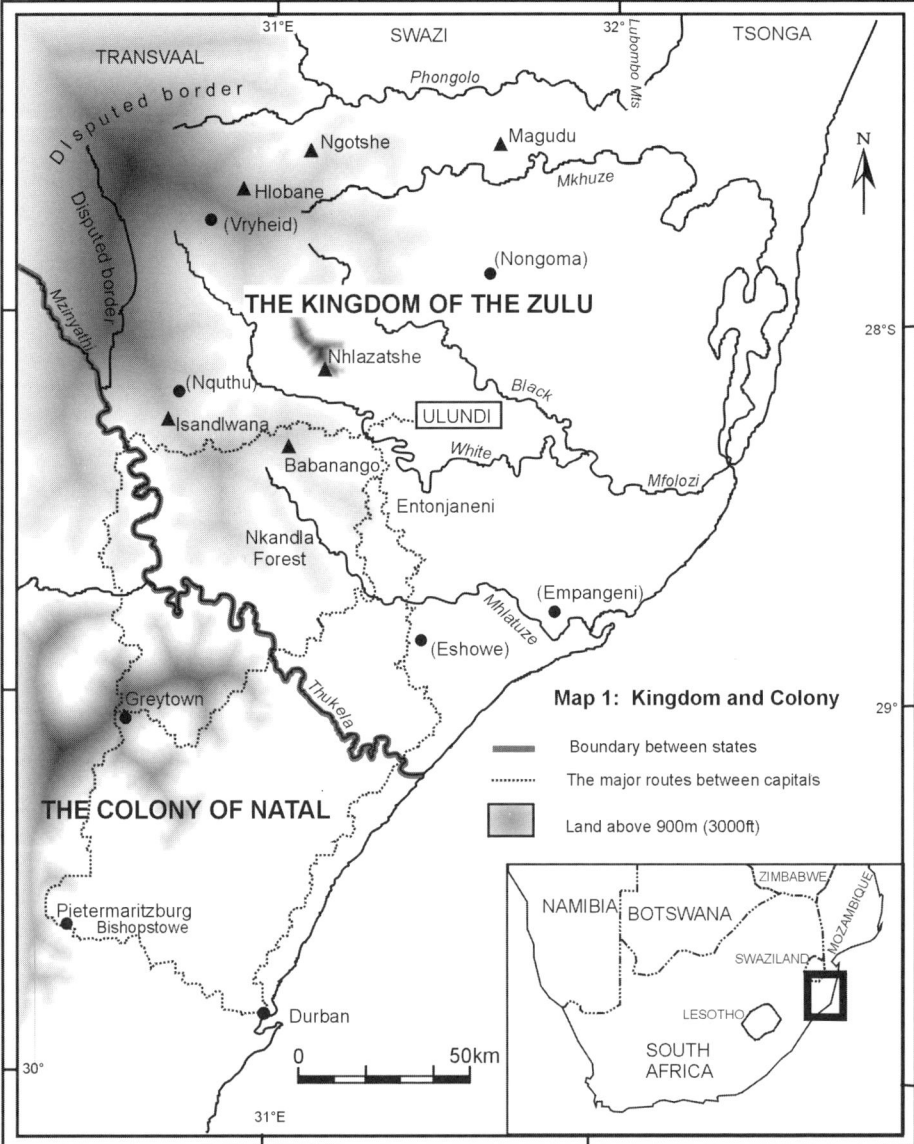

31°E SWAZI   32° TSONGA

TRANSVAAL

Disputed border

Phongolo

Lubombo Mts

▲ Ngotshe ▲ Magudu

N

Disputed border

▲ Hlobane   Mkhuze

● (Vryheid)

● (Nongoma)

Mzinyathi

THE KINGDOM OF THE ZULU   28°S

▲ Nhlazatshe

● (Nquthu)   Black

ULUNDI

▲ Isandlwana ▲ White

Babanango   Mfolozi

Entonjaneni

Nkandla
Forest

Mhlatuze ● (Empangeni)

● (Eshowe)

Thukela

● Greytown   **Map 1: Kingdom and Colony** 29°

           Boundary between states

           The major routes between capitals

THE COLONY OF NATAL   Land above 900m (3000ft)

               ZIMBABWE

● Pietermaritzburg   NAMIBIA BOTSWANA MOZAMBIQUE
  Bishopstowe

               SWAZILAND

               LESOTHO

● Durban

0   50km   SOUTH
           AFRICA

30°

31°E

THE HOUSE OF SENZANGAKHONA

'And when I die I shall not be altogether dead'

O n the morning of 11 February 1884 seven Zulu men appeared at the British Residency in Eshowe, the administrative centre of the Zulu Native Reserve. It was not an impressive building: five rooms, an out-side kitchen, 'the walls of the house are clay plaster, the roof of thatch, and verandah of iron. There is nothing permanent about the building. It is emblematic of the settlement itself',[1] wrote a visitor. The British Resident was Melmoth Osborn, isolated, disliked, uncertain of his official status, unhappy 'in this land of violence and blood'.[2]

The men waiting on the Resident had been amongst the best known in the land: the *abantwana*, the 'children', the princes of the Zulu kingdom, the leaders of the Usuthu, the royalist party in Zululand. But they were now humbled. Five years of war, treachery and violence had brought them down. In 1879 the British had invaded the Zulu kingdom, defeated the Zulu army in battle, exiled the king, Cetshwayo kaMpande, and then divided the kingdom into 13 chiefdoms. Political protest by his supporters in Zululand, Natal and Britain had led to his return in 1883. But the enemies of the Zulu royal house refused to accept this and in July attacked the king in his homestead, killed the leading men of the kingdom and thousands of their followers, and drove Cetshwayo first into hiding, and then to seek the protection of the British Resident in the rudimentary administrative settlement at Eshowe. There, on 8 February, at about 50 years of age, he had died.

Among the seven men waiting to see the Resident, Ndabuko was full brother to the dead king. He was a fine-looking man, princely, but taciturn and withdrawn. He bore heavily the responsibility for the terrible military defeats the Usuthu had suffered in the last few years during the civil war. It was said that at Msebe in March 1883, more lives had been lost than in any other battle in Zulu history. The Usuthu force had been ambushed by the Mandlakazi under the

3

1

2

3

The men who made the statement vesting the Zulu succession in Dinuzulu kaCetshwayo.

Photo 1. Ndabuko kaMpande, full brother to Cetshwayo kaMpande, guardian of Dinuzulu kaCetshwayo, leader of the Usuthu.

Photo 2. Sitheku was another prominent son of Mpande from the southern portions of the kingdom.

Photo 3. Shingana kaMpande, in Pietermaritzburg, after 'jumping over the precipice'. Spokesman for the Usuthu, leader of the resistance at Hlophekhulu in 1888, exiled to St Helena in 1889. The special friend of Harriette Colenso.

Photo 4. The man who heard the statement on the succession 'in this land of violence and blood'. The great enemy of the Usuthu, Malimade, Melmoth Osborn.

leadership of Zibhebhu kaMaphitha. Zibhebhu was an aggressive, younger member of the Mandlakazi lineage of the Zulu royal house, who asserted that he had been nominated guardian of the exiled king's young son, Dinuzulu. Ndabuko, as full brother to the king, had objected to this and assumed the guardianship. It was to these conflicts amongst members of the royal family that the origins of the civil war were traced.

Shingana kaMpande was lighter in character, intelligent and good humoured. Ziwedu kaMpande was from the north-east of the kingdom where he had been placed under Zibhebhu, while Mahanana kaMpande from the north-west had been involved in bitter fighting with his brother Hamu, who was considered by the Usuthu to be a dissolute renegade. The royal brothers were accompanied by Bhejana and Melelesi, *izinceku* or personal aides to the king, as well as being senior officials within the Zulu kingdom. The spokesman for the *abantwana* was Dabulamanzi kaMpande. Before the war his personal homestead had been near Eshowe. He was an independent and aggressive man, who had been in close contact with missionaries and traders and therefore also with guns and spirits. He was hated in neighbouring colonial Natal for his outspoken confidence and for the leading role he was supposed to have played in the 1879 war. It was he who announced the message to the British Resident, Melmoth Osborn.

5

We, the brothers of Cetshwayo, who is now no more, come to tell you the words spoken by Cetshwayo in the forenoon of the day on which he died. Cetshwayo said:

I am now in this state you see me in, and I want you, my children, to tell Mr. Osborn the words I now speak. I say that when Mageba died he left the country to Punga; Punga, on his death, left it to Ndaba; Ndaba, on his death, left it to Jama; Jama, on his death, left it to Senzangakhona; Senzangakhona, on his death, left it to Shaka; Shaka, on his death, left it to Dingane; Dingane, on his death, left it to Mpande; Mpande, my father, left it to me, Cetshwayo; I, Cetshwayo, leave the country to my son Dinuzulu for him to have when I am no longer here.

I have become the son of the Queen; when I die there is my son Dinuzulu, who I leave in my place. I say my words and my writings are with my mother, the Queen, and when I die I shall not be altogether dead, as my son Dinuzulu will live. The questions about my country are not ended yet. They exist still, and will remain until the Government settle them; and about the people having stabbed me – I wish the Governor to settle those questions even when I am no more as if I were still present. Take these, my words, to Mr. Osborn, and ask him to send them to the Governor, with the request that he would send them to the Queen.[3]

The British Resident took down the message, and read it back to them. The royal brothers listened and agreed that it had been correctly transcribed.

After the delegation had left, Osborn translated the statement into English and sent it to Sir Henry Bulwer, who held the dual office of Special Commissioner for Zululand and Governor of Natal. It reached him two days later at Government House in Pietermaritzburg, some 300 kilometres away to the south-west across the southern border of the Reserve, the huge valley of the Thukela River. Bulwer telegraphed the gist of the message on the succession to the Colonial Office in London[4] and began immediately to draft his official reaction for the consideration of the Secretary of State for the Colonies.

The Usuthu statement on the Zulu succession marks, literally, a crucial point in the history of Natal and Zululand. It was made at a time when the House of Senzangakhona, the father of Shaka the founder of the kingdom, was in disarray and Zululand in utter turmoil. When Zibhebhu had followed up his victory at Msebe with a dawn attack on the royal homestead at Ulundi in July 1883 most of the izikhulu – the great men of the kingdom – had been killed. Their people were now scattered, hiding in forests and caves, while their enemies ranged freely over the fire-blackened land. When the king died early in 1884 under the reluctant protection of Melmoth Osborn at Eshowe, the Zulu royal house was faced with the real possibility of extinction. Political authority was diminished and divided and, while the king's brothers had gathered around his body in the south of the country, the few surviving Usuthu of note elsewhere did what they could to keep their people together and alive.

It was out of this devastation – out of the 'Ruin of Zululand' which had followed the British invasion of 1879 – that this statement on the succession, this assertion of the continuity of the Zulu royal house, was made by the *abantwana*. It was a conscious attempt to create a sticking point, foot- and finger-holds, as Zululand slid out of their control in an avalanche of violence which threatened to bury them.

By their statement they sought to assert the right of the House of Senzangakhona to rule the country and to confirm the links between the royal house of the Zulu and the royal house in England and the obligations that these involved. The Zulu held that this relationship had been established by the founder of the kingdom, Shaka kaSenzangakhona, who, over half a century before, had protected the British citizens who arrived in the kingdom and then sought to establish diplomatic relations with his counterpart in England, an attempt which failed only because of the first Zulu king's death in 1828. Nothing that Shaka's successors, Dingane and Mpande, had done was considered to have finally prejudiced these attempts to open friendly diplomatic relations, and they had been revived and consolidated by the fourth Zulu king, Cetshwayo, when he agreed to allow the Secretary for Native Affairs in the neighbouring colony of Natal, Theophilus Shepstone, to formally confirm Cetshwayo's succession to the throne in 1873. The British invasion of 1879 was depicted as an inexplicable rupture of these relations, a tragic error which the British had attempted to make good by Cetshwayo's restoration in 1883. Although this had failed catastrophically, the *abantwana*, by their statement, were reminding the British of their obligation to recognise and affirm the right of the Zulu royal house to rule Zululand.

The statement was therefore an attempt at a significant historical intervention. But it was not only this. It *is* also a history – an account of the succession of the Zulu kings over the centuries, a chronological narrative and a historical argument made to justify their descendants' claim to authority. And furthermore, it is not just a claim to royal authority but a record of that claim – an attempt to make the oral statement permanent by demanding that it be taken down in writing.

Like the king, his brothers had grown up in an oral society in which the forces of modernisation had been consciously kept at bay. But the Zulu kings had been well aware of the contradictions in this policy and the vulnerabilities it created.

Photo 5. The king in whose name the abantwana made the statement on the succession in February 1884.

Thus, although they were without writing themselves, they were all very aware of its power.[5] Consequently, the royal brothers requested the British Resident, whom they mistrusted profoundly but through whom they had no choice but to act, to transcribe and translate the king's last message, and transmit it to London.

While they agreed that Osborn's reading of his transcription was a true record they were not in a position to control the English translation. For this they would have to trust that their literate allies, white and black, would check its accuracy once it was made public. But the *abantwana* had done what they could for the moment – and this was considerable. They had created a historical document which was now moving up the imperial administrative system and would leave its mark in the Residency at Eshowe, Government House in Natal, and in the Colonial Office in London. Their request then came before the British Cabinet, and exists today for consultation as an enclosure in a dispatch in the relevant British Parliamentary Paper. As such it is a successful attempt to use the technology of the conqueror, the power of literacy, documentation and written precedent, of the permanence of the printed word, to create a statement which reached beyond the ramshackle collection of huts that formed the Residency at Eshowe on the southern borders of Zululand just over a century ago, projecting their words into space and time, as a record of the claim of the Zulu royal house to political power. They had invoked the power of writing to give permanence to the passing historical moment, to create a record external to individual mem-

8

Photo 6. Dinuzulu kaCetshwayo, the prince in whose name the claim to the succession was made. He is bedecked with charms, the iziqu *being especially prominent, to ward off the influence of those who wished him harm.*

ory. And in so doing they gave a voice to the silence that death imposes: 'I say my words and my writings are with my mother, the Queen, and when I die I shall not be altogether dead, as my son Dinuzulu will live.' It is a claim to political power which moves beyond the immediate, local, transient world of orality and memory, into the future, made just at the time when, for the Zulu royal house, these historical links were on the point of being smashed.

'Historical facts'

But the statement was also an assertion of African autonomy and a claim to sovereignty, and as such it had to be countered. Sir Henry Bulwer did this from Government House in Pietermaritzburg using the literate's conventional weapon – close documentary analysis.[6] He demonstrated that there were internal inconsistencies in the princes' account of the circumstances surrounding the king's death and his alleged statement. He then turned to legal argument. According to the terms under which Cetshwayo had been restored to the kingdom, succession was to be 'according to the ancient laws and customs of my people ... subject to the approval of the British Government'. As Cetshwayo had only one son,[7] Dinuzulu, there could be no disagreement about his successor – but the question was wider than this. Should there be a succession at all? And it was the British government's prerogative to decide this question, not that of the

defeated Zulu royal house.

Then came history's turn. If there were to be a succession, it had been stated that it would be 'according to the ancient customs of the native tribes of which the Zulu people proper were one before the reign of Shaka'. But, Bulwer pointed out, it could not be 'according to any precedent in the dynasty of Shaka itself; because, with regard to the Zulu Kings dating from Shaka, there has been, strange to say, no order of succession according to ancient custom or in any other way'. Succession in the Zulu royal house had been determined not by custom, law and precedent, but by treachery and violence. Shaka had seized the throne by force and was succeeded by his brother and assassin Dingane in 1828. He 'left no son to succeed him, for he had caused all his children to be put to death to prevent any chance of their ever plotting against him'. Dingane also died violently 'but was succeeded by his brother Mpande, who, at the time of his death [1840], was with one portion of the Zulu army in open revolt against him'. Mpande was in alliance with the Boers at the time 'and to their support he mainly

10

Photo 7 (opposite page). The Zulu chief who led the forces against the Usuthu in the civil war which brought the royalists to the edge of extinction: Zibhebhu kaMaphitha, of the Mandlakazi lineage of the Zulu.

Photo 8 (left). The great enemy of the Usuthu and the Qulusi in the north-west of Zululand: Hamu kaNzibe, of the Ngenetsheni of the Zulu.

owed his succession'. Cetshwayo's succession had been decided in 1856 by civil war and the invited intervention of Theophilus Shepstone on behalf of the government of Natal.

Bulwer drew his conclusion with icy contempt. The uncomplicated history of direct succession presented by the *abantwana* was invalid:

> This way of stating the manner of the past successions hardly represents, it will be observed, the historical facts to which I have just referred.
>
> In point of fact there has been no constitutional or customary precedent as to the mode of succession in the dynasty of Shaka. The succession has been kept in the family, but it has been a succession in every case secured by force or by right of force rather than by any other right.

To recognise the succession of Dinuzulu as the princes' statement proposed would be to recognise the arbitrary exercise of power, not custom, and 'have the effect of prolonging the existing disorder in the country'. The petition had to be rejected.

'Tortured to death'

Although this version of Zulu history – of the tyranny of the Zulu royal house over the people of Zululand – was dominant in Natal, it did not go unchallenged. On 9 February 1884, when Sir Henry Bulwer heard the news of the death of the king, he had sent a message to inform F.R. Statham, editor of Pietermaritzburg's newspaper *The Natal Witness*. Statham immediately passed it on to Harriette Emily Colenso.

She was deeply saddened by the news, but not surprised. For her it was just the final act of the horrifying tragedy being played out in Zululand since the British invasion of 1879. Just a few months previously her father, John William Colenso, the Bishop of Natal, 'Sobantu' to Africans, had died in his seventieth year. He had led the campaign for the king's restoration, and cruel disappointment, overwork and official harassment, she felt, had killed him. Whatever the specific cause, the Zulu king's death was not dissimilar.

> There is no reason for surprise, they have just tortured him to death, as they did his Father seven months ago, only that he has been able to endure it longer, being younger and stronger. He said, when he heard of Sobantu's death, that it was his own death-warrant; then came Ulundi, and since then blow after blow, indignity upon indignity, has been heaped upon him – it is difficult not to say with the intention to break his heart.

That evening back at Bishopstowe – the Colenso homestead and mission station a few kilometres to the east of the colonial capital – she broke the news to the two Zulu men staying there undercover in order to take any urgent news back to the Usuthu in Zululand. They had their own explanation: as with Bishop Colenso, the king had been poisoned by his enemies. Nothing Harriette Colenso said could dissuade them: '"Yes Nkosazana, you think and suppose but we know. Has he not died now in the hands of Malimade [Melmoth Osborn] who took him from the Nkandla, saying that it was to protect him? ... Did we not tell you that Cetshwayo's turn would come next when Sobantu died, who went into Maritzburg and came home only to die?"'

They also knew where the blame ultimately lay – with the House of Sonzica. Sonzica was the father of Somtsewu, Sir Theophilus Shepstone, official in charge of African administration in Natal for nearly thirty years from 1846, now in retirement but still a force in the politics of the region. No Governor dared act on African matters without the advice of the ex-Secretary for Native Affairs – and his relatives, friends and appointees were to be found in positions of authority

12

throughout the colony. '"Truly, it is the House of Sonzica who are powerful!" the Zulu continued. "They are the mighty chiefs! and as for the Queen she is nothing! A mere name!"'

Harriette Colenso wrote all this to her brother Frank in England. The length of the letter, and the sense of urgency it conveyed, reflect the depths of her feelings on the subject. It had to be remembered, she told her brother, that the king's death, terrible as it was, did not signal the end of the struggle for Zululand and the Zulu royal house. It was now their responsibility, as the children of Bishop Colenso, to carry on his task, to articulate and publicise an interpretation of events in Zululand which countered the official one. Together with their supporters outside Zululand they had to continue the struggle for justice for the Zulu people and its legitimate rulers. Bulwer's interpretation of events could not be allowed to go unchallenged. Shepstone's history of the Zulu kingdom as a despotic tyranny had to be countered. She had already told the *abantwana*:

> that we shall still follow Sobantu's path, that if we are stopped, we shall stand looking that way, so that if we are struck down we shall fall with our eyes pointing that way. And you, Frank, must help ... Of course the howl for annexation will now rise louder and louder, and the only way to arrest the complete triumph of evil in this part of the world, and the utter destruction of the Zulu People, seems to be to attack vigorously their weakest point ...
>
> Even many of our friends will be liable to think that 'it is all over' now that the King is gone. You, however, know that this is not the case, there is still their fine nation, being trampled out of existence by a pack of rascals in the name of England, the only difference is that the Zulus want help – want light thrown into this Pandemonium more than ever now that they have lost both Sobantu and Cetshwayo.[8]

It is the story of Harriette Colenso's determination to throw light into the pandemonium of civil war, of how the Colenso family, the women especially, and their African allies, sought to stop a fine nation being trampled out of existence, to force history in another direction from that chosen by the colonial authorities, with which this book is concerned.

CHAPTER 2

THE HOUSE OF SOBANTU

Sarah Frances Bunyon

Sarah Frances Bunyon[1] was born in 1816, eldest daughter of Frances Bignold and Robert Bunyon, who managed the London office of the insurance company Norwich Union, founded by his wife's father. Sarah Frances spent her earliest years in the City. Many years later, in Africa, she remembered the view through her bedroom window, where she could see the dome of St Paul's, which 'with its ball and cross, was an object ... which I looked at with some pleasure, and which seemed to belong rather to the moon and stars above it than to the hideous grove of chimneys below it, and how I used to long for one tree to look at'.[2]

She was a keenly intelligent, intensely serious girl on whom 'every pretty thing in the way of dress was quite thrown away'.[3] She was shy, but showed an independence in her thinking which caught the attention of those around her. She was particularly sensitive throughout her life to the pretensions of those with power. In her old age she still remembered, with all the precision and detail that pain etches into the memory, the crushing effects of male bullying let loose in an academy for young ladies in the early nineteenth century. And in writing of it sixty years later she also revealed the sharp intelligence of the girl who saw through this man's posturing and who quietly told him so, as well as the rebellion in her heart. She hoped that her granddaughter would be able to escape what she had experienced; and for this she needed love:

> *plenty of love* so that she may have no *mortification* ever inflicted on her – once when I was a girl at school (perhaps 14) and sitting at my desk in the great drawing room with one other favoured pupil Miss Finch came in with her guest, a Mr John Brown (Father of one of the pupils) whom we all *knew*, i.e. from Miss Finch's report as not only a religious teacher of a high order but as a genius, a poet, philosopher something superhuman, who could see thro' the

veil of flesh to the bottom of our souls. Well this being came and stood behind me as I went on with my copying (an abridgement of Plutarch's lives by Miss Finch herself). Presently Mr Brown asked me whether I thought I could look ferocious? I could not answer that question – except by saying that I did not wish to do so. After a few solemn moments the great Mr Brown said 'Do you know what it is to feel mortified?' Of course I did ... [4]

The narrow evangelical spirit of her upbringing caused her much agony. Thus at 14, from the same academy for young ladies in Cheltenham that Mr Brown had visited, she could write, in desperate confidence, '(Dear Mama, pray for me, for I do find it so very difficult to come to Jesus. I cannot feel the reality of religion. I cannot love the Saviour or feel that He is *my* Saviour nor even feel the weight of my sins).'[5] In time she found her own answer to the guilt she felt for not feeling guilty, first in the writing of Coleridge, and then in that of the Anglican divine, F.D. Maurice. On her own initiative she wrote to Maurice asking him how he would answer certain questions on belief because 'Mr Maurice's voice would command respectful attention when those of young ladies talking about philosophy, or a philosopher, would not be listened to, even if they ventured to raise them'. They began to correspond and then became acquainted. But his attempts to persuade Sarah Frances Bunyon to give expression to some of her own ideas to a wider audience met with a characteristic response: 'I can only smile at the idea of my publishing my opinions or feelings and if you knew me my dear Sir you would smile also.'[6]

John William Colenso

In 1842 she met John William Colenso, a man who could match her seriousness and intensity. He was then a Cambridge tutor teaching mathematics and writing textbooks in order to work his way out of debt caused by a catastrophic fire at Harrow where he had been a master. The loving relationship which developed between them not only satisfied his longing for 'the cheering, humanising, satisfying feeling for the actual wants and sorrows of my fellow men', but also changed the fundamentals of his religious thinking. It was she who introduced him to Maurice and his circle, and led him towards a personal, felt, religious belief beyond argument and external evidence – a faith which was to allow Colenso to accept without qualms the discoveries and theories of the revolutionary age in which he lived.

Maurician theology, as well as the Broad Church within which it developed, was a reaction to both the narrow and sombre strictures of the evangelicals and

Photo 9. The family of John William Colenso before they left England in March 1855. Harriette Colenso is on her mother's left; Frances, two years younger, is on her father's right. Robert and Frank in front.

the privilege and social irresponsibility of the conservative church establishment. It was also part of the Romantic reaction to the utilitarian spirit of the age. To this way of thinking God's existence was perceived, not proven: it was to be found not in argument nor in the blind acceptance of the Scriptures or the rules of the church, but in human beings themselves, in their thoughts and their actions, in the desire for good and the individual conscience. God was to be found in humanity: in the selfless deed, in the expression of love and the act of sacrifice; it was in fact present, if one cared to search for it, in all people, at all times. This approach to religious thinking was also in part a reaction to the grime, poverty and social distress of industrialising Britain. It sought amelioration for social evils through social action which demonstrated the love of God by ministering to His children. Once Colenso had succeeded in shaking off the more severe aspects of his evangelical past he moved, under Sarah Frances Bunyon's influence, into this theological universalism which stressed the existence of God in all humanity, and the unity of God's people on earth, rather than the divisions between them.

Through Sarah Frances's friendship with Maurice, the young couple also

Photo 10. Sarah Frances, Harriette and Frances Colenso, soon after their arrival in Natal.

moved onto the fringes of the mid-Victorian, middle-class intellectual world, sitting nervously around the Carlyles' tea table as their friends discussed the issues of the age. In 1846 they were married, and moved away from London when Colenso took a college living in a small village in Norfolk. Here four of the Colenso children were born: Harriette Emily in 1847, then Frances Ellen two years later. Robert John was born in 1851 and Francis Ernest, or Frank, in 1852.

Although now somewhat isolated by distance, domesticity and the demands of the parish, Colenso edited a mission journal and his name was brought to the attention of Robert Gray, Bishop of Cape Town, when he was in England preparing to establish the diocese of Natal. Gray invited Colenso to become its first bishop. Sarah Frances was consulted: if Natal were safe for their children, then she would go. In 1853 Colenso had sold the copyright of his mathematics and arithmetic books. Financially free at last, he accepted Gray's offer to become Bishop of Natal.

In March Colenso preached at Great St Mary's in Cambridge and outlined his ideas on missionary teaching. The world was not divided into the enlightened and the benighted, the saved and the lost. The love of God redeemed all human beings: Christians of course had particular insights and therefore special responsibilities, but they had also to learn from the heathen about the God who was 'witness in *their* hearts'. They had to be met 'upon the ground of our common humanity ... that we are all redeemed, not accursed'. Conversion should not be made by attempting 'to uproot altogether their old religion, scoffing at the things which they hold most sacred, deriding the fears, which alone have stood to them, for many years long, as the representatives of the spiritual world'.[7]

In January 1854, in his fortieth year, John William Colenso, the newly consecrated Bishop of Natal, landed in Durban for a ten-week assessment of his diocese. Here he met the official responsible for Native Affairs, Theophilus Shepstone, who introduced him to the colony, its history and its people. A strong friendship developed between the two men. At first this might seem surprising. The one came from a thoroughly colonial background with only the most basic schooling in out-of-the-way mission stations, and from his teens had worked as interpreter and colonial administrator. The other had had a brilliant academic career and was a personal acquaintance of some of the great figures amongst the metropolitan intelligentsia. But in discussion they found an immediate affinity. For both Colenso and Shepstone, the potential disorder implicit in situations of inevitable and rapid social change was best answered by the conscious adaptation – and this implied the preservation – of existing elements within society.

Colenso's religious thinking was influenced by the broad response to the upheavals that were part of the experience of industrial revolution. The disorder provoked by the experience of change and massive social abuse had to be met with active social intervention to ameliorate individual suffering, together with acts of charity and appeals to the discipline inherent in the patriarchal domestic order. Similarly, in the colonial context, Shepstone attempted to avert a violent response to the changes that colonialism was demanding of Africans by advocating and implementing a system that allowed the continuation of aspects of African social life. And so he developed a policy by which the African homestead continued to structure agricultural production, and this implied access to land, recognition of the laws which ordered the homestead, patriarchal dominance, polygamy and, at a local level, the authority of the chiefly political order. Thus, in response to the potentially destructive social environments in which both men worked, they advocated, in their respective fields, radical philosophies which at the same time saw the need to conserve in order to negotiate the hazards implicit in change. As a result, neither Shepstone nor Colenso was prepared to dismiss or ignore African traditions. Whatever their ends and motives, both men worked for policies which recognised aspects of African custom, procedures and structures of power in a colonial situation.

The bishop established himself in Natal in 1855, and with his family built his home at Bishopstowe, a few kilometres outside Pietermaritzburg. Their fifth child, Agnes Mary, was born a few months after their arrival. The mission was attached to the bishop's house. It was called Ekukhanyeni, the place of light. It was here that training centres would be set up. Not only would there be a school for the sons of the chiefs who would be trained in the best traditions of English education, but also a centre of religious instruction and industrial, mechanical and agricultural training. Here the mission's energies would be concentrated, and in time their achievements would radiate throughout the colony.

Sarah Frances Colenso lived at Bishopstowe till the end of her life, but she had little to do with the settler community, and never accepted what she saw as the crude self-seeking physicality of colonial existence. She ran the home, taught, and wrote letters to her friends in England full of insight and penetrating judgement, and on occasion bitingly humorous, often at the expense of the men who strutted into her world. Her husband escaped the sharp edge of her judgements. She could tease him gently, and when necessary stand between him and their children, protecting them from his demands and expectations. But in her eyes her husband, her Lord, was brave, modest, intelligent, high-minded, and energetic in the cause of justice and truth. He had, in fact, all the qualities Natal, a colony 'so thoroughly matter of fact and nineteenth century',[8] lacked, and she decided 'never to thwart him or worry him, my Lord and Master, my superior in every way, morally and intellectually'.[9]

Sarah Frances was mid-Victorian and middle-class, but this did not prevent her from looking on her own prejudices with some detachment and amusement. She never became reconciled to African nakedness, emphasising class differences rather than racial ones, being 'not myself partial to savages of any colour, I am too fond of soap and water and clean linen'.[10] The mission station, she felt, should be 'a centre of civilisation, and clothing is a first step in it. Our Church Natives, William [Ngidi], Jonathan [Ngidi], Magema [Fuze] etc etc are all decently clothed. They have been accustomed to it so long, their wives have to get up their shirts and mend their things, but they are gentlemen, landed proprietors, teachers.'[11] This was the ideal, the family of the *amakholwa* – the believers – but as the years passed, her African experience enabled her to develop her own pertinent critique of the consequences of such changes.

'A complete Revolution'

Learning Zulu was a priority at Bishopstowe. Colenso within a few years established himself as a Zulu scholar of repute, publishing a grammar, a dictionary, readers, basic texts in science and hygiene, and of course translations of the

19

Photo 11. Colenso, the first Bishop of Natal, before the great biblical controversy of the 1860s; energetic, confident, determined to build a great Christian, English educational centre for the Zulu of Natal at Ekukhanyeni.

Scriptures. His assistant in this was William Ngidi, a convert from the American Mission, first hired as a wagon driver, but who then became a close confidant of the bishop. Together they worked through the biblical texts, interrogating them and one another, each gaining insights into the other's thinking, difficulties and beliefs. Colenso admired Ngidi's perception, intelligence and originality, and Ngidi the strength of Colenso's faith which seemed not to fear the frankest expression of opinion and had an answer for the most difficult question.[12]

But there was a wide range of practical problems which soon impinged on Colenso's ambitions as a missionary in Natal. The men and women with whom he had to work quarrelled amongst themselves and with their bishop. Not all had the commitment or the abilities which Colenso required, and they in turn found him unsympathetic. The religious differences between teachers, clergy and congregations hampered his work. Settler congregations resented the imposition of a bishop over them, his access to the seat of power, and the public funds his plans diverted and absorbed. White craftsmen opposed the training of black ones. Other missionaries preached God's word, but not as the glorious tidings of love and liberation: theirs was a fearful message which condemned those who would not hear, to eternal fire and damnation. As Colenso's knowledge of Zulu increased so did his awareness of the real problems of translation, the difficulties

Photo 12. William Ngidi, John Colenso's assistant in translation, through whose words Colenso began to create his own vision of Africans and African thinking in Natal.

in conversion and belief experienced by African converts, and the shortcomings of the missionary enterprise. Steadily Colenso became more dissatisfied with the conventional approaches to the religious teaching of the time.

But it was not just the problems he faced as a missionary bishop: his individual problems were also specific manifestations of the general crisis of religious belief in the mid-nineteenth century. Notoriously, Colenso asserted that he became aware of the difficulties confronting contemporary belief through the questions of an 'intelligent Zulu' – William Ngidi in fact. He had questioned Colenso closely on the difficulties he found in the biblical material on which they were working. For example, there was the story of the Flood. How could he persuade an African congregation to accept what was often obviously contradictory and even ridiculous? Colenso cast about for an answer. He was a well-informed man. He was aware of the scientific achievements of the age and the contemporary debates resulting from the increasing incompatibility of scientific discovery with conventional religious thinking. He had on his own admission avoided confronting these issues for many years; but the demands of missionary teaching generally, and Ngidi's searching questions specifically, forced him now to search for acceptable answers.

This search for contemporary truths raised more than intellectual questions. By July 1861 Colenso realised that his thinking on the Bible was in serious con-

flict with the accepted ideas of the church in which he was a bishop. By the end
of the year he was prepared to tell his most trusted friends that it was no longer
possible for him to teach that the Bible was the literal word of God. This for
Colenso was not a negative position, and he always rejected any suggestion that
he had fallen prey to that danger which stalked the mid-nineteenth-century religious thinker – doubt. Rather, Colenso believed, he was working for a new mission to replace the old – he was attacking conventional religious ideas in order to
save religious thinking. The missionary had to develop an approach which
brought to the heathen the glory of the Christian message, the light in all
humanity, to replace the conventional message of darkness, division and damnation. Religious belief would survive the discoveries of science only if it were
placed on a firmer basis. It could no longer demand the unqualified acceptance
of the writings of bygone eras, which although they surely contained, were in a
scientific age demonstrably not, the word of God. His experiences as a missionary bishop had created within him a vision which reached far beyond the borders
of his diocese of Natal. The time had come for him to share his African experience with the progressive thinkers of his day in order to effect 'a complete
Revolution in the religious tone of England'.[13]

In May 1862 John Colenso closed up Bishopstowe, left William Ngidi and
Magema Fuze in charge of Ekukhanyeni, packed his possessions and the printed drafts of his researches onto a wagon, and with his wife and five children
began the journey to Durban where they would embark for England. The mood
was one of excitement and anticipation. In her old age Sarah Frances remembered this journey under the brilliant African night sky while Colenso told them
stories associated with the different constellations. It was in fact the beginning
of a journey through notoriety into oblivion.

He published the first volume of *The Pentateuch and Book of Joshua Critically
Examined* in October 1862 and it caused a sensation. In it Colenso exposed the
contradictions, the obvious inaccuracies, the impossibilities, in the first five
books of the Bible. The author of the most widely used mathematics school textbooks used arithmetical demonstrations to do this. For some it was an honest and
convincing demonstration of the impossibility of accepting the Bible as the literal word of God. But for many others it seemed that a bishop of the Church of
England was working against the beliefs he was under oath to propagate and
defend.

The clergy howled, his brother bishops fumed, and most of his friends deserted him. The Church of England turned on this ambitious, talented man and
wasted him. No bishop, from within the church, could call the beliefs of its ministers shallow and challenge their congregations to reform them. No Englishman

in his position could acknowledge, as Colenso had done so publicly and prominently, a debt to African thinking. The mission societies deprived him of funds in an attempt to frustrate his plans and drive him out.

Any explanation for the extraordinary energy and viciousness of the attacks on Colenso has to go beyond the contents of the books themselves. It lies in the role the Bible played in the legitimisation and exercise of authority in mid-Victorian times. By questioning the truth of the Bible, Colenso was questioning recognised authority. Indeed he addressed his books not only to the clergy but also, specifically, to the informed general public, including members of the working class – its 'intelligent operatives'. As a consequence, the guardians of public opinion attempted to silence him. Characterised as a naïve and shallow, almost comical, publicity-seeking controversialist, he became one of the most notorious figures of the time: the bishop who had been sent to convert the Zulus had, instead, been converted by them.[14]

In response he turned a calm and reasonable face to the world. He came back to Natal in 1865 in order to demonstrate that a bishop in the Church of England could hold, indeed should hold and publicise, views which he believed were true and necessary for the further education of the Christian community in which he lived. In his farewell to his readers in England he looked forward to the day when his 'fellow-Countrymen and fellow-Churchmen' would be 'ashamed of that religious fear and frenzy, which has raged so furiously in these our times'. He did not comprehend, even then, the depth of the anger he had aroused and the determination of his opponents to silence him.

Winnington Hall

The furious three years spent in England during which Colenso published the first five of the seven volumes of *The Pentateuch and Book of Joshua Critically Examined*, and then defended in the courts his right to express these views and retain his diocese, were of profound significance not only to him but to his wife and his children, particularly the two oldest girls. When they left Bishopstowe for England in May 1862, Harriette was nearly 15 and Frances two years younger. They were to return to Natal after three years of excitement, varied experiences, new friends, and above all with the knowledge of what it cost to work for an ideal, for something perceived as more important than their own comfort and personal satisfaction, of sacrifice for a cause.

Once in England, Colenso made his base in London in Bayswater. Here he met and consulted with many of the progressive thinkers of the age, men and women of science, philosophy, social reform and literature. His schedule was

13

14

15

Photo 13. *Bishop Colenso with his sons Robert and Frank.*

Photo 14. *Sarah Frances Colenso with her daughters at the time when Harriette and Frances were at Winnington Hall.*

Photo 15. *Harriette and Agnes in England. Inseparable throughout their lives.*

crowded and made life for the family in London unsettled and unsuitable for the children. Sarah Frances had an old friend, Margaret Bell, 'an extremely clever woman, of a powerful and masterful turn of mind',[15] principal of Winnington Hall, a school for girls, in Cheshire, who offered help.

Winnington Hall's objectives were to provide middle-class young women with a wide range of educational experiences which included the sciences, music and art, self-expression through dance, and debates on topics such as religious belief. Amongst its visitors were some of the most progressive thinkers and artists in England of the time. In 1859 Miss Bell took some of her girls to hear John Ruskin lecture in Manchester and he became a frequent visitor and teacher at Winnington Hall.[16]

Ruskin's influence on the school and its pupils was profound, and in one of his best-known lectures he described the essential features of conventional contemporary education for girls – with Winnington Hall as the implicit inspiration for an approach which broke with convention:

> Let a girl's education be as serious as a boy's – You bring up your girls as if they were meant for sideboard ornaments, and then complain of their frivolity. Give them the same advantages that you give their brothers – appeal to the same grand instincts of virtue in them; teach *them* also that courage and truth are the pillars of their being: do you think that they would answer that appeal, brave and true as they are even now, when you know that there is hardly a girl's school in this Christian kingdom where the children's courage or sincerity would be thought of half so much importance as their way of coming in at a door; and when the whole system of society, as respects the mode of establishing them in life, is one rotten plague of cowardice and imposture – cowardice, in not daring to let them live, or love, except as their neighbours choose; and imposture, in bringing, for the purposes of our own pride, the full glow of the world's worst vanity upon a girl's eyes, at the very period when the whole happiness of her future existence depends upon her remaining undazzled?[17]

Miss Bell offered to support the Bishop of Natal by offering Winnington Hall as a retreat for the whole family, and a place of learning for his two older daughters. The broad education, the high-minded goals, the absence of conventional prejudice, greatly appealed to them – especially to Sarah Frances Colenso. It was just this that she felt her family had missed in colonial Natal.

At Winnington Hall the Colensos met Ruskin. He encouraged the bishop to continue to publish and declared that he himself went much further in his rejection of religious orthodoxy. He watched the children with interest, engaging

Harriette in intense if intimidating conversation, extracting from her an admission that missionary endeavour was self-interested, and the voluntary statement that African children were well behaved and willing to learn, unlike English ones in their 'misery and filth'.[18]

Harriette at 16 responded well to the Winnington environment, taking part not only in conventional studies but also in music and theatricals. She was serious in her work and intelligent. But she was shy and this was exacerbated by the acne which forced her back to her room and her books. And before the Colensos left England to return to Natal, Harriette had been called to 'keep house' for her father. Such duties in the service of her family and her father were to take up a large part of Harriette's life.

Eight-year-old Agnes was too young to spend time on her own at Winnington Hall, and it was upon Frances that the school had the greatest influence. She was more forthright than her sisters and, even now at 13, brightly confident. She was considered prettier and drew attention away from her sisters, and one suspects that she was rather spoiled. She was entranced by Winnington Hall, admired Miss Bell, and was anxious that her self-contained but frank and opinionated mother might give voice to ideas not in harmony with those of the school. She made close friends there, both amongst girls of her own age like Dora Livesey, and with some of the older visitors including Ruskin and Georgiana Burne-Jones, wife of Edward, the Pre-Raphaelite painter.

Although excited by Winnington Hall and its attempts to stimulate artistic and spiritual as well as strictly academic interests, Sarah Frances watched closely all aspects of her daughters' development. 'Dearest Harriette's present disfigurement is felt more than at home, by her Mama, and for herself it makes her even more retiring than she would otherwise be', she wrote, while Frances was 'growing towards the critical age now, and the narrowness and undevelopedness of her figure makes me a little anxious about her. But it is no use fretting before the time' and her 'perfectly free and natural manner amuses them all'.

But her mother's attempts to see Frances's outspokenness and enthusiasms in the best of lights cannot hide her concern at the strength with which her daughter expressed herself:

> I am glad indeed to hear such a good account of our dear Fanny, she is now quite impregnated with Winnington ideas, in harmony with all around her there – She will have to learn to give up her own will at home! I don't mean that she has not been learning anything with you of that most important lesson for young women, but that a change again to another atmosphere will bring more opportunity for practising that virtue.

A bright and slightly undisciplined girl whom she loved for her enthusiasm but feared for her outspokenness – this is how she appears in her mother's eyes. What about her own? Ten years later Frances wrote a novel, *Two Heroes*, and there are some hints at how she felt during these vital years at Winnington Hall.[19] The heroine, Katie Travers, has grown up in the colonies and is sent to school in England – to Willenden Grove. She is unconventional in her appearance, 'Such a wild-looking creature ... And so terribly brown ... and her hair fizzled almost like a negro! not at all pretty ...' She was unusual in her behaviour and independent in her thinking. Her relationships with men, and with women, are painful, for she loves with a fervour and frankness that they misunderstand and find hard to return. She differs from the world in her resistance to the self-seeking attitudes and the pursuit of worldly wealth which so dominate it. Kate gives her view of what life should be about: '"I think it means doing something in the world that will not be forgotten when one is dead" she said, with some hesitation, and then with sudden excitement, "and oh! it means, finding just one person, only one, to love with all one's might and to die for."'[20]

But in spite of her resistance this wild, spontaneous, different girl is tamed and the experience is a painful one. The themes, the emotions, the goals and ideals for which Frances lived in her life are here in the novel. Except for one. The novel has a projected happy ending in which love will transform this unconventional and independent girl from the colonies to a mature woman, fit to take her place in Ruskin's England. 'The full force of the love that was shortly to sweep her away in its strong irreversible current, changing her from the untutored passionate child into the noble and helpful woman, fit to be guardian of her husband's honour, his true help-mate in a worthy life, had not broken upon her as yet.'[21] And in life it was never to do so.

Bishopstowe

On their return to Natal all members of the Colenso family took with them the enthusiasms and friendships they had developed in these intense three years in England. The sons were interested in science, physical education and music, the bishop in his biblical criticism. Beyond their conventional studies in classics, mathematics and modern languages, the daughters of the house had their individual enthusiasms: Harriette studied botany and its practical application in the Bishopstowe garden and orchard, while acquaintance with Sir Charles Lyell had created an interest in geology and archaeology. Frances wrote and drew. Agnes was the one daughter for whom the killing of insects for an entomological collection held no fears, and also the one who resisted schooling most determinedly. All three girls had special responsibilities in the mission school, and in organising and participating in the housework.

While in England the Colensos had lost some of their closest old friends as a result of the controversy, including Sarah Frances's mentor, F.D. Maurice. But they did make new ones; and especially important was Katherine Lyell with whom Sarah Frances corresponded, thereby leaving us with, if not an intimate record of these years, then at least a deeply informative one. Katherine Lyell was in turn a friend of the curator of Kew Gardens, Sir Joseph Hooker, and Sarah Frances began a series of paintings of Natal flowers. They all assisted in collecting ferns for Katherine Lyell, who became an authority on the subject, and Hooker sent 500 kinds of flower seeds to Bishopstowe. Harriette organised the planting: 'Harry takes a great interest in them, but indeed she has many interests, and so much to do just now, that she is quite worn out every evening of her life. Her spirits never flag, except if she fancies her Papa is overdone ...'[22]

And he often was. The conflict within the church in Natal was carried on with a mean-spirited enthusiasm. Demonstrations took place around the cathedral and churches, doors were barred by one side and forced by the other, writs and warrants for arrest were served. Bishop Gray in Cape Town tried Colenso before an ecclesiastical court in St George's Cathedral, found him guilty of heresy and in 1866 excommunicated him. Colenso's victories in the courts forced Gray to replace him with a bishop of a diocese without any legal existence – 'Maritzburg, the conventional abbreviation of the name of the capital city. But the greatest difficulties for Colenso were created by the withdrawal of the funds upon which he depended to attract a competent clergy. When he was able to escape from working on the obscurities of ecclesiastical law, and the quarrels amongst colonials and clergy, he sought refuge in biblical criticism. Against this, however, his opponents now used the most effective weapon of all – they ignored it.

Sarah Frances Colenso became even more determined to retreat to Bishopstowe and observe the conflict from a distance. Intellectually and socially Natal offered her little. Music and painting were important to her and she was responsible for her children's general education, about which she had strong ideas: 'Agnes is very anxious to learn German, but I allow none of that until Latin first, and French next have been done ...'[23] The bishop intended to tutor his sons but given the other demands being made on him he was unable to do so. Once they could ride into Pietermaritzburg, attempts were made to find tutors for them there. His wife did what she could to foster an atmosphere of culture and learning at Bishopstowe, following the writings and debates of the age as best she could through the newspapers and periodicals. She and her husband attempted to cultivate those in the colony who might bring to Bishopstowe an atmosphere of enlightenment and learning. But it was not easy. They had visitors, of course, and Colenso made a point of inviting the officers of the regiment stationed in Pietermaritzburg to Bishopstowe. Sarah Frances accepted that it was a necessary concession to society, for 'the officers are apt to be, some of them, sporting characters, and some of them frivolous, but there is generally a small residuum of intelligence in the persons of one or two'.[24]

The overall responsibility for running a large domestic establishment consumed much of Sarah Frances's time, even with the help of her daughters and servants. Although only a few kilometres out of town the trip there and back filled the day. Bishopstowe tried to be as self-reliant as possible and this made more demands on the women of the family: 'All our garments are home made,' she wrote, 'and the fashions are preposterously complicated, as if invented to neutralize the benefits conferred on womankind by the sewing machine.'[25]

Yet there was an ambivalence in Sarah Frances Colenso towards life in Natal. The isolation of Natal, and her isolation within Natal, were compensated for by the peace she found at Bishopstowe. Their home was on high ground looking over the Mngeni valley towards the flat-topped Table Mountain. This view was part of their lives, so often framing their thoughts. The bishop called it his altar and arranged the furniture in his study so that he had an unrestricted view when he raised his eyes from his work. And although Sarah Frances found Natal mentally restricting, she became increasingly responsive to the space and the views at Bishopstowe.

> This is the place to enjoy the society of your friends (when you have any). In England, in London rather, there really is no time for it. How I should enjoy having you here for a week or two and to take you on a ramble in a certain direction where there is smooth walking and a glorious view towards Table Mountain all the way. It was very pleasant to sit and stroll in the gardens of the Crystal Palace, but there was not room there for me. Rattling about in cabs and railways used always moreover to make my head ache, dully at least, and that takes off the edge of any pleasure.[26]

The house was built over the years, the different elements determined by the needs at the time, but the main part with its veranda and gables, using African materials where possible, reflected the domestic architectural styles they knew in England. For their children it was home and school, the geographical location of the formative experiences of their lives. Many years later an American journalist visited it and described coming upon a wooded thicket, behind the 'leafy curtain' of which 'lies the most delightfully old-fashioned house imaginable, part

Photo 16. The home at Bishopstowe which those who grew up in it could never forget.

brick, part stone, part wood with peaked roofs and antique gables which would have pleased Nathaniel Hawthorne himself. House, garden and grounds, secluded from the world mid these lonely hills, seem the very embodiment of peace and repose ...'[27]

'Secluded from the world', a place of retreat: Bishopstowe came to mean this for the whole family. But it was not a retreat into idleness. The worthwhile life was one of hard work. After his return in 1865 the time-consuming, enervating ecclesiastical dispute gave Colenso little time with his family, but they made the most of it. The great treat for the growing children, and especially for the young women, was to be allowed to go with their father on horseback on one of his journeys through his diocese on visitation. They hugely enjoyed the adventure, the physical rigour, the hours on horseback without a rival for their father's attention. He was then able to bring them into his life, and share with them his high ambitions, his projects and his ideas.

As the 1860s drew to a close the two eldest daughters entered their twenties and began to participate in the social life of Pietermaritzburg. Harriette enjoyed dancing ('just for dancing's sake', her mother noted) but her father had to accompany her to the balls given by the military in Pietermaritzburg and then leave her with a chaperone. The girls made friends, but they were few and it was not easy to keep in touch. Harriette was very close to Kate Giles, who in time came to live with the sisters as a generous and dear friend. Frances, with memories of artistic friends in England, was rather above it all but also developed close friendships in Pietermaritzburg. One of these was Helen Bisset, daughter of General Bisset, who at 15 had married Shepstone's son Offy. Agnes was younger and remained, of her own choice, tied to Bishopstowe, the daily life of the farmers around the mission, and the mission school, Ekukhanyeni, attended by the children of the African neighbours and tenants.

Sarah Frances Colenso retained her dislike of colonial life. 'To be out of P.M.B. society too (though I must not say so here!) is quite as well for our girls, who have been accustomed to something better. So much is thought of dress, and the officers are so interesting to the young ladies, who seem to me not to go to the band to hear the music, but to show themselves!'[28] This high-minded seriousness was a feature of Bishopstowe, and in their different ways the children were moulded by it. It was an ambivalent legacy. It left the daughters with high ambitions and many interests. They were well educated and well informed. They counted amongst their acquaintances some of the leading thinkers, artists and scientists of the age. They were conscious of their position in colonial society and a sense of superiority based not on their material but on their intellectual and moral standing.

And yet, how were these interests and ambitions to be satisfied and sustained? Ruskin had said of daughters: 'Give them the same advantages that you give their brothers – appeal to the same grand instincts of virtue in them; teach *them* also that courage and truth are the pillars of their being ...' The bishop and his wife had succeeded in appealing to these grand instincts in their daughters – but they were not able to give them their brothers' grand advantages. In 1869 Frank and Robert were sent to England to be prepared for Cambridge and Oxford, and subsequent independent careers. It was painful to break up the family – so painful in fact that the parents did think momentarily of the possibility of using the money to set one of them up as a farmer in Natal. But it was a hesitation only. Sarah Frances reminded herself 'that their welfare is the chief thing for us to care about' and asked, if one of her sons stayed in Natal, 'Will he not regret all the rest of his life that he had not the opportunity which going to college offers, of becoming free [?citizens] of the republic of letters, forming friendships amongst those who are engaged in scientific pursuits, and even engaging in them himself? I could not bear the idea of him sinking into a lower stratum of mankind – I don't mean the least as to position in society.'[29]

This is typically high-minded. There was also the fact that the university degree provided the basis of a male career which would ultimately support the boys and their families. But as far as the daughters were concerned, unless they married they had only their interests and their voluntary mission work. All Harriette's learning, her scientific collecting, her obvious intelligence, remained personal attainments without practical application or the capacity to provide a basis for a career and an income, and therefore for an independent existence.

Harriette's and Agnes's energies were spent at home. Frances searched for a wider field. When her brothers left for Oxford and Cambridge she was allowed to accompany them to England for a visit. She was now 19. The ostensible reason for her journey was to get treatment for her eyes, but clearly memories of England and the friends she had made there were in her mind. And we have to suspect that more than one person in the Colenso family was thinking of her future and the advantages to be gained if she could meet men from a wider range of social backgrounds than the colonial and military men of Natal. But I doubt if this was ever expressed beyond some vague reference to her circle of friends and acquaintances – although the extant documents don't even have this: 'Papa thinks of her making Winnington her headquarters, where she will not lose her time but have some lessons.'[30]

Although troubled by unwanted male attention on the journey, once in England Frances was made welcome by Margaret Bell at Winnington Hall, and spent a year travelling and renewing acquaintances. She visited Ruskin, the Burne-Joneses, stayed with Maurice and the Lyells once again. She saw a lot of her friend from Winnington, Dora Livesey, a friendship so close that her mother felt she had to 'combat it rather, but with as much sympathy as possible, for I was just the same when I was young'.[31] Again we hear that slight criticism which probably hides a much deeper concern, but also suggests how parental love and commitment to grand virtues also trapped and stultified these young women: 'It is a very pleasant life, no doubt, floating about amongst friends and relations, but it must not go on too long. She has work to do out here, which will make her more truly happy in the doing of it than all the more passive existence in England.'[32]

Frances, however, was reluctant to return to Natal and even tried to persuade her parents to leave the colony. Her father had been thinking the same way. The forces ranged against him were great. Although they could not break his will, they were able to impose financial strictures which limited his activities and were hard to counter. Desperate to get some help in running the diocese but without the means to do so effectively, he made serious errors of judgement and hired an extraordinary number of men who turned out to be incompetents and crooks, who left him only more beleaguered than before. In 1869 Colenso was struck down by what was called rheumatic fever. He could not ride or use his hands, and now wondered how he should continue his duties if he lost his physical strength. But there was nowhere to go. His reputation in England was low. The fifth volume of his criticism had only just covered its costs. Longman was reluctant to take responsibility for the sixth, which was now ready. His friends, influential as some of them were, could not help. Colenso, as always, put on a brave face to the world and hid his feelings: 'I quite acquiesce in the judgment of yourself and my other friends, that there is no opening for me at present in England, and that I must be content to stop here ... [but] with increasing age and infirmity I feel that my work in this country is drawing year by year more nearly to its close.'[33]

Thus by the opening years of the 1870s the Colenso family in Natal were being forced to restrict their plans, get on and make the best of things. The bishop watched the development of the country closely, particularly the diamond mines where so many of the younger colonists had gone in the hope of fortune, and the Africans for a wage or a gun. His sons were now in England being prepared for admission to Oxford and Cambridge, not finding it easy, although secure enough in the professions they had chosen, law and medicine.

But his daughters were at Bishopstowe with no clear vision of their future. Frances had returned from England in 1870 and was 'working now vigorously at her school'.[34] At about this time a romance developed between her and Louis Knollys, one of the officers stationed in Natal. We don't know how it ended, but years later Frances was to write that 'there was no blame anywhere, but simply misfortune – to both of us'.[35] Agnes, by 1870 in her sixteenth year, was showing signs of rebellion by withdrawal. She was tall, shy and fiercely independent: refusing to show an interest in what was considered to be feminine, working with the farm animals, dispensing medicine, teaching at the school, she resisted participating in the social life of the young people in town. Her mother only partly opposed this: 'The little girls of P.M.B. seem to me too womanly by half and they and Agnes do not take to each other.'[36] For companionship Agnes looked to Harriette. As they grew older they grew closer and closer. Agnes supported her older sister as she took on more and more duties in the family, not just the domestic work but responsibility for the budget, the collection of rents from the tenants on church land, and the affairs of the mission station.

By the opening years of the 1870s there is a sense that the lives of the Colensos left at Bishopstowe were beginning to drift. Then, very suddenly, the situation changed. In the closing months of 1873 a series of events took place in Natal which were to radically alter the lives of all the Colensos, reviving their sense of purpose which the opposition to the bishop's attempts to revolutionise the religious thinking of the time had almost crushed.

CHAPTER 3

THE HOUSE OF SONZICA

Theophilus Shepstone

From the time John Colenso arrived in Natal, he and Theophilus Shepstone had been close friends. Although their backgrounds were very different they were both intelligent, interested and informed men, whose general approach to the social challenges with which they were confronted – conservation to control change – was in harmony. In practical ways both men gained from their friendship. Theophilus Shepstone was a member of Colenso's congregation and gave him unequivocal support in the most difficult years of his struggle with his church. Shepstone was also able to keep Colenso informed about the inner workings of colonial politics, settler and African. In turn, Colenso gave Shepstone access to the ideas and the leaders of the country from which he had been taken as a child, and which loomed so large in the lives of the settlers with whom he lived and worked.

Theophilus Shepstone had been born in England in 1817, grown up in a missionary family beyond the eastern frontier of the Cape, and become a fluent Xhosa speaker. From the age of 17 he had worked as an interpreter on the Governor's staff, and experienced directly some of the ugliest scenes of violence and cruelty which characterised the wars of dispossession on the frontier. In his twentieth year he was appointed Resident Agent at Fort Peddie, where he played a desperate game of pitting the Mfengu against the Xhosa until 1845 when he believed he had become the target of an assassin. Shepstone resigned his post and was offered the position of Diplomatic Agent to the Native Tribes of the recently annexed colony of Natal.

From 1846 to 1875 Shepstone dominated the African administration of that colony and his career has attracted considerable attention.[1] Though he is widely recognised as a man who played a significant part in the history of colonialism in Africa, pioneering a system of indirect rule and segregation, assessments of his character differ widely. For some he was a wise colonial administrator whose

Photo 17. Somtsewu, Sir Theophilus Shepstone.

ideals were frustrated by the parsimonious policy of his imperial superiors; for others he was a ruthlessly opportunistic overlord. A first step towards understanding Shepstone is to understand the African chiefs and officials through and with whom he worked, the *amakhosi* and *izinduna* whom he supported in order to secure white power in a colony which had never been conquered, and in which the settlers were a tiny minority in a huge African population – 2000 or 3000 amongst perhaps 100,000 at the beginning of his term of office, 16,000 amongst 300,000 at the end. It was a situation in which, Shepstone realised all too well, 'our destruction is inevitable the moment they become unanimous in determining it', and the keystone to his policy was to find ways to ensure that such unanimity never developed.

He was an exceptionally skilled man and a devious one, who used his insight into men and their affairs to institute a system of colonial overrule which drew on African patriarchal support from both chiefs and commoners to hold off the voracious, and above all dangerous, demands of settlers. This meant recognising African rights to a certain amount of land – the Native Reserves of Natal, which ultimately made up some 12 per cent of the colony's territory – and permitting African occupation of white-owned farms and Crown lands. On this land African homesteads, the *imizi*, were built – cattle enclosures surrounded by the rough circle of houses in which lived the male head of the family, his wives and children. These homesteads, and their associated arable and grazing lands, were now protected and organised under customary law, and grouped under the control of chiefly authority. Within this structure the African population of Natal grew the agricultural produce needed for their subsistence and an increasing surplus for the colonial market, and provided sufficient labour to earn the wages to pay the hut tax and the levies on the imports for the African trade which supplied the financial underpinning for the colonial administration.

For Shepstone it was a system that ensured a degree of continuity in African society while still allowing for change. But for Natal's settlers it was a system that permitted Africans to live independent lives instead of forcing them out of the reserves to experience the discipline and dignity acquired through sustained wage labour. From the point of view of most colonists, the Shepstone system starved them of the labour to which they were entitled and upon which the colonial economy had to be built. As a consequence, the settlers felt they were denied the opportunity to establish themselves and flourish in their new colonial environment.

Much of Shepstone's term of office was spent in applying and defending his ideas on segregation against settler attack. He did this with great skill and considerable ruthlessness. He gained control over the African population by deliberately dividing its leaders, recognising and rewarding the chiefs who obeyed him, and using them against those chiefs who showed signs of recalcitrance. His praise-poem recognised all these qualities. It lists the Africans raised to power by 'Our white man of the Town of Pietermaritzburg'

> Who washed his hands and they dried on certain men ...

It evokes in suitably hyperbolic metaphor the violence with which he treated those who opposed him:

> He attacks and the heavens thunder

And his deviousness is praised at length:

> He who appears as if he were not an expert,
> Inquiring about the rivers whereas he knows all about them
> For he would ask about the Msunduze, knowing it well,
> Doing it of set purpose ...[2]

Shepstone made sure that his own position amongst the African communities was unchallenged, and that they fully recognised that he was the source of their power, independence and security. At the same time, he acquired a considerable purchase on the colonial political system. In formal terms he was only a member of the colonial executive and an official within an administration headed by the Governor, who was 'Supreme Chief' under customary law. But it soon became apparent that no Governor could work in opposition to Shepstone, who was, in effect, the supreme authority on African affairs.

He was known to Africans as 'Somtsewu kaSonzica'. Somtsewu would appear to be a Sotho–Nguni hybrid which can be translated as 'father of whiteness'.[3] Sonzica was his father's name and the House of Sonzica referred to the Shepstone family, male members of which could be found holding official positions throughout Natal. His rule was a personal one: he heard cases and implemented decisions directly, in imitation of the court of an African chief, following custom and tradition, with African aides, advisers and police, *imbongi* and snuff-box carrier in attendance. Yet Shepstone's effectiveness as an administrator lay not only in the way he exhibited power but also in the manner in which he controlled information. The Africans with whom he had to deal lived in an oral culture. Their access to knowledge of the doings of government, the new laws, the structures of power, was determined by Shepstone. At the same time he also controlled the colonists' knowledge of African affairs. It was he who transcribed, translated and presented the words of Natal's African population to the broader colonial public. The long, detailed reports he wrote on the important official events with which he was associated, in which he spoke with such authority on African opinions and attitudes, were in fact Shepstone's often very subjective views, promoted to advance very particular personal objectives.

For many years there were few who could challenge this authority. For most of his time in office he was able to ensure that the oral *isiZulu* world did not mix with the written English one, and vice versa; he of course bestrode both and decided what the one side would know about the other. To both he presented himself as the great white chief, stern but just, remote but accessible to even the lowliest of his people, if they showed the required deference and respect. To the one he was enigmatic and reserved, privy to the innermost mysterious secrets of African character and African politics. To the other he was the representative of the Queen herself whose power, if she chose to use it, was unchallengeable.

It is from this consciously ambiguous world that much of the mystery around Shepstone has its origin. For Rider Haggard, who did more than anyone else to create the myth of Shepstone as the great white chief, he was 'a curious, silent man who had acquired many of the characteristics of the natives among whom he lived. Often it was impossible to guess from his somewhat impassive face what was passing in his brain.' In the written, colonial world it is Sir Bartle

Frere's assessment which is most often quoted: 'shrewd, observant, silent, self-contained, immobile'.[4] To Africans he was just the opposite. His 'desire [was] to speak with all people'.[5]

He justified his policy on the grounds of survival. In the face of the massive demographic imbalance between black and white, the only way in which the colony's security could be maintained was with the support of the African population, and this depended ultimately on African access to land. But this also involved Shepstone in a fundamental contradiction. Land was in short supply and any economic advance increased the pressure on land. Consequently, throughout his life Shepstone was looking for ways to extend the colony's territory and thereby gain land upon which to place Natal's Africans and in so doing reward his supporters and bind them closer to him. His gaze wandered southwards to Pondoland and west to Lesotho, and then to the north-east, to the territory lying on the western borders of the Zulu kingdom. Through here lay not only possible land for Natal's 'surplus population' but also a road to the fabled riches of the African interior. He travelled in 1861 to Zululand where he recognised Cetshwayo's claim to the Zulu throne, and again in 1873 to recognise his accession to that position. Cetshwayo, concerned about the pressure coming from the west from Natal and the Transvaal, felt that he needed an ally amongst one of his neighbours, and Shepstone, as the Secretary for Native Affairs (SNA), became 'his father' and protector.

The break-up: Langalibalele

It was towards the end of Shepstone's official career that social and economic changes in southern Africa began to threaten the system that he had built up in Natal. The discovery of diamonds in the interior at the end of the 1860s and the subsequent creation of new sources of wealth and markets were of great interest to Natal. Its leaders began to search for means to raise the capital for railway development, including borrowing against Crown land, much of which was occupied by Africans. Africans from different parts of southern Africa travelled to the fields to work in return for cash, and also for that commodity which had obviously played so important a role in the spread of European civilisation during the century – guns.

Instructions were given in 1872 that guns held by Africans be registered with their local magistrate. This order was treated with suspicion, particularly by the Hlubi, under Langalibalele, who occupied a large reserve up against Natal's western border on the Drakensberg. Langalibalele was ordered to attend the office of the SNA in Pietermaritzburg. He prevaricated and it was decided to enforce the order, and early in November 1873 a force of 200 colonial volunteers, with 200 British regulars in support together with 5000 African levies, was moved towards the Hlubi location. The Hlubi and their chief began to move out of Natal into Lesotho, and on 4 November in Bushman's Pass they clashed with a body of colonial troops under the command of Colonel Anthony Durnford, of the Royal Engineers. He was wounded, and a Mosotho, three colonial volunteers and Elijah Khambule, trusted emissary of Theophilus Shepstone, were killed. They were the men who stood with Durnford. Most of the colonial volunteers had already fled.

This was the first violent upheaval in colonial Natal in which settlers had lost their lives. The Natal force moved in and sacked the Hlubi location with such enthusiasm that the momentum carried them into the neighbouring Ngwe location as well. Women and children who had retreated into the caves and the rocks were driven or smoked out and their male protectors killed. The survivors were marched from the locations for distribution to farmers as labourers.

Langalibalele was brought to trial in Pietermaritzburg on 16 January 1874. A Special Court was set up under customary law and its proceedings were managed by Theophilus Shepstone. The presiding judge was the Governor of the colony, Sir Benjamin Pine, in the role of Supreme Chief; and Theophilus Shepstone's brother, John Wesley, prosecuted. When Bishop Colenso read an account of the proceedings in the press he began to be concerned. The evidence of one of the chief witnesses, Mahoyiza, messenger from the office of the SNA, whose report that he had been humiliated and stripped by the Hlubi had precipitated the order for the troops to march into the location, was inconsistent.

Mahoyiza was induna to the magistrate's court in Pietermaritzburg. He had been a tenant at Bishopstowe for fifteen years and the bishop knew him well, and found him 'slippery and doubtful'. Colenso decided to investigate further and obtained accounts of what happened between Mahoyiza and the Hlubi. Harriette was present when witnesses spoke with her father, and Magema Fuze, the bishop's printer, wrote down their accounts and collected additional statements. It was soon clear to Colenso that although the situation in the Hlubi location had been very tense, and Langalibalele had indeed refused to come in to the office of the SNA, there was no substantiated evidence that Mahoyiza had been humiliated, stripped or starved as he had stated.

Colenso contacted Shepstone, telling him that he had information which suggested that he, and now the court, had been misled. Shepstone called Colenso, Magema Fuze and the four witnesses on 27 January 1874 to his office, where he and some of his most important indunas did what they could to expose contradictions in the testimony. But Magema stood his ground. After some noisy debate the meeting ended, if not in agreement, then with the general feeling that Mahoyiza had indeed lied.

But the victory held no comfort for Colenso. He had become involved initially in order to assist the office of the SNA by pointing out an apparent weakness in its case. However, instead of finding his friend's intervention useful, Shepstone had treated his attempt to assist as unwarranted interference, and attacked Magema and intimidated Colenso's witnesses. Moreover, it now emerged that there was even more to the alleged stripping of the SNA's messengers. Incredibly, it seemed as if the Hlubi had suspected that Mahoyiza might have been concealing a weapon – that he was in fact an assassin. As a Hlubi had said, 'We too know that little trick of the white men, we too were there at Matshana's affair.'[6] And Magema had been told by Hlubi women at Bishopstowe that 'an ugly rumour went abroad that "a stern man was coming (meaning Mahoyiza), who would kill the Chief Langalibalele with the well-known pistol."'[7]

'The well-known pistol'

Colenso began to ask more questions of the Africans at Bishopstowe. It was public knowledge that in 1858 there had been a clash when Theophilus's brother John had attempted to arrest Matshana kaMondise, chief of the Sithole. What was not so well known, by white Natal at least, was that during peaceful negotiations John Shepstone had produced a concealed gun. In the fracas that followed, 30 men were killed. In the light of this experience of the office of the SNA at work, the Hlubi request that Shepstone's messengers remove their outer garments was only a sensible security check.

Colenso was profoundly shocked. As the trial of Langalibalele progressed, he was forced to reassess the view he had held for so long of the system of native administration in Natal, and the man who controlled it. The Special Court was clearly inadequate. On the bench were men whose impartiality had already been compromised by their circumstances and public statements. The African assessors had themselves been involved in the charges. The accused's guilt was assumed before evidence was led, and although he was made to plead he was not allowed counsel. And a defence counsel was certainly required because, as Colenso interpreted it, evidence was emerging that this was not a case of rebellion at all: Langalibalele had not resisted the constituted authority but had retreated from it.

Nonetheless, Langalibalele was found guilty, and sentenced to banishment. Colenso was determined to act. Ordinance 3 of 1849, by which customary law and the powers of the Supreme Chief had been promulgated, gave the right of appeal to the Lieutenant-Governor advised by the Executive Council. Colenso asked two elderly Hlubi men, Ngwadla and Mnyengeza, if they would sign a petition for an appeal. On Sunday 1 March, while the bishop was away in Durban, Harriette Colenso, William Ngidi and Magema Fuze met the old men, and explained the terms of the appeal before they put their mark on the document.

On Wednesday the petitioners were summoned to the SNA's office where they were threatened with imprisonment. Mnyengeza, who was very old and frail, said he had been forced to sign the petition. 'After this Mr. Shepstone together with the white and black chiefs and the Indunas laughed at him.'[8] When Colenso wrote asking for a response to the petition, Shepstone replied that it had been repudiated by the petitioners.

The next Saturday William Ngidi and Magema Fuze, also witnesses to the petition, were called in and interrogated. Every attempt was made to get them to admit that the appeal originated with Colenso or with Harriette, and that it had been foisted on the old men. Colenso protested in a fierce exchange of notes with Shepstone: he objected to the SNA's suspicion that he was party to a 'frivolous and fictitious petition'; of course the wording of the ordinance would have been difficult for the Hlubi men to understand – but they had no difficulty in comprehending the principle embodied in the appeal.[9]

But there was little frivolous about Theophilus Shepstone when he was crossed. In April the petitioner Mnyengeza, who had retracted when bullied by Shepstone and his indunas, was found guilty of moving cattle during the rebellion and sentenced to two years' hard labour. Colenso protested, not only against the conviction but at the very idea that someone so old should be sentenced at all, let alone to hard labour. He was released in May but, trying to get from the gaol to Bishopstowe, lost his way and died, probably of exposure.

To the shocked Colenso family the Langalibalele affair had revealed a Shepstone quite different from the man who had been their friend and ally for twenty years. Sarah Frances wrote to her brother:

> John is again at issue with the world in which he lives! It is useless to say to him, would it not be wiser to leave things take their course. You cannot bring the dead to life, nor restore the thousands of victims of official cowardice and cruelty to their homes. John *can not but* lift up his voice against injustice. The feeling of the typical colonist towards the natives is hardly that of man to man, but rather that the 'niggers' are to be utilised by the white settler, or else to be suppressed altogether. English feelings, I hope and trust, however, will always be something very different ...
>
> For so many years John has regarded Mr. Shepstone as the incarnation of

justice to the natives, as standing between the typical colonist and the tribes settled in Natal. And now that confidence has given way *altogether*! ...

Bishopstowe saw things so differently from their fellow colonists who

want to drive them out to forced labour, not content to wait for the action of natural laws to induce them to sell their muscles to the planter or farmer. The colonists want to increase the taxes. Well that might be done gradually. They want to suppress polygamy by legislation – which is as foolish a thing as they can do. And in fact there is, I suppose, some natural antagonism between black and white, which makes the latter absolutely jealous of the relative freedom from wants and from cares, which makes the native comparatively independent.

It is all nonsense to accuse us of 'negrophilism' etc., etc. We can only want simple justice, and believe that with that and with time and patience all things would come right.[10]

Harriette was deeply involved in assisting her father as he built up his case against the colonial authorities and did what he could to ameliorate the effect of their actions against the Hlubi and the Ngwe. It was in this day-by-day struggle, working with her father, that she gained the commitment and practical experience that were to give shape to so much of her life. She watched and learnt as he developed the legal arguments which exposed so thoroughly the inadequacies of customary law. Her spoken Zulu was better than her father's, and she not only was able to deal with interviews and translations but assumed responsibility for the welfare work Bishopstowe carried out amongst the victims. She also took over much of the administration of the mission estate, paying wages and collecting rents. To the Zulu she became known as Udlwedlwe – her father's staff, his guide and support.

When the friendship between Colenso and Shepstone ended finally in July 1874, it was Harriette Colenso who served as intermediary. She had just turned 27. When the conventional distance required by their differences in gender, age and status, and the notorious remoteness and reserve of the SNA are considered, it is an indication of the high regard in which she was held that the task was given to her. 'Good God!' Shepstone wrote in a note that he asked to be destroyed, 'I never could have supposed it possible that the close friendship, aye, love, of 20 years could thus easily have been shaken and wrecked.' Harriette protested at the word 'easily'. For her father the break meant that 'the light had all gone out from his life in Natal'. She reminded Shepstone that her father entered upon this Langalibalele controversy at first ... solely to defend and support you, being convinced that thereby he was best serving the cause of Truth and Justice ... And, as once in theological matters he risked everything ... for the sake of what he believed to be the truth, so now for that same conscience' sake ... he must give up even his dearest friend.[11]

The Bishopstowe faction

But these developments in the opening months of 1874 were more than just a dispute between two old friends over the failure of justice in a colonial situation. They mark in fact the end of the monopoly that Shepstone had over the African voice in Natal and Zululand. For here, in the sources that document these disputes, we have some of the first public African statements which challenge the official point of view of events in Natal and dispute the information coming from the office of the SNA. This process was to intensify and expand in the years to come, but these are the first signs of the activities of what was to become known as the Bishopstowe faction.

It was founded on the fact that at Bishopstowe there existed an environment where men and women could communicate news, ideas and opinions without the conventional colonial restraints. It was a consequence of years of work at the mission – in the Zulu language, in preaching and discussion, and in day-to-day communication which had created relations of trust. It carried with it many risks. Not only had Bishopstowe little to offer its members in terms of material reward, but those who were associated with it had much to lose if they attracted the anger of the office of the SNA.

At its head was the bishop himself. He was assisted by Harriette. Essential to the process was the co-operation of literate converts, the *amakholwa*, or believers, associated originally with the mission work at Ekukhanyeni. Most prominent was Magema kaMagwaza Fuze. Magema had come to Bishopstowe as a boy in 1855 to attend the school there. He had been sent to the printer's shop where he had learnt his trade of compositor. He was particularly important, not only because he provided a link with local African news and opinions, but also because as mission printer it was his job to put the bishop's researches and translations into a form suited for wider distribution. Although a convert, he lived in a polygamous homestead, but because he was a printer not a preacher this was allowed. William Ngidi, however, was no longer at Bishopstowe. In 1869 he had taken another wife and Colenso had dismissed him. Ngidi retreated to the countryside but remained in touch with Bishopstowe. His correspondence with his friend Magema provided an important source of information for the bishop and his helpers, and when they needed help in their protests against the actions of the authorities, he gave it.

There were other *amakholwa* at Bishopstowe who gave their assistance. Jonathan Ngidi, William's brother, was a teacher there, together with Mubi Nondenisa, who had been brought up at Ekukhanyeni and educated at the mission school, and was close to Harriette especially. There were a few white supporters in Natal, and a handful at the Cape, but more important were Colenso's liberal friends in England, most of them members of the Aborigines' Protection Society (APS), a comparatively well-funded and influential pressure group with access to a wider public through the London *Daily News*. The way in which the APS characterised as prejudiced and brutal the actions and attitudes which the settlers saw as necessary and just, infuriated Natal, especially when these accusations were made before a metropolitan audience whose authority Natal resented but whose esteem it sought.

The bishop brought to these projects a confident and quick mind and exceptional analytical skills. His appeals against Langalibalele's sentence, and his subsequent attempts to use imperial statutes to block his banishment to the Cape, show a remarkable grasp of the law. They failed of course – but he wrote up his researches in the form of an annotated and documented history of the events which was also a sustained critique of Natal's actions towards the Hlubi chief. Eventually it was published as British Parliamentary Paper C1141, which countered the official account from the office of the SNA. Through it Magema Fuze and William Ngidi's evidence and commentaries on African perceptions of the way they had been treated by the colonial authorities reached an important and influential audience.

The imperial factor

Theophilus Shepstone's control of the voice of Natal's Africans was being challenged at last. Both he and Colenso travelled to London in 1874 as a result of the Langalibalele affair: the SNA ostensibly to explain to the Secretary of State the Natal government's actions, but in fact to exonerate himself; and the bishop to expose the wicked injustice inflicted on the Hlubi and the Ngwe by the Natal government and to appeal for redress.

They arrived in London at that significant juncture in official thinking towards South Africa, when the Secretary of State for the Colonies, Lord Carnarvon, was considering a radical new policy. The Langalibalele affair seemed to exemplify the hazards of a situation where the region was fragmented amongst different and increasingly embattled systems of government – British colonies, Afrikaner republics and African chiefdoms. The creation of a South African political union – a single, politically stable, administratively efficient, militarily secure, economically productive South African state – seemed to Carnarvon to be a worthy goal for an imperial statesman.

Shepstone made a very favourable impression on the Secretary of State. His calm assurance, administrative experience, and intimate knowledge of South Africa and South Africans could greatly assist Carnarvon in his plans. As a result Shepstone returned to South Africa with a knighthood, and secret instructions to advance the new initiative that Carnarvon was considering in South Africa – the confederation scheme.

In April 1877 Shepstone annexed the Republic of the Transvaal to Britain and became its Administrator. He did so on the assumption that the bankrupt republic, increasingly unable to assert its control over its African population, would accept its loss of independence in return for the stabilising effects of British economic and military assistance. But Shepstone had miscalculated. For the boy from the mission station, the desire to walk the imperial stage had been too great. A growing number of Boers resented being brought under British control and began to make their opposition known. In an attempt to gain their support Shepstone now turned to the people whom, in different circumstances, he had chosen as his allies, the Zulu. And when they refused to assist him by sacrificing their land to the Boers, he turned against them.

Bishop Colenso had also impressed Lord Carnarvon. But whereas Shepstone was a pragmatic administrator with whom he could do business, Colenso was an idealistic missionary with a philanthropic pressure group at his back, and had to be treated very differently. Carnarvon listened to the bishop carefully and promised him privately that he would take steps to ameliorate the lot of those who had suffered at the hands of Natal's officials. He also indicated that he was about to reform native administration in Natal. Colenso returned to Natal with a private letter of congratulation from the Queen, persuaded that he should be patient: unnecessary protest and agitation would only make it more difficult for the British government to bring about reform in Natal.

Bishopstowe watched and waited for signs of these reforms. Shepstone, however, was the man of the hour, with a key role to play in the confederation scheme. He gained the ear of the new Special Commissioner in Natal, Sir Garnet Wolseley, and successfully shut Colenso out. Bishopstowe's numerous attempts to draw the administration's attention to individual acts of injustice which required amelioration in terms of Carnarvon's promises were rejected or sidestepped. The legislation to reform native administration was insufficient. Whatever Carnarvon's intentions, his promises of reform were not carried out.

Bishopstowe took the brunt of settler anger. It was depicted as the centre of a philanthropic conspiracy. Harriette Colenso angered the authorities with her attempts to get action taken on behalf of those still suffering from official harassment. Wolseley was infuriated when Bishop Colenso, dining at Government House, appealed on behalf of two of Langalibalele's people. Then, after visiting Bishopstowe, Wolseley wrote in his diary:

> Never will go there again for I was attacked by the whole family about the native policy in very bad taste, the Bishop losing his temper and in fact becoming so excited that his voice quavered so that he could scarcely utter. He has lost all position among the white people so he is now endeavouring to constitute himself the great protector of the black people, and to come between the Governor and them, a position that I will never sanction as long as I am here. His place is pretty but in bad order. Mrs. Colenso seems to be a drivelling idiot and to be tolerated by her family as such: all the lot have Kaffir on the brain and to be really mad on the subject viewing everything from one side alone and being incapable of taking a broad view on any matter where the interests of Kaffirs are in any way concerned.[12]

Sarah Frances Colenso in turn formed her own views on General Wolseley, 'this little featherhead of a fighting man'. Although her daughters attended the official functions thrown by Wolseley in an attempt to gain settler support, Harriette argued with him in public. 'Somehow', Sarah Frances wrote, 'we seem out of harmony with the society of the place …'[13]

One of the very few whites who stood with Bishopstowe was Major Anthony Durnford of the Royal Engineers. He had been the officer in command of the force which had confronted the Hlubi at Bushman's Pass. The settlers blamed him for the incident and he did not increase his popularity by being a close friend of the Colenso family.

And there was more than friendship in his visits to Bishopstowe. He and Frances Colenso had fallen in love. It was a relationship which in practical terms stood little chance of success. He was in his fifties and she was half his age. He was already married, with a daughter, although separated from his wife. Frances was considered the beauty of the family, was artistic, a romantic, on the fringes of the Pre-Raphaelite circle. Her juvenile stories had been printed privately and in local journals. They are tales of a girl of intense emotions, independent and wild, who expresses her feelings frankly and thereby opens herself to misunderstanding by her friends and the disapproval of the staid and unromantic figures of authority. She found in Durnford a brooding, wronged, chivalrous knight:

stern, upright, suffering the spiritual wounds of his unfortunate marriage, the physical ones he gained on Bushman's Pass, and the unjustified abuse of Natal's settlers. The attitudes of her parents, brothers and sisters to this relationship, if they ever dared to express them in writing, have long since been removed from their surviving letters. He remains 'our Major Durnford', one of the Colensos' best friends.

In 1874 Durnford initiated a project which sought to rehabilitate the Ngwe, who had been dispossessed in the attack on Langalibalele. But this identification with the views of Bishopstowe only increased Wolseley's antagonism towards him. Magema Fuze and Harriette Colenso were held to be responsible for a petition to Wolseley from a number of Natal *amakholwa* requesting that they be exempted from customary law. Wolseley, whose motto was 'homo homini lupus' – man is a wolf to mankind – was undoubtedly unhappy at being depicted in the petition as 'the same as a hen, which does not mind any kind of chicken, whether of a duck or turkey, or for any other bird, she does keep them all under her wings'. But, no matter how it broke the conventions of a properly drafted and presented petition, it is an important document in the history of African political protest, the ideas behind it reflecting real concerns of the emerging literate class of converts, whose experience enabled them to see that the application of customary law and procedure was an unfair and unjust means of control. Colenso depicted it as 'a genuine utterance of a semi-civilised native mind'. 'As such, especially considering that some of their alleged grievances are by no means "purely imaginary," it appears to me not unworthy of consideration.' For Harriette, 'They asked for bread and he [Wolseley] gave them a stone.'

In 1875 Bishop Colenso defended himself against the charge that he had libelled John Shepstone when he exposed details of the treacherous manner in which Shepstone attempted to arrest Matshana in 1858 by firing at him with a concealed pistol. Again, Colenso was only able to do this with support from the Africans of Bishopstowe, and witnesses brave enough to testify against members of the Shepstone family. The Zulu king, Cetshwayo, sent men to give evidence for Colenso. William Ngidi assisted his old friend and mentor in spite of being desperately worried by the consequences of becoming involved in a quarrel between the impulsive Sobantu and ruthless Somtsewu.

Colenso's witnesses told substantially the same story, but the bishop was unable to convince the inquiry of criminal culpability on the part of John Shepstone. Thus it was decided that while it was true that John Shepstone had fired the pistol, it could not be proved that he fired it at Matshana. The chairman of the inquiry admitted that the evidence went against this interpretation; however, he took into consideration the well-known fact that oral testimony 'crystallises in an accepted form', that Colenso had conducted his case far more effectively than John Shepstone, and that a well-known sportsman like Shepstone would not have missed Matshana if he had wanted to hit him. Colonial opinion felt that John Shepstone had been vindicated.[14]

Colenso was disappointed and angry. But they all had to be extremely careful. The office of the SNA resented any interference in what it saw as its sphere of activity. Its informers justified their employment with ridiculous stories of the bishop's and Harriette's activities. But, no matter that the connections had to be hidden, the links had been made. Amongst the men watching the situation carefully was Cetshwayo kaMpande: 'Messengers from the Zulu King were here the other day,' Sarah Frances Colenso wrote,

> on their way back from the office of the S.N.A. (they know their way here very well: Papa is his Father, and Harrie his sister, but tell it not in Gath!) and they assured the Bishop that only 8 persons had suffered death in Zululand within the last two years, and they for certain offences recognised as such by Zulu customs, nothing like the destruction of life which has been perpetrated in the eating up of the poor Amahlubi by our Christian and civilised government here. These rumours of wars in Zululand, help to keep up the notion of danger from any interference with the prestige of the Native Department ...[15]

CHAPTER 4

THE DESTRUCTION OF THE ZULU KINGDOM (JANUARY 1879 – JULY 1884)

Names

These rumours of wars were gaining intensity. Sir Theophilus Shepstone's annexation of the Transvaal had heightened Boer antagonism and unsettled the border with the Zulu. Shepstone tried to use his influence with the Zulu to mollify Boer fears and asked for a meeting with the Zulu to discuss the disputed border area between the Transvaal and Zululand. If he could persuade the Zulu to make some concession here it might increase his standing with the Boers, and decrease their opposition to his decision to annex the Transvaal.

They met near the Ncome, or Blood, River on 18 October 1877. It was immediately clear to the Zulu delegation that Shepstone the Administrator of the Transvaal was not Shepstone the SNA in Natal, and they accused him of treachery towards their king. For Shepstone, to be accused in this way was an unforgivable insult. The Zulu had forgotten the forms of respect to which he was entitled. As the king was later to relate, the meeting ended when Bhejana accused Shepstone of betrayal and addressed him by his name, not by his title. 'Somsewu then got in a rage and said, "Who is that that calls me by my name and does not address me by saying 'King'?" Then the other chiefs said, "No king in our country; although a man be a king, we chiefs call him by his name."'[1]

Furious at being publicly crossed, Shepstone broke up the meeting. He was never to forget what had happened, and he made sure that the Zulu generally, and the men in particular who had so insulted him, were to suffer for it. The Zulu, quite rightly, were to see this meeting as the beginning of the conflict that was to end their independence.

Meanwhile, Sir Bartle Frere had been appointed High Commissioner in order to facilitate the process that would bring into being the new South African confederation. It was clear that an independent Zulu kingdom was the most immediate obstacle to this. Throughout 1878 Shepstone played a central part in providing the High Commissioner with the arguments he required to mount the

49

charge that the independent Zulu kingdom was an imminent threat to progress, peace and security in South Africa. He turned to African history, law and custom to substantiate his argument. The Zulu kingdom was an aberration. Shaka, the founder, had terminated African chiefly rule and replaced it with a centralised autocracy, supported by a military system which oppressed its people and terrorised its neighbours. In the violent upheavals of the early decades of the century such a system might have been necessary, but now with civilised rule in much of southern Africa this was no longer the case. Cetshwayo, however, had revived the rule of Shaka, and rebuilt the regiments and the military despotism of the Zulu royal house. The Zulu king was seen by the forces of barbarism in southern Africa as the natural leader of all who opposed progress and change.

The bulk of the kingdom's people, it was asserted, opposed this reversion to the horrors of Shaka's rule but they dared not show it. In fact, Shepstone argued, it was on behalf of these oppressed and silenced Zulu that Britain should act. For ultimately the case against the continuance of Zulu independence did not depend on the character of any one individual or a particular policy. The Zulu threat to peace and progress in South Africa was a consequence of the historical structure of the kingdom over which no individual had control; it had to be looked upon as

> an engine constructed and used to generate power, the accumulation of which is now kept pent up in this machine, while the process that produces that power is as actively going as ever.
>
> The Zulu constitution is essentially military, every man is a soldier, in whose eyes manual labour, except for military purposes or in furtherance of military schemes, is degrading, he has been taught from his very childhood that the sole object of his life is fighting and war, and this faith is as strong in the Zulu soldier now, and is as strongly inculcated, as it was 50 years ago, when it was necessary to the building up and existence of his nation ...
>
> But the engine has not ceased to exist or to generate its forces, though the reason or excuse for its existence has died away; these forces have continued to accumulate and are daily accumulating without safety valve or outlets.[2]

At the same time, the threat was not an insuperable one: a demonstration by the imperial power that there was an alternative to this military despotism would result in its collapse.

While there were hints in the newspapers, in rumours and gossip, and in the movement of troops, to suggest that the Zulu kingdom was coming under threat, the evidence was not sufficient for Bishopstowe to do much more than express its concern at the way in which events appeared to be moving, and warn of the consequences. Thus, when Magema Fuze made a trip to Zululand in 1877 and had an audience with the king, the bishop arranged for his account to be published in *Macmillan's Magazine*.[3] The article presented a favourable account of a monarch aware of the dangers encroaching on his kingdom but determined to avoid a confrontation with the British.

The immediate impact made by the Bishopstowe faction was, however, only slight: a handful of men and women, white and black, monitoring and publicising events in Natal and Zululand had little effect on colonial opinion or imperial policy. Nonetheless, in the longer term the implications of the emergence of literate African voices are significant; and the officials, whose final line of defence was their control of African utterance through their control of language and writing, found it infuriating. Moreover, the High Commissioner, Sir Bartle Frere considered the voices from Bishopstowe of sufficient significance to attempt to control them.

In October 1878 Frere visited Bishopstowe and asked Colenso to criticise his policy. Momentarily the strategy succeeded. Ignored and isolated for so long, the bishop believed that his opinions and views might now be taken into consideration in the formulation of policy towards the Zulu. But as the year drew to a close Colenso came to realise that it was not a genuine appeal for criticism at all, but an attempt to muzzle the critical voices coming from Bishopstowe while the attack on the kingdom was being prepared. For even as he was asking Colenso for his views, Frere was building his case against the Zulu king and finding the pretexts he needed for war.

On 11 December 1878 Zulu emissaries were presented with an ultimatum which in effect demanded that Cetshwayo relinquish his sovereignty over the Zulu kingdom. It was assumed that he would reject it. On 11 January 1879 a force of some 18,000 men, one-third of whom were British regulars, half were African auxiliaries from Natal, and the rest colonial volunteers, invaded Zululand from Natal and the Transvaal. But instead of fragmenting the kingdom as Shepstone had predicted, the invasion had the effect of uniting the Zulu people in defence of their autonomy. On 22 January the Zulu army attacked the headquarter's column at Isandlwana. The Zulu force mounted charge upon charge into rocket, artillery and rifle fire, and suffered terrible casualties. But it eventually reached the British camp and slaughtered its defenders.

When the news of the defeat reached England there was an outcry from the liberal and radical press and the opposition benches. Under attack, the Conservative government began to move away from the policy which had brought about the war. But by now the invasion had generated its own mo-

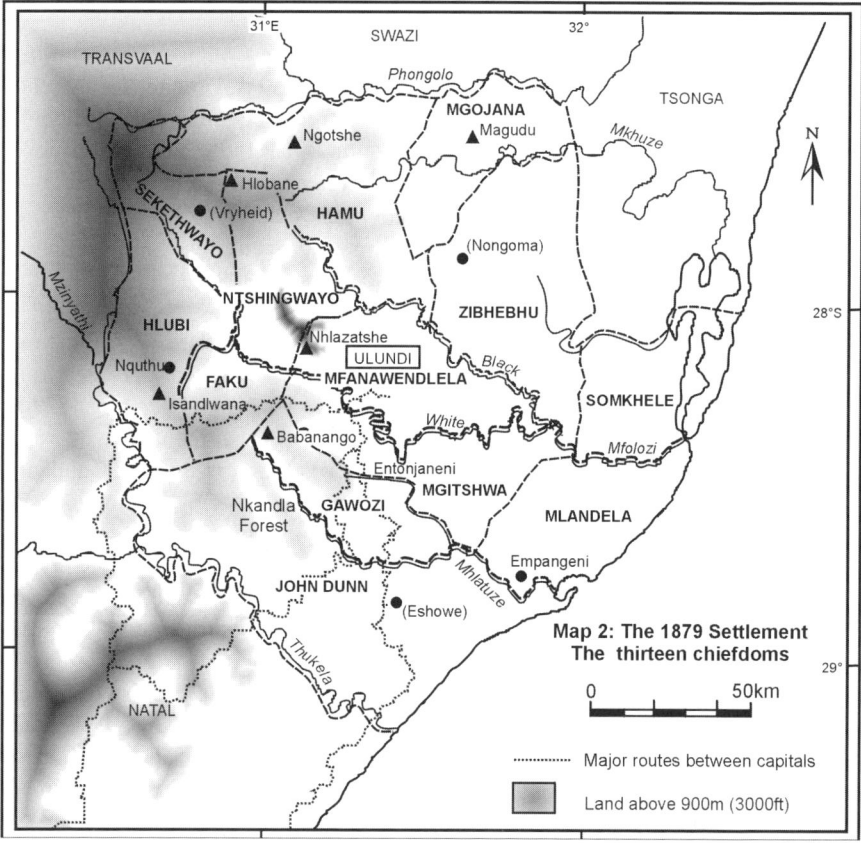

Map 2: The 1879 Settlement
The thirteen chiefdoms

0   50km

·············· Major routes between capitals

Land above 900m (3000ft)

mentum. The defeat suffered by the British at Isandlwana demanded that the war be continued. National pride had to be restored. Before there could be peace, a military victory was needed to restore Britain's imperial reputation.

The invaders retired to Natal to await reinforcements, and the slow crawl into Zululand began again. In July 1879 the British force reached the centre of the kingdom, provoked and drove off a Zulu attack, and depicted the action as an overwhelming military victory, which became known as the Battle of Ulundi. With the British military reputation secure, Zulu resistance was brought to an end: the Zulu people were informed that if they laid down their arms and returned to their homes they would be left in possession of their land. The war, it was stated, had been against the Zulu king, not the people.

Although the Zulu people were left independent, the Zulu monarchy was to be terminated. The rule of the Zulu royal house and its military system was declared to be at an end. In August the Zulu king, Cetshwayo, was captured and then exiled to the Cape, and the country divided amongst 13 independent chiefs. A half-hearted attempt was made to provide a rationale for their selection – that these were the chiefs of the major tribes of the region before their subjugation by the Zulu under Shaka. But the argument was specious in theory and dishonest in practice. Most of the chiefs did not represent these 'ancient tribes'. Some of the most important of them – like John Dunn, the trader whom the king had made a Zulu chief; Hamu kaNzibe, the king's close relative; and Hlubi Molife, the Sotho mercenary – were given their territories as a reward for assisting the British during the war. The arrangement was in fact a hurried act of retreat dressed up as a settlement. A British Resident was appointed, without authority, to monitor the situation. His name was Melmoth Osborn, close friend to Sir Theophilus Shepstone, who had served in the latter's administration in the Transvaal.

With the rest of Natal, Bishopstowe had been devastated by the losses at Isandlwana. Many of the young colonists who died there had, with their parents, been members of Colenso's congregations. But it was not only these personal and private tragedies that the bishop mourned. From his cathedral pulpit in March 1879 Colenso urged a congregation and a community, deep in mourning and terrified by the fear of a Zulu counter-invasion, to reflect on their own sins, on how the invasion had come about, and to remember those in mourning on the other side as well as their own. It was a sermon remarkable for its courage and humanity.

He analysed the events which had led to the invasion. They showed that the British had acted neither mercifully nor justly. As a consequence, thousands of their fellow human beings had died. 'We ourselves have lost very many precious

Photo 18. Anthony Durnford. Friend of the bishop and lover of Frances Colenso.

lives, and widows and orphans, parents, brothers, sisters, friends, are mourning bitterly their sad bereavements. But are there no griefs – no relatives that mourn their dead – in Zululand? ... And shall we kill 10,000 more to avenge the losses of that dreadful day?'

His anger and distress were deep. The invasion had struck away the very foundations upon which he had built his life in Natal. It denied the value of Colenso's life and work as the missionary Bishop of Natal. His task had been to bring justice, progress, hope and peace to the ignorant and uncivilised. The war had inverted the whole process. The British invasion of Zululand had annulled his sacrifices for the truth, debased the service he had given for God and Country. This had to be rectified.[4]

His first task was to expose the men who brought war to Zululand and the manner in which it was done. He stopped writing to Frere, realising that the invitation to do so had been an attempt to co-opt him, but continued his critical analysis of the events which led to the invasion. He was in contact with F.W. Chesson of the APS, who made sure the latest British Parliamentary Papers were posted immediately from London. In return, Colenso kept Chesson supplied with information that might possibly be used as the basis for a question, or an answer, in parliament, or a paragraph in a sympathetic newspaper. Colenso searched the dispatches for inconsistencies and discrepancies, and compared

Photo 19. Frances Ellen Colenso, from a set of portraits taken in 1881 which she felt 'are the best I ever had and I have not yet altered much since they were taken, and, as I do not mean to be taken again I should like to keep this one'.

them with other accounts in the press, with local gossip, and with information given to him by those officials and military men still prepared to talk with him.

More and more of the responsibility for the research and secretarial work was falling on Harriette. Short of funds and therefore of clergy, the bishop was called down to Durban to officiate at the Sunday services. Apart from running the home and the mission farm, Harriette organised the correspondence on Zulu affairs which was posted every week to England. Sunday evenings were always hectic as the Colenso family wrote the covering letters and made up the packets of documents to catch the weekly mail to sympathisers, supporters, and men and women of influence in South Africa and Britain.

A major part of their work was to put significant documentation, annotated where necessary, into printed form for circulation amongst their supporters and sympathisers. The closely printed pages went under the heading 'Extracts from the Blue Books'. For the first months Magema Fuze was solely responsible for the printing – his assistants had all been conscripted. Colenso was to close the 'Extracts from the Blue Books' at the end of 1880. It contained 855 pages of close analysis, a magnificent historiographical monument to Bishopstowe's intervention in imperial politics.

'A vast grave-yard'

This public intervention, however, hid private grief. Amongst the British dead at Isandlwana was Colonel Anthony Durnford, friend of the bishop and lover of his daughter Frances. She was to mourn him for the rest of her life. The circumstances of his death were particularly bitter because Durnford's superiors let him carry the blame for the disaster. It was said that instead of falling back on the British camp at Isandlwana he had impulsively ridden out and provoked the Zulu charge, leaving the British force spread too wide to defend its position effectively.

For Frances it was the final injustice suffered by her knight-at-arms. The defeat at Isandlwana was the consequence of the arrogance and incompetence of Lord Chelmsford and his staff. They had failed to set up the strong defensive position which was absolutely essential to counter a mass charge by the Zulu. They had then, in an iniquitous attempt at a cover-up, shifted the blame onto the heroic Colonel Durnford. This abuse of Durnford's memory could in some ways be compared to the way her father was treated: their nobility and their efforts for the truth brought to nothing by inadequate men pursuing violent ends and using deceitful policies to cover their own failings. In her grief and anger, the causes of Colonel Durnford and Bishopstowe began to merge in a campaign against all those in authority, the civil and the military powers, who used their positions to blind and mislead the public so as to protect their own cowardice and misdemeanours.

Natal, for Frances, had become a 'vast grave-yard'. Personally devastated, she gathered the mementoes of her love affair with Durnford, her paintings and manuscripts, and her father's 'Extracts from the Blue Books', and left for England in October 1879. She travelled with her brother Frank. He was also in great distress. His engagement to Sophie Frankland, daughter of the famous chemist, Sir Edward Frankland, was being threatened by the strain of separation. Frank left Natal in an attempt to save the relationship; Frances to escape the nightmare of Natal through art, her paintbox and her writing.

On the boat she turned to the 'Extracts' and began to write a history of what had happened in Natal since the Langalibalele affair from the Bishopstowe point of view. Once in England she made contact with the Durnford family: his father, the General, and his wife at Southsea, and Anthony's brother, Edward Durnford, of St Albans. Together they planned to write the memorial they felt was deserved by the man they loved – a book which would show not only how the war had come about, but also the manner in which it had been so wickedly suggested that Anthony Durnford was responsible for the defeat at Isandlwana.

Edward Durnford added a history of the campaign to her chapters on the causes of the conflict, and *The History of the Zulu War and Its Origin* was published in 1880. They both then edited Durnford's letters home and published them as *A Soldier's Life and Work in South Africa*.

Frances also published *My Chief and I*, a semi-fictional account of Durnford's attempt in 1875 to rehabilitate the Ngwe by using them on an expedition to destroy the passes over the Drakensberg.[5] To do this she assumed the authorial persona of a young man, Atherton Wylde, living an aimless existence in Durban until a meeting with Durnford gave his life meaning and a moral objective. In this way Frances was able to express her love and admiration for her 'chief' without going beyond the bounds of convention.

Frances was determined to lead an independent life in England – but she was hampered by lack of funds and the capacity to earn them. Her wealthy uncle Charles Bunyon strongly disapproved when she tried to borrow money from him against a proposed advance from her publisher. Her position wasn't made easier by the fact that her brother Robert had already drawn on Bunyon for financial assistance. Frank too had sought his influence for the job he needed to persuade Sir Edward Frankland that he had the means to marry his daughter. But Frances did have friends to draw on from her school days at Winnington Hall. Dora Livesey, now married and wealthy, sponsored the publication of the books. Frances wrote to John Ruskin of her plans to enrol at the Slade College of Art and asked him to bring the Colonial Office's attention to Bishopstowe's pamphlets. Her close friend in London was Georgie Burne-Jones, and Frances stayed with the Burne-Jones family at 'The Grange' in West Kensington before renting a cottage nearby.[6]

But now, just when she had escaped Natal, its restrictions and the pall cast over the colony by war and the death of her lover, Frances's physical strength collapsed. She was sent to Rome with friends for the winter of 1880 but in the summer of 1881 her doctor confirmed that she was suffering from consumption. It had affected the upper half of her right lung, and she was advised not to spend another winter in England.

Her restlessness and profound unhappiness intensified with the realisation that she might not have long to live. The numbers of those she saw as her enemies increased and, always outspoken with decided opinions, she became increasingly difficult even to her friends. She lashed out at those around her, at the narrowness and middle-class complacency of her relatives, the Bunyons in particular. They failed to understand her, then gossiped and reported their exaggerated fears back to Bishopstowe where they caused unnecessary distress. And all the while the continued injustice to the memory of her lover and to the wronged people of Zululand cast a deepening shadow over life itself :

> I don't know why we mortals should always think a continued life in this
> world of pain and sorrow a 'brighter prospect' than a new life in a 'better
> world'. We all *call* it a better world, but we do not seem to think it so. I sup-
> pose this curious love of life is implanted in us just because without it, none
> of would stay down here at all; we should all be helping everyone dear to us
> out of it as fast as possible.[7]

But she also answered this pessimism with work, work for 'the cause'. Wider
publicity had to be given to Bishopstowe's view of South African affairs. This
was not perhaps done in the way of which the bishop or her sisters approved, and
she believed that her family at Bishopstowe did not wholly support her publishing ventures. She chose to interpret this as a desire to publish the 'Extracts'
themselves. It is more likely that her father, mother and sisters feared the emotional intensity of her responses. Although Frances imbued her relationship with
Durnford with ideas of chivalry, selfless love, commitment to duty, and the sacrifice demanded by love which went beyond convention, her family were well
aware of what convention demanded. They must have feared scandal, not only
for Frances herself, but also because it might impair their pursuit of justice for
the Zulu.

There was also something about Colonel Durnford of which Frances was ignorant. In August 1877 her chivalrous knight had in the strictest confidence written Sir Theophilus Shepstone a letter in which he expressed his regret that circumstances had hitherto made personal communication impossible. Now that
the annexation of Zululand seemed a 'State necessity', however, he wished to
place himself at Shepstone's service.

> On the annexation of Zululand, I should hope for the post of Resident, and
> for this I am prepared to give up the Military Service of the Crown, if
> required.
> Many causes influence me in making this offer, but perhaps to you I need
> only say, that I am ready to devote my life to the Work for which I now pro-
> pose myself.[8]

Shepstone accepted the offer of support but did say that he doubted whether
Durnford had the patience needed for 'Zulu diplomacy'.[9]

There is no evidence that Frances ever knew that her lover, a man she
believed possessed a moral integrity matched only by that of her father and her

other hero, General Gordon, had fraternised with the enemy in this way. But we do know that Frank and Harriette discovered that Durnford was not to be trusted.[10] It is a monument to the loyalty between the Colenso children, a misplaced loyalty some would say, that they seem never to have told Frances, and supported her to the end in her struggle to vindicate 'our Colonel'.

The king in Cape Town

For the Colensos there seemed to be no ending to the outrage begun by the invasion. During the time between the Battle of Ulundi in July 1879 and the capture of the king in August, they waited anxiously for news. But they were deliberately excluded from official sources of information and were largely dependent on accounts in the press. They were furious at the way the public was being fed with what they knew were demonstrable untruths about the warlike and barbarous king and 'the spirit rampant here just now: Every accusation in it against the King is false'.[11] They feared, with reason, that someone would solve the problem posed by the king's future by assassinating him, and his capture was thus both a relief and a tragedy. Harriette found one of the two Zulu at Bishopstowe in tears at the news that their king was detained, and both

> quite overcome, 'only', they say, 'it was still worse when it was said that they were bringing him down here. Now we know at last that he is dead' – and dead to them he is if these wicked men are to have their own way – our only comfort concerning him is in remembering that he is capable of feeling (as he said two years ago ...) 'And if we have done no wrong, it will not be so hard to die.'[12]

Harriette's string of letters to Chesson at this time are breathless with anger and anxiety. There was talk of Cetshwayo being sent to Robben Island: 'Please, please, protest with all your strength against the King's being sent there ...'[13] For Harriette the war, and the way it was brought about, could not now just be forgotten as the newspapers and the politicians desired:

> Over indeed! while the King, who, if the war was unjust and unnecessary, is assuredly a most innocent and injured man, is a prisoner, cut off from all friends, all help, without being allowed to speak a word in his own defence.
> It is like a hideous nightmare to us, and I only wish that we would make all our friends as miserable about it as we are.[14]

More had to be done. We must be ready, the bishop said, 'with our battery as soon as Parliament meets'.[15] As a vehicle to publicise his research on the invasion Colenso purchased, translated, edited and annotated the journal of a trader who spent the war in Zululand. Chesson and Frank Colenso saw it through the press. Using sympathetic military officers, the bishop made contact with the Zulu king, now in exile in Cape Town, sending him a telegram: 'Sobantu greets Cetshwayo, he is grieved for him, and does not forget him.' The king replied: 'Cetshwayo thanks Sobantu for his message and is glad to learn he does not forget him. Hopes Sobantu will speak well for him.'[16]

Letters as assegais

Across Natal's border, in Zululand, supporters of the king – the Usuthu – had been deliberating on his future. As a result, early in February 1880 two men arrived at Bishopstowe. Mgwazeni of the Zungu was uncle to the king, and Mfunzi of the Mpungose was a trusted royal messenger before the invasion and well known at Bishopstowe. They said they had been sent by some of the most important members of the old Zulu kingdom: Ndabuko, full brother to the king; his brothers Ziwedu, Sitheku and Shingana; the prime minister, Mnyamana; and some of the other great men of the nation.[17] They had been ordered to report that members of the king's family were being ill-treated by the appointed chief Zibhebhu, and asked the bishop for his advice on this. They also wanted Colenso to send some medicine to the king. Thirdly, they carried with them a Blue Book – the presentation copy of British Parliamentary Paper C1137, Shepstone's *The Report on the Expedition to Instal Cetewayo King of the Zulus*. It had been taken from Ulundi when the British attacked the royal homestead, but dropped in the flight. The *abantwana* had organised a search and it was found in the grass, only slightly damaged. Could Colenso tell them, they asked, which of the stipulations the king was alleged to have contravened?

While the messengers were visiting the officials in Pietermaritzburg, Colenso prepared a summary of the charges that had been made against the king and used to justify the invasion. Mfunzi and Mgwazeni rejected them, and in the process gave Bishopstowe detailed information on the king and the politics and history of the kingdom. They left with official instructions to make all such complaints in future to the British Resident in Zululand, Melmoth Osborn. But they left behind at Bishopstowe a Zulu interpretation of the invasion of their country. For Bishopstowe its implications were clear: Cetshwayo's reign had been unjustifiably and cruelly cut short by the British as the result of an underhand campaign of vilification led by Sir Bartle Frere and Sir Theophilus Shepstone.

In April 1880 came the news that the Liberals had achieved a great electoral victory in Britain. Colenso felt that the Conservatives' disgraceful policy in South Africa was a factor in their defeat. It renewed his confidence: perhaps 'we were all mistaken in supposing that the English People were drugged and dead to their old principles of truth and justice. The heart of England, I trust, is still beating rightly ...' Now at last a new departure could be made.

The Usuthu then played their part. As the sun was setting on 24 May a party of some 200 men appeared over the hills at Bishopstowe. They were led by Ndabuko, who represented his brother's young son Dinuzulu, and Shingana. These princes were supported by some of the leading men in Zululand, members of Zibhebhu's Mandlakazi branch of the Zulu house; Ndabankulu kaLukwazi, chief of the Ntombela; and Mahubulwana, the chief of the Qulusi.

It was a quite unprecedented event, the physical presence in Natal of many of the Zulu kingdom's leaders. It was a journey taken only after great consideration. Shingana described the action as a jump over a precipice with no idea what they would find at the bottom. They had come, they said, to petition Government House in the cause of the Zulu king. The official response was immediate and predictable. They were again ordered to leave Natal and return to Zululand and make their statement to the British Resident.

Before they left, however, the Usuthu delegation visited Bishopstowe. Here they talked at length with the bishop and Harriette Colenso about recent Zulu history and Zulu politics. In response to the Colensos' questioning they gave evidence which repudiated in detail the charges made against the king before the war. And they went further than this – they asserted that far from his being a hated oppressor, it was widely recognised that Cetshwayo had been a benevolent ruler. One only had to consider the men present at Bishopstowe – they were sons of Mpande. The previous Zulu kings had got rid of their fathers' children whereas 'on his accession, Cetshwayo introduced an excellent practice, by allowing all his brothers to marry, and sharing with them his father's property, nothing like which has been done by any former Zulu king ...'[18]

Here then was direct testimony in support of the conclusions that the Colensos had reached independently. Here was evidence from the Zulu themselves in support of the call for justice for the Zulu king. Their presence at Bishopstowe gave the lie to the accusation that the Colensos were negrophiles in search of publicity, who in their misguided attempts at philanthropy imposed their views on the natives. Here was evidence of the Zulu voice – and of the official attempts to silence it.

In an article published in *Macmillan's Magazine*, based on information from her sister, Frances Colenso wrote an article on the progress of the royal brothers

Photo 20. Harriette Colenso and her father in Grahamstown in 1881. Looking back from the next century at this photograph, Alice Werner was to write that it depicted 'the Bishop and his daughter seated side by side – she habited in the fashion of the seventies, no longer "early Victorian" enough to have acquired charm in these days: bonnet with modest ostrich-feathers, and long satin ribbons, and so forth. Those who knew her in later days only will recognise the familiar face in its younger stage, not yet carved and modelled by the often bitter and cruel experience (which yet did not embitter) of the years.' The image of the stern instructor and compliant pupil was belied by Harriette's Zulu name, Udlwedlwe, her father's staff and guide.

around the house at Bishopstowe. Its object was to introduce the Zulu leaders to a wider public and point to their 'courtesy' and their 'good behaviour'. Ndabuko was 'a very dignified and rather silent personage' but Shingana they found 'irrepressible', 'a lively individual, with plenty to say for himself'. Without being patronising, Frances managed to communicate something not just of the fascination that the Colensos' house had for the royal visitors, but the humour of the visit as well. The leaders of the deputation, 'very great men ... in both senses of the word', explored a double-storey house for the first time in their lives, listened carefully to the stories behind the prints on the walls, and moved with great apprehension about the creaking upstairs loft, full of admiration at the speed with which the Colenso girls moved up and down staircases which for them was 'a very solemn undertaking, involving long pauses at every step'.[19]

But there was work to do as well. Harriette listened with deep concentration to their statements, translating and transcribing them for printing in the 'Extracts'. This was her first meeting with the brothers of the king, Ndabuko and Shingana. It was an important occasion. It was the beginning not only of a political alliance, but a personal friendship which was to change their lives and, despite the immensity of the forces ranged against it, was to continue until their deaths.

In November 1880 Harriette travelled with her father to the Cape. They stayed first in Grahamstown where they were photographed together. Harriette is dressed in the fashion of the time – in the years to come she and Agnes preferred styles which were better suited, they felt, to the practical demands made on them by their missionary work. The photographs depict a very definite relation between father and daughter: the bishop is the instructor, and points to the book he is holding while looking at the audience for approval; the pupil concentrates on the book whose pages reveal the truth through the instructor's mediation. It is an image of a relationship which Harriette herself would have confirmed. But we should remember that their roles had already been inverted by those who knew them – her Zulu name was Udlwedlwe – her father's guide and support.

At Cape Town they visited the exiled king and were allowed an unsupervised interview. They had no need, of course, for an interpreter. Harriette Colenso had never met the king, but 24 years before, in the Zulu kingdom, the bishop had visited him at the huge Emangweni *ikhanda* situated in the widening valley of the Mhlatuze as it approached the sea, with the young prince surrounded by his chiefs and advisers, as 'fierce, wild creatures as I have ever seen'.[20] The contrast could not have been more stark. Now they met in the cramped spaces formed by makeshift partitions in the military quarters of the Castle at Cape Town. On the first occasion Ngidi and Colenso had debated at some length on which conventions to follow and who should initiate the formal greeting, the Zulu prince or the English bishop. This time the king 'rose to welcome us, and clasped the Bishop's hand as if he could not let it go'.[21]

Family news, the fighting in Zululand, the Usuthu deputation, were discussed in detail. The king's appearance and demeanour confirmed for father and daughter that they were right in their conclusion that he was a man of stature who had been deeply wronged. It was incumbent on them, in the unique position in which they had been placed, to do what they could to rectify this. The first practical step that the Colensos felt should be taken was that he should petition to be allowed to visit England and make his case there. They had no doubt of his capacity to advance his cause before the highest authorities, and they would make sure he was assisted by the philanthropic lobby. They set up a secret network which allowed communication to take place between the king in detention in Cape Town, the Usuthu leaders in northern Zululand, the Colenso family at Bishopstowe, and the offices of the APS in London. From here information could be passed to potential sympathisers in England and the liberal press. He was encouraged to continue to dictate letters to people of note, drawing attention to his predicament and the injustice with which he had been treated by the British. The king agreed: as he said, letters were 'now his only assegais'.[22]

Real assegais

But real assegais were now doing their work in Zululand. Ndabuko and Shingana, joined by Mnyamana, appeared as instructed before the British Resident to make their complaints against their appointed chiefs, Zibhebhu and Hamu. Melmoth Osborn, Shepstone's friend and confidant, had only one answer – the terms of the settlement had to be obeyed, the rule of the royal house was over, its members had no authority to protest to anyone but the chiefs the British had appointed over them.

It was an inadequate answer to what was becoming an increasingly dangerous situation, and gave the appointed chiefs more confidence in their bids for power and property. John Dunn began to demand the payment of a hut tax, and appointed his own district magistrates. Hamu and Zibhebhu imposed further fines on the Usuthu on the ground that they had defied their authority. The violence spread, and the royalist and anti-royalist factions began to define themselves more clearly. Mnyamana kaNgqengelele of the Buthelezi had been Cetshwayo's first minister. A formidable man of great intelligence, he was a power in the north-eastern corner of Zululand where, in alliance with Cetshwayo's most committed supporters, the Qulusi, he had to protect the Usuthu from the violence of Hamu's Ngenetsheni on the one hand, and pressure from Zibhebhu in the east on the other. Zibhebhu, Hamu and Dunn headed the anti-royalist forces. Dunn had once been the Zulu king's friend and ally, and had been established by him as a Zulu chief on the coast in the southern part of the kingdom, from where he had built up an extensive trading network along the coast, which included supplying labour to Natal and running guns into Zululand. He was close to Zibhebhu, whose own chiefdom lay across the important trade route from Zululand to the north.

The Usuthu began to look increasingly to Mnyamana and Ndabuko for leadership. By the end of 1881 order in Zululand was breaking down. Zibhebhu tried to drive the Usuthu from the northern districts; Hamu and the Qulusi were involved in major conflicts. There were scenes of very severe violence and bloodletting, Hamu's attack on the Qulusi being particularly brutal with about one thousand casualties.

In the two years since the end of the British invasion there had been more violence and death in Zululand than during the whole of Cetshwayo's reign, and the

64

casualties were mounting. The officials followed Osborn in characterising it as violence caused by a royalist faction unable to accept its fall from power. For Bishopstowe it was the continuation of the theme which had typified the region's history for the past decade: the determination of certain officials to ignore or falsify African opinion as they pursued a policy which they believed would serve Natal's interests. The terrible violence in the north and Dunn's oppressive activities in the south of Zululand were, the Colensos had come to believe, the consequences of the official determination to quash all expressions of loyalty to the king. And this had the effect of further encouraging the appointed chiefs to loot the resources of the royal house and its supporters.

A block of territory

In an attempt to gain influence and impose order the British Resident, Melmoth Osborn, with Shepstone's support, tried to get Britain to increase the authority at his disposal. Britain, however, had no intention of allowing this. Zulu assegais in 1879 and Boer rifles in 1881 had destroyed the plan for a united South Africa, and confederation had been replaced by withdrawal and retrenchment. August 1881 saw the retrocession of the Transvaal to the Boers. This did, however, draw more attention to Zululand, which was becoming a disturbed and unstable territory lying between a now independent Boer republic and the sea. Although the information reaching London as to who was responsible was contradictory, there could be no doubt that the level of violence in Zululand was beginning to threaten British interests. If the situation in Zululand broke down altogether, it was possible that Boers would get involved. And if this happened, then Zululand's major function in the imperial scheme, to form a block of territory between the Transvaal and the sea, would be impaired.

The Colonial Office began to think of developing a fresh policy towards Zululand. There was still to be no annexation – but the idea was mooted that it might be possible for the king to be restored to his kingdom in order to stabilise the south-eastern seaboard by re-establishing an African-ruled territory between the Transvaal and the sea. 'Cetshwayo promises to be ... most amenable to advice, if returned, and I do not doubt that through him we could exercise the strongest influence without incurring the responsibilities of Annexation, and we should have a chance of re-establishing a self-supporting Zulu nation.'[23] This would not only be an economical solution but would also salve the Liberal conscience about the way in which the king had been treated. Hopefully it would also bring an end to the harassment of the Colonial Office and the government by the APS and Bishopstowe.

In 1882 Sir Henry Bulwer was appointed Governor of Natal. It was an appointment received with cautious optimism by Bishopstowe. During his previous term of office in Natal, Bulwer had shown some resistance when Sir Bartle Frere and Sir Theophilus Shepstone were driving the colony towards war with the Zulu, and an independent spirit of this kind was desperately needed now. From the start, however, Bulwer was opposed to the idea that the king should be returned, and very antagonistic towards the role being played in African affairs by Bishopstowe. Consequently, Bulwer's position was a very difficult one. By disapproving of the king's return he also disagreed with the direction that London's policy towards Zululand was taking – a policy he would have to implement.

Shepstone also opposed any policy based on the return of the king. Yet all the information available to him suggested that this was being considered seriously by the British government and, always the pragmatist, Shepstone now sought ways to turn any plans for restoration to his advantage. In a long memorandum drafted early in 1882, Sir Theophilus wrote of the trepidation he felt when looking at the situation of Africans in Natal. They had been deeply disturbed by the shifts and reversals in policy which characterised recent South African history. But at the heart of their distress was another even more serious factor – the shortage of land. 'The truth is that the colony contains a larger native population than, with its white inhabitants, it can conveniently or safely under present conditions of native life accommodate.' And the answer to the problem was clear: 'The Zulu country is the only direction in which relief can be looked for ...'

This 1882 memorandum was yet another version of that solution which Shepstone had been recommending for forty years – the need to assume authority over more territory in order to settle Natal's excess African population. But now he proposed that the return of the king be exploited in order to do this: 'In the event of Cetywayo being allowed to return to Zululand, a contingency which, under the circumstances I cannot help regarding as probable, another opportunity will present itself of doing something to avoid the agrarian difficulty that is so rapidly coming to a head among the natives in Natal; and as far as I can see it will be the last.' Cetshwayo should be allowed, Shepstone asserted, to have authority over only a part of the country, and he should be excluded from the territory between the Thukela and the Mhlatuze rivers – the territory in fact over which Dunn and Hlubi had been appointed in 1879. This could be

set apart for the redundant population of Natal, or more correctly, for that portion of the population of Zululand that has from time to time been driven by the past barbarism of Zulu rule to seek protection in Natal, the dangerous tension that now exists in this Colony would at once be relieved, and a source of safety be created that no other measure could accomplish.[24]

Shepstone therefore felt that the return of the king had to be used to get the southern portion of the country at least, under the control of Natal. The Usuthu and Bishopstowe were making plans in just the opposite direction – to persuade the British government to return the king to a Zululand united under his authority.

As far as the new Governor, Sir Henry Bulwer, was concerned, he had no choice but to go with the retired SNA. Soon after he arrived in Natal, Bulwer was confronted with just the situation to which he objected so strongly in London. In April 1882 a huge Usuthu deputation arrived in Pietermaritzburg. Of the 2000 Zulu present, Colenso calculated that some 646 were men of note. They were led by men who were either themselves, or represented, the most important groupings in Zululand. At their head were Ndabuko, Shingana and Dabulamanzi. Bulwer refused to receive them. This, he felt, was not a deputation from the Zulu people but a demonstration by a faction within Zululand, the consequence of massive interference by the agitators at Bishopstowe.

Colenso of course disagreed, and wrote at length about the deputation to prove it. He had resumed printing his comments on reports in the newspapers and the Blue Books. He called it 'The Digest on Zulu Affairs' and it was to total well over 800 pages before it closed. Sunday after Sunday the bishop, his wife and their daughters posted their letters to London with Magema Fuze's printed slips analysing official documents and newspaper accounts. They spoke of massive injustice, of the refusal of officials to listen to the genuine attempts at expression on the part of the Zulu people, of their commitment to their king, and their oppression at the hands of the appointed chiefs.

Although the bishop was fully aware of the hostility of officials towards Bishopstowe, he was not aware of its extent and the exact opinions of the various individuals in government who decided on policy. In fact, information had been passed to him that Sir Theophilus Shepstone had come round to agree that the king should be allowed to return, and that it was Bulwer who was most hostile to the idea. Increasingly Colenso was coming to accept that, if the king were ever to see Zululand again, then some accommodation had to be reached with Shepstone. No one had more knowledge and experience of Shepstone's skill at manoeuvring behind the scenes than Colenso. And yet by 1882 the bishop had begun to think that, if the cost of Cetshwayo's restoration was the recognition that Shepstone still had a role to play in African affairs, it was price that had to be paid.

Cetshwayo did not disagree with this – he too knew where power lay. Without

Shepstone's support little could be achieved. 'Sir T. Shepstone knows all the affairs of my country,' the exiled king wrote to Lord Kimberley, Secretary of State for the Colonies, 'and I want him to receive my people always when they visit Natal, and to convey any word from the Government to them. I want Sir T. Shepstone to take care of me, and to be my mouth in Natal.'[25]

It was Harriette Colenso who found it hard to adopt this pragmatic approach to the realities of power and influence. Events were rapidly changing her attitudes, and she found it more and more difficult to find sympathisers for her criticisms of policy towards the Zulu. British action in South Africa over the past few years had been totally unacceptable, and the Liberal government did not seem to be able to change this. She was furious at what was happening – the subjugation of African independence throughout South Africa by the power which posed as their protector.

> And what Tribe among all the South African Natives may we count on as a friend. The best and the bravest, the Basuto, the Zulus, the Bapedi owe their most terrible losses – in the two latter cases their destruction as ~~nations~~ peoples not to the Boers, but to the English, who first professed to be their friends – the Swazies, and the Pondos still remain, but the former are (we have always heard) more friendly to the Dutch than to the English, and there are the Natal natives – with the memory of Langalibalele's wrongs, and his people scattered through the other tribes.[26]

She could not agree with her father that support for the Shepstones would assist the cause. His 'natural instinct is always to hope, to suppose – that each man means to do the right thing, until each in turn has unequivocally proved the opposite'.[27] History, however, had shown 'that any scheme involving Shepstones ... *means virtual annexation*'. She knew that if the Shepstones were involved, 'they would overreach somehow or other, I should think it a great pity – a great mistake – for any white man to try to rearrange "Zulu domestic affairs."'

But Harriette was young and a woman. In spite of her disagreement she still felt she had to apologise to Chesson, albeit ironically, for differing with two men whom she so admired and respected. 'I wouldn't write such treason to any one else, but I know that you are as prudent and as anxious not to lose the "Shepstone influence" (while it is useful) as the Bishop is. But they are dreadfully cunning, and will play false somehow, and it makes my heart sick to see them at work.'[28] And she was right. They were cunning and they were playing false.

In September 1882 Cetshwayo left Cape Town for his visit to England. The politics surrounding the journey were intense. One of the Shepstone sons was appointed guardian and interpreter to the king. Bishopstowe's clandestine links with the king were exposed by the over-enthusiastic activities of one of its less scrupulous supporters, Lady Florence Dixie. In spite of the publicity and the attentions of well-wishers, and being mobbed in the street, and an audience with Queen Victoria, the king and his Zulu advisers were well aware that it was the negotiations at the Colonial Office upon which their future depended.

Here Bulwer and Shepstone succeeded in putting Cetshwayo at a great disadvantage. Bulwer confronted the problem of having to make recommendations on a policy of which he fundamentally disapproved by procrastinating. With the king about to arrive in England, Bulwer's recommendations for his future had still to be received. The Colonial Office demanded that Bulwer telegraph his 'main conclusions'. He did so: if the king must return, then it could only be to a part of the country; a portion had to be excluded from his rule for those Zulu who objected to his return; this portion should be in the south of the country and placed 'under Natal Government rule'.

The British government rejected this. There was to be no suggestion of annexation – not even of the creation of a protectorate. However, it did agree that a part of Zululand should be alienated from Cetshwayo's authority and reserved for those who objected to his rule. A Resident Commissioner should be appointed but he would have no authority, and the British should be under no obligation to defend the area or its residents. The territory would be called the Zulu Native Reserve.

Cetshwayo was therefore informed by the Secretary of State that he would be returned, but not to all of his old kingdom. Cetshwayo was unable to extract from Lord Kimberley any information on the extent of the territory from which he was to be excluded – because Kimberley himself did not yet know. Bulwer was given discretionary powers to make the final arrangements.

In London the king tried to protest but he was in no position to bargain. He left for Cape Town on 1 September and on the journey crossed with Bulwer's dispatch detailing his and Zululand's future. It may well have been written by Theophilus Shepstone himself. The basic problem in Zululand since the end of the war, it asserted, had been the absence of an 'adequate paramount authority'. It was impossible that this authority should be restored to the king. The Zulu military system was only 'dormant' and should be compared to 'a time-piece, which has been suffered to run down' and 'needs only to be touched by the master hand of whoever is recognised by the Zulu people as the supreme chief, and straightway the whole machinery is put in motion'. In addition it was obvious that there could be no peace in Zululand if the chief who led the opposition to the Usuthu was now brought under the king's jurisdiction – and it was therefore recommended that Zibhebhu be awarded an independent territory.

The Colonial Office saw quite clearly what had happened: the local officials were determined to turn the restoration to Natal's advantage. But London could do little about this beyond keeping imperial responsibilities to the minimum. Thus Her Majesty's Government, which had begun with a plan to restore the exiled Zulu king to his kingdom, now was forced to approve of the division of the country into three: Zibhebhu's territory in the north, Cetshwayo's territory in the centre, and the Zulu Native Reserve in the south with Melmoth Osborn, on Sir Theophilus's recommendation, as Resident.

No one was satisfied: not the Colonial Office, whose plan to create a stable African ally on the south-eastern African coast had been brought to nothing by the foot-dragging of a colonial Governor under the influence of a local faction; not that local faction who, failing to bring all Zululand under its power and influence, were now refused even sufficient authority to bring the Reserve territory under proper control; and especially not the Zulu king and his allies and sympathisers, who had so nearly succeeded in restoring him to his country, only to have their plans subverted at the last moment. But, for the majority of the Zulu people, it was more than a matter of who should rule whom and how – it was a matter of life and death. And for many thousands it was to be death.

When the final conditions were put to the Zulu king in Cape Town in December 1882 he claimed that they were not the same as those put to him in London. He would sign because he had to get back to his country, but he would do so under protest, 'merely … to put my name on the paper'.[29]

Sir Theophilus travelled to Zululand to arrange the king's restoration. At Entonjaneni, on the hills above the Mahlabathini plain where the new Ulundi was to be built, he announced the conditions of the king's return to the assembled Zulu at the end of January 1883. It was now approaching half a century since he had interpreted at the huge tense meetings on the eastern frontier of the Cape. This was to be his last such meeting, and arguably it was the most disastrous.

The Usuthu had organised their protest well. The king sat back as his orators first welcomed Somtsewu of the House of Sonzica and then berated him.

> We thank you, son of Sonzica, for bringing back the 'Bone' of Senzangakhona. But even to-day in bringing him back you are killing him, killing him, I say, as you have done all along! Did you not set him up at first and then destroy him for nothing? Did you not take him to his Mother (the Queen) and bring him back, and now do you cut off the land, saying 'it is for those dissatisfied'? Where are they?[30]

The meeting was long, it was humiliating for Shepstone, and when it broke up he rode immediately for Natal to write the dispatch which would successfully cover up the fact that he had played a major role in instituting a system in Zululand against which there had been a massive and well-planned protest. The Usuthu messengers also made their way into Natal, to give their version to Colenso, for printing and dispatch to London. But it was now too late. Events had proceeded too far, creating antagonisms too deep, for there to be a peaceful resolution. There had already been too many losses, too great a desire for retribution and revenge. As the king was to put it, 'I did not land on a dry place. I landed in the mud.'[31]

The destruction of the Zulu kingdom

After the installation Cetshwayo moved onto the Mahlabathini plain to rebuild Ulundi. Cetshwayo relayed his protests to his supporters outside the kingdom but they could do nothing for him. In the north, conflict broke out almost immediately between the Usuthu and the people of Hamu and Zibhebhu. In March 1883 the 5000 armed Usuthu under Ndabuko and Tshanibezwe, son of Mnyamana of the Buthelezi, launched an attack on Zibhebhu. The Mandlakazi caught them on the march, unprepared and in the open, at Msebe. As the Usuthu tried to retreat and gain cover, Mandlakazi horsemen broke up the force with accurate rifle fire, allowing the Mandlakazi foot soldiers to get in amongst the fleeing Usuthu, killing thousands as they tried to reach their homes. It is said that more were killed than in any other battle in Zulu history. Mnyamana lost ten sons. Ndabuko lost five, and the memory of his defeat at Msebe was to haunt him for the rest of his life.

At Bishopstowe they listened in horror as the reports of this violence reached Natal. It seemed that events had proved Harriette Colenso to be correct. Again the bishop had been outwitted. This was confirmed when the 1882 Blue Books arrived in Natal. While Colenso had been led to believe that there was no collusion between Theophilus Shepstone and the Governor, it now became clear they were working closely together. John Shepstone, the acting SNA, was using gossip collected by his informers to implicate the bishop and his daughter not only in the politics but in the violence which was taking place in Zululand. If the voice from Bishopstowe could not be silenced, then it had to be discredited.

Colenso protested. It was intolerable. The office of the SNA was determined to keep control of all sources of information on what was happening in Zululand. News with an anti-Usuthu bias moved freely across the border to be published in Natal newspapers as statements of fact. Usuthu messengers to Bishopstowe were stopped by the border police. But while these differences over just what was happening were contested in the Blue Books and the newspapers in London and Natal, in Zululand itself they were fought out on the hillsides and in the valleys, causing disruption and death as the homesteads of northern Zululand were burnt, and families and stock fled from raid and counter-raid.

By the beginning of 1883 Harriette Colenso was carrying more and more responsibility. Her father, the most energetic of men, was now beginning to feel the need for rest 'before I go hence'. For the first time he began to express his unwillingness to confront the Natal newspapers' abuse of their 'monomaniac' prelate. And the news of the deaths in Zululand, mounting now into thousands, demanded even greater efforts from the few who knew that those who were being held responsible were in fact the victims.

But in the winter of 1883 Colenso's efforts to publicise the truth he discerned in these dreadful events were brought to an end. In June he returned ill from Durban and it was soon clear that this was not just a passing fever. On the night of 19 June he became delirious, talking intermittently about getting the packets of documents ready for the English mail. He lost consciousness and the next morning he died. The Usuthu believed that his death had been brought about by their enemies. His family believed that overwork and deep disappointment had broken his heart.

At Ulundi the king had gathered around him the great men of the nation. Many of them were old – the contemporaries of Cetshwayo's father, the most senior men in the land with whom the king had ruled the independent kingdom. At dawn on the morning of 21 July, when Ulundi was just stirring, Zibhebhu's army, with white traders and mercenaries in support, attacked the royal homestead. The slaughter was terrible. Many were caught inside the homestead itself while others were hunted down as they attempted to escape across the Mfolozi valley. Women, children and the aged, unable to protect themselves, formed a large part of the casualties – and with them the *izikhulu* of the nation – the great men whom the British in the invasion of 1879 had failed to destroy. It is the slaughter here, the second Battle of Ulundi of July 1883, which marks the end of the independent Zulu kingdom.

Zibhebhu and Hamu rampaged through the country north of the Mhlatuze River. The local people retreated into the forest and the caves. It was a terrible situation. War in 1879 and the disturbances in the years that followed had severely disrupted the agricultural cycle, causing disease and starvation. Now the armies of Zibhebhu's Mandlakazi and Hamu's Ngenetsheni were burning and looting what was left. It was thought that the king must have been killed. Shepstone, now in England, was asked for his expert opinion and informed the

Colonial Office that he was sure Cetshwayo kaMpande was dead.

He was in fact alive. As the Mandlakazi entered Ulundi the king had escaped through an exit at the back of the homestead. But his horse was brought down by rough ground and he was overtaken and stabbed in the thigh. His personal authority saved him when he challenged his assailants and asked how they dared stab him, their king. Accompanied by some of his wives and attendants, he found a hiding place near the White Mfolozi River as Zibhebhu and Hamu burnt northern Zululand black.

CHAPTER 5

UKUSHONA: THE DEATHS OF FATHERS

Gone

W ithin six months the dream of a new Zululand headed by an African
king restored to his inheritance by an English queen was in ruins.
Thousands of Usuthu had died at the hands of Zibhebhu, his Zulu
allies, and white mercenaries. The only comfort for those at Bishopstowe was
that the man who had led them and given shape and meaning to their lives was
not alive to receive the news of the horror at Ulundi on 21 July 1883.

His death had been unexpected – a fever and some pain while in Durban, and
a sudden slipping away at Bishopstowe. We can still feel Sarah Frances Colenso's
shock in the letter she wrote soon afterwards to her friend Mrs Lyell: the composure of her writing has gone as she wanders from fragments of memories to
grief, hurrying to finish her letter in time for the mail.

> I cannot regret having religiously adhered to my own law to myself, i.e. never
> to thwart him or worry him, my Lord and Master, my superior in every way,
> morally and intellectually. O, what will become of me now. He is gone – but
> that is a matter of very little consequence. I am anxious about Harry, his
> 'Walking Stick' as her Zulu name indicates, i.e. the rod held in his right hand,
> partly to guide, partly to support his steps, because naturally her power in the
> way of colloquial Zulu was beyond her Father's after all these years.
>
> It is almost beyond the power of any woman's brain and heart to bear the
> strain of painful anxiety about the Zulu King and his Kingdom ... O, England,
> what iniquities are perpetrated in thy name, and how can teachings of
> Englishmen pass for Gospel to the black man. Lying and treachery are already
> stamped with the Hallmark of England in Zululand.[1]

It was the women of Bishopstowe upon whom the responsibility fell for continuing his work. The sons helped but they had other priorities: their own fam-

ilies, futures and careers. Frank had trained as a barrister and was now married to Sophie Frankland, and she was pregnant with their first child. With the help of his uncle Charles Bunyon he had obtained a post as actuary with Norwich Union Life. He was close to Frances and worked as hard as he could to assist her with her books and on Zulu matters. Robert was never deeply involved in Bishop-stowe politics and rather different from his brother and sisters, looking on the world with an ironic frankness that they at times found rather brutal. He lived in Beach Grove in Durban, building his medical practice. His wife Emily had just given birth to Eric, the first Colenso grandchild.

Bishop Colenso felt that he had already provided for his sons by giving them a university education. He stated this in his will, which left the bulk of the estate to his wife and daughters. However, he had not been able to leave them particularly secure or prosperous. But it was his moral legacy which was their overwhelming concern, for, when he died, his work had been left unfinished. They had to complete it. His life had to end, not in isolation and defeat, but as they had experienced it – a life victorious in its faith, courage and humanity. They had to work actively in their father's cause – the cause of justice for all the people of Natal and Zululand, and most urgently the cause on whose side he had been fighting – that of the Zulu king, his family and their supporters, the Usuthu.

Three sisters

Frances had returned to South Africa in 1881 to escape the English winter and was 34 years of age when her father died. With tuberculosis steadily taking its toll, she had been wintering in Durban when the news arrived that her father was ill. She followed her doctor brother up to Pietermaritzburg:

> I suddenly felt that I *must* go by the next train, so I packed a few things as
> soon as the dawn came, and started by the early train. And when I reached
> home I was already two hours too late. I sometimes think I shall never get
> beyond that – never reach the comprehension of our great loss – that I was too
> late is in itself too much sorrow to be borne.[2]

She expressed the feelings of all three daughters at the loss of the man who 'has been the very light of our existence for years. Harrie and Agnes ... have never had any interest in life apart from him, while to me my Father has been the great comfort of my life and for whose sake I have cared to live.' In her grief she thought of the last time she had seen him – just a momentary greeting as their trains passed between Durban and Pietermaritzburg. The last time they

75

had in fact spoken was a few weeks before that when her father was leaving Bishopstowe for Durban. She now returned to that occasion repeatedly in her mind: the carriage was drawn up outside the house; Agnes had checked and double-checked every buckle and strap of the harness; the rest of the family were on the veranda waiting to say their farewells, holding his brushed coat and his hat. In saying goodbye, Colenso suggested to Frances that she consider writing a sequel to her book on the Zulu War. This farewell remark now became a charge, an injunction from her father that she use her particular talents to continue their work.[3]

Most of Frances's books were collaborative projects. She actively sought the assistance of men and clearly found great comfort in the correspondence, company and friendship this provided. She also made great demands on them, insisting on her independence and autonomy while at the same time demanding from them hard work and frank appraisal. Increasingly, as she became weaker and the time left to her became shorter, so her demands became more urgent, even obsessive.

F.W. Chesson, secretary of the APS, was sympathetic and supportive, and tried to guide and control her when he felt that her efforts were misdirected. Frances's letter to him after her father's death became a eulogy: 'He died for the cause in which he has fought for so long, the cause of justice, truth and mercy, for truly it was the overwork in that cause, and the sorrow of seeing it still trampled underfoot that wore away his strength, and took him from us ...' And she apologised for both the length of the letter and the intimacy it assumed:

> I did not mean to write all that when I began – indeed I think I forgot to whom I was writing, but it does not matter, for you valued him greatly, and I have but to remember your kind face, and sympathetic manner to feel that I need not fear to have written too much. Still I have a real separate purpose in writing to you. Now, more than ever, I must set myself to do that work of which he spoke to me.

Most important in her mind was Colonel Edward Durnford, brother of Anthony, the man with whom she had collaborated on *The History of the Zulu War*, who she was sure would be eager to help with this new book.[4] Chesson consulted with Edward Durnford. They sought to calm her and persuade her to conserve her energy by writing not a book but an article summarising the events since the restoration. But before she had even received his letter her manuscript was already over 200 pages long. Durnford then told her that he lacked both the material and the physical resources to carry out what she required of him.

Frances was unsympathetic and put Durnford's reluctance down to opposition from his materialistic wife, and pursued the writing of *The Ruin of Zululand* with even more energy.

Protected by her family from physical stress and overwork, she was able to concentrate on her research and writing. At Bishopstowe she had her own room, carefully decorated, and an interleading one which served as her studio, coming downstairs to a fireplace when the weather was cold. When this was insufficient she moved to her brother's house in warmer Durban. She was more productive at Bishopstowe, however, because there Harriette was always on hand to be drawn on for details of Zulu history and politics.

But it was never easy. Confined and often isolated, Frances Colenso thought of the future and brooded on the past. The fact that the military hierarchy still asserted that Durnford was responsible for the disaster at Isandlwana was a source of the most bitter anger. She continued to search for evidence to prove that Durnford had received an order, not to defend the camp, but to leave it and join in an attack on what was thought to be a Zulu force. By 1882 she had come to believe that such an order had in fact been found on Durnford's body but was removed. And the man who had done this, she became convinced, was an officer amongst the Natal volunteers, Theophilus Shepstone's eldest son, Offy. He was also the husband of Frances's dearest friend in Natal, Helen Shepstone. Frances began to track down possible witnesses, hoping that she might confront Offy Shepstone with the evidence and force him to confess.

Despite her illness Frances lived her life at a high emotional pitch. She wrote that she despaired of achieving happiness, at least in this world where the unjust prospered and the good went under. She was extremely sensitive to what she saw as criticism, particularly of her father. At the same time she was outspoken in her own criticisms of others and her correspondence is marked with many misunderstandings, some reconciliations, and frequent furious argument. She was unable to reach the physical springs of her longing and unhappiness and could only express them as romantic ideals of the most ethereal kind. And as the 1880s progressed, so her behaviour appeared to become increasingly extreme, testing even her closest friends and those who loved her.

Harriette Colenso was the one to whom everyone turned: strong, determined to protect the memory of her father and protest against injustice, but her anger feeding commitment to the cause rather than public outbursts, and always a calming influence. She was 36 when her father died. Not only did she have to ensure that 'the cause of peace and justice in Zululand would not be abandoned in England'[5] but she also had to handle the estate, and the enormously difficult problems of the future of the congregations and the property of the Church of

England in South Africa, her excommunicated father's church. She had to guard the interests of the people who had remained with her father, first in his ecclesiastical and then in his political disputes; she had to protect the legally vulnerable pieces of property still attached to the Church of England; she had to try to find a replacement for her father as bishop in the Church of England in the face of the opposition from Bishop Gray's Church of the Province of South Africa. Frances watched with pride at the way Harriette got her way amongst the members of the church council, with Sir Theophilus at their head, while at the same time preventing 'these men from finding out that she is managing them, if they once *do* find it out they will become restive'.[6]

And always just behind Harriette, giving support, working in the house and the school, looking after the animals, nursing the sick, was Agnes, her youngest sister, now 28 years old, tall, shy and unconventional. An attempt to give her the opportunity to broaden her experience just before the war ('I rather wish her to be a little weaned from her devotion to the native children – but I only mean that she should be interested in other matters – and not have any cold water thrown upon her pitiful [?] care for them')[7] by sending her to England had not been a success. Her brother Frank had tried to introduce her to the world in which he and his fiancée, Sophie Frankland, were living in London, but Agnes left England more convinced than ever that life was best spent at Bishopstowe.

Frances voiced her distress; Harriette was reserved but vocal when the situation demanded it; Agnes was withdrawn, silent, uncompromising, and already almost a recluse. She and Harriette had now taken to wearing the same, rather severe, style of dress, suitable for the hard work of teaching and nursing. Frances, for whom pretty clothes were one of life's pleasures, disapproved. Agnes lived with and through her eldest sister, who in her letters addressed Agnes as 'my child'.

Brothers and sisters

When her father died, Harriette Colenso called a Zulu messenger, working at Bishopstowe as a gardener to escape the attentions of spies and informers, to see the bishop's body before leaving with a letter for the king:

> This worn-out-garment of his which he has left with us, we have allowed Melakhanya to see, as your eyes, because you too are Sobantu's son.
> Listen well to these words of mine, my brother, knowing that I come from him, that it is not I, but Sobantu who speaks to you saying 'Do not despair my son'.

And I too, although I am now weak through the flesh, seeing our great support removed, am nevertheless strengthened at heart, seeing how very many are the hands which wish to help his orphans, and his work too, for love of him.[8]

The king replied to his 'sister' saying:

You see, the death of my Father Mpande was a great distress to me. But there remained to me Sobantu who gave me courage, and spoke for me, setting things straight. And now it is Mpande's death over again. I pray you send word to all your friends that I may be supported. And report also our distress for the loss (*ukushona* lit. setting, used also of the sun) of our Father, to our friends, both at Durban, and at the Cape, and in London, to the whole company of them: and tell them that our hope is in them that they will stand up for the Zulu People as Sobantu did.[9]

The use of these terms of close kinship was not required by Zulu custom although they resonate with it. By using the word brother, and accepting the king's acknowledgement of her as sister, Harriette extended her family now to include the Zulu royal house, united in their fathers. Harriette was, however, well aware of the prejudices of colonial society. She told Chesson, if he used these letters, to 'prune judiciously': if it got about that she and the king referred to each other as brother and sister, Natal 'would abuse us both outrageously, and many in England too would sneer at the idea of such a relationship'.[10]

Harriette also showed a remarkable broadminded, commonsensical tolerance. One of the first problems she had to confront after her father's death was the political capital the newspapers made of the rituals carried out to strengthen Usuthu soldiers, including the cruel mutilation of a live bull. She pointed out that the use of body parts, including human ones, for ritual purposes in times of war was widespread and that it had been carried out by Britain's African allies during the 1879 war without shrieks of protest. She had good evidence that the king's enemies in the civil war had recently used the body of a woman for the same purpose. But Harriette was not a mere apologist for such practices, and it is the way in which she encouraged tolerance towards tradition without surrendering her abhorrence for cruelty which is striking.

I have no doubt that great capital against the King will be made out of that horrid ceremony of cutting off the bull's leg before killing it. It is a horrid practice, and it is one which the Bishop had set his heart on getting rid of ...

Cetshwayo could not be expected to do away with a custom so universally practised with the country in its present state, though it is one of the things which I shall beg him to consider if ever a time of peace comes.[11]

She was equal to Frances in her anger towards the way in which the Zulu kingdom had been treated. At the same time she was always calmer and more practical. Thus, after the terrible losses of the winter of 1883, Harriette felt that what was wanted was not another book but the means to take direct action – 'the sinews of war'. 'What', she asked,

> did it profit us to expose Sir Bartle Frere, to overpower Sir Henry Bulwer (in the matter of the King's return) since these underlings were left – the Shepstone Family – to weave again their wicked webs. The exposure of that case [assaults initiated by John Shepstone in the Reserve] would do far more to help Papa's work, than publishing the rest of the digest in any form. The real difficulty has hitherto been the want of the sinews of war – and now it would almost seem that they are forthcoming. And I would rather spend them in this way *for his work*, than *for his honour*, in reprinting his struggles and vic- tories all along.[12]

There is an implicit critique here of Frances with her plans for books and her male recruits. Indeed, as we shall see, there were significant differences between these sisters, founded in their very different personalities. It is not easy to dis- cover – the hands that pruned their huge correspondence did what they could to leave a record of children united in the love and the cause of their father. But it is there nonetheless. Beyond her differences with Frances, Harriette's call for sinews of war also suggests other feelings that she could not state openly: that the Usuthu should retaliate against their Zulu enemies and establish themselves in the country by force. The defeat at Ulundi and the flight of the king were being depicted as proof of Usuthu weakness. In order to retain its own credibil- ity Bishopstowe, and its allies like the APS, needed an Usuthu victory – a mil- itary one.

Strict control

But it was not forthcoming. Although it was widely believed that he had been killed, the king, after his escape from Ulundi during the Mandlakazi attack of July 1883, had holed up near the White Mfolozi River. He had been found at his hiding place on the White Mfolozi by his brothers Shingana and Mahanana, and

Sigananda, the son of Zwekufa, and Luhungu, both of the Shezi. They had brought a horse with them and moved the king at night safely out of the Mfolozi valley past KwaMagwaza to the Nkandla forest.

On the evening of 6 August a messenger arrived at Bishopstowe. He had been sent by the king's brothers to Harriette Colenso to say that he had survived the massacre and that he asked for an inquiry to be held into the attack that had been made upon him. On 7 August Harriette telegraphed the APS with this information. Privately the king asked Harriette for advice. She sent the messenger back to Zululand with bandages, medicine and the message

> that it seemed to me that there were two courses before him, either to come into the Reserve, in which case his head might be safe, but his Kingdom would be gone, as he would be counted a Refugee, or to remain in his own Territory, and call his people to him as their king. They scouted the notion of his being a 'Refugee' but I cruelly said that I really did not know, if the Zulus were going to run away and leave him in this fashion, it *would* perhaps be the wisest course for him to take.[13]

Meanwhile, although she did not yet know it, Harriette's own messengers had made contact with the king. Although Melakhanya had taken the news of Colenso's death to the king, Zulu custom required that formal notification be made as well. On 24 June 1883 Harriette had written a letter to the Governor, full of barbs, seeking permission to do this.

> Dear Sir Henry Bulwer,
> My Father has told you that he has never sent any Natal native as an emissary to Zululand, but now it is right that we should send messengers of our own to tell the Zulu King of what is his loss as well as ours. We should like that these messengers (two in number) should have a safe-conduct from you, to prevent their receiving let or hindrance on their sorrowful journey while they are beyond Cetshwayo's protection, and I write now to ask you for such safe-conduct in my Mother's name.[14]

To carry this out she selected a man of standing at Bishopstowe, Thwayisa Mabaso, with his own attendant, and Mubi Nondenisa, teacher and printer at Bishopstowe. Mubi had his writing case with him and kept a diary of the journey.[15] As formal emissaries they moved slowly through Natal, accepting hospitality and condolences at the homesteads they passed. On 25 July they had reached the border with Zululand and were preparing to cross the Thukela River at Middledrift when they heard rumours that there had been a terrible battle in Zululand – in fact, news of the attack on Ulundi by Zibhebhu and the Mandlakazi four days previously.

The Bishopstowe messengers were urged by their friends not to cross into Zululand, but they decided that they had to get more definite information. On 27 July they forded the Thukela. In Zululand they saw 'the passing and repassing of people lamenting with one another', and it was clear that there had been a terrible catastrophe. Some said that the great men of the land, men with huge followings and responsibilities, had been killed; some that the king's small son was dead, stabbed with his mother; others that, after urging his closest followers to save themselves, the king himself had been killed.

On 28 July they heard that Shingana kaMpande was nearby. He had been to Bishopstowe twice with the Usuthu deputations, and the Bishopstowe party went in search of him. They moved along the edge of the Nkandla forest, traditional place of refuge on the northern rim of the Thukela valley, to the homestead of Zwekufa of the Cube or Shezi. Here they found Shingana and another son of Mpande, Mahanana, and the king's oldest son, the 13-year-old Dinuzulu, who had survived the flight from Ulundi. The king, they said, was alive, although this fact had to remain a secret for as long as possible.

The Nkandla was a formidable part of Zululand. Thick forest covered steep and broken terrain out of which numerous streams had cut deeply incised valleys. It had been a stronghold and final place of refuge many times in Zulu history. Paths, complete with blind alleys and dead ends to confuse assailants, were hacked through the forest to connect the homestead in which the king was to live with the caves near the waterfall in the Mome Gorge. The remains of this place of refuge were still to be seen in 1970.

The report that the king was in the area had begun to spread and people were gathering in the vicinity, waiting for news. The messengers from Bishopstowe were told that the king was nearby, that he recognised their courage in coming into Zululand at such a time, that he wanted to see them, and they should prepare for an interview. They were given food and a place to stay. In the early hours of 6 August[16] they were taken to the hut in which Cetshwayo was resting, and delivered first their condolences and then their message. 'The King replied "No! I died on the day when Sobantu died, I felt then that it was all over with me."'[17] It was the same response that they had received from so many Zulu. The death of Bishop Colenso was an indication that the forces that opposed the Zulu royal house were in the ascendancy. Mubi sent for his writing case and put Harriette Colenso's questions on recent events in Zululand to the king.

The Zulu Native Reserve (henceforth the Reserve) where the king had taken refuge existed, unhappily, from 1883 to 1887. It was Natal's bridgehead into Zululand, the price the office of the SNA had exacted for agreeing to the king's return. John Wesley Shepstone, Sir Theophilus's brother, had been appointed to prepare the way for the arrival of its first Resident Commissioner, Melmoth Osborn, Sir Theophilus's best friend. 'Misjan' (Mister John) had no conception that, in the eyes of his superiors in London, the Reserve was 'independent native territory'. For him it was 'ours', and those Zulu living there who went to visit the king without his permission were 'intriguers'. Travelling with an entourage of indunas and African policemen from Natal encouraged by the promise of land and chieftainships, Misjan announced that the territory was now under British rule and ordered that all those who did not accept this should cross the Mhlatuze into the king's territory. Most of the inhabitants of the Reserve had no wish either to leave their ancestral lands or give up their loyalty to the king. John Shepstone insisted that they do one or the other. Those Zulu in the Reserve discovered going to visit the Zulu king were arbitrarily 'fined', and were warned that continued residence in the Reserve would be treated as rebellion.

Sir Henry Bulwer soon found that, despite the confident predictions of Zulu loyalty from his advisers, John Shepstone was unable to produce evidence for substantial support for the new administration. Bulwer was deeply concerned, but kept his nerve and the policy that he had been persuaded by Theophilus Shepstone to adopt. Steadily he applied the pressure on London and, notch by notch, permission was granted for the exercise of added authority: the British Resident should not merely represent but exercise 'paramount authority', and the collection of hut tax was authorised 'as an outward and visible sign' of that authority.[18] And when Cetshwayo sought refuge in the Nkandla, London was again asked for troops, 'chiefly for moral support to give assurance in the Reserve of our intentions and for defence. If active measures are necessary I should principally rely on the natives if expense which would be moderate was authorised.'[19]

It was a deadly policy: divide and rule taken to its extreme. First, rigid opposing political categories – loyal or rebel – had been imposed upon the people. It was then demanded that everyone give public expression to these divisions. Those who had sided with the colonial authorities were then ordered to demonstrate their loyalty by driving from the territory those who had not. To encourage them in this they were given 'moral support' by parading British troops, which had the effect of provoking the conflict. It was a policy that ensured that the price of subordinating the people of the Reserve, in money and in lives, was paid by the people of Zululand themselves and not by the British. This was the effect of the policy we see emerging in the Reserve in the first year of its existence and which was to be further developed in the years to come throughout Zululand, with disastrous consequences for its people.

On 20 September 1883 British troops crossed into the Reserve. As he set foot on Zulu soil the commanding officer was bitten by a snake – and died. London was nervous for other reasons. 'We are drifting into another Zulu War. With this attitude of Cetshwayo on the one side and the authorities on the other we may find ourselves committed at any moment to a course of action for which we are physically unequal.'[20] But there was to be no war. The idea that the king might use the Nkandla as a base to rebuild his power by attacking those who supported the officials was never a reality. Mubi Nondenisa and Thwayisa Mabaso's visit was to a ruler whose material power had been stripped from him, whose followers had been decimated, and who lived in daily fear of attack, but who was still hoping against hope that the British government, with which he had so recently negotiated in London, and with whose Queen he had just had an audience, would intervene on his behalf.

By October 1883 it was clear to Cetshwayo that the British troops who had entered the Reserve had not come from the Queen with orders to restore him. Moreover, it was becoming increasingly difficult to sustain himself in health and safety on the forest margins of the Nkandla. On 17 October Cetshwayo placed himself under the protection of the British Resident, Melmoth Osborn, at Eshowe. And it was here in February 1884, after months of accusations by Osborn that he was planning rebellion and warfare from the safety of the precincts of the Residency, that Cetshwayo kaMpande died.

On 12 February his brothers made the statement that the dead Zulu king had lodged the succession to the Zulu throne in his son, Dinuzulu.

II

THE
INHERITANCE

CHAPTER 6

A HARD PRICE
(APRIL–AUGUST 1884)

The threat of extinction

The loose cohesion of the Zulu kingdom had gone, destroyed by military invasion, greed, private ambition and political manipulation. The consequence was social, economic and physical devastation. But there are degrees even of devastation and the Zulu were well aware that, terrible as the situation was, it could get worse – even to the point of their extinction. Television has shown us something of what this means, at least in its contemporary manifestations: the burnt villages with the old waiting to die and the children staggering with hunger; babies clasped to dry breasts; heavily armed young men, looting and scavenging, their weapons turned against anyone they do not know.

The politics of pre-industrial societies cannot be understood without an awareness of how rapidly disorder can turn into disaster. For these were societies without forms of easily stored wealth, foodstuffs and resources, or the means to transfer them to secure areas in times of social stress. The homesteads, which were spread throughout the land, were not in normal times sited with security from a surprise attack in mind. When violence forced the inhabitants to retreat to the mountains and forests, the cost to their well-being was immense. Livestock demanded daily access to grazing, and water and health depended on proper sanitation, drainage, fresh water, secure food stores and proper preparation, all of which were difficult to maintain while in hiding. Above all, there was the steady and demanding rhythm of the seasons, the cycle of production, which meant that the land had to be prepared in the winter, planted with the spring rains, reaped in the summer and the grain stored in the homesteads for consumption through the year.

When the king died in February 1884 the continuity of these essential productive processes had been broken – in many parts of Zululand this had happened in every season since the British invasion at the beginning of 1879.

Something had to be done if the process of devastation was not to continue and intensify. It was a situation in which social survival demanded hard decisions and immediate action, with short-term objectives in mind. It is the lack of awareness of the overwhelming urgency of this situation which makes most contemporary commentaries and subsequent historical analysis on Zulu loyalty and rebelliousness at this time, so vacuous. As the 1880s progressed, not only were Zulu material independence and political sovereignty reduced, but with them the luxury of political choice – denied by the uncompromising demands of survival.

Once the threads of social order and material continuity had been broken they had to be rapidly rewoven: political leaders had to act quickly and find the means, the allies and the strategy to restore continuity and stop the situation from degenerating into further anarchy. It was this necessity for immediate action which drove the situation on, making neutrality impossible. The British government's reluctance to come to any decision on the political future of Zululand, its attempts to remain uncommitted until further developments suggested a suitable policy, might have worked towards keeping a parliamentary majority in the House of Commons, but it had near-genocidal consequences for the Zulu.

From his hideout in the Nkandla the king had protested: 'The planting season is advancing, and unless my people can cultivate with some sense of security, the additional misery of starvation will be added to their troubles.'[1] Reports from travellers in Zululand spoke of consequences of prolonged stays in the forests and caves, of malnutrition, enteritis, bronchial disease and scabies. They saw burnt homesteads with food stores deliberately fouled with faeces and dead animals. Raiding of resources regardless of ownership had now begun in the north. And violence of this kind breeds its own fury, which finds expression in more violence. Zibhebhu taunted the Usuthu by reminding them of their dead brothers and sons. Moreover, he had seized many women and children from the Usuthu, and this was 'a lasting stain on their character to let their women live in adultery and fornication with Zibhebhu and his headmen'.[2] Some Usuthu were heard saying they would kill until they were killed or there was no one left to kill.

Mfanawendlela, chief of the Zungu, one of the 13 chiefs cursed by Wolseley's gift of a territory in 1879, was exposed as an enemy of the Usuthu when his homesteads in central Zululand escaped attack by Zibhebhu. In September 1883 he appealed for effective intervention:

> I ask them to send an English Chief into the country to exercise supreme rule; unless this is done, there will be still greater troubles for the people to endure. Among other things famine will result next year, as because of the

unsettled state of the people, they cannot put in crops, and the planting season is now set in ... if something more be not done soon, we shall think we are
abandoned by the Government, and the stronger will attack the weaker.[3]

His turn came in December when he was killed by the Usuthu on the banks of
the Black Mfolozi River. Zibhebhu sent a message to Mnyamana: '"Father, I
intend visiting you to lament the death of Mfanawendlela."' Mnyamana sent, in
reply, the following: '"Son, come, and you will find me outside the gate."'[4]

But this was the fighting side of Mnyamana, the Buthelezi chief, after four
years of violence and death, caught between the Ngenetsheni of Hamu and the
Mandlakazi of Zibhebhu. He knew better than anyone that some way had to be
found to bring the violence to an end, and was in secret communication with
Osborn in Eshowe on how to do this. Mnyamana asked that an authoritative
instruction come from the British for a cease-fire, which would allow the people
to leave the caves and forests as a first step towards negotiations. This had to be
done. There was a lawlessness abroad that even he with his tremendous authority could not control. 'If the Government ... does not take action soon all the
people will be destroyed and it is not in my power to prevent this as the people
no longer regard my orders or advice.'[5] Bulwer sent to London a range of suggestions on how the British might use their influence to bring this anarchy to an
end – including the extension of a protectorate over Zululand beyond the
Reserve. But the Secretary of State, Lord Derby, gave succinct expression to his
feelings on this: 'I don't want more niggers.'[6]

This was the view from London; the view from the Ngome, the Nkandla,
Eshowe or Pietermaritzburg was that intervention of some kind was absolutely
imperative. After the king's death, it seemed as if Mnyamana might be willing
to agree to use his influence amongst the Zulu in favour of an extension of the
borders of the Reserve to the north. On 28 March two of Osborn's confidential
messengers were sent to Mnyamana, to urge him not to carry out a threatened
Usuthu attack on Zibhebhu. They reached Mnyamana at the Ngome, consulted
with him, and were returning to Eshowe when they were set upon and killed.[7]

It was an event unprecedented in Zulu history. The violation of a messenger's
immunity was a serious breach of custom. In the shocked aftermath of this murder all contact between the British authorities and Mnyamana came to an end –
and with it the initiative to extend British authority. The inference has to be that
they had seen or heard something at the Ngome which had to be kept secret –
and the evidence strongly suggests that they had come across another political
initiative, one which had to be hidden from the colonial servants of the Queen
whose friendship with the Zulu king had served the Zulu people so badly. They

had, one must suspect, discovered that white men, *amaBhunu* – Boers – were in consultation with Zulu leaders about the future of the country.

AmaBhunu

Some months before, at the end of August or early September 1883, while the Zulu king was still in the Nkandla, he was visited by a group of *amaBhunu*. They travelled in great secrecy to the hiding place in the forest above Mome Gorge and were believed to have made an offer to the king which they said would give him the chance to halt the cycle of violence in the country and allow him to regain his position as effective ruler of the Zulu by getting rid of Zibhebhu.

No one with any knowledge of Zululand or Zulu history had to be told of the significance of such a consultation, or the drift of their discussions. From the time the Boers had arrived in Zululand in 1837, their history and that of the Zulu had been intimately and often violently intermixed. It was not only that the Boers had inflicted a defeat on the Zulu army at Blood River; it was also that the Boers, as they often reminded the Zulu, had in 1840 helped place Mpande, the father of Cetshwayo, on the Zulu throne, where he remained until his death in 1872. In 1877 the Boers of the Transvaal had lost their independence when Shepstone annexed the Republic. In 1880–1 they had risen up against the British, inflicted a serious defeat on the British military, and forced the Liberal government to negotiate a peace and restore their independence by the Pretoria Convention of August 1881. It was the terms of this Convention that lay behind much of the thinking which led to the decision to return Cetshwayo, for it was thought that he could assist in containing the Boers by establishing a solid block of Zulu territory between the now independent Transvaal and the sea. Instead, after the return of the king the situation had only deteriorated further. It was feared that the pattern already emerging on the Transvaal's western borders, where Boers had invaded Tswana territory and set up the 'Robber Republics' of Stellaland and Goshen, would be repeated in the east. This would not only threaten Natal's future interests, but also affect imperial strategy in south-east Africa generally. Even before the secret visit to the king there were rumours of Boer activity in Zululand, and the threat of Boer interference in Zululand was a potentially explosive issue of which all sides were aware.

But there are particular difficulties in moving beyond rumour and reconstructing the Boer movement into Zululand. From the beginning the participants, Boer and Zulu, wanted to obscure the historical record. We do, however, have one account of the visit to Nkandla, made near to the event before subsequent developments influenced the telling of the story.[8] It was told to Harriette

Colenso by the king's brother Shingana. He confirmed that such a visit had taken place. He did not know then who the men were: they might have been officials from the Transvaal, or they might have been private individuals. But they had told the king that 'they had sympathised greatly in his troubles, and offered to assist him, and clear out Zibhebhu for him'.

The king refused. Harriette was told that the reason for this was that it 'would be displeasing to the English'. Yet 'many of the Chiefs wished him to agree, and the Dutchmen quite begged him to do so, saying "It shall be our affair altogether, we will not make you responsible, we only wish to get you out of the difficulty and set you in your place again where the Queen put you." But still he refused.'

But the king had died in February 1884. His death was followed by upheaval and distress in the Reserve caused by attempts to collect the hut tax and the dispute between Osborn and the princes over where the king should be buried. The territory was consequently in uproar when, in the last week of March, a small party of Boers arrived in the Reserve making their way to the Nkandla asking for information on the whereabouts of Cetshwayo's son, Dinuzulu. They said that they had come to take him to the Transvaal, and would make the declaration of Dinuzulu's succession a reality. However, when they reached the Nkandla they discovered that the prince had already left. On the night of 3 April Dinuzulu, in great fear and distress at the confusion all around him, had been spirited out of the forest to the north towards the Ngome forest, where he was placed under the protection of Mnyamana kaNgqengelele of the Buthelezi. The Boers turned north in pursuit of the young Zulu prince.

Dinuzulu kaCetshwayo

Dinuzulu was now 14 years old.[9] His mother Nomvimbi had been captured at the battle of Ndondakusuka in 1856 when the prince Cetshwayo had overcome his rival to the throne, his brother Mbulazi. Her father, a commoner, had died in the battle and she became Cetshwayo's attendant. Cetshwayo was given permission to marry in 1867 and Nomvimbi became one of his wives in the next year. In December 1869 a boy, Marelana, was born. He was taken to Gqikazi, the homestead of his father's mother, Ngqumbazi, who died in 1871. The boy was seen by Mpande, his grandfather, before he died in 1872.

Cetshwayo had had other children but they died when they were very young. Cetshwayo, it was said, had had a dream about this in which he was told by Ndaba and Dingane that these deaths were the result of his ancestors' concern over the propensity of the Zulu royal family to kill one another in disputes for succession to the kingship. After this dream Cetshwayo gave Marelana the name

Dinuzulu, 'he who wearies the Zulu'.[10]

Dinuzulu's boyhood was spent during the closing years of the independent Zulu kingdom, and, although there was no formal ritual to mark his status as successor, he was present as Cetshwayo's only son at the major ceremonies. He was 10 years old when the British invaded the Zulu kingdom and terminated the rule of his father's house.

But, as we have seen, the post-war settlement did not reflect the realities of power in Zululand. The people around the boy were very much aware that those who had control of his person, and gained his confidence, could also make a claim on his inheritance. It was on his shoulders that the hopes of the Zulu royal house and its supporters rested, and a major factor in the outbreak of the civil war was the struggle over the guardianship of the boy.[11] He entered his teens in the care of his uncle Ndabuko and with violence all around him. Too many times in the opening years of the 1880s he was woken by warning shouts before being bundled to safety by his father's wives and their attendants. When Zibhebhu attacked Ulundi in July 1883 it was the chief Sitshitshili who left his own aged father Mnqandi behind to his death to make sure the 13-year-old boy got a horse on which to ride to safety.

Dinuzulu was taken to the Nkandla forest where his father was in hiding, and he was here, at Luhungu's homestead, when Cetshwayo died and his uncles placed on record their statement investing the succession in his son. And it was from here that he was taken on the night of 3 April to Mnyamana in the north. The move was secret and the details remain unclear; but the possible outcome was obvious to all who heard about it – 'the Boers' would assist 'the Zulus' to defeat their enemies, and recognise Dinuzulu as Cetshwayo's successor and place him on the Zulu throne – as they had done with his grandfather, Mpande. In return they would receive a grant of land. The ground rules were in place for the next stage of the tragedy.

Boers and Zulus

The immediate sequence of events which led to Dinuzulu's flight from the Nkandla to Mnyamana's care can be traced to a meeting at a store in the northern corner of Zulu territory, on the Pemvane River in February 1883.[12] A group of men had gathered here to discuss the situation in Zululand. Prominent amongst them was Coenraad Meyer, a border Boer of long standing and well known in the kingdom. His father had played a leading role in the installation of Dinuzulu's grandfather Mpande over forty years before, and Meyer himself had been a Transvaal emissary to the Zulu until 1874, and was an authority on

Zulu–Boer relations. Meyer had land and property, and was described as well-off but uneducated. He was known to the Zulu as Khuneladi. Also present was Rudolph Wilhelm.

The men were meeting as a result of the violence on the Transvaal–Zulu border and certain messages that had been received from the Usuthu. Meyer said that Cetshwayo had been in contact with him about the 'low Boers' who were settling in the area and meddling in Zulu affairs. If there was going to be interference in Zululand it had to be kept in the control of the more responsible of their Boer neighbours, 'influential Boers' – men of standing with experience in Zulu affairs.

But it was necessary that the political consequences of such an interference be properly considered, and it was suggested that another well-known borderer who 'had a great deal of influence with the Boers', Jacobus van Staden, be consulted. He was present at the next meeting on 22 February. By now the situation had changed as a result of the death of the king. It is likely that Van Staden had also made contact with political authorities in the Transvaal, men like the landdrost of Wakkerstroom, J.C. Krogh, and Lucas Meyer, who were in turn in contact with Piet Joubert, Acting President of the Transvaal Republic. Such links had to be kept secret. The Pretoria Convention prohibited any move by the Transvaal beyond her eastern border, and a delegation was in London at that very moment trying to renegotiate this. It was the men on the border who were trying to devise a way to become involved in Zululand, but they did so with a degree of political sophistication and timing which suggests that the initiative had support and advice at the highest level in the Transvaal.

Before direct intervention was undertaken some exploratory moves had to be made. It was decided that Wilhelm should travel to Natal and use his contacts there to canvass opinion on possible British responses. In particular he should contact the representative of the APS in Natal, William Grant, and sound him out. Wilhelm stopped first at Pietermaritzburg where he spoke with Natal's Attorney-General, Michael Gallwey, and then with Theophilus Shepstone. From them he gained the impression that Britain would not interfere. He then went on to Durban where at the end of March he approached William Grant, representative and correspondent of the APS. Wilhelm wrote to his Boer associates saying that he had gained the impression that the APS would not be a threat to their plans.

With the disappearance of Dinuzulu from the Nkandla at the beginning of April 1884, we enter a dark period of Zulu history. The messages to Bishopstowe were now infrequent, and Harriette Colenso turned her attention to church affairs and Frances to writing her account of recent Zulu history. The Usuthu were now negotiating another alliance, a difficult and most dangerous one. A bargain was about to be struck. In its fundamentals it was straightforward: one party wanted land, and the other wanted mounted gunmen. The proclamation of Dinuzulu as Zulu king would give the deal historical legitimacy. But because it was a dangerous bargain, with an underlying contradiction in the objectives of both sides and many possible pitfalls and unpredictable consequences, everything was done to cover their tracks – thus making it difficult for the historian to trace exactly who travelled where and when, and what they did there.

In addition to this problem of obscure and even fabricated historical sources, there are other difficulties. One is the categories used by contemporary observers and subsequent students of these events to describe the two parties involved – the 'Boers' and the 'Zulus' – concepts which in their conventional usage are just too crude to reflect accurately the social groupings at the time and to understand the events in which they were involved.

For example, the Boer movement of the 1880s into Zululand was never just a movement of Dutch-speaking farmers but was made up of men from a range of different backgrounds and social groupings. They represented various interests, and in time were to struggle increasingly amongst themselves for power, influence and control. Eventually a cohesive leadership did emerge, consisting mainly of Boers from the Transvaal; but to recognise that the Transvaal eventually gained control does not mean that we must accept the over-simplified caricature of a monolithic movement into Zululand implied by the easy label 'Boer'. For to do so makes it impossible to understand the specifics of these events, and especially the nature of the relationships between these men with the Zulu.[13]

The men who were said to have begun 'the Boer movement into Zululand', Meyer and Van Staden, were 'border' Boers. That is, they were defined in terms of their local identity and their associations with the people of this particular part of southern Africa – men from families who had traded, negotiated, supported and fought with the Zulu authorities for nearly half a century. They were 'uneducated' perhaps, but well informed, canny, with substantial local knowledge and contacts, influential, and wealthy in terms of the land they controlled, their herds and the African labour living on their land. They considered themselves to be responsible individuals, with a prior right to the resources of Zululand if there was going to be a scramble for them.

These border Boers, residents in the tense tract of land stretching to the northwest of the kingdom, can be distinguished from the Boers from the highveld who moved their sheep and cattle to graze during the winter. Louis Botha, who was to become South Africa's first Prime Minister, born in Greytown in Natal, now lived in the Free State, moving in the winter with the family flocks to take advantage of the winter grazing over the edge of the escarpment into Zululand. His first experience of public life was gained with the Boer movement into Zululand. Boers such as Louis Botha, men with land or the prospect of land, were therefore concerned about the activities of the 'low Boers', as they were described by Coenraad Meyer: these were landless, often younger men, horsetrading, running guns, stealing grain from the deserted Zulu homesteads, squatting on the lands vacated as the result of the civil war, searching for opportunities amongst the Zulu which they could exploit. And there were men considered to be lower than even these low Boers. These were the 'mean whites who with two or three pounds' worth of goods go trading as they call it. Lazy good-for-nothings, they settle down at some kraal or other, get a kafir wife, and become white niggers ... These fellows are the curse of the country ... the native becomes a prey to their specious schemes.'[14]

On the other hand there were the Transvaal officials, salaried, formally educated, and wealthy at least in land and labour holdings, keeping in the background because of the political situation, but determined to gain some control over and benefit from the activities in the borderlands. Grant, writing later, believed that the Transvaal officials as high as the Acting President, Piet Joubert, were trying to control the movement from a very early stage.

Wilhelm, the man who went to Natal to report on the possible political reaction to the movement into Zululand, was 'of German descent', a failed sugar plantation owner. The store where the meetings were first held was owned by men with English names, and suggests the attraction the situation had for the entrepreneur, the storekeeper and trader. And there were soon to be many more men in the region with no qualification to be Boers at all but hoping to be included in their number and get some pickings from it. Harriette Colenso copied into a notebook a letter from an eyewitness who detailed the differences in age, religion, morality, class, wealth, motive and nationality in the confusion of the 'Boer' camp. She drew her own conclusions: 'What the Zulus' friends have to understand is that the word "Boer" is again being used to a large extent as a red rag & blind, the object is to complete the destruction of the National party, that Natal may enjoy the spoil.'[15]

Equally, the 'Zulu' who struck the bargain were not representative of the Zulu people as a whole. Initially they were not even the Usuthu – they were leaders of a faction of the Usuthu – younger men of chiefly families living on the border. They had grown up on the western borders of Zululand, geographically exposed to trade and colonial life. They were experienced traders, rode and owned horses, could use firearms, and had close relations with the border Boers. They were also more headstrong, more willing to take risks than the conservative and wary Usuthu leadership. This faction of Usuthu who first made contact with the border Boers was led by Ndabankulu kaLukwazi, chief of the Ntombela, who had worked for a time for Melmoth Osborn, and Mehlokazulu kaSihayo of the Qungebe, whose pursuit of his father's wives into Natal had been a pretext for the invasion. Amongst their number was Maphelu kaMkhosana, whose father had been the king's closest adviser during his exile. Maphelu and his Usuthu allies, who included the Qulusi, lived and fought in the north-west corner of Zululand where it abutted on the Transvaal. From the time of the British invasion they had fought with the Ngenetsheni of Hamu, mounting raids from the huge caverns to be found in the mountains on the watershed of the Mfolozi and Mzinyathi, and the Phongolo rivers. It was a vicious and bloody conflict. Maphelu worked closely with whites who supplied him with horses, arms and ammunition, and his reputation was that of a murderous border ruffian.[16]

It is from Maphelu that we get an idea of the divisions within the Usuthu leadership on the initiative being taken by the Boers and certain Usuthu. Zulu opposition to an agreement with the Boers was led by the most senior and respected man of the kingdom, Mnyamana of the Buthelezi.[17] Once the word had come from Wilhelm in Natal that he felt that Grant and the APS would not be a threat to the movement, together with the news that the London Convention had been signed, Meyer and Van Staden entered Zululand and made their way to the Ngome to find Mnyamana. In the Buthelezi chief's hiding place they suggested to him that they be allowed to take Dinuzulu from Zululand into the Transvaal, raise a force of Boers, install Dinuzulu as his father's successor, and demand the submission of his enemies.

It was a dreadful situation for the Buthelezi chief. The *abantwana* were still in the south, in the Reserve, trying to get possession of the king's body. Mnyamana feared that if he did not act, then other less circumspect Usuthu would – without his discretion or concern for the consequences. Even now he realised that his formidable authority was waning. 'Everything has gone wrong. I know not what to do' was a translation of one message he sent. The desperate violence which survival made necessary was exacerbated by the desire of his people to avenge their losses of land, homes, crops, cattle, women and children. Under this pressure the Usuthu were fragmenting. And Mnyamana knew that the group of younger men like Ndabankulu and Mehlokazulu were in close contact with the Boers, and threatened to break away with unpredictable consequences. There was also fear amongst the Usuthu that if the Boer offer of assistance was refused, then elements amongst them might offer firepower to their enemies. Some action had to be taken. The British government might be able to let the situation drift, but for the Usuthu it was a drift towards extinction.

At the same time, of course, Mnyamana knew exactly what lay behind the Boer offer to install Dinuzulu and force the submission of his enemies – the desire for the land of the Zulu – and the great difficulties the Usuthu would have of ever controlling their demand for land once the Boers had become actively involved in the Zulu civil war.

Mnyamana prevaricated, trying desperately to find a way out. The possibility of regrouping the Usuthu in order to attack Zibhebhu again was being considered, but given the recent history of Usuthu defeats and the fact that many of the Usuthu supporters lived across the border in the Transvaal and required Boer permission to enter Zululand, this was a faint hope. Mnyamana informed the Boers that he could make no decision without the *abantwana*, the king's brothers, and this meant waiting until Cetshwayo had been buried and Dinuzulu's succession had been formally announced.

It was at just this moment – with Coenraad Meyer and Van Staden urging Mnyamana to act – that Osborn's messengers, who were trying to open negotiations with Mnyamana, were killed.[18] Consequently, just at the time when he had to face Meyer, Van Staden and their Usuthu supporters, Mnyamana found that he had been cut off from the outside world – and most significantly from the British officials trying to find another option. But Mnyamana still opposed the plan. In reply, 'The two Boers ... got on their feet, saying "We shall take him! Are we to go on talking from day to day, while you continually make difficulties? You will be the death of him [Dinuzulu], you wretched little cowards! as you have been the death of his father. If Zibhebhu's *impi* were now to appear would you not fly, and leave him?"'[19]

In the end, unable to find support amongst the Usuthu, and under protest, Mnyamana gave Dinuzulu up to the Boers and their Usuthu allies, sending with the prince his oldest and most trusted induna under orders to report all developments directly to him.

The crown prince

In the Reserve meanwhile, once they had learnt of developments in the north and that some Boers were searching for Dinuzulu, the *abantwana* agreed to bury the king at Dabulamanzi's homestead, not far away from Eshowe. However, Osborn insisted that the burial take place at Eshowe itself, but gave way after the king's widows attacked his house, roughed up a messenger, and threatened to seize the king's body and carry it off themselves. On 8 April it was placed in a packing case on a wagon, and in the evening moved off in the direction of Dabulamanzi's homestead, but then continued towards the Nkandla. Amidst rumours of an impending attack, and the arming of forces on both sides, the body was taken to Luhungu's homestead in the Nkandla and on 23 April the burial took place. The *abantwana* were now free to move north to Mnyamana and get on with the business of forging an alliance with the Boers.

Dinuzulu had been taken first to the farm of Coenraad Meyer, and then moved to the protection of Krogh, the landdrost of Wakkerstroom. Here a force of some 200 men was raised amongst the border Boers, calling themselves 'Dinuzulu's Volunteers'. The bare rumour of the gathering of a Boer force, as news passed from homestead to homestead in Zululand, was enough to break the stranglehold the Mandlakazi and Ngenetsheni had over the Usuthu.[20] As a Zulu–Boer alliance became a possibility in April 1884, so the Usuthu began to emerge from their hiding places and hideouts and make their way towards Mnyamana in the Ngome. In response the people of Zibhebhu and Hamu began to fall back towards the homesteads and strongholds of their chiefs.

At the end of April the armed force began to move from the Transvaal borderlands into Zululand. There were about 200 Boers accompanied by an Usuthu force, many of whom came from Transvaal territory north of the Phongolo which had been excised from Zululand by the 1879 settlement. They were led by Lucas Meyer, a Transvaal official, but whose participation was kept in the background at this stage. Once in Zululand the Boers drew up their wagons and formed a laager at Hluti, between the Hlobane and Ceza.

On 1 May letters were sent to Zibhebhu and Hamu informing them that the Boers were going to install Dinuzulu as king, as they had done with Mpande in 1840, and instructing them to lay down their arms and enter negotiations with the Zulu prince and his allies.[21] Many Usuthu supported this move. But they could not get the agreement of the most influential man in the land, Mnyamana kaNgqengelele of the Buthelezi. He warned of any precipitate alliance with the Boers. It was an extremely dangerous move and the Zulu risked losing their land. There was still, Mnyamana believed, the possibility of organising an independent Usuthu attack on their enemies. Furthermore, no long-term decision could be made while the country was so disturbed. Dinuzulu had fled to the Boers for his own safety in the face of attacks from the authorities in the Reserve. It was no good the Boers waving letters at them and stating that they had widespread support for their actions, including that of Harriette Colenso, or demanding that agreements be signed. 'What is the use of that? I cannot read. Sirs! you have got me in a corner, and are throttling me!'[22] The Usuthu needed trustworthy literate advisers, he continued, before taking far-reaching decisions. Proper procedures should be followed. Cetshwayo's last wishes should be formally announced and the response of the British, who had restored him to his territory, should be received and considered.

But Mnyamana could not carry the bulk of the Usuthu with him, nor could he get the support of the *abantwana* who had just reached the northern districts after the king's burial. Even his chief induna, Hemulana of the Sibiya, argued against him, pointing out that although the Usuthu were numerically superior to the Mandlakazi, they had been seriously weakened physically by their long sojourn in the caves and by starvation. And, he asked, how could Mnyamana argue that they would lose their land? As they were at the moment, eking out an existence in caves and forests, they were no longer in possession of the land.[23]

On 21 May, seated on a packing case on a wagon under the flag which was said to have been flown at his grandfather's installation, Dinuzulu was anointed with oil and declared king of the Zulu by the Boers. A number of documents were drawn up, the essential features of which were to proclaim Dinuzulu's succession to the Zulu throne, while the Boers bound themselves to bring 'peace, law, and order' to the country. In return for this they would receive from the Zulu a tract of territory as large as they 'may consider necessary for establishing an independent self-government'. All Zulu would be excluded from this territory, and all relations with other powers would have to be conducted with the Boers' consent.[24]

On the same day there had appeared in *The Natal Witness* in Pietermaritzburg a report of Gladstone's statement in the House of Commons in London on 19 May, in which the Prime Minister declared that after much consideration his government had decided not to intervene militarily outside the Reserve. And thus the Grand Old Man gave the men forging the Boer–Usuthu alliance the confidence to continue.

It also brought an end to Zibhebhu's aggressive dominance in Zululand. Ndabuko, always silent and morose, arranged the details of the attack on the Mandlakazi. The nightmare of Msebe, when Zibhebhu had used surprise, horses and guns to sow panic and then slaughter the fleeing, traditionally armed Usuthu, was not going to be repeated. Ndabuko wanted horses and guns, and men who knew how to use them, on his own side this time.

By early June the Usuthu–Boer force was on Zibhebhu's western borders. He pulled his people eastwards so they could fight with their backs to the Lubombo. At Etshaneni, where the Mkhuze River flows through a narrow poort in the Lubombo range, the 3000 Mandlakazi prepared to face an Usuthu force double the size. Rifles, fired over the heads of the attacking Usuthu by the 200 Boers in support, broke the Mandlakazi defence, and Zibhebhu's men were slaughtered, by the Usuthu this time, on the banks of the Mkhuze. In the hours before sunset the Usuthu and the Boers plundered the Mandlakazi cattle, and captured the women and children who had been hidden on the Lubombo.

Zibhebhu escaped to the Reserve where he made an impassioned complaint against the English who had set him up, encouraged him in his opposition to the Usuthu, and then failed to support him.[25] He formally requested assistance to return to his territory and save what he could of his property, and rescue the women and children left behind. Osborn and Bulwer backed this appeal from a loyal chief 'who has proved himself to possess as chivalrous and gallant a nature as the history of the Zulu nation can show'.[26] But, in reply, the British government admonished Zibhebhu and its own officials who encouraged him to think that he was an 'ally from whom aid, to which he is justly entitled, has been withheld'. There was not, and never had been, any formal basis for such a view.

> The condition of Zululand since 1879 has been one of chronic war, carried on by barbarous reprisals, and opinion is hopelessly divided as to the degree of blame to be assigned to each chief or party. Zibhebhu at least has often acted on his own responsibility; his recent defeat was the consequence of his victory of 1883, and his ambitious projects of the present year, and Her Majesty's Government has never entered into any engagement to aid or defend him. All, therefore, that he is entitled to is an asylum in the Reserve ...[27]

But the British Resident in Zululand, Melmoth Osborn, did not agree. The refusal of the British authorities to intervene in some way on behalf of Zibhebhu kaMaphitha, the man who had actively carried out British policy by his refusal to support the pretensions of the family of Cetshwayo, was a rank injustice. And the presence of Zibhebhu in exile in the Reserve was a visible humiliation to the officials who had backed him. Osborn in Zululand, and the Shepstone family in Natal, were not to forget the debt that they believed the British owed Zibhebhu. In time, they would try to repay it.

The pound of flesh

In northern Zululand there was also payment to be made, and the leaders of the Usuthu waited uneasily as their allies prepared to demand the reward for their services. They had reason to be worried. An increasing number of whites were entering the territory. The movement had been begun by a handful of men from the Zulu borderlands, most of them well known to the Zulu. They had raised a force of some 300 men, who had accompanied Dinuzulu back to Zululand. But by the time that Zibhebhu was defeated there were over 500 in the country. The committee that asserted it was in charge of the movement had declared that no more land grants would be awarded, but still they came, from the Free State,

Natal and the Cape, not only men who could be called Boers, but traders, land speculators, drifters, many bankrupted by the recession. By the end of June there were six or seven hundred with more arriving daily.[28]

They built two laagers, one near Hlobane, and the other on the upper reaches of the Mkhuze River, which by July consisted of 120 wagons placed in double rows. From these impregnable, mobile centres of intimidation and coercion the Boer committee called on the Usuthu leaders to negotiate a cession of land.

Mnyamana had to carry the burden. The Usuthu still had a confidence in him that they didn't have in the *abantwana*, who were much younger and had grown up in the shadow of their brother Cetshwayo. Dinuzulu was a figurehead and he was closely guarded by the Boers. And he was also too young: the customary physical event marking the onset of manhood and the rituals associated with it, his first nocturnal emission, was only to occur later in the year in November. On 7 July, unable to procrastinate any longer, Mnyamana and the royal brothers made their way to the Boer laager.

According to Usuthu sources, they resisted giving any land grants for three days. They argued that any demand for land was premature. Hamu was still at large, Zibhebhu had been defeated but not yet conquered, and anyway it was not their land to give but the Queen's, by right of conquest. But when the Boers threatened them with violence, Mnyamana agreed to grant them a narrow strip on the north-western border – it amounted to little more than the old disputed territory, land which had already been taken from the Zulu when the border was laid down at the end of the war in 1879.

The Usuthu offer was of course rejected. Mnyamana and the princes continued to resist but, even as they did so, circumstances narrowed the options open to them. There were now nearly 1000 armed men in the two laagers, backing the demand for land. Meanwhile the planting season was approaching and a settlement had to be reached.

It was at this desperate moment in Zulu history, on 23 July 1884, that there appeared at the laager the man who was to force a conclusion and break the deadlock. William Grant, friend of Bishop Colenso, correspondent of the APS, representative and adviser to the late Zulu king, confidant of Harriette Colenso, arrived in northern Zululand at the laager to give the Usuthu and the Boers the benefit of his advice and assistance.

William Grant

William Grant had been a trader in Zululand before establishing himself as a businessman in Durban, as a partner in the firm of Grant and Fradd. By the time of the invasion Colenso counted him a friend, and in March 1880 provided him with a letter of introduction to such leading liberals in England as F.W. Chesson, Sir Charles Dilke and Leonard Courtney. 'He is', wrote Colenso, 'the best representative I could send to you, being both experienced, and well-informed, and a lover of light and justice.'[29]

On his way back from England, Grant visited the exiled king in Cape Town, but in Durban he returned to misfortune. Like so many business enterprises at the time, his firm had suffered in the devastating recession of the 1880s. In July 1882 it went bankrupt. Grant had ten children and was desperately in need of funds. The Zulu king had just been returned and, in the opinion of Colenso, urgently required an honest and independent secretary to 'conduct his correspondence'; and Grant was the obvious man to undertake such work. He would be not only adviser but purveyor to the Zulu court as well. The bishop advanced him £50 when he set out. As Harriette wrote, 'I imagine that Mr. Grant's bad fortune was our (the Zulus) good fortune.'[30]

In retrospect it is clear that from the start Grant's perception of the post was not the same as Colenso's. He seemed to have no awareness of the political implications of his visit – either for the king or for Bishopstowe. Before he had even left for Zululand his intentions were published in *The Natal Mercury*. Colenso could not believe that Grant could have been so indiscreet. Grant then suggested that he should inform Shepstone and Bulwer that he was about to proceed to Ulundi on the king's invitation. Colenso's reply was sharp: such a move would not only be bad strategy and pointless, but it would also be 'wronging the King', who had made no such invitation.

Grant stayed at Ulundi from 2 to 16 June 1883. During this time he managed to extract from the Zulu monarch – at the height of the civil war when the king's time was being taken up with the most appalling difficulties – a document which appointed Grant as 'my Resident Adviser and Counsellor to confer with me on all matters affecting the Constitution of my Country and the government of my People and to act as a medium of communication and faithful representation between myself and Her Majesty's Government'.[31]

While at Ulundi, Grant was able to give the king lessons on the strengths of constitutional government. He sent passages from his diary to his friends:

> I entered into a long explanation of the construction of our own House of Parliament and the Cabinet as well as the part our Queen took in the Government of the Country in all of which he manifested a deep interest asking many pertinent questions that clearly illustrate his intelligence ...
> I remained outside, playing the part of the Queen.

> This meeting was a doubly interesting one ... it was the first effort of the
> king's in the direction of Constitutional government.[32]

Colenso's death at this moment deprives us of his reaction to this, but we can
be sure that he would have been strongly disapproving. The tone of Grant's writing is that of the narrowest of secular missionaries, blinded by his own sense of
intellectual and cultural superiority, giving the natives gratuitous advice. There
is nothing of this kind in the writing of Colenso or his daughters. Harriette did
not approve of his calling himself 'Resident Counsellor', and would have preferred 'Secretary'. And she was shocked to read of the little lectures and sem-
inars that Grant set up for the king – and the fact that he was pleased with himself about it. She felt that he 'rather overestimated his position there, from a
Zulu point of view. I don't think that they feel that there is any necessity for
Cetshwayo to have a whiteman to help him to govern the Zulus.'[33]

It is here that we have Harriette Colenso's strength: in her refusal to patronise
her African allies, and her faith in their competence and right to independent
political judgement. Nonetheless, despite their failings, Harriette needed such
local white male allies. In her letters to Chesson she tempered her disapproval
of Grant's actions by asking Chesson not to pass on her comments – 'For this is
high treason'.[34] But Harriette should have followed up her criticisms of Grant
instead of subduing them for the sake of his friendship and support, for he was
a man incapable of disinterested political judgement or of subordinating his own
obsessive search for publicity to wider interests. On his way back from Ulundi
he quite unnecessarily called on Osborn at Eshowe – who understandably told
him it was just like his 'damned impudence'. He then, again quite unnecessarily, submitted the document of appointment as adviser to the king to Bulwer
who, again quite understandably, refused to give it any official recognition. This
only provoked Grant into lengthy complaints that he had been slighted and that
he refused to return to Zululand – something one suspects he had no desire to
do anyway. And it was from Durban, as we have seen, that he led the initiators
of the Boer movement into Zululand to believe that the APS would not agitate
against their involvement in Zulu affairs.

The descent of the hawk

In July 1884 Grant made his way to Zululand once again. One can only suppose
this visit was the consequence of Zibhebhu's defeat and the possibility of a
change in Usuthu fortunes. He arrived in the northern districts where hundreds
of whites were concentrated around the Boer laagers and demanding that the

Usuthu give them land. The Usuthu, now in desperate trouble, welcomed Grant's return. Here at last was a literate man who might take upon himself some of the pressure being applied by the Boers.

But Grant fundamentally misunderstood the situation. He interpreted the Usuthu welcome as a recognition of the confidence they had in his abilities. Grant's self-importance and his propensity for self-delusion were quite extraordinary. 'I find myself', he wrote to Chesson, 'in the position of being the practical successor of Cetshwayo, and this before I have arrived at headquarters. They say "Dinuzulu is yours, the people are yours, the country is yours, we look to you as our father."'[35]

He reprimanded the Usuthu for making an alliance with the Boers without first taking his advice. They explained that they had believed the Boers when they said they were acting with his consent. However, he 'forgave' Mnyamana for what he had done through 'ignorance' and 'fear', if he promised never to act again without Grant's advice and insisted on his presence at all future meetings.[36] The Boers called the Usuthu to just such a meeting the day after Grant arrived, but they refused to have anything to do with this representative of the notorious humanitarian lobby in England. Grant, however, persisted and followed the Usuthu to the meeting place. His arrival, he said, was 'very like the descent of a hawk in a farm yard'.[37] Here, Grant related, he began to use his political acumen to create divisions and confusion amongst the Boers: 'in two or three hours I succeeded in creating a buzz and if you will allow the expression "establishing a funk" ... I soon learned that I had in the Volksraad a majority who disagreed with the action of the Executive – this was the beginning of the working faction which I succeeded in maintaining in the majority to the end.'[38]

What seems in fact to have happened was that a number of Boers realised that instead of having to deal with a threat, they were dealing with an incompetent. In his over-estimation of his own powers, and under-estimation of theirs, Grant could be manipulated with ease. Instead of the interfering, potentially dangerous representative of a powerful humanitarian pressure-group they had expected, they found a pompous, ineffectual individual, completely lacking in political judgement.

On 16 August a document was put before Grant and Dinuzulu. By this proclamation, as it was called, the Boers were awarded 1,355,000 morgen of land and 'the right to establish there an independent Republic, the New Republic'. Furthermore, 'the remaining portion of Zululand and the Zulu nation shall be subject to the supervision of the said New Republic'.[39]

Mnyamana and the two *abantwana* present did not 'hold the pen', and thereby avoided direct responsibility and retained a possible future negotiating position. Dinuzulu put his mark to the document, and Grant his signature, and in so doing signed away what was left of Zululand's sovereignty. The document gave the Boer leadership what it needed to proceed with its plans – an agreement, signed by a person who was literate, publicly proclaimed as adviser and counsellor to the Zulu royal house, backed by the late Bishop of Natal, his family and the APS, to a massive tract of Zulu territory. It meant that in the years to come the Zulu had to negotiate from the weakest of bargaining positions when they were confronted with a document which vested Zulu sovereignty and an extensive but undefined tract of Zulu land in a group of Boers – signed by the prince who they had announced to the Queen was his father's successor, and their white counsellor and adviser.

Grant's signature had also, of course, the most serious consequences for Bishopstowe. For the officials, whom Grant had already provoked by his insistence that his work in Zululand receive some sort of official recognition, the proclamation of 16 August 1884 was a public demonstration of the effects of irresponsible interference by Bishopstowe and its emissaries in African affairs. As Bulwer was to write, 'If Mr. Grant and the other friends of the Usuthu party had been the bitterest enemies of that party, I venture to say that they never could have inflicted on the Zulu country one-half of the injury which was the result of their friendship.'[40]

Grant was to argue that when he arrived in Zululand in July he had found the Usuthu intimidated, demoralised and without effective leadership. Zibhebhu had been beaten but was still in possession of his territory. The planting season had arrived and the Boers refused to settle affairs themselves or allow the Usuthu themselves to settle them. The Zulu were on the brink of losing all their country: by signing the proclamation he had saved two-thirds of it.

There is little validity in these arguments. While his signature did take the immediate pressure off Mnyamana and the *abantwana*, made the way for the final attack on Zibhebhu, and allowed the Usuthu to plant their crops for the coming season, it was no real answer to the Usuthu's problems. Grant interpreted the proclamation as a successful compromise made against tremendous odds: it was in fact a complete surrender to Boer demands. The determining factor in his decision to sign was that the proclamation seemed to award him with the recognition and status he had always desired. The prospect of becoming formally the 'representative and adviser of the Zulu Nation'[41] and informally, he believed, 'the responsible head of the people'[42] turned this bankrupt trader's head and clouded his judgement even further.

Colenso is often said to have been a bad judge of character. He certainly appointed a long list of dipsomaniacs and incompetents to his diocese.[43]

Nonetheless, Colenso's misreading of men and their motives was not a mere personal failing. The withdrawal of financial support instigated by those who opposed his religious teaching meant that it was hard to attract men of quality to his diocese. Some came to work with him because no one else would have them. Others attached themselves to him for the attention it attracted – to work with Bishop Colenso at least meant one was noticed, even if not admired. The very independence of Colenso's thought made the unconventional attractive to him – as Sarah Frances wrote of one family, they 'were so odd that they were impossible even to us, who are apt to think there may be something exceptionally good in odd people'.[44] But above all, in a community determined to isolate him socially and exclude his ideas and ideals, he was drawn to those few who offered him companionship, political conversation and a sense of community, and who were prepared to take some share in the consequences of his politics of protest.

But, in the case of Grant, it was the women at Bishopstowe who had to pay the price for their father's isolation and consequent failure of judgement. Grant's correspondence and journals reveal a man whose attitudes to the Zulu stand in stark contrast to those apparent at Bishopstowe: where the Colensos were informed and unpatronising, Grant was ignorant, bombastic and patently self-interested. Grant pontificated; Harriette always sought, to use the phrase which appears throughout her correspondence, 'the Zulu point of view'. This is not to say that the Colensos always got it right – but in their writings they are seldom uninteresting and always informative. Grant's letters and journals are so permeated with self and so restricted in judgement that their value to the historian is very limited. Frances Colenso described his letters exactly when she complained of a tone of 'really insufferable assumption ... He writes as tho' he were the King of Zululand himself.'[45]

As 1884 progressed, Grant was to discover that, far from being indispensable, he was disposable. He left Zululand in December 1884, angry that the Usuthu still looked to others for advice, and because he believed that they had not reimbursed him sufficiently for his labours in their cause. Early in 1885 he admitted to Chesson that the Boers had in fact never addressed him in his official capacity of Representative and Adviser of the Zulu Nation.[46] To the last he could not see beyond his own obsessive search for personal recognition.

CHAPTER 7

THE SCRAMBLE FOR ZULULAND
(AUGUST 1884 – MARCH 1885)

The northern districts

The years 1884 and 1885 were dark ones in the history of Zululand, a time of conspiracy and secrecy, from which the women at Bishopstowe, although they would have to suffer the consequences, were to a large extent excluded.

With the coming of the spring rains in 1884, those Zulu who could, tried to do something to repair the damage inflicted on their society in the five years since the British invasion, to consolidate what remained of their resources and begin again the processes of agricultural production. Many starved as they waited for the crops to ripen.[1] In the remote northern districts, which had suffered most severely in the civil war, people were forced to live on bulbs, roots and wild grasses. In the more accessible southern and central districts Natal traders brought in grain, but took out cattle. The new authorities in the Reserve offered food for labour on public works and distributed a certain amount of maize.

After Zibhebhu's defeat, Ndabuko, Mnyamana and Dinuzulu led the Usuthu attempt to establish order in the districts north of the Reserve. Mnyamana was the most respected, influential and politically astute of the three. But he was now approaching 80 years of age and had been physically weakened by the privations of the preceding years. Although he had personally opposed the alliance with the Boers, he could not escape the consequences of the actions of his superiors in the royal house who had overruled him.

Ndabuko, as full-brother of Cetshwayo and regent for Dinuzulu, retained his prominent position in Zulu affairs and was consulted on all important issues. Yet he appears to have shown little positive political initiative, exerting himself only under extreme provocation. His ward Dinuzulu was still too young to make independent political decisions. His 'coronation' by the Boers was not recognised by either the British or the Zulu. However, as Cetshwayo's eldest son in whom the *abantwana* themselves had vested the succession, and the individual upon whom the Boers rested their claims to Zululand, Dinuzulu's status was considerable,

107

and he was treated with great respect by both the people of the country and the whites who sought concessions in Zululand. Young and impressionable, keenly aware of the importance of his position, he responded to flattery and accepted gifts with little regard for the consequences.

His position was not an easy one. One obvious way to weaken the proclamation of 16 August would have been to get rid of the Zulu signatory, and there were rumours that factions amongst the Usuthu were considering abandoning Dinuzulu in favour of Manzolwandle, the posthumous son of Cetshwayo by the daughter of the hereditary Magwaza chief Qethuka.[2] But despite many difficulties, the vulnerable triumvirate of failing elder statesman, impetuous adolescent heir and morose regent was for the moment to hold together.

Under it the Usuthu were able to repair at least some of the damage they had suffered since 1879. Once the threat of Ngenetsheni and Mandlakazi attack had been removed, Usuthu began to move out of their strongholds and places of retreat to reoccupy the valleys and plains of northern Zululand. Others moved in after being forced off their land by Boers in the west. Dinuzulu followed the practice of his royal ancestors by establishing royal homesteads in the area, and appointing a new generation of *izinduna*.

Mnyamana and his immediate followers were able to leave the strongholds of the Ngome and surrounding hills to occupy the valley of the Black Mfolozi. Ndabuko reoccupied his KwaMinya homestead in the lower Ivuna valley. Higher up the same valley, Dinuzulu established his homestead Osuthu. On the rim of the valley, at a higher altitude where horse-sickness was less prevalent, Dinuzulu built Emahashini – the place of horses. The valley of the Ivuna River and its environs became, from 1885, the political and administrative heartland of the Usuthu.

Amongst Cetshwayo's brothers, Ziwedu was now also able to reoccupy his lands in the lower Ivuna valley. Dabulamanzi built a homestead just north of the Mhlatuze, not far from his brothers Sitheku and Shingana at KwaMagwaza and Emakhosini respectively. Mahanana, the induna in charge of the Mphangisweni section, occupied an important position amongst the Usuthu, but his homesteads were at the sources of the Black Mfolozi and therefore threatened by the Boers.

It did appear, at least in the spring of 1884 as people moved into the land freed from Mandlakazi dominance, as if the deal with the Boers had brought some material advantages to the Zulu. But this momentary relief was not allowed to continue: the Usuthu had incurred a debt. The mercenaries had still to be paid – and they were now joined by hundreds of other men, from a variety of backgrounds, hoping to take advantage of Zulu vulnerability and gain something from the situation.

There was a Zulu saying which referred to these years following the death of the king: *Kwafa enyoni enkulu kwabola amaqanda* – When the great bird died the eggs became rotten. The metaphor refers to the protective aspects of the centralised kingship upon which social continuity depended, and the desolation and decay which followed when this nurturing authority was destroyed. For many Zulu, any long-term vision of the future had gone and decisions were opportunistic and pragmatic, made in order to survive. The deliberate destruction of the central political power by the British in 1879 had exposed its people and their resources, its rich and fertile lands, full of promise and rumours of wealth, to their enemies. These were, by the 1880s, many and varied – but the most immediate were the oldest, and were to be found amongst neighbours of the Zulu – in the colony of Natal, and the Boer republic of the Transvaal.

The Zulu Native Reserve

Natal had already made its claim in setting up the Zulu Native Reserve, where Osborn's new administration was trying to establish itself. At Eshowe, George Mansel of the Natal Mounted Police was appointed to form the Zululand Police, soon to be known and feared as the 200-strong 'Nongqayi', many of whom were recruited from Natal. His second-in-command was Dick Addison, from a leading Natal family and already exhibiting the arrogant racial attitudes of the Natal civil service. A detachment of British troops, authorised to give 'moral support' only, set up its camp on the high ground beyond the Residency. Osborn had the resentful support of John Dunn on the coast in the east; and beyond the Nkandla on the north-western borders of the Reserve at Nquthu, the Sub-Resident, A.L. Pretorius, established himself, with the support of Hlubi Molife and his hundred armed and mounted followers. Osborn also had with him a number of African assistants from Natal – his indunas, led by Yamela who, in the tradition of the loyal Natal induna, had already formed a considerable chieftainship on the lands around Eshowe.

Osborn worked hard to show that his administration had the general loyalty of the Zulu chiefs as well. This was best demonstrated by their prompt payment of the hut tax, which would repay the imperial advance and satisfy the pressing demands of the Treasury in London. But a significant proportion of the Reserve's chiefs, especially those living in inaccessible areas with proximity to the forest retreats of the Nkandla and Qudeni, prevaricated and kept in contact with the Usuthu to the north. In so doing they provoked first severe warnings, and then attempts at coercion by the new administration of the Zulu Native Reserve.

The Reserve was also a place of refuge for those Zulu beyond its borders who were unable to defend themselves against the Usuthu. Thus, in March 1884 when Zibhebhu had to attend to a disturbance on his western front and left his allies on the coast in the lurch, Sokwetshata of the Mthethwa was driven south into the Reserve by the coastal Usuthu.[3] By April 1884 rumours of the coming alliance between Usuthu and Boer began to spread across the country. This was followed by the removal of Dinuzulu to the north and the burial of the king, after which the *abantwana* themselves moved to the north, followed by large numbers of Usuthu. Dabulamanzi remained behind to organise the Usuthu forces left in the Reserve. It was too much for the Resident Commissioner. By the end of April Osborn had decided that the Usuthu in the Reserve should finally be removed and the loyal forces consolidated: he ordered that all the cattle of those Zulu who had left the Reserve be confiscated.[4]

Through the winter of 1884 Osborn attempted to crush the Usuthu in the Reserve. But his efforts turned into a fiasco. His police and his allies seized cattle so indiscriminately that they had the effect of turning loyals into rebels as Zulu tried to defend themselves against the authorities. There were violent clashes with fatalities, panic in the Nquthu district, and John Dunn eventually refused to risk his men by allowing them to become involved in actions of such incompetence. Eventually Bulwer himself had to visit the Reserve to establish lines of command. Then came the news of Zibhebhu's defeat at Etshaneni.[5]

The Zulu Native Reserve, Shepstone's safe haven for all Zulu who did not want to come under the rule of the king, was threatened with collapse. In the panic which followed Zibhebhu's defeat, the officer in command had telegraphed for instructions with the question, 'Am I to see loyals destroyed and Reserve overrun?' In July, Osborn and the officer in command of the British detachment received permission to undertake a 'reconnaissance' along the borders of the Nkandla. Bulwer was horrified to discover that this reconnoitring party was preparing an attack on the Usuthu. Angrily Bulwer called the troops back, protesting that they had been 'moved for one definite purpose' and were now being 'employed for another and wholly different purpose'.[6] London was also worried:

it is evident that Mr. Osborn was preparing to commence a little war against the Usuthu in his District ... the telegram shows that Sir H. Bulwer and Mr. Osborn are by no means as much united in points of information and opinion as we supposed, and leads to the conclusion that we may be being totally misinformed, as we have been in other places and on other occasions, and that we are much nearer to a Zulu war than we suppose.[7]

Bulwer was eventually forced to insist that Osborn face the reality of political loyalties in the Reserve: that it was not made up, as he alleged, of loyal Zulu intimidated by an Usuthu minority. Thus, when Osborn recommended the expulsion from the Reserve of all Zulu guilty of 'hostile proceedings' and their replacement by Africans from Natal, Bulwer demanded a policy based on informed analysis of the situation.[8] The Colonial Office was also getting impatient. Derby telegraphed Bulwer on 30 August asking if there was any 'prospect of permanent pacification [in the Reserve] British authority being now definitely established there?'[9]

The failure of official policy was dramatically demonstrated when on the evening of 7 September, over 5000 Mandlakazi crossed into the Reserve, the men carrying their shields and assegais, the boys with their sleeping mats and the women with their children and household possessions, and driving the herds they had saved from the Boers and the Usuthu. Osborn demarcated territory between the Nkandla and the Thukela for these people, their presence a demonstrable slight to his authority and a living manifestation of his political failure and that of the House of Sonzica with which he was associated.

The time had come for a change of approach. Bulwer had now lost faith in Osborn's capacity to deal with the Usuthu in the Reserve and asked the commander of the British forces, General Smyth, to see if he could take the initiative. The General sent a message to the Usuthu urging them to submit 'in order that you may live in peace, so that you and others can go on with the planting of your crops, and thus prevent famine in the land'.[10] He then moved his troops to a position close to Luhungu's homestead and waited.

For the Usuthu it was important that their people be allowed to regain access to their agricultural land and begin to plant without harassment from the authorities. By the end of September a number of representatives of leading Usuthu had pledged their submission. Osborn now had no choice but to go along with the process. Even if he had the authority to use regular troops, the rainy season had begun, which made it impossible to move men, guns and wagons along the razor-backed ridges on the margins of the Nkandla forest. But to allow the Usuthu to 'submit' was a hard choice and a humiliating one for Osborn, for it was clear there had been no successful 'pacification' or effective assertion of authority. He went along with developments because he had to, not even demanding the most basic guarantees. Thus Smyth himself observed on Luhungu's submission: 'The result of the talk was satisfactory to Mr. Osborn, though, judging by the expression of their faces, it was not so to the loyal chiefs present. But what was to be done? It was impossible to attack people who had submitted, and there was no one else to fight.'[11]

For the Usuthu this was a qualified victory. They returned to their land to try to make good their losses. The descendants of the major Usuthu groupings like the Magwaza under Qethuka, the Ntuli under Godide, and the Shezi under Siganda live in the Nkandla district to this day. But of course their submission to the administration only gave them a breathing space before the next call for payment of the hut tax as a demonstration of their loyalty. Nonetheless, their submission in 1884 did allow the people of the Reserve to settle down for the moment and plant their crops – and attend to developments across the Mhlatuze in the northern part of the country where the Zulu had to confront other threats to their independence.

The scramble for Zululand

For many whites from the Transvaal, Zululand was their historical inheritance, in particular the fine winter grazing in the valleys which cut back towards the Transvaal's borderlands. For forty years the power of the Zulu kingdom had kept them out – but now this power had been broken by the British, and fragmented further by civil war. By their intervention in this conflict between the Usuthu and the Mandlakazi, some of these men – Boers – had succeeded in setting up defended positions in the northern districts, and were now ready to give their claims to the northern districts some substance.

Furthermore, the long-standing pressure on Zululand's borders was now intensified by a more modern phenomenon. In the first half of the 1880s, colonial southern Africa had slumped into deep recession: 'Just as 1882 had proved to be worse than 1881, so 1883 was described as "the worst ever experienced," and 1884 in turn as "the year of greatest depression."'[12] Natal was hit particularly hard after the boom induced by the war of 1879 had passed, and because of the loss of speculative investments made in the Transvaal. The discovery of gold to the north intensified the feeling that there might be pickings to be had amongst the devastated homesteads of Zululand. Men with nothing, and nothing to do, began to move towards the Boer laagers to see what they could find. Many Zulu leaders, trying to re-establish themselves, uncertain of the future, in need of advice, and of guns, ammunition and horses, and very often grain for their starving people, were very vulnerable to the increasing number of traders, concession-seekers, fortune hunters, adventurers and gunmen moving into their territory.

The international context was also changing significantly. These events occurred during the 'scramble for Africa' – the intensified interest and expansion in Africa on the part of the major European powers as they manoeuvred for what they perceived as diplomatic, strategic and economic advantages over their rivals. In 1884 Germany had unexpectedly made claims to the coast of south-west Africa. Soon afterwards a traveller, said by some to be a bankrupt watch-maker from Port Elizabeth, informed Sir Henry Bulwer that he was Dr Augustus Einwald, leader of a scientific expedition to Zululand. He wore a Prussian uniform during his meetings with African chiefs, flew a German flag from his wagon, and hinted that he was in communication with Bismarck.[13]

Although he antagonised most of the Boers, Einwald did succeed in creating an alliance with another German, Adolf Schiel, who had been chosen by the Boers as Dinuzulu's minder and secretary. On 13 November 1884 Schiel and Einwald obtained from Dinuzulu, in return for some trinkets and the promise of German protection, a document which purported to give them rights to 60,000 acres at St Lucia. Schiel wrote to Bulwer repudiating the Boers' actions in Zululand.[14] He then appears to have borrowed money from Einwald to get to Europe, double-crossed him, and at the end of 1884 signed over his rights to St Lucia to the German merchant-adventurer Lüderitz.

While interesting perhaps as a footnote to the history of the scramble, and characteristic of this period of economic recession when opportunism and fraud reigned, it is difficult to take the German incursion into Zululand too seriously. But it was felt in London that neither parliament nor public opinion would tolerate another surrender to Germany in southern Africa and that 'Natal and the Reserve would be much weakened if foreigners had St. Lucia Bay'.[15] The matter was handed to the Foreign Office, and the German Chancellery was informed of Britain's long-standing claims to St Lucia. On 18 December 1884 the commander of HMS *Goshawk* reached St Lucia, raised the Union Jack, fired a 21-gun salute, and gave a written statement to a group of Zulu onlookers.[16]

But while the presence of the Royal Navy at St Lucia might have meant little to the Zulu watching from the sand dunes, it was very significant to the men waiting to make their claims to Zululand. It suggested to them that there was a possibility that Britain might even now assert its rights to the country. The slaughter of the Zulu, the devastation of their homesteads, the occupation of their land, did not appear to be sufficient grounds for British intervention. But the possibility that German interference in south-east Africa might antagonise the British electorate and threaten British dominance in the region had led to immediate action. And Britain had the capacity to go further. In spite of all the remarks about the bumbling of her generals, the Liberal capitulation in the Transvaal, the death of the true British spirit at Majuba, Britain, everyone knew, was the power in the land – if she chose to exercise it. The Boer leadership feared that over-enthusiastic expansion into the land of the Zulu would provoke

British intervention. This concern held them back, forcing them to dissociate themselves from the wilder elements amongst their followers.

At the same time the Boers knew that they could not hold back for too long: if there were ever to be negotiations over Zululand's future, claims based on occupation would be more telling than paper ones. A town – Vryheid – had been laid out near the Hlobane mountain, and plots were surveyed and put on the market. In December 1884 a deputation was sent to Sir Henry Bulwer in Pietermaritzburg to assure him of the New Republic's friendly intentions and ask for recognition while a 'survey commission' was set up to demarcate farms. Hundreds of farms were to be laid out, the prime sites on the Transvaal borders for the initiators of the movement, others for those who had arrived before Zibhebhu's defeat, with smaller farms for the latecomers. Surveying began on the Bevane River and, by the beginning of 1885, 300 farms had been surveyed and distributed by lot. The commissioners then moved down the Mhlatuze River, marking out farms until they reached the sea before turning north. By March it was reported that the survey party was in the vicinity of St Lucia.[17]

This was just what Bulwer and settler Natal had feared would happen. The Mhlatuze formed the northern border of the Zulu Native Reserve. It was a move that would 'close the outlet from Natal to Zululand and beyond' and be 'fatal to us'. It was the culmination of the long-standing desire of the Boers to overcome their geographical isolation and reach the sea. It would deprive the Zulu of their land and preclude the possibility of Natal using Zululand to reduce its 'excess native population'. 'With great solicitude' and backed with a petition from 1900 Natal whites, Bulwer urged Her Majesty's Government to intervene.[18]

The Zulu watched the Boer surveyors as they moved amongst the homesteads threatening the occupants, marking trees and setting up their sod beacons and piles of stone. But they could do little beyond protest. They were rebuilding their homes, gathering their stock, preparing their crops for the harvest. There was no way in which organised physical opposition could be mounted without the possibility of fearful reprisal. The leadership, weak and divided, was unable to take direct physical action. Without a political centre from which to organise resistance or the military capacity to expel the Boers from their country, the Usuthu leaders began to make the first tentative moves to see if they could find other allies beyond their borders. Amongst these were the more responsive of the Transvaal officials; the office of the SNA through which all dealings with the Governor of Natal had to pass before a message could reach the Queen; and Dlwedlwe, Harriette Colenso, who was ignored while the ruthless deals over guns and land were being cut but who remained the staff that the Bishop of Natal had left behind to guide them.

CHAPTER 8

PLAGUES

Fire

T he death of Bishop Colenso had left the people at Bishopstowe and Ekukhanyeni with an array of difficulties which tested to the full their capacity to sustain themselves as an effective and organised group. As Sarah Frances wrote, 'The fact is it is because his work was left in such a terribly tangled state, owing to the wickedness of the world, that we cannot bear to leave off doing all we can.'[1]

Harriette Colenso's level-headedness and her grasp of the legal complexities of such intractable questions as how to appoint a successor to her father's See were widely recognised. But these seemingly irresolvable church matters took hours and hours of her time, and it had therefore been a relief to let William Grant in Durban deal with Zulu affairs. Frances was working hard on *The Ruin of Zululand*, using the 'Digest' as the prime source of information, checking details with Harriette before sending it to Frank for final editing prior to submission to the printers.

One of Harriette's responsibilities was Bishopstowe's security. Built near the crest of a range of hills, the property was particularly vulnerable to runaway grass fires, and the bishop had almost lost his life in one in 1862. The long dry winter of 1884, increasing stands of timber, and the reduction of cultivated land around Bishopstowe meant that Harriette had to take special care in burning firebreaks. On two occasions fires had jumped the gap and, but for Harriette's care, her mother felt 'we should have been swept off the surface of the earth ... I grumble at her having to spend 2 or 3 hours every afternoon to superintend these burnings! It is a great drag upon her strength – and if her strength gave way I don't know what would become of us – perhaps our enemies mean to burn us up as heretics!?'[2]

On 3 September Harriette was working in her father's study when an African rushed in saying another fire was approaching. Harriette went out and, to her horror, saw 'towers of smoke rolling towards' them, driven by a violent wind. It had already jumped the firebreaks, and was soon in the trees around the house. There were five women and children inside when the front of the building began to burn: Frances and Harriette, her friend Katie Giles, Robert's wife Emily and her son Eric. Helped by a neighbour they were hurried out of the house and taken to a grove of mulberry trees through which the fire had already swept. Frances and Katie then got the horses out of the stables while women of the family of Langalibalele living on the farm drove the cows to safety.

But the house was now on fire. A desperate effort was made to save some of the contents. The top floor was burning and they lost all their clothing and linen. Frances's bedroom and studio contained notes, letters, her paintings – some by Burne-Jones – and the preliminary notes for a third volume of *The Ruin of Zululand*, the proofs of the first volume having just arrived, and the manuscript of the second sent safely away. She also saved her notes on the 'case' – the evidence which she believed showed that a deliberate attempt had been made to make it seem as if Durnford had been responsible for the defeat at Isandlwana. The box containing the letters that passed between John Colenso and Sarah Frances before their marriage, was saved. From the downstairs rooms they managed to salvage some of the family's most treasured possessions – paintings and books, some vital church documents, the bishop's own copy of the 'Digest'.

Photo 21. September 1884: Bishopstowe destroyed by fire.

116

But much more was lost than was saved: many of Sarah Frances's paintings of Natal flowers, and the music she had collected from the time of her youth – Beethoven, Mendelssohn, Schubert – which she and Frank still played. The next day Harriette went up to the ruins of the house, already being searched for 'relics' by trippers from Pietermaritzburg, to retrieve coins and the melted lumps of metal which had been jewellery and watches. Agnes was in Durban and had therefore saved what for her was of least significance and most easily replaced – her clothes. Instead she lost what was irreplaceable – the gifts from her father. We can only guess at the correspondence which went up in flame – and what documents and photographs on Natal colonial life, mission work, Zulu history and the Zulu language. The next day Harriette walked through the ashes heaped in the foundations.

> The walls stand a great deal better than I should have expected – you remember how we used to walk about on a windy night to 'hold the house up'. But it is rather a ghastly sight. The bare walls – every scrap of wood gone, every door plate and window frame, and nothing visible in the heaped up ashes at the bottom of the foundations but a few tin boxes and numerous iron bedsteads twisted in all directions, as if they had been tortured to death.[3]

Not only the study where the bishop had worked for thirty years, but the chapel was gone. And so was the instrument so vital to the work of Ekukhanyeni – the printing press, the type still molten the day after the fire.

Frances, Eric and his mother were sent back to Durban. The others spent two nights on a neighbouring farm where they received many offers of help and shelter – including one from Government House. But Sarah Frances, Harriette and Agnes decided not to be separated and to remain on Bishopstowe land. They moved with Katie Giles into an empty farmhouse, down the hill a few hundred metres from where Bishopstowe had been. It was a run-down structure consisting of two small cottages, built in a row of three and five rooms.

They were determined not to treat this catastrophe as a catastrophe: 'none of our whole party mopes', wrote Sarah Frances.[4] They would not complain: they had their lives still, they had one another, and they had the memory of the man most important to them. And they had his work to complete, for the Church of England in South Africa, for the people at Bishopstowe, for the Zulu. They also had the task of preserving his memory – the memory of what he had been to those who knew him, not as he appeared to the world.

Sarah Frances called the cottages 'Seven Oaks', giving an ironic pastoral dignity to the rooms without ceilings under the thatch – only two with floorboards

Photo 22. Robert Colenso, his son Eric (or 'Nondela') and his wife Emily seated next to his mother. Harriette Colenso is standing and Agnes is present but, as always, on the margins. Guy is asleep on the veranda on the left.

and papered walls – with stable doors, and glass window panes replaced with brown paper. The four women lived in one room with a corner screened off for washing, until Katie Giles cleaned and whitewashed another and moved into 'White Hall'. The stove, damaged but working, was dragged out of the Bishopstowe kitchen and installed in another room. One more room, 'Blackfriars', was set aside for the African men of the household, and another, the 'Museum', for items salvaged from the ruins. There was a sitting room and a pantry, and the room at the end housed the family's calves.

Although Sarah Frances was determined not to complain, the family had suffered a heart-breaking loss, and behind the outward resolve there was the private grief:

I got dear Mrs Lyell's letter ... and she seems quite to understand my feeling about the little worth of *things* following on *the loss* of Him who went first – yet every now and then when as this afternoon Harriette and Agnes and I have been up to the Ruins a feeling of desolation comes over one just for a little while – Neither of *us* 3 would indulge in fretting, for the sake of each other – but, the view of the Mountain from the old site is so *beautiful* and I must allow

Photo 23. Mother and daughters at Seven Oaks, c.1885. If the woman in the dark dress is Frances, then consumption has wrought its changes. The dress appears to be the same as that worn by Emily Colenso in photo 22. Perhaps Frances wore it because she had lost her own clothes in the fire. Harriette Colenso wears a man's hat, practical but extremely unconventional.

that such a view, particularly when familiar for many years does inspire affection – it is more than a thing, or collection of things.[5]

Harriette feared that if they left Bishopstowe's environs it might be interpreted that they were relinquishing their claim to the property of the Church of England. If they could somehow establish their legal rights to a portion of the property at least, and raise the money, they could go back up the hill, rebuild if not the whole house then a part of it, and from there establish a mission station, a school, farm some land, set up a printing press and, with the support of local Africans, teach and care for the people who joined them, produce books in Zulu – all in the traditions that their father had established.

Pestilence

On 13 November Frances came up from Durban to stay at Seven Oaks. She was tired, sick, menstruating, and quite appalled at the conditions she found in this

'Valley of Humiliation'. She told her mother and sisters that she would '*give and take no rest*' until they left. Harriette calmed her down for the moment, talking of how necessary it was, for the present at least, that the Colensos make a public demonstration of their resolve by remaining physically at Bishopstowe.

But Frances was to find it increasingly difficult. Harriette and Agnes were able to put up with the rough makeshift conditions. Their mother was able to do so as well, for her daughters' sake and because they looked after her. Frances, although proud of her willingness to sacrifice material things for justice, for art and for her independence as she had done in London in 1880 and 1881, found the conditions at Seven Oaks too rough. She was used to comfort and domestic assistance. She loved what she saw as beautiful things about her, she did not like ready-made clothes or the coarse underwear that she had to wear after her clothing had been destroyed in the fire. Tuberculosis drained her strength. Then, soon after arriving at Seven Oaks, she suffered an attack of shingles. Dressing in all but the lightest clothing exhausted her: she was just too weak to pull on and off her heavy garments. Her sisters tried to make her life as easy as they could. A new bed with a spring mattress was moved into Katie Giles's room. In her search for privacy Frances hung a cloth partition across it, and her mother draped the bedstead with lace that had been given the family for curtains. But it was all too much for Frances and she quarrelled with her sisters. Harriette tried to repair the damage that was done, but Agnes was unsympathetic to Frances's outbursts.

Frances found it harder and harder to summon the energy she needed for her projects. But as her physical strength flagged, so she drove herself harder. She had finished the second volume of *The Ruin of Zululand*, and was contemplating the third. Harriette discouraged her and, in an aside with a hint of criticism, noticeable because it is so rare, wrote that she, Harriette, could not afford the time for another of Frances's books.

Frances also began to plan the family project to produce their father's biography – the book that was going to bring his true character and worth to the attention of the world. After some debate it was decided that the book should be written by Sir George Cox, scholar and classicist. Cox was an authority on the religious struggle – the political struggle in the later part of Colenso's life would be dealt with by his children and the whole would be checked by his wife.[6]

All the while, however, occupying Frances's thoughts was the deep, persistent grief she felt at the death of Anthony Durnford and her determination to clear him of the blame for the British defeat at Isandlwana. She received a tremendous boost when, in the latter part of 1885, she recruited a new ally – Colonel Luard, officer commanding the Royal Engineers in Natal. He went over her

research, was persuaded that she had a case, and promised to assist her in exposing Offy Shepstone as the man who had removed the vital documents from
Durnford's body.

Frances pursued the campaign to exonerate Durnford without regard to personal or physical cost. Those who declined to help her were labelled weak and
cowardly. Frances's dearest friend from the time they were girls was Helen
Shepstone, Offy's wife. She urged Helen to persuade her husband to confess.
Helen did everything she could to convince her that Offy had nothing to confess.

But Frances had no such fears and was scornful of Helen's desperate efforts to
halt what she saw as the persecution of her husband. Helen's father-in-law, Sir
Theophilus, saw the origins of her ruthlessness in the character of her father, and
in a bitterly moving comment on his old friend and foe said of Colenso that 'the
pity is not that he took the view he did, for that was the result of an ardent love
of justice, but that he looked upon every one who could not take the same view
as he did in the light of a personal enemy, and bequeathed that blasting legacy
to his children'.[7]

The strain on the women at Bishopstowe was great and there was a frightful
quarrel between Frances and her sisters at Seven Oaks, probably during her visit
at the end of 1885. Evidence of this escaped the posthumous guardians of her
correspondence and, in another fragment of a letter to her mother, Frances complained of the way they all smothered feelings which are natural to women and
of which they should not be ashamed. For example, even to refer to

> the 'dreary time in women's life etc' will, I fear, be in your opinion a sort of
> sign of inferiority – something which it is beneath one's dignity to feel, still
> more express but, you know, I don't think so – to my mind that kind of feel-
> ing is natural and womanly (not of course, to be expressed except to one's
> mother) and I don't wish to be more than a woman, or see any inferiority in
> what *is* her nature.

It was the same with her feelings for Durnford. Why should she not give expression to them?

> I do not see any reason why one *should* smother or be ashamed of that longing
> for love which makes its object the first thought in everything, never forgot-
> ten, never unobserved, and which, after being once experienced, leaves the
> need of it behind – which is at the bottom what I believe you sometimes
> [take] to be pride and self-love in me. I think I feel its loss, and regret more
> passionately the days when I had it, and only half prized it, every year I live,

as I grow older, and realise more fully what life *might* have been to me by this time but for the loss of a noble life, and the preservation of our unworthy one.

Then, again, you never like my speaking bitterly of my own lot because you say it is the same for all three of us, and that in regarding my own life a failure I am saying what is infra dig and for Harriette and Agnes. But it seems to me so different. Neither of them have had my particular experience and grief, and they cannot bitterly regret (as I do) the loss of what they have not tried. And they have each other, which is not saying little. I think few sisters are so entirely at one as they are. They really are like husband and wife.[8]

Frances was able to cope with this conflict between the mores of the time and her feelings for Durnford by representing their relationship as a moral cause – a noble man, cruelly wronged by the ignoble, a wrong which she had to redress. Taking up the ideas of the teacher of her youth, John Ruskin, together with the popular concepts of late Victorian chivalry, she depicted herself as someone who tried to live Woman's essential role: to infuse male desire with spiritual purity; to give courage and conscience to her knight as he confronted the terrors and temptations of the quest. She depicted her love for Durnford in terms of her love of justice, and it was the nobility, not the physicality, of the man for which she fought with such intensity. And she extended this to other men like Edward Durnford and then Colonel Luard of the Royal Engineers, who offered to assist her – bringing them onto her side and involving them in her projects.

Although her relationships with these men gave her some comfort, and were sufficiently close to alienate their wives – who consequently earned Frances's scorn for their inability to discern the purity and nobility of her motives – they could of course in no way replace what she had lost by Durnford's death. It was Frances's bitterness at this loss, at the absence of love, at the passing of the opportunity for love, at her own mortality, together with a terrible sense of failure at not having the man through and with whom she could live fully, which drove her on to the end.

But to the world, her friends and often to herself, she expressed her furious regret at the loss of a lived and sensual life in other terms – in terms of her dedication to bringing justice to a man who had been treated unjustly. And this was part of a wider struggle for justice. She sought to demonstrate to the world the good in those whom it sought to discredit: of the Zulu, who had been invaded and conquered by the British for no just cause; of their king, who had been made to suffer for the devotion of his people; of her father, 'the most Christ-like man of modern times'; of her lover, a man of courage and a noble spirit, whose reputation had been besmirched to cover the military inadequacy and moral frailties of others.

And in her anger, during that exceptionally wet, unseasonably cold summer of 1884–5 in the uncomfortable cottages at Seven Oaks, with their dusty earthen floors and lack of privacy, she made the lives of her mother and her sisters even more difficult. As they watched her getting thinner and thinner, and through the mud walls heard her struggling to breathe, they grieved at the frailty of her body and the fury of her spirit, but could do little to help her.

Vermin

Through all this Sarah Frances tried not to despair, not to complain. She presented their lives at Seven Oaks with a wry humour. They had been visited during their time in the cottage by a number of plagues. First the rats which woke them 'between 3 and 4 with rushing and squeakings – light the candle and you see a huge grey thing rushing along the top of the wall not far above you – People in general use some poison but what are we to do, "tradition" of the family forbids the use of any thing which would cause suffering even to vermin.' A cat solved this moral question, but then came the plague of flies. Their old mangy dog, called, regrettably, Guy, scratched and smelt and insisted on sleeping in their overcrowded and badly ventilated bedrooms, bringing with him a plague of 'bounding chamois' – the family reference to fleas.

Serpents

As she tried to write herself out of her sorrow, and away from 'my poor little Frances ... really too frail to be exposed to roughness', Sarah Frances began to dream of a future at Bishopstowe – an African future.

> Our idea is, a modest home with sufficient stabling, a good strong cattle kraal, so that our horned friends may be hindered from walking about at night amongst our poor neighbours' mealie gardens – and sufficient space for our oldest and most valued black friends to pitch their tents, i.e. rear their huts under our wing, i.e. as our tenants. We should of course belong to the Jacobite party in Zululand and the other side (whether filibusters, or Boers or tools of the Shepstone faction pretending loyalty to the Imperial Government! and having betrayed or destroyed their native monarch). Monarchy is surely the 1st step upwards from anarchy, from a chaos of selfish wills regardless of general good – to the perfect state of the rule of the wisest!

At this point in her letter-writing she was interrupted by Kate Giles inside the cottage, who had heard a 'boiling sound' and seen a snake disappear down one of the rat holes. 'There was a position for us! I began to think the "plague of serpents" would turn us out eventually, but it struck me to try what smoke would do' – and Mubi and the other Africans smoked the snake out and killed it.

Sarah Frances was surprised at her own sense of relief: not just at the death of a possibly dangerous reptile, but at what the Africans had told her – that the snake was an emissary of the House of Shepstone, and the evil messenger was now dead. Her own reaction to this piece of information rather surprised her:

> O what a relief that was to my mind! It is odd that we had all been more or less uneasy and restless of a night *without knowing why*, Sunday, Monday, Tuesday, – now we think we do know why, having sunk so deeply into superstitious notions about snakes, and evil influences acting on human beings without the intervention of their senses! We do not *quite* share the feeling of our poor people about the long list of misfortunes which have befallen our house ascribing them as they do to the hostility of another more powerful house – that of Somsewu! ...
>
> I must have tired you out with so many small details – but I think the death of that snake has taken a weight off my mind, it seems like a victory over the powers of darkness.[9]

Shepstone had a capacity to instil dread in those with whom he was in conflict. Sarah Frances in her musings on the subterranean powers of Shepstone was drawing on fears that had emerged in the dark days at Bishopstowe in the winter of 1883. Just before he died, even the bishop, his hopes for peace and justice again turned to bloody violence, wrote, 'I have a sort of superstitious dread of him and his influence.'[10] And soon after her father's death Harriette wrote that 'I sometimes feel that my dear Father must have been taken away from some great evil to come – and certainly the Powers of Darkness seem to be having their own way just now. I hear that Sir Theophilus Shepstone is coming back suddenly. Has he got leave to annex Zululand entire, I wonder?'[11]

For years Sarah Frances had called Shepstone the Old Serpent. She was of course smiling at the idea, but there was dread behind the smile as well. There was a sense of the presence of evil in Shepstone – manipulating, planning and plotting, seeking out his enemies – penetrating even this poor place of refuge, recognisable to them all, regardless of their traditions and beliefs, African or European, in the guise of a serpent.

CHAPTER 9

THE PRICE OF BLOOD (1885)

Messengers – in touch once again

But leaving aside these fantasies on the supernatural power of the House of Sonzica, there were very tangible reasons at the beginning of 1885 to be fearful of what the year would reveal. For by now the Usuthu leaders were beginning to have to confront the implications of their alliance with the Boers. Large numbers of white men were moving into the country, taking advantage of the confusion and the absence of organised African leadership. Many of them disregarded both Zulu protests and the instructions of the New Republic.

The Usuthu knew that some new initiative would have to be taken. Wearily, they began once again to try to revive their contacts with the British through the Natal authorities. They also made contact again with Harriette Colenso. At the end of December, Melakhanya arrived at Bishopstowe, instructed by the Usuthu leadership to tell her what had been happening in Zululand since the death of the king. Over the next few weeks Harriette took down his account, translated it, and eventually put it into print.

Since her father's death and the burning of Bishopstowe, Harriette had been unable to give Zulu matters the attention that she would have liked. Nonetheless she had assumed that William Grant was actively keeping watch. But by the beginning of 1885 she was concerned at the way things were going. Grant, 'Representative and Adviser to the Zulu Nation', confidant of Bishop Colenso, essential ally in the next stage of the struggle, appeared diffident. He was not forthcoming with the information Harriette urgently needed to understand the situation. He seemed to be feeling slighted. The Boers, once they had got his signature to the land grant, had broken their promise and ignored him. The Usuthu had not deferred to him as his official position warranted. He felt that they should confirm their commitment to him with a gift of cattle – one hundred head.

She travelled down to Durban with Melakhanya and Mubi to visit Grant and they went through Melakhanya's version of recent Zulu history. During the interview she discovered that William Grant, signatory to the land grant on which the New Republic had been founded, which had signed away over 2,000,000 acres of Zulu land, was unable to comprehend and communicate what this figure meant in practical terms.[1]

It was all very disturbing. But Harriette, only too aware of how important Grant was to the Usuthu and to Bishopstowe's reputation, could do no more than express a passing concern. Nonetheless, it was clear that Grant was reluctant to act and that any fresh initiative would have to come from her. It was a heavy responsibility at a time when many others, in her family, in the church, at the mission, were drawing on her resources. She turned for assistance again to two of the Bishopstowe Africans, Thwayisa Mabaso and Mubi Nondenisa, asking them to travel to northern Zululand on her behalf to interview the Usuthu leaders and obtain more reliable information on recent Zulu history.

Here, the men from Ekukhanyeni found the Usuthu determined to protest against the occupation of their country but divided on how to carry it out. Dinuzulu, escorted by a mounted detachment of Zulu, appealed to those whom they saw as the most responsible and authoritative amongst the Boer leadership. On 15 March 1885, in Wakkerstroom, they met the Transvaal officials Joubert and Krogh to complain about the actions of the New Republicans. They were received sympathetically but could extract no assurances from the officials, and negotiations broke down.

Mnyamana advocated another strategy – an appeal to the Queen through Natal. Early in March 1885 two Zulu messengers arrived in Pietermaritzburg to make a statement to the Natal authorities. The Boers, they said, 'have gone through the country, beaconing it off in farms down to the sea'. But Zululand, they continued, belonged to the Queen, whom they urged to 'step in and relieve them of their difficulties and the troubles'.[2]

Bulwer had been anticipating this moment. Here was a statement from the men who had turned their backs on the authorities in Natal, who had plotted with Bishopstowe, who had killed two messengers on an errand to bring peace, and who in an attempt to re-establish their tyrannical rule had made an alliance with those who were clearly their enemies, in order to destroy Zibhebhu. Now that these allies were demanding their blood-money, the Usuthu had the effrontery to appeal to the British for assistance. As he told the Secretary of State, 'To intrigue against the forbearance and lenity of English authority in the Reserve Territory was an easy thing to do; but to resist the acts done on behalf of 800 Boers with rifles in their hands, who are not troubled by ideas of constitutional government or leniency or forbearance, is another thing.'[3]

126

Bulwer turned on the Usuthu messengers: their leader, the dead Cetshwayo, had 'let go the hand of the Government'.

> They gave themselves and their country to the Boers, and now they wish to be rid of the Boers, saying, that they had no power or right to make the promises they did, as both they and the country belonged to the Queen by right of conquest. One day it was one thing, and another day it is another thing; so that the Government never really knows what is meant ...
>
> Let Mnyamana and the Chiefs say clearly what they mean, so that their words may be known to the Government, and that I may send them to the Queen.[4]

Bulwer of course knew clearly what the Usuthu messengers meant – it was that he found their message far too presumptuous. It was time for the Zulu leaders to show contrition and some humility. If they were to save anything of their land, their power, their dignity, this could only be done with the assistance of the British. But before any request for help could even be considered, the Usuthu had to admit to their faults, their indiscretions, their massive irresponsibility towards their people, and what they had cost them in blood. The Usuthu, neither then nor later, were ever to give the Natal authorities that satisfaction.

Turned away by the Transvaal officials and rebuffed by Bulwer in March, the Usuthu leaders tried to plan their next attempt to appeal to Britain more carefully. First they had to overcome the real problems created by their dependence on oral communication. They accepted Martin Luthuli when he offered his skills in English and written Zulu. He had been brought up and educated at the American Board Mission at Groutville, had also suffered financially during the recession of the 1880s and had been hired by William Grant to look after his interests in Zululand. Harriette Colenso was soon to come to believe that Luthuli had been drawn far too close to the office of the SNA. This was probably true, but the power and influence of Somtsewu was formidable. Harriette would have been shocked to know that even Magema Fuze was corresponding confidentially with the Shepstones, who passed his letters on to the Governor.[5]

The Usuthu were to make many appeals and petitions to the British from 1885 to 1887. They were always contested and difficult occasions, which created difference and controversy. For Bishopstowe there was the fear that the Zulu message would be misinterpreted – as they believed the office of the SNA had done repeatedly. Control of Africans meant controlling the African voice. The challenge for Harriette Colenso was how to break this monopoly of the word. It was her task not to speak for the Zulu, but to discover and relate the situation from 'the Zulu point of view'. And her particular fear in 1885 was that their appeal for intervention by the British would be characterised in the official reports as an appeal for intervention by Natal.

Usuthu messengers usually reported the content of their messages to Bishopstowe on their arrival in Pietermaritzburg, and the response of the officials and their replies on their departure. Harriette Colenso was thus able to get a Zulu account to Chesson in London at about the same time that the official dispatches arrived at the Colonial Office. The secretary of the APS could therefore take informed action on his own initiative in England if necessary. But there were disadvantages to this. Firstly, it attracted official wrath. Secondly, it helped little unless the authorities decided to leak their version to the newspapers, for, if the official accounts were published, they only appeared months later in the Blue Books, when it was far too late for a correction or counter-statement to have any significant effect. Harriette did all she could to carry out her role as watchdog for the Usuthu – but more often than not, she could only bark long after the damage had been done and the culprit fled.

Although the Usuthu messages and petitions from 1885 to 1887 were not entirely consistent, the differences were in matters of detail rather than on major points of argument. They asked that Dinuzulu be recognised as his father's successor. They insisted that the Boers had never been invited by the Zulu and that it was only after considerable resistance on the part of the Usuthu (especially by Mnyamana) that the Boers' offer of assistance was accepted. Only a limited number of fighting men were given authority to join the attack on Zibhebhu – just enough to counterbalance the white mercenaries on the Mandlakazi side. Despite Usuthu protests, however, hundreds of whites had subsequently entered northern Zululand. It was alleged that the Boers had been promised a reward in cattle for their help. Grants of land had been refused because it was no longer theirs to give – it belonged to the Queen. The Usuthu denied any knowledge of the contents of the document signed by Grant and Dinuzulu; and as allies of Britain from the time of Shaka, and as subjects of the man whom the Queen had returned to Zululand, they asked for protection from the Boers who had entered their territory by fraud, and were attempting to occupy it by force.

In June 1885 they sent such a message to the authorities. Its mode of delivery mixed the old with the new: Luthuli put it into writing in Zulu, but he was accompanied by Mfunzi, the most experienced of all Zulu messengers. And to make sure it reached England unaltered, they asked Harriette Colenso to translate it into English. This of course infuriated the authorities. Luthuli's letter 'purporting' to be from the Usuthu leaders was, Bulwer hinted strongly, really the product of Bishopstowe, or Bishopstowe in cahoots with Luthuli's employer,

William Grant. The Governor ignored the messengers and their gift of leopard skins. He got the Zulu letter translated again, by the SNA, Henrique Shepstone, and sent it to England in a dispatch different from the one forwarding Harriette Colenso's translation. Bulwer was clearly furious: if he could not stop Harriette's interference in official dealing with Africans, then he could at least discredit it.

The messengers, who arrived a little later to ask for the formal recognition of Dinuzulu, were treated with the same angry scorn: 'The Governor will send the words of Mnyamana and the Chiefs to the Government of the Queen: and he will also send these his own words.'[6] He sent his own words indeed – completely undermining their petitions. The pattern was set for the future.

Building a wall around us

Dispirited and demoralised, the messengers left, not feeling themselves sufficiently confident to deliver to their chiefs such an antagonistic message. They went to Bishopstowe and showed Harriette the envelope which contained the written version of Bulwer's reply.

She thought long and hard. Then, knowing full well the consequences, she opened the letter and copied it. She then wrote to Bulwer protesting at the way the Usuthu's message had been misinterpreted and misunderstood. But this only confirmed what Bulwer had already written to the Colonial Office: the Usuthu were influenced by 'injudicious advice of those who have for so long ill-advised them; but it is exceedingly difficult to deal with a people who are in such misfortune and yet whose leaders advance such unwarrantable pretensions'.[7]

The Natal authorities tried to do something practical to stop this by implementing a Native Passes Bill to restrict movement between Zululand and Natal – it was popularly called the 'Colenso Extinction Bill'. In such situations Harriette quoted her friend amongst the sons of Mpande, the *mntwana* Shingana, who had once said, 'They want to build a wall around us.' The pressure was beginning to tell on the people of Bishopstowe: the hostility from Government House; their deepening fear that William Grant was not to be trusted; the crippling consequences of the Usuthu agreement with the Boers; the apparent impossibility of finding a way out.

Frances suggested that it was perhaps time to think of leaving Natal. Her sisters disagreed. Her mother, desperately concerned that Frances might somehow get to hear that she was going behind her back and thereby breaking the sense of family solidarity, wrote to Frank about it: 'Frances says we have given up enough of our lives and our means to these *dark skinned* people – it is time now for us to turn our means and opportunities to the best account for ourselves!!'

But the hold of Bishopstowe and Natal was too strong:

> If you could walk so far with us from this little 7 Oaks hole to the dreary
> Ruins on the top of the hill and feel as we do how one's heart clings to the
> prospect of trees, not all burnt by any means, the beloved mountain over
> [which] we saw the Comet hang in awful glory and He was with us always
> indeed it was He who called us up to look at it whenever there was a clear sky
> at that exceptional time for crowding together on the verandah if you my dear
> Son could see all these things and every other thing small and great, so famil-
> iar and dear so impregnated as it were with His presence almost with His
> smile you would not wonder at our longing to be allowed to build a nest there
> again ... Besides our own mere *sentiments* on this matter there is the feeling,
> which is very real, that unless we remain as centre to the Mission work of this
> diocese, which has but few sympathizers in the Colony, it will soon fall to the
> ground.[8]

And this could not be allowed to happen. There was work to be done in South
Africa.

A warning

The deep concern at Bishopstowe, the desperation of the Usuthu, the anger in
settler Natal and at Government House at the Boer occupation of Zululand,
meant little in London. Although the possibility of German intervention
rumbled on in the press, London was convinced the Zulu were a spent force and
they would ultimately come to accept that, if they were to save anything from
their disastrous compact with the Boers, they were dependent entirely on British
goodwill. That they should appeal to the British for assistance was expected. If
Britain could do something towards saving a portion of their territory without
jeopardising other interests, she might possibly do so, but the pleas of a powerless and broken people could not be a significant factor in London's calculations.

But even then the permanent officials in the Colonial Office found it difficult
to persuade the Cabinet to make a positive move. The consequences of British
attempts to intervene on the Transvaal's western border at the time were not
encouraging. The Foreign Office was dealing effectively with the possibility of
German involvement. Gladstone's second administration, beset with a host of
more important problems, did not take any action in Zululand, and at the end of
June 1885 the Liberal government fell with no decision on the future of Zululand having been made.

Derby was replaced as Secretary of State for the Colonies by his brother, Colonel F. Stanley, and the Colonial Office was determined to get some decision from the new Cabinet. Edward Fairfield, the astute expert on southern African affairs in the Colonial Office, wrote a memorandum that argued that to avoid 'a fresh Zulu war' which would flood the Reserve and Natal with refugees, and to reduce the cost of keeping British troops in the Reserve, a protectorate, even annexation, of Zululand should be announced. Once this was done, Bulwer could be authorised to recognise the New Republic behind a boundary of 'reasonable limits'.[9] But the British Cabinet was not prepared to go that far: 'Annexation is, I conclude, not contemplated at the present time.'[10]

Unable to devise a way in which to control Zululand without incurring the responsibilities implicit in annexation, the British government continued to procrastinate. Confusion, violence and despair amongst the Zulu did not threaten imperial control and dominance in this rather obscure corner of the Empire. Consequently it was decided that, as Bulwer's term of office was coming to an end, he should consult directly with the Colonial Office when he was back in London. On 23 October Bulwer left Natal, leaving Sir Charles Mitchell to act as Administrator of the government until the arrival of Sir Arthur Havelock, the new Governor of Natal and Special Commissioner for Zululand, who would be responsible for any new initiative.

In Zululand further policy drift meant greater material deprivation. Winter was always a difficult time for the Zulu living on the western borders, as they came under pressure from the Boers moving down from the highveld in search of the sweet grazing in the bushveld of the river valleys to the east of the Transvaal. In the winter of 1885 this seasonal pressure became a dispersed invasion. Many Boers began to erect dwelling places. In a consciously provocative move a township was marked out at St Lucia, despite an official warning from Bulwer.[11] A traveller reported that 'the Zulus were very much excited by the numbers of Boers encroaching on ... the land, burning and devouring all pastures before them ... I saw many Boers busy building, tree planting etc. ...'[12] It was this man's view that the Boers seemed unsure of their rights to the country, and the Zulu were in 'Ebb and Flow', and asked him repeatedly when the English were going to intervene.

From her discussions with Zulu messengers at Bishopstowe, Harriette Colenso realised what this meant. The appeal for recognition of Dinuzulu was not, as the Natal authorities treated it, a mere rhetorical flourish in a political game. Recognition would give Dinuzulu added political standing, which would make it easier for him to build the centre of royal power from which to set up the administrative structures necessary for effective control. At the moment, everywhere there was 'confusion and sending about from one chief to another'.[13] The exercise of political authority needed a geographical centre at a time when processes of division, alienation and interference in Zululand undermined any chance of re-establishing order. In all parts of the country, which less than a decade before had been securely in the control of the Zulu king from Ulundi, any attempt by the Zulu authorities to take a positive political initiative was undermined by the freebooters, mercenaries, Boers, traders, concession-seekers and adventurers moving into the country. It was occurring on all sides – in the south in the Reserve, in the west in the mooted New Republic, in the north along the Phongolo and the boundaries with the Swazi kingdom, and in the east in the Lubombo along the still-permeable border with the Tsonga.

Over the next few months reports of eviction, demands for labour, whippings and crop destruction by the New Republicans began to reach Natal, together with some cases of Zulu resistance. Many Zulu retreated under the pressure, moving east towards the Lubombo into the region recently occupied by the Mandlakazi, where they tried to clear arable land and prepare for planting.

But then the New Republicans overstepped the mark. On 26 October 1885 they issued a proclamation which defined the boundaries of the New Republic. A copy reached Mitchell in Natal; and Henrique Shepstone, the SNA, and his uncle John, together with some Africans who knew Zululand, set to work to transfer the boundaries onto a map. They came to the conclusion that the Boer boundaries left the Zulu about one-sixth of the territory outside the Reserve.[14]

London was informed of this conclusion on 26 December 1885. The Colonial Office was already concerned by reports of the Boer activities at St Lucia, and the estimate of the extent of the New Republic's claim persuaded the Secretary of State to act. Early in January 1886 a warning was sent under flying seal to the New Republic's leaders that their activities were being viewed by Her Majesty's Government with concern.[15] Melakhanya, who had been waiting at Bishopstowe for just such a development, hurried back to Zululand with the announcement confirmed in writing by the newspaper clipping Harriette Colenso gave him.[16]

'The Zulu people are sinking away'

The New Republicans were, of course, furious. It appeared that the restraint they had shown in the past eighteen months had only given the Usuthu the opportunity to go behind their backs and complain to the British government. Already copies of the British Parliamentary Paper C4587, with its expressions of Zulu loyalty to the Queen and petitions for British intervention which the Usuthu made in 1885, had reached the New Republic. For the Boers this was traitorous behaviour by which the Usuthu were attempting to renege on their agreements; the boundaries of the New Republic had to be finally demarcated immediately – and confirmed by the Usuthu.

Commandos were called up and the Usuthu leaders ordered to accompany them as witnesses as they rode along the newly proclaimed boundaries.[17] The Boers moved as a commando up the Sikhwebezi valley, which lay between Mnyamana's and Dinuzulu's homestead, set up camp, and ordered all the Usuthu to a meeting. With the Boers armed and in amongst their homesteads, fields and grazing lands, there was little they could do but obey. On 22 January the Usuthu leaders and many of their followers arrived as instructed. Dinuzulu, however, was not present. The Boers picked out the leaders and escorted them into the camp where they were accused of trying to set up a rival to Dinuzulu – and when they denied it the Blue Book was produced as proof. They were ordered to sign a document by which they pledged their loyalty to Dinuzulu. The Usuthu leaders refused, arguing that they had, and could have, no knowledge of what they were signing. The Boers abused and taunted them. They read out the appeals the Usuthu had made to the officials in Pietermaritzburg and accused them of being traitors who would be tried and executed. A bugle was blown, a troop of mounted men surrounded the camp, aimed their rifles at the Usuthu, and snapped the bolts. Mnyamana told them to shoot. They would still not sign. Ndabuko and Mnyamana were arrested, and released only after hostages had been taken and hundreds of cattle paid as bail, and the Boers then rode off towards Vryheid.

This meeting in January 1886 was for the Usuthu leaders the most bitter of humiliations. A string of reports about how they had been treated reached Natal in February, with the messengers under instructions to 'impress' upon the authorities that

> the Zulu people are sinking away; they are dying; their trust is in the English and unless the English come between them and the Boers soon, at once, they fear it will be too late ... Tell the Governor and the other Chiefs of the Queen that Mnyamana, the Zulu chiefs and people are in great trouble and they call loudly to the English to whom they and the country belong, not to delay, but to come at once and save the Queen's people and land from the Boers.[18]

The price of blood is a hard price

In London, Zululand matters were under consideration, but at a very different pace from that which the Zulu desired. Bulwer was now in England and submitted his lengthy 'Memorandum on the Situation in the Zulu Country ...' to the Colonial Office early in January 1886.[19] It reflected the view of the colony of Natal, in particular that of the office of the SNA – or, as Bishopstowe saw it, the opinions of the Old Serpent and his offspring. The memorandum traced the history of events in Zululand from the time of Cetshwayo's restoration and took the form of a sustained attack on the Usuthu and its leaders who, in their determination to retain the 'old hard, bad Zulu system',[20] had brought such misery on their people. Cetshwayo and Bishop Colenso were to a large extent responsible: the king was 'a man unfortunate both in the manner of his life and of his death, but most unfortunate of all in his friends and partisans who had identified themselves with his cause and who, wanting in judgment and transgressing what was right, led him fatally to his ruin'.[21] By means of this unholy alliance the royalists had defeated their enemies in battle,

> but at what cost! – at what a cost to the Zulu people, to the generation of today and to the generations of the future! The price of blood is a hard price; and to compass the destruction of Zibhebhu the Usuthu leaders bartered away the best part of the inheritance of the Zulu people, an inheritance, let it be remembered, which was left untouched by the British Government after the war of 1879.[22]

The British should intervene: for the sake of the Zulu north of the Reserve, for the Reserve itself, and for the colony of Natal. Bulwer's argument was one version of many made by Theophilus Shepstone for years now. 'The solution of the [Natal native] questions lay in the Zulu country': the major problem confronting Natal at that moment was its 'large and increasing native population', which demanded the 'return' of the 'Zulu' in Natal to Zululand. This was the 'natural and legitimate solution of the native question in Natal'.

However, if the Boers were allowed to retain the land which they claimed, this would

> shut the door upon the rightful settlement of the native question in Natal by closing the great part of Zululand to the Zulu people; and it will, in fact, alter the whole situation in that part of South Africa, because in affecting the native question in Natal, it will affect every other question that, directly or indirectly, nearly or remotely, is connected with it.
>
> The outlet for the native question of Natal lies in Zululand; and I will go further and say that the outlet for every native question in that part of South Africa lies through Zululand and the native territories that adjoin it to the vast

African continent beyond the region of European occupation.

That way lies a golden bridge for the native questions of the future. But let that outlet be closed, let that golden bridge be destroyed, and there will remain, pent up within our limits, unable to escape, the elements of burning questions which, for want of their natural outlet, must someday be kindled into flames in our very midst.[23]

Bulwer, however, stressed that he did not believe the Usuthu should 'gain all and lose nothing by the Boer compact'.[24] The Boers had been in Zululand for eighteen months now and had acquired certain rights. The extent of these should be decided in negotiations between representatives of the New Republic and the British authorities, the negotiators being instructed to keep in mind the interests of Natal, and of the Zulu generally, for their present predicament was a consequence of the recklessness of their leaders. In order to secure Britain's various interests in the region the negotiators should attempt to restrict the Boers 'to the country lying west of the Babanango and Nhlazatshe hills; leaving the coast country entirely for native purposes'.[25]

There was general agreement with this amongst the permanent officials in the Colonial Office.[26] However, before any further action could be taken, the Conservative government fell and the new Secretary of State for the Colonies, Lord Granville, had to be briefed. A draft dispatch on Zululand was prepared for the consideration of the Cabinet in March 1886.

Thus in London ministries fell, cabinets were shuffled and reshuffled, and peers of the realm were appointed as Secretary of State for the Colonies, while in northern Zululand an African society was being irretrievably shattered as the Zulu suffered further occupation of their land, loss of ownership, expulsion, and the humiliation of their leaders. As Melakhanya had said 'somewhat in despair' to Harriette Colenso – 'it is all talking, talking. The Queen is up in the sky, and the Zulus are on the earth being killed ...'[27]

III

DIVIDING THE INHERITANCE

CHAPTER 10

MATTERS OF HISTORY
(FEBRUARY–OCTOBER 1886)

Sir Arthur Elibank Havelock's instructions

Sir Arthur Elibank Havelock was in his early forties when he arrived to take up the post of Governor of Natal and Special Commissioner for Zululand. He had spent much of his youth in India, gone to Sandhurst, and left the military to join the colonial service, serving in the Seychelles and then Fiji. Before coming to Natal he had been in West Africa and involved in the demarcation of borders there during the scramble.

Natal was to test his abilities to the full. There was the settler factor for a start. The colony had still to emerge from economic recession, the Legislative Council was fractious, demanding and always ready to blame the representative of a haughty and remote imperial administration for its problems. Thus, the failure of Britain to restrain a rabble of adventurers from laying claim to a rich territory that rightly should have fallen to Natal caused huge resentment, which was directed towards the Governor.

Soon after Havelock arrived, the powerful figure of Sir Theophilus Shepstone, predictably enough, offered him his services. Havelock needed allies and advisers in Natal and accepted gratefully.[1] Nonetheless he did not intend to be just Shepstone's man, and made a point of also establishing friendly relations with Bishopstowe. There was social justification for this as well. One of Havelock's friends and associates from his military days was Louis Knollys, who had been in Natal at the end of the 1860s and become involved with Frances Colenso. Subsequently Knollys had been posted in Mauritius where he had been on the same staff as Havelock.

When the Havelocks visited Seven Oaks to call on Sarah Frances Colenso they brought with them their private secretary, Gerald Browne, whom Knollys had introduced as a special friend. He and Frances immediately got on well – and one gets a hint of the confidence she had in her relations with men, who in turn found her stimulating and attractive. The women at Seven Oaks were amused by 'Brownie' and his devotion to the Governor and his family. In time the laughter was to stop and they were to test Brownie and his patron Havelock severely. But it is remarkable that the women of Bishopstowe still had the resilience to laugh, for the summer of 1885–6 had been particularly trying. First Robert's son and then his wife contracted typhoid. Agnes, followed by Harriette, rushed down to Durban to nurse them. It was just at this time that the messengers came from Zululand with their appeals for intervention, which Harriette felt she had to monitor carefully. Then Agnes at Bishopstowe became ill. Frances was frightened by this because she was unable to nurse the headstrong Agnes, who would only listen to her eldest sister, Harriette. Then lungsickness in their cattle caused heavy losses, and not just monetary ones, for they all – and Agnes especially – cared deeply for the animals on the farm.

They recovered from typhoid but their work continued to drain their energy. Frances was absorbed in the Durnford case – and there is a hint of disapproval in her mother's letter to Frank: 'It would be *quite useless* to attempt to persuade Frances to give it up – It is now what she lives for – so she thinks ...' Both Harriette and Agnes worked too hard and stayed up too late, to their mother's way of thinking – but their reasons were characteristically different: 'their only complaint is "insomnia" but that is because Harriette writes so long at night and because Agnes is so late amongst her little rabbits and chickens seeking to intercept the wild cat who is always interfering with some little party just arrived.'[2]

But regardless of the other demands being made on Harriette, something had to be done in Zulu affairs now that it seemed that William Grant was unwilling to take any initiative. On 23 February 1886, the day after Sir Arthur Havelock took office, Harriette picked up her unfinished letter to Chesson, put aside five weeks previously when typhoid struck. A few days later Mfunzi and Luthuli, the old and the new, the confidential messenger of the Zulu kings and the literate *kholwa* from Groutville, reached Pietermaritzburg to make another appeal – this time to the new Governor. Luthuli avoided Bishopstowe but Mfunzi kept in touch and told Harriette of the intensification of Boer violence against his chiefs. There was now no going back. The two-year interval since the death of the king, during which the Usuthu had attempted to solve their predicament by an alliance with Boer gunmen, was over. The consequences had been disastrous. They now turned again to the women of Bishopstowe who, although they had no guns, did possess moral courage, integrity and their letters.

On 5 March the Zulu messengers were introduced to the new Governor. John Shepstone was present to advise Havelock on the complexities of native diplomacy. Mfunzi and Luthuli asked, on behalf of Mnyamana, Dinuzulu and Ndabuko, that Dinuzulu be recognised by the British as Cetshwayo's heir, that

the Boers be removed from Zululand, and that the Zulu be allowed to 'live under the Queen who has always ruled over us'.[3]
A week later Havelock was sent a telegram from London giving him the gist of the official instructions regarding Zululand. Boer rights were to be recognised, but only over a portion of Zululand. The extent of this territory was to be arrived at by friendly negotiations, and Havelock was to invite the New Republic to participate in these.[4]
Havelock called Luthuli and Mfunzi to Government House. He informed them that Britain could not accede to all their requests. The Zulu, he said, were 'not ignorant of the importance which white people attach to signing a paper' and could therefore not 'expect to escape the effects of their own acts'. 'The utmost that, in my opinion, the British government may be induced to do is to bring about an agreement with the Boers, by which a portion of land may be secured for the Zulus; and this I will be prepared to recommend. If the Queen's Government will consent to do this much, the Zulu should be thankful.'[5]
It was a most disconcerting reply – but Mfunzi and Luthuli were never able to deliver it to their leaders because even more worrying was the news coming in from northern Zululand. After the unsuccessful attempt to coerce the Usuthu into an agreement in January, the Boers stepped up their violence against the Usuthu. More and more reports of floggings, evictions and the destruction of crops reached Natal, together with threats to capture the leading Usuthu. On 17 March, Ndabuko, Shingana and a number of their councillors fled their homes, crossed into the Reserve, and asked Colonel Cardew, Acting Sub-Commissioner at Nquthu, for the opportunity to put their grievances to the authorities. Mnyamana was unable to join them and Dinuzulu had refused because 'the people would become completely demoralised and take flight' if he did. But the 'nation which was built up by Chaka is being ruined'.[6]
For Havelock it confirmed the incapacity of the Zulu to act as viable agents in the dispute. They were clearly powerless. The solution lay in negotiations not with the Zulu but with the New Republicans. Early in April the dispatch with his instructions arrived in Natal. Her Majesty's Government, it declared, had never surrendered 'its rights and the obligations of its position as the paramount power in the portion of South Africa [beyond the Reserve]'. If the New Republic's claims in this area were recognised 'it might cause the most serious inconvenience' to independent Zululand, to the Reserve and to Natal. As far as the agreements alleged to have been made between the Boers and the Usuthu were concerned, not only were the Zulu under treaty obligation with Britain not to alienate land, but, Granville continued, Her Majesty's Government was not satisfied that the Usuthu had fully understood the contents of the documents

signed and therefore 'cannot be held bound by the instruments on their full literal effect'. Nevertheless, there could be no doubt that the Usuthu had promised 'to alienate some portion of their land [and] after all that has happened, and having regard to the time which has elapsed, the occupation of a part of Zululand by the Boers ought to be recognised on reasonable conditions'. Havelock was instructed to open communications with the New Republic with a view to reaching an agreement on the extent of territory to be placed under its jurisdiction. Once this had been achieved, Britain would come to a decision on the political future of the remainder of the country.[7]

The main intention behind the instructions is clear enough. Britain wanted to make sure that the Afrikaner republics were to be confined to the interior and isolated from access to the sea. The Zulu, under a form of colonial overrule which could be decided in the future, would be used to confine the Boers to the interior. Recognition of the New Republic would be justified by arguing that Britain was saving at least something for the Zulu from the consequences of their disastrously unwise agreement with the Boers.

To carry out these instructions Havelock needed to begin playing a game of diplomatic bluff. Basing his first move on the assertion of the rights acquired by conquest in 1879, he presented the New Republicans with the apparent choice of losing all the land they claimed, or securing a portion of it if they came to the conference table. As far as Natal was concerned, although deprived of the chance of acquiring all Zululand, she should be satisfied with the fact that a good proportion of the country's land and labour would be secured for future colonial exploitation. The Zulu, faced with the possibility of losing everything to the Boers, or retaining something through this British initiative, should be satisfied as well. It was true that the Zulu royal house and its supporters appeared dissatisfied, but they were too intimidated and divided to resist. They were responsible for their predicament and were after all only a minority representing the old order, which had to change. Officials reported that it was only the continued encouragement they received from Bishopstowe which raised their hopes and persuaded them to hope for a major concession. Havelock believed that as long as the Zulu feelings were sensibly and firmly handled, Usuthu opposition to negotiations with the Boers need not be a major consideration.

Havelock was wrong.

'Matters of history'

Harriette Colenso realised from the information she had gleaned from newspapers, from Mfunzi's reports to her of his interviews at Government House, and from general gossip in town, that an announcement on the future British policy towards Zululand was imminent. It was essential, therefore, that Havelock was properly briefed and not just dependent on whatever information the SNA chose to send him. The Usuthu perspective of events had to be placed on record.

But she was very restricted in what she could do. She had so few allies. She tried to revive the link that her father had established (to Frances's discomfort) with Dr Jorrissen, State Secretary in the Transvaal. 'The Zulus too tell me that they believe certain of the original party who are Transvaal Boers to have been honestly their friends throughout', she wrote. 'I have always called the "New Republicans" "filibusters" in order to keep clear the distinction between them and "the Boers."' While many laid the blame on the Transvaal Boers for land-grabbing, she always believed that many of the men were Natal merchants from some of the largest firms and that the Natal government was just as much to blame. If only the Usuthu would give evidence that there had been just a hundred men involved originally in the movement, that in its initial conception it was not a movement of wilful aggression but a necessary defence against Zibhebhu and his mercenaries, then 'something can be done to prevent the Zulus from being "eaten up" by Natal doings, and also by the strong desire expressed by the Jingoes here that, the New Republic should be annexed to Natal'.[8]

It was a brave attempt and a clever letter – but more important was the one she wrote to Havelock. He received it on 30 March 1886 together with a number of enclosures, all of which she felt would have to be part of any arbitration process. In the covering letter she pointed out that evidence would have to be taken from William Grant on the circumstances surrounding the signing of the treaty.[9]

Frances meanwhile tried an informal approach. Havelock had fallen down some stairs breaking an arm and dislocating a shoulder. Frances's book, *The Ruin of Zululand*, which took the history of the kingdom up to the king's return, was now published and she sent him a copy to read while he recuperated. Harriette reported that Havelock 'has written a private friendly note to Frances thanking her for the Ruin of Zululand which she had lent him to amuse him in his illness! and which he says that he has read and wished to talk with her on the subject some day. May he be strong enough!'[10]

On 9 April the sisters were asked to Government House for lunch and in the afternoon they talked Zulu politics. It marked a great change. After years of its being excluded from consultation on African matters, the Governor was attempting to bring Bishopstowe into the process. Havelock hoped to be able to work with and not against the bishop's daughters.

Nonetheless, although she was gratified by the attention, the visit did not make Harriette any easier about the future of Zululand. To her great concern, it appeared as if Havelock wanted her 'to persuade my poor friends not to *expect* much!' 'There was no use in inquiring how things had come about, they must *be taken as they are*, no force would be allowed, the most that could be done would be to save a small part of the country for the Zulus, to draw a hard and fast line and stick to it.'

In Harriette's opinion the Usuthu position had to be rooted in the history of the last ten years and the sustained attempt to misrepresent the Zulu royal house. It must include the unjust war that the British had forced on the king and the settlement of 1879, which excluded the true representatives of the Zulu people from power. Any intervention would have to take into consideration the numerous attempts of the Usuthu to avert the approaching disaster in Zululand and the way in which their efforts had been dismissed by the officials. It should take into account the different interest groups that had encouraged civil war, and the attempts of the Usuthu leaders to defend their people – a defence which in the end only brought more violence. It could be proved, Harriette believed, that the history of the Boers in Zululand was a history of deceit and fraud. Above all, no decisions about the future of Zululand could be made over the heads of the Zulu leaders – if negotiations were started, they had to be represented.

But from their first meeting it appeared to her that Havelock felt 'the rights of the case don't matter – *that's* the answer we get when we try to urge them to some Inquiry', 'these things were now matters of history'.[11] The Usuthu and Harriette were never to accept this view. If there was to be a settlement in Zululand this could only be done if the history of the decade of violence and its causes was thoroughly examined. History could not be treated as an irrelevance.

The hawk

And there was someone who could give substance to this history, an eyewitness to many of the events, and signatory to the agreement between the Boers and the Zulu upon which so much depended – William Grant. But his attitude had worried both Chesson and Harriette increasingly through 1885. They accepted his argument that he had signed the document only because the Usuthu were being threatened with violence and because they were already so compromised that all he was able to do was to save them from further disaster. But it was an uneasy acceptance, made possible only by averting their eyes from other aspects of his account which suggested that he had been extremely unwise, perhaps even fraudulent.

If he had acted from any but the highest motives, then their whole project was threatened. The responsibility Grant had assumed by signing the document was immense, and it extended beyond Grant personally to those who had backed him – to Bishopstowe and the APS. As Bulwer had written:

> The Boers, wise after the wisdom of this world, had taken precaution against future denials by recognising Mr. William Grant's claim to be considered as the adviser of the Zulu nation, and by admitting his right to take part in the agreement: and hence we see Mr. Grant's signature to the paper. If Mr. Grant had not been there, if no European had been there to read the paper and explain its purport to the Usuthu Chiefs, then the latter might have been able afterwards to deny all knowledge of it, or, at all events, a complete knowledge of what they were doing. But, as it is, that way of escape is closed to them.[12]

And there *were* problems in Grant's explanations and in his actions. There was his insistence that he was still owed cattle by the Usuthu. Harriette felt that in principle he was correct to make the claim – the Usuthu should not enter into such agreements and promise payments lightly. But there were persistent rumours that he had already been paid, some said in cash, some said in cattle. Martin Luthuli, his own emissary, now working for the Usuthu, believed he had been well paid.

The more Harriette Colenso tried to build a case upon which the Usuthu could negotiate by uncovering the circumstances under which the agreement of 16 August had been signed, the more evasive Grant became. But once Havelock arrived in Natal, and it became clear that he was going to negotiate with the New Republicans, the difficulties with Grant could no longer be avoided. He was needed immediately: his account had to be marshalled on the side of the Usuthu.

But the new Governor got to him first and in April he had an interview at Government House. Grant wrote to Harriette about it, still aglow with the light of official recognition at last. And, he suggested, further assistance on his part would depend upon adequate reimbursement. 'As I have already told you it is impossible that I can waste any more of my time over the question. I have however promised the Governor replies to certain questions he has put and generally to give him any assistance in my power. The rest remains with the Zulus. If they want my services they must acknowledge them in a substantial form.'[13]

On 2 May, Ndabuko and Shingana, the two most prominent brothers of the dead king, arrived in Pietermaritzburg with their advisers to make their statement on conditions in Zululand before the Special Commissioner. Not wanting to prejudice their mission in the eyes of the authorities, they kept away from Bishopstowe. They were, however, in clandestine contact with Harriette and she passed on to Grant their urgent desire to meet him and discuss the position they should take, before they met the Special Commissioner.

Her letters to him were still friendly despite the fact that she was well aware that there were differences between Grant and the Usuthu and that the meeting would be difficult – not only for the Zulu involved, but for her: 'They want him [Grant] to come up and talk over the matter with them, before me as umpire before going to His Excellency. A nice position for me, especially if they finally disagree.'[14] Grant, however, had no desire to meet the Usuthu.

> As I have already explained to you it is impossible for me to waste further time upon those who place no value upon my services. I have done my friends, and family, and self a gross injustice in my efforts to help the Zulus, and in the absence of any recognition by them I cannot believe there is any genuine wish on their part that I should continue to represent them.[15]

Harriette Colenso's reply was controlled and courteous. For her, the issues at stake were so much bigger than the squabbles amongst those who participated in them. She urged Grant, for her sake, to make the comparatively short journey to Pietermaritzburg and meet the Usuthu on matters 'in which you have already taken an important – if not vital part'.[16] Grant refused. He would attend a meeting with the Usuthu only if called to do so by the Governor. This opportunity came on 7 May 1886, when the Usuthu – led by Ndabuko, Shingana, Santingi, Martin Luthuli, Makhedama – met William Grant and the SNA, Henrique Shepstone, on the invitation and in the presence of the Governor, Sir Arthur Havelock.[17]

For the first hour Shingana and Santingi went over the history of the relations between the Usuthu and the Boers. It was in essence the same interpretation of events that they had used in their previous petitions: the Boers, through force and fraud, had entered Zululand, and the Usuthu had signed documents either because they were misinformed of their contents or because they had been forced to do so. Then came the major issue of difference. The Usuthu declared that the contents of the 16 August proclamation had never been explained to them. It was only recently that they had discovered that a huge area of land had been ceded. Grant asserted that he had explained it fully. The arguments continued until dark, with Grant and the Usuthu flatly contradicting one another. Grant was furious – he lost his temper and there was an 'explosion', as Harriette put it. It was exactly the situation that she had hoped to avoid – a wrangle between former allies in the presence of Havelock and his officials.

Three days later, without William Grant, the Usuthu delegation met the Governor, who asked them to state what they wanted of the British. Shingana answered with a call for an inquiry. He wanted the presentation of evidence and open and direct confrontation with those with whom they differed – an investigation, in other words, suited to members of a society aware of the power of the document but still dependent on oral communication.[18]

Havelock gave the same noncommittal reply that other Usuthu deputations had received. He found it hard to believe that Grant had not explained the terms of the agreement to them. The Usuthu had 'let go the hand of the Government, and it is not to be surprised that they have suffered for it'. As Special Commissioner he felt he could not do more than save a portion of the country for them – and if that was possible 'they should be very thankful'.

After the interview Ndabuko and Shingana considered that it was safe to meet Harriette Colenso. They told her that they had been received with kindness and consideration by Havelock. However, he had warned them 'not to expect to recover the whole of their country'.

> You see, they, poor things, go back to the Queen's promises to Cetshwayo, and looked at straightforwardly – not politically – it is a very ugly story for England of treachery, and cruelty.
>
> Well I'm very cross, you see I have been hearing the Zulu side of the case for some hours, and it's so unanswerable and I am so ashamed to be an Englishwoman before them.
>
> I have not yet quarrelled with Mr. Grant, but I expect he will with me, because I can't believe him against Ndabuko and Shingana without evidence on either side, and I have not enough yet.[19]

A few days later the Usuthu made their formal farewell of the authorities. They took the opportunity to tell Havelock of the violence that had taken place in Zululand since they had last met, and their fear for their safety once they returned. They also informed him of something about which they were greatly concerned. They had heard rumours that Zibhebhu was attempting to get permission to return to his lands in the north. 'We hope', they told Sir Arthur Havelock, 'there is no chance of his wish being complied with, as we are sure it would only lead to more bloodshed. It would be like putting a half-dead snake into your bosom which will, when warm, turn and bite you.' But in the end they hid their disappointment and very real concerns, and expressed

> our thanks to the Governor for the kind and considerate treatment we have

received while in Natal, and we thank the Governor also for his words, which
give us hope that we will be taken care of ...
    We have expressed no request as to what we would like; we trust to the
Government to do the best it can for us. We know that we will be safe in the
hands of the Government, without whose help we will become dry bones.[20]

They left. Harriette Colenso now had to act. It was up to her to persuade the
authorities to give the Usuthu a place at the British–Boer negotiating table. If
that failed, as it well might, then the position as viewed by the Usuthu had to be
placed on record. The situation demanded a quick, effective, but careful
response, and Harriette showed a hard-headed political realism in her approach.
Grant had told her that he had had a private meeting with Havelock. He
described it as a '"most satisfactory interview" and that Sir Arthur "pretty clearly realises" the whole case'. Harriette turned this piece of typical Grantian bom-
bast against him. In this situation then, she wrote, 'it behoves me to omit no
morsel of evidence which I possess, as I by no means "realise the whole" – in the
sense which Mr. Grant intends.' Ten days later she submitted to Havelock her
'notes' – annotations on a letter of Grant's which demonstrated that, despite
what was being said by Grant and the officials, the dispute was immensely com-
plex and full of difficulties. There could be no quick negotiated solution as the
officials clearly hoped. What was required was a detailed inquiry into the different points of view of the participants, and a careful sifting of the evidence, before
any judgement could be made. She was taking it upon herself to make this intervention because

    it is to be feared that the Zulus must now plead their cause alone, and at a ter-
    rible disadvantage, where everyone but themselves has the assistance of writ-
    ing and printing. Before a just tribunal, however, their very weakness will pro-
    cure them consideration, and I will therefore make no further apology for
    troubling you with the enclosed notes ...[21]

Heart sickness

By the end of May 1886 Harriette was exhausted. During the course of the year
she had had to deal, over and above her usual responsibilities at Bishopstowe,
with typhoid in the family, lungsickness amongst their cattle, the continuing difficulties over the future of the Church of England, the arrival of the Usuthu deputation, the decision to take up its case with Havelock, and the break with
Grant. And at just that moment another crisis broke, a family one.

Offy Shepstone, determined to stop Frances Colenso and her advocate Colonel Luard's investigations into the allegation that he had removed documents from Colonel Durnford's body, succeeded in persuading the military authorities in Natal to hold an inquiry. It found in favour of Shepstone. Frances was absolutely devastated. She suffered a relapse, and decided to leave Natal immediately for England. Her mother and sisters were trapped, fearful of the consequences both of opposing her and of letting her go – not wanting to treat her like a child, but at the same time desperately worried about sending her to England with insufficient funds and care. But Frances assured them that, once in England, she could stay with her friends and relatives. With her mother and sisters it was agreed that she should have an allowance of £5 a month. It was clearly insufficient for someone who was by now an invalid. But Frances was determined to leave, and on 9 June 1886 she sailed from Natal.

Through all this, Harriette had to come to terms with the quarrel with Grant, her own and her father's failure to read his character, and the way that this had undermined the attempt to build a solid negotiating position for the Usuthu. Grant had also compromised the sober, sensible lobbyist F.W. Chesson in London. On 30 May Harriette began a letter to Chesson to bring him up to date. After a few lines she was unable to continue – 'so far I wrote and then stopped, partly because my head ached too much to write sense, partly from heart sickness, because if Mr. Campbell is right as to [Grant's] "honesty of purpose" I can't help feeling that in other matters ... Mr. Grant is proved unreliable ...'[22] She was able to admit, albeit in her reserved way, what one senses she had come to realise for some time but could not acknowledge: that they, her father included, had been wrong about Grant, and in their error had severely damaged the Zulu cause.

Harriette was now more isolated politically than ever, but not alone. There were her family and friends, of course: Agnes and Katie Giles, and her brother Robert and his family in Durban, supported her emotionally, materially where they could, and gave her secretarial assistance. But they could not provide the legal, political, strategic advice that she needed so badly. And they, in turn, were so dependent on her. Just at the time when the 1886 crisis was at its height and Harriette was being weighed down by work and disappointment, her mother wrote, Harry 'is just a sunbeam amongst us'.[23]

There were also the Usuthu leaders and messengers, with whom she talked, to whom she listened, and who informed her in ways direct and indirect on affairs in Zululand. Although Magema had been away on family affairs in Zululand, he was soon to return to help in the printing. Mubi Nondenisa was not only her confidential messenger to Zululand but increasingly a trusted adviser and companion. There were the men and women and their families of Bishopstowe: the tenants, white and black, in whose lives they became involved, the Hlubi especially. This had advantages and disadvantages, giving her the warmth, but also the distractions, of domesticity. As she wrote in a letter to Chesson, apologising for the scrappiness of a letter: 'we have only one sitting room here, and my little nephew and a grandson of Langalibalele are playing hide and seek in it.'[24]

Some of the leading white men in Natal were able to separate the public and the private sufficiently clearly to remain friendly and supportive. Although her attitudes were widely considered to be not just extreme but inappropriate for a woman, she was still able to elicit respect from some of the prominent people in the colony, who clearly admired her efficiency and her integrity. Harriette was quite prepared to make use of these contacts, the quiet friendships she had with some of the leading professional men in the colony, the frank exchanges made in confidence in the Attorney-General's office, even over the Governor's table. Without breaking the strict conventions pertaining to confidential conversations and private correspondence, she took the opportunities they provided to receive and pass on important information on Zulu matters.

Nonetheless, the final decisions on how to act and promote the cause of what she now called 'the Zulu National Party' were her responsibility. And the material resources she had to do this were few. In an attempt to revive her father's 'Digest' and place the Zulu case on record, she purchased a small second-hand printing press with a very depleted set of fonts. With the help of Magema and Mubi she set it to work to produce annotated statements and analyses of documents which she believed would facilitate an understanding of Zululand's recent history. She sent copies to Havelock and to her supporters in South Africa and England, in the hope that they would assist in the inquiry which she and the Usuthu still believed had to precede any final agreement between Boer, Zulu, imperial Britain and colonial Natal over the future of Zululand.

The Agreement: 22 October 1886

In July 1886 a deputation from the New Republic, led by Lucas Meyer, arrived in Natal to negotiate terms with Havelock. They met on 5 July, and to his surprise Havelock learnt that Meyer refused to accept the conditions laid down in April as the basis for any negotiations. Instead he published an alternative set: recognition of the New Republic's sovereignty over 2,260,000 acres of land, and 'suzerain rights' over all Zululand outside the Reserve.[25] Havelock had no choice but to suspend the meeting. He wrote to London that 'it is not easy to discover the object or the motive which induced Mr. Meyer and his colleagues to incur the trouble and expense of making the journey'.[26]

But it seems unlikely that Meyer and his colleagues were acting out of ignorance. Their position in the territory north of the Reserve was strong. Divided politically, devastated economically, the central organising features of the society broken, the Zulu were unable to rally around either a military or a political strategy. The Usuthu adopted a passive response: they would 'sit still' and appeal to the 'Queen' for intervention.

They had little choice, but it was a weak response indeed. The coming of the 1886 winter had seen another influx of Boers seeking winter grazing in the lower parts of Zululand. More land was occupied and the Zulu were pushed eastwards once again.[27] Beyond the January warning that the occupation of Zululand should cease, Britain had done nothing to hinder this movement. It was clear that the more land that could be occupied and farms established, the stronger the New Republic's bargaining position would be. To the horror of the Zulu, the Boers moved into the valley of the kings, Emakhosini, where the Zulu royal ancestors were buried, and in the search for loot despoiled the grave of Senzangakhona, the father of Shaka, Dingane and Mpande.

Rumours of the meeting between the New Republicans and Havelock reached the Usuthu, together with reports that a Babanango–Nhlazatshe line was being mentioned. A meeting was called, and Luthuli wrote down an urgent message for transmission to Havelock. Even in Henrique Shepstone's translation it was one of the most eloquent of the Usuthu petitions.

Like Harriette Colenso, the Usuthu feared that a decision would be reached between Boer and Briton without Zulu participation. They asked to be kept officially informed of what went on between Meyer and Havelock 'because there is much that troubles [us] in the air'. They reported with horror the desecration of the graves of the Zulu kings, together with the continued efforts to drive the Zulu from the country 'which was given to us by the House to which we belong, to be the inheritance of our children's children'. They reported that they were being denied access to their lands by Boers, who were 'settling in the midst of us', and now that the planting season had arrived they were threatened with famine. 'O, Chief, we lived through last year, as we still had cattle, with which we bought sacks of mealies; this year we have no cattle, they have been taken by the Boers. We shall die, and the country will be desolate. We cannot, O Chief, live in the same country with the Boers.'[28]

In his reply, Havelock reminded them they were largely responsible for their situation. The line mentioned was only a basis for negotiation, but Havelock would keep the content of their message in mind. Yet whatever happened, they must 'take a firmer hold of the guiding hand of the Government than they have ever hitherto done'.[29]

But it was a confusingly changing guiding hand. By the time the news of the suspension of negotiations had reached London, Gladstone's third administration had been defeated and the Conservatives were in power once again. Edward Stanhope became the new Colonial Secretary of State, to be replaced by Sir Henry Holland, soon to become Lord Knutsford. And, from the Zulu point of view, it was a weak and palsied hand as well. It was felt in the Colonial Office that if the New Republicans were reluctant to negotiate, then they should be encouraged by the offer of more land.

> I should not see any great objection to a considerable extension of the Boer country ... to the Eastward ... provided that (1) a good width of country along the coast is kept under British control, so as to secure an outlet through British territory to the northward [and to prevent interference with the coast and St Lucia Bay] and that the Boers are bound in the strongest terms to give free passage through all parts of the country ...[30]

However, it was important to act quickly: it was far easier to refute paper claims than those based on occupation. Havelock was informed by telegram on 4 September 1886 that Her Majesty's Government

> attach great importance to a settlement of Zululand without any avoidable delay; and that subject to the retention of sufficient land for the Zulus, and, above all, of a sufficient belt of country between the territory of the Boers and the sea, they consider the establishment of some boundary as of more importance than the precise limits of the territory reserved.[31]

The New Republicans were to be informed that unless they entered into communication with Havelock, a line might be drawn unilaterally. This ultimatum was sent to Meyer on 6 September,[32] and a month later he and members of his executive arrived in Pietermaritzburg to renew negotiations.

But the rumours and the delays were creating tension and stress in Zululand itself, increasing the possibility of violence and tragedy. There were reports that Dabulamanzi, brother of Cetshwayo, differed with the other sons of Mpande on matters of policy. Grant, resentful of his former associates, exploited this, and forwarded a message to Havelock from Dabulamanzi repudiating Ndabuko and Shingana's petition to the Governor. On 22 September Dabulamanzi was arrested by two Boers called Van der Berg and Joubert and ordered to ride with them, in the company of his son, to Vryheid. As they passed close to the border with the Reserve, Dabulamanzi broke away from them and galloped into 'British territory'. The Boers followed, there was an argument and a scuffle, and Dabulamanzi was shot three times. He died the next morning.[33]

There is evidence that the shooting was in fact a political assassination, instigated by the Usuthu leaders and carried out by Boer hit men. It was believed that Dabulamanzi was trying to take his own initiative in Zulu affairs at a time when the Usuthu leaders had to present a united front to the threat offered by the British–Boer compromise over the future of Zululand. However, Dabulamanzi's death was not allowed to hinder the progress of the negotiations, where the Boers took a very hard line claiming a huge tract of land. Havelock insisted that whatever territory was left to the Zulu had be contiguous with the Reserve and that the wagon road from Eshowe to Ulundi should remain in British territory. Meyer countered by stating that this was land heavily settled by Boers, and that he could not guarantee their support if he handed it over. Instead he offered a compromise. The area need not be incorporated into the New Republic as long as it remained in the possession of the white farmers. To compensate for this, however, the British had to make a further concession: the territory in the north between the Mkhuze and the Phongolo (which, in 1879, Wolseley had awarded Mgojana of the Ndwandwe) had to be incorporated in the New Republic. Under pressure from his superiors in London to reach some agreement, Havelock felt that he had little choice and 'I finally, though unwillingly, accepted the compromise'.[34]

For the Zulu people, the line eventually agreed upon was a disaster. The highlands of Zululand passed from their control, as well as the rich mixed grazing around the upper reaches of the major rivers north of the Mhlatuze. By the 'compromise' they lost a huge wedge of territory in the north-west stretching along the Phongolo to the Lubombo mountains. Moreover, the tract of land which was to remain outside the New Republic but in possession of the whites – it was called Proviso B – was a legal nicety which brought no advantage whatsoever to the Zulu. They lost their land no matter who had authority. And within Proviso B was Emakhosini – the place of the kings – the cradle of the Zulu nation.

Thus, with the signing of the Agreement between the British and the New Republic on 22 October 1886, the Zulu lost control of half the territory which had remained in their possession. And Britain still had to decide the conditions under which the territory left to the Zulu was to be ruled.

CHAPTER 11

THE LIMITS OF PROTEST

Worse things than death

Frances Colenso had arrived in England at the end of July 1886. She and her family believed that her already fragile health had been weakened further by her disappointment over the outcome of the inquiry into Offy Shepstone's actions, and her distress at the way her friend and advocate Colonel Luard had been treated. Desperately unhappy as she already was, her defeat in the Durnford case now pushed her to the edge of despair. But she was determined to continue her work: to vindicate Durnford, to assist in the completion of her father's biography, and to keep Zulu affairs in the public eye. But she was physically very weak, and she suffered relapses which left her even weaker – and as she lashed out at the wrongs and injustice, the blows fell often on the people closest to her.

When she arrived in England she found that Major Louis Knollys was there also, passing through on his way to take up a post in the Jamaican police. Beyond the fact that it existed, we know nothing about their love affair in Natal twenty years before. But to be able to see him again was a surprise and a pleasure for Frances. Their time together was brief and intense, and she found a sympathetic listener to her story about Durnford and the stolen documents.

In order to be in London with Knollys she changed arrangements and delayed the visit to her brother Frank. He wrote her a letter in which he expressed his disappointment and disapproval. Frances turned on him. His letter, she wrote,

has given me extreme surprise and pain to find myself so completely misunderstood where I should least have expected it. I think you forget, dear Frank, that I am no longer a girl, but a middle-aged woman who has seen something of the world, and much of sorrow ...

I have *not* 'thrown you overboard to please a major' (or anyone else), nor has he 'imposed his wishes' on me and 'frustrated your hopes' ...

She was angry to think that Frank believed that Knollys and she were meeting 'or are likely to meet on "warmer terms," than those of old and valued friend-ship'. And then, purporting to demonstrate to Frank the nature of her feelings towards Knollys, she wrote:

> No one lives *less* likely to credit me with anything short of the purest and highest motives for all I do than Louis Knollys, but, as perhaps you will not accept my judgement on that point, I have made up my mind to tell you that he knows, what I did not mean to tell you abruptly or without tender prepara-tion, that my life is not now as 'good' a one even as it was when I left England, five years ago, with one injured lung.

Her doctor had just confirmed what she had already suspected. Tuberculosis had spread from her right to her left lung. But to tell Frank in this way, in response to his mild protest at her wish to stay in London to see Knollys, was cruel.

The spread of the infection meant that the coming winter was a real threat. There were not many options open to her, but she was thinking of being admit-ted to a consumptives' hospital on the Isle of Wight.

> And now, dearest Frank, I trust that after this letter you will see that the whole of yours is written under a misapprehension, and will feel justified in withdrawing what are – forgive my saying so – very serious accusations to be brought against a woman of my age and position by her brother. Unless you can do so I fear that we shall not have a very happy meeting, for it would be intolerable to me to be with those I love so dearly, but who so completely mis-judge me as you have done, unless the misunderstanding can be removed ...[1]

Her closest friend at the time was Georgie Burne-Jones, a figure who has attracted some attention from biographers as one of the MacDonald sisters, as the wife of Edward Burne-Jones, as intimate friend of William Morris, as well as a spirited woman in her own right. She was older than Frances. They had met at Winnington Hall in the 1860s and Frances had kept in contact and renewed the relationship during her last visit to England. By now it was a deep friendship which made great demands on Georgie's kindness and concern as Frances grew emotionally, and physically, increasingly dependent upon her.

There were many others who depended on Georgie at the time, not only her children, but her husband Ned, absorbed in his painting and his private worlds, and also William Morris. Georgie's world was one to which Frances aspired – the artistic world of the Pre-Raphaelites, its ethereal women, chivalrous knights, their literary friends. They had a mutual acquaintance in John Ruskin, and Georgie had been a close friend of George Eliot, whose writing was greatly admired at Bishopstowe. When Frances was still in Natal, Georgie had tried to evoke her life in London:

> It is just upon 11 a.m. and Mr Morris is here as usual, and Edward is drawing a cartoon for stained glass, and the two are smoking and talking and rather enjoying themselves. Now Mr Morris is reading Silas Marner aloud to Edward, and with that background I am trying to go on a little with this letter. It is to my mind the most beautiful book that George Eliot wrote. I have just been reading 'Middlemarch' and thought it far from beautiful.[2]

Both women saw themselves as radicals – and Georgie went further:

> Dearest Nelly, Your letter this evening reached me as I was so to speak, *reeking* from the perusal of socialist literature, and was an extraordinary echo in parts of my own thoughts and emotions. About Edward I agree with you – *his* work is so clearly defined in the world that I could not have him troubled by anything else – but with me it is not so, therefore I read much to myself but talk little to him on the subject of socialism. In truth I *am* a socialist and yet nothing could induce me as I now feel to join any sect of the movement.[3]

Once Frances had arrived in London, Georgie invited her to share in this atmosphere, to rest and recuperate. Spend all Sunday with us, she wrote, 'you shall write or rest, as you please – just as if you were alone – only we shall be in the background for when you have finished'.[4]

And she needed support like this. On his arrival in England, Luard, her spokesman in the Durnford case, told Frances that he would not continue, and also advised her to give it up – in what she saw as the most brutal terms (Frances's furious interpolations are in italics). Luard wrote,

> You assume that you must be right, and that every one else must be wrong, that all the world are either knaves fools or cowards, and, by the terms in which you now express your deep sorrow for me, I can only conclude that I am now included in some section of that category.
>
> Ask yourself – are *you* the person whose duty it is to do whatever has to be done? *Certainly – if those whose duty it is more than mine, will not do it …*
>
> What will the world think of you then for publishing this matter independently? They will say, and will say rightly, that it is the act of a very 'strong

minded female' (however much you may dislike the term) *Let them. I do not care so [long] that the 'act' succeeds* and they will perhaps not think any the better of the late Col. Durnford when they fathom (as they probably would do) the reason for your taking so exceptional an interest in his cause.[5]

He urged her to stop working on the case, to rest, and to work instead on her father's biography and gather her strength.

In the end Frances could only lapse into melodramatic cliché: '*Oh! self-condemnation. Alas! how are the mighty fallen.*' But the betrayal only persuaded her to work harder at the case. As she wrote to Chesson,

> my point is a suggestion from some of my kindest (military) friends – '*What will the world think* of me, of my motives, and of my dead friend, if I persist in following up this matter on his behalf, when his own corps, and even some of his own brothers are satisfied to let it drop?'
>
> My answer is 'the world – I hope – will say that I am a Colenso, implying sympathy or contempt according to their own views of life etc – and, if not, the world must think what it pleases'.
>
> I do not profess that I 'do not care', being but a woman I care acutely, but in no sense which could induce me to fore-go what, on other grounds, I have thought right, for fear of 'what the world may say'.[6]

In November 1886 Frances was admitted to a consumptives' hospital near Ventnor, on the Isle of Wight. It was a hard decision to make. Life in an institution made heavy demands on a woman who prided herself on her independence and, while she might dismiss the world's opinion on conventional morality, was conscious of her class position as a bishop's daughter, and appreciated good food, wine and comfortable surroundings. There was a stigma attached to such institutions as well – it was felt that patients were admitted because their families lacked the will or the means to provide the necessary support at home. Frances consequently feared that outsiders might think that her father had not provided adequately for his daughters.[7] But, she argued, it was not financial stringency which persuaded her to go to Ventnor – it was the fact that the hospital provided an 'artificial atmosphere' for its patients – heated air was ducted into the room. She depended on this to survive the winter.

And there was another reason: the terrible fear, hardly spoken of, that she was dying. It was this which made it so difficult for her friends just to open their homes to her, as they would have liked.

On 19 November 1886, Frances inspected her new room in the Royal National

Hospital on the Isle of Wight, with its balcony and view of the sea, and the 'hot-air apparatus, which sings perpetually like a kettle, and keeps the room charm-ingly warm'. The kindly doctor who had arranged her stay

> came back to say goodbye to me, and I told him *to go away at once.* For just a
> few minutes I felt my courage shaken, and that as he *had* to go, the sooner he
> went the better, or I should break down. I need hardly say that when he saw
> the tears coming into my eyes he shook hands warmly but hastily and fled. I
> felt for a little as tho' my last friend were lost to me, and I alone on a desert
> island ... But do not you be unhappy for me sweet. Left alone, my courage
> soon returned I knew it would and now I'm as cheerful as possible, and I feel
> sure I have done the wisest thing.[8]

In a letter to Harriette, remarkable not only for its consideration and sensitiv-ity, but the grace with which it speaks of what could not be said, Georgie Burne-Jones wrote 'thinking you might like to hear *of* Nelly [Frances] as well as *from* her'.

> I hear from her very often, for she has truly the pen of a ready writer, and I
> saw her up to the day before she left London. The weather has been so very
> severe this last month or two that I am very glad she is breathing an 'artificial
> atmosphere', for the natural one has been often quite unfit to use. We very
> much enjoyed her visit to us: the drawback of course is the anxiety we cannot
> but feel about her health – but, as she says, there are things that are worth
> more than life, and I am sure you were right to let her come over. I have
> promised to go to her at once at any time if she should need me, and she
> knows she need not scruple to call me – but I do not think there will be any
> need for it. I only mention it to let you know that there is something like a
> substitute for a sister at hand here in this distant England for her ...
>   Please use me in any way, always, that would relieve your minds about
> Nelly – and send anything (of course) here for her – and ask me to do any-
> thing as if I *were* the sister I only pretend to be.[9]

Manufacturing consent

Her sisters in Natal also needed courage as 1886 closed. The Agreement of 22 October 1886 between the New Republicans and the British signed away a huge portion of Zululand without reference to the people who lived in it. Indeed the one reason for completing it so quickly was to avoid having to consider repres-entations from the Zulu. Harriette Colenso was therefore deeply shocked to read an outline of the Agreement in the Natal press on 25 October. Her formal letter of protest was completed on 1 November. It was made, she wrote, because she felt 'bound, in my father's name, as an old friend of the Zulus, and in their absence and helplessness, to protest, respectfully, but most earnestly'. She went over yet again the circumstances by which Britain had destroyed the capacity of the Zulu to defend themselves, and then refused to take responsibility for the appalling consequences of this action. She ended by placing on record her protest 'against the term "boundary dispute" being applied to a transaction, which would seal the extinction of the national life of the Zulus ... and add yet another to the examples, bitterly stored up in the minds of the Natives, of the uselessness of trusting to the word of the English nation'.[10]

But Havelock now needed to implement the Agreement. And for this he had to try to manufacture, if not Zulu consent, then at least some form of Zulu recognition of its terms. Melmoth Osborn was called from Zululand for consultation. Sir Theophilus Shepstone was, of course, always on hand with advice. Their conclusions were predictable. The Zulu had to be instructed that the terms of the Agreement were final and permanent. All protests had to met with firm and unequivocal rejections. The Agreement had to be implemented immediately so as to present the Zulu with a *fait accompli*. Any suggestion that Her Majesty's Government might be prepared to consider an appeal had to be dismissed. There could be no protests against what had happened, or petitions for reconsideration.

However, the Usuthu were not going to be so easily controlled. On 9 November, Shingana kaMpande arrived in Pietermaritzburg to protest – not initially against the 22 October Agreement, the news of which had not reached the Usuthu when he left Zululand, but against the rumour, now months old, that the British were considering a line drawn between Babanango and Nhlazatshe. Havelock refused to see him. Shingana, though, was accompanied by Martin Luthuli, who saw a report in the newspapers not only of the Agreement itself but also of its confirmation in London. Havelock now had no choice but to hear the Usuthu response.

Shingana's position was difficult. He obviously could not have had permission from the Zulu leadership to protest against the Agreement – they had had no knowledge of it when he left Zululand. At the same time he knew he would have to take some personal initiative even if this opened him to the charge of acting without due authority. Havelock, advised by Osborn, did just this. Shingana's protest was then used as an opportunity to inform the Zulu officially of what had been decided and to crush, once and for all, any expectation they had that the boundary line might be reconsidered. On 9 November, Havelock called Shingana and Luthuli to Government House. Melmoth Osborn was in attendance. They were informed of the boundary and that it would be pointless to inquire into the decision or to protest against it. 'No good could come of it. I have heard both sides; one says *black*, the other says *white*.'[11]

It was only by his sheer perseverance, by risking and receiving the Governor's wrath, that Shingana made his protest. He pointed out, to Havelock's discomfort, that the line placed Emakhosini in the possession of the Boers. But he was ordered to return to Zululand where Zulu representatives should be selected to serve on the Boundary Commission: 'The Queen's word is spoken, and the work has been done. It is their duty now to go back at once and tell the Chiefs to select a representative to accompany Mr. Osborn. Mr. Osborn, Colonel Cardew, and that representative will go with the Boer Commissioners to mark the boundary line. They must make haste.'[12]

But Havelock was not simply going to silence him. Shingana persisted and managed to make two more appeals. Luthuli was instructed to write a letter of protest to the Queen and ask Havelock to forward it. Like the statement on the succession of Dinuzulu, it is based on the awareness of writing's capacity to give permanence to a petition. In translation the language might seem overly paternalist, even sycophantic – but if we keep in mind the strongly patriarchal nature of Zulu society and its effect on terms of respect, authority and deference, then the message is strong enough to penetrate the hierarchical layers imposed on it by Luthuli's transcription and Henrique Shepstone's translation:

> We are your children yesterday, to-day, and to-morrow, and for ever. We cry to you as children who have been injured. (We cry) in the name of the Zulu people. We bear earnest witness that this cutting off of the Zulu country, without our having been given a single opportunity of answering or being listened to, we do not willingly accept. We desire that these words may not be obliterated, but always remain known for ever and ever.
>
> We now return to the Zulus, that we may tell them what we have heard, and they also will answer for themselves.[13]

Making the best of it

In spite of Havelock's warning that they should not listen 'to mischievous people who tell them lies and make mischief',[14] Shingana stopped at Bishopstowe. He gave Harriette Colenso his account of what had happened and asked her to obtain transcripts of the Zulu statements made at Government House.[15] She did so, but Havelock specifically instructed that the documents should go directly to Shingana and they were placed in an envelope addressed to Martin Luthuli. The messengers, however, brought it to Harriette.

It placed her too in a most difficult position. She was already worried that Martin Luthuli was too close to the officials. The issues here were so important – the Zulu protest had to be accurately reported to London. She knew, of course, that if she opened the envelope she would give substance to the allegations of unauthorised interference. But she felt the situation demanded that she know what was in the documents. It was pointless to make her protests after the records of the interview appeared in the Blue Books perhaps six months later when the issue was already dead. She decided to open the envelope and take the consequences. She copied the documents for herself and for the Usuthu, and returned the originals to Havelock, drawing attention to errors and criticising points of translation.

But just as she feared, when Shingana's statement was sent to London, its contents were undermined by the official comments which accompanied it. Osborn wrote a dour minute which dismissed the protest as unauthorised and unrepresentative of Zulu opinion. Havelock repeated this charge and attacked Bishopstowe for raising 'delusive hopes' amongst the Usuthu.[16]

Against the official weight of disapproval Harriette had few options open to her, but she tried to use those she did have effectively. One of these was that Havelock was still prepared to talk unofficially with her on Zulu matters. On 10 November she had complained personally to Havelock of the terms of the Agreement. He replied that 'the Zulus "must make the best of it."' Harriette rounded on him and suggested that 'they might prefer to die – fighting'. Havelock, apparently shocked, hoped that she and her friends would never advise them to take such a course. 'I replied for myself, that I could not advise them to fight; but that they were, at any rate, free to die for their liberty, and that I could not blame them if they chose to do so.' Even to mention the possibility of violence against the constituted authorities was, of course, very dangerous talk indeed. Harriette realised this and wrote to further explain her position to Havelock: firstly that she had wanted to impress upon him her fear that the Zulu would now try physically to upset the agreement; and secondly, that to one who knew the history of events in Zululand since the 1879 invasion, such a response was entirely understandable. It was these points which placed her in what 'is my (at present most unenviable) position' –

> to represent, in my father's name, the last shred of a reason which the Zulus
> still possess for believing in English good faith, and for continuing to appeal
> thereto by constitutional means, before making what must, nevertheless, be

the last appeal – to the assegai ... [and this] lays upon me the most solemn responsibilities towards both sides.

My object in touching upon this point on Wednesday was to convey to Your Excellency my apprehension that ... it is not improbable that before many weeks are over the Zulus, desperate, may turn, at bay, at last; and our crime against them becomes quite irreparable.[17]

There was much huffing and puffing from the officials at this. As Osborn commented, 'If the Zulus should, by any unfortunate turn of events, be induced to be guided by the advice which she so strongly indicates has been given them, then I say let the responsibilities of the consequences rest with those who gave the advice.'[18]

The matter of violence, and whether Harriette had actually advised the Usuthu to use violence, was to remain an issue, officially and unofficially. Knowing that she was going to be criticised, she put her ideas forward in letters to those she felt might be able to understand her response. The range of correspondents from which she had to choose was small indeed – but to a liberal Dutch biblical critic who had supported her father, she wrote that it was wrong to attach all blame, as Natal did, to the Boers:

The English and Dutch conspire together to crush the Zulu and divide the spoil. And, if the Zulus make an attempt to stand for their liberty, they will be mercilessly butchered by either or both of these civilized and Christian nations.

And I want you to understand the real nature of the transaction, and the cruel injustice of thus wiping out the national existence of the Zulu people, by robbing them of their country, whether the robbers are to be ruled in future by Dutch or English law.[19]

The boundaries of debate

Frances, on reading Harriette's formal letter of protest against the Agreement, found it 'splendid'. 'Is she not her Father's own daughter.'[20] But Frances would have gone further:

Whether the robbers and tyrants are called Shepstone, Osborn, Natal Colonists or Boers is 'only' a difference of degree not of kind, and personally I think it would be better for our poor friends to die to a man, than to be made subject to any rule by colonists, or that brings them into contact with the colonists. There are many things worse than death.[21]

Frances felt that she had had to confront such things too often. She also found life in a consumptives' hospital restricting and difficult. She tried not to complain, fearing to distress her family even more than she had already, but she did find living by the rules of an institution hard to tolerate: 'Of course they must have rules but it doesn't do to treat everyone equally blindly, i.e. all patients must have a bath once a week – which is interpreted as one bath a week not more.'[22]

She felt, she said, imprisoned. She lashed out – even at her friends. She attacked the jurist John Westlake for a passing remark he had made about her father which Frances felt misrepresented him. Colenso had helped Westlake in his youth, and in return Westlake gave his advice, support and his expertise to the bishop. The attack that Frances made on him was undeserved and ungrateful but he rose above it and remained a good and active friend to the sisters for many years to come.

When news of the Agreement between the New Republic and the British over the future of Zululand reached Frances, Chesson urged her to be calm, to conserve her energy, above all to be realistic in her demands:

> You write under a complete misapprehension as to what the government here can be induced to do. They will not send a force into Zululand in order, by driving out the Boers, to establish an independent Zululand under Dinuzulu ... If the course you advocate is carried out I believe that nothing will save the Zulus from complete destruction and enslavement ...

Perhaps, as she said, it was because she felt her own loss of liberty so deeply that she was more sensitive to the loss of liberty in others. But certainly the antidote to her unhappiness and isolation was to lose herself in work. The preparation of materials for the revived campaign to clear Durnford's name took much of her time. She also had work to do on her father's biography. And she watched Zulu matters closely, supporting Harriette when she could, trying to get letters published in the English press, and corresponding with Chesson, who in turn had his contacts in the establishment.

It was therefore devastating when her illness made it difficult for her to carry on with this work. Up to the end of 1886, intermittent attacks made her so weak that it was impossible to keep her pen steady enough to compose a legible letter. By 1887 these attacks had become worse, her temperature rose, and she lost the capacity to work at all. This terrified her. If she couldn't work, she felt, she would lose the will to live.

But when the crisis passed, the letters began to show optimism again. 'I begin again to think that I shall get thro' and do my work. Now, what is there that I can do in Zulu matters? These splendid (but atrociously printed) letters of my sisters ought to be used in some way, ought they not?'[23]

So she began again the debate over Zululand – and she drew others in. Although she never lost her anger she did find it possible to be more tolerant, at least with Chesson: 'You will of course fully understand that however *hotly* I may write about *things*, there is never a word meant to vex you. The fact is I have neither time nor strength to think of anything but my matters, and my manner has become too abrupt, I fear. Please not to mind.'[24] Not quite an apology – but certainly an explanation warm in its appreciation of his continued interest in her and in Zululand.

The debate travelled between Chesson in the office of the APS in London, Harriette Colenso at Bishopstowe, Gerald Browne at Government House, and Frances Colenso in her room in the consumptives' hospital on the Isle of Wight. It was about the limits of political action: about if, and when, protest should be cease, and violence could begin. Chesson, always cautious and constitutional, pointed out that British rule, no matter how compromised, was better than Boer tyranny or the consequences of hopeless resistance. Frances and Browne debated where responsibility lay for the partition of Zululand. Browne put the view that Havelock had no choice, the Zulu stood to lose everything to the Boers, and the British intervention, inadequate as it was, saved them something. Frances accepted that Havelock did think he was helping the Zulu – but that he was trapped by his instructions and therefore objectively he was failing them. But then it needed a truly exceptional man to escape the limits imposed by official policy – only a Gordon, a Durnford, a Colenso, would have had the courage and faith to act independently and rise above the equivocating spirit of the age.[25]

In the end Frances rejected the very terms of the debate. For her it was not a question of who should rule over the Zulu, but about restoring self-rule to the Zulu. But Frances was at a great geographical and psychological distance from the events. Harriette was working in direct contact with the people involved. She tried to assist the Zulu in their protest but knew all the while that it would not be sufficient. She was desperate at not being able to suggest a more effective strategy. And she was haunted by the point Frances had made: that perhaps Bishopstowe should have stood aside while the Zulu fought for their land, unencumbered by any idea that the British would in the end be just. For 'when grey headed men put their case earnestly to me, and ask what can be said against it, I can only cover my eyes and admit that there is no answer – no real honest answer'.[26]

For Harriette the questions were immediately personal and agonising. But, Chesson argued, she was misreading the situation. If she was to continue to play an effective role in Zulu affairs, then she had to move to a new starting point, no matter how compromised she felt. Steadily she was forced into recognising that the Zulu had to accept the existing situation and work within it – although the idea that violence would have been a better option still worried her:

> My very existence as my Father's daughter tended and *still tends* to hold them back from resorting to force – from the demonstration – which might – (who can tell) ... 'have been their chance'...
> I could not advise them to fight because I could not share the responsibility or the consequences – because I could not sufficiently judge of their chances of success, because, as an Englishwoman I had no right to believe that England would not in the end – when she had heard – do right.

What was doubly unjust was the fact that she was still being depicted as someone who had advised the Zulu to fight. It was not just the accusation to which she objected, but the foolishness of the idea that Zulu resistance would be the result of an outsider's advice: 'Why should the Zulus need anyone to "advise" them that they have been shamelessly treated? No only do they feel it plainly and bitterly, but so does every tribe in South Africa – and will remember it, I fear, long after I am unable to "remind" them.'[27]

Chesson, at the centre of imperial power, knew that if the Colenso daughters advocated violent resistance, then neither they nor he could hope to influence imperial policy. He wrote to Frances about it:

> The Blue Book, just published makes it clear that the Zulus were in no sense parties to the new boundary, but protested against it to the last. I suspect that they have since accepted the new arrangement, for the simple reason that they have no other alternative but to fight. This latter course, it would appear, your sister rather advised them to take. She is of course perfectly entitled to give such advice, and no one can respect her motives more than I do, but it is fatal to her influence at the Colonial Office.

As he wrote to Harriette herself:

> It would be fatal to us if the impression got abroad that one so closely associated with the [Aborigines' Protection] Society as you have been had stirred up the Zulus to acts of hopeless resistance ... You see what colour Mr Osborn puts upon your letter. It is calculated to create a prejudice against your action the existence of which we should deplore, because we all fully appreciate the righteous and generous feelings by which you have acted.[28]

Frances rejected Chesson's interpretation:

> Will you tell me *how* it appears that my sister rather advised the Zulus to fight? Only on her word would I credit such a change in her principles of what it is right for *her* to do, and if it has been *made* to 'appear' by anyone else it is, of course, in order to destroy 'her influence' at the Colonial Office ...
>
> Sir Henry Holland is powerless because he *chooses* to be – he could at the very least send out a Royal Commission to give back to the Zulus all the land held nominally by Boers, but actually by British subjects.
>
> On what grounds do you believe that the Zulus have acquiesced? ... that is to say *not having showed fight.* You will find that their having *still* waited for England to help them, and *not* having fought, is the only sense in which they have acquiesced – and this is made another excuse for England's vile conduct to them.
>
> My hand is shaky in the morning – firmer later in the day.[29]

This is the last letter by Frances in the Chesson file. Although she kept the information from her friends, she had been bedridden for a month. The hospital was for convalescents, not for the terminally ill, and in the week she arrived 'a poor little girl of 14 left ... When patients *cannot* be cured, altho' they are not turned out they are advised to go to their friends; it is bad for the other patients to have deaths here.'[30] Now, at the end March 1887, it was Frances's turn to leave.

Georgie Burne-Jones made contact with Frank and told him of the severity of Frances's condition. There was no way she could travel or stay in an ordinary household. They arranged for her to take rented lodgings in Ventnor for April. Georgie Burne-Jones planned to visit her there. There was, however, considerable concern about the risk of such a visit to Georgie's own health. Desperately concerned not to hurt Frances, Georgie's letters tread delicately around the whole question of how private, and how physically close, they could safely be during this last time they would have together.

When Georgie left in the middle of April, Esther Clarke, sister of a young soldier whom Frances had nursed on his deathbed in Natal in 1879, came to help, and a maid was hired. Frances wrote bright and chatty letters to her mother – of her plans to go to London, where she intended 'to look after those dawdling men'. There she intended to make recruits to the Durnford cause again:

> If I *had* but been a strong person with good lungs I might have done *such* a lot of pricking on in London this past winter and spring! But there! if it had been

best so it would have been so. Well, I hope I shall be strong enough as the summer comes on, to do all the work I want to do before coming back to you.[31]

A week later Esther Clarke, terrified, wrote an urgent letter to Georgie Burne-Jones. Frances was much worse, unable to get up, drifting into unconsciousness, and could not stop coughing. She was frightened to leave her alone. Frank cabled Bishopstowe – shocking them deeply because they did not know how ill she had in fact been. As her mother wrote, 'these cablegrams are cruel cruel things'.[32] Harriette wrote, realising that her letter would probably never reach her: 'And so Darling, I will just write to you as usual of the things that I know you will long to hear about if you can hear about anything.'[33] Edward Durnford, whom Frances so admired, would not visit her: 'Do not be vexed about me dear Nelly, but try and think of me as I do of you in the former days, and let these be our thoughts as long as we both remain on earth.'[34] The Bunyons came down to Ventnor with plans for her to return as quickly as possible to Natal.

On 27 April she began a letter to her mother saying that she had decided to come to Natal in June. She didn't finish it. On the 29th Frances Colenso was being dressed by her maid when she put her arms around her, rested her head on her shoulder, and after a few minutes stopped breathing.

The letters of condolence all spoke of her courage. Chesson wrote to Sarah Frances Colenso:

At the present moment I will not intrude upon you with many words of mine. Your dear daughter has laid down her life in the cause which she loved so well; and no friend of hers or of her family can feel more deeply than I do the loss which you and we have sustained. Her letters to me from Ventnor show the indomitable spirit and the high sense of duty by which she was actuated up to the moment her failing powers compelled her to rest from her labours. She has gone to her just reward: this is the one reflection which will be certain to comfort you in your sorrow.[35]

Harriette comforted Frank by reminding him that she had 'been brave, and she has been allowed the blessedness of dying in harness like her Father, of keeping on at his work ... to the last. And what better can one wish.'[36] Africans in Natal with whom she had grown up had a different message of sympathy but one which comforted Sarah Frances greatly: 'The poor natives overwhelm us with condolences – They say Sobantu wanted her so sent for her!'[37]

She was buried on the Isle of Wight. Harriette suggested an inscription on her tombstone that would include the words 'like her Father' and that Frances 'gave up her life on behalf of the helpless and oppressed in Zululand both of the Zulu and of the British Army'. But she hoped that someone would find words 'more telling' than 'helpless and oppressed'. No one did; the final inscription reads:

> Following her Father's example she sacrificed
> her life on behalf of the helpless and oppressed.

'No unclaimed lands'

When Frances is remembered, there has been a tendency to concentrate on what were considered to be her excesses: on her outbursts of anger, on her relationship with Durnford – often with a nudge and a wink; the bishop's daughter and the colonel, you know – and the extremes to which she was driven to vindicate him.

We should also remember other aspects of her protest: at the colonial and the imperial world in which she lived – so rare at the time and valid today. Thus in February 1886, when she already knew but still would not accept or speak of the gravity of her illness, she read an article in the *Pall Mall Gazette* which recommended European emigration to South Africa as a remedy for its problems. As far as she was concerned, the suggestion 'makes out the blacks the aggressors, which they have never been, only the most outrageous conduct on the part of the whites ever rousing them to resist'; consequently the effect of this 'remedy' would be simply to make the whites strong enough to trample on the natives safely'.[38] In a letter to the press she made the good and little-acknowledged point 'that there are no unclaimed lands in South Africa any more than in other parts of the world, and that he [the author] could only make room for his proposed thousands of white emigrants by displacing the rightful native possessors of the soil'.[39] And when the news of the boundary was coming through and the reality of the future facing the Zulu was becoming clearer, she wrote: 'Better to die to a man, as the brave men they have always shown themselves to be, fighting for their rights, than to die out slowly as a degenerate race in the wretched unhealthy worthless corner left to them.'[40] Such views address the realities of imperialism as few others had the insight to do at the time. They might be emotional, they might be extreme, but they give expression to a valid vision of imperialism, a vision whose absence negates the value of most contemporary commentaries, and even now mars many histories.

CHAPTER 12

THE BLANKET BREAKS
(NOVEMBER 1886 – AUGUST 1887)

Dismembering the beast: November 1886 – May 1887

Shingana and his party made their way back to northern Zululand in November 1886, stunned at the boundary line that the Governor and the Boers had negotiated. Harriette Colenso wrote: 'They have been shockingly treated. They came down knowing nothing of this "agreement," and get it suddenly fired off full in their faces, and are forbidden to speak in reply ... and are ordered to start next morning.'[1]

In just under a fortnight, Shingana had reached northern Zululand and a meeting was called at Mnyamana's homestead. Here the Zulu learnt of the catastrophe with which they were being threatened. The effect of the Agreement was to exclude them from nearly all the highland grazing, the valuable mixed- and sour-veld of the upper reaches of the major river systems, and the strongholds of the Ngome forest, together with the country between the Mkhuze and the Phongolo. Much of the territory that remained was not habitable. The lower reaches of the major rivers were swampy, heavily wooded, infected by tsetse, and malaria was endemic towards the coast. The northern half of the proposed boundary passed just north of the main homesteads of Mnyamana, Ndabuko and Dinuzulu, then travelled due east along the Mkhuze River before running north along the Lubombo, thereby excluding territory in which lived the Qulusi, Sebeni and Mphangisweni sections, as well as the Mdlalose, Ndabankulu's Ntombela, Hamu, and many of the Buthelezi. Between the Mkhuze and the Phongolo, the emGazini of Masiphula and the Ndwandwe also fell within the New Republic. The southern section of the line (including the Proviso B district) placed the homesteads of Shingana, Ngobozana, Sitheku, Faku and Qethuka in Boer territory. The graves of the pre-Shakan kings were now on white farms.

This great incision made through Zulu territory was likened to the dismembering of a beast and the distribution of the choice cuts of meat. As with the Boundary Commission before the invasion – whose findings were in favour of the Zulu but kept secret while the invasion was planned – the hide, it was said, had been thrown over the heads of the owners, while the butchers divided the carcass amongst themselves. Shingana's return from Natal to the northern districts was followed closely by the arrival of Osborn. He had been instructed to organise the demarcation of the boundary. The Proviso B territory, the area left in possession of the Boers though excluded from the New Republic, was the lung – that portion customarily left to the herd boy after the animal was butchered. It was Melmoth Osborn who was responsible: the village which was to grow around the magistrate's court and residence was named after him. As Maphelu kaMkhosana said: 'Melmoth had been given this land by the government as his reward for his work dividing the land. Just as a herd boy is always given a lung when a cow is slaughtered, so Melmoth has received his share.'[2]

The Usuthu leaders decided that they would refuse to co-operate with any official attempt to divide the land. At the same time they would try to raise funds to send a deputation to England for a final appeal. Regardless of the Governor's instructions, they would still protest, and they did so repeatedly. As Mnyamana said:

> I do not do this for the purpose of going contrary to the orders of the
> Government or to do anything which may cause offence. I only wish to protest
> and to express the feeling of the Zulu People about the boundary you have
> told us of, so that, even if the Government does do the thing you have told us
> about, it may be known what our feeling and views are in the matter.[3]

From early December 1886 to mid-January, the Boer and British commissioners moved through northern Zululand placing their beacons. There were no Zulu representatives in attendance. Harriette Colenso followed the proceedings as best she could from Pietermaritzburg, and derided official statements in Natal which tried to give standing to the commission by asserting that the Zulu participated in it. Because of the watch she kept on the situation, Osborn dared not invent representation. She was experienced in Zulu methods of communication and accreditation, and was clear on the differences between a Zulu messenger, a witness, an observer and a representative. Now that she was in close contact with the Usuthu, she was a very substantial challenge to officials like Osborn who feared the possibility that even his most confidential asides, made in the depths of Zululand, would ultimately form the basis of a report in a London newspaper, a question in the House of Commons, or a Blue Book. The traditions of native administration in which Osborn worked depended on the control of the African voice. But it was proving impossible to silence the Usuthu, as long as they could relate their version of events to Harriette Colenso.

In order to smother this alternative view, the officials advanced even faster in the hope that unequivocal, public action would quash the Usuthu protest. They were only too aware that the laying down of the border was just the start. The next stage of the process, the nature of the new government and administration to be imposed over the territory to the east of the New Republic, had still to be decided and, after that, implemented.

Havelock, on Osborn's advice, had recommended the immediate extension of 'British Protection [over the] remainder of Zululand'. He believed that the Zulu were 'ready for it'.[4] The British government, however, was not ready for it. Having successfully confined the Boers to the west, the officials paused to consider the future policy towards the Zulu in the east. They had had their fingers burnt before. Stanhope cabled Havelock saying that he would be prepared to recommend British protection, but it would have to be shown that the Zulu agreed to this. And in a secret postscript the Colonial Secretary added: 'Act with caution as to matter of Protectorate. Take great care to satisfy yourself it will not meet with opposition from the Zulus or any substantial portion of them, and if in doubt inform us.'[5]

This was the test. Havelock, giving Osborn as his authority, admitted that there might be some dissatisfaction on the part of Cetshwayo's family 'as it will tend to diminish their power, and control the exercise of their privileges'. However, it was not thought 'that this dissatisfaction will induce opposition, or that it will be felt outside the circle of the late King's family'. Moreover, this dissatisfaction could be ameliorated by paying the Zulu leaders 'stipends ... subject to good behaviour'. Havelock ended the telegram by assuring Stanhope that 'I will most carefully keep before me your injunctions, as to caution and discretion in the matter of the proposed Protectorate over the Zulus'.[6]

Osborn, still on the Boundary Commission, made every effort to get an expression of Zulu support for the extension of British authority. He called a meeting on 3 January 1887 and it was attended by all the major Usuthu.[7] Here he formally announced the decision regarding the boundary, and the granting of territory to the Boers. Then, following instructions from Havelock, he asked whether the Zulu would prefer to be governed by Natal, or to be ruled as the Reserve was.

The antipathy towards Osborn on the part of the Usuthu was very deep indeed. It was felt, with reason, that his personal antagonism towards the royal house had been a major factor in the disasters which had overtaken them since 1879. The very proximity of men like Osborn and Zibhebhu was dangerous, as it was believed that they were in possession of powerful supernatural means to promote their ends. The Mandlakazi repaid the Usuthu fear and hatred in kind. The Usuthu refused to answer Osborn's question about their future government. Instead they mounted a swingeing personal attack on the man they felt was more responsible than anyone else for the loss of their land. It was Osborn who had betrayed them from the beginning by distorting their appeals and petitions to the British. He had harassed them in the Reserve when they were trying to bury Cetshwayo. He was the guardian and protector of their greatest enemy, Zibhebhu. He had divided the country in the face of their protests and was now trying to get their agreement to this. Dinuzulu and his people were being forced to live amongst the Boers because of him. Using a metaphor that was often to be repeated, Ndabuko told him: 'Chief, you will kill this child of Cetshwayo, inasmuch as, if you put a calf in the kraal and it sees its mother a short distance away, will it not get over the fence to its mother? Then the calf will be killed, on the plea that it has run away.'[8]

It was a public humiliation comparable to the one suffered by Osborn's patron, Theophilus Shepstone, on Cetshwayo's restoration in January 1883. Osborn, like Shepstone on that occasion, hid this fact from his superiors, informing Havelock that he felt the Zulu were 'acting on the advice of irresponsible Europeans'.[9] Havelock repeated this allegation against Harriette Colenso in his dispatch to London, and repeated the official line: once the Zulu realised the decision was final, they would agree to it. 'The Zulus are, however, gifted with much shrewdness, and some common sense. I think there is little doubt that when convinced that the settlement arrived at is irrevocable, and has the authority and sanction of Her Majesty, they will see the futility of their present attitude with regard to it, and will accept it.'[10]

Havelock asked for, and received, an authoritative statement from the Secretary of State declaring the settlement would not be reconsidered, and that the Queen was not prepared to receive a Zulu deputation to protest against it.[11]

After the Boundary Commission had finished its work on 17 January, Osborn remained in the north of Zululand to settle 'other political questions'.[12] There was a note of anxiety and impatience in Havelock's confidential request that Osborn do his 'best to obtain confirmation of the previous admission that they are under the Queen, and consent to incorporation with the British Empire'. And, Havelock continued,

> You should endeavour to ascertain the wishes of the Zulu people at large, as distinct from those of the chiefs of Cetshwayo's family, with regard to the assumption of British rule over them. I shall hope to receive information from you on this point. During your journey through Zululand on your present mission, there must have been abundant opportunity of ... ascertaining the real wishes of the Zulu people.[13]

Osborn tried, but was unable to obtain any such evidence.[14]

But Osborn could not now go back. Despite Usuthu protests, he was committed to annexation on the ground that it was what the Zulu really desired. Trapped now by his own predictions, he could only proceed more resolutely with his plans for annexation, hoping to gain the initiative by advancing further and faster. Thus, on 5 February, Osborn announced that Zululand was under British protection. He sent his messengers to inform the Zulu chiefs

> that taking into consideration the circumstances in which the Chiefs and people in Eastern Zululand are at presently situated, which subject was thoroughly discussed at the different interviews lately had by them with me, I deemed it my duty to notify to them that owing to the urgency of the situation, British protection carrying with it the supreme authority of Her Majesty's Government, was, subject to your Excellency's approval, extended over Eastern Zululand and the chiefs and people therein ...[15]

His justification for this action was, he asserted, his conviction that Zululand was in imminent danger of a complete social breakdown. There were reports that the Boers were attempting to cross the border, and that the Zulu might alienate more land. There was the danger of civil strife amongst the Zulu themselves. Zibhebhu could well attempt 'to retake his territory by force of arms from the Usuthu and at the same time ... punish them with terrible and barbaric severity for having brought the Boers against them'.[16] Osborn insisted that the Zulu desired the extension of British protection. The only possible exception was Ndabuko. The standard explanation was given: Ndabuko 'harboured schemes for his own personal aggrandisement'. Havelock was informed that 'after the most careful inquiry I have strong reason to believe that both the Chiefs and people are glad of the step taken'.[17]

But he still had to explain the fact that he could produce no evidence for this statement. It existed, Osborn argued, but it was impossible to obtain. The answer to this conundrum lay in Zulu custom, for

> by Zulu tradition and law, no Zulu, whether a Chief or not, may ... voluntarily consent to the transfer of the country or any portion thereof, or of the rights and position of the paramount Chief, to any power or person ...
>
> They could not, even in self-preservation, make any offer to be taken over by any friendly power, nor could they openly consent to any measure involving such a condition. They would, however, submit cheerfully to any act, even of total absorption by such a power, and especially by the British

Government who had conquered them, and to whom they still admit they belong. But they could only so submit on the initiative of that power, as they would thereby be at once relieved of the responsibilities imposed upon them by their own tradition and law.[18]

This is obviously nonsense. In essence, Osborn replied to the instruction that British authority should be extended if it could be shown that the Zulu would consent to such a move, by arguing that the Zulu would consent once Britain extended her authority. Havelock asked Sir Theophilus Shepstone for his opinion.[19] It came promptly. Havelock cabled London, 'I have conferred with Theophilus Shepstone. He considers that Osborn's action was necessary under the circumstances. I have full confidence in it myself. May I confirm?'[20]

The new Secretary of State, soon to become Lord Knutsford, gave his approval.[21] His predecessor, he felt, had committed London already. Harriette Colenso's letters of protest were rejected with impatience.[22] But there were expressions of disquiet in the Colonial Office nonetheless. Fairfield realised immediately that Osborn had not been honest in his presentation of evidence for Zulu support, and may well have made a dangerous move, for he had

> obtained no hearty or unequivocal consent; and it may be doubted whether he would not have acted more in the spirit of Mr. Stanhope's instructions, and in the interests of this country, if he had abstained from action and reported so as to give us an opportunity of washing our hands of this nasty mess, for such Eastern Zululand may well prove to be ...[23]

But other officials disagreed, and the next few months were spent trying to decide whether Britain should establish a protectorate or extend its authority over Zululand. Eventually it was agreed that, while a protectorate necessarily created responsibilities, it did not provide the means to honour them, and consequently annexation was recommended to the Cabinet. With a little help from Osborn and Shepstone, the question of Zulu support for the move was skirted over: 'The Zulu have tacitly acquiesced in this step. For various reasons, those best acquainted with Zulu law and custom consider that a hearty and express consent was not, under the circumstances, to be expected of them, but their attitude implies no intention to offer resistance of any kind.'[24]

On 7 May 1887 the British government agreed to the annexation of Zululand subject to Her Majesty's pleasure. On 11 May 1887 authority was granted to Havelock to annex both the Reserve and eastern Zululand to Britain. Shepstone and Osborn had managed it. They had carried first Havelock, then the Colonial

Office, and now the British Cabinet, with them. At last they had the authority to establish order in Zululand and demonstrate that annexation had the support of the bulk of the Zulu people. The beast had been slaughtered and dismembered; it was time to dine.

Feeding on the carcass: June–July 1887

By royal commission, Sir Arthur Havelock was declared Governor of Natal and Governor of Zululand as well, with the authority to proclaim the law and to appoint officers of the law. The laws of Natal were extended to British Zululand 'so far as applicable' and in so far as they were compatible with the laws and regulations for the government of Zululand, which Havelock went on to announce. Law No. 1 'vested in the Governor of Zululand all and every powers and prerogatives hitherto attaching to the position of Supreme Chief over Zululand and its Native population'.[25] This was Somtsewu's specific legacy to the government of British Zululand. Thus the central tenet of native administration in Natal, as first devised by Theophilus Shepstone forty years before, was extended to British Zululand. In this way, an invalid conception of the nature of African government invested absolute authority in the Governor of Zululand.

In Zululand itself, the senior official would be the Resident Commissioner and Chief Magistrate, whose court would be the court of appeal. Zululand was to be divided into six districts, each under the control of a Resident Magistrate. They would be responsible for good order in the districts, and their courts would try civil and serious criminal cases like murder, rape and 'pretended' witchcraft.

Original jurisdiction, in certain cases, would lie with the chiefs of Zululand. If there was to be security in Zululand, wrote Sir Theophilus Shepstone in a memorandum which embodied the arguments he had used to justify his policies for nearly forty years, there had to be an element of continuity. To deprive the chiefs of their powers would be a 'violent innovation':

> the Chiefs would suddenly find themselves disrated; sympathy and loyal co-operation with the ruling power that had thus degraded them could not be expected; the people, incapable of seeing the advantages, if advantages they might prove, that were intended to be conferred upon them, would look upon their Chiefs as martyrs, and thus, at the very outset, estrangement and distrust would be created, where confidence was so essentially necessary ...
>
> Any injustice or arbitrary exercise of power would at once be checked by the exercise of the privilege of appeal to a white magistrate ...
>
> Practically this provision at once establishes a process of gradual ameliora-

tion in the administration of justice, and renders improvement in the laws of the country a matter of natural growth.

It may be accepted as an axiom, I think, that it is impossible to govern effectively a Zulu population, such as that of either Natal or Zululand, without the aid of their own institutions, at the head of which are their Chiefs or Headmen.[26]

It was Natal's Attorney-General who asked the obvious question: who were to be the chiefs and what was to be the role of the Zulu royal house? Shepstone was not specific in his answer, but he pointed out that the Zulu population was made up of a number of tribes which had 'more or less' kept their individuality, and that there were important individuals who might be recognised: 'These sub-divisions and these ambitions will, I think, furnish the chief executive authority with ample means of reducing to a safe minimum the power for mischief of the members of the Zulu Royal Family, and their loss of power with its corresponding advantages and privileges might be compensated by an annual money allowance.'

The Natal system of native administration, as devised by Theophilus Shepstone, had been extended to Zululand. Henrique Shepstone, as the SNA in Natal, and Sir Theophilus Shepstone were retained as advisers, formal and informal respectively. Most of the men appointed to the administration had received their training in the Natal civil service or its offshoot, the Zulu Native Reserve. Melmoth Osborn was appointed Resident Commissioner and Chief Magistrate of Zululand with the highest recommendations from Sir Arthur Havelock.[27] The British Residency, with its small garrison, high court, gaol and new gallows, remained at Eshowe with the headquarters of the new Zululand Police, the 'Nongqayi', known and feared for their strong-arm tactics on and off duty. In spite of a deficit in the accounts for which he had been censured by the Secretary of State,[28] George Mansel of the Reserve Territorial Carbineers was placed in command of the Zululand Police with Osborn's son John as a lieutenant.

Eshowe the frontier town gave its name to the Eshowe district lying between the Thukela and the Mhlatuze rivers and stretching from the coast, still dominated by John Dunn, to the wet forested hills that extend towards the Nkandla district to the north-west, with its precipitous slopes and deep forests running down to the hot dry bushveld in the Thukela valley itself, bordering on Natal. A.L. Pretorius, previously Sub-Resident at Nquthu in the Reserve, now became Resident Magistrate of the Nkandla district. A British military officer, Major A. McKean, was appointed in an acting capacity at Nquthu in the high open country towards the Mzinyathi, where Hlubi Molife and his Tlokwa could be relied upon to give energetic support to the magistrate. These three southern districts, Eshowe, Nkandla and Nquthu, had been created out of the Zulu Native Reserve.

The Proviso B area was incorporated into the magisterial district of Enton-janeni with its magistrate's office in the town called Melmoth, on the road north from Eshowe. J.L. Knight took charge. He had been clerk of the court and inter-preter in Natal, and had once been found guilty of illegally flogging Africans. Bulwer described him as 'a colonial-born young man, who knows the Natives and their language but is rather inclined to treat them arbitrarily'.[29] But he did speak Dutch, which was necessary for the magistracy to which he was appointed.

On the coast between the Mhlatuze and Mfolozi rivers, the Lower Mfolozi dis-trict was demarcated. It was placed in the charge of Arthur Shepstone, son of Sir Theophilus, on the strong recommendations of both Bulwer and Havelock. This was his first official post. It was a region of strong Usuthu loyalists, but also the important anti-Usuthu faction of the Mthethwa under Sokwetshata, and had been deeply divided and disrupted in the civil war.

Richard Addison was also Natal-born, from one of its best-known settler fam-ilies, and had been clerk and interpreter in the Natal civil service before becom-ing second-in-command of the Reserve Territorial Carbineers. He was appointed, on Osborn's strong recommendation,[30] as Magistrate to the northern district called Ndwandwe, probably to emphasise the pre-Zulu historical traditions of the area. This district was crucial to the success of the new colony, for it was here that the civil war had caused the most disruption and here that the Usuthu presence was concentrated. It abutted on the New Republic and contained within it the home-steads of the most important members of the Usuthu. Ndabuko's KwaMinya, Dinuzulu's Osuthu and Mahashini, and Mnyamana's Buthelezi homesteads lay in the valleys of the tributaries running into the upper Black Mfolozi. In the eastern districts lay some of their most important supporters like the Hlabisa and the Dletsheni of Msushwana. This area had been Mandlakazi, and large tracts had been occupied by Usuthu once they had driven their enemy south to official pro-tection in the Reserve in 1885. Addison moved first to the Nkonjeni ridge, which was in heliographic contact with the military post at Eshowe, and established a police post. It was the first step before moving to the Nongoma range to the east of the Ivuna River where the Usuthu were concentrated.

Public expressions of loyalty to the Crown had to be obtained from the chiefs, who would receive in return formal recognition of their status. These new offi-cials were totally unaware that such expressions of loyalty to the new order would be seen by many Zulu as evidence of treachery to the old. They were equally unaware of the fact that they were themselves bound by the laws and regulations just proclaimed. They moved into Zululand blindly and brutally, categorising the people placed under them as either loyal Zulu or rebels. They were either supporters of the new order and desirous to share in its blessings, or supporters of the Zulu royal house and its desperate attempt to perpetuate its tyranny. And the more events suggested that official perceptions were in fact invalid and wrongheaded, the more they placed the responsibility for their failures on the Usuthu and their outside advisers.

The Queen's Golden Jubilee, 21 June 1887, would be a fitting day, Havelock felt, to celebrate publicly the royal commission which conferred upon the Zulu 'those blessings of peace, good order, and good government which are secured by British rule'.[31] The British military detachment at Eshowe and the Zululand Police were on parade when, by Osborn's account, the 9000 Zulu present heard the official announcement proclaiming Zululand's formal incorporation into the Empire. They were then marched around a flagpole flying the Union Jack and gave it the royal salute 'Bayete'. In his report of the occasion, Osborn annexed the names of 48 'Chiefs and Headmen' who were present. Of the 21 on the list who can be readily identified as men of rank and significance, eight were either chiefs unfortunate enough to have been appointed by Wolseley in 1879, or their successors. Osborn included on his list three obscure sons of Mpande, his own induna, Yamela, and the best known of the loyals in the Reserve.[32] There were no significant members of the Zulu royal house in attendance.

Inflating the attendance list could not hide the fact that most of the important Zulu leaders were absent.[33] Osborn was ordered to go to the northern districts and repeat the ceremony. He was not to be confrontational, and Havelock expected him to 'endeavour to conciliate those chiefs as much as possible, and … adopt every means of explaining to them their present position'.[34] Dinuzulu, his most prominent uncles and Mnyamana were to be offered stipends ranging from £60 to £300 a year, backdated six months. But Dinuzulu declined to receive Osborn's messengers or accept the documents proclaiming the annexation. All the Usuthu leaders were ordered to attend a meeting[35] but Dinuzulu refused again. The senior Usuthu, however, decided they had no choice, and Ndabuko, Mnyamana and Shingana led a few hundred followers to Nkonjeni. On 7 July, after being coached by Osborn's induna,[36] they saluted the flag. Osborn spoke on the system of government now in force, and introduced the two men who were to administer the two northern districts, Dick Addison and Arthur Shepstone.[37] The *abantwana* and Mnyamana were then informed they were to receive stipends to compensate them for their loss of power and prestige.

The blanket breaks: August 1887

The crisis was now upon the Zulu. Their leaders could procrastinate no longer. The authority of the chiefs had been usurped, and a new system of law had been proclaimed over them and was now about to be implemented. The new magistrates were moving with their indunas and their police into Zululand looking for healthy sites for their residences, courts and police posts. Orders were beginning to be sent for the chiefs of Zululand to assist the new administration and attend the courts of its magistrates – these young white men from Natal. The common Zulu reaction was to refer the orders to the Usuthu leaders – to Mnyamana, Ndabuko or Dinuzulu – an action which the new magistrates considered insubordinate and suggestive of an incipient rebelliousness.

The Usuthu leadership, however, had to find a response more effective than protest, boycott and non-participation. Mnyamana called a meeting of the Zulu people and their leaders. A new royal council, an *ibandla*, would meet at Dinuzulu's Osuthu homestead. Here it would discuss the situation and devise a response which could be announced to the assembly of Zulu.

It met early in August. Mnyamana did all he could to revive the political traditions of the old kingdom, so tragically disrupted for the last eight years. It was time for those who had reached maturity since the invasion to learn something of the political life of the Zulu kingdom. In spite of the disruptions in their lives, the Zulu of the northern parts of the country had had something of a respite since the defeat of Zibhebhu in 1884. Many had moved in the face of Boer interference towards the east, occupying territory out of which Zibhebhu's Mandlakazi had been driven. Dinuzulu had begun to attract a following of young men, forming them into regiments, and they tried as best they could to serve the young prince. They attended the August meeting as members of new regiments. Dinuzulu's own bodyguard was mounted and armed. Mnyamana found them noisy and undisciplined, and ordered them to leave the area where the great men of the *ibandla* were about to hold their discussions. Dinuzulu was ordered to join the latter. A Zulu prince had many skills to learn: 'Mnyamana sent Dlova, son of Vubela of Mkheswa to go and call Dinuzulu who was giving food and beer to the people to come and sit with chiefs not with boys, so that he could learn the art of talking from great men.' Mnyamana was hoping that he could bring Dinuzulu on to his side – by evoking tradition and playing on a sense of royal responsibility. But Dinuzulu was too young and enthusiastic a prince and wanted to spend time with the regiments, not talking politics with the old men. As desperate as the situation in Zululand was with an alien government imposed on the people of Zululand, Dinuzulu, now 18, was playing the role of an independent Zulu prince.

Mnyamana whispered to the prince, using the noble title 'Ndabezitha', reminding him that even if he serves food, he must not forget to come and sit with men as his father used to select men to talk with, and draw wisdom from them.

After a while, as they were still sitting there, Mnyamana again allowed the prince to go and see his people.[38]

The immediate question before the *ibandla* was whether to accept British annexation. Mnyamana argued that they had no choice. No matter how badly the British officials had treated them, they had to accept the changes, and then perhaps attempt to improve them. There was simply no other option. Mnyamana found support in two of the leading sons of Mpande, Sitheku and Ziwedu, while Shingana was sympathetic but not committed.

Ndabuko argued that there was another option – a further appeal to the Boers. It had to be taken into account that some of the most important of Dinuzulu's supporters were now in Boer territory – men like Ntuzwa of the Mdlalose, the redoubtable Ndabankulu of the Ntombela, and Mabhoko of the emGazini who had lost his territory in the region between the Mkhuze and Phongolo. Sikhobobo, it was said, had secured some land from the Boers for the Qulusi. Some of the chiefs had already reached agreements with their particular Boer landlords which they believed might work to their advantage – for the moment at least – for as patriarchs and homestead heads they did not themselves have to carry out the labour required as rent, and could pass it on to the younger members of their families and their followings.

Mnyamana made the obvious response – surely they had learnt by now that the Boers were their enemies, not their friends? The answer came back that some of the Boers had been their friends – those who had actually fought on their side against Zibhebhu, as distinct from those who took advantage of the situation to seize their land. And they had to deal with the Boers anyway, in their day-to-day existence in the New Republic where their people still lived. And so the argument continued. Mnyamana asserted that they had no choice but to make efforts to contact the Queen and her ministers in an attempt to win some concessions. His opponents only had to point to the north and the west, towards the highlands and new boundary cutting them off from their homesteads, and then to the south and the east where the new magistrates were moving in to establish their magistracies, supported by their detachments of Zululand Police, many of them men from the followings of John Dunn and Zibhebhu. And soon there would be calls for payment of the hut tax, and the demand to attend their courts. This was what English rule meant. They had to oppose Mnyamana's decision 'to go to the English, to Malimati, the *umtagati*, (bewitcher) who killed the chief [Cetshwayo]'.

There could be no agreement: they could find no common ground. Mnyamana, after all the years of keeping the nation together, was now isolated from the Zulu leadership, which itself was split. It was a division amongst the royalists which was to have profound effects. The man who for so long had held the Usuthu together through the terrible years of civil war could no longer carry them with him.

And yet, as important as the fact of this division is, it must not be oversimplified. I have discussed earlier the way in which historians, following their contemporary colonial sources too closely and too uncritically, have imposed on their subjects – as in the use of the terms Boer and Zulu – ethnic and racial categories which are far too exclusive and rigid. This division amongst the Zulu leadership is another example. The officials at the time soon categorised the differences as those between loyal and rebel. But behind these apparently stark choices of 'going to the Boers' or 'staying with the Queen' was ambivalence, reluctance and the heartbreak implicit in being forced to abandon deep personal bonds and historically rooted, emotional and culturally charged loyalties. It is true that accusations of treason were made, that violence between the factions did break out – but there was also, especially amongst the older generation who had experience of Mnyamana's role in Zulu history, the recognition that he remained an honourable man of exceptional ability. And it was also recognised that the division amongst the Usuthu was a tragic consequence of a colonial policy that viewed the national cohesion of the Zulu as a threat and hindrance to effective domination, and had therefore to do everything it could to fracture it.

The tragedy which had overtaken the Zulu is exemplified by a statement made at the August meeting by Mankulumana kaSomphunga, of the Ndwandwe. He was to become Dinuzulu's chief induna, and his loyalty to the prince and the Zulu cause through the many years of trouble to come was quite remarkable. He supported Dinuzulu at the August meeting – *and* at the same time defended Mnyamana, in an ambiguous but richly revealing statement on attitudes to the Zulu royal house and Zulu national sentiment: 'Why are you blaming Mnyamana, who has been looking after *the child?* you did not tell him, when you took the child to the Dutch; you Zulus will never be satisfied.'[39]

But there could be no reconciliation. Ndabuko and the faction with him decided they would make another journey to Vryheid to appeal to the Boers. The younger, less controlled elements amongst the Usuthu began to act provocatively towards their old comrades. At last officials had succeeded in weakening the bonds of unity within the Usuthu: they now began to call for authority to protect their new Zulu allies and to discipline their opponents, these Zulu rebels.

IV

RESISTANCE

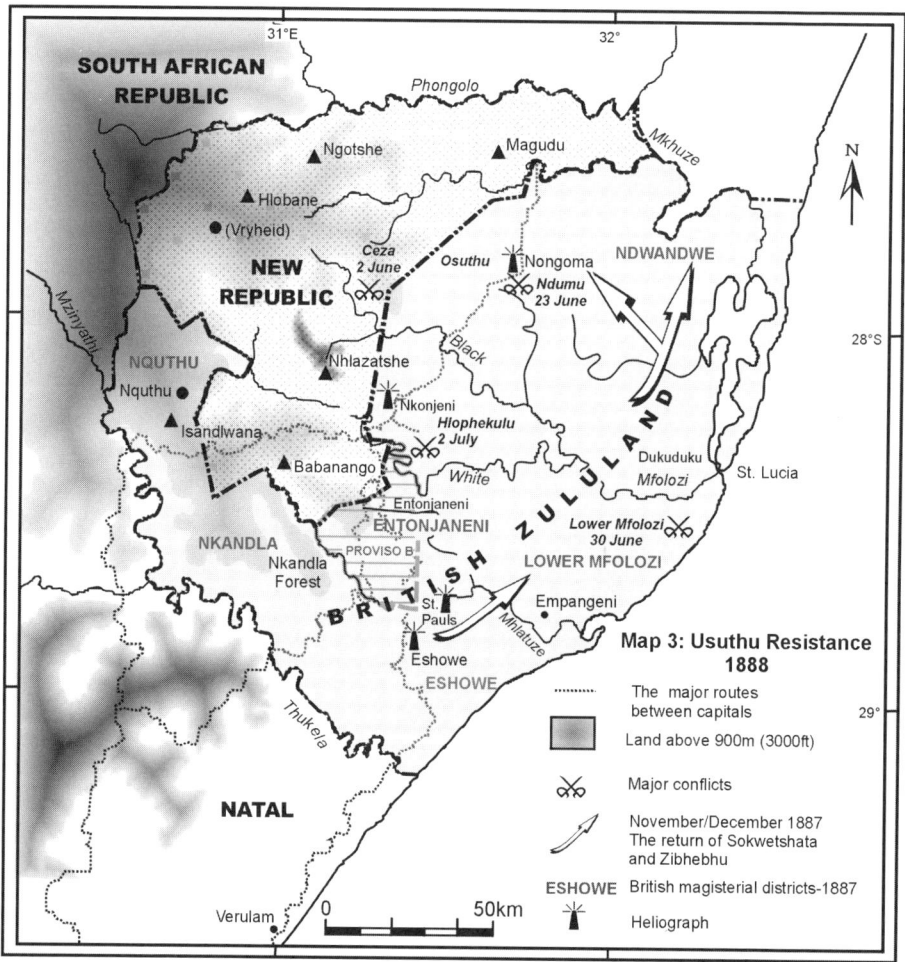

SOUTH AFRICAN
REPUBLIC

31°E

Phongolo

Mkhuze

Ngotshe

Magudu

Hlobane

(Vryheid)

NEW
REPUBLIC

Ceza
2 June

Osuthu

Nongoma

Ndumu
23 June

NDWANDWE

32°

N

28°S

Mzinyathi

NQUTHU

Nquthu

Nhlazatshe

Black

Isandlwana

Nkonjeni

Hlophekulu
2 July

Babanango

White

Dukuduku

Mfolozi

St. Lucia

Entonjaneni

ENTONJANENI

PROVISO B

NKANDLA

Nkandla
Forest

Lower Mfolozi
30 June

LOWER MFOLOZI

B R I T I S H   Z U L U L A N D

St.
Pauls

Mhlatuze

Empangeni

Eshowe

ESHOWE

NATAL

Thukela

Verulam

0   50km

Map 3: Usuthu Resistance
1888

.... The major routes
between capitals

Land above 900m (3000ft)

29°

Major conflicts

November/December 1887
The return of Sokwetshata
and Zibhebhu

ESHOWE British magisterial districts-1887

Heliograph

CHAPTER 13

TAIL LASHING
(SEPTEMBER–NOVEMBER 1887)

Contumacy: 9 September 1887

The officials of the new colony, British Zululand, watched developments with increasing concern. Although Melmoth Osborn, now Resident Commissioner and Chief Magistrate, had assured his superiors that the Zulu as a whole would be thankful and prepared to pay for the privilege of British rule, he had been unable to produce any convincing evidence for this from the Zulu themselves. While the officials had had to compel attendance at the official meetings to proclaim the new order, thousands of Zulu had of their own volition moved through northern Zululand to attend the August *ibandla* at Osuthu. For the officials this meeting was, in effect, an Usuthu mobilisation and a threat to peace. Then came the news that after the meeting a huge Zulu deputation under Ndabuko had travelled to Vryheid to consult with Lucas Meyer.

For the new administration this was an act of treason: a typically reckless act by an untrustworthy and unscrupulous minority who, in pursuit of their goals, did not hesitate to recognise two authorities and simultaneously attempt to play them off against one another. It was also profoundly embarrassing to have their public assurances of Zulu loyalty contradicted in this way, and infuriating when Meyer claimed that the Zulu nation had requested the protection of the New Republic. But the Usuthu gained nothing from their attempt to get support from the Boers. The deputation to Vryheid was berated for making complaints to the English.[1] And soon after the visit came the announcement that the New Republic had on 14 September 1887 been incorporated into the Transvaal.[2]

Moreover, the situation in Zululand was becoming increasingly difficult. Mnyamana's argument that the Zulu had no choice but to accept British rule had created tension between his followers and the other Usuthu. This in turn gave officials the chance to argue that Mnyamana's loyal Buthelezi had to be protected from the wrath of their former royalist allies. Addison wrote that he feared that if Mnyamana's people were attacked they would fall back on the police post at Nkonjeni for protection, where they might be followed by the Usuthu.[3] He believed that 'unless immediate steps are taken by the Government to suppress Dinuzulu and his followers and the former severely punished for his wilful disobedience of your orders, there will be disturbances and fighting in a very short time similar to those in the Nkandla in 1884'.[4]

Police were moved up to Nkonjeni, and Osborn asked Havelock for troops. The troops were not, of course, to be used in action. As Osborn wrote: 'I do not think that the slightest chance exists of the natives coming into conflict with the troops ... but the moral support which the presence of troops will afford the Assistant Commissioner in preventing disturbances or restoring order will be of incalculable value.'[5] The parallels between this situation and the one in the Reserve in 1884 are quite clear: moral support in fact meant intimidation. Havelock authorised this request for troops, as Bulwer had earlier. Osborn accompanied them to Nkonjeni, arriving there at the end of August – just when the Usuthu leaders were returning from their meeting with Lucas Meyer in Vryheid.[6]

Now with a detachment of troops at his back, visible and threatening despite the fact that they could not be used for direct action, Osborn tried to force the Usuthu into submission. He ordered the leaders to attend a meeting at Nkonjeni. On 3 September Mnyamana, Ziwedu and Shingana appeared before him.[7] But Dinuzulu and Ndabuko refused to attend, and Osborn chose two incidents on which to challenge their authority. The first concerned the destruction of the homestead of one Mfokozana accused of bewitching Mankulumana. Mfokozana had escaped but his wife had been killed and, according to reports, her body had been mutilated for medicinal purposes. In the second case Dinuzulu and Ndabuko had fined the participants in a fight over cattle. Osborn, arguing that they now lacked authority to do this, demanded that the cattle be returned, and imposed a fine of 30 head on Dinuzulu for 'contumacy'.

Early in September, Osborn ordered Addison and John Osborn to go to Osuthu with 60 Zululand Police and retrieve the cattle. Osborn assured Havelock that 'there will be no resistance to police, and this decisive assertion of authority will put an end to further pretension by Usuthu'.[8] Early in the morning of the 9th, the police lined up in front of the homestead and Addison demanded to see Ndabuko and Dinuzulu. Senior councillors were sent out to try to negotiate. There was no way, they said, that Ndabuko and Dinuzulu could leave the protection of the homestead and speak with a magistrate with 60 men armed with rifles at his back. Their own people would never allow them to do so. Instead, Addison should either enter the homestead and interview the *abantwana* personally, or negotiate outside with their representatives. As Hemulana said to Addison's induna, 'How can we go out there, when you are armed with breech-loading guns and you are red (referring to the red cartridge-belt)?'[9] But Addison refused to negotiate. That day and the next, he and his police raided homesteads in the Sikhwebezi valley seizing 2000 to 3000 head of cattle. That evening Osborn reported that because the fine was not paid, an equal number of cattle were taken in their place, and that all was quiet.[10]

It was not. The effect of these raids was immediate and dramatic. Ndabuko and Dinuzulu refused even more adamantly to attend the Resident Commissioner. The Usuthu, believing that their leaders were now threatened by official attack, moved towards Osuthu to protect them. Such mobilisation heightened the level of general rowdiness and war-talk, and increased the risk that foodstuffs would be looted for subsistence. Cattle were moved and steps taken to make sure that women and children could be got to places of safety. The younger men began to show their hostility to the most vulnerable members of the new administration, the African messengers from the magistracy.[11] One of Osborn's messengers was assaulted. The rift between Mnyamana and his following on the one side, and Dinuzulu and Ndabuko and theirs on the other, became wider. The general tension in northern Zululand increased.

Under orders to 'conciliate' Dinuzulu and Ndabuko, Osborn and Addison had tried to intimidate them. Havelock was now beginning to worry. The contradictory nature of the news coming from northern Zululand – that active measures had brought peace, but that further active measures were necessary – was clear. He refused Osborn his request to use British troops and informed London that he had told the Resident Commissioner 'that it is most undesirable to incur any risk of collision between the troops and the Natives, and that I shall be unable to authorize the employment of troops in an advance on Dinuzulu's kraal till every other expedient has been exhausted'.[12]

Protests and appeals

Dinuzulu managed to get a number of messages out of Zululand to publicise his predicament and ask for assistance. One was written by Paul Mthimkhulu. He had been born in Zululand but raised in the Cape, and it was his skills in traditional medicines which had led to his being invited to Zululand by the king.[13] However, before he arrived Cetshwayo had died, but he had remained with the royal family. He wrote a letter for Dinuzulu to the Trappists at Mariannhill in Natal:

> I send to you, of Rome, to ask how it is that we should be allowed to die here ... Help Help You of the Chief in heaven. Come and help us. We are dying from the acts of Mr Osborn. I am like one who is in Gaol ... The whole Zulu

nation has come to grief, through the acts of Mr. Osborn and the Chiefs of
Maritzburg. They are people who cause great trouble. The whole country is
disturbed without cause. My request is this, come to help us to reconstruct
the whole Zulu country with the help of God ...

It is not right that there should be any division between the Romans and
the Zulus. The people are being shot with guns like wild animals. I send
greetings to you, my Chiefs. I, Dinuzulu, say do not let any one know you are
coming here. Come, and let us see one another and consult together alone
because if they heard of it, they would cause great trouble.[14]

A deputation to the authorities in October claimed that Dinuzulu was being

destroyed by Malimade without having been in any way told what wrong he
had done ... His father left him fully clothed, but Mr. Osborn has unclothed
him, and left him naked ... a large part of his country has been cut off in which
his fathers lived ... these are the clothes which have been taken from him.
What is he to do now; he has nothing; is he to wear the leaves of trees of the
thorn country left to him ...

Dinuzulu complained of Osborn's interference in Zulu disputes, and the confusion which the placing of white magistrates in the country was causing
amongst the Zulu. 'This Proclamation has entrapped him; it has deprived him of
his inheritance, left him by his father, and makes him a common person, as it
takes away his Chieftainship, which Malimade has now usurped.'[15]

Already embarrassed by the letter from the New Republic stating that the
Zulu nation had asked for protection from the Boers, angered by Osborn's
reports of 'contumacy' on the part of Dinuzulu and Ndabuko, and sickened by
the accounts of the mutilation of the body of the wife of Mfokozana, Havelock
reacted strongly to this message. He told the messengers to inform Dinuzulu
that Osborn had not taken Dinuzulu's chieftainship. He had been placed over
the country by the Queen for the benefit of the Zulu who, by their actions, had
shown themselves incapable of either ruling or defending themselves. Osborn
had taken cattle because the law had been broken. The Zulu could no longer do
'what they like in the country, by killing and eating up the people'.[16]

'A sort of Orangeman'

Behind this bluster and his determination to put the Usuthu in their place,
Havelock was worried. He had been instructed not to make any moves that

might be resisted by the Zulu. But the pattern of the news coming from Zululand was just too familiar: promises from Osborn of peace – once there had been another demonstration of force. Bishopstowe had warned him to beware of the influence of the office of the SNA, present and past, on any policy for which he would be responsible. Frances Colenso had been told that on his arrival in Natal Havelock had been determined to take a new initiative, and that he had 'the whole series of our books read aloud to him ... I *know* that he held that office [the SNA] and its doings in contempt, and was determined to prevent such doings during his term.'[17] The Usuthu delegations had noticed signs of a change in attitude at Government House: rather than the conventional gift of shin bones, in order, they joked, to strengthen their legs for the journey back, a whole beast was given them to slaughter. After Havelock's arrival no objections were made when the Zulu visited Bishopstowe, and their deputation did not necessarily terminate at the office of the SNA, but at Government House itself.

But Havelock could not develop these new departures. Steadily the local experts, led by Sir Theophilus Shepstone and his friend Melmoth Osborn, supported by members of his family and their associates in Natal's native administration, had gained their hold on him. And the Governor needed this support, for in obeying instructions from London, he had also alienated a large body of Natal's settler community as represented in the Legislative Council. In its eyes Havelock's agreement with the Boers over Zululand was a betrayal by a weak-kneed Governor in collaboration with an ignorant home government. Labour from Zululand was needed for Natal's farmers, the land of the Zulu was required for the excess native population, and Zulu tax payments should accrue to Natal. It was through Zululand that Natal should make contact with the goldfields being opened to the north at this very moment, and gold had been found in Zululand itself. But Natal's Governor had ignored the interests of the colony and capitulated to imperial interests and the Boers. The Legislative Council passed a vote of censure on Havelock and eventually refused to ratify that portion of his salary for which the colony was responsible.[18]

The Colonial Office did not take the colony's protests very seriously. Natal was unable to balance its budget and a deficit of £250,000 was expected for 1886. She depended upon imperial troops for her security and defence. Britain was not going to hand the political initiative in Zululand to colonists and yet still remain responsible for good order and defence. Settler Natal remained angry with Havelock but Shepstone was there to give advice and support to the Governor, at his shoulder to remind him that the bulk of the people of Zululand were not Zulu at all and, once assured of the permanency of British rule, they would abandon these upstart remnants of a defunct royalist tyranny. But in the months that followed the annexation, these explanations were beginning to wear thin. In London the Treasury was reminding the Colonial Office of its fiscal obligations. It was hardly right that these chiefs of the old order should receive pensions before the first substantive act of the new order – the collection of the hut tax – had been carried out. It was time for the officials in Zululand to demonstrate the efficacy of the new administration, and for the Zulu people to demonstrate their loyalty and appreciation by paying the tax. Under pressure, the local officials sought for a way to bring this about. It was clear that London was never going to allow direct force to be used against the handful of Zulu who continued to obstruct the new administration. The time was therefore coming closer for them to utilise one of the basic strategies of Natal's native policy: the selection of African forces within Zululand to put an end to the pretensions of the Zulu royal house.

The forced exile of Zibhebhu to the southern districts of British Zululand was not just a disaster for the Mandlakazi, but a standing insult to the officials who had backed him so publicly. As long as the Zulu royalists occupied his land in the north, so the commitment of the colonial officials to the recognised chiefs and their capacity to support them must appear unconvincing. Osborn had backed Zibhebhu's many appeals for permission to return to his lands in the north, and Shepstone had supported him. But Havelock did not agree. He felt that such a move would be far too dangerous. Yet his advisers kept up the pressure. When in July 1887 he received another set of memorandums asking for Zibhebhu's return to be reconsidered, Havelock passed it on to Shepstone, asking for his comments. Sir Theophilus responded by recommending Zibhebhu's return in a memorandum that could rank as a classic in the history of imperial divide and rule.

It is not inconsistent with the most sanguine view of the success of the Zulu Administration to recognize the presence of disturbing elements which will require something stronger than moral influence to repress.

The organized police force is, and must always remain, too small to do more in serious cases than to represent the power that is behind it, and the military must be felt more as the ballast of the ship than as intended to actually interfere in the management of it; the real and effective force of the country must be furnished by its own population under the direction of Government.

At present, as far as I am able to judge, there is no such force in Zululand except that commanded by Zibhebhu; things are at present too new to rely entirely upon the support of Chiefs, who, however loyal they may wish to be, find it difficult to realise that the last arrangement is a permanent one; their co-operation will be more tentative than zealous; and this will apply to the great majority of the Zulu Chiefs.

Shepstone then went back to his own early experiences in Natal: at that time he had found it necessary to appoint a few chiefs who owed their positions solely to the patronage of the colonial government. They were then used to offset the power of the traditional chiefs. Zibhebhu should be used in the same way.

> The return of Zibhebhu to his people will at once throw the balance of Zulu power into the hands of Government; it took some time to do this in Natal, because the process was one of growth, but from the moment it was seen that Government was furnished with such power, the necessity for using it seldom arose, and so it will be in Zululand in proportion to the weakening of the savage instincts of the people, which their previous Government only served to keep alive.

Zibhebhu, Shepstone concluded, 'is capable of affording great assistance or great embarrassment to the Government; his existence cannot be ignored, and the best policy is, I think, to use him for the good of the country'.[19]

Havelock informed Shepstone that he had sent the memorandum 'to the Secretary of State, and am earnestly urging the adoption of the course advised by you'.[20] In London the proposal that Zibhebhu be returned to his country as 'a sort of Orangeman' divided the Colonial Office. Fairfield felt, wearily, that he had been here before. At the time of annexation he had suspected that the wording of Osborn's dispatches 'may foreshadow his [Zibhebhu's] use in some punitive plan of campaign against the Usutus meant to punish them for their uppishness in 1884–5'.[21] Now, five months later, the memorandums disclosed 'the possibility of dangers as to which we were pretty well kept in the dark hitherto; but this is our usual fate. It seems to be a choice of evils. Mr. Osborn says that if we don't give Zibhebhu leave to go, he will go without leave.'[22] But Bramston supported the suggestions for Zibhebhu's return and Herbert felt that the elder Shepstone's 'opinion is almost irresistible'.[23] The Secretary of State for the Colonies was not so convinced, but in the end he felt he had to bow to the men on the spot. 'Upon the whole then, looking to the strong opinions expressed by those qualified to form them, I am prepared to leave Sir Arthur Havelock full discretion to act as he thinks best on the matter.'[24] It was now up to Havelock. He decided to return Zibhebhu and take responsibility for the consequences. Sir Theophilus had won. All Zululand was to lose.

'Lashing his tail': 24 October 1887

Harriette never despaired – it was against her philosophy and her theology – but when the news of her younger sister, Frances's, death reached Pietermaritzburg at the end of April 1887 she was close to it. She broke both her own and Zulu conventions on mourning by going to see an Usuthu deputation in Pietermaritzburg to tell them reluctantly, bitterly, that she could not see how they could challenge the terms of the annexation. There were legal implications on which she could not advise them, and it was arranged that they should seek advice from W.Y. Campbell of Dumat and Campbell in Durban. Harriette stood surety for their fees. Although she kept in touch with the Usuthu during the winter of 1887 she concentrated not on the present but on the past, and the spirit of the past to which they were all committed, and worked on completing the biography of her father.

Havelock remained in private contact with Bishopstowe, going through the motions of cordiality. But politically they had less and less to say to one another. However, when the Usuthu deputation of October 1887 made its statement on how the annexation had stripped Dinuzulu of his inheritance and which attacked Osborn directly,[25] Havelock sent transcripts out to Harriette at Bishopstowe for her consideration.

She responded by urging Havelock not just to accept the information that came from his officials. She pointed out that there was a great difference between the message as transcribed and translated by the SNA and the Usuthu messages given to her. Henrique Shepstone's translations, for example, apart from specific errors and omissions, gave the wrong impression because the long, necessary, formulaic introduction was presented, in the translation, as the body of the message. Havelock did not accept her criticisms, but he did ask to see her and rode out to Bishopstowe on 24 October.

For Harriette the meeting was most disturbing. This gentlemanly and courteous Governor was in a fury, 'lashing his tail'. Dinuzulu was 'positively defiant' and had been acting in a most appalling manner. The murder of Mfokozana's wife was so horrific that he could not give her details. If he could pin it on him 'he would have the greatest pleasure in hanging Dinuzulu in Maritzburg Gaol': in fact he was also quite ready to hang Ndabuko, who he suspected was behind it all. But he was going to Zululand, to Eshowe, where he would meet them and give them just one more chance to abandon the course they were following and which would inevitably lead to their destruction.

Harriette had to think quickly to formulate a response. She was angry too. She had just seen the Blue Book in which Osborn's memorandum accusing her of stirring up the Usuthu had been published. Havelock should never have forwarded this to London without giving her a chance to reply, and she told him so. At the same time she knew the issues at hand were too important to be jeopardised by her personal objections. One of Havelock's motives, she suspected, was to try to frighten her into persuading Dinuzulu to be more amenable to the new authorities. And although she treated the threat of hanging seriously as an indication of the Governor's state of mind, she also suspected that it was 'intended to alarm me and possibly Dinuzulu (I have underground communication with him, you know, as the Bishop was said to have during the war ...)'.[26]

She tried to persuade the Governor to be more critical of the evidence that he was receiving from the officials. Who exactly were these messengers whom the Usuthu were treating so badly? Was he sure that they weren't Dunn's or Zibhebhu's men with a history of antagonism towards the Usuthu? It was not good enough for him to dismiss her comments on the grounds that 'this is a mere matter of detail of which he "knew nothing," he did not know the names of the chiefs, he "could not be expected to" understand'. As Governor of Natal he was not expected to know such details, but as Governor of Zululand he certainly was. Instead of just reacting with horror and fury at the report of the use of the woman's body for medicinal purposes, it would be far more useful to learn a lesson from the incident – of how important it was to have 'a good Doctor' in places like Zululand, who 'would have done much more to weaken the belief in "witchcraft," or poisoning than would be accomplished by hanging all the Zulu Chiefs together for murder'.

But behind Havelock's show of temper Harriette suspected there was also unease: he was beginning to realise that, just as she and her sister had warned him, he was being led into a trap.

What shocked me is Sir A. Havelock's tone. I can only suppose that the Shepstones (to use their name for them and their party especially Osborn) have been too many for him, and have committed him beyond recall to their mischievous policies ...

At the end, when he broke out about hanging I could not help saying that of course he could hang them both, but that could not alter the Zulus' belief in the justice of their cause, but might injure Her Majesty's prestige. It occurs to me that he may report this as a threat that I know the Zulus will fight. What I mean, and please say so for me, if desirable, is that Her Majesty's prestige for *justice and mercy* to the helpless and ignorant will be injured in all South Africa.[27]

'A dog on a string': November 1887

Havelock then left for Zululand where Addison and Osborn, desperately worried that the Usuthu would ignore the instruction, had to threaten them in order to persuade Ndabuko and Dinuzulu to attend the Governor at Eshowe. Ndabuko arrived first on 4 November, but to the local officials' fury and embarrassment it took another ten days before Dinuzulu was brought by his uncles and his councillors before the Governor. For refusing to obey Osborn's summons, Ndabuko and Dinuzulu were each fined 50 head of cattle. But as significant as this was for the officials, it meant little to the Usuthu, at least when compared to the manner in which the Governor reprimanded them and the tone in which he spoke of the changes that had been brought about by the annexation. In a speech which is quoted to this day, Havelock said that

> Dinuzulu must know, and all the Zulus must know, that the rule of the House of Shaka is a thing of the past. It is dead. It is like water spilt on the ground. The Queen rules now in Zululand and no one else. The Queen who conquered Cetywayo has now taken the government of the country into her own hands. The Governor is sent to represent the Queen, and to maintain her authority in Zululand. Let Dinuzulu and Ndabuko and everyone know that the Governor is determined to do this. The Queen has taken the rule of the country out of kindness for the Zulu nation. The Zulus can no longer stand by themselves ... and others would come and take the whole country down to the sea ... It is to save the Zulus from the misery that must fall upon them if they were left to themselves that the Queen has assumed the Government of the country.[28]

To have to sit and listen to this view of their present predicament and of Zulu history, and be denied the opportunity to answer, was not just frustrating but utterly humiliating for the Usuthu. To hear such opinions pronounced in the presence of the very men they believed were responsible for the disasters which had overtaken them was both unjust and degrading. But the meeting was more than a humiliation. It was also intimidating and frightening. For example, the acceptance of stipends had been made by some of the Usuthu leaders in confidence. Havelock chose this moment to break this confidence. He announced that Mnyamana, Sitheku, Ziwedu and Shingana had agreed to accept the payments. To many of the Usuthu present it seemed as if there were traitors amongst their most trusted leaders. The memory of this moment was vivid: 'The chiefs all kept silence from bewilderment, and their eyes became large as they looked at one another.'[29]

Ndabuko was in physical pain as well. He had fallen from his horse while at Eshowe and dislocated his shoulder. In spite of being warned of the consequences, he had refused to let the army medical officer put the joint back in place. It was said by the Usuthu that the accident was the result of Ndabuko sitting on a chair which had been treated with medicine by his enemies in the official camp. Dinuzulu was more astute and refused the chair offered to him, and escaped injury as a result.

But neither the evil effects of the medicines spread around the meeting place, nor the humiliation of a public tongue-lashing from the Governor, nor the deep unease caused by his public revelation of confidential negotiations with their leaders, could be compared with what happened next, at the final meeting. On 15 November Havelock announced that Sokwetshata of the Mthethwa and Zibhebhu of the Mandlakazi, whom the Usuthu had driven from their territories into the Reserve, were to be allowed 'to return to their old lands and to re-occupy them ... There is no longer room for them here. They understand that they are subjects of the Queen. They are loyal to the Queen, and will obey her laws. The Governor wishes to have loyal Chiefs and people in Zululand, those who will obey the laws and help the Government.'[30]

The rumour that Zibhebhu was to return had been passed about in Zululand for years, and always created fear amongst the Usuthu and hope amongst their enemies. Now, however, it was confirmed. Zibhebhu was to be restored: the man who in 1879 had turned on the Zulu royal house to which he belonged, who had seized its cattle and despoiled its women, who had slaughtered the great men of the kingdom in 1883, whose actions had led to the death of the king and forced the Usuthu to protect themselves by using the Boers, which led directly to the partition of the country amongst their enemies, was now going to be returned to his lands by Malimade, the friend of Somtsewu, the man who, although officially the representative of the Queen, had all the while been on the side of the Mandlakazi chief. The Usuthu listened to the announcement in shocked silence. *This* was the consequence of taking the hand of the English – Mnyamana's advice.

But they could not dwell on their grievances, for the injustice of the move to the Usuthu, severe as it was, was nothing compared to its danger to the Zulu people as a whole. They had to try to bring the potentially catastrophic implications of the decision to the Governor's attention immediately. Havelock, however, had no intention of hearing their too predictable response and he left immediately for Natal. And so it was left, once again, to Osborn, the Usuthu's prime enemy, to hear their reply.

In his official letter about his meeting with the Usuthu, Osborn reported that the atmosphere had been generally friendly. It was true that the Usuthu leaders had complained that they had not been given the opportunity to reply to the Governor, but there was 'only one thing they were not satisfied with' –

Zibhebhu's return: 'it would have been better to keep him and them wide apart so as to prevent disputes and troubles arising. But, they added, as the Governor has seen fit to allow Zibhebhu to return, the Governor will, they trust, see that they are not molested by Zibhebhu.'[31] This letter was written to reassure an angry Governor. Dinuzulu and his councillors were undoubtedly courteous – the prince was being trained by his elders to conduct negotiations in a seemly manner, and the Usuthu had no wish to antagonise Osborn unnecessarily at this moment. But to characterise the meeting as 'friendly' was disingenuous in the extreme.

A year later Dinuzulu gave his account. Havelock's abrupt termination of the meeting and his departure had left him feeling 'gagged'. He had asked Osborn to ask the Governor

> how is it you have returned him [Zibhebhu] when you knew he had attacked and killed my father who had been returned by the Queen. Zibhebhu was driven out by us and the country in which he used to live has been occupied by my people. Besides the land on which he lived, Maphitha's [Zibhebhu's father], belonged to the King although he lived in it, are you putting us against one another? If a fight occurs between Zibhebhu and myself know that you will have caused it because he destroyed me and mine.[32]

The Usuthu left Eshowe and, travelling northwards, spent the first night at the homestead of Sitheku. He was Mpande's oldest surviving son, and a man held in great respect. He had a private discussion with his nephew. His advice was to keep his anger under control and not react violently to Zibhebhu's return. He had to avoid putting himself in the wrong with the British.

> 'My Child, as the Government are bringing back Zibhebhu, you had better remain quiet and not do anything: Mnyamana has removed, because he sees that Zibhebhu is brought back again by the Government.' Such were the words of advice given by Sitheku to Dinuzulu, advising him not to do anything against Zibhebhu although he, Zibhebhu, thirsting for the land, had always been acting violently in the land. Then Dinuzulu replied, 'I cannot bear to live so close to Zibhebhu, it was he who killed my father.'[33]

This private consultation was followed by a general meeting. The gathering was tense. Opinions on the general strategy to adopt in the face of the news of the return of Zibhebhu were divided. Some Usuthu advocated force – Zibhebhu had to be stopped at the Mhlatuze River. Others, including some of Dinuzulu's senior councillors, sided with Sitheku. Zibhebhu should not be confronted by violence. Diplomatic pressure had to be applied: no responsible authority could accept such an outrageous decision as that to return Zibhebhu. Mankulumana argued it was ridiculous to say that Zibhebhu should be stopped at the Mhlatuze when the Usuthu were so divided amongst themselves. The argument became more intense, with one group accusing Mnyamana and Ziwedu of destroying Dinuzulu by deserting him, and the other saying that the best way to destroy Dinuzulu would be to encourage him to resist Zibhebhu.

In the end the Usuthu did not attempt to stop Zibhebhu. Mnyamana's advice at this time has become part of oral tradition: 'Zibhebhu was like a dog that the British government was leading by a piece of string, and if you struck the dog, naturally the British government would become involved, perhaps even taking up arms against you.'[34]

On 19 November, Dinuzulu returned to Osuthu to await developments. The next day, some 12 kilometres to the east of Osuthu, Addison arrived on the Nongoma ridge to establish the new magistracy there, with the major Usuthu homesteads lying in the valleys to the west, and the land occupied by the Usuthu and claimed by the Mandlakazi to the east. On 24 November, Zibhebhu and Sokwetshata left the Eshowe district. They had no women and children with them, were drawn up as an armed column, and took the coast road, marching northwards, to reclaim their lands.

The warnings – Bishopstowe's many attempts to persuade Havelock not to follow his predecessors' policies in Natal, the huge effort and expense of getting *The Ruin of Zululand* published in order to expose what had gone before and get a fresh policy devised for Zululand, the Usuthu protests documented in the Blue Books and in the hundreds of pages printed by Magema Fuze, Frances's heroic efforts to keep her pen steady and strong during her last winter – had failed. The Old Serpent had wriggled his way into Government House yet again, and another catastrophe was about to overtake Zululand.

CHAPTER 14

EAT SORROW
(DECEMBER 1887 – APRIL 1888)

An invading army

On 24 November Zibhebhu kaMaphitha of the Mandlakazi section of the Zulu, and Sokwetshata kaMlandela of the Mthethwa, left the Reserve. For Osborn and the officials around him it was a triumph 'dictated by justice, good policy, and by expediency'. To the Zulu watching, it was an invading army; and for the Zulu now living on the land to which it was marching, it was the next chapter in a decade of disasters. For Zibhebhu, Sokwetshata and their followers, it was the revenge for which they had waited for over three years. They marched without supplies. It was midsummer and the fields were thick with unreaped grain.

Zibhebhu had been given permission to return to the land he had occupied in 1879. Apart from the fact that the extent of this territory had been in dispute since then, the Usuthu had, since Zibhebhu's defeat at Etshaneni in June 1884, not only reoccupied their old homesteads but built new ones throughout the territory and prospered. Osborn, however, in a statement so muddied with qualifications that the Governor should have been warned, informed Havelock in July 1887 that 'is at present, or, rather was to within a few weeks ago, almost, comparatively speaking, entirely unpopulated'.[1]

It was thickly populated. The occupation of Mandlakazi land was one of the fruits of Usuthu victory.[2] Dinuzulu had built homesteads in the territory which had indisputably been in Zibhebhu's control in 1879 and placed some of his most important councillors in charge of them. On the perimeter of this area were homesteads of Zulu who had given their allegiance to the Usuthu largely as the result of their harassment by Zibhebhu earlier in the decade. The *ikhohlo* branch of the Mandlakazi, now in the charge of Fokoti after the death of two brothers at Zibhebhu's hands, occupied the north-east portion, north of Nongoma. Near the magistracy itself were the Nzuza and Mgamule's Ntombela. Towards the southeast, keeping above the unhealthy middle reaches of the Black Mfolozi valley, were tracts occupied by Mfinyeli's Xulu, intermixed with Mandlakazi who had deserted Zibhebhu. To the east again were the rich Hlabisa highlands where Mthumbu of the late Mbopha's section of the Hlabisa was in charge. The 'legitimate heir', Somfula, shared Zibhebhu's exile. East again was the large Dletsheni clan under Msushwana. Caught on the borderlands, they had suffered repeatedly in previous years when Zibhebhu had driven them into the lowlands. Here Somkhele of the Mpukunyoni had given them protection, and been drawn himself into the fighting, spreading it down into the coastal areas – now the Lower Mfolozi magistracy.

For Zibhebhu it was far more than a return to the lands of the Mandlakazi. It was a move which would re-establish him as the dominant power in a huge area running down the eastern flank of Zululand. Travelling with him was Sokwetshata, the man who claimed the Mthethwa chieftainship between the Mhlatuze and the Mfolozi. Also there was Somfula, claimant to the Hlabisa chieftainship. From the moment the force crossed the Mhlatuze, they were marching into an area thickly populated with their rivals.

Zibhebhu's force reached the office of the magistrate, Arthur Shepstone of the Lower Mfolozi district, on 28 November. The magistracy had already had its share of violence and upheaval, most of it, however, kept out of the official record. It had been established in July 1887 by Sir Theophilus's son, over an area that had been swept by violence during the civil war, ending with the expulsion of Zibhebhu's ally, Sokwetshata of the Mthethwa. There was a concentration of Usuthu chiefs living just north of the Mhlatuze, around where Empangeni is today. Most of these chiefs had initially been associated with the Emangweni military homestead in the area, and established themselves in its vicinity. Amongst them were some of the men who had been close to the Zulu king Cetshwayo including Somopho, induna of Emangweni and chief of the Thembu, and Bhejana of the Cebekhulu. Lokotwayo and Ndabayake were also considered Usuthu leaders in the region. Just to the north of the Mfolozi in the Ndwandwe district lived Somkhele of the Mpukunyoni. Linked to the royal house by marriage, his power reached south into the Lower Mfolozi district. On the arrival of Zibhebhu they all made for their hiding places in the swamps near the coast, including the Dukuduku forest.

Arthur Shepstone had wasted no time in asserting his authority and there was no shortage of men willing to assist him. His civil case book shows a series of claims made by loyal chiefs and policemen against the most important Usuthu chiefs resident there. The first signs of hesitation met with summonses and fines, repeated and increased every time they failed to appear before him. Behind their recalcitrance Arthur Shepstone saw Usuthu plots and incipient rebellion. But there was more to his hostility than this. Somopho of the Thembu and Bhejana of the Cebekhulu were depicted as being in direct contact with Dinuzulu, who encouraged them in his disobedience. But the Shepstone family had other reasons to be antagonistic towards them. Somopho of the Thembu had publicly attacked Arthur's father, Theophilus, when he visited the royal homestead in 1861,[3] and Bhejana of the Cebekhulu was the man who in 1877 had accused Shepstone senior of deserting Cetshwayo, the son of his friend Mpande. It fell to Shepstone junior to make the Zulu chiefs pay for these public insults.

The arrival of Sokwetshata gave Arthur Shepstone the confidence to attempt to do this. On 21 December Shepstone mobilised an armed force made up of nearly 400 of Sokwetshata's men, some traders and Zululand Police, and dragged Somopho from his hiding place and then forced Bhejana to surrender, for their refusal to obey civil summonses. Shepstone not only fined all the leading Usuthu chiefs for 'contempt of court and defying the authority of the Supreme Chief', he gave Bhejana and Somopho, two elderly and highly respected men, the additional sentence of three months' hard labour in Eshowe.[4]

After leaving Sokwetshata to reassert himself in the Lower Mfolozi district with the help of the young Shepstone, Zibhebhu had continued northwards with his 700 men.[5] By 1 December the *impi* had crossed the Black Mfolozi and ascended the north side of the valley into the Hlabisa district. The Hlabisa people fled, and the Mandlakazi helped themselves from their grain stores. Galloway, the official appointed to accompany Zibhebhu, reported that the Mandlakazi were 'nearly starving and there is great difficulty in keeping them from their [!] kraals, Zibhebhu wishes me particularly to ask if you can help him soon for the grounds he requires for gardens are at present in the hands of his enemies'.[6] Galloway depicted Zibhebhu as a victim because the Usuthu did not support him in their own spoliation:

So here is Zibhebhu returned by the Governor, denied by the people in consequence of Dinuzulu's report and *order*, with about 700 men in the midst of thousands of enemies, and no food, and yet tied by the order received from the Government, not to help himself. I therefore consider it *absolutely necessary* that he should be supported by an armed force.[7]

Zibhebhu then moved his force through the district occupied by Mfinyeli's Xulu people. Three days later he was at Msebe nearing the centre of the old Mandlakazi district. Usuthu fled before him to the east or across the border into the Transvaal, and the Mandlakazi seized the food stocks they had left behind. Hemulana, a leading Usuthu councillor and orator who had been placed in charge of one of Dinuzulu's homesteads, was ordered to leave by Zibhebhu and 'eat sorrow', as he had done at Msebe. Three of his sons had died in that battle.[8]

By 5 December, only three weeks after Havelock's official announcement that he was to be returned to his territory, Zibhebhu had reached the site of his chief homestead, Bangonomo. He left behind him a trail of terrified people, deserted homesteads and empty grain pits. Refugees had begun to cross the Ivuna on their way to Osuthu to seek the protection of Dinuzulu and Ndabuko. Other Usuthu joined them from different parts of the country, gathering around their leaders, to prepare for the coming crisis, whatever form it was going to take. Dinuzulu made his complaints personally at the magistracy at Nongoma on 8 December.

Zibhebhu claimed not only the land that his people had occupied but that of his allies as well – Somfula's sections of the Hlabisa, for example, and Mgojana's of the Ndwandwe. The officials gave him active support in this. Addison depicted Usuthu east of Nongoma as 'squatters' and used his police to evict them, and interpreted the fact that Usuthu were gathering around Dinuzulu as evidence of an impending attack on Zibhebhu. He advocated further coercion.

By early January 1888 northern Zululand was in crisis. Zibhebhu's force, reinforced by Mandlakazi who had been living in the north, was now well over 1000 strong. It had moved westwards from Bangonomo, re-establishing homesteads in the direction of the Nongoma magistracy. On 2 January the force reached Addison's office at Nongoma, where it triumphantly sang 'war songs'. Mnyamana rose above the split between himself and the Usuthu leadership, to protest 'against removal of Usuthu Kraals from Zibhebhu's location and dispute Zibhebhu's right to the Country, that it belonged to Senzangakhona and now consequently to Dinuzulu. Mnyamana says he cannot be held responsible for any warlike movement that may take place.'[9]

More Usuthu gathered for safety in the vicinity of Dinuzulu in the Ivuna valley. Addison and Osborn chose to depict this as an Usuthu mobilisation in preparation for an attack on Zibhebhu, and asked for a forward movement of British troops. Havelock agreed, and also instructed Dinuzulu and Zibhebhu to disperse their men. On 10 January the troops arrived at a point midway between Nongoma and Osuthu. The Zulu gathering at Osuthu began to disperse and Zibhebhu moved his force off in a north-easterly direction, paying off a number of scores on the way. Nkowana, chief of the Nzuza, had his crops trampled, and Fokoti and the Mandlakazi *ikhohlo* were ordered either to give their allegiance to Zibhebhu or leave the territory. Hlomuza received the same instruction, and one of Dinuzulu's homesteads was destroyed.

For some time Havelock in Pietermaritzburg had been aware that there was trouble in Zululand about which his subordinates were not keeping him informed. In mid-December he sent a stinging rebuke to Osborn on the 'imperfect and meagre information' which was reaching him, and demanded reports 'constantly and promptly', and that the Resident Commissioner give Addison 'imperative and precise directions'.[10] As the situation developed it became clear to him that, despite the interpretation of his Zululand officials, the mobilisation of Usuthu around Dinuzulu was best explained as the result of fear created by Zibhebhu's movement in the direction of Nongoma, not as part of a plan to attack the Mandlakazi. He gave orders that all Dinuzulu's complaints about the seizure of grain be investigated. If they were proved, then the Usuthu had to be compensated. He also informed Osborn in a public dispatch that he was

> reluctantly compelled to think that more care and greater discretion might
> have been exercised in the earlier state of Zibhebhu's re-settlement. I cannot
> too strongly express my earnest desire that you, and those serving under you,
> will use every effort to further a settlement of the difficulties that at present
> exist by a firm and judicious exercise of powers conferred by law, seasoned by
> a conciliatory and forbearing spirit.[11]

But Addison was not the man for this. He was too ignorant of the law he was supposed to implement. He had no idea that he was formally bound by Zululand's laws and regulations. He had been brought up in Natal and was imbued with settler attitudes towards Africans. At the slightest provocation he used violence, ordering his police to terrorise those Zulu he believed were disobedient, flogging and driving Usuthu out of territory he assumed was Zibhebhu's. In December, while investigating an alleged case of murder, he flogged the respected Usuthu messenger Siziba for refusing to answer questions. He then tried to extract information about a murder by pretending to shoot witnesses. He stopped this investigation only when the murder victim appeared on the scene to find out what the fuss was about.[12] In January 1888 Addison and his police chased down a group of men he believed were moving from Osuthu to the Transvaal without a pass, threw them to the ground and flogged them.[13]

When it was pointed out that these sorts of actions were not legal, he explained that he 'was dealing with men who had no inclination to keep the law':[14] he had flogged them because 'the acts for which these three men received the lenient punishment were dealt with under native law, according to which any native guilty of the same offence was, under the regime of Cetshwayo, put to death without any further inquiry'.[15]

At the end of January Addison laid down the boundary which was to define the western border of Zibhebhu's territory. Amongst the homesteads it left in Zibhebhu's territory were those of the Mandlakazi *ikhohlo*, the followers of Mthumbu of the Hlabisa district, and most of the land occupied by the Dletsheni.[16] Addison and the police then moved through the territory ordering the Zulu there either to give their allegiance to Zibhebhu or to leave. Some did so, moving into the Transvaal, or crossing the boundary to settle near Dinuzulu. Mthumbu of the Hlabisa was given a pass to go and live in the Lower Mfolozi district. Msushwana, the old chief of the Dletsheni, was told that if he found it impossible to live under Zibhebhu he should go there too. Both the Hlabisa and the Dletsheni had suffered immensely when they were driven into these low-land areas in the fighting of previous years. Highland Zulu could not just trans-fer into the lowlands without their people and their stock suffering from diseases to which they had no immunity. 'It is impossible to live there,' a brother of Msushwana was reported to have said, 'I lived there once and lost all my chil-dren. Only people who are born and bred there can live there; we people from the highlands cannot. [But the officials] They said, "You must go."'[17] Msushwana went to complain to Addison at Nongoma and was arrested.[18] Mthumbu destroyed his pass and fled to Osuthu.

Osborn persisted in his interpretation of events: the Usuthu were gathering around Dinuzulu to resist the Queen's authority and attack Zibhebhu.

The return of Zibhebhu to re-occupy with his people the place upon which his tribe had up to 1884 dwelt for generations past, was made the ostensible cause of serious dissatisfaction, and a large body of armed men were assem-bled by Dinuzulu, and kept at his chief kraal, the Usuthu, with the avowed object of attacking Zibhebhu.[19]

In Pietermaritzburg Havelock, at last, found the confidence to disagree. There was nothing in the information that he was receiving, he said, to suggest that it was Dinuzulu's 'avowed' object to attack Zibhebhu. The Usuthu mobilisation appeared to be a response to Zibhebhu's force moving westwards towards Nongoma. The Governor had by now realised that he could not rely on official information coming out of British Zululand. But it was already too late.

'A fairy tale (*Inganekwane*)': March 1888

At Osuthu the Usuthu leadership discussed the situation. It was serious and frightening, but it also provided them with an opportunity for effective protest. They had warned the authorities repeatedly about the consequences of the return of Zibhebhu, pointing out that although Havelock had promised that it would take place 'under the law', Zibhebhu was a man whom the law could not easily control. And now the Governor's word, solemnly given them in November, had, in December and January, been flouted. What they had predicted then, had now happened. Zibhebhu had entered the territory, seized property and driven out those who refused to recognise his authority.

The Usuthu strategy seemed clear. They should establish the facts of Zibhebhu's return, build a strong case against him and the Zululand officials, and present it to the Governor for transmission to London. This could work to their advantage and possibly divide the imperial from the colonial officials, and thereby perhaps even open the way for a new policy towards Zululand.

It was a sound strategy. The young men at Osuthu were kept firmly in control to avoid damaging the Usuthu case. Four men were chosen to present the case, with Mtokwane as their chief spokesman. They kept strictly to formal procedures, going first to the Resident Commissioner, Melmoth Osborn, at Eshowe. He heard their statement on 3 March, and gave them permission to repeat it before the Governor in Pietermaritzburg.[20] Osborn did so with the greatest reluctance but he realised that he was now much too vulnerable not to accede to their wishes. Zibhebhu had dragged him into the northern Zululand mire. He had lost the Governor's confidence over his handling of Zulu affairs, and the gist of the Usuthu message confirmed the Governor's interpretation of events. Osborn might suppress the Usuthu statement, as he had often done in the past, but this would not stop it getting out, if not through the colonial press, then through Bishopstowe.

Up to this point Osborn had procrastinated. On his desk were the details of Addison's boundary line. They had been there for a month. Two days after the Usuthu deputation had made its statement, Osborn informed Havelock that he could not confirm Addison's boundary on the grounds that 'I consider the tract of land included therein is unnecessarily large for the requirement of Zibhebhu and his people, and further that the location has not been made in terms of Your Excellency's permission to Zibhebhu which was that he could reoccupy only the old tribal lands and sites occupied by his tribe before the war of 1879'.[21] The Usuthu strategy had gained its first success.

In Pietermaritzburg the messengers went first to Harriette Colenso. She had not had direct contact with the Zulu leaders for a year now, although she had watched and commented upon reports coming from newspapers, stood up for them to the Governor, and kept Chesson informed on Zulu matters. But most of her energies had been spent on completing the final chapters of her father's life, and trying to deal with the enormously complicated affairs of the Church of

England in South Africa. Completing the biography of her father had been emotionally very demanding. It was a standard two-volume Victorian memorial – letters interspersed with text to vindicate the life of a great man. Sir George Cox dealt with the theological matters and the religious disputes, Colenso's daughters with African matters.

Now that the manuscript had been finished, she felt 'spent' and the need to rest, even a holiday. But she was not going to get it. The Usuthu messengers arrived at Bishopstowe on Sunday 11 March. For the next three days she took down their statement, and translated and annotated it. It was clearly a significant document. Magema put it into print and a copy was sent to Havelock on the 18th. From his response Harriette realised immediately that something had changed at Government House. Havelock asked for permission to use it officially and forwarded it, together with the official versions, to London.

Despite the differences in detail, the substance was clear: Zibhebhu had been returned in a manner which Havelock had not authorised and in circumstances of which he had not been aware. The deputation gave the names of the Usuthu who had been plundered and evicted and the homesteads which had been destroyed. They related the story of the arrest of Msushwana, chief of the Dletsheni, and Mthumbu of the Hlabisa, ordered by Addison to the swamps of the Lower Mfolozi. They spoke of Arthur Shepstone's arrest of Somopho and Bhejana, both 'working on the roads ... We heard that it was because they had delayed when summoned by Mr. Arthur Shepstone. They are both hoeing, watched by policemen (at hard labour) as convicts at Eshowe. Somopho is an aged man; he was enlisted in the Dlambedlu Regiment, under Dingane.'[22] 'In the days to come,' the Usuthu messengers told the SNA,

> when we of this generation are all dead and the affairs of our nation are being related, this story of Zibhebhu's present behaviour will appear to our children to be but a fairy tale (Inganekwane); when they are told that Zibhebhu, who has killed Cetshwayo, the father of Dinuzulu, was allowed to eat the food of Dinuzulu, and was practically nurtured and fed by the son of the Chief who he had slain, they will not believe it, or if they do they will look upon Dinuzulu as having been a very foolish, weak Chief.[23]

The message had the anticipated effect on the Governor. Its bearers were told that Zibhebhu and his people were 'only allowed to re-occupy the kraals and the land which was theirs before the war'. Those Usuthu who had suffered crop losses would receive compensation. Moreover, a new departure would be made. Assistant Magistrate John Knight, from the Entonjaneni district, would be instructed to investigate the land dispute: he had never had anything to do with the affairs of Zibhebhu and Dinuzulu, and he would be instructed to make 'strict inquiry about the rights of Zibhebhu and Dinuzulu's people, and not to allow to Zibhebhu any lands which cannot be shown to have been occupied by him and his people before the war of 1879'.[24] Havelock's message to Dinuzulu was read to them. He enclosed a copy for Osborn and instructed him to read it to them and to send a copy to Addison, who was also to read it, in their presence, to Dinuzulu. Havelock had taken control of the word out of the mouths and hands of his subordinates. He then tried to follow this up. On 21 March the Governor, his wife and private secretary visited Bishopstowe.

'Many a slip'

Havelock might have tried to give the impression that his visit was a social one, but in fact he had important political business with Harriette Colenso. He had not paid her a visit since they had clashed in October the previous year, when he had threatened to hang both Ndabuko and Dinuzulu. Since then, there had been no private communication between them on Zulu affairs. But he took her into his confidence. He told her that 'things had been done up there lately of which he did not approve'.[25] He intended to compensate the Usuthu for their losses and he was going to try to win Dinuzulu's confidence with an inquiry, carried out by someone unconnected with the northern districts.

Havelock also wanted some assistance. The meeting was, of course, strictly confidential but he hinted that these efforts to conciliate Dinuzulu had been done against the advice of the men around him in Natal. He asked Harriette if she could use her influence to persuade Dinuzulu to accept his invitation to come down to Pietermaritzburg and see him.

It was immediately clear to Harriette that events in northern Zululand had proved Havelock's advisers wrong and placed the Governor in a difficult position. But she was not one to crow over his discomfiture. She told him that she probably could help to persuade Dinuzulu to visit – but only if Zibhebhu was brought under control. At the same time she was not particularly optimistic of the outcome. To her brother she wrote, 'It remains to be seen, how far he can carry out his intentions *in spite of* the Shepstone clique – whether the Governor of Zululand in fact, is more powerful than was the Secretary of State when he meant to do rightly by Cetshwayo.'[26] She was pleased that the Governor was now prepared to talk with her but she did not hope for much. As Harriette told Chesson, she felt the forces ranged against the Zulu royal house were simply too great, for everyone from Sir Theophilus Shepstone downwards are interested in pre-venting things from settling down under Dinuzulu, in preventing him and his uncles being in favour with the Governor, and in preventing his coming down to be received in PMB as the head and representative of what is left of the Zulu people. So I am not too sanguine and see that many a slip may be arranged for us between the cup and the lip, but at any rate the present posi-tion is more hopeful.[27]

This letter was in fact one of the last letters that F.W. Chesson received from her. In May 1888 the secretary of the APS, and good friend and supporter of John Colenso and his children,[28] died at the age of 57. It was a severe blow: 'please let me know', she asked Frank, 'is there anyone left to write to? on these matters besides yourselves'.[29]

They needed allies desperately. In spite of the Usuthu success in convincing Havelock of the wrongs associated with Zibhebhu's return, there was no ques-tion of a sudden reversal of policy or of fresh appointments. Thus when Havelock's 'independent investigator', the magistrate John Knight, arrived in the northern districts in the company of Osborn, 'Ndabuko and Hemulana exclaimed, lamenting, "Maye! Alas! is Malimade coming! then we are undone; for he will twist the words till they become evil."'

Knight's insensitivity to their feelings and their situation only confirmed their fears. He called the Usuthu to a meeting. Here they found to their horror that their deadly enemy was also present. They had to confront Zibhebhu in person: they 'were set face to face with Zibhebhu, only some few yards apart looking one another full in the eyes'.[30]

The investigation into the various views on the boundary is interesting for what it reveals of the complexity of the land claims[31] that had developed in the area from Mpande's time. But it was beyond Knight's competence to reach an adequate judgment even if Havelock's instruction that Zibhebhu return to the lands he occupied in 1879 had not been so vague as to be open to widely differ-ing interpretations. For beyond bias and imprecision were more fundamental problems of perception, because the very concept of a spatial definition of land ownership did not apply. People gave their loyalty to certain chiefs, who were obliged to grant access to land in recognition of this political allegiance. This land could be described loosely in spatial terms – this side of that river, beyond that mountain, in this valley – but ownership of this land was defined in terms of personal affiliation, not in spatial terms. The inscription of lines on the land was possible, and explicable: it could be used to describe where people lived; but it did not, could not, reflect land rights. This needed first a revolution in concepts of land ownership – and indeed from this perspective, the misery of Zibhebhu's return, the violence, the threats and the hatred laid up for the future, can be seen as that revolution in progress, being forced into existence by the colonial authorities blindly from above.

We can see Knight blundering towards an understanding of Zulu concepts of land ownership but not reaching it – in the word 'network' in the quotation below, for example – in his reaction to the Usuthu complaints against him. Yet the dim realisation that his instructions and conceptions are flawed is resolved not by a deeper understanding of what he and the officials were bringing about in Zululand – but by the invention of an Usuthu conspiracy:

> It is obvious that if the various claims set up for portions of the Mandlakazi location [by the Usuthu] were acknowledged, the remainder would form a network so useless as to practically mean the extinction of the location as a whole.
>
> Take for instance the ground claimed by Msushwana. To acknowledge his claim would be to place him over a fourth of the location, right in the very heart of it, on which stands and always has stood Maphitha's chief kraal, *Xedeni*. There can be little doubt, from the nature of the claims, that they were got up with the object of cutting up Mandlakazi tribal lands in such a manner as to render them useless to Zibhebhu and his people as a whole.

Knight's line was unacceptable to the Usuthu.[32] They withdrew their representatives from the boundary inspection team and made formal objection to Knight's constant communication with Addison and Osborn, and angered the officials by refusing to accept cash in compensation for the crops which had been destroyed. How, they asked, were they to eat money?[33]

Havelock decided to give Knight's line a four-month trial. It was in fact overtaken by events and never ratified. Havelock's new-found critical approach turned to hesitation. The situation in northern Zululand began once again to drift out of his control. Immediately after Zibhebhu's return, the senior Usuthu leadership had been able to enforce strict discipline amongst their followers and avoid reprisals. This now became much more difficult when it appeared that their strategy of bringing the Governor onto their side was failing. Despite Havelock's promise of neutral intervention, Usuthu were still being forced to leave their homes by the Zululand Police. More and more Zulu moved westwards to take refuge in the vicinity of the Osuthu homestead in the Ivuna valley, eventually numbering well over 3000 from the time of Zibhebhu's return.[34] They brought with them problems of discipline, and raised fears amongst those Zulu who had not committed themselves to the Usuthu side and whose cattle and crops in their fields were a standing temptation to those who had been dispossessed.

It was a volatile situation, and late in April Osborn decided to settle northern Zululand once and for all. To go back to Eshowe now would mean going back to yet another round of Usuthu complaints and demands for explanation from an increasingly unsympathetic Governor. At the same time, the situation in the northern district would only deteriorate as Zibhebhu attempted to establish himself and the Usuthu congregated around their leaders. For Osborn and Addison it was time to come to terms with the two ringleaders, Ndabuko and Dinuzulu, the men whom they were under orders to conciliate but who were quite clearly beyond conciliation.

On 26 April Osborn wrote officially in optimistic terms of the peace and order which annexation had brought to Zululand, except of course for those districts under the influence of the recalcitrant young Zulu prince and his embittered uncle. Although their actual following was small, it had been increased by the return of Zibhebhu, which had provided the two Usuthu leaders 'with an ostensible cause for discontent, and a plausible reason for their conduct in collecting bodies of armed men'. Only 'severe measures' could put a stop to their intrigues, and Osborn informed Havelock that 'steps are now being taken to enforce, if necessary, the magistrate's authority, according to law'.[35]

Osuthu, enforcing the law: 26 April 1888[36]

On 24 April a force of nearly 100 Zululand Police, commanded by John Osborn, son of the Resident Commissioner, and accompanied by the magistrate Dick Addison, had made its way from the Nongoma magistracy into the valley of the Ivuna.[37] It was under orders to collect the balance of the cattle fines which Havelock had imposed on Dinuzulu and Ndabuko the previous year at Eshowe. It was also to arrest four men who, it was believed, had taken refuge at Osuthu. One was Mthumbu, the Hlabisa chief who had fled to Dinuzulu rather than move his people to the Lower Mfolozi district. The other three had refused to appear before Addison to face civil charges brought by a member of the Zululand Police, a follower of John Dunn and a man belonging to Zibhebhu. As had happened in the Lower Mfolozi district, men loyal to the new authorities found the magistrate's office a useful weapon in their personal disputes with other Zulu.

The police left in the evening and took a circuitous route so as to arrive in the Ivuna valley without warning. Consequently, before the cattle had even been driven out to graze, 70 head had been taken from the Ekubaseni and Ekubazeni homesteads, and Ndabuko's KwaMinya. The Nongqayi then terrorised the inhabitants of the homesteads. At the Ekubazeni homestead they surprised Makhedama and his uncle, Mgamule, one of the most senior men in the country. Zibhebhu had apparently brought charges against Makhedama for having taken horses at Etshaneni and he was arrested. Mgamule panicked and tried to run away, but was clubbed to the ground by Nongqayi rifle-butts.

Before dawn the next morning, 26 April, John Osborn, Addison and the police moved towards Osuthu to serve warrants on the men supposedly in hiding there. When it was within 50 metres of the main entrance, a detachment was sent to surround the homestead and cover the exits.

At this moment they were seen from within Osuthu. There were over 1000 Zulu in the homestead at the time, and the men poured out of their huts scrambling for their weapons. No one could have forgotten Zibhebhu's dawn raid on Ulundi in July 1884 and the massacre that followed.

Dinuzulu was not at Osuthu at the time, and Ndabuko was in charge. The moment he saw the surrounding force was in uniform, he sent his *izinduna* to try to keep their men under control. Most of them returned to the homestead and formed up around Ndabuko, his councillors, and the women and children. Mankulumana and two other senior men were then sent to parley with the police.

By now both sides were angry and frightened. Each accused the other of intending to attack. The Usuthu were so furious that it would have been impossible for Ndabuko to surrender the men even if he had wanted to. As he told Addison and Osborn, 'Those [Usuthu] men you see armed are armed by you, the men you want are armed amongst them, your system of arrest has defeated your own object.'[38]

As the argument continued, the police became increasingly concerned for their own safety. Parties of armed Usuthu were placing themselves across the track leaving the homestead. Osborn asked Ndabuko for an escort to ensure their safety when they left. He was given one. But as they left, numbers of young men followed them shouting insults, threatening them, and slapping their horses.

The Zululand Police were extremely fortunate to get away from Osuthu without violence. It was the active presence of the older Usuthu, Ndabuko and Mankulumana in particular, which saved them from a severe mauling. Given the state of tension within the district, the raids and assaults of the previous day, the fact that there were women and children in the homestead, and the dreadful memory of a dawn attack five years before which destroyed their fathers and the kingdom, the official attempt to arrest the men by means of a dawn raid was a highly irresponsible provocation.

The retreat from Osuthu, however, had been a humiliation. And the response of the officials to a humiliation was an attempt to reassert their authority with more aggression. Thus, Ndabuko's refusal to surrender was depicted by Osborn as

> a case of open resistance to the authority of the Resident Magistrate, requiring
> the serious notice of the Government ...
> I would recommend that a movement of troops be made in support of the
> Zululand Police, who should be sent again to execute the criminal warrant of
> the Resident Magistrate, and, if necessary, enforce the authority of the law.[39]

Havelock tried, but it was now too late to appeal yet again for an attempt at reconciliation. Neither Osborn nor Addison had any intention of doing so. The Usuthu on their side knew that the incident of 26 April would be interpreted as a serious breach of the law and that an attempt would be made to punish them. They could not risk having their women and children living unprotected in such circumstances, nor leave their cattle grazing freely in the valley. On the night of 26 April the inhabitants of Osuthu and nearby homesteads moved up the Ivuna and Sikhwebezi valleys, and hid their non-combatants and cattle in the forests or amongst their sympathisers in the Transvaal. Once this was completed, the men returned to their homesteads to await developments. In the eyes of the authorities, the Usuthu were now preparing for armed resistance.

'Am I to go away from Shaka?'

When the news of the attempt to arrest the men at Osuthu reached Dinuzulu, he was in the Transvaal residing with the emGazini, under the authority of the chief Mabhoko, near the Magudu mountain. With him were Mabhoko's son Sithambe, Sikhobobo of the Qulusi and Ndabankulu of the Ntombela.

It was said by the officials that he was in the area to recruit 'fighting men' with whom he intended to resist the Queen's authority in Zululand. There was, of course, much more to Dinuzulu's motives and intentions than this.

Dinuzulu was now nearly 18 years old and physically in his prime. Since 1884 he had lived in the shadow of his uncles and Mnyamana. During this time Dinuzulu had not been allowed to make independent political judgements or act without reference to his councillors. Nonetheless, he had at times escaped from their close supervision, particularly when the tug-of-war between his uncles and the Boers diverted their attention and gave him the opportunity.

By 1887 he had begun to assert himself and take a somewhat independent line. He had built homesteads in the Mandlakazi district in which his followers were allowed to live, and he was gaining increasing recognition as son and successor to Cetshwayo kaMpande, the last Zulu king. Later, in 1889, Hemulana, who had fought under Dingane and served Mpande and Cetshwayo, gave expression to the feelings of many of the older Usuthu when he said:

How could I *khonza* [give allegiance] to Zibhebhu, while Shaka's people are still alive? Maphitha was the son of my father's sister. [?yet] I would rather *die* with Dinuzulu: while he is alive, I will not leave him: the kings ... in Zululand, fed me. Am *I* to go away from Shaka? I belong to the Queen, under Dinuzulu: he is the Queen's son, and *I* follow *him*.[40]

But it was the young men of Zululand who formed the heart of his following. He had revived the Falaza and formed the Mbokodwebomvu regiments, and young men from all parts of the country came to his main homestead Osuthu to serve him. For Dinuzulu and his age-mates, the tragedy of the events developing in Zululand was, to some extent, mitigated for the moment by the opportunity it provided to march and ride through the country, feast and drink, and court young women, as befitted the heirs of Shaka. While their contemporaries elsewhere in southern Africa, including southern Zululand, were entering adult life as house-boys or railway labourers, or working on the new mines in the Transvaal, Dinuzulu and his followers moved through the valleys of northern Zululand, trading cattle for horses, rifles and ammunition. And in so doing, they gained for themselves and their leader the reputation of rebels attempting once again, as Dinuzulu's father had done, to revive the House of Senzangakhona.

Yet in significant ways Dinuzulu's followers were unlike those of their predecessors. Many of them were horsemen, and Dinuzulu created an escort and bodyguard which exemplified the changes overtaking Zulu society. They were divided into two sections: the *amagagana* – the emaciated ones – numbering about 20, all mounted and dressed in black with braid on their coats; and the *amahuza* – the stealthy ones – dressed in light-coloured clothing. They marched with a bugler who transmitted commands from Dinuzulu to his men.

Paul Mthimkhulu was his chaplain. He was an independent preacher who mixed his knowledge of Christianity with Zulu custom, travelled with the Usuthu, shared their predicament, combined biblical readings and prayers with appeals to the Zulu ancestral spirits, and used his knowledge of traditional medicine to treat their ailments and injuries.

So, in the valleys of British Zululand, Dinuzulu and his young men gave expression to their spirit of military adventure. On the intervening ridges the magistrates and police watched the movements of the Usuthu beneath them with concern. The supporting troops established safe lines of communication and flashed heliograph messages from the crests of the hills for transmission to

Pietermaritzburg and London. But for the son of Cetshwayo and his young followers these few precious months in 1887 and 1888, during which they moved in military formation across colonial borders, were a time to celebrate Zulu tradition and a freedom made more valuable by the fact that it was about to be brought to an end.

For their activities were deeply resented and feared by the authorities. Spies reported them to the magistrates, and their fathers were summonsed to the new courts and fined. The continuing charge made by the officials now, and increasingly later, was that the Usuthu were not only rebels but traitors: that they were not only resisting the British, but were also in contact with the Transvaal Boers, who encouraged and assisted them in their plan to overthrow the authority of Her Majesty's Government itself.

The movement of Usuthu and Dinuzulu into the areas to the north of British Zululand confirmed this. Particularly attractive was the wedge of territory between British Zululand and Swaziland, now part of the border area of the Transvaal. Much of it was valley bushveld, low-lying, useful for winter grazing rather than permanent Boer occupation, at least in these early years of white occupation. Here Dinuzulu was able to ride with his mounted escort, visit his followers, and find refuge from the Zululand Police and from the real fear that Zibhebhu was being encouraged to exterminate the Usuthu leadership. There was considerable sympathy for Dinuzulu, especially amongst the older border Boers, who had initiated the move into Zululand. Local officials like Lucas and Coenraad Meyer, Louis Botha in the west, Paul Bester from the central area and J. Ferreira from the eastern districts, gave Dinuzulu advice and permitted him and his followers to cross the territory under their control.[41] Here Dinuzulu could exchange cattle for rifles and horses, chat with visiting traders and adventurers, talk about land with visiting Boers, about British tyranny and injustice, and smoke dagga, drink beer and court the girls in the homesteads of his people.

When Dinuzulu crossed into the New Republic on 6 April 1888 it was alleged that he did so to recruit an army to attack the Mandlakazi. It is most unlikely that this was true. Some of the most senior men still on his side were urging him to keep back, if only because he lacked the manpower to go against Zibhebhu. Nonetheless, the possibility of war with the Mandlakazi must always have been a consideration. The fear that Zibhebhu would attack was real. The area beyond the British Zululand boundary therefore needed to be reconnoitred, and its people consulted. The 26 April raid on Osuthu by the British magistrate and the Zululand Police showed clearly that Havelock's attempts at conciliation were not going to be carried out by his officials in Zululand, and the Usuthu might well need a place into which to retreat before too long.

CHAPTER 15

FLIGHT (MAY 1888)

The move to Ceza: May 1888

When the news of the 26 April raid at Osuthu reached him at Magudu, Dinuzulu decided that he should return with his followers. It was widely believed that Zibhebhu had mobilised again in preparation for an attack. Dinuzulu was able to raise about ten companies – that is, 500 to 600 men – drawn from the central and eastern portions of the district, the bulk of them from the emGazini, and he began to move with them to the south, towards the Ivuna valley where Osuthu was built.[1]

At Osuthu, Ndabuko and his followers were waiting for the British reaction to the humiliation that Osborn junior, Addison and the Zululand Police had suffered on 26 April. It came soon enough. On 12 May it was reported that a squadron of soldiers was making its way from Nkonjeni to Nongoma. These were the British regulars authorised by Havelock to support the civil authority. The next day Ndabuko and his followers from the Ivuna valley and its surrounds, supplemented by men who had been evicted from the lands now claimed by Zibhebhu – about 13 companies strong – abandoned their homesteads. Meanwhile Dinuzulu and his men from the north had crossed into British Zululand. On 14 May they met with other Usuthu and moved towards Ceza, the mountain stronghold bordering on the Transvaal.

Dinuzulu and Paul Bester had examined Ceza twice before its occupation in May. It was situated on the eastern extremity of a huge spur that juts into the valley of the Black Mfolozi, which describes an arc around it some 15 kilometres away, and about 600 metres beneath it. On the eastern summit of the spur, at about 1500 metres, a beacon had been placed by the Boundary Commission, and it now marked the border between the Transvaal and British Zululand. From this point the border travelled to the north-east in one direction, and south in the other. Most of the spur was therefore situated in the Transvaal, but its eastern extremity jutted out into British Zululand at Ceza.

Just below this, within Zululand, was a steep rocky slope, covered with thick bush that formed a dense band of vegetation through which a few narrow paths had been hacked. Below this, the ground levelled before it fell away steeply again towards the Black Mfolozi River. The Usuthu built temporary shelters in the bush below the summit, using the open level space as an assembly ground for the 1000 soldiers who gathered there.

Geographically and politically, Ceza was ideally situated as a retreat and for defensive action. From their hideouts in the bush the Usuthu commanded a huge stretch of territory. On the southern horizon they could see Nkonjeni police camp with its military heliograph flashing messages to the Nongoma magistracy 50 kilometres to the east of them but out of sight. Below them stretched the upper reaches of the Black Mfolozi River, and through its broad valley, amongst Buthelezi homesteads, passed the track linking Nkonjeni and Nongoma. Nobody could approach Ceza from the south or the south-east without being observed as they toiled over steep, open ground. The Usuthu flanks and immediate rear were protected by the bush-covered, rocky slopes, while behind them lay the boundary with the Transvaal, offering, as long as the arrangements between Usuthu and the local Boers remained sound, a retreat if they were attacked by the British and their Mandlakazi allies.

Ceza was an excellent defensive position. But there were factors beyond topography and political geography which had to be covered as well. This was left to Paul Mthimkhulu. He sent men into the thornveld to cut and bring to Ceza logs of wood.

> These poles were sharpened at both ends, and were to be used on the suggestions of Umtandalaza, the prayer-reader, that, on being struck by a bullet, the pole would turn round and the other end would still be prepared, as it were, for battle. Those poles were to be as good as fighting men: when struck, the piece would fly off and would strike the party who had fired. That was the suggestion of the praying-man, who does not confine himself to praying. Those poles were brought up from the thorn-country, and they were put down very carefully and reverently, not simply thrown down anyhow.[2]

After Dinuzulu and Ndabuko's men had made their way to Ceza on 14 May, their numbers were augmented by Zulu from the western portions of the Vryheid district – the Qulusi, Mphangisweni, Mdlalose and Ntombela. To the officials, of course, there was nothing defensive about the move. It was mobilisation for resistance, made in preparation for an attack on the British authorities in Zululand. There is no solid evidence for this. There were undoubtedly a number of aggressive, boasting young men in the force, with nothing more to lose and a little to gain – if only their military reputations – if there were a successful armed clash. Nonetheless, there were also many senior, responsible men, who were well aware of what the consequences would be of a reckless attack mounted by the Usuthu. The move to Ceza was primarily a defensive one made by the Usuthu leadership because it was felt that they would be unable to protect or control their people if they were to suffer further aggressive raiding by the Zululand Police, especially when their families were in the homesteads. There was also the genuine fear that the British would use, or lose control of, Zibhebhu. It was primarily a responsible measure taken in the face of the irresponsible manner in which British authority was being imposed over them. It placed the Usuthu in a strong defensive position, without their leaving the territory and thereby perhaps forfeiting their rights of domicile within British Zululand. At the same time, if they were heavily pressed they could retreat into foreign territory into which they could not be pursued by the Zululand authorities.

Despite this, a retreat to defensive strongholds had its own destructive dynamic. It made it impossible to maintain a neutral position. Divisions which initially were not deep – over matters of strategy rather than commitment – became unbridgeable with the move to the stronghold in May. Those Zulu hitherto with Dinuzulu in spirit, now had to be with him in person – in the caves and forest at Ceza. Those who remained in their homesteads, for whatever reason, were seen as being against him – like the people of Mnyamana – now characterised by the officials as loyals, in contrast to the rebels in the hills. Dinuzulu sent messages into other parts of Zululand, instructing the chiefs to give him their support, in particular by sending their young men to join the force at Ceza.

The move to Ceza marked the beginning of a crisis of commitment for the people of Zululand. Public expression of commitment to the Usuthu meant harassment by officials and, it was feared, an attack by Zibhebhu. Public commitment to officials meant being branded as a traitor to the Zulu royal house, and perhaps ultimately an attack by an Usuthu – perhaps even, rumour had it, by an Usuthu–Boer force. Most of the Zulu people, after eight years of civil war and disruption, hoped to maintain some sort of neutrality during which time they could build up their strength and resources. But circumstances in 1888 did not allow this. Instead, the struggle for power between the new colonial and the old Zulu authorities forced the Zulu into the crude categories of the officials: those who were not demonstrably loyal had to be rebels.

There were material factors as well which made a safe neutrality impossible, exacerbating the divisions between the Zulu and driving them further apart. The mobilisation of men, and the movement of women and children to safe retreats, disrupted the agricultural cycle yet again. Only a limited amount of grain could be carried to places of refuge. The rest remained in the deserted homesteads, exposed to the increasing number of hungry marauders. It was difficult to keep cattle in places of safety and still ensure that they had access to water and grazing. The decision to vacate homesteads created severe hardship, and the problems of inadequate sanitation and disease were made worse by the debilitating effects of inadequate diet. Men from the strongholds would spend much of their time foraging in the surrounding homesteads for grain or searching for cattle, and in so doing they clashed with others on similar errands, increasing the level of violence.

Sir Theophilus Shepstone had argued that the return of Zibhebhu would provide ballast to stabilise the Zululand ship. Instead it drove it listing and out of control onto the rocks. For, while it irrevocably alienated the Usuthu from the authorities, it drove the uncommitted Zulu in both directions for different reasons – to the Usuthu and Ceza as the finest defensive position in the country against a possible attack by the British or Zibhebhu; or to the authorities and the magistracies in the hope that the Usuthu or the Boers would not attack them in the presence of British troops and under the guns of the Zululand Police.

The Ndwandwe district: May 1888

Before 14 May the differences between Ndabuko and Dinuzulu, and their old allies Mnyamana and Ziwedu, had been tense but not violent. The move to Ceza, however, gave physical expression to their differences, and as the Usuthu passed through Mnyamana's and Ziwedu's homesteads they took cattle from them on the ground that these cattle had been taken at Etshaneni and therefore, as the product of an alliance now terminated, belonged to Dinuzulu.

But even at this stage the animosity between these erstwhile allies was not intense. They were closely related by history, residence, kinship. Until a few weeks before they had been comrades-in-arms. Some of the men who had lost their cattle went personally to Ceza, and the Usuthu leadership heard their complaints. Some were told that the cattle had been taken by young men without authority and had already been slaughtered. Others had their cattle returned and they were escorted to safety from the stronghold.[3]

But neither Mnyamana nor Ziwedu felt safe in their homesteads. On 19 May both men moved to the vicinity of the police camp at Nkonjeni. It was a move that was to have significant consequences. Up to this point Havelock had been resisting the interpretation of events which was coming from his subordinates in Zululand. The débâcle associated with Zibhebhu's return, together with

Harriette Colenso's injunction that he be more critical of the evidence he was receiving from Zululand, was still having its effect. But on 23 May Osborn cabled Havelock that Mnyamana had told him that over 100 of his cattle had been slaughtered at Ceza for the Usuthu *impi* there on Dinuzulu's orders. Osborn asked Havelock for authority to protect Mnyamana's and Ziwedu's people – if not, he argued, they would be forced to cross over to the Usuthu for their own safety. Havelock consulted with the officer commanding the British troops in Zululand and on 25 May he gave Osborn authority to arrest the men at Ceza responsible for the robberies.[4] British troops were to support the police when they served the warrants. Three months later Havelock informed Osborn that, on examining the documentation of events at the time with the intention of building a case against the Usuthu, neither he nor the Attorney-General was able to find the evidence for 'the information which finally induced me to authorize the arrest of Dinuzulu and other ringleaders'.[5]

A national party – 'a rope of sand'

Serving a warrant of arrest with the support of British troops on the Usuthu leaders while they were at Ceza was just the sort of action which Harriette Colenso had been urging Havelock to avoid since his visit to her only two months before.[6] She was sure he was wrong in his overall interpretation of the Usuthu motives – he was being used by his advisers and subordinates – and she was determined to keep pressure on him.

Havelock saw it differently, of course. He believed he had done everything he could to encourage Dinuzulu to behave otherwise. He had urged Osborn not to antagonise him. The consequence had only been further resistance, robbery and even murder. Dinuzulu headed a small but violent faction in Zululand deter-mined to challenge the British administration there. Thus, Havelock objected when Harriette Colenso used the term 'the Zulu National Party' to describe the Usuthu. Dinuzulu, he felt,

> had wilfully and irretrievably committed himself to a course of lawlessness. The only thing to be done was to put the law in motion against him and his associates. Warrants have been issued, and they must be executed. If there is resistance and loss of life in executing them, the blame must rest with Dinuzulu and the other responsible parties ... There is no national party with Dinuzulu. His followers represent an insignificant section of the Zulus ...[7]

The arrival of Blue Book C5331 at this time gave Harriette a clear idea of the sort of pressures Havelock was under and the ideas that he was receiving from his advisers. In August 1887 Sir Theophilus had written a memorandum for Havelock in response to protests that the Colonial Office had received from the APS (and therefore from Harriette Colenso) on the boundary of the New Republic generally, and specifically about the alienation of Emakhosini, the graves of the pre-Shakan kings. For Havelock it was an important document, for political reasons and for the historical record. The Zulu royal family, Shepstone reminded his readers, were the descendants of a tyrannical conqueror, and their victims could not be described as a 'nation'. It was all a question of history:

> There is a liability to attach too much importance to representations made by messengers from the Zulu Royal Family, and this is caused chiefly by a mis-conception of the actual condition of the Zulu population, from the first estab-lishment of Zulu power until now.
>
> It is believed that the Zulus are a nation properly so called, and that the rep-resentations sent from the Zulu Royal family are really sent by the Zulu nation.
>
> This belief is not correct in the sense in which it is adopted. The Zulus were originally a small tribe; accident and the military genius of one of their Chiefs, Chaka, enabled them to subdue and incorporate their tribal neigh-bours. Knowing the danger to his power if he left alive the reigning families of these incorporated tribes, Chaka tried to extirpate them, but failed ... These conquered tribes retained their tribal names, and it became convenient for the purposes of control that they should retain them ...
>
> The yearnings of these tribes have always, and naturally, been for their ancient separate existence, relieved of the terrible incubus of the Zulu Royal Family. The Zulu nation is therefore a collection of tribes, more or less autonomous, and more or less discontented; a rope of sand whose only cohes-ive property was furnished by the presence of the Zulu ruling family and its command of a standing army.[8]

'Rope of sand' is an interesting metaphor – something of apparent substance but in fact vulnerable to the waves of history – the waves of history which had swept over Zululand since the British invasion. It had become, as Havelock said in that other often-quoted phrase, 'like water spilt on the ground'. But it is a metaphor which reflects a very particular view of Zulu history – the viewpoint of the authors of the destruction of Zulu independence – and the basis of an argu-ment over the nature of the Zulu royal house which is still alive to this day.[9]

The opposing point of view was put at the time by Harriette Colenso. She was infuriated:

I really can't go near Sir Theophilus Shepstone again until I've thoroughly
answered and shown up his impudent memorandum on the non-existence of the
old Zulu Kings. He flatly contradicts my despatches published the end of 86 and
beginning of 87, and he is as *wrong*, as ignorant throughout, as he can be.[10]

She traced the history of Shepstone's use of this argument from the time he
began to cite it to justify the 1879 invasion. Events had proved his interpretation
of Zulu society and history wrong time and again. In 1879 Shepstone had pic-
tured the kingdom as a 'ball of sand' that would collapse when touched:
Isandlwana should have put paid to this. In 1882, 646 chiefs and headmen had
come to Pietermaritzburg to petition for the king's return. She herself had questioned chiefs about the history of the royal house and discovered that the graves
of nine generations of Zulu chiefs were known in Zululand; that a large number
of tribes, including the Mandlakazi, were of Zulu origin; that some of the most
important tribes had originally been Zulu; and that many of the great chiefs'
mothers and wives were from the Zulu royal house. It was impossible to make
sense of events in Zululand since the invasion unless one realised that a substantial proportion of Africans in Natal as well as Zululand saw themselves as followers of the Zulu royal house and members of the Zulu nation. The Usuthu,
those Zulu who actively pursued the interests of the Zulu royal house and its followers, were, she felt, indeed a national party. Shepstone's depiction of Zululand
as a collection of conquered and discontented tribes made no sense at all. The
evidence showed

> that the deeply rooted and widespread attachment to their reigning Chief
> which was proved to exist, is just what might be expected towards the heir of
> their race, the representative of their Kings and ancestors, for whose sake they
> believe that these old spirits still protect them or punish them. Such I believe
> to have been the origin of the National Party now called the Usuthu because
> identified with Cetshwayo's own tribe during his imprisonment. That its
> power of resistance should now prove insignificant would only be natural,
> since to crush and efface it has been the object diligently pursued since 1879,
> by those who imagine its heads to be a 'terrible incubus' on the Zulu People.
> But I believe that the sentiment which it represents is still deeply rooted and
> wide spread, and that sympathy for Dinuzulu is now being strongly felt among
> the natives of Natal, and as far north as Umzila's country.[11]

But, however misleading, at least Sir Theophilus's many memorandums on the
nature and the future of the Zulu royal house were presented as serious

attempts at political analysis and African history. One wonders, though, how Zulu matters were discussed around the patriarch's dinner table. Henrique Shepstone, SNA, son of Sir Theophilus, adviser to the Governor, the man who had dealt with Shingana's insistent attempts to protest at the annexation in November 1886, wrote to an officer in Zululand about this brother of the king: 'Shingana will cause trouble unless he is snuffed out at once and I gather from your letter that you intend doing so when Hlubi comes ... if there is the slightest chance of doing so shoot him. There would be no greater mercy to the Zulu people than to shoot the whole of the Royal family at once, everything would then settle down quietly.'[12]

The central districts: May 1888

By the end of May, with the situation deteriorating in northern Zululand, the officials had gone a long way in persuading the Governor that the Usuthu could never be brought under the law. Peace in Zululand required an unequivocal assertion of authority. Havelock now began to try putting some distance between himself and Harriette Colenso. She had

> not heard again from Sir Arthur Havelock and I much fear that the enemy will be too strong for him, and keep the Usuthu in perpetual hot water till they've quashed them finally ...
> However His Excellency's eyes are half open and he will not like being balked, and it would be my fault if it is not plain to him![13]

For this reason it was essential that she try to make contact with the Usuthu and offer them some way to escape the slide into more violence and the possibility of despair. Her options were obviously very limited, but she asked Thwayisa Mabaso and Mubi Nondenisa – the same two men whom she had sent to Cetshwayo in the Nkandla in 1883 – to try to reach Ceza and deliver a message from her to the Usuthu.

It invoked, of course, the memory of her father. 'It is I, Dlwedlwe, daughter of Sobantu, who am now sending to you. I send to you Heads of the Zulu People, to Mnyamana, to Ndabuko and to Dinuzulu. I send because of our friendship, in the name of my Father Sobantu, Sokukuleka (Father of Counsel) concerning a matter in which I see that you should receive counsel.' She informed them that their account of events which occurred on the return of Zibhebhu had now appeared in the latest Blue Book – 'a book which has come from over the sea'. As a result of this message the Governor had invited them for consultation, and she urged them to take it up 'that they might meet, and come to understand one another, and become acquainted'. This was necessary because it was being said that they intended to attack Zibhebhu and were asking for Boer help to do so.[14]

In Zululand Mubi Nondenisa and Thwayisa Mabaso found tension and danger. Even before the move to Ceza, groups of Zulu from the central districts between the Nkonjeni ridge down to the Nkandla had been moving surreptitiously to the north to join the Usuthu, thereby evoking the anger of the authorities. Dinuzulu's messengers travelled through the country and the magistrates seized cattle from the homesteads of men who it was reported had gone to join him.

Shingana had moved to this central district after abandoning his homesteads when the Boers occupied the land upon which they were built. He had accepted a stipend and was considered loyal, but from the start he came under pressure from local people who had previously been members of the royal homesteads which were once scattered through the district. They looked to him for advice and at first he had told them to sit still. But as May progressed, Shingana had become increasingly worried. He had the reputation of being the wiliest of the *abantwana*, and it was his particular fear that Zibhebhu had a grudge against him and was waiting for the chance to attack.

But it was impossible for Shingana to go to Ceza without abandoning his women and children and his stock. The distance was too great and anyway the police post at Nkonjeni dominated the line of communication. On 28 May he decided on a compromise plan and made a dash for Hlophekhulu, a mountain rising steeply from the northern banks of the middle White Mfolozi valley on the southern rim of the Mahlabathini plain. In its precipitous, bush-covered southern face he hid himself, his people and his cattle. Again it was a defensive position although, being open to attack from the north, it was not as secure as Ceza. But by retreating to Hlophekhulu, Shingana was better able to protect his following and at same time satisfy the Usuthu that he had not, in the end, deserted them.

Once at Hlophekhulu, the same pattern of events occurred which had taken place in the vicinity of Ceza a few weeks previously. Young men with Shingana raided cattle of those Zulu who had not joined them, on the grounds that the beasts belonged to Dinuzulu. Attempts to hurry the animals to the protection of the magistracy were intercepted, and the animals driven back to Hlophekhulu.

On the same day that Shingana went to Hlophekhulu, Magistrate Knight moved to intercept Qethuka of the Magwaza who, his spies had told him, was preparing to march to Ceza and kill the magistrate on the way. Qethuka was one of the last of the old *izikhulu* left alive in the country after the decade of violence since the invasion. Knight tried to arrest him, a 'fracas' broke out, a man was killed, and Qethuka imprisoned. In the Nkandla Arthur Shepstone, recently moved to this magistracy from the one at Lower Mfolozi where his arrest of the senior chiefs had created so much resentment, reported that Siganana was preparing to give support to the Usuthu in the north. Siganana was also detained. When, months later, the Attorney-General read the evidence against these chiefs, he decided that they could not be charged.[15]

Ceza: 2 June 1888[16]

By early June the officials believed they had sufficient forces under their command to impose their authority over the Usuthu. Before dawn on the morning of 2 June, 64 Zululand Police under Mansel, and 164 British soldiers from the Dragoons and Mounted Infantry, left Mfabeni to serve warrants on Ndabuko and Dinuzulu. The troops were under orders to act only 'in support of the civil power, to be employed only on the request of the Resident Commissioner or of a magistrate, and conflict with Natives was not permissible except in self-defence, or to cover the withdrawal of the police, should the latter be placed in difficulties'.[17]

From the start it was expected that Zulu should demonstrate their loyalty and support the police and troops. Thus 400 or 500 men from Mnyamana's and Ziwedu's people were drafted as levies. Those who evaded the order risked being singled out as rebels and losing their stock. Those who joined stood a chance of acquiring some cattle as loot. The levy system, used without hesitation by the local officials and accepted gratefully by their superiors as a necessary part of decreasing both the costs and the risk to British troops, had the potential for turning, at a stroke, allies into enemies and minor differences into blood feuds.

It was still dark when the force reached the Black Mfolozi. The wagons were left here and the police and their supporters began to move towards Ceza, 15 kilometres away and 700 metres above them. By mid-morning they had covered half the distance, and from a ridge the Usuthu could be seen gathered in the open space at the foot of Ceza bush. It was decided that the troops should approach from the south-west along a spur, while Mansel and the police would take a more direct route across the valley. Mansel ordered the levies to accompany him but they refused. They were not going to fight men who until so recently had been their comrades.

The Usuthu numbered between 1000 and 1500 men. As they saw the police moving quickly towards them, orders were given for them to retire up the narrow paths through the bush, to the open country on the top of Ceza from where they were within a short distance of the border with the Transvaal Republic. On seeing that the Usuthu were 'trying to bolt', Mansel urged his men even faster across the valley. In their efforts to escape, the Usuthu jammed the narrow paths to the top of Ceza, and by the time Mansel arrived within range about three companies were still in the clearing below the bush. Most of them belonged to Dinuzulu's younger regiments.

Mansel was to allege that at this point the Usuthu began to manoeuvre in preparation for an attack, throwing out horns to the right and left. But there is little evidence to support this. 'I did not know what to do,' Mansel said later, 'our position was most precarious. Seeing that there was nothing else for it, I dismounted the men and opened fire.'[18]

What appears to have happened was that the three companies, trapped at the base of the bush by the crush in the paths to the summit and the speed with which the police moved across the valley, had searched for cover.[19] A young Usuthu then panicked, stood up and shouted at the police, 'Why is this being done, have you come to kill our people?', and was hit by the first shot. The Nongqayi were later to boast that it was fired by Mansel. The police then fired a volley and the Usuthu returned it, killing six horses. The Usuthu charged, were hit by another volley, took cover again, and began to fire at the police. By this time the troops had reached their position on the ridge. Addison formally asked them to protect the civil authority and they began to fire at the Usuthu as well.

By now most of the Usuthu had reached the summit of Ceza and were moving off when they heard these first volleys. They turned, some of them berating Ndabuko for ordering them to retreat while the young men were being killed down below. They rushed back down the paths to give their support to the companies confronting the police and now the British soldiers.

Captain Pennefather, who led the regular troops, felt the position was becoming dangerous and refused Mansel's request to bring up his men so that they could confront the Usuthu together. Mansel's whole approach had been far too provocative for a policing operation and Pennefather's orders were to protect the police, not engage in a battle with the Zulu. He informed Mansel that he was going to withdraw and that he would do so independently if the Zululand Police did not join him.

Reluctantly Mansel agreed. It appears that he was unaware of the orders under which the troops were operating, and even of the distinctions between the functions of a military and a police force. And he remained ignorant of them. Months later, when giving evidence at Ndabuko's trial, he said that he 'reluctantly, was compelled to give the order to retire ... I was disgusted because ... if [the troops had supported us] we should have beaten them, the Usutus.'[20]

Once the police and troops began to retire, the Usuthu, increasingly confident now, began to harass them. The British soldiers had to cover the police in their retreat, and for much of the way the ground was broken and difficult for horses. When it was sufficiently level and open, however, the troops mounted charges on the Usuthu. Although later accused of leading the attacks on the retreating forces, Dinuzulu claimed that he was in fact trying to turn them back.[21] But it was only when the force reached the river that the Usuthu left them alone and they were able to make their way back to Nkonjeni in the darkness. It is not known how many Usuthu had been killed, but three members of the British force were injured and two regular soldiers were dead.

For the Usuthu leaders it was an unwanted skirmish for which they knew they would be made to pay. Despite attempts to avoid a fight with the British and thereby sustain the argument that they had occupied Ceza for their own protection, Mansel's precipitate charge had incited an Usuthu attack. British blood had been shed. The Usuthu knew they would be held responsible and it would be avenged.

But for many of their followers it was a stimulating victory. They had confronted an attacking force of police and regular soldiers and sent it scurrying back to the magistracy. Many Zulu, hitherto hesitant, now joined the victorious Usuthu, often to preserve their own lives and property. In the days that followed, bands of men moved through the Black Mfolozi valley seizing cattle and looting grain. Some of them were beyond the control of the Usuthu leaders, and others entered British Zululand from beyond its borders looking for loot. Two white storekeepers, father and son, Dirk and Klaas Louw, despite being associated with the Usuthu, were killed, mutilated and their shops plundered. Mubi Nondenisa held responsible 'those burrowing (people taking by stealth the corn which had remained in the deserted kraals)'.[22] Zulu who had hoped to escape from the disputes by taking refuge in the rocky fastnesses of the Black Mfolozi were driven out and killed. Eight years of violence in the region had created many desperate men, who saw the retreat of the authorities from Ceza as an opportunity for pillage. It was just the sort of situation the Usuthu leadership had hoped to avoid, and no matter how it was treated militarily, they knew it was a serious political reverse for which they would ultimately have to take the consequences.

CHAPTER 16

THE CONQUEROR OF TWO BULLS[1]
(JUNE–AUGUST 1888)

Levies

When the news of the Usuthu repulse of the Zululand Police and the British troops at Ceza spread through Zululand, many Zulu who had previously sought security by committing themselves to the magistrates began to waver and consider whether they should go over to the young man who was proving himself to be such an effective leader of the Zulu. As Havelock reported to London, the events at Ceza appeared 'to the eyes of the natives, not only as successful resistance of the police, but as a repulse of the regular forces, and as such is calculated to give confidence to Dinuzulu and to his followers and sympathisers, and to induce uneasiness in the minds of those natives who are loyal to the Government'.[2]

Throughout June the civil and military authorities floundered as they tried to build up a force of sufficient strength to make a concerted attack on Ceza without running the risk of another retreat. The mustering of large numbers of African irregulars – levies as they were called – from Zulu allegedly loyal to the administration was essential to this. Politically this was important: after all, from the start it had been argued by the officials that the great bulk of the people of British Zululand desired the peace and the order of British rule – this was their chance to demonstrate their commitment to the idea. There were economic and tactical reasons as well. The Zululand Police were not sufficiently strong in numbers to execute this sort of task without support, but the officials did not want to risk British regulars skirmishing over the broken ground and amongst the boulders and bush of the Usuthu strongholds. Native levies were needed to precede the professionals and drive the Usuthu out of their hiding places. There was great reluctance, however, to carry out this duty despite the promise of looted cattle. A major reason for the very existence of the loyals was that they sought peace and order. Now they were supposed to flush their brothers out of their strongholds so that the armed police and troops could deal with them in comparative safety.

226

Osborn had intended to draw most of these levies from the south – the old Reserve territory.[3] But he discovered in June that he could not raise the force. Dunn felt that his people believed that the disturbances had been caused by Zibhebhu 'for whom they do not care to risk their lives',[4] and there were many others in the Reserve who were still able to resist the instructions of the administration, if only by refusing to go to its aid in other parts of the territory. The Resident Magistrate had to leave the Eshowe district and attempt to raise the levies from Africans living in Natal.[5] Eventually Havelock ordered that levies should be promised 'deferred payment in cattle or money on liberal scale'.[6]

Ndumu: 23 June 1888

But there was one loyal Zulu upon whom the authorities could depend. On 31 May, Addison had ordered Zibhebhu and his men to come to the Nongoma magistracy to protect it while he accompanied the police and the troops to serve the warrant on Dinuzulu at Ceza. The Mandlakazi chief had bivouacked near the magistracy with eight companies of his men. Although in complete command of the Black Mfolozi valley, the Usuthu left the police post at Nkonjeni, and the magistracy at Nongoma, well alone.

Havelock was worried after 2 June that Zibhebhu might become directly involved in the struggle against the Usuthu on the side of the authorities. He therefore instructed Osborn 'not to employ him actively, and merely to make use of his presence in his location as a moral support to the force actually engaged'. Osborn's reply was typical: Havelock's warning was 'apparent to me from the first' and he had instructed Zibhebhu to occupy the Ndumu hill opposite the magistracy and within his location and 'not to move from the spot'.[7] Did Osborn forget that he told Havelock on 7 June that 'Zibhebhu's men patrol daily from Ivuna towards the Black Umfolosi'?[8] Or did he just no longer care?

Msushwana, chief of the Dletsheni, had suffered directly as a result of the return of Zibhebhu. He had been excluded from much of the territory in which his people had lived, and then forced to move beyond Zibhebhu's new boundary. The antagonism between the Mandlakazi and the Dletsheni was intense. Zibhebhu had a particular hatred for Msushwana, who he believed had been directly responsible for bringing the Boers into Zululand. For the Dletsheni the return of Zibhebhu was a horrific tragedy. On 11 June two Dletsheni men, one of them a son of Msushwana, killed two of Zibhebhu's followers. Zibhebhu asked C.C. Foxon, the clerk at the magistracy, for permission to punish the offenders. It was refused. Zibhebhu nonetheless set out to find them.

Early the next morning the homestead in which Msushwana was sleeping was

Photo 24. The levies used against the Usuthu in 1888. Seated in front: the chief Hlubi wearing the braided cap on the left; Major McKean with the dog; and the man with the long moustaches is identified as Arthur J. Shepstone.

wakened by a warning shout. The villagers made a rush for the bush, only to discover that they were surrounded by Zibhebhu and a Mandlakazi force. As he passed through the main entrance, Msushwana was shot and speared. Following custom, Zibhebhu jumped over the old man's body.

Msushwana, like Qethuka, was one of the few *izikhulu* left alive in Zululand. He was closely related by marriage to the royal house. His territory had formed a link between the Usuthu of the northern districts and those of the coast, and his death was warning to them all. The news had a devastating effect on the Usuthu generally, and particularly on those still gathered around Dinuzulu and Ndabuko at Ceza. They were infuriated. The Governor had promised publicly that Zibhebhu would return 'under the law'. He had instead pillaged Usuthu homesteads, driven them from the land they considered their own. Now he had killed one of the few great men of earlier times who had escaped his earlier attack on Ulundi in 1883.

By the third week in June there were about 4000 men at Ceza. On the evening of 22 June they were addressed by Dinuzulu. Zibhebhu had killed again and it was time that he was punished; and they, the Usuthu, should do this. The defended position at the magistracy, however, should not be attacked. It was then the turn of Paul Mthimkhulu. Before 2 June he had read them the story of Hezekiah, who had remained passive in the face of the Assyrian attack and trusted in the Lord. Now he turned to the Bible again, to Deuteronomy XXX verses 1–20.

His text had meaning for the many Usuthu whose ancestors' land was now in the possession of others, whose homesteads had been broken up, whose people had been destroyed in the years of civil war, whose cattle had been seized, raided or used to buy guns, ammunition and horses. It gave hope to those who had had to listen to the Governor tell them that the House of Shaka was like water spilt on the ground. The prayer showed that other peoples had suffered, just as they were suffering. And, like them, the Usuthu should

> return to the Lord your God, you and your children, and obey his voice in all that I command you this day, with all your heart and with all your soul; then the Lord your God will restore your fortunes, and have compassion upon you, and he will gather you again from all the people where the Lord your God has scattered you. If your outcasts are in the uttermost parts of heaven, from there the Lord your God will gather you, and from there he will fetch you; and the Lord your God will bring you into the land which your fathers possessed, that you may possess it; and he will make you more prosperous and numerous than your fathers ...
>
> And the Lord your God will put all these curses upon your foes and the enemies who persecuted you ...
>
> The Lord your God will make you prosperous in all the work of your hand, in the fruit of your body, and the fruit of your cattle, and in the fruit of your ground; for the Lord will again take delight in prospering you, as he took delight in your fathers.[9]

On the night of 22 June the Usuthu left Ceza and moved up, and then out of, the Ivuna valley. By first light they were a few kilometres north of the Nongoma magistracy. Inside the fort there were about 50 Zululand Police, in the charge of Addison and Foxon. Zibhebhu and his men, about 800 in all, were on Ndumu hill, a kilometre east of the magistracy across a valley.

At six in the morning a bugle was sounded, and the Usuthu advanced towards Ndumu. A thousand men, most of them from the Qulusi and emGazini, kept moving to the right in the direction of the fort. It was their task to intercept the Mandlakazi if they rushed westwards across the valley in an attempt to gain its protection. Meanwhile the main force advanced down the ridge towards Ndumu hill and the Mandlakazi. At half a kilometre they charged. The Mandlakazi met them but, outnumbered four to one, their ranks broke. Meanwhile, when they were within 500 metres of the fort, the Usuthu right came under fire from the police guns. They wheeled left across the valley, successfully cutting off the Mandkalazi from their protectors. Zibhebhu and his men fled, with the Usuthu in pursuit. In their retreat the Mandlakazi lost about 250 men, and cattle, women and children were captured. Ziwedu's small supporting force was also attacked.

Victorious, the Usuthu moved north, keeping well to the east of the magistracy before reassembling out of range. A party of Nongqayi pursued them and retook a number of cattle but the Usuthu did not put up a serious resistance, and retired in the direction of Ceza. The Usuthu leaders had been successful: they had wreaked their revenge on the dog, leaving the owner, still holding the string, humiliated but unharmed.

Amongst Zibhebhu's casualties were nine of his brothers; Mgojana of the Ndwandwe, appointed a chief by Wolseley in 1879; and the son of Somfula and heir to the Hlabisa chieftainship. The Usuthu had avenged their losses at Msebe and Ulundi. Dinuzulu has scored a decisive victory at the head of his troops as befitted the descendant of Shaka.

The coastal districts: June 1888[10]

Meanwhile, Havelock's attempts to raise a force with which to make a move on the Usuthu at Ceza received another reverse with the arrival of the Commander-in-Chief of the British forces in South Africa, General H.A. Smyth, together with his aide-de-camp and nephew, Captain Robert Stephenson Baden-Powell. Smyth ordered that all military operations should cease until he reached Zululand.[11] A dispute broke out between the General and the Governor over the limits of civil and military authority. In the end Havelock managed to retain political control, but the running dispute between the civil and the military authority about who was to have control over the deployment of troops in Zululand bedevilled the operations for the next month and a half.

Arthur Shepstone had been transferred from the Lower Mfolozi district, possibly as a consequence of his aggressive actions towards its chiefs. But up to the beginning of June the people of the coastal district had decided that the safest strategy was to make a show of allegiance to A.L. Pretorious, the new Resident Magistrate. They had already learnt the consequences of not mollifying the authorities. But the defeat of the Mandlakazi at Ndumu was followed by messengers coming from the Usuthu, allegedly from Dinuzulu himself, urging the coastal Usuthu to follow his example and attack Sokwetshata of the Mthethwa, who filled the same role on the coast as Zibhebhu did in the north. The Usuthu chiefs gathered in the bush to discuss these developments. It was decided that an attack should be made on Sokwetshata but, as in the case of Ndumu, the Resident Magistrate should not be harmed. Orders were given to their people to move to the vicinity of the Lower Mfolozi magistracy where they would rendezvous.

Meanwhile the magistrate Pretorius had ordered Sokwetshata to leave his homesteads and come with his people and cattle to the magistracy. Sokwetshata refused at first: he was well aware that such a move would be interpreted as a provocative action, which would increase the general tension in the area and the possibility of violence. But in the end Sokwetshata did move towards the 'fort' – earthworks thrown up to give some protection for the rifles of the Zululand Police. And predictably his brother, the Usuthu Mthatheni, 'cut off' some of the Mthethwa cattle as they were being driven towards the fort. Equally predictable was the tragedy implicit in this policy of encouraging and then exploiting division amongst the people of Zululand. Thus, when Mthatheni captured some of Sokwetshata's Mthethwa followers, he sent them back to the magistracy with an escort saying, 'We have all come from the same birth, we are the same people; I cannot have them killed ...'[12]

But it took a brave man to make such a decision, for there was fear, anger and violence in the air. On 29 June, the day Sokwetshata arrived at the magistracy, two traders, White and Knight, reached it exhausted. They had been at Somkhele's the day before and decided to leave when they saw the Mpukunyoni arming. Knight was already unpopular as he had helped Arthur Shepstone arrest Somopho and Bhejana. Once they began to move south, the Mpukunyoni started to pursue them. They had with them African women and another trader, ill with fever, whom they abandoned to be killed before fighting a running battle with parties of Mpukunyoni, which stopped only when they reached the protection of the fort.[13]

On their way south, the Mpukunyoni were joined by the Sokhulu people under Dlemudlemu and more of the pro-Usuthu Mthethwa of Mthatheni. The chiefs, older and slower, kept themselves apart from their men, and the force skirted past the Lower Mfolozi magistracy and assembled at Bhejana's homestead to the south on 29 June. Here it made contact with some of the Emangweni people who had come up from the south. They were the followers of Somopho, who was too old to accompany his men, and Somlomo, chief of the Mbonambi people, who joined them once he had secured the safety of the family of the local Norwegian missionary.

The next day, 30 June, the Usuthu force moved to the hills near the magistracy, where they saw that Sokwetshata and his people were within the perimeter of the fort with Pretorius and his police. The two most senior men present

Photo 25. British officers who led the suppression of the Usuthu in 1888.

were Somlomo and Bhejana. They were under orders to avoid any conflict with the officials and so, as long as Sokwetshata remained in the fort, it seemed to them that no attack could be made.

But there were other opinions amongst the Usuthu. The Mpukunyoni, for example, had been on the march for three days and were hungry and impatient. And the Mthethwa cattle, grazing a kilometre from the magistracy, were such a temptation. With Bhejana and Somlomo and the older men standing on a near-by hill, ten companies from the Mpukunyoni and ten from the Emangweni moved in on the cattle, to the left and right respectively, and, assisted by the Nongqayi fire from the fort which panicked the herds, swept them off. Magistrate Pretorius did not believe that there had been an attempt to attack the magistracy. Osborn, however, had to have a rebellion – and it was an 'attack' 'upon the station itself'.[14]

The Usuthu force then withdrew to Bhejana's homestead, where a meeting was held. Mafukwini, the messenger said to be from Dinuzulu, addressed the men and suggested that they follow up their victory by guarding the drifts between the Lower Mfolozi magistracy and the Mhlatuze River in order to prevent Pretorius from making contact with Eshowe. But the Mpukunyoni refused on the ground that this exceeded their orders, and left for their homes in the north – with a share of the captured cattle. Others followed their example but some groups did go to the drifts and the situation remained disturbed. When Sokwetshata and the Zululand Police tried to regain the cattle they were driven back to the fort. A small group of men, the followers of Lokotwayo, tracked down a white trader who was making his way to safety in the Eshowe district, killed him and plundered his wagon.

Such incidents of violence were largely the responsibility of local groups acting on their own initiative. In time, attempts were made to show that they were carried out on the instructions of Dinuzulu as part of a rebellion, one of whose objectives was the murder of all whites. In fact, the violence of 30 June and the days that followed had its origins in the intense hatred and fear the local Usuthu had for Zibhebhu's ally Sokwetshata and their belief that it was in their own interests to show support for Dinuzulu, especially after he had been victorious against Zibhebhu. There was no intention to attack the authorities, and those in charge had tried to avoid an attack on Sokwetshata. But the officials had to have their scapegoats, and in time six of the Usuthu chiefs were to stand trial for public violence associated with the events of 30 June.

Hlophekhulu: 2 July 1888

By the end of June the fortunes of the Zululand authorities were at their lowest ebb. Twice they had had to retreat from the Usuthu when they attempted to arrest their leaders. Zibhebhu, the man who they thought would cow the Usuthu and throw the balance of power on the side of the authorities, had only provoked them further, and he had now been decisively defeated. Large numbers of Zulu living in what had been the Reserve since 1884 and who had been depicted as people who welcomed the security of British rule, resisted being drawn into the disputes, which they saw as the responsibility of the authorities. There was conflict between the civil authorities and the military command, with the latter demanding unrestricted control over the means to be used to put down the rebels.

However, on 29 June the long-awaited levies from the southern districts arrived at Nkonjeni. They were drawn from some of the best-known loyals from around Eshowe. It was decided that before any attack could be made on Ceza it would be necessary to secure the rear, and this meant dispersing Shingana and his followers from Hlophekhulu.

Hlophekhulu mountain lies on the banks of the middle reaches of the White Mfolozi. It has a narrow summit running roughly east and west, the highest points being at the east and west extremities, which are connected by a lower ridge. Approached from the north, that is from the Mahlabathini plain, it appears as a long low hill rising above the plateau. Its southern side, however, drops precipitately 600 metres to the thornbush-covered White Mfolozi valley below. It was in the dense vegetation which grows amongst the cliffs and boulders on the southern side that Shingana and his followers had hidden with their women, children and cattle. In the bush they had built low retaining walls to stop the cattle from straying and to give themselves some protection. Whereas Ceza's northern approaches were protected by a political boundary, Hlophekhulu was vulnerable to an attack from this direction. It was essentially a place of refuge, not a stronghold.

On 2 July, 200 regular soldiers, 180 Basotho followers of Hlubi, 100 Zululand Police, and 2000 levies drawn from Mnyamana's Buthelezi, together with those from the Eshowe district, left Nkonjeni for Hlophekhulu.[15] Although it was not admitted publicly, Zibhebhu was with the force. Colonel Stabb was in charge of the military, and Addison represented the civil authority. At midday they approached Hlophekhulu from the north and saw groups of Usuthu on the long ridge ahead of them – that is, on the northern aspect of Hlophekhulu. Orders were given for the levies to surround the mountain by working their way to its base on the southern side. The Eshowe force went round to the east, and Mnyamana's men to the west. The Zululand Police under Mansel and John Osborn, the Basotho force and some British troops then moved to the centre of the ridge itself.

The Usuthu scattered. Some went over the top, scrambling down the steep sides of the southern face into the bush below. Others moved east and west along the ridge. Once on the summit, the troops peered over the edge. A British officer was hit in the head and killed by a huge charge from a muzzle-loader. Perched in the centre of the Hlophekhulu ridge, the force fired wildly into the bush below, where many of the women and children were still hiding. The eastern summit was taken without resistance, but when the police tried to move to the west a small Usuthu force made a stand amongst the rocks. Reinforced by regular troops, the Nongqayi drove the Usuthu off the summit with a bayonet charge and then pursued them over the edge into the bush. Mansel lost control of his police as they rushed after the herds of cattle they could see in the valley below.

Meanwhile the Eshowe levy and Mnyamana's troops had moved round the mountain and were in amongst the Usuthu and their cattle at its southern base. Here they were joined by the Nongqayi, and there was a scramble to get hold of the Usuthu cattle. Most of the Usuthu, however, seem to have remained in the bush, desperately trying to protect the women and children, and stop their herds from stampeding into the open ground where they would be looted by the levies

Photo 26. The Nongqayi, the Zululand Reserve Territorial Carbineers, later to become the Zululand Police, with Addison on the left and Commandant Mansel in the centre.

and the police. The white officers and the troops remained on the summit, rolling boulders into the Usuthu beneath them or, like John Osborn, 'taking pot shots at Usutus scuttling through the bush'.

It was estimated that 200 to 300 Usuthu were killed. Perhaps 60 of the levies died keeping the regular troops out of danger when they took the first impact of Usuthu attempts to defend themselves. At sundown the attacking force was recalled. Taking thousands of head of cattle with them, the levies began to drift off to their homes. Shingana sat tight in the bush and that night he and his people, together with about 1000 head of cattle, moved off to the east, crossed into the Transvaal Republic, and then made for Ceza to join the rest of the Usuthu.

Although Hlophekhulu was now cleared of Usuthu, the advance to Ceza was held up by the presence of Usuthu blocking the line of communication between the Lower Mfolozi magisterial district and Eshowe, which meant that the magistrate Pretorius was effectively under siege. A flying column under Major McKean was appointed to open communications. John Dunn now agreed to join the column and brought 2000 of his men with him. The column left on 7 July, 'relieved' the magistracy on the 9th, and returned to Eshowe on 11 July, burning deserted homesteads on the way and seizing cattle. The Usuthu chiefs left their homesteads once again and hid themselves in the bush and the forest. Somkhele, Bhejana and Somlomo chose the impenetrable Dukuduku. But apart from a small skirmish involving a group of Dunn's followers, the Usuthu did not resist. General Smyth attributed this to the 'fitness of [McKean's] dispositions and the celerity of his movements', which meant that 'the enemy was never quite bold enough to stand and fight'.[16] To the last, the General was unaware that the vast majority of Zulu were not prepared to treat British troops as enemies.

'A good effect on the native mind'

With the Lower Mfolozi district secure, the way was open to move against the Usuthu at Ceza. Troops were moved up to Nkonjeni and a two-pronged attack was planned. One column was to move along the coast road past the Lower Mfolozi magistracy and force the Usuthu leaders there to submit. It would then swing north-west towards the Ndwandwe district. There it would make its rendezvous with the column from Nkonjeni at a point near the Black Mfolozi and Ivuna rivers, and, having secured the territory in the rear, it would move on Ceza.[17]

Havelock had been successful in his struggle with General Smyth and still kept political control. While he had no objections to the two-prong advance on Ceza, the Governor insisted that before any move was made against the stronghold itself, the Zulu there had to be given the chance to disperse. The only exceptions to this were Dinuzulu, Ndabuko and Shingana, together with any other Zulu accused of specific crimes.

Towards the end of July, Smyth got his two columns under way. By the end of the month the coastal force had reached the Lower Mfolozi without opposition.[18] Its commander, Major McKean, examined the Dukuduku forest, where Somkhele was hiding, and reported that it could only be taken with the assistance of gunboats. John Dunn sent instead a messenger into the forest, who returned with Somkhele, Dlemudlemu, Mthatheni, Somlomo, Lugoloza and Ndabayake, who all expressed a desire to surrender. Pretorius imposed a fine of 2000 head of cattle on Somkhele and 100 head on the other chiefs, and then sent them to await trial in Eshowe. Somkhele also turned over to the authorities five of his people, including his chief son, who were alleged to have been responsible for the murder of the trader Ashby. Somopho and Bhejana had already experienced the Eshowe gaol and did not surrender, remaining in hiding.

The column then continued towards Nongoma burning deserted homesteads and shooting the occasional 'Usuthu' on the way. The levies, who included some of Hlubi's Basotho, Zibhebhu's Mandlakazi and Dunn's following, looted cattle and captured women and children belonging to Zulu now characterised in reports as 'the enemy'.

In the west the levies supporting the other column behaved in much the same way, terrorising the inhabitants. In the Entonjaneni district a large tract of territory was swept by such a force, the homesteads burnt and the cattle taken. It was under the direct command of men employed by the Zululand government as levy leaders, supervised by the magistrate Knight. On 28 July a report in the Natal press read: 'Just returned to Knight's with about 300 head of cattle, some kafir sheep and goats, and a good supply of grain, the result of three days' looting. A great many huts were burnt, and the disloyals will find the aspect a very bleak one.' Havelock demanded an explanation and discovered that the article was written by a levy leader. Further explanations only gave Havelock more reason to be furious at this flouting of his instructions. 'The proceedings of McAlister's levy as recounted by Mr. Knight are certainly most extraordinary. It is difficult to understand the effect which is attributed to those proceedings in the following words: – "it has undoubtedly had a good effect on the native mind in this District generally, and has fully established my authority over them."'[19]

By the first week of August, the coast column had reached Nongoma and the western column was setting up a base on the Black Mfolozi, with the territory to their rear clear of all 'rebels'. From the high point of Ceza, Dinuzulu, Ndabuko and Shingana had watched the progress of the British troops moving towards them, and its trail of burning homesteads, looted cattle, and captured women and children. It was no longer so easy to reach comparative safety by moving northwards across the border of the Transvaal Republic because Pretoria, under diplomatic pressure from the British High Commissioner, was trying to bring its local officials under greater control. Slowly the Usuthu force on Ceza began to break up as men drifted back towards their homesteads in Zululand and the Transvaal Republic.

It was time to abandon Ceza. Ndabuko left first, then Dinuzulu. They travelled at night, moving northwards towards Mabhoko's across the border. On the evening of 7 August there were about 1000 Usuthu still on Ceza. A 'war song' was sung and they put their huts to the torch. Keeping military formation, they moved away from Ceza, to the east.[20] They marched across the Sikhwebezi river, moved north, and spent the night at the Qanda mountain. The next morning they began their march again till they crossed the Mkhuze River into the Transvaal Republic. Here the force broke up. Ndabuko and Dinuzulu, together with the latter's bodyguard and his most senior councillors, kept moving in a northerly direction.

The last gathering of the Zulu organised on a military basis under the direct control of the Zulu royal house had dispersed. It had done so voluntarily. It was not going to allow itself to be attacked by the advancing forces, and thereby give the authorities in British Zululand the chance to say they had put down a rebellion – the rebellion they needed, to justify depriving the Zulu leaders of their autonomy and Zulu people of their independence.

'Got them'

British Zululand was devastated. The army of regulars, loyals, levies and general hangers-on – Dunn's, Zibhebhu's and Hlubi's men – had moved through the country north of the old Reserve seizing cattle, burning homesteads and scattering its occupants. Time and again those Zulu attempting to gain the protection of the forests and hills around them were indiscriminately attacked as Usuthu rebels. Havelock still kept overall control of the political objectives, and the order was that only the leaders should be arrested. But there was nothing he could do to stop individual acts of pillaging and looting in the more remote parts of the country.

One such incident is worth mentioning. On 11 August a small troop of British mounted regulars and levies, moving towards Ceza and in the vicinity of Fig Tree Store on the Transvaal border, were told that there were Usuthu nearby. The next morning they prepared to confront the enemy and, when local people began running from their homes to hide with their cattle in the hills and caves nearby, they were called upon to surrender. They refused, shots were exchanged, and the levies were sent in to attack.

Over 100 cattle were captured and at least three people were killed, one of them a woman described as half-witted. It was then discovered that the enemy were in fact allies, Mnyamana's people, and that they had taken cover across the border in the Transvaal. Then came the cover-up: reports spoke of inaccurate maps, stressed that it was the levies not the troops who had crossed the border, and characterised the incident as regrettable but understandable. It should also be called memorable. The officer in charge, Captain Robert Stephenson Baden-Powell, was to become one of imperialism's greatest heroes, the founder of the Boy Scout movement. But one must not suppose that the author of *Scouting for Boys* had just misread or been misled by his map as the official account had it. Years later he recounted that 'the Usutus had tried to save themselves by crossing into the New Republic. However we disregarded the border and followed them up, attacked, and got them.'[21]

CHAPTER 17

TWO ROADS TO DEATH

The lesson of the law

Zululand was now pacified: driven to exhaustion by the new magistrates and their police supported by British troops and thousands of African levies demonstrating their loyalty to the new colonial state by looting food and livestock, settling old scores, killing the men they could find, and capturing women and children. For the authorities the struggle for the dominance of Zululand and its rulers was over: they now turned to its people.

The Governor and his Chief Magistrate discussed the merits and cost of keeping a military garrison or increasing the size of the Zululand Police, and the six Resident Magistrates began to put a working administrative system into place. Loyal chiefs had to be identified and their areas of jurisdiction demarcated in preparation for the activity upon which the viability of British Zululand was predicated – the collection of the hut tax. The colony had been established on the assumption that it would be self-supporting. There were advances from the Treasury in London which had to be repaid. Urgent messages were sent to the chiefs and their homestead heads informing them that arrangements were being made for the collection of hut tax. Men without cattle for sale should make sure their sons went out to labour for wages. The migrant labour revolution was about to begin and the Zulu to enter the stream of modern South African history.

But there was an ideological, even a psychological, victory which the authorities had still to attain. It had to be demonstrated publicly, to the Zulu people and those who identified with them, that the pretensions of the Zulu royal house and their Usuthu followers were at an end. It had to be shown that the fundamentals upon which the policy towards Zululand had been based since the invasion of 1879 had been valid: that there was no such thing as a Zulu National Party, only a tiny faction of self-interested royalists; and that no Zulu in British Zululand could behave, as the royalists had done since annexation, in a way that implied that history invested in them an independent authority. This demonstration should be carried out in the courts of Zululand. It was here that an example could be made of the royalist rebels: here their guilt could be established and their misdeeds punished as a clear warning to anyone who still hoped that the Zulu royal house might yet play a part in British Zululand's political future.

It was this desire to make an example of the Usuthu leaders, to uphold the law and punish them through the courts, that gave Harriette Colenso her chance. For she could also use the law, in her case to mount a challenge against the Zululand administration, its policies, its officials and activities since annexation, and to assert the justice of the cause of the Zulu royal house and the legitimacy of its claim for a place in the government of Zululand.

Messages

Harriette Colenso had been watching events closely, but with rebellion and military operations to control, the Governor had little time to consider her protests. They were significant, nonetheless. Mubi Nondenisa and Thwayisa Mabaso, carrying their message inviting Dinuzulu to come to Pietermaritzburg for consultations with the Governor,[1] had crossed into Zululand on 6 June. It was while they were at the Nkandla magistracy that they heard the news that their destination, Ceza, had been the site of a skirmish on the 2nd between the authorities and the Usuthu, and that the northern districts were in turmoil. They pushed on to find the man they knew so well from his visits to Natal, the messenger Mfunzi, and to ask his advice. His homestead was deserted, the chickens roosting on the roofs of the huts and the dogs howling. Mfunzi had left, crossing for safety into the Transvaal, where Nondenisa and Mabaso found him.

They discussed Zulu affairs. Mnyamana should never be written off as a traitor, Mfunzi said. No one should jump to conclusions about him: 'When all is known it will be found that he was right.'[2] Regardless of what had happened he felt it important that Harriette Colenso's emissaries should deliver their message. They moved off towards Ceza. It was a tense and dangerous journey but when they were threatened they identified themselves as Sobantu's people and were given safe passage.

Even in this country of desolation and fear, Nondenisa and Mabaso followed protocol. At a homestead occupied by Cetshwayo's widows they were given a man to introduce them formally to Ndabuko. The interview took place on Ceza in a rough grass shelter with the rain driving under the matting roof. At night it froze. Both Ndabuko and Dinuzulu expressed their pleasure at being able to put their point of view. But they both felt their situation was hopeless. In their experience, the more effectively they put the justice of their case to the British

Governor, the more vigorously they were attacked by the local officials. Nonetheless, they called a meeting of the Usuthu leaders and made a lengthy statement on recent events, which the Bishopstowe men took down. They also instructed two men, Sifo and Soni, to proceed with them to Pietermaritzburg to repeat the statement to the Governor.[3]

But while the men were on their way back to Pietermaritzburg, events in Zululand changed the situation irrevocably when the Usuthu defeated Zibhebhu at Ndumu on 23 June. As a result, when the messengers arrived in Pietermaritzburg they found a hostile Governor totally unsympathetic to messages from men who pledged loyalty to the Queen and asked for reconciliation while they were preparing to attack the constituted authorities in Zululand. He did not therefore 'attach much importance' to the Usuthu message,[4] and when he did send it to London he did so together with official denials of its contents, and the opinion that it was 'in most points inaccurate and misleading, and in others untrue'.[5]

For Harriette Colenso, however, the message confirmed what she had suspected: 'the Usuthu feel themselves driven to bay, the Government has brought Zibhebhu back in order to destroy them'.[6] And as important as the message was, there was much more to it than its contents. It also showed that Bishopstowe's influence still existed in Zululand: that her father's mission had not died with him. It was for this – justice to the Zulu – that he had laboured in Natal and devoted his final years. She had no choice but to continue what he had begun.

'Turning the tables'

First she had to find an effective strategy: was there a legal solution to the Usuthu's predicament? If they surrendered, would they stand a chance in the Zululand courts? And if so, could they be persuaded to appear before a Zululand court? Or had their confidence in British justice been so shattered that they would resist to the end?

She turned to Harry Escombe, Natal's most prominent lawyer, member of the Legislative Council, and leader of the movement in Natal for responsible government. The Colensos had long recognised his abilities and standing, and had employed him professionally. But they had been unable to recruit him to their cause. Harriette believed him to be too much of a political opportunist. But now she needed his help desperately. She accepted that Escombe's primary motive would be neither a sense of justice nor a commitment to the Zulu royal house. Yet if the débâcle in Zululand could be used to demonstrate the incapacity of the imperial government to direct colonial affairs effectively, this might provide him with a political opportunity to advance the cause of responsible government for Natal.

She wrote Escombe a private and confidential letter. In the message just delivered from the Ceza stronghold was confirmation of what she had always suspected. In the face of the charges made against them, the Usuthu 'practically turn the tables, and charge the local authorities with various atrocious acts, culminating in the attack on Ceza, (alias an attempt to serve a warrant on Dinuzulu)'. The initial fines had been imposed on the Usuthu leaders without due investigation. The accused themselves had no idea of the substance of the charges against them. The laws and regulations of British Zululand had been ignored. The application of the law in Zululand was in fact the application of selective violence. Dinuzulu, who said he would 'rather die than be treated like his father', asked for an inquiry. Please advise me, she asked with some irony,

> Is there not any course of legal procedure open to the Zulus to counterbalance the disadvantages of being British subjects. The Governor retains the *powers of Supreme Chief* which as we know are *most elastic*, and cover practically anything (as interpreted by Natal officials.)
>
> Can they not appeal against Mr. Osborn or – seeing that under sec. 28[7] they might be hung drawn and quartered for such offence, can I do anything for them? bring some counter charge ...
>
> And I ask your advice on the too probable supposition that it may only result in a direction to 'surrender to Mr. Osborn who will be directed to investigate' etc. They can't and won't surrender to Osborn, and they would not attend to me if I were to advise them to.[8]

In the closing days of July, Harriette Colenso and Harry Escombe met to discuss the Usuthu case. For Harriette it was a desperately important moment. She brought with her a message she had drafted to the Zulu chiefs and they went over it together. Moved by the intensity of her commitment, and seeing the possibility of turning it to his political advantage, Escombe agreed to defend the Usuthu if they voluntarily surrendered. It was a rather impulsive promise, and one which in time was to make great demands on the ambitious and busy lawyer.

A struggle in the courts would be expensive. Harriette Colenso had few resources beyond the support of her family, friends, and her African assistants at Bishopstowe, the wary goodwill of a handful of Durban lawyers, and the now beleaguered and scattered Usuthu leaders from the Zulu royal house. It was her task, in the winter of 1888, to organise and consolidate these resources, and find the means to drive the case forward. As an executor of her father's estate she had access to the comparatively small legacy upon which she, Agnes and her mother lived. Colenso's sons, however, were also drawing on it. Robert's Durban practice had not been financially successful, and he had moved to Johannesburg, taking with him some of the Colenso capital, which he invested and lost. Frank, in spite of just being appointed to the post of secretary and actuary of the English and Scottish Law Life Assurance Association, had just moved to London and found himself financially straitened as a result. But although shortage of funds was a matter of some anxiety, and was to become more so, Harriette was not prepared to let this stand in the way of providing the Usuthu with a proper legal defence. As she said to her worried brother: 'I am not "demented" in money matters. How could I – given Sobantu's influence – stop short of using it.'[9]

'Two roads to death'

There could, of course, be no defence of the Usuthu leaders without their participation. But they were on the run, out of touch, ignorant of their legal strengths and weaknesses, and convinced that the Zululand authorities were determined to destroy them. The message which Harriette Colenso drafted had to put the options before them fairly, and allow them to make up their minds. It was a remarkable document. The written version, even in English, has the directness of the oral statement, and Harriette's parenthetical amplifications of the Zulu, the dialogue she constructs with the recipients, enable the reader to get closer to the oral discourse than is usually possible with a written text. There are many points to make about this message. One is the very real awareness of the urgency of the situation and the tragedy that might well overtake them all unless they tried to wrest the initiative from the hands of their enemies. Another is Harriette's refusal to assume that she knows what is best for the Zulu. She gives her own opinion, but at the same time indicates that she will support the Usuthu in their decision, whatever it might be. She recognises fully their autonomy: their right to choose their own destiny, even if that choice is death. She, nonetheless, wants them to live – so that they might fight on. It is a document which speaks, almost literally, for itself: it has to be read in full.

> To the HEADS of the ZULU PEOPLE, to DINUZULU and to NDABUKO, and to SHINGANA (TSHINGANA), Princes of the Zulus, and cared for of SOBANTU (the late Bishop Colenso).
> I send to you to-day, friends, because I see death (destruction) on all sides of us, for I have been trying to examine all the (courses) roads open to you. And, although I am sending, it is not for me to advise you to-day, because it is

not I who have to choose to-day among different (kinds of) deaths. Forasmuch as my suffering is of the heart alone, and it is you who are marked out to suffer both in your hearts and in your bodies.

It is therefore for you to choose.

For your choice, then, there are two roads that I can see, and perhaps you will choose the death in which you may yet die (free) holding your weapons; saying, forasmuch as you are merely throwing back the spears flung at you (returning the blows struck at you) when you had done no wrong, but were being pursued by that old enmity (of white influence from Natal making use of Zibhebhu) which has for so long been hunting down the house of Ngqumbazi (mother of Cetshwayo and Ndabuko, and grandmother of Dinuzulu), and forasmuch as you believe you can see for yourselves that this is now your day to die (that your death is intended and inevitable), and because, for the Zulu people generally, if you must die, it would be less hard that you should just die among the weapons (fighting), and that they too should die with you, in a heap, as a funeral pile.

If you should decide thus, I can say nothing; I can only mourn, and these messengers I have then sent as mourners.

Here, however, is the second road – to death (destruction) – concerning which I bid you choose.

It is that you should go of your own accord, giving yourselves up to the English authorities. This too is death (destruction), because, although we know for ourselves – you and I and those with me – that you would give yourselves up believing that you had done no wrong to begin with; yet now there is a wrong, that of returning the blows of the authorities, a matter concerning which you are charged with a crime, that of rebellion against the Queen's rule, so that it comes to be similar to the charge against Langalibalele.

Ah! no! It is here that you will interrupt my words, saying, 'Rather than that (rather than be treated like Langalibalele) we choose to die in a heap together!' I can understand that feeling, for I too do not forget (lose sight of) all the long persecution and the treacheries with which you are hemmed in to this day, nor the hardships of bonds for you, and, for the people, their bereavement of the stem of their Chiefs who are their (*amadlozi*) guardian spirits; since we may even be reached by that disaster, I will not hide the truth from you.

Let us bear in mind, however, that that funeral pile of yours, in which you might die, whether of Zulus or of English, would just be the thing which would fill the air, and cover over and conceal all those (slanders) treacheries against you, and also (smother) any word with which we might have

attempted to justify you. So that you would have died, your complaints having
been stifled, being accounted evil-doers.

Whereas even yet, even among all dangers, certain points shine out to me,
to wit:–

1. That his Excellency the Governor has told me that he personally does
not wish to cut you off, stifled. He says that, were you to surrender, he should
wish that your case should be examined.

2. That his Excellency went so far as receive the words brought by Sifo
and Soni, and, in replying, said pointedly, according to Mr. Shepstone's translation, that he understands that you impeach Mr. Osborn and other officials.
That is an important word, for even by English law there is no one who can
try himself his own case in which he is accused.

3. That just as your dying in a heap will cover up and make things smooth
for those who have slandered you, the other road, that of putting yourselves in
bondage that the case may be tried, will enable us to expose the treachery by
which you are hemmed in. So that it shall be, that though you may be condemned, since your returning of the blows cannot be denied, but can only be
mitigated by that ground on which you appeal, to wit, that the white authorities themselves were at variance, you will yet bring to punishment at the
same time those who are destroying and slandering you and the Zulu people,
and who destroyed Cetshwayo.

Might it not be said in this case too that you had satisfaction in your
(death) ruin; that you did not suffer in vain?

And even as I write there have appeared words from the headmen (M.P.s)
inquiring on our behalf over in England, and one of them has actually spoken
out, laying the blame on your (local) white authorities ('colonial officials').

4. Further, a trial does not means [sic] destruction inevitably, and, as to
Langalibalele's case, Sobantu did not know about it at first, he went into it at
the end only, and your counsellors can begin with the beginning of the case.
Again, we have seen that if but the spark (of life) remains, it may be protected,
and, under Providence, may live even after crossing the seas, but from the
grave there is no bringing back.

5. Again, the case of a man who is seized, fighting, is very different from
that of one who gives himself up, believing in his own innocence, and bearing
witness to it.

These words of mine to-day, I write with difficulty. They are all bitter to
me, by reason of the trouble that you are in; and I am also ashamed of being
English, that you should be thus treated by the English. I speak them,
however, according to Sobantu's heart, which would throw light even on ways

leading to the grave.

And since the words are so heavy, and also so long, I ask you to tell Mubi to repeat them, reading them to you twice or perhaps three times, and to examine them and consider them well before you choose your road. And if, perchance, you should have the great, the excellent courage, to choose the road of bondage, you can take these men, who are my eyes, along with you, and let them see you to Nkonjeni, to the military officer in command there.

I can say no more to-day, but be well assured that whatever happens, I, and all Sobantu's family, still grieve for you, and protest for you also,

> It is I who write,
> Dlwedlwe, Daughter of Sobantu.
> H.E. Colenso[10]

She then tried to make the prospect of surrender by the Usuthu less terrifying. They were informed that Escombe had promised to defend them if they gave themselves up. She tried to convince the messengers that there was no need to fear the letters they carried with them, for it was the Governor's normal practice to write in red ink.[11] She knew that the officer commanding the troops in Zululand, Colonel Stabb, had gained the respect of the Zulu, and hoped that he would receive their leaders personally if they surrendered. She got in touch with Stabb, telling him 'privately, as a friend' that the chiefs 'are dreadfully afraid of being poisoned by their enemies (especially by Zibhebhu) as they firmly believe that Cetshwayo was'. She created a picture of a fearful world in which

> not the ground they tread on, the air they breathe, whatever they are likely to handle, let alone food, are all likely to be rubbed or sprinkled or otherwise imbued with some poisonous property. They would not have this fear, or not to anything like the same extent, among 'the red soldiers of the Queen' alone. And it would immensely add to the confidence felt by people as well as chiefs, if their own people could be allowed, *directed* to bring them food ... At home only certain duly appointed persons are allowed to touch their food.[12]

The Usuthu did not surrender immediately. The area into which they had retreated was a remote and distant borderland of the Transvaal over which the central authorities had little control. While Havelock was assured Dinuzulu was about to be confined, it appears that the initiative lay with local officials and private individuals who had been close to the Usuthu. They kept the situation and the territory about the Mkhuze and the Phongolo, between Zululand and Swaziland, in confusion; and this gave rise to a string of rumours, and contradictory newspaper reports, of Dinuzulu's intentions and his whereabouts.

Harriette Colenso's message, that she would do all she could to support and defend the Usuthu leaders if they surrendered, presented them with a strategy. But first their cattle and their people had to be settled and secured in so far as that was possible. However, on 16 August Ndabuko surrendered to the military authorities in northern Zululand and was taken under escort to the military post at Nkonjeni. Already some of Harriette's warnings were having their effect. The appointment of Stabb excluded Addison from the legal process. With great circumspection Harriette made contact with Stabb, thanked him for the consideration with which he had treated the Zulu prince, and for reassuring her – 'this "suspicious and distrustful Usuthu."' And she wondered if, without 'instigating you to a conspiracy', she could pass a message of reassurance on to Ndabuko himself.

'A poor woman and a rich man'

At this critical point, however, Escombe began to backtrack. He had other commitments. Surely she did not expect him to take up on his own the enormous amount of work that any defence of the Zulu chiefs would involve? Comments like these were unfair and testing for Harriette. It would have been understandable if she had reminded him sharply of his promises, just two months old, and of her own considerable sacrifices. But this was not her way – indeed it couldn't be. She was too vulnerable, too dependent; as always, she had to keep these men with her. And, without sufficient material resources to do so, or even the conventional feminine ones, she had to use tact and moral persuasion, ignoring the lawyers' inconsistencies and prevarications in order to play on their better feelings – to persuade without pleading, to insist without demanding.

Thus at the end of September 1888 Harriette wrote to Escombe that 'I quite recognize'

> that I have responsibilities in this matter which cannot be shifted on to your, or on to anyone else's shoulders, if I wished to do so (and how devoutly should I wish it if it were possible!) I know that I must 'follow my conscience' and play 'off my own bat' in the main. But I may not always perceive at the moment where our promises separate, and if, in consequence, I refer to you when you think I should not, you have only to tell me so, please.

The collecting of witnesses would of course be a tremendously difficult logistical task. But this was just a beginning: 'And when we have got them – what will you expect of me? To take down their statements? You will not forget – by any chance – that I am not a proper solicitor. You won't expect a brief from us in proper style?'

Meanwhile 'Ndabuko himself, and the Zulus generally must be most painfully watching since his surrender, for some sign of our promised intervention'.[13] And she reminded Escombe of the circumstances under which it was made:

> You will remember that you said after reading my revised message to the
> Zulus, that you believed I should never regret sending it. I do not, for I
> believe that we both followed our consciences then; and I still think that we
> did what was best; but I could not have presumed to take the position which I
> did take, bringing my Sacred Ark into the field (the Bishop's influence) with-
> out the full confidence which I possess that you will stand by us, and I doubt
> whether had I known then how important it was to you to go to England with-
> in the next month or two I should have had the courage to accept a position
> involving the possibility of so much distress to you, and from which I could
> not release you even did I think it right, being equally bound with you.

Then came the gently flattering appeal to his conscience: 'I may, it is true, be permitted to share the belief that this would not be the first occasion on which you have placed a public good before a private happiness, but I know also that the want of the latter may be none the less keenly felt therefore.' Then she reminded him that she was not so caught up with moral duty as to be incapable of seeing possible political advantages for Escombe if he undertook to defend the Usuthu:

> I cannot help hoping, however, that though your promise is to the Zulus, –
> and we are grateful to the full – yet the result of your present action may also
> be to help forward another public matter which you have at heart, I mean
> Responsible Government for Natal. And in saying so, I mean also that I can
> go with you in that matter as far as I am able to grasp it ...
>
> Am I perhaps wasting time in writing all this? At any rate I wish you to
> understand that my sympathies are not all absorbed by the Zulus.[14]

It worked. Escombe turned his attention to the documents and two days later told her that 'I have been at work on the Zulu Land papers for many hours yesterday and to-day and think that I see a course of action which you will approve. I will explain it to you on Tuesday if you will call at my rooms.'[15]

But again the question of money came up. The lawyer W.Y. Campbell had told

Escombe of Mr Grant's experience of Usuthu unreliability in money matters. Harriette objected. In her own experience, and she gave details, the Usuthu had always paid their debts but they had so little experience of money that they had difficulty in comprehending its magnitude. For example, they had just sent Harriette six pounds and five shillings towards legal costs. But of course the defence had to confront the question of the expense, and 'comparatively speaking', she wrote to Escombe,

I am a poor woman, and you a rich man. And the fact that when you do take an interest you need not be balked by an immediate want of funds, is certainly one of your virtues in this case. You are also a political magnate and the benefit of your countenance to the Zulus, which I solicited, is far and away out of the region of payments – save by gratitude. But I did solicit it, and your professional assistance into the bargain, and you don't suppose that when I was asking and you were giving of so much greater value that I intended that you should reverse the usual position with regard to fees ...

... it is Sobantu's influence which began this struggle, it is Sobantu's estate which is finally responsible tho' Agnes and I might have to be your debtors in this matter also, while my Mother lives. For several reasons I gratefully accept your arrangement that you for the present should be responsible for Mr. Campbell's fee but I could find £200 at once, besides the £6/5/0 and £1,000 at short notice without reference to the Bishop's Estate.[16]

It was a start.

V

A SORT OF PARADISE

CHAPTER 18

THREE JOURNEYS
(12 NOVEMBER 1888)

The Court of Special Commissioners

Towards the end of August Sir Arthur Havelock, Governor of Zululand, informed Lord Knutsford, Secretary of State for the Colonies, of the legal process by which he proposed to try the Zulu leaders for murder, high treason and public violence. While he felt that the constituted courts of Zululand should be used, the fact that the Zululand magistrates might be called as witnesses meant that judicial officers from Natal should be appointed for the task: Justice W. Wragg of the Supreme Court, with two Resident Magistrates as assessors, G. Rudolph, who could speak Dutch, and Bernard Fannin, who was fluent in Zulu.[1]

Harriette Colenso had already begun a series of testing letters to Havelock formally asking him for information on how the court was to be set up and then, taking advice from Escombe, challenging the answers. Havelock had to fall back for help on the Attorney-General, Sir Michael Gallwey, who resented Harriette's presumption in implying that the courts of Zululand were not qualified for the task before them.[2] It was thus all the more galling when the Secretary of State for the Colonies took the same line. From newspaper reports, questions in the House and letters from the APS, most of which had their origin in Harriette's reports, the Colonial Office was forewarned not to accept without careful consideration the official recommendations coming from Natal. London was not sympathetic to the Usuthu. Nonetheless there was sufficient weight in the charges that Harriette and the APS were making to suggest that the Colonial Office should create some distance between itself and the officials in Natal and Zululand.

As a result, the Secretary of State decided that the constituted Zululand courts should not try these cases. Using the excuse that he did not wish to disrupt the normal judicial procedures of the colony, he ordered that a Special Commission be set up. It would have the powers of a judicial commission to pass sentence on those arraigned before it, and they would have the right to be defended by counsel. Wragg, Rudolph and Fannin were appointed as commissioners.

This was clearly a setback for the Zululand administration. The very term 'Special Commission' had a particular, contemporary resonance. It was a Special Judicial Commission which the British government was using in an attempt to prove Charles Parnell of the Irish Nationalist League guilty of criminal political activity in Ireland. In fact the Zululand proclamation which established the Court of Special Commissioners was copied from the documents which set up the Parnell Commission, except that in the Zululand case the clauses which exempted witnesses from subsequent prosecution were omitted. In the view of some local observers, London, by drawing on precedents set by one of the great public issues of the time, had given an unwarranted significance to a minor trial of local upstarts in the outposts of Empire.

But there was more to come. After the sentences had been passed, the judge's notes of the evidence would have to be submitted to Her Majesty's Government for consideration. The sentences would then be reviewed by the Secretary of State before being implemented. Knutsford went on to give a warning. The court should be more than just a means of punishing the Zulu. It should stand as an example of the new order and what could be expected of it. 'No question', wrote Lord Knutsford, 'can arise as to the impartiality of the tribunal which it is proposed to create, and its freedom from local influence.'[3] In effect, by deciding to prosecute the leaders of the old Zulu order before a Special Commission, by allowing the accused counsel, and by insisting that all sentences were to be reviewed before implementation, London had also put the Zululand administration on trial. The Zulu defence team that Harriette Colenso was at the moment putting together was to make this point many times, and take the fullest advantage of it.

On 16 October 1888, the Court of Special Commissioners was promulgated by Proclamation IV of British Zululand. It was to begin sitting on 15 November. Harry Escombe would be on his way to England on a previously planned trip at this time, but he arranged for two lawyers to be in Eshowe when the trial began.

Durban: 12 November 1888

At seven o'clock on Monday morning of 12 November, Harriette Colenso, Frank Dumat and W.Y. Campbell boarded the north-coast train at Durban station, with tickets for the railhead at Verulam. Their support staff had left the day before with the baggage: Magema Fuze and two Zulu messengers were making their way to the Umvoti Mission Station at Groutville to see if they could make contact with Martin Luthuli and hire a wagon from him.

At Verulam a carriage and pair was waiting for the defence team. Dumat took the reins and the party continued towards the ferry on the Thukela River. There were others travelling along the coast road making for Eshowe. One of the journalists remembered that it was exactly ten years before that British troops were moving in the same direction in preparation for the invasion of the Zulu kingdom. Then

> Zululand was, to the general public, a sealed book, whose contents were by no means made any clearer by the romantic information afforded by persons professing to be experts. Naturally this state of ignorance gave place to terror when it was found that the Zulus were capable of annihilating half a British column. All through the subsequent stages of Zulu history, more and more has been gradually learnt about the Zulus and Zululand, and now that the independence of the race has finally disappeared, solid fact has taken the place of romance.[4]

Harriette Colenso would not have agreed. She was on her way to Zululand to try to establish and place on record some solid facts; she had also arranged for a shorthand reporter to be present at the trials, and had given her mother and Agnes at Bishopstowe instructions to keep all the press clippings and her letters as a record.

While they were having lunch at a roadside hotel, the postcart from Natal arrived with two of the commissioners and the interpreter S.O. Samuelson – her antagonists in the coming struggle. She knew Fannin and he bowed to her. She shook hands with Samuelson and introduced herself to Rudolph, who told her that he had known her father well. The rest of day's journey passed quickly as the three members of the defence continued northwards discussing the events in Zululand which had brought them together. It was a long time since Harriette had had the opportunity for uninterrupted, concentrated conversation on Zulu matters and to share her experiences with others. The times ahead were going to be difficult and harrowing. But she was also excited, exhilarated at the prospect of direct participation in the cause after working alone for so long.

That night they stopped at lodgings a few kilometres on the Natal side of the Thukela, and Harriette wrote a long letter to her mother. She had hardly been away from her since the bishop's death, and Sarah Frances was becoming increasingly frail and dependent on her eldest daughter. Harriette did what she could to calm her mother's anxieties about the cost of her intervention and her absence, writing with a sensible optimism, stressing that even the worst of people are not wholly bad (except for Osborn), and pointing out that she had no choice but to go on with the Zulu defence – her father's life and memory demanded it.

'It is just 9 o'clock', she wrote, 'and I am tucked up in a clean and comfortable bed ... Today has been just one luxurious picnic for me, lovely weather, Mr. Dumat driving, two horses, Mr. Campbell in the back seat, and Zulu talk going on most of the time' – Zulu talk through the day: after years of isolation, of writing about Zulu affairs to London, but with so little Zulu talk beyond the circle of her family. 'Our party is rolling together ... my two legal escorts are really good fellows, and *could not* take more care of me than they do.'[5]

And they needed to. The next morning, after they had crossed the Thukela and were ascending a steep hill on the rough track to Eshowe, their carriage rocked forward, the *disselboom* dug into the ground and snapped, and the impact threw Harriette out of the carriage under the hoofs of the horses. To her companions' surprise she was only lightly bruised. An hour later the party reached Eshowe.

Eshowe: 12 November 1888

Eshowe, Osborn's place of residence since the establishment of the Zulu Native Reserve and now the administrative and judicial centre of British Zululand, was still an outpost, little known in Natal, on the broken high ground between the Thukela and Mhlatuze rivers above the coastal plain. Coming on the track from the Lower Thukela, the first building to be seen was Brunner's Store, then further to the left the Residency, the courthouse and the gaol. The military camp was a few kilometres further up the road, with its huts converted into suitable accommodation for officers, tents for the men, and a sod fort. Direct communication with Natal was established by a light military cable, frequently broken by careless wagon drivers. Heliographs kept contact with the outposts to the north, flashing messages to the military and the police at the high points at Kwa-Magwaza, and from there to the post at Nkonjeni and the magistracy at Nongoma, newly established at so much cost.

Eshowe was beautifully situated, the climate fresh and healthy, the open ground broken by stretches of forest. But for many Zulu it was a place of terror and evil. It was here that the king had died – killed, it was widely felt, by his enemies. Zibhebhu could be found near the town, drinking with the police and the indunas who had settled under the wing of the officials. The most important of these was Yamela, induna to Melmoth Osborn, his standing with the government of Zululand indicated by the large number of his homesteads in the surrounding hills.

Osborn, the Resident Commissioner and Chief Magistrate, silent and despond-ent, was now drinking heavily. His ten years in Zululand had been marked by disaster, and a sense of personal failure weighed on him. Piles of correspondence lay unanswered in his office. The setting aside of his own courts for the Court of Special Commissioners questioned publicly his authority. The dangers of this could never be understood by the shuffling politicians in London, who had been persuaded to allow, within the precincts of the government of Zululand, attor-neys, lawyers, journalists – that is, all the trappings of civilisation – amongst a people who had not reached the stage where the public criticism of those in authority could be understood as anything but weakness. Proper deference to authority was the rock on which the effective administration of natives was built. Bishop Colenso had flouted this when, during the prosecution of Langalibalele in 1873, he had publicly questioned the actions of the authorities. Now in 1888 his daughter was doing the same thing, and had come to Eshowe with her entourage in order to misrepresent what had been happening in Zululand for a philanthropic audience in England.

There was still time, however, for a public demonstration of official authority in Zululand. At the moment that Harriette Colenso was leaving Durban, a party of officials, police and onlookers made its way out of Eshowe to a piece of open ground on its margins where the gallows had been built.

They were escorting three Zulu convicts. One of them had been found guilty of murder and mutilating the body, another of murder for robbery. The third was called Nkowana, a chief of the Nzuza people living in the northern part of Zululand. He was an Usuthu who had suffered with his people in the years of violence between the Usuthu and Mandlakazi, and when Zibhebhu had returned to the north his crops had been trampled. He had reported this to Addison. In March 1888 two men from the Mandlakazi walked past Nkowana's homestead. He confronted them, and there were some sharp words. Nkowana was told that the damage to his corn was just a start and that Zibhebhu was deter-mined to destroy him. Nkowana said that the Mandlakazi had come to spread the necessary medicines before this took place. Others believed they were spies preparing the way for a Mandlakazi raid. On their return they were ambushed and killed. On his arrest Nkowana had made no attempt to deny that his action was part of these disturbances. For him the violence was part of the history of conflict that had been taking place for years between the Usuthu and the Mandlakazi. Osborn sentenced him and the two co-accused to death.

Harriette had read garbled reports of murder trials in Zululand at the time. It was difficult to know what to do without more accurate information, but she sent the Governor her 'protest ... against any further destruction of human life on account of a state of lawlessness for which, before God, England is responsible, and I claim the remission of all death sentences arising out of the recent disturbances'.[6] But when the case came before Havelock he confirmed the sentence on Nkowana and commuted the other two to life imprisonment.

Nkowana, it would seem, comprehended the terrible situation he was in only after the sentence of death had been passed. Now he tried desperately to save his own life. He declared that he had been obeying Dinuzulu's orders, and asked to call witnesses in his defence. Osborn, usually only too ready to allow evidence on Dinuzulu's participation in acts of violence, denied it in this one. The court followed the letter of the law and declared Nkowana's appeal irrelevant, and received the backing of the Attorney-General for this.

There were obvious reasons to be worried about the sentence. The Attorney-General felt there was substance in the claim that Dinuzulu had ordered the killing, and recommended clemency. But Osborn, determined to get the death sentence, treated the offence as a common murder, not a political killing. On the morning of 12 November 1888, at Eshowe, Nkowana and the two others accused of murder were placed above the two-metre drop, and hanged. They met their fate, the correspondent for *The Natal Witness* wrote, with fortitude.[7]

The officials in the Colonial Office were disturbed by the hangings, and the correspondence did not become public. The Usuthu defence came to call Nkowana's execution a judicial killing. It was that, and more. It was a demonstration of official power by means of a public execution. It was done to show the Zulu what could happen to those who decided to take the law into their own hands and avenge themselves on official favourites – loyals, Zibhebhu's followers. The timing was all-important – the day before Harriette Colenso's arrival in Eshowe in the company of lawyers who were going to defend the Usuthu leaders in the coming trial. This too would be carried out in public. Lord Knutsford had insisted on it. It was possible that the defence would put Zululand's officials in the witness box and subject them to cross-examination. The behaviour of the Resident Magistrates, officers in the Zululand Police, trusted chiefs and indunas, might well be called into question, their accounts contradicted perhaps, in open court. When that happened it would be salutary for the people of Zululand to remember also Nkowana, the man who killed two of Zibhebhu's men, swinging from the Eshowe gallows.

Pietermaritzburg: 12 November 1888

On the same day, 200 kilometres to the north, another group of travellers were also making a journey that was to end in Eshowe. It had begun in the Transvaal,

Photo 27. 'Rebels' in Pietermaritzburg in November 1888 after months on the run. Dinuzulu kaCetshwayo seated in the centre with Paul Mthimkhulu wearing the hat standing on his right, and Ndabankulu kaLukwazi to his right in the light coat.

continued across the north-west corner of Zululand, crossed into Natal near Rorke's Drift. This journey, however, was made unobtrusively, the men avoiding settlements and sleeping in the open. Its leader was Dinuzulu, 18-year-old son of the last Zulu king, Cetshwayo kaMpande. For the past six months, he had been crossing and re-crossing the borders between Zululand and the Transvaal. Accompanying him were some of the most respected men in Zululand, his trusted advisers and the most faithful adherents of the Zulu royal house, together with a young Afrikaner called Meyer. They were now skilled in tactics of evasion. They had just escaped a party under orders from Pretoria to detain the prince. In Natal the group split, one portion reporting to a magistrate that the young prince was on his way to Ladysmith, while he in fact made his way to the railhead at Elandslaagte.

On being informed of Dinuzulu's arrival in Natal, Havelock issued a warrant for his arrest for entering the colony without a pass. He was determined to deny Dinuzulu the opportunity of appearing in public in Natal meekly asking how he had offended his father, the Governor, and his mother, Queen Victoria. He had to be arrested, not allowed to surrender. For his part, Dinuzulu was determined not to be seen as a fugitive. He wanted to surrender to the Governor, declare his innocence, and await the just decision of the Queen. And he believed that Harriette Colenso would help him in this.

On 14 November, at four in the afternoon, Dinuzulu and a few followers caught the train at Elandslaagte, arriving in Pietermaritzburg at 1.30 on the morning of 15 November. They slept in the streets for a few hours, under the walls of Government House, and at first light began the 12-kilometre walk out to the farm at Bishopstowe. They were tired and the older men fell behind.

Agnes Colenso and her mother were in the cottage at Seven Oaks. Just after eight, a servant announced that there was a white man to see her and that he had Dinuzulu with him. Agnes found the idea hard to believe but went to investigate. At the back of the house she found an elderly Zulu, Meyer and a young African sitting on a bench. Meyer presented the young man to her as Dinuzulu, the son of Cetshwayo. Agnes gave the men soap, water and fresh towels, and asked them to come into the house after they had washed. Meanwhile she sent an urgent message to an African who she knew had once seen Dinuzulu. When the interview began, Agnes apologised for the absence of her sister together with all the Africans from Bishopstowe, who were more knowledgeable on Zulu affairs. As she spoke she noticed there was something familiar about the older Zulu and she asked who he was. He reminded her that he had in fact been to Bishopstowe years before on a deputation, and 'as he spoke and smiled I remembered him more'.[8] Then one of the stragglers entered the room. It was Paul Mthimkhulu, the preacher and doctor to the Usuthu. He was to be followed by Ndabankulu kaLukwazi, chief of the Ntombela on the north-western border, who had been deeply involved in the negotiations which brought the border Boers into Zulu politics.

Agnes was now convinced. She got up and shook hands with Dinuzulu, apologising for her suspicions saying '"it was far too important a matter for me to allow myself to be deceived." "What," he said, with a smile, "did she think she was being deceived?" and we were from that moment the best of friends.'

They were taken into the dining room, the stragglers swelling their number. Agnes, thrilled and touched but shy and lacking confidence, confined herself to the briefest welcome, hiding her deeper thoughts,

for I could not bring myself to say, 'I am glad you have come here to us.' Though of course his father's son will always be very welcome where we have a home, and we shall always be glad to be allowed to do anything we can do for him, and I was proud of the lad for coming down in his courageous innocence, right into the lion's mouth. But the knowledge of the will and power of his enemies made my heart ache to think he was in their clutches, because he still had faith in that far off, and apparently for the Zulus unattainable justice of England.

Agnes knew that she would have to report his arrival to the Governor. She was anxious, not wanting to leave the house, fearing that the police might arrive while she was away and rough him up, or march him into Pietermaritzburg handcuffed, exposing him to abuse from the public as had happened many years ago to Langalibalele. But she had to go, and contacted a neighbour, asking him to come over and make sure there was no violence if the police came.

Before leaving, she introduced Dinuzulu to her mother. He noticed the tusk in the corner of the room sent to the bishop by a chief in Mozambique. He tested its weight and told them it was the first tusk he had ever seen. He examined the photographs of Bishop Colenso but declined to look at those of his own father.

In Pietermaritzburg Agnes cabled Eshowe to tell Harriette what had happened, and informed the evening newspaper of Dinuzulu's arrival. She then went to Government House and waited for Havelock to finish luncheon before sending in her letter. Gerald Browne came out and told her that Sir Arthur had no reason to see her or Dinuzulu personally, that he knew of Dinuzulu's whereabouts, and that steps had been taken to secure his arrest. Agnes only had time to say that she hoped the police would not use handcuffs, and that it was a disgrace, and that it would be seen as such in England, before she hurried away.

She drove the carriage back to Bishopstowe herself, not waiting for the driver. The police passed her on the road, and she was relieved that they waited to see her safely across a stream – an indication, she hoped, that they would treat Dinuzulu with equal courtesy. They did, waiting for her to return before they made the arrest, and providing him with a horse to ride to the police barracks. She and her sister were to remember this act of consideration on the part of the Natal Mounted Police. Dinuzulu said his farewells and 'having taken leave of Mother, he mounted the fine looking horse on which he looked quite at home, and rode off, and in three minutes not one of his men was on the place, they hastened so to follow him'.

Havelock moved as quickly as he could to get the young man out of Pietermaritzburg and the colony of Natal, and into British Zululand where he would stand trial. On 22 November 1888, on the border between Natal and Zululand, Dinuzulu kaCetshwayo was handed over to Mansel of the Zululand Police, and taken to Eshowe.[9]

CHAPTER 19

ESHOWE
(15 NOVEMBER – 5 DECEMBER 1888)

The Court of Special Commissioners:
15 November – 5 December 1888

The Court of Special Commissioners sat in Eshowe from 15 November to 5 December 1888, then reconvened from 23 January to 27 April 1889. It heard nine indictments in all, against 17 different men. Some of these were for particular cases of murder made against individuals, but most of the time and attention was spent on the cases involving the Usuthu leadership and the members of the Zulu royal house in particular: Ndabuko kaMpande, Shingana kaMpande and Dinuzulu kaCetshwayo.[1]

There was no room in the offices at Eshowe big enough for the court, so Brunner's newly built store was hired and adapted for the purpose. Considerable effort was made to give it a suitably imposing judicial character. The tables were covered with red and green baize, and the walls of the store hung with blue gauze. At the one end the three commissioners were seated at a long table, Mr Justice Wragg in a red robe, and his assessors in black gowns – their petticoats, Harriette Colenso called them, for, apart from their fussy pretentiousness, they had a ritualistic quality which earned her Low Church scorn. There was a raised table for the registrar, H.C. Campbell. Then came the tables for the prosecutor, W.B. Morcom, who had been involved in the Langalibalele trial, and others for the defence counsel and the press. Harriette Colenso was allowed to sit here so that she could advise the defence on matters of fact and translation. The dock, with the accused guarded by the Zululand Police, was placed behind them, and there were chairs on either side for white visitors. A partition then segregated the court to create a space for African spectators, and this was divided in turn to separate loyals from rebels.

On the first day of the trial there were nine men in the dock. The proclamation and the charges were read out and translated – except for the phrase 'high treason'. It was alleged, in the archaic English of the law, that they did

Photo 28. Brunner's Store in Eshowe, where the Court of Special Commissioners sat.

with divers other persons, to the Prosecutor unknown, and being all and each or some one or more of them armed with Firearms and Assegais, and divers other weapons, wrongfully, unlawfully, maliciously, and riotously assemble and gather together to disturb the public peace, and wickedly, seditiously, and trait-orously did encourage and conspire with certain persons to the Prosecutor unknown to resist the authority of the Supreme Chief and of the Government of Zululand, as by law established ...[2]

W.Y. Campbell immediately put in a request for an adjournment to give the defence time to prepare its case. The prosecution, believing that an adequate defence of the first of the accused would necessarily have implications for the Usuthu who would stand trial later, argued against this. The court decided to proceed and Campbell withdrew from the case.

Somhlolo kaMkhosana: 16–22 November 1888[3]

The first man to come to trial was Somhlolo kaMkhosana, the Biyela chief, wide-ly believed to be the legitimate heir to the huge chiefdom straddling the middle reaches of the Mhlatuze River. His father, Mkhosana, had died at Isandlwana – he was one of the few men of the highest rank within the kingdom to have been killed in the war of 1879. Somhlolo had been bypassed by Wolseley in favour of his

263

brother Mgitshwa, who, predictably, had become a favourite of the authorities, and a loyal to be used against the Usuthu. But Mgitshwa had been forced to retreat into the Reserve during the civil war, leaving Somhlolo dominant north of the river, where Zibhebhu had burnt his homesteads and killed his relatives in 1883.

In June 1888 Shingana had asked Somhlolo to support him by joining the Usuthu at Hlophekhulu. While he hesitated he received warnings from different quarters. First Shingana sent messengers saying that Zibhebhu might well attack him. Then he received information that the Boers were about to attack those who had deserted the Usuthu. Unsure that Resident Magistrate Knight had the capacity to protect him if he refused, he tried to compromise. Leaving the bulk of his people in their homesteads, he went with a handful of followers to Shingana at Hlophekhulu on 13 June. The move, however, split his people. Some followed him to the mountain stronghold; others went down to the coastal district and became involved in the conflict there; and another faction took the children of the late chief Mkhosana, of whom Somhlolo was guardian, to Magistrate Knight's office. At Hlophekhulu Somhlolo quarrelled with Shingana and, when Hlophekhulu was eventually attacked by the authorities, Somhlolo remained in hiding a few kilometres away. For this he was charged with 'high treason, rebellion, and public violence', 'or some one or more of the said crimes'.[4]

A good-looking, unassuming man, he chose not to assert himself or the Usuthu cause in court. He agreed with the witnesses the prosecution used against him. He had indeed gone to Hlophekhulu but he had not been involved in the clash with the authorities; he had no wish to defy the authorities, and his overwhelming motivation had been his fear of all the parties involved. He told the court:

> Yes through fear I ran away and left my people. I thought that my people would be saved, that I would save them by going away from them, that the impi of Dinuzulu, on finding that I was no longer amongst my people, would not come to my people. I went out through fear, not because I was angry or because I was going to fight with the Government ... my head did not think of war, it thought only of death and I went out to hide myself.[5]

On 24 November Morcom, the prosecutor, began his address to the court. He outlined the history of Zululand from 1879. He spoke of a conspiracy by the Usuthu to resist the return of Zibhebhu. It was true that Somhlolo had not been at Hlophekhulu at the time of the fight. But he had nonetheless been there previously when he should have been at the side of the authorities, and he was therefore liable in law. Fear was no justification whatsoever. Morcom cited Lord Denman in *Regina* v. *Tyler*: 'The law is that no man from fear of consequences to

himself has a right to make himself a party to committing mischief on mankind.'
Justice Wragg agreed.

> Your evil example caused very many of your tribe to arm themselves and with
> those arms to fight against the Queen's Government in Zululand ... We unan-
> imously find you guilty of the crime of High Treason. You have broken your
> words of allegiance to the Queen's Government in Zululand, you joined those
> who were resisting, with arms in their hands, the Queen's authority, you caused
> men of your tribe to fight with and to kill the Queen's loyal men, and all this, we
> are convinced, with intentions hostile to Her Majesty's authority in Zululand.[6]

Somhlolo was sentenced to five years' hard labour.

The Court of Special Commissioners had been sitting for less than a week, but
some of the major features of the trials had already emerged. There was little
evidence of a massive conspiracy – rather a general fear of the consequences of
Zibhebhu's and Sokwetshata's return, and concern that a refusal to commit oneself to one side would invite attack from the other. As a Crown witness said,
'Could a person have stayed at home and not have been killed? We were all
afraid, we were afraid of each other ...'[7] Mobilisation, whether for attack or for
defence, tended to cause general disruption.

Most significant was the way in which the prosecution had used a narrow legal
argument to get a conviction. Somhlolo had disobeyed the authorities by going
to Hlophekhulu and was convicted for this act. Neither the general atmosphere
of intimidation, insecurity and the demands for mobilisation from both sides, nor
his own motives or sense of responsibility towards his people, nor even the fact
that he had not participated in the violence, was seen as a mitigating factor.

Harriette Colenso watched and listened from her place at the table halfway
down the court. She was one of the few who could follow proceedings in both
Zulu and English. She thought the translations were bad, and checked the
record being made by the shorthand writer she had employed. Nonetheless it
was clear that the evidence already emerging confirmed her interpretation of
events in the recent history of Zululand: '"the Crown" did not, I think, reckon
with Zulu loyalty to their chiefs, and the witnesses *as it is* have done a good deal
to tell our story, and let out the truth, although naturally frightened'.

'Cruel work'

Already Harriette was making her mark at Eshowe. Just before she left Durban
she had received a stiff, awkward letter from the commandant of the Zululand

Photo 29. The Eshowe gaol with the Resident Commissioner's Office on the left, the gaol to the right and what appear to be the tents in which Dinuzulu and his uncles were allowed to spend the day during their detention in Eshowe in 1888–9.

Police, George Mansel. He had been a friend of the Colensos when they were younger, of Frances in particular. It was he who had told Frances of Durnford's death, and arranged for Durnford's horse to be brought to Bishopstowe. When he heard Harriette was coming to Eshowe, Mansel wrote to her.

> As there is no place that I know of that you could possibly stop at, I write to offer to put you up ... Of course I dare say your views on politics may differ, but I do not see why that should interfere with private matters, and politics need never be mentioned between us. At any rate I hope you will take the offer in good part, as it is intended to be made. I wish to tell you that I am far from being an enemy of the Usutos, and really feel great sympathy for them, and as I have often stated, if I were a Zulu, I would be a [?] Usuto myself ...
>
> For the sake of your dead Father and sister and for auld lang syne I hope you will let me do this much for you.[8]

She accepted the invitation. Indeed, she made a point of behaving courteously to the officials at Eshowe. Although she was unable to establish personal relations with either Osborn or Wragg, she did so with all the other officials and the military as well. She even accepted an invitation from Dick Addison for luncheon. This frightened the Usuthu, who urged her not to spend too long with him. She survived by avoiding political topics and keeping, she wrote, to such

Photo 30. Osuthu at Eshowe, called the 'rebel camp' by the authorities. The gum trees separate the camp from Brunner's Store. The wattle-and-daub rectangular shelter was built by the lawyers, and eventually occupied by Harriette Colenso.

subjects as 'elephants, wild-dogs, and porcupines'.[9]

She soon established her routine. She got up early, rode from the Mansels' house to visit the prisoners, which she was allowed to do while they were still awaiting trial. The gaol was small, the extensions being made were incomplete, and the weather was hot, and the princes spent the day in tents pitched in front of the building. These visits were important. It was here she got to know Shingana and Ndabuko better, and Dinuzulu for the first time. The first, quick and intelligent, was always a favourite and had been to Bishopstowe on a number of occasions since the invasion, and they were close friends. Ndabuko she grew to admire increasingly, discerning resolution and strength of character in what others saw as a dour and uncommunicative man. Dinuzulu was 'the lad' – a version of the term of respect by which princes were known, *mntwana*, and which avoided 'child', with its paternalistic, and 'boy', with its dismissive and racist connotations. They also became friends, and Harriette was pleased that Agnes and her mother had already met him.

After seeing the prisoners she rode to the small camp behind the gum trees Brunner had planted, known as Osuthu, the place of the Usuthu, where the rest of the defence team lived in tents. Soon the number of people at Osuthu increased as visiting Usuthu, witnesses and supporters, put up temporary shelters there. This greatly annoyed the officials, who called the encampment, Harriette related with pride, the 'rebel camp'. But they did not dare to touch it.

After visiting Osuthu and talking with the defence lawyers and the Zulu who were there, Harriette would move on to the court to get ready for the day's proceedings. She had established herself as a presence in the court, checking the translations, passing notes to her colleagues, making sure she had an independent record of events. Of all the people in court she was the most knowledgeable of the total situation, and as each day passed so she became better informed of the detail as well. Her presence as a critical observer deeply disturbed the prosecution – which pleased her greatly.

It was soon clear that Somhlolo's case had been used to prepare the way for the trial of three major figures: Shingana, Ndabuko and Dinuzulu. But Harriette could do little for Somhlolo. His defence – that he had gone to Hlophekhulu out of fear not just of Zibhebhu, but of the Usuthu as well – was ill-advised, she thought, and the consequence of pressure put on him by the officials. He should have dwelt solely on his fear of Zibhebhu, and this would have allowed the Usuthu defence team to come in on his side. At the same time she felt sorry for him, frightened and isolated as he was, in the control of the police, bullied by the court, and without sound legal advice. And she was able to intervene, in a way, even for Somhlolo. 'It was a horrid drizzly old day', she wrote,

> and 'the prisoner' Somhlolo had been left to get through the midday hour as best he could while Judges and lawyers etc all refreshed themselves with luncheon – I could not stand it, so asked McAlister (it would amaze you to see the terms I am on with many a rascal) to get me a cup of coffee for him. No coffee to be had but he got tea for me as he thought – so we got a loaf and emptied the sugar basin into the cup of tea, and poor Somhlolo was grateful, and I sent for another cup and had some tea tar as it was then.[10]

A small incident, but indicative of Harriette Colenso's awareness of Zulu feelings, and in the phrase 'I could not stand it' revealing, behind the formal courtesies towards the officials, how distressed she was at what was going on in Eshowe. As she wrote of Somhlolo's trial, 'It is cruel work ...'[11]

Somkhele kaMalanda and the coastal chiefs: 16 November – 1 December 1888[12]

The next case was that of Somkhele and the five other chiefs from the Lower Mfolozi district, who were alleged to have mobilised their forces with hostile intent and attacked the magistracy there on 30 June 1888. We have seen how, as a consequence of the return of Zibhebhu and Sokwetshata, the whole coastal region had mobilised and there had been violence in the vicinity of the magistracy, which had been interpreted as a direct attack on the authorities.[13] However, there was no evidence that the chiefs had anything directly to do with the acts of violence which had taken place or that they had intended to attack the magistracy. Some of the accused had not even reached the area where the attack was supposed to have taken place. The evidence in fact strongly suggests that the only violence had been the raiding of cattle belonging to loyals, and that the hunger of men who had been in the field without support for days was a major reason for this. Somkhele said that they had done so 'because they are human beings'.[14] Eighty years later, old men in the area told me that the reason that the men attacked was because 'they ate meat'.

'We admit to fighting', Somkhele pleaded, 'but we fought when we were summoned ... to do so by the sons of our King. We wish to have an attorney to represent us in this matter.' Once again W.Y. Campbell agreed to defend them, asked for an adjournment in order to prepare the defence, and when this was refused he withdrew. The authorities had on this occasion provided the accused with an attorney but they refused to co-operate with him. It was embarrassing for the court, and the judge felt that the defence had worked on the accused behind the scenes. As it was, Somkhele found it difficult to forget his senior position within the Zulu kingdom and he did not treat the court with the required deference. 'Why don't you speak up, boy?' he shouted from the dock at one witness. 'You have been told to speak so that we may hear you.'

Like many of the Zulu who were to appear in the court, as accused or as witnesses, they misunderstood their position and spoke with a self-incriminating frankness. It was hard to view obedience to the son of Cetshwayo as a crime. One man, on the capital charge of murder, had reported to the magistrate who was searching for him. When one of Somkhele's own witnesses tried to conceal the fact that he was armed, Somkhele corrected him. Much of the evidence appeared to observers tediously long, especially as it had to be translated. Witnesses, used to oral discourse, with its memory-reinforcing repetitions and back-looping, resisted attempts by the court to bring them to the point. Visitors and journalists began to get weary, and their interest in the cases began to wane.

But not Harriette Colenso, although she could only observe, give advice when she could, and sometimes intervene informally. For the most part she did so calmly but lost her temper on occasion, once returning to the courtroom, her hand still

> shaking a little because I let myself get angry, and *ran* to get food for the
> prisoners who were brought up without breakfast. It was worth showing anger

about, and has made some impression and they got their food, bread and coffee. They made a great protest yesterday, 'harassed' the Court, we can hardly
expect them to stick to it and keep silence through *all* the slanders, but that
will not matter much, *the protest has been made* ...[15]

In the case of Somkhele and the coastal chiefs, the charge of high treason was
abandoned; they were found guilty of public violence and sentenced to five
years with hard labour. Somkhele still managed to have the last word. He had
done wrong, he told the court, in assembling his men – but he had admitted this
already months ago, when he left his stronghold in the Dukuduku and paid a
fine of 1800 cattle to the magistrate Pretorius. In this way Mr Justice Wragg, and
the outside world, discovered that Somkhele had already been heavily punished
for the offence for which he was now being tried.

Ndabuko kaMpande:
15 November – 5 December 1888[16]

Ndabuko's turn came next. The charges focused on four specific incidents. The
first was the unsuccessful attempt to arrest men on 26 April 1888, when the
Zululand Police surrounded Osuthu before dawn.[17] It was held that Ndabuko on
that occasion 'did disobey and defy the Resident Magistrate placed over him,
and did insult and treat with violence and contumely the Messengers and Police
sent, in the execution of their duty, to arrest certain persons then and there
being'. The second referred to the move to Ceza in May,[18] 'the better there to
conspire against and defy the said Government of Zululand, and to wage, levy,
and carry on the insurrection, rebellion, and war aforesaid'. The clash on Ceza
formed the basis of the third charge, when on 2 June Ndabuko 'did then maliciously and traitorously attempt and endeavour, by force and arms, to subvert
and destroy the said Government of Zululand'. The final charge concerned the
attack at Ndumu hill on 23 June,[19] when Ndabuko with others 'did attack,
wound, and wrongfully, unlawfully, and maliciously kill and murder certain of
Her Majesty's subjects and forces ... and unlawfully steal certain Horned Cattle,
the number, description, and ownership of which the Prosecutor is unable to set
forth with certainty'.[20]

On 28 November Campbell asked again for an adjournment in order to prepare his defence. When it was refused he withdrew from the defence, and made
his way to Johannesburg where he was planning a business venture. The trial
began with Ndabuko refusing to answer questions on the ground that he was not
properly defended.

The defence played what it saw as its advantage with great energy. Telegrams were sent to Escombe, now in London, and he in turn wrote terse and angry protests to the Colonial Office. Harriette Colenso worked hard to keep all parties on the same track in a situation which was becoming increasingly tense. She presented a controlled and confident image to the world, which stiffened the morale of the Usuthu. Her behaviour annoyed the officials and worried the African loyals, and some began to fear that they had perhaps backed the wrong horse. She was able, she wrote, to 'manage among the enemy' although 'often on the point of exploding, amiable as everyone (almost) is to me'.[21] And her own confidence increased as the evidence coming from Crown witnesses supported the argument that she had been developing from the time when she first heard of the disturbances in Zululand: there had been no rebellion, the Usuthu leaders had done what they could to restrain their people, and would have succeeded had it not been necessary to defend themselves by making a pre-emptive attack on Zibhebhu.

But more was demanded of Harriette Colenso than time, energy and good judgement. Her financial costs were still increasing and she had to draw again on her father's legacy. It was clear that there was a long battle ahead, not just in Zululand and Natal, but in England as well. They had decided to challenge the legality of Dinuzulu's extradition from Natal before the Judicial Committee of the Privy Council. The legal expenses would be large. She believed that in the end they would be successful and they might then be able to claim for them. But unless they could raise the funds now, they would fail and, as she told her mother,

> this must not be – you know Darling that you said you would not stop me if you could, and I should be stopped with a vengeance if I could not produce certain monies presently ... I will be very careful, and I do not believe that we shall lose it – or much of it, in the end, but even that would be better than losing the lives of these poor trusting ill used Zulu friends, and therewith all Zulu faith even in Sobantu ...
>
> And try not to be anxious on the money points, please my Mother, we won't be ruined, I promise you – and we will circumvent the enemy just where they think that they've got us.[22]

Her mother did not object – but she did offer a very tentative warning on a possible non-monetary pitfall: 'I fear, my own child, the powers of this world are arrayed against you. God bless and keep you. Perhaps I ought to remind you that the powers that be are ordained of God.'[23]

'Our fathers'

On 1 December, following her usual routine, Harriette rode up to the tents of Ndabuko and Dinuzulu pitched in front of the gaol. They weren't there. The previous night 'some idiot started the idea that the chiefs meant to try to escape and so they were hustled out of their tents into one of the cells'.[24] She found Dinuzulu angry and demoralised. He had had enough. He told Harriette he was not going to go on. He had never been captured. He had surrendered voluntarily. He would not be locked up night and day. Harriette tried to calm him down and got him to accept one more night in the hot cell, and promised she would come and see him the next day.

They met at ten on Sunday morning. She talked about what had happened in Zululand and in Natal since the annexation a little less than two years ago. She told him about Havelock: about how he had been pushed into a corner by his subordinates. She talked about the difficulty of their present situation, of how she believed that legally their position was strong. But Dinuzulu would have to co-operate if its strength was to be realised. If he did not, then the whole plan to challenge the court and its decisions would fail. She told him that it was only because she knew the sort of men his uncles Ndabuko and Shingana were that she had dared commit herself to this course of action. She also felt she knew his father's son and 'we talked of our fathers, and he said he was quite sure that unKulunkulu [the Great Great One] exists or he would never have got safely to Bishopstowe and we lunched together ... and he took all I said as nicely as possible, and assured me that he understood, and I think is making up his mind to – even the gaol. He is a dear boy.'[25]

Her commitment was increasing. It was to bear heavily on her then and for many years to come. But she was convinced it was worth it, indeed she felt she had no choice but to go on. As she wrote to her mother and sister:

> I should like you to see beautiful Zululand, but Eshowe as it now is, is too sad altogether – and only endurable when one has so much fighting that one has not time to think about it ... Dear Ndabuko is behaving as usual, perfectly, 'No Sirs, I mean to ask no questions' says he each time, and sits down again, to the increasing discomfiture of the Bench.[26]

Defences, legal and moral

Not only was the Bench discomforted but so was the Colonial Office. At this moment the officials were considering the activities of Harry Escombe, now in

London. On Monday 3 December he had been interviewed at the Colonial Office where he had justified the defence's decision to withdraw on the ground that it had insufficient time to prepare. On 5 December he had sent a letter to *The Times* enclosing the latest telegram from Durban, telling him that the defence team had discovered that over 3000 people had been expelled to make way for Zibhebhu: 'Many killed; bulk in forest starving; present trial sad farce; impartial Imperial inquiry imperative. Facts now disclosed barely credible (as happening in) British territory.'[27]

It was one thing to hear this from the APS but quite another to read it over breakfast in *The Times* on the authority of Natal's leading advocate and politician. Havelock was asked by cable if the court could not be adjourned in order to give counsel time to prepare its defence. The Natal authorities were furious and protested, but the Colonial Office insisted. A face-saving excuse was devised and on 5 December the court, under protest, adjourned until 23 January 1889, and its members made their way towards the Thukela to spend Christmas in Natal.

The adjournment gave the Colonial Office time to reconsider its policy towards the Zululand trials. Edward Fairfield put the problem to the other officials. It was clear that there were two aspects to the case. First there was the legal one. The defence could not deny that their clients had violated the law. Technically they would be found guilty. On the other hand there was the question of their 'moral guilt'.

> What the Zulus wish to show apparently is that Zibhebhu and his tribe came galumping back into Northern Zululand, boasting and threatening slaughter and revenge – utterly unprovided with a commissariat and therefore obliged to live on the country as a conquered country – and that when they arrived at their destination they ejected five thousand Usutus – and that it was under the stress [?] of the panic and resentment caused by this series of events that the Usutus took up a fighting attitude. All this is no legal defence, because the Government had a right which the Court cannot question to shift the Tribes about at its will; but it is a very weighty moral defence, especially as we were told that the restoration of Zibhebhu would not injure any legitimate vested interests, the country being almost uninhabited.

By adjourning the trial, the British government had given the defence time to construct a lengthy case detailing the way in which the Usuthu had been provoked, thus making it possible to shift from the legal to the moral ground. The time had therefore arrived, Fairfield believed, for London to take some counter

273

action. If the trial was going to be embarrassing for the officials, it would also be lengthy and expensive for the defence. Perhaps a bargain could be struck? After all, Her Majesty's Government had retained the right to review the sentences. If Escombe could persuade his clients to plead guilty on the lesser charges, then the Colonial Office might agree to reduced sentences. The 'only real question', Fairfield felt, 'is what, as a matter of political expediency, ought to be done with Dinuzulu and the other leaders for the next few years'.

Not everyone in the Colonial Office agreed. The whole matter needed further investigation before any negotiations with the defence were even considered. After all, there had been resistance to Her Majesty's officers, civil and military, and there had been casualties. The Colonial Secretary, Lord Knutsford, went with this and instructed that Escombe be reminded that it was time for him to return to defend his clients.[28]

In spite of this rejection, it is clear that Escombe's protests, based ultimately on Harriette Colenso's months of hard work, had had an effect. Official abuses in Zululand were now being reported in the British press and catching the attention of radical MPs. The officials in London, aware that subordinates in Zululand had acted carelessly, in a partisan fashion and perhaps illegally, were already taking evasive action, making plans for a safe political response to the trial after the convictions and before the confirmation of the sentences: 'It is very important from a political point of view that the Zulu people should have no ground of complaint in respect of these trials.'[29] Public opinion was going to be on the side of the Zulu chiefs, and 'we shall not execute them, and shall not be able to imprison them closely, or for any long period'.

This was a note made in passing, an assumption at the Colonial Office, accepted with hardly a comment. One can only speculate, however, what the case might have been without Harriette Colenso's interventions over the past few years and the publicity Bishopstowe had brought to Zulu affairs. And while mitigation of sentence after conviction was already assumed in the confidential comments at the Colonial Office, this was not known in Zululand where the possibility of hanging still appeared very real. The contrast was stark between the urbane, rather cynical debate in Whitehall over policy towards the accused Zulu, and the terror with which the officials and their policy were viewed in Eshowe. In London, officials hoped to get themselves out of a rather awkward situation by a combination of political argument, pragmatic recourse to the law, and the knowledge that, ultimately, power lay with them. In Eshowe the magistrates still looked to the gallows – and the Zulu accused of high treason lived in fear of them.

Nonetheless, the instruction from London to adjourn the court for six weeks was a hopeful sign that the defence was making a mark and that the three main accused, the surviving leaders of the Zulu royal house, were not just going to be got rid of – another violent episode in the history of imperial expansion, another sad story of the deaths of kings like Hintsa, Sandile, Moorosi, Sekhukhune, Cetshwayo. Much of the credit for this lay with Harriette Colenso, working through the night on her letters to London, to the lawyers, to the Governor, listening heartsore to Zulu accounts of betrayal and death, waiting anxiously for answers to her messages to the men in hiding in the north, sitting day after day in the Court of Special Commissioners, noting the mistranslations, the rudeness, the intimidation, discomforting the officials as she recorded her observations which might soon be included in another letter of protest to arrive at Government House, the Colonial Office, or the editorial offices of a London newspaper.

CHAPTER 20

ESHOWE
(DECEMBER 1888 – APRIL 1889)

Osuthu

During the adjournment more and more Zulu began to arrive at Osuthu. Magema Fuze was there, and so were Mubi Nondenisa and Thwayisa Mabaso, in Harriette Colenso's employ. Fokoti, brother of Zibhebhu, arrived, and Mankulumana of the Ndwandwe, who was to become Dinuzulu's chief minister. Mtokwane, the trusted messenger, joined the camp. Some of these Usuthu stayed with friends and relatives in nearby homesteads. Others found protection under the storekeeper Brunner's wagon in the lee of a plantation of young gum trees. When it was clear that the trials were to continue for a lengthy period, Dumat built a small, thatched, wattle-and-daub hut amidst the tents and makeshift shelters of 'the rebel camp'.

Osuthu became a place from which the authorities could be challenged: where the Nongqayi could not just stroll in, fists and rifle-butts flying. Here the defence discovered more and more about recent events in Zululand. Here Zulu from all over the country were able to relate their experiences over the past few years to sympathetic listeners. In the process a huge amount of information was uncovered about the specific events associated with the 1888 disturbances and British rule in Zululand in general. Harriette Colenso was horrified when she heard about what had happened in the more remote parts of north-eastern Zululand after the Usuthu had left Ceza and the disturbances were declared to be over. She was told of people who had been captured, not only by the Mandlakazi, but by Hlubi's Basotho, the native levies, even the Zululand Police; that women and children had been distributed amongst these official allies, and how they were then abused, or held to ransom, to be redeemed, at times with the assistance of the Zululand civil courts.

By the beginning of 1889 many of the people gathered at Osuthu were gaining confidence in themselves as members of what Harriette Colenso saw as the Zulu National Party. It was reflected in their demeanour and their dress as well – when she persuaded the male witnesses and visitors not to dress themselves in the cast-off clothing of the whites just because they were in Eshowe. She found them 'a grand dashing set of men, and [they] have quite fallen in with my idea of having dirty rags to be the sign of the other side and appearing in Zulu costume'.[1]

Eshowe, its horrors notwithstanding, allowed her to escape from the isolation in which she had worked for so many years. Her friendship with Dinuzulu and his uncles grew. She enjoyed Shingana's perceptive commentary on events and shared his fears, and came to admire Ndabuko, for his stoicism and the respons-ibility he assumed for his brother's child. She felt Ndabuko understood and appreciated the work and sacrifice that her support for the *abantwana* entailed.

It was not just the developing friendship with the prisoners, and the men and women who came to visit Osuthu; it was also the men involved in the defence. She could talk law with Campbell and Dumat. Legal debate had been part of life at Bishopstowe and it was a world into which she moved easily now, and the male lawyers soon came to respect her insights and ability. Together they discussed strategy. They knew it was unlikely that the accused would escape being con-victed, but the evidence that was emerging only confirmed what she suspected from the first: that the accused had been trying to control the consequences of reckless and irresponsible maladministration. The trial would only be a first step: the next could be an appeal to the Privy Council, or perhaps an independent inquiry into what had occurred in British Zululand.

The Zululand officials were to discover that, within a few hundred paces of the court set up as a working demonstration of the new order, a centre of protest and resistance was to be found. In November 1888 Dick Addison, Resident Magistrate of the Ndwandwe district, had been called to give evidence at Eshowe, and was replaced by L. Tyrrell, another young Natal man. On discov-ering a party of men building and preparing land for planting in what he believed to be Zibhebhu's territory, Tyrrell had fined and flogged them. Osborn quashed the sentences, but only after he discovered that the incident had been reported to the defence. In January Harriette Colenso had managed to get an account published in a Natal newspaper, which she copied to Charles Hancock, a lawyer on the committee of the APS. He in turn published a letter about the illegal flog-ging in the London *Daily News*. It was just the sort of evidence of 'maladminis-tration' that formed the foundation of the defence's case, and its publication infuriated the officials at every level, including those in London who had to pre-pare the answers to these charges in the House of Commons.[2]

Although the officials fumed at the 'scandalous impertinent, unintelligible' statements of the defence and the 'very Home Rulish style of harangue', the damage being done to the officers administering the Zululand government by the defence team was considerable. On 24 December Harry Escombe, still in London, forwarded to the Colonial Office a telegram from Harriette Colenso and Advocate Dumat, demanding that the proceedings of the court be suspended because defence witnesses were being terrorised by the officials. London cabled Havelock for more information and discovered that three Usuthu witnesses had been arrested when they had arrived at Eshowe. One of them was the Colensos' old friend, Mfunzi, the royal messenger. Havelock was furious and reprimanded Osborn in a public dispatch.[4]

This incident marks the beginning of the end for Melmoth Osborn. Herbert at the Colonial Office felt that 'we *must* replace Mr Osborn by some other officer (not South African or white Kafir) in Zululand ... I should like to pension Mr. Osborn on the abolition of his office.'[5] Rumours of his drinking and intended resignation had reached London. Now the officials at the Colonial Office began to plan for that event. Fairfield wrote: 'It is lucky that the latter intends to retire. The arresting of two comparatively obscure men, who were charged with nothing but public violence, but who were also known to be witnesses for the defence, has an ugly look.'[6]

It was another victory for Harriette Colenso – but the work it entailed was exhausting and distressing and the cost was high. She decided not to return home during the six-week adjournment. It was a blow to her mother – 'I can't tell you how tired I am of her absence – but of course I would [not] risk interfering with any of her plans. – I seem to have been in a very doleful mood when I began this letter, do not regard it ... I shall be quite a different person when Harriette comes home ...'[7]

The Colensos' financial situation worsened: at a time when Harriette's expenses were increasing at Eshowe, both the Colenso brothers asked for additional financial support from their mother and sisters. In some ways hardest of all, *The Life of Bishop Colenso*, in which they had invested money and so much more, had been ignored or dismissed by the critics as laboured, long and partisan. The publisher was now calling for further payment towards its costs. Frank asked Uncle Charles Bunyon for help, which he provided but, in the opinion of Harriette and her mother, with bad grace. But, Harriette wrote, they should take the money thrown at them, for the sake of the Usuthu.[8]

Sarah Frances Colenso, after a fall, was unable to walk unassisted and, often very depressed, sat quietly in her corner at the desk Harriette had brought for her after the fire, still reflecting on the world of words in which she had lived for so long: 'with my Harry still away at Eshowe we (Agnes and I) seem to be in a state of suspended animation (if those words convey any distinct or indistinct meaning), day by day we look for news from Eshowe'.[9]

Harriette did what she could to celebrate Christmas at Eshowe. Dinuzulu had presented her with an ox and was hurt that she had not yet slaughtered it, and Harriette decided to use it for the Christmas dinner. Somkhele was not in the gaol but confined in a nearby police homestead. Out of consideration, Harriette sent him a sympathetic message saying he had been excluded from the gift of meat only because he himself had said he feared that if he got too close to the lawyers he would injure himself with the authorities. She was expert by now at extracting concessions from them. She asked for permission to hold a Christmas service in the gaol, and in so doing gave the officials the choice of allowing the Usuthu to gather with their leaders, or appearing in the press as Scrooges or worse.

Paul Mthimkhulu had followed the young prince to Eshowe. The officials depicted him as a war doctor – combining Christian teaching and prayer with the dark barbarism of Zulu ritual. But the more Harriette discovered of Mthimkhulu and his prayers before the skirmish at Ceza and the attack at Ndumu, the more convinced she became that he was a force for moderation – urging the Usuthu not to kill women and children and to avoid gratuitous and uncontrolled violence. Here amongst the Usuthu there were perhaps signs of emerging Christian influence which did not do violence to African religious idiom and beliefs.

On Sunday 16 December, Mthimkhulu had gathered nearly 50 Zulu round him in the grove of gum trees which flanked Osuthu. Harriette noted how the service followed the liturgy of Morning Prayer, the importance that was given to the prayer for the Queen, and the selections he made for readings from the Bible. No one missed the significance of the story of Daniel saved from the lion's den, nor the three saved from the fiery furnace.

> Stress given with great effect. Finally an appeal to congregation if that was not the sort of help that we needed now. Unani now assents with uplifted finger. One Ndungemya adding that it was quite certain that we were in a fiery furnace here and a lion's den into the bargain, and that the help which got Daniel and the others out was the only help which would be of any use to us here – so we sang a hymn and broke up.[10]

It was Paul Mthimkhulu who ministered at the Christmas day service in the new gaol yard at Eshowe. Although the walls were now high enough to prevent any attempt at escape, the congregation was closely guarded by the Zulu police and they were not allowed to converse. But, wrote Harriette Colenso,

> even I was not prepared for the very obvious and genuine comfort and satisfaction that this little meeting and service afforded prisoners and witnesses,

for these too were allowed to take part. Paul took for his text Hebrews XI 1–6, and I fear that there were few present who did not promptly personify the 'mountains' which we hoped to see removed.[11]

Harriette felt she could not leave Eshowe – not even for Christmas. 'I do want to come home too, very much, but I think you would see that I can't, yet, if you could see the poor anxious faces here, reading mine daily, and having so little visible to trust to.'[12] But in her victories, and in the confidence she was creating around her, there were, her mother realised intuitively, dangers too:

> Well it does seem unwise to give one's heart away (so much of it) to those over whom one can have so little influence. Yet stay – when I think of the influence my 2 dear Daughters have over all the people of this country first as the children of Sobantu and then when they are known on their own account – there must be some meaning in it.[13]

Ndabuko kaMpande: 23 January – 9 March 1889[14]

Ndabuko's trial resumed on 23 January 1889. He continued to refuse to allow the court to appoint a lawyer on his behalf, or cross-examine the 52 witnesses called for the Crown. He sat silent in the dock except for the few occasions when he was provoked into an angry outburst: for example, when he protested at evidence being led on the murder and mutilation of the trader Klaas Louw.[15] 'I have nothing to say to all these lies which are spoken. What I wish to say is that we are very angry with those who have killed these storekeepers. Klaas was one of us, and, in killing him, they killed us.'[16] He also got involved in an altercation with Mnyamana's son Tshanibezwe, whom the officials had persuaded to give lengthy evidence for the Crown, hoping to prove treasonable intent in the Usuthu's dealing with the Boers. After Mansel had given his evidence, Ndabuko was again sufficiently angered to speak again: 'this disturbance', he said,

> was caused by the rulers whom the Government has put in this land, as it is their object to wipe out the Zulus. I, a leading man of the Zulus, have been forced into this disturbance; the guilt is on those who are backing up Zibhebhu. They have taken no notice of what Zibhebhu does and rather support him. I and my people have been driven into an awkward position. It is not I who fought against the Queen, it is not I who started the disturbance. This is a case which requires thorough investigation; my case is not ready, I am still wanting certain evidence. I am sorry for what has been done to the Zulus,

greatly grieved. I am grieved that the Queen wishes this case to be tried in a way which the people object to. I say that Dinuzulu is one who should not be brought into this matter; he is still a child; his matters are in the hands of others, I am in charge of them. That is all which I wish to say. I do not wish to put any questions to this witness. I finish with what I say.[17]

Harriette Colenso listened and watched from her place in the court. The evidence was rich and fascinating. Amongst the witnesses were some of Zululand's most important men. There were officials like Addison, John Osborn, Mansel, Zulu chiefs like Tshanibezwe, magistrates' indunas and policemen like Yamela and Vusindlu, storekeepers and traders. The defence team came to the opinion that there was no reason why even this mass of evidence should unduly disturb them. Enough was coming out which supported the line they were developing. The accused would be found guilty, but the evidence emerging in Ndabuko's case, even from the witnesses for the Crown, without cross-examination, confirmed the defence's case and should become part of the public inquiry that was needed to bring justice to Zululand.

Shingana kaMpande: 13 February – 9 March 1889[18]

Shingana was brought before the court on 13 February 1889. Dumat and R.C.A. Samuelson agreed to appear for him. Unlike the other accused, he had accepted the £5-a-month stipend and had been told that he would hang for this. Nothing that Harriette Colenso told him could rid him of his fear of the gallows. The Crown called 28 witnesses, messengers and policemen, but now that the accused was defended, none of the white administrators were called to give evidence and thereby risk cross-examination. Again, nothing in the evidence suggested any great mendacity on the part of Shingana, and under cross-examination Crown witnesses spoke frankly and openly, often to the discomfort of the very officials who had briefed them. It appeared that Zibhebhu, despite all the instructions and assurances to the contrary, had taken part in the official attack on Hlophekhulu, that the force had indulged freely in looting on the way, and that some of the captured women and children were still not released.

The defence called 42 witnesses to show that Shingana had retreated to Hlophekhulu to protect his people and that he had particular reasons to fear Zibhebhu because that chief felt Shingana was far 'too cunning'. From the point of view of the Zulu who had retreated with him to Hlophekhulu, the fighting of 30 June was a desperate attempt to defend their cattle, women and children against an official attack which killed over 200 people. The witnesses told of individual acts of violence by the police and by Zibhebhu. In spite of the objections of the prosecutor the defence managed to place on record evidence of the killing of Msushwana. It was particularly harrowing, with its description of the mutilation of his body when parts of his scalp and his genitals had been removed to make medicine. When the case closed on 9 March, the defence was satisfied that whatever verdict was passed, the evidence against the Zulu administration could not be ignored.

Dinuzulu kaCetshwayo: 14 March – 24 April 1889[19]

The status of Eshowe, as the developing administrative and judicial centre of British Zululand, meant that it had to have not only its gallows and a larger gaol, but also a hotel. It was completed while the trial was in progress. Harriette described it as 'the new Tin Hotel' – corrugated iron, divided internally with wooden walls. One of its first guests was Harry Escombe, just returned from London and who had come up from Durban to appear for the last of the Zulu leaders to be brought to trial, Dinuzulu kaCetshwayo.

The specific charges against the 19-year-old prince were of high treason, rebellion and public violence, and concerned the withdrawal to the stronghold at Ceza in May, the incident at Ceza on 2 June, the attack on Zibhebhu at Ndumu on 23 June, and responsibility for the general violence from May to July 1888. The attack at Ndumu was the obvious centrepiece of the prosecution's case but it also spent much time dealing with the events at Ceza on 2 June, including the allegation that Dinuzulu had murdered a boy at the time.

The Crown called 47 witnesses. The responsibility for establishing the basic narrative of events was given to Vusindlu and Yamela, the indunas attached to Addison's and Osborn's magistracies. With the exception of Mansel, the white officials were not put in the witness box: now that so much was known of their activities they did not dare face cross-examination under oath. A number of the witnesses belonged to Mnyamana's Buthelezi, who because of their proximity to Ceza had suffered particularly from stock losses at this time. Even here, however, it was hard to sustain personal charges against Dinuzulu: indeed evidence emerged of the attempts made by the Usuthu leadership to keep their followers under control and in some cases make reparations for stock losses. But although the Crown was unable to fix specific acts of violence on Dinuzulu, it did what it could to present evidence of acts of cruelty and violence, and associate them with him by implication.

Escombe used all his skills, and his authority, to expose the Zulu administration and its officials. He requested that official records be admitted as evidence, drew attention to the administration's ignorance of the law, cross-examined with vigour, weakening further the prosecutor's case. His impact on the court was obvious even to those who could not understand his language. As Dinuzulu said, 'Our people are always glad when Mr. Escombe is standing up and speaking. We do not know what he says, but when he speaks we see that everyone is listening and drawing in his legs.'[20]

Harriette Colenso was exhilarated by the energy, the commitment, the shared responsibility, that his participation brought to the defence team. Here at last the injustices and the indignities which she had known for so long were being placed on record: and the man doing this was one of Natal's most influential and eloquent public figures. The day after Dinuzulu's trial began she shared her excitement in letters to Bishopstowe, and to Frank in England. 'All well here,' she wrote, 'Mr Escombe and Dumat full of fight and confidence.' Where he had once been aggressive and dismissive, the attitude of the prosecutor was now deferential. Harriette enjoyed the contrast immensely. Above all, Harry Escombe was sharing the burdens which had been pressing on her for six years now, since the death of her father. 'Since Mr Escombe has been here I have been more at ease, more relieved of responsibility – helped in bearing it rather – than ever before, *since 1883.*'[21]

CHAPTER 21

A SORT OF PARADISE

'Watching and learning'

But this active involvement had its price, and not just a material one. Escombe was an ambitious man, and a politician, and his own plans began to influence Harriette from the very beginning of Dinuzulu's trial. She told her brother that

> Mr Escombe ... bids me call your special attention to the point that this is a *colonial defence of natives against officials, not a case in which the Home Government has been called on to protect the natives from the colonists.* Surely England will not hang back under such circumstances, or even support the wrong doers because officials, when the whole population white as well as black cries out against them?[1]

Harriette did what she could to persuade herself that this was indeed a colonial bid for justice against imperial abuses: she was not very convincing at the time,[2] her knowledge of the colonial abuse of power in Natal was too immediate, and her commitment to an ideal of English justice was too deep. But Escombe had sown the idea. It grew in time, with disastrous consequences.

Although Harriette found it hard to move from the moral high ground to the pragmatic plains where the political battles were fought, she did not doubt Escombe's ability. She admired the self-discipline with which he mastered his brief, and the energy with which he confronted his opponents – so much so that, she told her brother, it 'makes me love him'.[3]

> Just a line to tell you that in the midst of all these horrors it is really a more heavenly state of things than I ever expected to experience, after 1883 – This having two such men as Mr. Escombe and Mr. Dumat working heart and soul, almost day and night, at the Zulu trouble. Some good must come of it, and I

don't see why, as Mr. Escombe expects, all good should not, but for this we must all *work hard*, you at your end as we at this.[4]

For someone who had worked so long on her own it was exhilarating. As she told her mother, Escombe

> kept me all this morning giving him the course of events in Zululand *from 1879*. When I got to Dinuzulu after lunch and told him how it was that I had not come earlier, he quite agreed that it was worth doing without me ... I am working at a list of dates of the course of events ... another on Dinuzulu's own movement for the last 2 years (partly from Blue Books, partly from evidence given before this Court) and stopping whenever Mr. Escombe asks a question ... It is a sort of Paradise for me.[5]

But a male Paradise for all that – confident and comradely, into which she was allowed to enter for a few short weeks in March and April 1889. After the court had adjourned for the day, the defence went down to the gaol and then to Osuthu for tea and discussion of the day's events and to plan for the next. She wrote that this had become 'quite an institution ... the only wonder is that I don't indulge in a pipe as well – yet. It's wonderful what an amount of smoking seems required by lawyers.'

To be able to share the responsibility allowed her to relax. She experienced the relief immediately and physically.

> Well they are doing the thinking for me, and that is probably why I have no headaches, and only one or two faint suggestions of one all this time. Agnes asks about my finger aches, well my right hand and arm are pretty stiff by the end of a day's work ... but then there is always Mr. Burgess to fall back on, if I do miss a few lines, and my hand has not cramped yet.[6]

She was writing this letter in court and had to stop as proceedings began. That night she took up her pen again after leaving the Mansels' table early, waiting in the hotel, with keen anticipation, for Escombe and Dumat to finish their dinner and begin work. 'I am comfortably settled in my own corner' of Escombe's hotel room, she wrote to her mother and sister,

> and can hear the voices of my 'co-conspirators', and the rattle of their knives and forks in the next room (the walls are only wooden, and our last hours' work is generally smoothed by a neighbouring snore). When they come in we

shall either write letters for England or work up Vuzindlu's evidence, I'm not sure which. Two of our 3 Boers – 'Miss Colenso's Dutchmen' in Eshowe parlance – have turned up and the 3rd is expected with Henderson.

Escombe paid tribute to Harriette's intelligence, commitment, zeal and unselfishness. But one can only wonder how conscious he was of his capacity to please her: 'Mr Escombe has a way of saying the nicest things – that glow all through one ... that I remind him so of my Father in my ways – of walking and of shaking hands of course. I have been shy of doing it ever since because I like it so much. Ah! well here's the court.'[7]

She was 42 when she wrote this, a woman aglow at being told by a man that she was like her father: an expression of feeling difficult to reach and appreciate one hundred years and a sustained revolution in sexual politics later. It was made privately and disingenuously but is still disturbing in its suggestion of the strength of the paternal embrace reaching out even from the grave. Yet it is made historically complete by the final exclamation with which she ends her reverie and turns to the work at hand. For while we can recognise how the memory of her father restricted and confined her, we can also recognise how it underlay her achievements – her keen perception of the predicament of the other, her courage, her selflessness. Historians have drawn attention to the female communities which women have created and which have sustained their lives and their work.[8] Harriette Colenso belongs with them. At Bishopstowe, she and Agnes, their mother and Katie Giles, taught, counselled, healed, and monitored the newspapers and the courts, intervening when they could. Nonetheless the responsibility which fell on Harriette, and the loneliness implicit in that responsibility, were immense; for although she would not have recognised it in these terms, repression and exclusion as a woman working in an African cause were also part of Harriette's life experience.

When her father was alive his demands on her had alleviated this, for these were 'the days when my father and Mr. Chesson worked hand-in-hand for [the Zulu], and when I was privileged to watch and learn'.[9] Now at Eshowe, some of the responsibility was lifted and she was able to watch and learn once more. In Eshowe she was able to participate again in that wider world, an African world, a man's world, a professional world, and while she had the chance she took it eagerly. We can sense her exhilaration and excitement from that first day in November 1888 as she travelled towards Zululand, talking about the case and the courts with the lawyers. It is there in the controlled energy of her interventions to protect the accused and the witnesses from the effects of official cruelty. She felt it at Osuthu and in the smoke-filled rooms of the wood-and-iron hotel at Eshowe, planning legal strategies with her allies, associates, comrades, friends, be they Zulu from the northern districts, Africans who had grown up at Bishopstowe, or the men who had left their chambers in Durban to assist her.

It gave her the confidence to take on the officials, and to score important points not only for the defence, but also as a woman over men. Consider the way she wrote about an incident in early March, while Dinuzulu was being tried. Harriette had been called to Pietermaritzburg where her mother had been taken ill. A rumour had gone about that she had 'run away' – but, she wrote to her mother, the moment she returned she 'proved that I'd come back worse than ever'. It was immediately apparent to her that she 'was much wanted, to steady things generally'. Dinuzulu told her that one of the defence witnesses was closeted with the officials. Harriette marched to Osborn's stables, where she found the witness and the magistrate Knight in discussion. She demanded that the witness report to the defence immediately and left her assistant Mubi Nondenisa to escort him there: 'to break up his confab was wholesome for the whole party, I notice that the police raise their hands half as high again in greeting me this morning.'[10]

Women hardly figure in the accounts of the time: Harriette Colenso changed this. An increasing number of women came to see her, to tell their stories, to ask for help to find children captured by the Mandlakazi or the British levies, and to share in her courage and her example in facing up to the officials. Harriette took down some of their statements and persuaded them to give evidence of their experiences. They are harrowing in their direct evocation of what in the official reports are vague and abstract accounts of violence. The following evidence from one of these women was led in Dinuzulu's trial and eventually formed the basis for an intervention in the British House of Commons:

> Early next morning, an impi came and surrounded the kraal and then killed us, and killed my eldest daughter, and the child, born before this one, was killed: it was stabbed in the thigh and then it crawled, as its *mother* fell, from her back to the fire-place where we had been. I heard the impi cry, *wa checha*, nothing else ... As to Msushwana, he was shot: as to the men who shot him, they were men of the *Inyoni-Mhlope* regiment. I heard Msushwana, when he was shot, say, 'My father! here am I dying! what have I done?' ... The impi took away women and children: they said that I could remain; what was the good of taking one so old as I was? ... that child was between me and my eldest daughter, and an *insizwa* came up, and said, 'What are you looking at?', and stabbed it.[11]

Harriette Colenso's reputation as a healer also grew while she was at Eshowe.

Some of the illnesses for which she received requests for medicine were well known to her, as was their treatment. Many others were not part of her medicinal experience and indeed outside conventional Western medical practice. She nonetheless accepted that they were genuinely held by her patients and that they suffered from them. Thus, she took seriously the predicament of the man who, dangerously ill because of his failure to carry out the purification rituals after killing at Ndumu, was cured by quinine and the effect of Harriette Colenso taking his pulse. Another patient discovered the extraordinary healing powers of her thermometer which, placed in his armpit, went 'straight to the spot'. She was pleased when she was told that although Zibhebhu's doctors had been brought down from the north to spread damaging medicine amongst the defence, they did not work. They found 'that something ... seems to stand in the way of their medicines and make them harmless'. But she remained concerned about the effects of such medicine on her friends, for it was 'a fear on the part of our poor prisoners, which I have to meet and fight the best way I can, however much one may smile at some features of it'.[12]

In Eshowe in 1888 and 1889, while the work of the Court of Special Commissioners was proceeding, and especially in March and April 1889 when Harry Escombe led the defence, others shared responsibility for the Zulu cause for a moment. In the years to come, in times of disappointment, the memories of what they had achieved in Eshowe in 1888 and 1889 remained an inspiration to her.

The struggle for authority

However, the situation for the Usuthu remained very serious. For the officials, London's insistence that justice be seen to be done in Zululand had been unscrupulously and dangerously exploited by the defence. Every incident that lifted Usuthu morale lowered that of the authorities. This provoked the officials into making counter-demonstrations to assert their own authority, which they felt was being reduced in the eyes of the natives. But they had to be careful how they did this, with Harriette Colenso listening carefully to Eshowe gossip, be it at the dinner table of the commandant of the Zululand Police, the ladies' tennis club, or when consulting with the Usuthu.

Tension had been increasing in the town since the trial had begun five months previously. Dinuzulu's own trial had lasted for over a month. Eshowe was filled with people, many of whom had been fighting a civil war for nearly a decade. Every effort was made to assert official power visibly during the trials. The Zululand Police were present inside and outside the court, with their bayonets fixed, according to the defence lawyers' protest. The defence team, with its few hundred witnesses, visitors and supporters gathered around Osuthu, looked angrily at the bayonets of the parading Nongqayi. They resented the presence of the men from Natal, official favourites, indunas, messengers, now being set up as chiefs and bringing their followers to settle in Zululand. They objected to the men who had proved their loyalty to the administration by raiding and burning Usuthu homesteads, and to the Zululand Police who roughed them up, broke their beer pots, maltreated their wives and children. Then there were the Zulu chiefs who had sided with the government, the most notorious of whom was Zibhebhu, the prime cause of a decade of horror, who, though charged with the murder of Msushwana, still rode his horse around Eshowe and joined in official processions.

The Usuthu, it was said, taunted and threatened those who were not on their side. They wore the symbols of the Usuthu openly and in defiance of authority: the *shokobezi*, the white cow tail; and as one of Shepstone's loyal chiefs pointed out, Dinuzulu was wearing the *iziqu*, the wooden beads to denote bravery, worn by those who had killed in battle.[13] Havelock put together a dispatch listing a series of complaints about Usuthu boasts of the imminent restoration to power of Dinuzulu and the Zulu royal house. Arthur Shepstone put his own fears into the mouths of the loyal chiefs of the Nkandla district. After experiencing the consequences of ten years' 'leniency, indecision, and weakness of the British Government', it seemed to them that the Usuthu's 'European supporters ... appeared to be too strong for the Government'.[14]

All sides were worried about the rising tension in Eshowe as the time for the verdict drew closer. On Monday 22 April 1889, Escombe called a meeting with the Usuthu, and it was attended by such important leaders as Hlomuza the brother of Zibhebhu; Ndabankulu kaLukwazi of the Ntombela; and Manku-lumana of the Ndwandwe. They had long been prepared for an adverse verdict. But they were hoping, in time, for a review of the sentences and perhaps a pardon. Whatever happened, Escombe told them, they must keep order.

There can be no doubt that the defence was genuinely concerned to do what it could to reduce the chance of Usuthu violence and that Escombe was making the speech in that light. At the same time it is clear that he also wanted to impress upon the Secretary of State that he was not just the ally of a well-intentioned but perhaps over-enthusiastic female agitator, but also a responsible and sober worker in the cause of stability in Her Majesty's possessions.

The Usuthu leaders were grateful for his words, but not that impressed. As Somcuba put it, '[We] thank you for telling us beforehand what is the kind of death by which we are to die.' Mankulumana thanked Escombe for what he had done, and said that he would not be surprised at an adverse verdict. 'For we were

289

already aware of what you had said and of what Miss Colenso had said that we were not to be surprised if the sky thundered for us. We have long been holding ourselves ready for that, and taking hold of our courage for it, knowing well for ourselves that there was no case which could ever end in our favour here.' But they feared the future. They had come to Eshowe, leaving their people on the hills, exposed, without land on which to build. 'This persecution is consuming us. We are made to pay taxes, and our cattle are eaten up on that account before we have any huts set up: we are still people carrying bundles, without huts, and we have to pay hut tax.'

Escombe promised to see what he could do about their problems. But he had little to offer in fact beyond the clichés of the time: 'What can be done shall be done, as far as I am concerned. They must remember two things, however; one is that there is a limit to my power – I can only represent. But there is no limit to the love which Englishmen have for fair play.' Imperial banality, no doubt. But he had used his legal expertise on their behalf and the Usuthu understood this. Mankulumana, already showing the diplomatic skills which made him a worthy successor to Mnyamana kaNgqengelele of the Buthelezi as the foremost political figure amongst the Zulu, apologised for subjecting Escombe to their complaints and their fears: 'Friends, it is time that we should cease. We are drawn on by the relief of being able to speak to you, so that we go over all the words that are most bitter to us.'[15]

The verdict

The Crown closed its case on 23 April and Escombe began his speech for the defence, which lasted the rest of the day and continued into the next. After much legal argument, he gave an outline of Zulu history before turning to the annexation, and analysing the various incidents which formed the specific charges against Dinuzulu. There had been no treason in Zululand. The accused had been provoked into defending themselves from the consequences of the destruction of their system of government in 1879 by an imperial government, and the subsequent abuses of a colonial administration. He closed by saying that

> The work has not been an easy one; I cannot say that it has not been in a
> great degree distasteful. I have had to do things I did not like; I have had to
> say things which perhaps I should have left unsaid. But I hope Your Lordship
> will give me credit for this – that my sole effort has been absolutely to vindi-
> cate the law in its fullest meaning ... we claim to have proved that the distur-
> bances are referable to a set of circumstances totally inconsistent with treason

and perfectly consistent with another cause. My Lords, we may fail, for all we know we may fail entirely. But even in that case this work will not have been thrown away, because it has enabled us to bring some light, though not full light, upon recent events in Zululand ... We believe it will answer the purpose of the Crown ... that it will enable the authorities better to understand the circumstances and the conditions of the people; and we who are taking part in the defence hope to find our reward in a more contented country – a happier Zululand.[16]

Harriette Colenso found it 'a grand speech, which under any other circumstances one would have enjoyed listening to – nay – I enjoyed it intensely, as it was. It was directed to people in England rather than these precious judges ...'[17]

On the day he left Eshowe, Escombe wrote to Harriette's mother:

> Your daughter has prepared the way for happier days in Zululand by work and sacrifice without a parallel in my knowledge of women.
>
> At my request she will yet stay so as to let the Zulus think that they have a true friend still at hand.[18]

Escombe did not wait for the verdict, and left immediately for Durban. There he sat down and wrote to the liberal Cape politician John X. Merriman:

> I am now clear of Zululand except as regards a letter home. I made a promise in an unguarded moment that if the Zulus would lay down their arms I would stand by them.
>
> Being a promise to savages I could not get a release from it – it has cost me in money £1000 in time many months, and yet I am not sorry that I became involved; I have got a better knowledge of Native affairs than was possible if I had not got the full confidence of the headmen.[19]

The difference in tone and intent of these letters written within days of one another is stark and striking. For the moment these differences were not revealed to Harriette Colenso. In time they would be forced upon her.

The sentence and the prayer

On 27 April in Eshowe, at nine in the morning, a troop of Scots Guards left their camp for the gaol where the Usuthu prisoners were under guard and marched the few kilometres to the courthouse. Harriette was already at Osuthu to make sure that only the *izinduna* went up to the court and watched it all. 'I was at Osuthu early', she wrote to her mother,

> turning back the Usuthu, and the band (drums and fifes) was then screaming and banging away over at the camp. I tried hard to believe that it had nothing to do with us, and was *not coming our way*. It presently came, close behind the trees, and stopped in front of the Court house out of our sight, while one company of foot soldiers marched past us up towards the gaol, then Mnyamana's and Zibhebhu's men went streaming by – then came from the gaol the procession of civil police, some 20, with assegais and knobkerries and an occasional gun and after a pause the whole force of Nongqayi, then the prisoners, our three and Somkhele's 4 boys, the soldiers following them, Mr Mansel and two or three mounted Nongqayi on the right hand ... and on the other Yamela, *Zibhebhu* ... and two or three other mounted men. Mr. Mansel kept hailing them all, and presently rode up to Mr. Dumat and me to ask for a 'tot' for Ndabuko, who was feeling ill. We might not go to speak to him, but might send it by one of Ndabuko's men, so I duly tasted the brandy and sent it by Mankulumana. He only took about a table spoon, and tells me today that it was cramp – they have kept him sitting still for the last 3 months and now expected him to walk a mile.

They were taken individually into the court room to hear the sentences. Ndabuko: guilty of high treason and sentenced to 15 years. Harriette was relieved. It wasn't the death sentence – perhaps passed as an act of intimidation, for Havelock, 'that little wretch, to "commute."' And high treason could be challenged outright – public violence would have to have been met with a plea in mitigation as 'we all admit to one another, that we were not very quiet that day at Ndumu'. Shingana: 12 years for high treason. Harriette 'began to breathe again ... His 12 years poor fellow, showed that we had been right to pooh-pooh his terrible bugbear, the fact of having accepted the pensions for which he had been freely promised hanging.' The murder charge against Dinuzulu was dropped: he got 10 years for high treason. 'They all behaved beautifully, quietly and with dignity, the dear lad giving his little head a half involuntarily shake, when it was assailed by all those cruel falsehoods.'[20]

They were marched back under escort, but not now to their tents. Although the sentences still had to be reviewed in London, they were now to be held in the cells. Their tents were pulled down and all their possessions were delivered to Osuthu, with the order that the camp had to be vacated and all the Zulu living there should leave immediately for their homes.

On Sunday 29 April, Harriette called the Usuthu for a final meeting. All told, 472 Zulu formed a circle around her. She thanked them for keeping away from the court on the previous day – it showed a mutual trust that she hoped would last in the difficult times ahead. There was nothing new to tell them about the verdict; it was what they had expected. She hoped they would now leave Eshowe (knowing that many of them had nowhere to live, she deliberately avoided the phrase 'go home'). This would enable her to concentrate on the important work still to be done for their leaders.

Paul Mthimkhulu was ill and unable to hold the usual Usuthu Sunday service. Harriette took his place, assisted by Magema Fuze, Mubi Nondenisa and R.C.A. Samuelson, who as a Zulu speaker with pretensions to the law, had been helping the defence. Harriette was worried that her voice would not reach everyone, but with the three men leading the responses the service went well. It was a suitable ending to the trials, a farewell undertaken in a mood of sadness but in the belief that something had been achieved at Eshowe which could be built on for the future. She had composed a prayer for the occasion:

Almighty God, Creator of mankind, Who hast made the heavens together with the earth, Who despisest nothing that Thou hast made; we, Thine unhappy Zulu people, cry to Thee for the great misery which is upon us to-day.

We lament for our people, homeless and scattered on the hill-side; we lament for our families, for our little ones who are wandering, hungry; and especially we lament for those the children of our Chiefs, whom we are leaving here in bonds and in misery, being condemned for matters said to be heavy, while we are driven away like wild animals.

We have no skill of books to help ourselves therewith, neither have we power to protect ourselves in any way. For us, darkness has come over us. Help us, O! our Father, for Thine eye is over all things, seeing the deeds of men and their hearts. Thou knowest our heart therefore, and the hearts of our Chiefs, that we do reverence the English rule. Thou knowest both our sins, and wherein we have not sinned, and also those things in which we have been wronged. We say, be Thou our witness.

Help us in this present trouble, and give these prisoners courage to endure for our sakes, who love them. And to us give the heart to restrain ourselves under all the wrongs done to us.

O Thou who hast all light, and all knowledge, enlighten us. Show forth to us Thy kindness in the midst of this darkness. We beseech Thee to help us, and protect Thy servant Victoria, our Queen, enlighten her that she may see the truth in this our matter, and may right it, that under her we may be goodly and quietly governed. And grant to all those in authority under her, that they may truly and indifferently minister justice to the overthrow of all wickedness and the increase of Thy worship and virtue. Amen.[21]

This is Harriette's translation, and it is worth reading with some care so as to reach beyond the surface of religious and royalist sentiments, to its human and political content, in order to imagine how the words sounded in Zulu to the 500 Zulu gathered around her. Harriette's prayer is a most fitting ending to the ten years of civil war in Zululand – a civil war brought about by the determination of colonial officials, inspired and supported by the person and policy of Theophilus Shepstone, to terminate the power of his greatest rivals, the descendants of Shaka, the Zulu kings; a civil war by which the Zulu themselves did the work that the British army and its colonial allies had failed to do in 1879. It is a prayer to a monarch and a god in whose names the independence of the congregation had been violently crushed. And yet it is in this prayer perhaps that we get closest to their feelings of loss.

The Usuthu prayer marks the end of an important stage in Zulu history. The invasion of 1879 removed the centralised political authority but left in place many of those Zulu with political power. This was undermined in the civil war and destroyed in Zibhebhu's attack on Ulundi in July 1883. With the political strength gone, it was possible to undermine the country's economic independence by the seizure of land, imposition of hut tax, and the recognition of limited local political authority of those African leaders – chiefs – pledged to recognise absolute white administrative supremacy. The Usuthu resisted this, in the Reserve in 1884, and then in the rest of the country in 1888. Now this had come to an end. The 500 Zulu around Harriette Colenso were the last gathering of the representatives of Usuthu resistance.

There were, however, two Zulu leaders who had not submitted to the new colonial authority, Somopho and Bhejana. They were both old men, who in the days of Zulu independence had publicly berated Theophilus Shepstone and then years later, in 1887, been gaoled by his son Arthur, and who were now hiding in the forest and swamps of Dukuduku, unwilling to experience the Eshowe gaol again. But in February 1890 even these two last resisters came out of the swamp and gave themselves up. They spent the rest of the year detained at Eshowe and were brought before the High Court of Zululand in 1891. Somopho's 'old age and feeble state' were taken into account, and he was sentenced to two years' imprisonment. Bhejana was given three. The Acting Resident Commissioner reminded Governor Mitchell that the President of the High Court recommended clemency when the sentence came under review.

From Pietermaritzburg, Mitchell was not sympathetic: given the crime, the sentences in his opinion were 'very light'.[22] They served as a warning: it was not wise to cross the House of Sonzica.

Defeat

The political defeats were also reflected in the material history of the past decade. The reference in the prayer to 'our people, homeless and scattered on the hill-side; our families, for our little ones who are wandering, hungry' is more than sentimental rhetoric: it was a reflection of the reality of a fundamental shift in Zulu life which went way beyond the immediate consequences of the violence of 1888. For during the 1880s, while the Zulu were struggling for and against one another and their conquerors, revolutionary changes due to the opening of goldfields in the Transvaal had been taking place in southern Africa as a whole. The surge this created in the development of the regional economy created a massive demand for cheap labour – African labour. Whatever the specific differences amongst the authorities, colonial or imperial, they were united in the opinion that the solution to all difficulties in Zululand lay in one direction – that of wage labour, by Zulu men, in the expanding southern African economy.

In July 1889 Sir Charles Mitchell visited Zululand and reported favourably on the progress that was already being shown. The road to Eshowe, the public buildings, were all improved. The Zululand Police were smart and efficient under Mansel's fierce discipline. Above all, £20,000 of the hut tax had been collected, already twice the sum that had been collected in the previous year. At the same time, from the same place, Harriette Colenso looked at Zululand and saw it very differently. She wrote to her brother of a conversation she had just had with Mansel, who had been hunting in the Mhlatuze valley near the coast.

> Mr Mansel said to me yesterday. 'I don't know what the people are doing there, they have got no mealies.'
> I said 'they are doing without – can't you see it by the holes in their faces?'
> These are the people belonging to the poor old coast chiefs ...
> It was then remarked 'Could they not go out to work, that people in Natal want labour?'
> But the old men and women and babies and sick people can't do this, and for a young man to do so means that he must leave all such for at least 6 months without any communication being possible, without their knowing if he is dead or alive.
> Many have done this, but if they have spent none of their wages they can

only bring back from 10/- to 20/- for each month, and 14/- a hut or in terms of the law 'that is to say a wife' is now being wrung out of them in taxes.

And you will presently be assured that the condition of the country is satisfactory, and the people paying their taxes freely and willingly.[23]

In the years to come Harriette Colenso's protests were to be met time and again with statements on the new-found prosperity of British Zululand and the satisfaction of the bulk of the Zulu people with their situation. By 1893 the imperial loan raised to set up the administration had been repaid, together with the costs of the Court of Special Commissioners, and a surplus of £20,000 had been invested. For officials in London there could be no greater achievement. No matter what sins, crimes or stupidities had been inflicted on the Zulu by the local officials, a surplus on the books outweighed them all.[24]

Labour migrancy, that overriding theme which marks the contours of South African history and moulds the private and social character of so many of its institutions and personalities, began in earnest in Zululand in 1889, and signals a substantial, irreversible change in its people's history.[25] But Harriette Colenso's letter shows that she, unlike so many commentators on South Africa then, and for a century to come, saw that labour migrancy was not just an opportunity to share in the opportunities of capitalist development, but also a social catastrophe. She was already able to perceive something of its human consequences. She was becoming aware of the human cost of balancing the imperial books.

The successful imposition of the hut tax and the beginning of widespread labour migrancy in 1889 mark the essential breach with the old order that Garnet Wolseley had trumpeted ten years before in his attempt to convince the world that the British army had defeated the Zulu. Much of Zululand, the independent kingdom, the chieftaincies within it, the autonomous homesteads within the kingdom, were now gone, and the labour of Zululand's young men was forced to become part of the wider capitalist network spreading over the subcontinent.

The verdicts of the Court of Special Commissioners mark the end of a stage of Harriette Colenso's struggle for the Zulu, and for the name Colenso as a tribune for freedom and justice in southern Africa. It was a great fight, with substantial victories. It has left in the historical record an alternative account of the history of KwaZulu-Natal and a record of an African voice at a time when every attempt was being made by the colonial authorities to appropriate and control it. It may well have saved the leadership of the Zulu royal house from the gallows and certainly saved numbers of their followers. It also enabled the Zulu royal house to continue its efforts to ensure that it remained a factor in South African history and South African politics when there were powerful forces attempting its eclipse.

At the same time there were many defeats. Tens of thousands had died; the ranks of traditional chiefs had been decimated; land had been lost and divided; political authority lay with outsiders, dominated by the interests of the neighbouring colony of Natal. Most important of all, the foundations of the independent Zulu economy had gone, and it was now in the process of becoming a subordinated, vulnerable part of a new, ruthless, expanding capitalism.

And it was this which so weakened Harriette Colenso as she entered the next stage of the long struggle for justice in South Africa. She fought in the name of the Zulu royal house, which she believed, rightly in so far as it represented social continuity, had the support of the majority of people in Zululand. However, the economic underpinning upon which that ruling house depended had, by 1888, been destroyed. It was now an adjunct to the developing capitalist economy in South Africa, which in turn was part of the growing world imperial network. The Zulu royal house had survived, and she had played a part in its survival, but materially it had been disastrously weakened. Its hold on the Zulu people was rooted in emotion, in ideology, in its history. This was strong and often effective. But it was not, and could not be, strong enough to combat effectively the forces ranged against it. Nonetheless, for many years to come, it absorbed the political and moral energy of its supporters as they attempted to restore to the heirs of Shaka kaSenzangakhona their lost prestige and autonomy.

CHAPTER 22

AS IRREPRESSIBLE AS EVER

The spirit of our dream

Two months after Harriette Colenso read her prayer at the Usuthu service in Eshowe on 29 April 1889, it was published in London. It was part of an article she wrote for the *Women's Penny Paper: The Only Paper Conducted, Written, Printed and Published by Women.* For some months now, the paper had been following her activities on behalf of the Zulu, 'who were apparently happy until we took them under our "Protection." Perhaps the Zulu are like women, who begin to find out that protection, when it does not mean self-protection, is a more than doubtful boon.'[1] Harriette followed this up with a series of articles on the trials at Eshowe of her own, her first piece of extended writing to be published. She wrote to her brother Frank for copies – after all, 'a fellow does like to see how a thing looks in print!'[2]

Harriette might well have treated the idea of a woman journalist with a touch of irony. But the *Women's Penny Paper* introduced her name to a number of liberal and radical women working actively in public causes – in particular in areas of local government where they had some freedom – whose significance in the broader movement of English history has been convincingly established.[3] Their interest and support for Harriette Colenso were to become of great importance to her. Even before the death of her father and of Chesson, the links between Bishopstowe and sympathetic humanitarian and radical personalities and groups in England had weakened. It was necessary that such links be built up again if the inquiry into Zulu affairs, which was now the prime objective of the Usuthu's supporters, was to be established.

But she knew very little about potential allies in Britain, and left it to Frank Colenso to find them. He had made contact with Dr G.B. Clarke, the radical pro-Boer MP for Caithness, who, together with Thomas Ellis, the Welsh nationalist, was prepared to put questions on Zulu matters in the House of Commons. From Eshowe, Harriette wrote detailed letters to Charles Hancock, which he used as a basis for the letters of protest he managed to place in sympathetic English newspapers. When Henry Fox Bourne became secretary of the APS, he took over Hancock's position and made contact with Harriette, promising to do what he could for the Usuthu cause.

Fox Bourne took up the appointment in January 1889. He was a talented author and radical journalist, and Harriette replied to his first letter, saying that she was 'indeed thankful to know that our dear Mr Chesson's work is to be continued in his spirit and avail myself at once of your permission to "use" you "as we used him" though I think I should have done so in any case on the one word "scandalous" applied by you to these Zulu "trials."' She felt that they had done all they could in South Africa, 'and it now rests with you in England, whether or no such convictions so obtained, be allowed to stand, to England's disgrace, and assuredly to throw back ... Christianity and civilization among the native tribes of South Africa for years'.[4]

They had to find more allies. By this time Frank could describe Walter McLaren as an 'amiable friend'.[5] He was a prominent Liberal MP and wealthy businessman, a supporter of women's causes, once married to John Bright's sister and now to Eva Muller, whose sister Henrietta was the founder and editor of the *Women's Penny Paper*. Harriette thought back on the men who had given them support when their father was alive. The eminent man of letters J.A. Froude was a long shot but Harriette tried it.

Leonard Courtney, now a Privy Councillor, 'used to be uSuthu somewhat' and she felt he might be one still. She had had some hope in Joseph Chamberlain who had once made a statement in the House which she saw as favourable to the Usuthu chiefs. In a letter to Frank Colenso, Chamberlain wrote with the voice of political experience. He said that he would do what he could

> to secure justice and consideration for the Chiefs of Zululand. But I am not willing to condemn the officials of Her Majesty's Government on *ex parte* statements in a matter of this kind however influentially and honorably supported. My experience convinces me that in a matter of this kind which does not involve party interests, the only way of benefiting the objects of our sympathy is by friendly representations not by accusations against the authorities. The Government Department is bound to defend its servants, and can always do so successfully in ordinary times.'[6]

'Representations not accusations': it was advice that the Colensos could perhaps have pondered upon.

Harriette continued to write for the *Women's Penny Paper* from Eshowe. She

had no journalistic experience, of course, and her articles show this. It is interesting to see how someone whose personal letters are so immediate, conveying
their meaning with accuracy, humanity and humour, whose knowledge of recent
history was so sure, found it so difficult to communicate this, at this early stage
at least, in her public writings. She weighed her argument down, smothering it
in detail, notes and cross-references. Her articles in the *Women's Penny Paper*
became an impenetrable history of Zululand since the invasion, and had still to
reach the topic announced in their title when she abandoned the series. Perhaps
it was the influence of her father's biblical criticism during her formative years
which lay behind her penchant for quoting and assessing her sources, to the
detriment of the onward flow of her argument. Part of the problem, however, lies
in the nature of Zulu history in the 1880s. As Frances Colenso found in *The Ruin
of Zululand*, and historians subsequently, the contradictory perspectives of the
sources, colonial and African, make it extremely difficult to construct a unified
narrative, and the fact that these sources themselves became part of the struggle
disrupts attempts at synthesis.

The edition of the *Women's Penny Paper* in which the Usuthu prayer was published also reviewed Ibsen's *A Doll's House*. Nora's predicament was compared
with that of Lyndall in Olive Schreiner's *Story of an African Farm*, the reviewer
noting that in both Nora's and Lyndall's case, 'the financial or economic independence of woman underlies her higher moral development; she can never be
free, in the fullest, finest meaning of that word, whilst she is in financial, slavish
dependence upon man'. One can only wonder whether Harriette Colenso's eye
fell on this passage and if she applied it to her own predicament. The costs had
already been heavy. There were her own expenses in Eshowe: her horse, messengers, interpreters, gifts to the prisoners, and the medicines which she was
continually asked to dispense. There had been legal costs in obtaining permission to make use of their father's legacy, and there were the wages of the five
African men from Bishopstowe who had accompanied her and formed part of her
team. Her brothers could not assist. Robert, from Johannesburg, had managed to
extract another £50 from his mother at the very moment when the trials were
coming to a close, forcing Harriette to intervene at a time when her energies
needed to be concentrated at Eshowe. All in all, she felt she had spent something over £3000 on the Zulu defence. Any future political and legal actions
would cost even more. A substantial part of the material legacy from their father
had been spent in pursuit of the moral and political one.

Everything depended on the appeal to the Judicial Committee of the Privy
Council. She did not, after her experiences through the 1880s, have much faith
in the Colonial Office, even if parliamentary and extra-parliamentary pressure

could be brought to bear on it. The APS was an important ally but it was too vulnerable to Tory and Colonial Office influence. The law, she felt, was a more dependable instrument. A favourable decision of the highest court of the Empire, one which exposed the illegality of the actions and policies of the present Zulu administration, would form the basis of a political appeal not only to free the Usuthu leaders, but also for a system of government in Zululand which recognised the claims of the Zulu royal house.

Harriette recommended that a Zulu Defence Committee be set up in London for the collection of funds to apply for the right to appeal to the Judicial Committee. Frank Dumat was on his way to London to brief counsel. Harriette left Fox Bourne and her brother in London to raise the funds by recruiting people who 'recognize a duty in politics beyond and above that of party'[7] and to work out a basis for an effective appeal:

> That was my ultimate trust in urging them to surrender. How strong in law as
> well as justice their case would prove and *could be proved* was the point on
> which we had to struggle here. It has been proved now almost beyond all my
> hopes, to the entire satisfaction of Mr. Escombe as lawyer and politician, and
> all that remains is to take the final step of laying our case before the Privy
> Council.

Frank Colenso and Dumat briefed Sir Horace Davey, a considerable legal and political figure, who had been briefly a member of Gladstone's ministry in 1886. He was, however, 'unavoidably' unable to attend the hearing, and Sir John Rigby QC, also a formidable lawyer, appeared instead. He argued the case on legal grounds: that in bringing the prisoners before the Court of Special Commissioners which he had constituted, Havelock had removed the accused from the general laws of Zululand, thereby discriminating against them unfairly and illegally. Lord Halsbury, the Lord Chancellor, known for his support of reactionary causes and who had been counsel for the notorious Governor Eyre, refused to grant permission to appeal. 'Nothing', he said,

> could be more destructive of the administration of criminal justice than a sort
> of notion that any criminal case which was tried in any one of our Colonies
> from which an appeal lies to this Committee can be brought here upon
> appeal, not upon broad grounds of some departure from the principles of nat-
> ural justice, but because some form or technicality had not been sufficiently
> observed. That is a principle which I believe never has been permitted, and
> never I trust will be permitted.[8]

For the Usuthu, for the Colensos, it was a catastrophic decision. One can only wonder at the quality of Dumat and Frank Colenso's briefings, and the decision to use legal arguments, when there was such a wealth of evidence to support an argument based on just the grounds the Lord Chancellor spoke of: 'some departure from the principles of natural justice'. There were suggestions that the case was 'rushed'. Frank Colenso does seem to have been overconfident. He was certainly crushed by the outcome: 'At times I can hardly believe that the whole affair of Tuesday was not an ugly dream', he wrote to Harriette, and he hoped that she would have the strength to deal with the decision, which closed off the fundamental objective upon which she had based her intervention on behalf of the Usuthu.

For Frank, 'A complete change has come over the spirit of our dream.'[9] Harriette, made of sterner stuff, hid her feelings and adopted an ironic colonial bravado: 'We here never had much faith in Lord Halsbury – and out here we never had one of our lawyers doing badly.'[10]

'Insane, and likely to get hanged'

With the trials over, the Zululand officials had hoped they could get on with the business of setting up the administration without the continual interference and agitation of the Usuthu defence. The last lawyer left Eshowe on 1 May. Immediately, the Zululand Police moved into Osuthu, removed the tents and pulled down the shelters. Only the hut which Dumat had built as a temporary shelter for himself and his wife remained standing.

For Harriette Colenso it was just another act of intimidation – unnecessary and uncalled for, a warning to the Usuthu. What particularly annoyed her was that she felt so badly compromised. She had tried hard to co-operate with official Eshowe. She could do so no longer. If she had to choose, she would choose the Usuthu. She left the Mansels and moved to Osuthu into Dumat's hut.

> I had tried to do my duty to society at Eshowe, and now society had returned the compliment by pulling down my tents. Well that decided me, and I told the Mansels that I did not think it right to leave my people alone with so many wild (civil) police about, so now I am *established* here, have made my bed, and bought candles and matches. Mrs Dumat has left all sorts of household necessaries, and luxuries, about 10 blankets, a lock up cupboard, an easy chair – even some cigarettes!

Harriette Colenso took the hut over. From now it was her base – and her occupation of it the symbol that the Usuthu struggle was not over.

It was in this spirit that she entered her next few months in Eshowe. It was often a distressing experience, made exhilarating at times by her victories. There was much unfinished business. Although the Usuthu leaders had been sentenced and the conditions of their detention made more rigorous, their sentences were not to be implemented until the British government had studied the evidence now on its way to England. Until the sentences were confirmed in London, Harriette believed she had to remain 'on guard' against any vindictive acts of the local officials. She also did what she could to ensure that Ndabuko, Shingana and Dinuzulu's detention was made as bearable as possible.

Her presence was a continuing annoyance to the authorities. For Melmoth Osborn it was an affront to have her in Eshowe watching and reporting, especially when she attended his courts. But they still had to treat her carefully. The investigation into the murder of Msushwana was not yet completed. And there were still Zulu facing the death penalty for specific offences during 1888. Harriette attended these trials, which were presided over by Osborn as Chief Magistrate, with Arthur Shepstone and Knight as assessors.

Later she wrote up these cases, either as a plea for pardon or in mitigation against the severity of the sentences.[11] The administration hoped to prove that there had been an Usuthu conspiracy to kill whites during the disturbances. But in order to sustain the charges, the prosecution used as witnesses men who had themselves admitted to having killed during the disturbances. Harriette argued that any competent defence would have successfully demonstrated the inadequacy of the witnesses used by the Crown to secure its prosecutions. But for Fairfield in the Colonial Office, her defence of some of these men was 'strong evidence of Miss Colenso's unreasoning fanaticism'.[12]

She was also needed in Natal. Her mother had been taken ill. She had to consult with Escombe about the legal future of the Usuthu, and about her own financial situation, which she treated with grim humour: her lawyer

> discovered that to use our money for the Zulus legally, the Trustees (S.F.C. and H.E.C.) must lend it to me on security, to afford which I have got to insure my life. I am going by Mr. Mason's advice, to do it in the Star – an office which allows the object of an assigned policy to die without injury to the policy either 'by suicide or at the hands of justice'. Rather a neat way I think, on Mr. Mason's part of recording an opinion that I am already insane, and likely to get hanged before I'm done with it![13]

The prisoners were most disturbed by her absences from Eshowe. Her parting meal was a gift of beef from Dinuzulu himself, 'bless him'. Women in the neighbourhood had supplied the 'delicious tshwala', though she also had a bottle of whisky to compensate for the absence of the sherry which she had enjoyed while staying with the Mansels. But there was no question now of her staying long in Natal. She was needed even more in Eshowe: 'I have said goodbye to our poor friends in gaol for 12 *days*, they say that they can't *think* of being longer left alone!'[14]

It was on one of her visits to Natal that she received a letter from Magema Fuze in Eshowe, with the news that investigation into the charge against Zibhebhu for the murder of Msushwana was completed – and that he had been released, 'whereat his people are all rejoicing over the uSuthu'. But Zibhebhu was not allowed to go back to his home in the north. His behaviour on the previous occasion made it far too risky, and Harriette did not allow the British officials to forget what happened then. The object of her attacks was the officials who had so used Zibhebhu, rather than the man himself.

Havelock was away from Natal on leave, but few people believed he would return. He was replaced temporarily by Sir Charles Mitchell, who was not sympathetic to the many requests forwarded to him by Harriette. But she was now getting expert at applying pressure on the officials, and extracting concessions. She brought her nephew Eric – 'Nondela' – with her to Eshowe, and he and Dinuzulu became friends and gave one another gifts – it was an unequal exchange, sweets for the one and a calf for the other. She obtained permission to teach the prisoners to read and write, and when she left Eshowe her place was taken by Magema Fuze. Dinuzulu of course learnt faster than Ndabuko and Shingana; by June 'Dinuzulu knows up to "ma" well, and his uncles both think that they can manage that page in less than a month.'[15] Five years before, the two older men had been members of the delegation which had dictated the message vesting the succession to the Zulu throne in the younger one. They were now able to gain another perspective on the formidable power of writing. 'Ndabuko remarked today, on my saying that I must go back to my writing, that he verily believes that when a person once really takes to writing it takes possession of him and he can't stop but must write write write always ...'[16]

She got some satisfaction in observing her effect on the officials. Castle, the Eshowe gaoler, found himself caught between Harriette's demands and the orders of his superiors:

> There's no use in being shy in these circumstances and perhaps the very novelty of being flown at may strike him as an interesting phenomenon in human nature. Castle says 'I don't know how you do it, unless you mean to frighten

everybody here, you never come but I get into hot water for something or other', 'and I'm coming every day, I promise you' said I and on the whole he grins and bears it well.[17]

While in Eshowe, Harriette was able to extend her knowledge of the people of Zululand, getting to know them personally, getting the details of their suffering during the civil war, details which had never reached the Blue Books. What worried her particularly were the many stories of women and children who had been captured by both sides.

The cases were often difficult and tested her diplomatic capacities to the full. Take, for example, the little girl belonging to the Mandlakazi who had been captured by the Usuthu in 1884. She was now claimed by her brother and ordered by the courts to return with him to his homestead. She, however, wanted to stay with the Usuthu – with one of Cetshwayo's widows – with whom she had been for the last five years. It was a difficult situation. After all, it had been the Usuthu defence who had exposed the practice of capturing women and children, and who had demanded that it be brought to an end. Harriette found the brother to be 'amiable', and suggested to the girl that she go with him. She promised, however, that she would stay in contact to find out how she was getting on. She then talked with the brother and told him how she and the Usuthu, Dinuzulu included, agreed with the principle that all captive women and girls should be released. But, she added, 'the child now belonged in one sense to me, being a small person in trouble, and that though I sent her home, she still belonged to me, and as I shall be here, he must bring her presently to let me see that she looks as well cared for as she does now'.[18]

Amongst the Zulu she got to know were the families of the prisoners who came to Eshowe to visit them. There was a wife of Ndabuko, dying of consumption. It was her experiences which heightened Harriette's awareness of the unwritten, unpublished sufferings that had taken place over the past ten years, especially the effects of the war on women and children. Ndabuko's wife had never seen a white woman before. The white men she had seen had been soldiers and officials, and were objects of terror. 'Poor thing, she looks ill and says she has felt so since 1879 – "However" said she, "I shall not die so quickly now that I have seen you. How do you manage not to be afraid of them all – and to laugh." I said it is right to laugh and to be of good courage.' After visiting the gaol she told Harriette that 'they too were laughing in there "but that's because they've got you to take care of them." It is a very quaint position altogether so are the different points of view taken of it. I am sometimes inclined to "turn round three times" to "make sure that this is I."'[19]

'They think so much of my having come here', Harriette wrote, and as a result 'this war horse feels inclined to prance a little'.[20] But perhaps the greatest satisfaction came when she observed that her actions were noticed not only by the Usuthu, but by their Zulu opponents as well: 'As a matter of fact several of the gaol police are quite friendly; *All* of them, I think greet me respectfully now, and I hear they speak of me as the Inkosazana who speaks for our Black House – us black people – What a dangerous letter this is growing [into]. Don't betray any of my co-conspirators, white or black.'[21]

'As irrepressible as ever'

As useful as her work was in Zululand, it became increasingly clear as 1889 progressed that the important decisions were to be made in England. Together with Fox Bourne, Frank Colenso had set up the Zulu Defence Committee and he had also made contact with the most formidable of the parliamentary radicals, Charles Bradlaugh, energetic spokesman for a clutch of causes including Indian nationalism.

The suggestion had been made that it was now perhaps time for Harriette to think of going to England to assist. There was no one who had her detailed knowledge of the situation. Furthermore, she was also becoming known in radical and women's circles through the *Women's Penny Paper*, and Fox Bourne had managed to get her portrait and a story placed in *The Graphic*. In October Harriette wrote and thanked him for it: 'I am ready to go wherever you like to take me, for the good of the cause, and have a sort of suspicion that I shall some day end on a platform (not the one under the gallows). But *The Graphic* picture is really a very good likeness, my dear people say.'[22]

The assumptions behind this idea that Harriette should come to work on the case in England were many and male. But the men involved in the struggle either demanded payment for their services or were on a secure income. Harriette, Agnes and their mother were not. They had spent much of their legacy on the defence, lacked any secure or suitable means of earning an income of their own, and had many other responsibilities.

A trip to England would entail further risks, not only to their income but to the health of their increasingly frail mother. The very idea that they should go terrified Sarah Frances. At first she resisted it: she could not be parted from Harriette, but if they all went they would never come back, 'and what would our poor natives do then?' 'No, no, we should be lost. England would be hostile.' And, 'Do you mean actually to mount the platform and speak in public? Do, if you wish to, my precious child, but what would Uncle Charles say?'[23] Above all, it meant increasing dependence on others – a cruel thing for women who so valued their independence. But even this had a bright side, wrote Harriette: 'The staying in other people's houses, is I agree a nuisance, but oh it's a compensatory blessing to have nothing to do with one's dinner but eat it.'[24]

By December Harriette had almost finished making arrangements,

> including making up my mind and other people's, to come over and – take English counsels' advice, says Mr. Escombe, in fact take whatever part I can in the next campaign, as the only uSuthu free to come over in person ...
>
> I have not quite fixed on my steamer yet, but shall leave as early as I can manage it in January, so as to be in London if possible, before Parliament meets, as I am glad to see Mr Bradlaugh means to be also.[25]

As the New Year opened, Harriette, Agnes and their mother were ready to leave. Harriette called on Sir Theophilus Shepstone to say farewell to the foremost layman of the Church of England in South Africa, and the man whose life had been so much part of her own. He was not in. She was never to see him again.

On 3 January the three women boarded the *Grantully Castle* in Durban. They went first class and, looking down the passenger list, discovered that General Smyth was to join them at Cape Town. He had just been awarded a CMG, his official 'pat on the back', wrote Harriette, 'for "suppressing the Zulu rebellion" – and here he will find it on board the same steamer, as irrepressible as ever! poor man'.[26]

'Much ado about nothing'

As all-consuming as they were to the Usuthu, for the officials in London Zulu affairs were a minor, but persistent, annoyance. There was a steady stream of questions in parliament on the misdemeanours, illegalities and brutalities perpetrated by the Zululand officials. The answers had to be researched and their political implications carefully judged. There was little sympathy for either Harriette Colenso or the APS in the Colonial Office as a result. This was political agitation. It had already lengthened the trial enormously, greatly increasing its cost – and by the same token reduced the possibility of compensation for costs to the defence.

Whatever shortcomings there might have been in the administration of affairs in British Zululand, there was no possibility that the Colonial Office could ever consider accepting the point of view of the Usuthu and their defenders. The fact that the Usuthu had broken the law could not be disputed. The Secretary of State would make sure that any local attempt at retributive sentencing which might prove politically dangerous would be checked. The officials examined the vast amount of evidence before them carefully for any hidden pitfalls, but they were confident that the remedy for the violent incidents of 1888 lay in limiting any adverse political consequences, not in further inquiry. 'It might save worry to explain this privately to the members who are having their feelings harrowed by Messrs Escombe and Dumat.' It was time to stave off any parliamentary embarrassment by doing some work in the lobbies and the clubs.

The difference in approach between the officials and the Zulu defence could not have been greater. For Harriette it was a life-and-death fight for justice; for the officials in London it was a matter of damage control.

> Nothing can be done on these [protests] until Mr Osborn's report is received, and probably until they can be taken into connection with the Notes of Evidence. But Baron de Worms might like to peruse them in the mean time. Mr Addison has been removed to an undisturbed district, and Mr Osborn's retirement on pension is under discussion; and no formidable or humiliating form of imprisonment is contemplated as regards the Chiefs – so that really it is all 'much-a-do about nothing'.[27]

The question of the sort of non-punitive punishment to impose on the Usuthu leaders was a difficult one, however. Osborn believed that they had to be deported because if they were imprisoned in Natal or Zululand, then 'dangerous intrigues' were 'sure to be carried on by partisans of the Chiefs'.[28] Havelock felt they had to be removed from southern Africa – even if they were sent to Bechuanaland, as had been suggested, 'Miss Colenso would intrigue with them there'.[29] The obvious place, Havelock felt, was St Helena. But the Colonial Office balked at this: it had no wish to give its critics the opportunity to make snide comparisons on British attitudes towards the House of Bonaparte and the House of Shaka: 'We have negatived proposals in other cases to send any petty offending savage to the Island of Saint Helena – for sentimental and international reasons. If we did so, we should never hear the last of it either here or in France.'[30]

However, London was unable to sustain this position, and by the end of the year was ready to make an interim judgment. On the ground that incarceration in Zululand would have to be 'strict and irksome', they argued that deportation would be in the best interests of the prisoners as it would allow them a larger 'degree of freedom from personal restraint'. Consequently it was decided that they should be sent to St Helena.

By this time, the end of 1889, Wragg and Havelock were in London and work-ing with the Colonial Office to draft a response to its critics over their actions in Zululand. The officials discovered from Havelock how difficult it had been for him to control his subordinates. It was clear that the return of Zibhebhu had been a grave miscalculation based on inadequate information and that it had been badly handled. Havelock had been 'seriously displeased' with Addison, his floggings, and his disregard of instructions. Osborn was dilatory and deeply hated by the Usuthu.

At the same time, there was nothing in these arguments which suggested there should be a shift from the general line of policy already taken. As Chamberlain had told Frank Colenso, government departments are bound to defend their ser-vants – and this is what the officials worked towards. The Secretary of State announced his conclusions in a series of dispatches in February 1890. He accept-ed Wragg's verdicts, commuted the death sentence, and made minor remissions to the sentences. At the same time, with Harriette Colenso on her way to England, and before the next parliamentary session, the three Usuthu leaders were hurried from Eshowe to board ship at Durban, on their way to St Helena.

The Colonial Office was now able to view the situation with some equanim-ity.[31] The officials had worked hard. Fairfield had a detailed grasp of the lengthy court record and the evidence that had been led. They had before them the writ-ten views of the Governor and the judge in the trials. They also knew from previous correspondence on what points the APS and their supporters in the press and in parliament would attack, and had prepared their defences with this in mind. They felt confident that they could defend the policy towards Zululand, in broad outline at least. There could be no doubt that the offences had been committed or of their illegality. When the broader moral aspects of the case were raised, these could be countered by citing the various acts of remission of sentence authorised by the Secretary of State – and this included deportation to St Helena rather than incarceration in South Africa.

Further inquiry – the main objective of the Usuthu protest – would not be considered. Those who insisted upon it could be referred to the printed pages of evidence, a hundred copies of which were lodged in the libraries of parliament, and the Blue Books, which as, Fairfield minuted, could also 'be used as briefs by the Government speakers in case of debate'.[32]

Of course, there were aspects which even the careful planning of the Colonial Office could not control. Every effort had to be made to ensure that the local officials no longer acted without authority or inflamed the situation. Thus, when Mitchell tried to get permission for Zibhebhu to leave Eshowe for the north once again, this was promptly vetoed. 'It is very necessary to let Parliament, Miss Colenso and the Press blow off their steam (after reading the Blue Books) before the restoration of Zibhebhu to his territory is discussed.'[33]

Havelock was approached to respond to the first of the formal protests from the APS and its call for 'a searching and unbiased inquiry'.[34] His reply was angry and effective. He had no doubt that an inquiry would exonerate him and his subordinates: he did, however, fear the consequences of such an inquiry in Zululand when exploited by the Usuthu agitators there. The enormous pains taken by the Court of Special Commissioners obviated any need for further inquiry. Where mistakes had been made, as in the return of Zibhebhu, these had been admitted. His own actions in Zululand had been examined by Her Majesty's Government and received its approval. The legality and the equity of the court he had established had been examined and approved of by the 'highest tribunal of the Empire'.

But his most telling points were given in his rejection of the attacks made on him by the APS. The society, he wrote, 'says that *an alienation of nearly half the country was forcibly effected by me*'. But it was 'not effected by *me, but by the Zulus themselves, advised by a counsellor sent to them by their friend Miss Colenso, acting also, it is believed, on behalf of the Aborigines Protection Society*. My part in the transaction was to extricate the Zulus, as completely as possible, from the scrape they had thus got into.'[35] William Grant still haunted Harriette Colenso.

VI

THE
QUEST

CHAPTER 23

HARRIETTE COLENSO IN ENGLAND
(1890–1891)

'A giant refreshed'

The refusal to consider an inquiry and the hurried removal of Dinuzulu, Ndabuko and Shingana to St Helena at the very moment when she herself was on the way to England, did not surprise Harriette Colenso. She had long since ceased to hope that any fresh initiative would be taken spontaneously by Downing Street, regardless of whether Liberals or Conservatives were in power. Her task now was to publicise what had happened in Zululand since the annexation, and provoke public debate in order to put pressure on the British government. She was in London not to plead in mitigation of the sentences, but to protest against the fact that the Usuthu leaders had been brought to court at all. As she told a journalist soon after her arrival: 'My object in coming to England is to present the cause of the Zulus as I understand it – the cause of the people as well as the Chiefs, because I hold that those now being punished as traitors and rebels are the very people who have done most to keep order in the country for a long time, especially during the late disturbances.'[1]

Most urgently, in the short term, every effort had to be made to ensure that Zibhebhu was not returned to the north. This was necessary for the immediate well-being of the people living there. It was also essential that Melmoth Osborn be removed from his post as Resident Commissioner. Without this there could be no change in the Shepstone policy of setting up chiefs whose main qualification was their opposition to the Zulu royal house and its supporters – that is, to the majority of people in the land. And until this policy was changed there was no hope for the return of the exiled leaders, three men whom she now considered her close friends, comrades and companions, bound together by their duty to the memory of their fathers, the King of the Zulu and the Bishop of Natal.

It was a campaign fought on a number of fronts with a range of allies. However, because it was a campaign in an African cause, carried out at the centre of Empire, at the height of imperial power, conceived and led by a woman, it

313

laboured under massive disadvantages. Very quickly after her arrival, Harriette had to make a number of radical changes in the way in which she worked. Life in London was not only different, but very difficult for her. She no longer enjoyed the independence she had in Natal. There she was a leader of the small but supportive community at Bishopstowe – her mother and sister, Mubi Nondenisa, Magema Fuze, Kate Giles, the African teachers, printers, assistants, the servants, the tenants, and all those who saw in Bishopstowe a place for worship, education, medical help and advice in handling the disadvantages imposed on them by the colonial state – all those whom Harriette Colenso referred to as 'my dear people'. They looked to her for guidance and took her instructions, wearying her with responsibility, but giving her the satisfaction of companionship and independence.

She lost this in London. She had to draw on others for shelter and support for herself and her mother and sister. Charles Bunyon, her mother's brother, and his wife Eliza were the obvious source of assistance. But the Bunyons had disapproved of the activities of Bishop Colenso, and they doubly disapproved of those of his children. Frank Colenso's relations with his uncle were good – as they had to be with the man whose influence had secured him his job. Robert Colenso was hopeless in money matters and was soon to arrive in London, where he persuaded Uncle Charles to assist him financially. It was the sisters who resisted the Bunyons. Frances had found their respectability and conventionality stifling. They believed that in her state of health she should never have been allowed to come to England in 1886, carrying with her, in her concern for the posthumous reputation of Anthony Durnford, the possibility of scandal. Now in 1890 Harriette had not only embarked on a financially catastrophic political venture, but brought with her to England her strangely withdrawn sister together with their mother, who clearly was too old to undertake such a visit. The difficulty for the Bunyons was not just that they found all this unconventional and irresponsible – but that their own conventionality obliged them to assist family. And Harriette knew that she would have to make use of this sense of obligation, for their mother's sake, and for that of the campaign.

Although, as the family of the Bishop of Natal, they never completely lost an aura of respectability, the priorities and the behaviour of the Colenso women were obviously not those of the circles in which the Bunyons lived and worked. As far as her Uncle Charles and Aunt Eliza were concerned, if Harriette insisted on leading a political campaign in London, then she had at least to follow conventions. From the start it was clear that her clothing was not suitable. Although, when she was photographed with her father in 1882 on their trip to the Cape, Harriette was dressed in the elaborate finery of the times, since his death Agnes and Harriette had developed, as independent missionaries, a more functional garb suitable for their work as teachers and nurses spending much of their time in the open, which included wearing a man's hat when necessary. Harriette simply did not have the clothes to lead the life of an active woman in London in the 1890s engaged in public affairs, nor the means to obtain them.

In the year that she died, Frances had warned her about this. It had taken Georgie Burne-Jones's advice

> not to let me, whether as myself, or as my Father's daughter, do anything that would be thought outrageous – as it would be for instance for a woman of my age and position to go about in a hat in London! You think such things absurd? Even you, dear, were you to come to England would find yourself obliged to conform to a certain extent if you are to *do* anything, to stir people up, and so on. When I go to the Colonial Office I shall dress my very best. I am not at all sure that my ulster and cap did not injure my influence at the War Office. They were too much in keeping with strong-minded action in going there. When one wants to do a strong-minded thing one should do it delicately.[2]

It was all very difficult: the formalities, the dress, the presence of her disapproving uncle. When Harriette, soon after her arrival, went for her interview with Lord Knutsford, Secretary of State for the Colonies, her uncle took it upon himself to introduce her. She was driven to Downing Street in Mr Bunyon's carriage, wearing a coat her aunt had given her for the occasion. The interview was awkward and little was gained by it. Bunyon insisted that Harriette bring up the matter of financial compensation, and Knutsford and Harriette sparred over whether the Usuthu leaders had surrendered or been arrested or been forced to give themselves up.

But it was not just the conventions of dress and manners which created problems for a single woman with limited means embarking on a political struggle in England. It was also her inexperience, her very limited knowledge of the conventions by which political agitation was conducted. While the *Women's Penny Paper* had been important in publicising her name, Harriette's attempts at political journalism had not been successful. As publicity material she carried with her the *Remonstrance on Behalf of the Zulu Chiefs*, a pamphlet based on Escombe's speech for the defence. But to Uncle Charles Bunyon it was a 'perfect puzzle' and reflected the confused and incomplete nature of his niece's whole approach. In what direction did she expect to work? Was she going to attack the government and demand that the officials be punished? If she was, then he could only disapprove. As far as he was concerned, her object had to be to gain amelioration for the chiefs – and with it some compensation for the money she had spent.[3]

Although not all her advisers adopted such a narrow approach, most agreed that the means that Harriette intended to use were inadequate. John Westlake, jurist, Professor of International Law at Cambridge, one of the number of men whom Harriette recruited to her cause, was also, like Bishop Colenso, from Cornwall. Westlake had been helped by Colenso when he was a young man, and in return gave selfless and unstinting assistance first to the bishop and then to the bishop's children. His wife, Alice Westlake, was an important figure in the women's movement, who in 1876 had been elected to the London School Board.[4]

Westlake too found the *Remonstrance* of little help. It was not succinct enough and assumed a detailed knowledge of recent events in Zululand. He gave Harriette advice on legal strategy – impeachment, he explained in some detail, was no longer an effective way of dealing with political opponents. It would be far more effective to find allies in the House who would be prepared to ask testing questions of the government. To assist her in this, he promised to introduce her to the Commons' library – it was true that he had never seen a woman there before but he did not think an objection would be made. While the *Remonstrance* was not suitable as a pamphlet, he did think it could be used to frame questions in parliament – but another article was required to put the Zulu case to the public. And this needed experience and skill.

> Is there no one who could undertake it, under your supervision? Or could you not write a draft of it, to be worked on by some one? Excuse my seeming to think that your draft would need being worked on, but of course I don't know how you would do it, and it might be all right as it stood, only it is not every one, however able that could without experience write any thing to catch the thinking public which read the principal reviews. It is the thing to set about without loss of time.[5]

She set about it with the help of Fox Bourne and soon ran into trouble. The *Universal Review* offered her space but Harriette, nervous and uncertain, delayed submitting the article, and then made changes when it was in proof, before trying to withdraw her name at the last moment. Harry Quilter, editor, journalist and art critic, friend of Edward Aveling, and as ''Arry Quilter' the butt of Whistler's attacks on contemporary artistic taste, had no hesitation in telling Harriette what he thought of her: 'You must allow me to say, that, in this matter, you have given me more trouble, and made more requirements than I have ever

Photo 31. Harriette Colenso in Birmingham. While her sister Frances consciously used the photograph to present her conventional femininity in appearance and her dress, Harriette had no intention of doing so. Instead she tried to communicate her dedication to the cause, but this proved difficult, and too often her attempts to convey courageous devotion were tense and awkward. Nonetheless photographs played an important role in her struggle for the Zulu royalist cause. In these photographs Harriette Colenso holds the symbol of the royalist cause – the white cow tail, the shokobezi, *and wrapped around the handle on which it is mounted is a string of* iziqu *– the carved wooden charms awarded to the brave, and which fend off the supernatural powers of the enemy. Any Zulu who saw these photographs would have had no doubt of Harriette Colenso's activities in England.*

experienced with regard to any article whatever which has yet appeared in the *Universal Review*.[6] It was a novel experience for the often forthright, but always considerate, Harriette to be addressed in terms such as these.

Leonard Courtney, the Liberal statesman, was at that time chairman of committees in the House and another Cornishman in whom her father had found an ally and who extended his friendship to the bishop's daughter. He and his wife, Kate Courtney, sister of Beatrice Webb, were significant and supportive figures in Harriette's life in London.[7]

The Courtneys conducted their political socialising over breakfast. Harriette attended one such breakfast at the end of March, wearing a dress with a train, over which she draped Aunt Eliza's long furry coat, which made it impossible to hold up the skirt as she made her way to the house and 'so I arrived with ½ yard of London mud on the tail which Mrs Courtney washed out before breakfast she and her maid with sponges on each side of me'.[8]

Harriette was a modest and retiring woman. She, and Agnes even more so, were soon to long for the comparative informality and freedom of colonial Natal. She would rather have spent her time and what money she had on the production of pamphlets than on meeting the representatives and demands of contemporary London social and political life. But the networking had to be done, and there was no one else with her knowledge of the situation in Zululand to do it. On first being asked for an interview for a newspaper she felt, at least to her closest friend, that she had 'no views on anything but the Zulu question. What shall I say!!' But the journalist arrived at Frank Colenso's house in St John's Wood and 'found her seated at her writing-table, surrounded by innumerable books, papers, reports, and photographs, all bearing upon the engrossing subject in which it is easy to see her very heart and soul are bound ... It is impossible to look in her kind face with its clear honest eyes and bright sunny expression without being favourably impressed.'[9] Like her father, she could not let her private agonies become public fears. Too many depended on it. Her friends and supporters, particularly those in Natal, had to be encouraged, and to them she had to appear confident. As she wrote to Katie Giles after an attack of flu, she was now ready 'to sally out ... like a giant refreshed to fresh adventures'.[10]

'The fag end of the session'

Harriette Colenso confirmed her mother's worst fears when she spoke in public on 17 April 1890, addressing the National Liberal Club. It was gruelling: she had so little experience and feared that her voice would fail. But it held out, and Fox Bourne assisted her when she faltered for a moment during the questioning. The women's drawing-room meetings at which she was soon invited to speak were a means of gaining experience without the intimidating presence of a large audience. Outwardly, and to the anxious watchers in Natal especially, she was bright and confident as she sought out allies amongst London's liberal set. 'Last night we went Sophie, Frank, Percy [Frankland, Sophie's brother] and I to a huge crush at the Westlake's (Bag – 2 MPs one Lord. Private) oh and a canon.'[11]

The pick of the bag was the formidable radical parliamentarian, Charles Bradlaugh, controversial, in some quarters notorious, but known through the land for his independence, courage and oratory. A generation previously, Bradlaugh had included John William Colenso in his series *Half-hours with the Freethinkers* with, amongst others, Socrates, Lyell, Strauss and Darwin.[12] He met with Harriette on a number of occasions in the first half of 1890 so that she could instruct him on the case. His responsibilities and commitments were enormous, but he kept in contact with Harriette, looking for a possible 'peg' on which to hang a parliamentary debate. It was thought best that Zulu questions should be asked on a non-party basis and it was decided that he should be supported by the Conservative member for Preston, Charles Hanbury. Harriette canvassed and found support in parliament amongst nonconformists, radicals, and Irish, Welsh and Scottish nationalists especially. She took great pains to make sure they were well prepared on Zulu matters. But the House was very busy and the proposed April debate was postponed.

By now Harriette Colenso had abandoned any idea of continuing the expensive process of appealing to the Judicial Committee of the Privy Council, and she concentrated her energies on parliament. This required a knowledge of the House, its members, the process of lobbying and briefing, and for this in turn she needed secretarial assistance. Here she got help from the women's organisations which were now such a significant part of political life in London, in particular from the Women's Local Government Society. This organisation had been founded in 1888 to facilitate the election of women to the county councils which recent legislation had made a possibility. It included women who were to become Harriette's staunchest allies, and some became her friends. Annie Leigh Browne, the organising secretary, gave time, advice and affectionate support to all three of the Colenso women. Eva McLaren, sister of Henrietta Muller of the *Women's Penny Paper* and wife of the sympathetic Liberal MP, was the treasurer. Jane Cobden Unwin, daughter of Richard Cobden and wife of the publisher, was one of the four women who stood for the London County Council; she became a good friend to Harriette as did Emma Cons, who was nominated as an alderman. The election and nomination of these women was, however, challenged, the whole controversy coming to a head in the very month that Harriette arrived in London.

The experience of her friends on the Women's Local Government Society, in the courts and as a parliamentary pressure group, was directly relevant to Harriette and her campaign.[13] They provided her with the names of MPs known for their support of liberal and radical causes. Harriette paid particular attention to individuals with a record of support for Bishopstowe's different objectives over the years. It was a completely new world for Harriette, one which required not only a knowledge of politics and the working of the House, but time, funds and secretarial assistance. Annie Leigh Browne tried to help but was herself already over-committed: her letters indicate some of Harriette's difficulties. 'I'm glad it's all right therefore with my 280 Whips, I will do the best I can, and the clerk shall address them first thing tomorrow. I have sent a packet of circulars to Mr Alfred Webb and a few to Mr Wicksteed. How many copies of the circulars wd you like? 500 have been struck. The type can be kept up for the present.'[14]

On 11 August Harriette was in the Ladies' Gallery in the House of Commons waiting for the beginning of the debate on the civil service estimates – the peg on which the Zulu question was to be hung. But her attempts to bring the case of the exiled leaders before the House had always to compete not only with the great issues of the age, Irish matters in particular, but with the normal mass of business. The debate was delayed again and again, and it was 3.30 the next morning that she returned to St John's Wood, Agnes still up waiting for her and the debate not begun. The next day was spent in the same way. By midnight the House was emptying and those present were exhausted. It was after 1 a.m. when Bradlaugh rose to speak. 'It would be absurd to attempt to do that at this period of the Session, in the present state of the House, and at this time of the night,' he began. Nonetheless something must be placed on record about the state of affairs in Zululand. He gave an account of recent events in the colony, following the briefing given him by Harriette – to whom he gave fulsome praise. He assured the House that the view he gave could be substantiated from the Blue Books.

> I do not pretend that I am not [*sic*] presenting the view I have arrived at in consequence of the examination I have made, and it is quite possible that my presentment is not an impartial one. It is impossible to go into the case fully at the fag end of a Session, but I give notice that an early opportunity will be taken next Session to put the whole case before the House. I trust that in the meantime the Government will not allow anything to be done to make the state of things more deplorable than it is now.[15]

Sir Richard Fowler, on the committee of the APS but far too close to governing circles for Harriette's taste, spoke briefly and hesitatingly. He was followed by Clarke, the pro-Boer member for Caithness, who moved the debate to Swazi affairs. Henry Labouchère, Liberal MP, followed and launched a swingeing and pertinent attack on the British South Africa Company. Alfred Webb, Irish member and pro-Home Ruler who had made contact with Harriette after reading about her in the *Women's Penny Paper*, brought the debate back to Zulu affairs, giving information, provided by Harriette, of famine, the inadequacy of the gaols, and the placing in Zululand of chiefs from Natal. Conybeare, an MP with Cornish connections, spoke at length but with some confusion, testing the patience of the few weary members still in their places, before the Under-Secretary of State, Baron de Worms, rose to answer. He treated Bradlaugh's intervention with respect but he insisted that he did not accept the validity of his statement on Zulu affairs. He did not, however, intend to go into detail – that could wait till the next session if the matter was raised again. But, De Worms continued, the contention that the present state of Zululand was

> most unsatisfactory is in no way supported by facts; the country is now perfectly tranquil and the people contended [*sic*], as the statistics which I will

give to the Committee clearly prove. The revenue for the first-half of 1890 was £34,225; the balance on the 1st of January was £8,175, making a total of £42,400. The expenditure for the half-year has thus been one of great prosperity. The Hut Tax has been paid in all parts cheerfully and satisfactorily and in coin. This is significant, as it is the first occasion on which no cattle have been tendered in lieu of cash. The tax has exceeded the estimate of £25,000, having realised £27,141. There has been no crime of a serious nature in any of the districts. The colony is out of debt.[16]

It must have been difficult for Harriette Colenso to have to wait silently behind the grille of the Ladies' Gallery and hear such a statement. It was precisely what she had predicted, and feared, would happen. A world and a year ago, in Eshowe, she had been told stories of starvation in the Zululand coastal districts, and she had immediately perceived the connections between this and the imposition of the hut tax, which was paid not 'willingly' but only after the cruel silencing of Zulu protests. Wages earned by labour migration were not a cure but an intensification of Zulu suffering. She suspected then, as we have seen,[17] that the authorities would present the situation as the desirable consequence of the successful implementation of the policies of an administration no longer thwarted by the activities of a small group of disgruntled Zulu royalists and white agitators. Now, a year later, from the Ladies' Gallery of the House of Commons at two in the morning, during the debate which she had initiated at such cost and in which she had invested so much energy and hope, she had to listen to Baron de Worms telling a handful of weary impatient members that 'the condition of the country is satisfactory, and the people [are] paying their taxes freely and willingly'.[18]

It was cruel to have her fears confirmed in this way, and her first parliamentary intervention was hardly a success. Hanbury, suffering from a migraine, had not even appeared, and the burden had fallen on Bradlaugh. He 'did all that was wanted', but it was all too rushed, and took place too late, to have the impact she had hoped for. It was hardly noticed in the papers, and there was little return for all her anxious preparations and printing, lobbying and letter-writing, which now, if she wished to continue, had to be begun again next session.

Nonetheless, her first six months in London had been an important introduction to what was required of a political lobbyist. She had spoken in public, published an article, been interviewed by the press, and briefed sympathetic members of parliament. She had built a small group of friends around her who offered advice and support. With parliament now in recess it was time to move out of London and meet the English public.

321

In June 1890 she had received a letter from Kate Ryley of the Southport branch of the Women's Liberal Association asking her to lecture in the autumn. Women's Liberal Associations had begun to make their appearance in the 1880s, in the aftermath of the hopes raised by the moral fervour of Gladstone's 1880 Midlothian campaign and the subsequent victory at the polls[19] – the event which also raised the spirits of the Colenso family in the belief that something would now be done for the Zulu and their king. The Women's Liberal Associations allowed predominantly middle-class women to give expression to a noncon-formist reforming zeal, to support local Liberal candidates, and to participate in a husband's or father's political activities. Many were also active in the move-ment for women's participation in local government, so there were many useful connections to be made. Thus Kate Ryley, herself a lively and controversial par-ticipant on the local school board, had heard that Harriette Colenso was to delay her return to Natal and hoped this would 'give some of the provincial "Women's Liberal Associations" the advantage of hearing your story from your own lips ... I may say', Kate Ryley continued, 'that I think the people here are absolutely uninformed about the African difficulties and you would be breaking entirely new ground.'[20]

Once it was known that she was prepared to speak publicly, invitations came in not only from other Women's Liberal Associations nearby, but local geograph-ical and lecture societies and church congregations. These were often Unitarian, sometimes led by a minister who had been influenced by John Colenso, or with some philanthropic or humanitarian interest. In the closing months of 1890 Harriette Colenso lectured in London and its surrounds, and then made several trips to the north. She spoke in Bradford, Leeds, Preston and Northampton, returned to London before travelling north again to Manchester, Nottingham, Sheffield and Coventry and back through Cambridge to London. She went to Manchester to speak at Upper Brook Street Church at the invitation of its min-ister, John Trevor, who was soon to move to London and found the Labour Church. In London she lectured to the famous South Place Ethical Society and the Progressive Association.[21] In Sheffield a Colenso Committee was formed. In Nottingham, Isabella Ford[22] made a major contribution to Harriette's lectures by converting her photographs from Zululand into lantern slides.

As 1890 drew to a close, the lectures continued, in London, its suburbs and the provinces, the north in particular, in lecture halls, meeting places and chapels. By November she had delivered 24 lectures and had 16 more to give to complete the schedule. People attended to be informed, as part of a need for greater social awareness; out of support for a woman fighting hard in a humanitarian cause; and, for many, out of respect for Bishop Colenso, still remembered as one of the great controversialists of the century, and yet so little known as a man.

The lectures were clearly important, and it would seem they were appreciated by most audiences. It put Harriette in contact with some of the leading women in the country, in the Liberal Associations at least. And yet, as interesting and inspiring as her talks seemed to many, they made little difference to the Zulu Defence Committee's finances. The organisers usually paid Harriette's fare, and gave her hospitality. Often, but not always, a collection was taken after the meeting, but the amounts collected were not substantial.

The political impact of Harriette's lectures is more difficult to estimate but it can hardly have been great. Even though she could number amongst her advisers public figures of considerable political and intellectual weight – Courtney, Bradlaugh, Westlake and, later, James Bryce, for example – they were not significant numerically. The women and their organisations who gave Harriette sympathy and support were, we can see more clearly now than then, very often people working in movements of contemporary and historical significance. But they also made up only a small portion of the contemporary political scene, and their activities were dwarfed by other political controversies of the time.

Ireland, from the time of the controversy over Home Rule in the mid-1880s, had always diverted attention from South African affairs generally and Zulu matters in particular. It is true that it was amongst Irish MPs that Harriette Colenso found some of her most active supporters. But it was Irish matters that took them away from her as well – no more so than at the end of 1890 when the scandal over Parnell's relationship with Kitty O'Shea broke, and ruined his political reputation. Harriette, like many of the leading liberals of the time, chose not to censure Parnell for sexual immorality – instead she cited his deceit as an indication of political untrustworthiness.[23]

But the cruellest blow was struck towards the end of the year. Charles Bradlaugh, with whom she had been working for their next parliamentary intervention, fell ill. To have on her side one of the country's best-known radical activists, a formidable debater and orator, was to have an ally indeed. His house was near Frank's in St John's Wood, and Harriette and Agnes walked to it daily to enquire after his progress. On 29 January they noted that straw had been lain on the street outside to soften the noise of the traffic. He died the next day at the age of 57.

By now Harriette had been in England for a year. During this time she had gained considerable experience as an independent worker for a political cause. But she must also have become aware of the enormous practical obstacles in the way of the project to bring justice to the Zulu people, and to their leaders in particular. Even if she was not prepared to think of failure, she must have come to realise that it was time to reassess the objectives of her project. And yet it is difficult to find evidence of either disappointment or even a change of tactics in her letters of the time. I have found no overt admission that the project, at least as originally formulated, was failing. One has to assume, however, that through the hard winter of 1890–91, perhaps on the long solitary train journeys to the small scattered audiences in the north, she must have come to realise that she would never be able to rouse the British public or its parliamentary representatives to take a major initiative on behalf of the Zulu – or at least one of sufficient scale to be more than a minor annoyance to the politicians and officials.

'Land or niggers'

But it was not just the limitations imposed on her by her gender, her background and the minute scale of the resources at her disposal: it was also the general political and cultural context in which Harriette Colenso worked. She had come to London in the spirit of her father – and therefore of mid-Victorian evangelical humanitarianism – to remind 'the English People' of 'their old principles of truth and justice'[24] and show them how these principles had been abandoned in British Zululand. But times had changed.

Historians agree that from the 1870s there had been a fundamentally important shift in British attitudes towards Britain's possessions overseas. It was a halting movement at first but the general direction was clear: towards an aggressive imperial policy made on the assumption that the economic strength and the social well-being of Britain were directly related to the possession of overseas dominions; a movement which saw Rosebery, a Liberal imperialist, succeeding Gladstone as Prime Minister in 1894. This was a situation in which Joseph Chamberlain, the nonconformist radical, could assert in the Commons his belief 'in the expansion of the Empire and we are not ashamed to confess that we have that feeling, and we are not at all troubled by accusations of Jingoism'.[25]

The wider context of this movement was provided by the challenge to Britain's position as the leading industrial power in an increasingly aggressive struggle amongst industrialising nation-states for world dominance. We have seen some of the manifestations of this process already in South Africa – in the German moves towards the South African coast in the mid-1880s, and the British moves to block the Transvaal from access to the sea, which was part of the decision to annex British Zululand in 1887. But the major development in South Africa which gives the imperial narrative its particular form was the discovery of the Transvaal goldfields in 1886 and their development in subsequent years.

In South Africa the new aggressive drive for English dominance was embodied in the character and the policies of Cecil John Rhodes. Born in England into a vicar's family of no particular standing, he had come to Natal as an aspirant farmer in 1870 at the age of 17 and after a year followed his brother to the Kimberley diamond mines. Before the end of the decade he was wealthy enough to continue as a South African businessman while financing his undergraduate career at Oxford. Here his imperial dream matured: the English were a superior race, and the boundaries of the British Empire should be further extended for the benefit of the rest of mankind. Cecil John Rhodes came to believe that it was his destiny to use his wealth, and the power and position that it bought, in pursuit of this end.

Through the 1880s Rhodes built up his financial base with the diamonds of the South African interior, and his political base in the Cape parliament. From here he looked to the north, to those areas which the scramble had left inadequately or loosely defined. The discovery of gold on the Rand only encouraged the long-held belief that in the African interior there were vast deposits of minerals, which, if they were not acquired by Britain, would be seized by another, inferior, European power. When in the mid-1880s the road to the north appeared to be threatened by expansion from the Transvaal (in a western movement reflected in the east in the events which saw the establishment of the New Republic), Rhodes was actively involved in ensuring that the way north remained open to British interests. By the end of the decade Rhodes was finalising the negotiations out of which De Beers Consolidated Diamond Mining Company was created, and with it a monopoly on diamond production and sale. This would provide the means for further expansion – the 'sinews of war' upon which his vision of conquest was based, reaching now across the Limpopo to the interior plateau, the southern portion of which was ruled by the Ndebele, under Lobengula, son of Mzilikazi, who had once been a member of Shaka's kingdom. Rhodes's idea was to obtain a charter from the British government, like those granted in West and East Africa, under which he could colonise the territory, for Britain, in the company's name. But in order to close off the ambitions of rivals with the same intention and to give his application substance, he had to obtain some evidence that the Ndebele king had granted him rights to the kingdom's resources.

It was these plans and activities, involving huge numbers of people, millions of pounds, international financing and plotting with men situated at the highest levels of the state, that created much of the political atmosphere within which Harriette Colenso had to work in London in the early 1890s. Of course the disparity between her means and objectives and her resources and those of Rhodes could not have been greater. Nonetheless, they did share a fundamental belief in the desirability of British rule. For Harriette Colenso, however, this implied equality and freedom under the law for all British subjects. For Rhodes, British supremacy was an end in itself. For the one it was the justice, for the other it was the power, implicit in British rule.

Their actions in the closing years of the 1880s and early 1890s sound an ironic counterpoint. At the end of 1888, while Harriette was persuading Harry Escombe to defend the Usuthu, Rhodes's agents were extracting from the Ndebele king a concession on which to base his bid for the charter which he would use to extend his financial activities into the area north of the Limpopo. On the last day of October 1889, Rhodes's agents obtained from Lobengula a document which they considered sufficient to form the basis for a claim to exploit the mineral resources of the kingdom. In 1889 Rhodes travelled to London in order to steal a march on his rivals, consolidate his allies and recruit supporters using the method which came so easily to him – bribery.

In the opening months of 1889, while Harriette Colenso was in Zululand assisting in the defence of Ndabuko and Dinuzulu, Rhodes arrived in London. Here he began negotiating the agreements, private and official, by which a charter would be granted by the Crown to the British South Africa Company, authorising it to assume control over the territory north of the Limpopo. The author of the monumental biography *The Founder* describes in fascinating and ugly detail the way in which this 35-year-old colonial politician and mining magnate, still on the margins of the metropolitan society, inserted himself and his vision of imperial conquest amongst those in positions of power in London.[26] Whilst many spoke of Rhodes's negotiating skills, his grasp of detail, his charm, it was his cheque book and share offers which seem to have been his most persuasive attributes. He and his agents made full use of them as they worked their way amongst the leaders and makers of public opinion. Editors and journalists, politicians Conservative and Liberal, bourgeois and aristocratic, English and Irish, were persuaded to give him their support. W.T. Stead, radical journalist of the *Pall Mall Gazette*, was recruited and founded *The Review of Reviews* with Rhodes's backing. Flora Shaw of *The Times* became a supporter. Lord Grey, Liberal aristocrat, was offered a directorship. The Duke of Fife, soon to marry the Queen's granddaughter, became vice-chairman of the British South Africa Company. In the spring the officials at the Colonial Office, and then the government itself, were persuaded to authorise a chartered company. Here, it seemed, was a way in which British influence could be extended, into an area in which Britain would probably be forced to intervene anyway in the near future, but without the British government having to carry the financial responsibility.

In January 1891, at a meeting at the Mansion House, the Duke of Fife spoke of the British South Africa Company's support for the King of the Belgians' efforts to put down slavery and control the arms and liquor trade in the Congo. *The Aborigines' Friend* reported favourably on his intervention and how he had emphasised that the British South Africa Company was 'not a mere trading company'. On 20 May the Duke of Fife was invited to take the chair at the annual meeting of the APS itself. 'I am here', he said in his address to members,

> because I am convinced that the members of the Board of the British South
> Africa Company are as anxious as any member of this Society to act justly
> toward the natives in our territory, and to do all we can to labour to ameliorate
> their conditions. Our policy has been to place ourselves in direct communica-
> tion with the native chiefs, and, by their intermediary, to work in harmony
> with the people, thus protecting the natives from being oppressed and demor-
> alised by rival bodies of white men; and I venture to ask what the most enthu-
> siastic member of your Society could wish us to do more?[27]

At least one member present wished it – Harriette Colenso. She was infuri-ated to see her old ally, the APS, and the philanthropic lobby fall under the con-temporary spell and promote a benevolent imperialism. She already felt that some of its members were far too close to the men who made policy in Downing Street, to be successful critics. She also felt that the organisation as a whole had not given her, and the Zulu cause, the support they deserved, leaving her to fight largely on her own for the year she had been in England. And now came the Duke of Fife, who spoke of the mission of 'the Anglo-Saxon race' to fill the 'unoccupied spaces of the world' – spaces which her dying sister had rightly argued four years before did not exist. If there was to be space, it had to be created over the bodies of the men, women and children who lived in it. This she knew from her own experience in Zululand.

In May 1891 she received a copy of *The Natal Mercury*, which provided all the evidence she needed to prove that both Rhodes and the British South Africa Company deserved only the unequivocal opposition of the APS. She copied it out in a letter to Fox Bourne with her own emphases. Rhodes had said that 'Pondoland was the one cloud on the horizon of the colony. He looked upon it as a swarming beehive. *Now he must say that he preferred land to niggers*; and before plunging into the Pondo war they had to consider the cost and the practical advantages.'

She was very angry. Rhodes had now demonstrated to the world the sort of man he was – a jingo, a filibuster, a man of murderous intentions whose mater-ial ambitions excluded humanity. His aristocratic, philanthropic supporters in

England notwithstanding, as far as she was concerned there could be no working relationship between the British South Africa Company and the APS, and if
she had to criticise the latter publicly on these grounds she would do so.[28]
  Fox Bourne tried to explain the role of a pressure group to her: it had to cultivate allies, it often had to compromise, and it sometimes had to ignore what was
unpalatable in its supporters if this meant gaining a degree of influence in the
corridors of power. Harriette Colenso, however, could not accept this. She had
direct experience of imperialism at work, she was too close to those whom
Rhodes called niggers, to accept the argument. In a published letter she wrote
how Rhodes's words were 'a glaring contradiction to the pleasant theory upheld
by the Aborigines Protection Society, and by the Duke of Fife' and that

> This Pondo business is only one incident in the South African drama, but it
> shows that Mr. Rhodes's avowal that he 'prefers land to niggers' was not a
> careless figure of speech, but is the expression of a principle already being
> acted on in deadly earnest. I do not believe it to be a principle on which the
> bulk of my fellow-countrymen and women wish to act in obtaining possession
> of any country, and, therefore, besides bringing the matter to the notice of the
> Aborigines Protection Society, I feel it my duty to lay it thus before the pub-
> lic, having met in my own small circle with more than one instance in which
> the proceedings at the annual meeting of the society had produced an entirely
> mistaken notion of the principles and action towards the natives of the char-
> tered South Africa Company.[29]

In her rejection of the tactics of the APS we see perhaps something of the depth
of her general disappointment. As she wrote to Fox Bourne,

> What I complain of is that instead of as you say making the Duke of Fife
> 'take sides with' the A.P.S., the result of the alliance is to make the A.P.S.
> 'take sides with' the South Africa Co. The Aborigines reap no benefit, nor the
> society, for the Duke of Fife is powerless over Mr C Rhodes; but the well-
> meaning 'negrophilist' section of the public is being led to believe that the
> Company deserves to be supported, as a blessing to the natives, and since you
> do not see your way to correcting this impression or inviting the Duke of Fife
> to do so, I cannot share the responsibility and must send the enclosed to the
> papers.
>   I am very sorry to have vexed you, but I do feel very strongly that while an
> A.P.S. exists, it ought not to have been left to me to protest against Mr.
> Rhodes' infamous declaration and to warn any portion of the public who have

consciences, of the danger they incur by investing in the S.A. Company while it is under his management. I may have spoken strongly, as I feel, of the attitude of the A.P.S. at this juncture, and if this is my offence, I am not the less sorry, but I cannot help it.[30]

The whole incident is an important one. It marks a change. There had been, as we have seen, differences between Harriette Colenso and the philanthropic lobby. Up to now these were differences amongst allies. But now there had been a fundamental shift, representing a change in the spirit of the age and those who dominated its ideas and thinking. Harriette was now working in the age of high imperialism, against a coalition of classes. She was unable to find a sufficiently solid base within British politics for her humanitarian project for the victims of imperial expansion. Rhodes, a man whose methods should have placed him beyond the boundaries of the philanthropic lobby and its liberal supporters, had intruded himself within it.

For Harriette Colenso there could be no compromise with Rhodes. It is true that she herself did not break with the APS. It was difficult to do this with Fox Bourne as secretary, for he defended with spirit her right to disagree both with him personally and with the society. But she became a difficult member especially when she criticised the organisation publicly. Gestures in the direction of humanitarianism were not enough, she felt. The APS should stand true to its name and attack Rhodes. She was also deeply disappointed with the half-hearted support it had given her attempt to bring the Zulu cause before the public. The Zulu Defence Committee, she felt, had to be wound up. John Westlake, Professor of International Law at Cambridge, audited the accounts. In two years the Zulu Defence Committee had collected a little under £350.

'A beautiful little debate'

The apathy in England, as reflected in the donations to the committee, had not, however, held Harriette Colenso back. She had spoken on platforms throughout the country, some of the leading journals had published her ideas, and she had built up a group of informed and supportive activists and MPs. The new generation of controversial Colensos was at work. She had to build on this publicity and these achievements.

But she also had to go on for other reasons – for in spite of all the energy she and her allies had expended, they had as yet made no substantial gains. She was now aware of how difficult it was to find a popular audience through the press or pamphlets, and, whatever the personal satisfaction derived from direct contact with sympathetic audiences, the limitations of the lecture tour were clear. But she could not give up. She could not go back to Natal, to her dear people whose high hopes in the English she had done so much to encourage, with nothing to show for her absence and all the energy and capital she had expended. She would never come 'sneaking home' – as had been suggested in the Natal press by her opponents – empty-handed. She had no choice but to stay and look for political openings and opportunities which might lead to some concessions for the exiled chiefs and for the people of Zululand.

In July 1891, even as she was putting a distance between herself and the 'Rhodes Protection Society', as she called it to Katie Giles, she attended 'a beautiful little debate in the House'. The approval of the civil service estimates again provided the opportunity, and while she was waiting for Zulu affairs to be introduced she had the satisfaction of hearing Labouchère attack the British South Africa Company, its financial structure, its mode of operation and the frequently stated idea

> that there was a very large black population in these territories who might then be put to useful work. We know, however, what has happened in Cuba and other places where a black population have been put to useful work in the mines, and I shall protest against this large black population in South Africa being put to 'useful' work of a similar kind.[31]

Alfred Webb, the Irish MP, opened the Zulu debate with a long detailed speech, prepared by Harriette, which gave a history of events in Zululand since the invasion: the war, the trial, the appeal to the Privy Council, the exile, and the role played by Miss Colenso and Mr Escombe in bringing the injustice to the public. Osborn, who was visiting England at the time, was also present in the House and must have been pleased to hear the Under-Secretary of State, Baron de Worms, reply that these were merely the views of Miss Colenso 'who, I am sure, is thoroughly sincere, but who for many years has played a part in Zululand which has not been conducive to the welfare of the natives or the peace of the country. (*Opposition cries of* "Oh!")'[32] He then referred to an 1882 dispatch of Bulwer's which blamed Harriette directly for inciting the Usuthu to violence: 'Not only have they rebelled against the authority of the Crown, but they have committed acts of great violence. They have been described as martyrs to British injustice and tyranny, when the fact is that they are rebels in the true sense of the word, and that some of them are actual murderers.' There was no question of their cases being reconsidered.

Most likely it was Osborn who reminded the Colonial Office of this dispatch:

Harriette wished that he and she had been allowed to fight it out in the chamber itself. But it was Dr G.B. Clarke, the pro-Boer radical, who objected with spirit to British policy and activities in Zululand, although without much grasp of the facts. T.E. Ellis, the Welsh nationalist, protested at the way in which Harriette Colenso had been attacked, as did J.A. Picton, a Liberal MP. He picked up the debate after the weekend and chose to tell the House of the death of Msushwana. He quoted directly from the evidence that Harriette Colenso had collected at Eshowe from the old woman of the Dletsheni.[33] It is dreadful in its detail of the callous violence against women and children, and Harriette chose it deliberately to try to make what happened, under British rule, have some impact on the tired gentlemen in the House.[34]

It was a cross-party debate, and Captain Bethell spoke from the government side of the House. Melmoth Osborn, he said, was a man for whom he had no particular animosity but whose public statements against the Usuthu should preclude him from continuing in his post. Osborne Morgan, another Welsh nationalist and Liberal of standing, defended Dinuzulu on grounds that Harriette must have found objectionable – but had to accept as part of the price of his support. 'We all know that in a country like South Africa human life is far less sacred than in a country like England,' he said of the country which had initiated the invasion of 1879, and 'It may be that Miss Colenso probably has indulged in some of that feminine exaggeration which probably we look for when we get female suffrage ... But Miss Colenso is thoroughly honest and generous in spirit, and she carried on with enthusiasm the work bequeathed to her by her father.'[35]

The quality of the debate improved when James Bryce, eminent barrister, academic and writer, soon to become a member of the Liberal Cabinet, took the floor. If Harriette Colenso was an agitator, he said, then the colonies needed more of them. In Ireland there was resistance to the police, but this was not depicted as high treason. The Privy Council had passed judgment on the legitimacy of the court, not on its sentencing, which was far too severe, and he felt that a division should be taken 'so that we may have an opportunity of recording our protest against the policy which has been pursued'.[36] The government received a majority of 42.

Parliament went into recession, and Harriette prepared her Natal audience for the accounts they would read in the press.

> So you have just got the first notice of the Debate. You will find it improve as you hear more of it. One prominent M.P. writes to me 'The debate and the division gave great pleasure to your friends, and *indeed* to all who had followed the question sufficiently to understand the questions of justice and humanity

involved: and we congratulate you on the success – for such it may certainly be called – which has attended your persevering efforts in the cause of right.' And I don't think that many of them labour under the delusion that this 'success' will affect me otherwise than to whet my appetite for more.[37]

The setbacks, mischaracterisations, even insults notwithstanding, the overall strategy was a sound one, and she wanted her friends in Natal to know this. But behind the letters of encouragement that she wrote and received was the still unstated realisation that whatever victories were gained, they were minor ones: it was now clear that justice was not going to be brought to Zululand on a wave of popular support in Britain.

We can sense the disappointment and concern lying behind the determination and grim optimism of her letters in her longing to return to Natal. England was never 'home' for Harriette Colenso, and she resisted the settlers' habit of using the word in this way. From the house in Somerset which her uncle had taken for the summer, she stared out of the window at the parkland and the rain sweeping across the Severn estuary and the 'beautiful big trees here, which it is a pleasure just to look at. One a plane tree towers and billows just in front of my window – but if it takes all this rain to keep them going – why, I prefer a gum tree ... Sala kahle Katie dear.'[38]

She travelled to the Lake District as a guest of friends and supporters. For a few moments her letters notice the wider world around her, before they move back to her family, and to the cause.

> The steamer crowded with all sorts of people, with gloves and without, botanists with tin cases, small boys with towels, maidens with sweethearts, and chaperons with ducklings, brass band playing, dancing dogs performing at the landing place. But the lake itself is beautiful, and the hills around, some of them not cut up by hedges.
>
> [Frank and Sophie have] just fresh papered and painted our rooms for us! So we think that we must let them dry before we go into them, and go back to our lodgings, which are rather fun ...
>
> Oh my dear, I must not go on chattering to you. I really ought to be taking a turn at Baron H. de Worms – or at church matters.[39]

Although she still had to work on her own, taking the bulk of the responsibility, she did find a radical, energetic young woman journalist who was prepared to help her. Alice Werner was another independent and talented woman whose journalism and scholarly ambitions were also rooted in the support given her by her

Photo 32. This picture conveys a message from the Colenso family in England in the 1890s to their Zulu allies – the exiled abantwana *on St Helena in particular. Mrs Colenso is in the centre together with all her children, their wives and children. Agnes at the back on the left holds the* iziqu *for the camera, and Harriette the* shokobezi. *Eric, or Nondenisa, who met the exiles while they were in gaol in Eshowe, also has* iziqu *around his neck and what appears to be a doll, which figures in other photographs and appears to have a special significance for him and the exiles.*

mother and sister. She was determined to make her own life and was in time to become the first Professor of African Languages at the University of London, and remained a close and supportive friend of the Colenso sisters all their lives. Harriette's brothers Robert and Frank were now both in London and tried to help, but they were unable to give the unqualified material and moral support that was expected of them as Colensos. Robert was financially strapped and Frank was unhappy and under pressure at work, and his wife Sophie, while sympathetic, was also very intense and nervous under the increased pressure on her family. Difficulties arose over the accommodation of these very independent but rather impractical women from Natal who were determined to pursue the cause regardless of cost. But the three Bishopstowe women were intensely involved with and protective of their grandchildren, nephew and nieces, and as soon as they could they rented rooms of their own, nearby but independent of their brothers.

While Harriette concentrated on the political work, it was Agnes who stayed behind to look after her mother. Strange and withdrawn, Agnes was not easy to live with. She hated London – 'a ghastly place – gorgeousness and misery, prancing carriage and weary cab horses all so near together' – but she had to be there, to look after her sister and for the sake of the cause. In their old age Agnes reminisced with Sophie Colenso about these days in London: of how she waited through the early hours of the morning for her sister to return from the debates in the Commons: 'I never see Orion without thinking of the balcony over your front door in St John's Wood from which I used to watch for the cab bringing Harry home from listening to Mr Charles Bradlaugh in the House of Commons when it was clear Orion was always there in the sky.'[40]

'A lizard in the sand'

On 19 January 1890 the men for whom Harriette and Agnes Colenso were working, Dinuzulu kaCetshwayo, Ndabuko and Shingana kaMpande, had been taken from cells in the Eshowe gaol to the Resident Commissioner's office, where they found the Governor of Zululand, Sir Charles Mitchell, waiting for them. Osborn had already told them that the sentences passed by the Court of Special Commissioners had been confirmed in London, and that they were to be sent into exile on the island of St Helena. Now the Governor wanted to confirm that they had understood these instructions, and to answer any questions they might have. The interview took over two hours. From the translated account of the meeting, it seems as if Mitchell thought it was best to communicate with Zulus in the biblical mode, with Queen Victoria standing in for Jehovah and the Governor his prophet:

> Now, the Queen with Her 'Indunas' has read over all the evidence and Her wise men of the Law and Chief men have advised Her that the sentences passed are right ones and consequently She has confirmed the sentences of the Court and you become like all other prisoners, and if you remained in Zululand you would be treated by the Law as ordinary prisoners.
>
> But then the Queen said, 'These men have been chiefs in their Land and it would not please me, that they should work like common prisoners. Therefore I wilt send them to a country in my dominions, where they can enjoy indulgences which it is impossible to grant them in Zululand, where they would be shut up in a cell and not be able to see the green grass.'[41]

They were to be allowed a male attendant each, the uncles to take a wife with them, and Dinuzulu two female attendants. Once they had gained confidence the *abantwana* began to take advantage of the Governor's presence, and used it well:

Dinuzulu: What will become of the people remaining here, I mean the women, my family?

His Excellency: Do you think anybody will molest them?

Dinuzulu: They will have trouble, not seeing us will be a trouble to them.

H.E.: It is a trouble to my people at home, not seeing me.

Dinuzulu: In your case it is different. You are not a prisoner.

H.E.: But then I have committed no offence to make me a prisoner.

Dinuzulu: Your people will have a hope of seeing you again.

H.E.: So will your people. You will not be much longer away from your people than I will be away from mine.

Dinuzulu: Is it likely that you will be away from your friends such a long time?

Governor: I am sent here for six years.

Dinuzulu, strongly backed by his uncles, asked that his own medical attendant be allowed to go with them. 'I am not strong. I want the medical attendant selected by my father to accompany me.' He was to get his way. Paul Mthimkhulu joined the exiles.

The prisoners were hustled out of the gaol at Eshowe at dawn on 3 February 1890, two days before Harriette Colenso arrived in England. The authorities took great care that the move through Natal for embarkation in Durban would be secret and secure. The mule-drivers, however, managed to steal Dinuzulu's stash of *insangu*. Its absence was to be a great trial on St Helena.

Dinuzulu was accompanied by Nyosana kaMdwala as his male attendant, Zihlazile, daughter of the chief Qethuka, and Umkasilomo, daughter of Ntuzwa of the Mdlalose. Ndabuko and Shingana were each accompanied by one of their wives and a male attendant. With them went a custodian, W. Saunders, and Anthony Daniels, an African educated at Lovedale, as interpreter.

Harriette Colenso had tried to get Magema Fuze appointed to the post of interpreter. He had already begun teaching Dinuzulu, having replaced Harriette when she left Eshowe. But the officials would have nothing to do with the 'notorious' Magema. The interpreters and guardians were to be changed often. Most were unsatisfactory, they became embroiled in petty squabbles with their charges, were dissatisfied with their wages and working conditions, and over-indulged in what would seem to have been a real hazard of St Helena life, alcohol.

Soon after they arrived, Dinuzulu dictated a long letter to his mother. He described the journey, the seasickness, and their first impression of the island. They were pleased to discover that they were not to be closely confined, and that the house, Rosemary Hall, in which they were to live was spacious and out of Jamestown. He asked her to arrange to send them things they needed. Dagga, tobacco and snuff, various eating utensils, a new gourd from Qethuka to replace the one broken on board ship, fibres to weave prepuce covers, various plants to be used as medicine, and money. He was, of course, desperately concerned to hear from his people at home, and passed his greetings and his concern for them in his absence, for

> you are at your homes drinking beer and happy, and I am thrown away, and yet you don't give me any news. I asked the Governor at Eshowe if a fence could be put up round the women's huts so as to protect them, remember me kindly to Boko, – Have Nenegwa's people built a kraal for my cattle? are all my horses alive? and are my dogs well?[42]

It was never easy for the authorities to decide what degree of control they should exercise over the exiles. They had been sent to St Helena to make it easier to control access to their supporters and to demonstrate the finality of their sentences, without having to detain them too closely. But they were still convicted rebels, and all letters and all parcels were checked by the authorities. The officials in Zululand were determined to make the restrictions on their communications with the rest of the world as severe as possible, but they found it impossible to control completely the information getting through to them, or their contact with the outside world.

Letter-writing was an important activity for the exiles. Until Dinuzulu learnt to write they were dependent on the interpreter or Paul Mthimkhulu for this, and soon large numbers of messages were going to Zululand, to relatives, to friends, missionaries, friendly Zululand officials, asking favours and enquiring after their families, their followers and livestock. They mourned the deaths in Zululand and gave advice on domestic disputes. Requests for money were a recurring theme. Paul Mthimkhulu could not continue accepting the offer of a St Helenian woman who insisted on doing his laundry. 'Send money,' he wrote, 'I feel ashamed that such a woman should wash my clothes and charge nothing. I will at least have to pay the children, who fetch the dirty clothes and bring the clean ones back.'[43] Dinuzulu had a monarch's expectations of his subjects' duties towards him: 'Concerning the money I will have no objections. The money *must* come. By Mpande! By Mpande! Wo Tya! You people are good for nothings.'[44]

And from Magema Fuze he requested a copy of the hymn book produced by the American Board Mission. 'I know you will loiter about it. Your movements are like of the Chameleon as a rule. Do for once try to act like the Lizard.'[45]

Magema Fuze, now employed to train printers at St Alban's mission in Pietermaritzburg, was already working hard for the Usuthu.[46] It was he who transcribed the messages coming from Zululand, working them into letter form, and collected the monetary contributions, for transmission to the authorities, who sent them on to St Helena. Osborn wrote a string of sour minutes pointing to the unwarranted assumptions of chiefly authority on the part of the exiles and their continued attempts at agitation.

Once they had gained some confidence at Rosemary Hall, the exiles began to test the limits of their detention. The question of their health became a matter of dispute, giving them a chance to protest. When they fell ill they objected vehemently to aspects of medical examination. Ndabuko refused to accept not only the insertion of a catheter but the taking of urine samples.[47] The great crisis came in September 1890 when the women were found to be pregnant.[48] Tradition demanded that they be secluded, and the men insisted that they should be sent to Zululand for their confinement. The Governor refused. It would cost too much, especially when 'there would appear to be every reasonable probability of a similar charge forming an annual item in the maintenance of the Zulu establishment in St. Helena'. The Bishop of St Helena tried to intervene. He suggested they be secluded on St Helena – but, Dinuzulu asked, who would then attend to the birth? 'They must be sent to the care of his mother, and other Zulu women. And the women themselves would die rather than be nursed by other than their own people, and that no suffering would induce them to be treated by a male doctor.'[49]

Osborn commented that the real reason for the request was that, according to custom, sexual relations were deferred for from one to two years after childbirth. Dinuzulu and his uncles declared that they had told the Governor in Eshowe that they would have preferred to have had only male attendants, but the Governor had replied that the women had to accompany them, on orders from the Queen. It was agreed that they should be sent back if Dinuzulu paid the passages – and recognise that they would not necessarily be replaced. But Dinuzulu refused to sign the document, and in the end the women remained on St Helena and a midwife was sent from Zululand. At the end of 1890 Shingana's wife had a boy, and Dinuzulu's attendants a boy and a girl.

The disputes went on. They had their own doctor in Paul Mthimkhulu, but he of course needed his own medicines – and this meant that they should be collected at home, which in turn meant communication with Zululand and Natal. For

Osborn it was just another subterfuge; for the exiles, a matter of life and death.

> He is a great medicine man. If Paul had not been with us, we would have been dead ...
> *Our* medicines are not like those of the Europeans, provided with labels and properly weighed in scales. A dose of our medicines is measured by a man, duly instructed by the doctor, and a person, who has been shown how the medicine has to be used, is the only one who understands the medicine.[50]

In the middle of 1891 another crisis began to emerge. Ndabuko and Shingana wrote about it to Harriette Colenso:

> we are greatly troubled in our minds, because we are like 'beasts' in our appearance. We are ashamed to show ourselves amongst people, as we are afraid of being laughed at ... Our marks of distinction, the headrings, are worn out, and therefore we write you, asking you to plead for us, that a person from Zululand might be sent to us to dress our hair.

Materials together with detailed instructions ('1. Twist the Usinga (back sinew fibre) into a cord about the size of sail-twine ...') arrived at St Helena. But the attempt was not successful, and when some of the attendants were exchanged later it was made sure that a skilled hairdresser was amongst their number.

The exiles made a favourable impression in St Helena. They attended social occasions – a concert in Jamestown, a picnic held by the Admiral and officers, a cricket match at the Governor's residence. Ndabuko, it is true, was withdrawn and morose, showing little interest in the events around him. But Shingana's good nature was commented upon by visitors to Rosemary Hall, and Dinuzulu kaCetshwayo was seen as an attractive and interesting young man. He was soon happy wearing 'English' clothing, had asked for a bed, and was working hard at his lessons. These had been begun with Harriette Colenso and Magema Fuze in the Eshowe gaol and were now taken up by the custodian and the bishop's wife. It was officially reported that Dinuzulu

> no longer dons the primitive garb of his native country (i.e. skintails and blan- ket) as he used to before my arrival at Saint Helena and as his uncles still do, but he takes a pride in being well dressed, at all times, even distinguishing the difference between gaudy – coloured apparel – so attractive in the eyes of savages – and the sombre but more becoming hues of the garments of civilised races.[51]

By 1891 he was writing letters in Zulu on his own. His first letter to Harriette Colenso complained angrily at the inadequacy of the education he was receiving – 'Can a candle give light, unless there is some one to light it?' – but ended with the postscript 'I, Dinuzulu have written it all with my own hand'.[52]

In December he wrote again to Harriette, in whose translation the letter is a document rich in association, fascinating in its choice of metaphor.

Rosemary Hall St Helena 13 December 1891

These to you, Madam, Miss Colenso, at the home of Gebuza ... in London, saying:–

See, now! here have I been writing although no one is helping me, and I am like an ignorant lizard sprawling through thick sand. Here are actually two letters written by me. And if I were not in bondage I should verily be over there now, where you are, and studying books. I greatly desire to learn, indeed, I am like one who has been long athirst, receiving no water, until he feels as if he must swallow the whole river. That is just the feeling I have. But then, too, I am like a fly wrapped round in the spider's web, though his heart is alive. I too am just like that, or I should be at school now, over there where you are, while you are there in London. We should be glad to know that you are all well, you and Nondela [Eric, her nephew, whom Dinuzulu had met at Eshowe] and my Grandmother [Sarah Frances Colenso], and your sister, and all your Father's house. As for us, we are all well; but O! Dlwedlwe could you not write to us just a single letter that we may learn if you are well. What troubles us in this land of St Helena is the rain. It is a daily affair here, every day, upon our word of honour. But our real trouble is the bad news which comes from home of much disease or death there.

And now an end. I salute you much, and my uncles salute you much, and all our party at St Helena send salutations.

Farewell, Friend of my Father. This is I, your Dinuzulu son of Cetshwayo of the Zulus.[53]

With a letter like this to drive her on, there could be no going back to Natal until something had been achieved for the Zulu prince, something to hold out hope for the future.

CHAPTER 24

HARRIETTE COLENSO IN ENGLAND
(1892–1893)

❦

'Absolute irresponsibility'

arriette Colenso was planning questions for the new parliamentary session. It was exacting work trying to contact, then persuade and, most
difficult of all, to inform the handful of MPs prepared to speak for the
Zulu cause in the House. They realised only too well how vulnerable they might
be if the Under-Secretary challenged their intervention on matters of fact and,
instead of promoting the Usuthu cause, they provided the government with the
opportunity to make a public statement against it. Harriette tried to interest
Chamberlain in the Zulu case, but he declined to see her and expressed his confidence in the present policy.[1] She was very disappointed but, as a friend reminded her, elections were imminent and 'you must always bear in mind that Mr
Chamberlain never does anything except he thinks it is for his interest'. Instead
she should 'bang away at these Tory members – they will be increasingly fidgety
as their term of life shortens in the parliamentary history'.[2]

The civil service estimates were again chosen as the peg on which to hang the
Zulu debate. On 18 March 1892, J.A. Picton, Liberal Unionist member for
Leicester, opened with a long account of recent Zulu history. It was a wearisome
experience for the members present and his reference to Britain's 'sacred duty to
these poor, uneducated, or, at best, half-cultivated people' shows once again the
extent to which Harriette was unfortunately at the mercy of her own parliamentary sympathisers.

In his reply the Under-Secretary at the Colonial Office said that he appreciated the member's concern. Nonetheless, it was unwarranted. Zululand was
peaceful and prosperous. Revenue was increasing, and there was now a surplus
on the current account. And he drew attention to a pamphlet that had been cir-
culated to members, written by Miss Colenso. It described the situation in
Zululand in the most alarming terms and stated that preparations were being
made to allow Zibhebhu to return to his territory in the north. This statement,

De Worms announced, was 'absolutely without foundation'. He then turned on Miss Colenso:

> If trouble ensues in Zululand, though it is now in a most peaceful condition, it will be in great measure due to the action of persons like Miss Colenso, who act with the freedom and recklessness of absolute irresponsibility. I had occasion last year to speak of the course pursued by Miss Colenso in severe terms, and in the responsible position which I have the honour to occupy in this House I repeat that condemnation of her action, and do not hesitate to affirm that documents such as she has circulated here to-day, when transmitted to Zululand, are more likely to bring about trouble there than any possible action of Her Majesty's Government.

Osborne Morgan, the Welsh nationalist, defended Hariette – although even then his attempt to treat all sides fairly must have been hurtful to her: 'It may be possible that Miss Colenso has indulged in a certain amount of exaggeration; but we must remember that she acts from the highest philanthropic motives.'

After extracting from De Worms the assurance that Zibhebhu would not be sent back, Picton then withdrew the motion. But he was not willing to let the attack on Harriette Colenso go unanswered, and he objected to the way De Worms had spoken about her. He was backed in this by Alfred Webb: 'Unfortunately, we Irishmen have too much reason to know this in our own experience. A person like Miss Colenso is often likely to be more accurately informed than officials in such matters, and instead of blaming her I think the whole nation is under a deep debt of gratitude to her.'[3]

The Liberals in power – stolid resistance to change

It was true that there had been certain gains for Harriette Colenso in this debate. A renewed attempt to return Zibhebhu had been vetoed from London; the Usuthu were not just going to be eclipsed by reports of peace and prosperity in Zululand: their view of events, the voice of the exiles on St Helena, had been heard and placed on record, and would have to be a factor in future decisions about the country. However, De Worms's defence had been effective, and his attack on Harriette Colenso must have suggested to many the sexist stereotype of an over-zealous, even hysterical, female. Some believed that the attack reflected badly on De Worms and the administration in which he served. But again – with all the work she had put into the debate – it would do very little to increase the chances of achieving even her immediate objective, the early return of the exiles to Zululand. Without this, or at least some firm indication that their lot was to be ameliorated, it remained very difficult for Harriette to return to Natal.

But in the summer of 1892, the Conservative government called a general election. Although she had little faith in contemporary Liberal administrations, a change of government might give her more opportunities to publicise the Zulu case. Her return to Natal was delayed once again. New lodgings were found for herself, her sister and her mother, while her friends in Natal, Katie Giles, the Africans at Bishopstowe, the Usuthu in Zululand and the exiles on St Helena, were told yet again to be patient.

Harriette worked hard for the Liberals in the election campaign of the summer of 1892. Dadabhai Naoroji, a founder member of the Indian National Congress, asked her (in a gratifyingly misleading letter) 'as a great friend and supporter of the Liberal party and of all oppressed peoples more especially of India'[4] to campaign on his behalf. It was a controversial campaign, but he was elected with the narrowest of majorities to became the first Indian MP.

Gladstone formed his last ministry in August 1892; in the opinion of the Queen, she entrusted her government 'to the shaking hand of an old, wild and incomprehensible man of 82'.[5] Harriette Colenso, after twenty years of attempting without success to persuade British governments, Conservative and Liberal, to act with justice towards all the peoples of the Empire, had no reason to be unduly optimistic that this particular administration would be the exception. Moreover, the aggressive chauvinism of the new imperialism was gaining a hold on increasing numbers of Britons. The Foreign Secretary, Lord Rosebery, who was to take over the government after Gladstone's retirement in 1894, was a Liberal imperialist, who believed that imperial policy demanded a continuity which should place it beyond the volatility of party politics. Nonetheless, the Colonial Secretary was Lord Ripon, who as Viceroy in India had gained a reputation for tolerance and liberal reform. His Under-Secretary, Sydney Buxton, was also considered to be more sympathetic to the first element in the concept of Liberal imperialism, and Harriette and her friends had hopes in both men.

Zululand, however, was not high on the administration's agenda. Ireland dominated the political life of the new government as Gladstone brought Home Rule – the issue which had beset and finally split the Liberals' last administration – before the House again. Southern African affairs were also becoming more and more tense, with attention being drawn towards the north-west interior, where the development of the goldfields of the Transvaal continued to transform all aspects of the subcontinent's social and political life, and Rhodes and the British South Africa Company were preparing for further acts of expansion and deprivation.

In Natal, the movement for responsible government was proceeding with some success. When the latest proposals were placed before the settler electorate they were accepted on a recount. As far as the colony of Zululand was concerned, it was agreed that the exile of the Usuthu chiefs had improved the situation. The budget showed a surplus. Most of the income was derived from the hut tax, which was collected from the cash brought into Zululand by young men working for wages outside the colony – an admirable state of affairs. As far as the permanent staff of the Colonial Office were concerned, there could be no radical change in policy towards British Zululand. Miss Colenso's agitation on behalf of the chiefs ('lecturing about them in every constituency in England for two years past') was not going to be allowed to play on the liberal consciences of the new administration and persuade them to reverse policy. Even as Ripon and Buxton were moving into their offices in Whitehall, the permanent officials began to prepare answers to the inevitable letters and petitions that Harriette and Fox Bourne of the APS were indeed at that moment drafting for the consideration of the new administration.

The expected letter from the APS was posted on 22 August. Fairfield, on the staff at the Colonial Office, informed his new Secretary of State, Ripon, that while he had tried to make his draft reply 'as conciliatory as possible',

> It seems to me important to dispel the sort of wild idea that as there is a new government they [the APS] and Miss Colenso are to be allowed to dance on everybody, and that these Usuthu who are really rebels although not a very sinister type, are to have their horn [?] exalted, whilst the Mandlakazi are to be bullied and reviled for adhering to the British side ...

Osborn, Fairfield advised, should

> not be thrown to the lions in his old age, as the scapegoat of the sins of those who made the Zulu War of 1879 and thus begat all this crowd of troubles.
>
> There was a time when he would have lost his situation if he had acted in the way to be approved by the A.P.S. and Miss Colenso, and it would strike at the whole civil service of this country to condemn him untried. There has not been a crisis in the history of Zululand for 10 years past when the Secretary of State could not have given a perfect turn to events by a scratch of his pen ... If the local authorities had been overridden ... decisively in 1887 when they proposed to restore Zibhebhu, the rebellion of 1888 would probably not have taken place ... Others must share the blame of that mistake with him [Osborn] – including myself.[6]

343

The situation, Fairfield felt, demanded a response based on practical policy, not sentiment. He was not averse to making concessions, even to proposing substantial changes in Zululand. There had undoubtedly been much that was injudicious in the behaviour of the local officials. But to admit this did not mean that Harriette Colenso was correct in her opinions and interpretations of events. The fact remained that the Usuthu had rebelled, and their return could well create disturbances once again. Their exile, Fairfield argued, was not so much punitive as a measure taken for the sake of peace. For the same reason Zibhebhu was confined to the south of the country. Moreover, the Usuthu

> could not be sent back to Zululand as long as Mr Osborn is Resident Commisioner, because that measure would utterly destroy his authority, and the Usuthus, in the triumph of their return, would 'go for' the Anti-Usutus and perhaps defy the British Authorities ... [Harriette Colenso] has been the great thorn in the side of the British Government in Zululand, and her messages of encouragement to the Usuthus, and constant prophesying that the late Government would be upset and that Sir Charles Mitchell and Mr Osborn would go to the wall with the Cabinet, has prevented things from settling down ...[7]

Even as Fairfield's minutes were being considered, the Colonial Office received two assessments on Osborn. The first summarised the colony's 'very healthy and satisfactory' financial situation. Fairfield used it to defend the Resident Commissioner:

> Mr Osborn is a cautious administrator and very successful outside the Ndwandwe district, where owing to his having been indoctrinated with the views of those who made the Zulu war, he has made mistakes. But his loyalty to his superiors is a virtue even where these superiors were grossly mistaken. I am preparing for consideration answers to attacks on him by Miss Colenso and the APS which take some such line as the above – our getting rid of him quietly on our own accounts is a different thing to throwing him to these lions.[8]

From the other side there was a pamphlet by Harriette Colenso, *Mr Osborn as a Source of Confusion in Zulu Affairs*. Fairfield minuted that it 'simply comes to this',

> that dating as he does from the time when every official was bound to act on the principle of pulverizing the Usuthus, he did it too well and that up to a short time ago his despatches had the ring in them of the words of Frere and Wolseley and the elder Shepstone. It was the way to get promotion in those days, and to avoid dismissal; and to make this unfortunate survivor of a past regime the

scapegoat for it all would be to strike at the root of the civil service system. There was a great change in Mr. Osborn worked by his coming here early in 1891, and although it would be well for all parties that he should retire with honour we cannot admit, and I should hope we will repel the principle of presumptive disqualification which Miss Colenso and the APS would have us enforce.[9]

In this manner, steadily and carefully, Fairfield ensured that, even though there were to be changes, they would not be immediate, and they would be sufficiently limited to ensure continuity in Zulu policy. Attempts to answer Harriette Colenso's long and detailed letters were for the most part abandoned. Instead she would be granted personal interviews not only with the Under-Secretary, Sydney Buxton, but with the Secretary of State himself. It was easier and quicker for them to use the personal interview, within the precincts of the highest offices of the Empire, to ingratiate themselves with her, than to allow her to challenge them point by point on Zulu matters in writing. As Harriette Colenso said, 'Of course they don't tell one anything, only they don't snub me, and they seem to listen carefully to what I say, and to wish to do *something*.'[10] Finally, the greatest of these great Liberal personages was called upon to play his part in silencing this persistent critic. He used the magnanimous gesture to do so: in October Harriette received a private letter from Mr Gladstone in which he told her that he was '"very sensible of your ... strong claims to respectful attention!"'[11]

Years before, Chamberlain had warned Frank Colenso of the propensity of officials to protect their own.[12] It was exactly this that the permanent officials responsible for Zululand did now. John Westlake, loyal and eminent friend, must have had sources within the Colonial Office of great authority, for his advice to Harriette at the end of the year summarised exactly what was happening in its corridors and committee rooms. He warned her that

> In estimating how far the Colonial Office has advanced, it will not do to take opinions [?] of the highest only into account, as the permanent service in that or in any government office is able to oppose a deal of stolid resistance to any change of policy, and often does so. The chiefs of a department often give good words to outsiders, which they really mean, but which they find themselves unable to give effect to when they have conferred with the permanent staff.[13]

Sir Melmoth Osborn

So by the end of the year, in the depths of the Colonial Office, it had been decided to continue with the old policy towards Zululand while making preparations for slow reform. Osborn was to be encouraged to retire, but at his own speed, and with no hint that he was being forced out. It was hoped that he would be knighted, wrote Fairfield, although he hesitated: Osborn 'has a wife living who had disgraced herself by forming an intrigue with a boy during her husband's absence on service' and such a decoration 'would therefore turn her into "her ladyship."'[14]

On 3 January 1893 Osborn wrote a private letter to Fairfield:

> I am now sixty years of age and after all the difficulties, worries and dangers I have had to encounter during so long a period I desire rest. Moreover it is clear to me that my continuing in office would add considerably to the task of the Secretary of State in governing Zululand owing, among other reasons, to the determined and implacable opposition I have incurred from the APS in their well meaning but mistaken interferences in Zulu Affairs. I should be much obliged if you would represent my wish in the proper quarter.[15]

After having extracted a promise of resignation from the man they wished to retire, the Colonial Office urged him not to rush. A replacement had to be found as Zululand's Resident Commissioner, someone upon whom they could rely to decide whether a new direction should be considered in the British policy towards Zululand. When Osborn's formal letter of resignation arrived in London at the end of May, it had been decided that he should be replaced by the present Administrator of Basutoland, Sir Marshal Clarke.

Clarke had been in Natal twenty years before as a military officer, during which time he had acted as a Resident Magistrate. He had served in the Transvaal when Shepstone was in charge and had been appointed as Administrator of Basutoland after it had been abandoned to the British government by the Cape following the 'Gun War' of the early 1880s. There he had developed a policy which recognised and worked through the traditional chieftainship, the family of Moshoeshoe I in particular. Already the idea of recognising existing African political authorities, rather than undermining them as the officials had done in Zululand, had caught the attention of Harriette Colenso. Early in 1893 she had written to Clarke to ask questions about the history of Lesotho, comparing it with the history of Zululand. She challenged Theophilus Shepstone's view that the Zulu kingdom had been created comparatively recently as a result of Shaka's conquests. Her research suggested that Zulu power predated Shaka, and that his conquests were a late development in a long process of consolidation. Shepstone, she suggested, had been unduly influenced by having grown up outside Zululand, amongst people who had suffered from Shaka's raids. She asked for information and sources on Lesotho history –

suspecting from what she had already read, and quite correctly, that Moshoeshoe 'was not altogether a man of peace, I think?'[16]

But, although she was in private correspondence with Clarke, Harriette Colenso was of course told nothing officially of what was to happen in Zululand. As a consequence she was forced to wait in London in an agony of suspense, searching the newspapers, asking in high places, putting questions in the House, for a hint on how policy was to develop. She was unable to plan her return to Natal, and had to continue drawing on the resources of her friends and relatives, and suffer the consequences of this. In some ways it was more difficult to have Liberals in power than Conservatives because it meant that she had to treat the officials as potential allies rather than proven enemies. She had to be circumspect in her comments on these men and yet suffer the delays they imposed on her. As she wrote to her new friend and supporter, Alice Werner (sharing a joke on the problems the Court of Special Commissioners had in translating legal terms into Zulu) 'I must not hurry the Col. Off over their Xtmas, that would be i-high treason.'[17]

Early in the new year her hopes were raised again when she learnt that Sir Charles Mitchell, Governor of Natal and of Zululand, was to visit England. Officially it was to discuss the introduction of responsible government for Natal. But, Harriette felt, Zulu matters must also be on the agenda.[18] For some time she had been writing a pamphlet which summarised the ideas she was developing on the exiles' role in Zulu affairs once they had been returned. It was time now to complete the document and submit it for inclusion in the internal discussions in the Colonial Office on policy towards the Zulu.

'Mostly old history'

She called her pamphlet *The Present Position among the Zulus (1893) with Some Suggestions for the Future.* It was 32 pages long, many of them taken up with a protest against the existing administration in Zululand. It objected to Zululand's fragmentation under an increasingly large number of petty chiefs, and to the application of Natal customary law. She argued against the view that the Usuthu party was just one tribe amongst many, and Dinuzulu one chief amongst others. She reiterated her defence of the Usuthu chiefs and her attack on the verdict and the sentences of the Court of Special Commissioners, before turning in the final pages to a proposal for the future. In keeping with the advice that was given her on all sides, it was a modest proposal and, although she did not say so overtly, it was clearly just a first step. She proposed that Dinuzulu should be returned to Zululand, not as just another chief but as a

Head Induna appointed in the name of the Queen at a salary of four hundred a year, who shall hold office during Her Majesty's pleasure.

Such Head Induna shall aid and assist in the government of Zululand by carrying out the orders and instructions of the Governor of Zululand as conveyed to him by the Chief Magistrate.[19]

Such a move would recognise Dinuzulu's unique position without undermining the authority of other chiefs. It would also be a move which would have the support of the leading Natal lawyer and politician, and friend of Harriette Colenso and the Usuthu, Harry Escombe. 'It is submitted', she concluded, 'that this good understanding between the principal native race, and a leader of the Forward party in Natal politics, is an influence on the side of peace and order in that part of South Africa which it would be difficult to over-estimate, and which deserves recognition and support.'[20] What she couldn't say publicly, however, was that the proposal was not just supported, but had in fact originated with the leader of the Forward party, Harry Escombe, himself.

She worked hard to get the pamphlet to the Colonial Office while Mitchell was in England, and had great expectations of it. But far from being an influence on future policy, Fairfield dismissed it as 'very jumbled'. His colleague Sydney Olivier felt more strongly:

Miss Colenso has no conception of how to write an effective pamphlet. I don't think any one but a member of an opposition in Parliament could read through this with enthusiasm. Half the energy she devotes to these brochures, directed to getting a journalist or two on an evening paper to take up her cause would help her very much more than all these labours. Perhaps, for the sake of a fair judgement of the matter, it is fortunate that she does not adopt this method.[21]

'To any one without extensive knowledge of the Zulu question I should think they would be quite unintelligible,' he minuted a week later. And anyway, another official wrote, it was 'mostly old history'.[22]

Convinced that an announcement on the Zulu question was imminent, she continued to wait. But while there was movement, it was not at a pace to satisfy Harriette. The Colonial Office was not going to be rushed. Meanwhile Harriette did seal some boxes of books ready for shipment to Natal, but had had to keep the most important documents accessible in case they were needed. Still no announcement came. When the lease on the house they were renting came to an end, they had to move again. They pushed their possessions to their new lodgings in a pram belonging to her brother's family.

Sir Marshal Clarke

It was on 2 May, in answer to a question from Baron de Worms, now on the Opposition bench, that the House was informed that Melmoth Osborn was to retire as Resident Commissioner in Zululand. A month later Buxton announced that there would be no changes in British policy towards Zululand until Osborn's successor, Sir Marshal Clarke, had taken up his appointment.

It was a victory – of sorts. The departure of Osborn at least meant that it was now possible to consider a change in policy. And in Clarke, the Zulu administration would have at its head a man unconnected with Shepstone's policy and who had a reputation of being independent enough to develop new directions with confidence. What this might be was, of course, still undecided. Yet again the future of Zululand, and that of the exiles on St Helena, would have to wait, first for Clarke's official investigation, then his report to London, after which it would have to be carefully considered before any policy could be formulated.

For Harriette it was time to return to Natal to await these decisions. But to the last she kept as much pressure on the Colonial Office as she could. She completed a pamphlet on the sentences passed on the less important Usuthu implicated in the disturbances. When *The Cases of Six Usuthu* arrived at the Colonial Office, Buxton commented wearily, 'I suggested that she should put them into writing – from this mouse this mountain.' 'Miss Colenso is just off ... to S Africa in order to keep an eye on Sir M Clarke!'[23] But it was all very well to comment in exasperation at her persistence: she had nonetheless made her mark, and whatever their precise impact, Harriette Colenso's protests would have to be considered when coming to a decision on the future of Zululand and its leaders.

'"Dish" (or dished)'

Before she left there was much to do and some important speeches to make. One was to the annual meeting of the Women's Liberal Federation in the Holborn town hall. By now she was well practised and showed little nervousness before a large audience. The other speech was at the annual meeting of the APS on 17 May 1893, when she was asked to move a resolution urging Her Majesty's Government to show a 'greatly increased watchfulness and energy ... to protect the aborigines of Africa from injury by the present extensions of European influence in various parts of the continent, alike under British and under other auspices'. It was clear that what in South Africa was called 'the native problem' was in fact the result of 'depriving African tribes – a huge majority of the population, keen-witted people, accustomed to manage their own affairs – of the democratic checks inherent in their own organization, while they are unable to take part in ours'. She reminded her audience of a recent statement by the Prime Minister, that 'it is impossible to govern a country in the interests of law and order without some regard to the sympathies and convictions and traditions of the people'.

Above all, she urged that the exiles on St Helena be returned while they still had their health, and asked that her audience 'watch Zulu affairs during the next few months with special interest'. 'We ourselves, my mother, and my sister, and myself, begin to hope that the object of our mission to England is, at last, in course of accomplishment, when we may return to continue some part of my father's work in our African home; and in that hope I bid you goodbye.'[24]

Privately she felt let down, deserted even, by the philanthropic lobby in England as manifested in the APS. It was not in her nature, nor in her philosophy, to show bitterness or recrimination. But her deep disappointment can be seen in the correspondence that passed between herself and Fox Bourne when he tried to organise a farewell gathering of the APS for her. At first she liked that idea – but she proposed a business meeting rather than the breakfast that he suggested. Fox Bourne disagreed: the amount of business in parliament, the midsummer heat, would all count against attendance at a formal evening meeting. Harriette, however, did not want a general invitation to be sent out: she was not even sure of the loyalty of all members of the APS to the Zulu cause. Instead, the farewell should be for those who had demonstrated their commitment: the Courtneys, the Alfred Webbs, Gertrude Russell, the son of Lady John Russell and her husband Rollo, the Westlakes, Captain Bethell; her friends from the Women's Liberal Association like Emma Cons, Mrs Bunting and Mrs Cobden Unwin, and Annie Leigh Browne and her mother. Fox Bourne still thought a farewell breakfast would be best: it would carry more weight and had

> a chance of being well reported, and giving you something like the representative 'send off' you deserve. There is, of course, the alternative of an afternoon 'at home' – but at this there could be no speeches, and it would have much less weight – *this* is what I want – something that would emphasize the importance of your past work …[25]

But the more he pressed, the further Harriette retreated, and in so doing revealed more of her disappointment. Her farewell could not be a celebration, for there was so little to celebrate. They had in fact achieved very little. Everything still remained to be done and her supporters in England had to be persuaded to continue the struggle, not to rest contented. In fact she would rather not attend a farewell at all – perhaps it could be held after she had gone.

I think that you really must let me off, please. Such a gathering as you pro-
pose partakes of the nature of a festivity. If we had the exiles here, now, off St
Helena on their way home, it would be different – or if we even had a fair and
square promise for them, but the permanent Colonial Office intention is as
deadly as ever ...

And as you say, most of our friends are too busy to come for the Zulu only,
some might come for the breakfast and some out of personal kindness to me, I
should feel myself to be the principal '*dish*' (or dished) – And really there is
hardly time. The above is between you and me, but may I not with all gratitude
decline the honour offered me by the Society on the ground of want of time ...

Couldn't you have a breakfast 'to my intention' as some say, when I'm
gone – I mean a breakfast on behalf of the Zulus.[26]

No farewell party was held. Early in August, Harriette, Agnes and their
mother travelled in a carriage lent to them by Mrs Browne to London docks to
board the *Grantully Castle*. Their brothers Frank and Robert came to say goodbye. Frank caught a glimpse of his mother through the porthole. He knew that
he was unlikely ever to see her again.[27]

'The Woman of the Future'

The letters which form such a wise commentary on the Colensos' life and times
hardly exist for the three and a half years they spent in London when Sarah
Frances Colenso was in immediate contact with her relatives and friends. But
they began again once she left England. She wrote to the Brownes of the journey. The captain was good-natured – but then 'Captains always are good-
natured'. Sir Horace Davey was on board: barrister and now Lord Justice of
Appeal, who at one stage it was thought would handle Dinuzulu's appeal to the
Privy Council. Harriette was soon speaking to him of Zulu matters. His daughters were travelling with him, 'very pleasant lively girls', wrote Sarah Frances, 'if
any one called them "jolly" they had not perhaps been offended'. They even
allowed her a glimpse of the contemporary cultural life that they had denied
themselves during their stay in London:

They afforded us one really considerable pleasure by acting, with the help of
some of the young men of the passengers who had perhaps seen the drama
acted in one of the London theatres. I am not acquainted with them so I
could not tell, but I was much diverted with that provided for us by our clever
fellow passengers. Its name is 'The Woman of the Future'.[28]

351

They arrived back in Natal in September. They were met by the Escombes and stayed with them in their house overlooking the bay. For Natal it was very grand, with white servants, thus letting the Colensos down gently from the civilised standards they had become used to in London, wrote Harriette, with a glance of mock horror towards Agnes for whom there was nothing civilised in London life. They travelled by train to Pietermaritzburg. Their mother wrote to Sophie of their arrival:

> Katie Giles met us at the end of the railway and vehicles belonging to this Hotel [the Imperial] being close at hand Katie saw us into it, no such easy matter for my ancient legs to climb, I did not know it was an *omnibus* until a little fat old man hopped in, and before we arrived at the Hotel, hopped out again so then I felt I was nobody which is a comfortable feeling.[29]

The cottage at Seven Oaks was in a dreadful state. Their possessions had been guarded carefully for their return, even the small pile of notepaper donated by the Usuthu for the letters to be written to St Helena. But there were white ants in the walls, fishmoths in their books and papers, and the thatch of the roof was down completely in places. Preparations were made to make it habitable. Agnes began the missionary work, attending again to the school and the health of the people on the farm. Harriette threw herself into the enormously difficult situation which had arisen over the governance and property of the Church of England, before journeying up to Eshowe to meet Marshal Clarke, the new Resident Commissioner.

It was strange not to have to confront the hostility of Osborn. Clarke found her 'very amiable' and believed that 'it is better to have such a clever partizan wishing to help instead of to thwart'.[30] It was indicative of the new mood in Zululand that she was invited to be his guest at the Residency, and while she was there she was able to meet the Governor, Sir Walter Hely-Hutchinson, as well. Floods then delayed her, and it was only on 7 December that she was able to return to Natal.

She had sent messages to the Usuthu not to organise any great welcome – for it might well be seen as a demonstration of royalist solidarity, and work against their interests at this delicate time in their history. Nonetheless, she was unable to stop a flood of personal messages and visits from the Usuthu.[31] She wrote to her mother, 'On walking over to the hut I found some 40 Usutu collected ... We strewed some of Mr. Mansel's rushes on the floor and put a chair for me, and they crowded in. The happiness in their eyes and the *trust* were worth coming from England for.'[32]

Back at Seven Oaks she found that her mother had not been well. Her daughters watched over her with concern, preparing her meals with great care, and reading to her in the evening. On Friday 22 December she was in some distress and Harriette sent a message to the doctor. That evening, at about 8.30, she

> seemed to be having a quiet sleep, and woke up quite herself, asked what we were doing, and drank off some champagne, but, a few minutes after, began to half cough, half choke, and while we put our arms round her, the dear head fell forward. I laid it on my shoulder, and we said His little prayer, which suits all times and places, but I knew already that she had left us, and so it was. It was then just half past ten.
>
> There had been no time for any last words, which is a pain for all of us; but for her it was so quick and so quiet that we can only be thankful. I think that she was the bravest woman I have ever known, but she was getting very weary.

With her death came the end of an incomparable commentator on the history of Natal and Zululand. Although her pen was not as busy in these final years, hundreds of letters from earlier years survive, to Katherine Lyell, her relatives and her children. They are marked with wit and shrewd judgement, poignant in their reflection of the failure of the Colensos' dreams and ambitions, and wise in their ironic comments on the world around her. They record long journeys: from the homes of the intellectual elite of early Victorian London to a vermin-ridden, tumble-down cottage on the estate of a colonial bishopric of doubtful legal status; from the close mental and physical confines of the narrow evangelicals at the school for young ladies in Cheltenham, to the humanism of F.D. Maurice, to the failure of the man she loved to introduce a theology of liberation in South Africa. She believed it had been her privilege to subsume her life in that of her husband but was never able to accept the narrowness of colonial life, settler prejudice, African nakedness or imperial violence.

By the 1870s she had come to question the ideals of the civilising mission itself: 'John Bull has been taught, it seems, that he is the Israel of this century, that every other of the many families of man on the globe ought to conform to his ideas, obey his laws, pay tribute to Queen Victoria etc. etc. But is it quite certain that the civilisation of Western Europe is good for Eastern Africa?'[33] Her support for her daughters' attempts to find an alternative mission which tried to understand and not impose, had consequences which make up the narrative in this book.

She was buried in Pietermaritzburg the day after she died. On Sunday Harriette and Agnes held a service at Bishopstowe:

our poor people were streaming over the hills to join us, many of them grey-haired, and all scantily clad, and, strangely enough for December in Natal, it was almost chilly ...

Tuesday, Dec 26. Today has been rather a trying one, through our poor friends coming to mourn, when one has to hear all they have to say, and reply.

The mourners continued to arrive in the days that followed. 'Today the Zulus and the Hlubis came, tomorrow we expect the *amakholwa* and perhaps the Table Mountain people, Manyosi, one of Somtseu's old Indunas sent today, he himself poor man, is half paralysed.'

Zulu beliefs distinguished between untimely death as the work of enemies and death which came in its time as another step on the journey home, and the fact that Sarah Frances Colenso's death was seen by their African friends as timely was a comfort to her daughters: 'They say, truly enough, that her appearance misled them, they had thought her looking well, when it was "the beauty of approaching departure." I am thankful to find, too, that none of those most interested think her death has been caused by the enemy.'[34] As Harriette told the exiles on St Helena:

To ourselves even the end came suddenly although we had long recognized that strength was failing her greatly and that, indeed, she had remained with us to bless us, for so long after our Father Sobantu had left her, only through the great courage that was in her, and her great interest in Sobantu's work.

One sign of her care for that work is her having crossed the sea, at her age, to lament to the English for the Zulu people; and again that she repeated that voyage, coming this way, though both her much loved sons, and all her grand-children remained there on the other side.

And, verily, the Almighty gave her strength to reach this land, and, further, to wait for me, until I had returned from Eshowe bringing good news which rejoiced her. And then she departed, being very tired and desiring rest recognizing both of us, her daughters and having seen in a dream on that same day, both Sobantu and Cetshwayo.

According to our English way of thinking that points to her feeling towards those two but I tell you about it knowing that it will lighten your grief and will mean to you that she has indeed been taken home by the word of our Father, without any evil deed or accident.

As to us two, we are well. What we feel is that our Mother has now laid afresh upon us the command to have courage to persist in the work of our Father Sobantu.[35]

CHAPTER 25

CLEMENCY AND OBLIVION

'The evil genius of the Zulus'

B ut the work of their father, Sobantu, was soon to prove even harder to pursue. With the new year, 1894, the daughters of Sarah Frances Colenso had to learn how to live without the woman around whom they had organised their lives for so long. They also had to find a way to fight their political, theological and church battles with very little money or support, and Harriette concentrated on finding legal and political strategies to protect the Church of England congregations from the inroads of the powerful Church of the Province.

Much had changed in Natal and in Zululand in the four years they had been away. In June 1893 Sir Theophilus Shepstone had died. For Bishopstowe it was Shepstone who, more than any other individual, had caused the 'Ruin of Zululand'. It was the work of the Old Serpent, bribing, intimidating, manipulating, hovering at the ear of the Governor, waiting to pour the poison of deception, that lay at the root of their troubles. As Harriette commented on receiving the news of his death, 'he has been the evil genius of the Zulus'.

Colonial Natal believed the opposite. The point has often been made that although the man and his policy were consistently attacked by the settlers while he was in office, after his retirement and death Shepstone's ideas on native administration were enshrined as the legacy left to the colony by a wise, far-seeing founding father. Natal's Legislative Council praised the man who more than any other had left his mark on the colony's history. The Colonial Secretary, moving a motion of sympathy in the Legislative Council for the Shepstone family, referred to 'certain services ... the knowledge of which was almost entirely confined to the inner circle of Government. From the days when the late Sir Theophilus Shepstone relinquished the cares of office, he had been distinguished for the willingness with which he had laid the fruits of his ripe experience at the service of successive Governors, and he had so rendered services of incalculable benefit to the Colony ...'[1]

To the very end Shepstone defended his particular interpretation of Zulu history – the Zulu royal house was an aberration, a military despotism which had violently torn power away from the local African chiefdoms and imposed its authority over them.[2] I have taken pains in this book to show that this interpretation is not only profoundly misleading but disingenuous in the way it hides the way he had to actively manipulate Zulu history so that events conformed to this view of the past. The kingdom did not fall apart under the impact of invasion as he had predicted; the 13 chiefs of 1879 did not represent the conquered chiefdoms of Zululand in any significant way; the power of the defeated Zulu 'military despotism' remained a force in the land despite the continual efforts, in which Shepstone played the major part, to undermine it.

In the last of his writings he extended this interpretation to cover events up to the 1890s. The fact that the Zulu royal house was still a political factor was the result, he asserted, not of its intrinsic strength but rather of the policy of a dilatory imperial government which allowed misguided humanitarians to encourage its pretensions. Like the man himself and his works, Shepstone's final statement on Zulu history is deeply dishonest – and yet contains real insight. The Zulu, he wrote, had been 'broken by conflict with a civilised power'; however, 'the policy that followed has tended to support the hopes of the ruling family; to disappoint the aspirations of the incorporated tribes, who had hoped to become free, and more unfortunately still, to suspect the idea of finality; so that the end of this political chapter, whatever it may be, has still to be looked for.' And is, over a century later, still being looked for.[3]

Zululand 1890–1893

Fundamental changes had taken place in Zululand while the Bishopstowe women were in England. The basic principles of the Natal system had been extended there during the 1880s with catastrophic results. But in the end, with the crushing of the resistance in 1888 and the arrest of the Usuthu leaders and the setting up of a compliant chieftainship, the officials had moved in aggressively to demand the hut tax, forcing the younger men into wage labour, largely on the gold mines of the Transvaal or for the Natal Government Railways on the line being forced through Natal towards the Transvaal.

In 1890 Colonel F. Cardew, Acting Resident Commissioner, obtained authority to set up a commission to demarcate and divide the area around what had been Zibhebhu's western border. Nowhere had the consequences of the attempts to divide and rule Zululand been more tragically apparent: the four attempts to draw a boundary since 1879 had in every case left members of the other party on the wrong side with disastrous consequences. The 1891 Boundary Commission was unlike any of the boundary commissions which had preceded it: its members were now aware of the sensitive nature of their work and the fact that any slip would be pounced upon by Harriette Colenso and her supporters. Even so, in its attempts to reflect political loyalties that had their origins in an older system and were subsequently fragmented by a decade of civil war with its cycles of eviction and reoccupation, while keeping evictions to a minimum the Boundary Commission created a mosaic of discontinuous petty chiefdoms, including one for 'the Usuthu'. Its decisions were accepted by the Usuthu under protest – but more out of exhaustion than agreement.

Responsible government[4]

There had been other changes as well. In 1893, while Harriette was waiting to hear finally from the Colonial Office about the possibility of political reform in British Zululand, the colony of Natal had been granted responsible government. It had been a long and confused struggle. The leading figure in this was John Robinson. He had arrived in Natal at a young age, and from the editorial chair of *The Natal Mercury* had spoken consistently for greater settler autonomy and the reduction of 'Home' interference in colonial affairs. In the 1880s Robinson was particularly vicious in his attacks on Bishopstowe and the exiled Zulu king. The demand for responsible government was a demand to reduce the influence of the imperial government, and also the humanitarian lobby, in matters which the settlers felt they knew best how to handle.

For many years Robinson's greatest political rival in Natal was Harry Escombe – but they had now become allies in their desire for more independence from London. We have already seen how this was a major factor in persuading Harry Escombe to defend Dinuzulu before the Court of Special Commissioners, and how he characterised his action as a colonial defence of African interests against the ineptitude of a remote imperial government.

As far as the British government was concerned, the considerations which militated against giving Natal's settlers greater political autonomy were obvious – its minute settler population, its weak finances and its native policy. It was not even clear that the responsible government movement commanded a majority amongst the white males who made up the voters in the colony, which meant that demonstrable support for the movement as a whole was pitiably small. The white population of Natal in 1887 was under 40,000 and the African over 400,000, and Britain remained responsible for Natal's defence. But to surrender overall political authority while retaining military responsibility clearly entailed an unacceptable risk for the British government. Until there was some indication that the men working for responsible government had some practical recommendations on how they would govern the population as a whole, they could hardly expect the British government to grant them overall control. Thus, in spite of the fact that the general direction of British policy was to increase the autonomy of its colonial dependencies, this could not be extended to Natal as long as it was feared that Britain might have to intervene if the huge African population in Natal were to be provoked into violence by the excesses of a settler government.

Natal deeply resented this. The imperial government, it was felt, failed to support the colony's real interests. For example, the Governor, Havelock, had handed over some of the most desirable parts of Zululand to the New Republic in 1887; the British government had refused to back the loan needed to develop the rail link with the Transvaal and did not give Natal the support it needed in negotiations over regional customs duties; and it was widely believed that imperial politicians were in the pocket of Cecil John Rhodes, whose territorial ambitions included Zululand.

The early 1890s saw intense negotiations between the Colonial Office in London and the Responsibles in Natal for a new constitution. When Robinson attempted to extract political concessions, London demanded assurances that Natal had the means and the will to accept and implement policies which took into account the substantial responsibilities implicit in greater political autonomy. Some of the most difficult debates were over questions of race, rights and native government: would the franchise be extended to people not of 'European descent'; and would the new government insist on retaining in some form the powers of the Supreme Chief which, in the name of African tradition, gave such immense powers to the executive? Nonetheless, in the spring of 1892 the Responsibles, after a successful appeal to the Supreme Court for a second election, were victorious. A year later the first responsible government was formed. The Governor, Sir Walter Hely-Hutchinson, retained the enormous powers of the Supreme Chief. The Prime Minister of the first Natal ministry was John Robinson and its Attorney-General was Harry Escombe.

Clarke's report

Harriette Colenso now had a friend in a key post in the new ministry. And, had she had known it, Harriette's political campaign in England in the opening years of the 1890s had influenced attitudes towards Zululand at the Colonial Office

Photo 33. Natal's first Cabinet. Seated in the centre is John Robinson, Prime Minister and enemy of Bishopstowe. Standing on the left is Harry Escombe, Attorney-General, who defended the Usuthu in 1888–9 and betrayed them and Harriette Colenso in 1895.

and was at the moment having something of an impact on policy. No matter that the officials disparaged and dismissed her in their confidential minutes, she had made an impression on them, and the Liberal administration which had come to power in August 1892 did intend to make some sort of break with the past policy towards Zululand. Melmoth Osborn had been eased out of his position as Resident Commissioner. His replacement, Sir Marshal Clarke, on his appointment in June 1893, had been confidentially instructed to investigate and report on Usuthu and anti-Usuthu attitudes in Zululand, not with the intention of 're-opening past controversies' but as the basis for a consideration of future policy, in particular in so far as the role and status of Dinuzulu were concerned.

The Secretary of State, Lord Ripon, had drawn on the language of the English Revolution when he instructed Sir Marshal Clarke to follow 'the approved principle that when after an insurrection, a country has quieted down – when the power to rebel is gone and the spirit of rebellion is extinct – a policy of clemency and oblivion should be adopted'. Clarke was to report whether he felt that this

Photo 34. Sir Marshal Clarke, 'one-armed Clarke', Resident Commissioner in Zululand from 1893 to 1897, with whom Harriette Colenso believed she could work, together with Escombe, to bring reform to Zululand.

was possible – for this was a subject upon which 'very decided opinions have been expressed, but you will examine the evidence and probabilities for yourself, and express your independent judgment as to whether those opinions still hold good'.[5]

By the end of the year Clarke felt that he could assess the mood of the country with some confidence, and in December and January he wrote three confidential dispatches which, as instructed, reported on the situation and made recommendations.[6] The first of these, significantly, was posted immediately after Harriette Colenso's visit to Eshowe in December.[7] Since the exile of the Usuthu leaders, Zululand had been peaceful, to be sure – but it was not a healthy peace. Zululand was exhausted; there was an atmosphere of intimidation and mistrust. As a result, expressions of political opinion by either the Usuthu or the anti-Usuthu could not be given any special credence. Twelve years of divide and rule made it impossible to extract a straightforward expression of political loyalty. There seemed to be no great animosity between the factions, at a social level at least. The chiefs were either sycophants imported from Natal and the creatures of the officials, or they were 'cowed' as the consequence of a policy which had made every effort to silence expressions of loyalty to the Zulu royal house and its adherents. The Zulu chieftainship, Clarke felt, had to be reformed. Its numbers had to be reduced, and the status and the extent of the chiefs' jurisdiction formalised.

Fairfield saw the significance of the recommendations immediately. This was the end of the 'Shepstonian system' by which 'the breaking up of tribes and exaltation of mere constables and hangers-on of the Magistracy Courts has been carried to a monstrous extent'.

> The tone of the Report is very good, and he seems emphatic in the opinion that loyalty is not the monopoly of those who have broken away from their hereditary chiefs. If poor old Cetshwayo were now alive he would see that his prayer has been answered that he might be 'delivered from the House of Shepstone', as Sir Marshal Clarke evidently thinks ill of the Shepstonian System, of which Sir M. Osborn was a mere disciple.
>
> One effect of Sir Marshal Clarke's policy of giving prominence to the tribal authority of the Chiefs will be to put Zululand in a position which will not be so acceptable to Natal as the present state of things if ever Natal succeeds in persuading us to hand over Zululand to her. But I think we need not let this consideration weigh with us.[8]

As far as Dinuzulu was concerned, Clarke felt there were many difficulties. Zululand could not be treated like Lesotho where Clarke had built his policy upon the dominant chiefly house of Moshoeshoe. Although the Basotho were of more diverse origins than the Zulu, their struggle against a common Boer enemy had made them, he believed, more cohesive. The Zulu had become divided as a consequence of the policies since the 1879 invasion. The non-hereditary chiefs who had come over from Natal would be fearful of the return of Dinuzulu, and he could not be placed over them. At the same time, to bring Dinuzulu back as just another chief over a discrete tract of territory would not be wise either. Like it or not, he was considered chief by a large number of people in many parts of the country, and they would attempt to give expression to their loyalty. Clarke consequently recommended a compromise. Dinuzulu should return in a dual capacity. He should be chief over the Usuthu in their territory around Nongoma at the north, but he should also have a special role to play in the government of British Zululand, as induna and adviser to the Zululand government. For this he would have a house built for him at Eshowe and a salary of £500 a year.

Although this could not be openly admitted, there can be no doubt that Harriette Colenso's many letters, and her visit to Eshowe in November 1893, had made an impression on Clarke and influenced his thinking. For Clarke's recommendation that Dinuzulu be returned to Zululand as 'Induna and Adviser' to the government is close to Harriette's that he return as head induna. And this in turn had been made at the suggestion of Harry Escombe.[9]

The Colonial Office was somewhat taken aback by the recommendations. It was widely recognised that there should be a change of policy towards Zululand but Clarke was now proposing a series of quite radical recommendations, the consequences of which he and the Governor admitted were not easy to predict. As Fiddes minuted, 'The letter is somewhat of a leap in the dark and there is decided risk in taking a second leap before we know where the first has landed us.'[10]

Incorporation before restoration

An added difficulty to devising a new policy towards Zululand was the long-standing demand coming from colonial Natal that Zululand should be incorporated into the colony. This had deep historical roots, as we have seen, but by the 1890s it was heightened by the general intensification of the expansionist mood across southern Africa. As the decade progressed, it seemed to Natal's politicians that the colony was about to be further confined by her neighbours as the expanding forces of imperialism, Cape colonialism and Boer republicanism manoeuvred for positions of greater dominance in South Africa. Rhodes, at the head now of both the British South Africa Company and the Cape, had moved along the western flank of the Transvaal, through Bechuanaland, and into the territory beyond the Limpopo. The British government was negotiating with the Boers, and with the African chiefdoms, like the Swazi and the Tsonga, to the east of the Transvaal to which Natal felt it had historical claims. Natal also considered that it had rights to the territory of the Mpondo to the south, but it was clear that the Cape was advancing here as well. It was widely believed in Natal that Rhodes was, in the words of a Colonial Office official, 'going to leapfrog over Natal and into Zululand' – a territory which the cattle farmers along its inland borders, the sugar planters of the coast, the gold prospectors and the labour agents believed was Natal's rightful inheritance. It could not fall into other hands. The new responsible ministry felt bound to find some way for Natal to make good its historical claim to the land of the Zulu. Its reputation amongst Natal's electorate depended upon this.

The Colonial Office, however, considered Natal's demands to be too strident and its fears hysterical. 'How can we deal with men like these', commented Ripon, when despite official denials he was told that Natal politicians remained convinced that Rhodes intended to wrest Zululand away from them. It was generally accepted in London that, in time, Zululand would be incorporated with Natal – but the timing and the nature of this incorporation were matters for future consideration. There was nothing in the behaviour of the new Natal government to suggest that it would safeguard the interests of all its people. The fears of Natal's Indians for their future under responsible government were confirmed in April 1894 when in the second session of the first parliament a Franchise Amendment Bill was introduced to exclude those of the 'Asiatic races'. The debates were vile in their expressions of economic and racial prejudice, the new Attorney-General, Harry Escombe, often being in the van.[11] In July a petition bearing 9000 signatures against the Bill was raised, with a young lawyer, Gandhi, playing an important part in organising the protests against the intended legislation on behalf of the newly formed Natal Indian Congress. There was nothing yet in the record of responsible Natal to suggest that it would be wise for the Colonial Office to hand over Zululand to the new Legislative Assembly, and much which advised against it. For the moment Natal would have to wait.

But Natal was not willing to wait. And it believed it did have a weapon which it might use: the apparent desire of the imperial government to return Dinuzulu and his uncles to Zululand. Hely-Hutchinson had been given to understand that the Natal ministry was preparing a memorandum recommending that Zululand be incorporated into Natal *before* Dinuzulu was returned. If this did not happen, then there was a real possibility that the colonists might attempt to disrupt Dinuzulu's return. As the Governor commented: 'I need scarcely observe that if the return of Dinuzulu were to be made the signal for strong political agitation, adverse to this return, in Natal, such agitation would be an obstacle to the peaceful settlement of existing difficulties in Zululand.'[12]

The Colonial Office strongly disapproved of these threats from the Natal ministry, as interpreted in the Governor's dispatch:

> Sir Walter Hely-Hutchinson seems to think that Her Majesty's Government
> are so anxious for Dinuzulu's return that they are ready to pay any price for it
> but I doubt if the solution would satisfy Dinuzulu or the Colensoites, as Natal
> would soon settle Dinuzulu ... I imagine that the Natal Ministers fancy they
> are in a position to squeeze Her Majesty's Government, their argument
> being:- 'You are anxious to restore Dinuzulu, we can stop it by an agitation
> here; therefore you must buy us off, on our own terms.'[13]

Nonetheless, there was one member of the Natal ministry who, it was felt, disagreed with this approach and supported the idea of the unconditional return of the chiefs. This was the Attorney-General, Harry Escombe, the most powerful member of the ministry. The Prime Minister, Sir John Robinson, dared not oppose Escombe directly, in spite of the fact that the electorate was also vehemently opposed to the return, and London could therefore pursue its own policy. Thus forewarned, when Natal's memorandum recommending incorporation before restoration was completed and dispatched on 3 May, the Colonial Office was not surprised.[14] But it was difficult to find a suitable response and the Colonial Office procrastinated. Clarke's proposals were accepted but no immediate effort was made to implement them. The London officials were greatly taken up with other South African matters – in particular, relations with Swaziland and other territories to the north and north-east of Zululand that lay between the Transvaal and the eastern seaboard. As a result, through much of 1894, Clarke's reports and recommendations moved slowly across the desks in Whitehall. And while this suited the pressed officials in London it left Harriette Colenso in Pietermaritzburg in an agony of apprehension as she waited for any hint of what Clarke had recommended in his report.

The officials denied her this information. Although Clarke listened to her with courtesy, when pressed he retreated behind the conventions of confidentiality. Harriette, in contact with the Usuthu in Zululand, the exiles on St Helena and radical humanitarians in England, was still seen as dangerous. The officials dared not give her the least idea of the developments which were taking place within the circles of government.

A decision

In London, background papers on the subject were prepared in July for the consideration of the Cabinet, and on 23 August Ripon was able to inform the staff at the Colonial Office that 'Her Majesty's Government has decided to adopt the course concerning the repatriation of Dinuzulu and his uncles which has been recommended by Sir M. Clarke and supported by Sir W. Hely-Hutchinson, and to allow the early return of Dinuzulu and his uncles on the terms under this arrangement sketched out by Sir M. Clarke.'[15]

It was necessary that the plans be kept absolutely confidential. If Natal got to hear of what was being planned, then settler outrage might mean that Dinuzulu and his uncles would be greeted in Durban by a lynch mob. And if the Usuthu got to hear of it, say through Harriette Colenso, then they might be persuaded to see the return of Dinuzulu as a victory to be celebrated by turning on their old enemies.

There were still more delays as other pressing South African matters, the situation in Swaziland, and the visit to London of the High Commissioner, Sir Henry Loch, pushed Zulu matters aside yet again. Then Natal's request that incorporation with Zululand should precede the restoration of Dinuzulu had to be answered. It was not acceded to, but not denied either. In September the Natal ministry was informed that in Lord Ripon's opinion, 'The time was not ... yet ripe for taking this question into practical consideration, but that they might rest assured that if and when it appeared desirable to remove the administration of Zululand from the immediate control of the Imperial Government, the prior claims of Natal would be recognised.'

It was only at the end of October that attention could be turned to Zululand once more and arrangements made for the details of the return. The logistics were difficult. Natal was in telegraphic contact with London, but St Helena was not. Merchant vessels called at St Helena, and the one from Natal left once a month, taking about a week to Cape Town and another week to reach the island. Premature disclosure of the return would give Natal time to mount a campaign against it, and so the interval between the announcement of the return and the event itself had to be carefully judged. Hely-Hutchinson felt he needed a week to prepare the Natal ministers to accept the news before it was made public. Meanwhile, the conditions under which Dinuzulu was to return would have to be translated into Zulu and this had to be done in Natal or Zululand. But more time would be wasted if these translations were then sent to London – and then back again to St Helena. Fairfield wrote to prepare the Governor at St Helena for the documentation which would reach him from Natal – making the whole process sound even more conspiratorial:

Dear Grey-Wilson 30 10 1894
    You will probably in a few weeks time receive from Hely-Hutchinson a long document in the Zulu language. Keep it under lock and key and say nothing to anybody about it until you receive instructions from Lord Ripon telling you what to do with it. It is a translation of a despatch from his Lordship, which in due course you may have to cause to be read to the Zulus. It contains the decision of the Government as to the future. Their exile is very shortly to terminate. In the mean time, go on treating the Zulus and making announcements as to current matters just as if they were to remain with you indefinitely. Some casual economy or shortening of sail often gives a hint as to future policy which Colonists are only too ready to decypher. EF[16]

The original idea was that the Royal Navy should transport the Zulu chiefs home from St Helena. However, the Admiral at Cape Town found that 'a suitable man-of-war cannot be spared' and a merchant vessel on the Natal route was commissioned in London to stop off at St Helena and pick them up. To make sure that information about the return did not reach England – and from there Natal – prematurely, Grey-Wilson was told to wait until the mail ship from South Africa had left St Helena for England on about 19 January before announcing to Dinuzulu that he was to return. Hely-Hutchinson was given authority to tell his ministers, in confidence, of the decision after 10 February, by which time the Zulu chiefs would be safely off St Helena and on their way to South Africa. London hoped that, confronted with a *fait accompli*, settler Natal would be less inclined to agitate against the return of the Zulu chiefs. But everything depended on secrecy and on timing.

CHAPTER 26

SHARP PRACTICE

Clarke caught

Early in December Clarke was in Natal to make the final arrangements with the Governor. On the 6th they felt confident enough to cable London that preparations were now complete. The next day, while walking in the streets of Pietermaritzburg, Clarke, to his considerable discomfort, came across Harriette Colenso and a visitor, her new friend and confidante, Alice Werner.

It was a year since Harriette had stayed with Clarke at the Residency in Eshowe and shared with him her hopes for the future of Zululand and the central role that Dinuzulu might play in it. Since then, however, no attempt had been made to consult her over the policy towards Zululand which was being formulated. She understood, she felt, the need for discretion on the part of the officials. She had done everything consistent with her commitments to the Usuthu to avoid being seen as interfering or presumptuous. But to be completely excluded, for reasons of protocol, from all official information by men who she felt had a degree of sympathy towards her, she found unnecessary and cruel. It was politically inept as well, although she dared not say so. She had waited for news of Clarke's report for too long: she was no longer just impatient, but angry, and she said so to the Resident Commissioner.

From Clarke's point of view, to emerge from highly confidential meetings with the Governor on the return of Dinuzulu and to be confronted in the street by one of the major protagonists demanding information was highly embarrassing. Harriette perceived this and immediately deduced that something was going on. According to Hely-Hutchinson, in a private letter to the Under-Secretary, Buxton, Harriette had 'caught' Clarke 'in the street yesterday, and went for him about Dinuzulu. She told him that she had waited and waited but that her patience was exhausted, and that she intended to write to the Colonial Office and ask that his report, which she was sure he must have made, should be published. So you know what to look out for.'[1]

The warning was not much help. It was an early indication that the imperial planners were not able to keep the tight control they intended over their plans for the return of Dinuzulu. Harriette Colenso, however, decided that she could not waste any more time waiting in Natal for developments. She had promised the exiles she would visit them and could not delay much longer. She would make arrangements to go to England to press the whole matter further at the Colonial Office, calling on the way at St Helena. On 30 December she wrote to Hely-Hutchinson informing him of this, and asked if he could give her some indication if there was any prospect of an imminent return of the exiles as she did not want to make a wasted journey.

Hely-Hutchinson knew that the documentation to authorise Dinuzulu's return had already been posted from London to St Helena. But he replied that he could not answer her question. This only made her more suspicious and determined, and she announced that she would be leaving for St Helena at the end of January. Hely-Hutchinson, realising that if this happened she would pass the chiefs in mid-ocean, telegraphed London on 10 January. He was not, he informed the Colonial Office, prepared to take her into his confidence and tell her what was going on. In his opinion she was 'unsafe'. Perhaps Ripon could ask her not to make the journey?[2]

Squeezing Her Majesty's Government

But the problems raised by Harriette Colenso's pending visit to St Helena were immediately overtaken by another more serious difficulty. On 11 January 1895 Hely-Hutchinson received a confidential minute from the Natal ministry, stating its 'unanimous opinion that Dinuzulu should not return to Zululand till after Zululand had been handed over to Natal; and urging on your Lordship the advisability of handing over Zululand to Natal without delay'.[3]

In forwarding the minute, Hely-Hutchinson stated that he did not think it had any direct connection with the plans to return the Usuthu leaders or that the Natal ministry had knowledge of London's intention to do so. Nonetheless, the Natal ministers were 'uncompromising' in their opposition, and if Dinuzulu were returned it would arouse 'strong opposition and agitation in Natal'.

This was serious. Here at the most delicate moment in their plans, with instructions already on their way to St Helena to inform the Zulu chiefs of their imminent return, the Governor of Natal was warning the Secretary of State in London of opposition from the Natal ministry and disruption and agitation from the colonists, who demanded the annexation of Zululand. Moreover, it was unanimous and was therefore supported by Escombe.

On 12 January the Governor had an interview with his Prime Minister and attempted to persuade him to retract the minute. Sir John Robinson agreed to ask his ministers to reconsider it but, he pointed out, it was a matter of great seriousness and he doubted that his ministry would survive if Dinuzulu was allowed to return unless Zululand was already in Natal's control. On 17 January Robinson returned to inform the Governor of his ministers' response. Not only was the minute practically unaltered but he had more news that was both disturbing and startling.

The source was Harry Escombe and it concerned Harriette Colenso. The evening before, she had told him 'that she is strongly in favour of handing Zululand over to Natal before Dinuzulu is brought back. She has written to that effect to the Aborigines Protection Society, and, if necessary, will proceed to England from St Helena to urge it.'[4] Escombe was called to Government House that evening. He assured Hely-Hutchinson that Harriette Colenso was indeed of this opinion; furthermore, the implications were serious, for it made it necessary for Harry Escombe to change his stance. Whereas he had previously insisted on the return of the exiles as soon as possible, it was now clear that Miss Colenso no longer agreed with him on this. And, because he could not oppose Miss Colenso, the Usuthu's confidante and adviser, he was forced to accept her view. The consequence was that he could now no longer oppose his ministerial colleagues either, and accepted that before the chiefs could return, Zululand had to be incorporated into Natal.

There was now a real risk that Dinuzulu's return would precipitate a serious political crisis in Natal. Hely-Hutchinson had previously described the ministry as divided on the question of Dinuzulu's return. Escombe's about-face meant that this was no longer so. At two o'clock on the afternoon of the next day, 18 January, the Governor sent a secret and confidential telegram to London summing up the situation:

> I learn that the Prime Minister intends to discuss to-day with his colleagues the advisability of making a definite offer to bring Dinuzulu back by a fixed date, provided Zululand is previously incorporated with Natal ... Sir J. Robinson informs me that serious agitation is sure to arise here should Dinuzulu be brought back without at least a public assurance that Zululand will be handed over to Natal ... Matters have been seriously complicated by Escombe's adopting the position described in last telegram.[5]

The telegram was considered in the Colonial Office that afternoon. It was clear that the Natal government was preparing to use the return of Dinuzulu, and even the threat of public disruption, to force the British government to authorise Natal's take-over of Zululand. Ripon was angry at being pressurised in this way, but it was difficult to see how he could counteract it. He could not risk returning Dinuzulu in the face of a political crisis in the Natal government, popular agitation from the settlers and, now, the possibility of protest and pressure from the humanitarian lobby in London, led by Miss Colenso, and even from the exiles themselves. At the same time, the matter could not be delayed: the announcement of the chiefs' return was already in St Helena and there was no way of cancelling the instruction that they be informed of its contents. But it would still be possible to stop them leaving the island. A Navy vessel was sent from Cape Town with orders to postpone the return, and the *Umkuzi*, which was to transport them to Natal but had yet to leave England, was now to carry a message informing the Zulu that their return was delayed. At 5.40 Ripon sent his reply. 'Your Ministers have chosen a very inopportune moment for again raising the question of transferring Zululand to Natal, as it has the appearance of an attempt on their part to put pressure on Her Majesty's Government. I have, however, for the present suspended Dinuzulu's return, in accordance with the wish expressed by you.'[6]

'Miss Colenso's interference'

Hely-Hutchinson's superiors in London were clearly most displeased, and the Governor had to find his excuses and scapegoats. Harriette Colenso was the obvious choice. It was she who had forced Escombe to change:

> Until a fortnight ago, Ministers were divided in opinion. Escombe was, and is, strongly of opinion that Dinuzulu should return without delay, but Miss Colenso's statement to him has enabled him to come into line with his colleagues. Ministers are now unanimous in their views, and if Dinuzulu were now to be brought back there would be an agitation in support of their policy. Prime Minister told Clarke on the 20th instant that Miss Colenso's movement had entirely changed the situation.[7]

But the Colonial Office was suspicious of this explanation. It was clearly possible that Harriette Colenso had been set up by members of the Natal ministry, or by Escombe in particular. Ripon demanded to know when the Natal ministers had been told that Dinuzulu was to return, and what Harriette Colenso herself knew of the plans, and whether Hely-Hutchinson had direct evidence of her position on the return or only the word of Harry Escombe. Ripon was assured that, even now, neither the Natal ministers nor Harriette Colenso knew of the plans that had been made to return Dinuzulu. On the second question it was true that it was Escombe who had been the source of the information about the fact that Miss Colenso had changed her mind. But Robinson had now provided the Governor with direct confirmation of her attitude. It was from an intercepted telegram she had sent on 24 January to the APS: it read: 'Tell Lord Ripon, Courtney, and friends, chiefs return better, if Zululand first and at once joined to Natal.'

Still Ripon was not satisfied. Hely-Hutchinson had placed his superiors in a most awkward situation. If only he had told London of the potential difficulties before Dinuzulu had been officially informed that he was to return, and

> that you saw objections to his return under present circumstances, I should
> have abandoned the idea, as I have acted in accordance with your advice in
> the whole matter; but now that he has been told, I do not see how, without a
> breach of faith, we can refuse for any length of time to carry these intentions
> into effect. Have you any observations to offer on the position considered in
> this aspect?[8]

Indeed Hely-Hutchinson had. Harriette Colenso's inconsistency and unpredictability had created the problem and should provide the solution: Dinuzulu should be informed that, although the British government wanted to return him to Zululand, Harriette Colenso and the APS had requested, on his behalf, that Zululand must first be incorporated into Natal. In so doing, it was she who had created the difficulties which now forced the government to delay their return. As Sir John Robinson added: 'Miss Colenso's interference has changed the situation, and her action has thrown obstacles in the way of the course decided on by your Lordship. She has acted, as it were, as Dinuzulu's representative and agent throughout, and she should therefore bear the responsibility for delay.'[9]

Ripon would have none of it: 'Miss Colenso's reported change of opinion has no effect on my judgment: and I cannot throw responsibility on her in the way you recommend, nor can I regard her as competent to bind Dinuzulu.'[10] Instead, the Natal ministry was now to be given full details of the proposals for Dinuzulu's return and their postponement. They were also to be informed that the British government was determined to treat incorporation and the return as separate issues.

Both sides had failed. The Liberal administration had been unable to make the break it intended with the old and much-maligned policy towards the Zulu royal house. At the same time the Natal government had failed to turn to its own advantage the imperial government's intention to return the exiles. But it was, of course, the exiled Zulu princes and their entourage who suffered the consequences of this deadlock most immediately. And in the midst of it all was Harriette Colenso who suddenly, and to her friends and allies inexplicably, was opposing the cause she had initiated and worked for so energetically – the return of the Usuthu leaders to Zululand – at the very moment that it was about to take place.

Jostling in the dark

On 24 January Dinuzulu and his party were told by St Helena's Governor that they should prepare to leave on 7 February on board the *Umkuzi*, which would then sail directly to Natal. Once in Zululand Dinuzulu was to be appointed chief of the Usuthu at Nongoma, and induna and adviser to the Zulu government at a salary of £500 per annum. The exiled party now numbered 18 and they had accumulated a considerable number of possessions in the five years they had been on the island. Hurriedly they packed what they could and sold the rest.

Then, to everyone's surprise and concern, on 4 February a gunboat arrived from the Cape with the news that their return was postponed. On the 7th the *Umkuzi* arrived, but instead of taking the Zulu on board it now delivered documents from London confirming the postponement.

Meanwhile, Harriette Colenso had left Durban on 26 January for Cape Town from where she would leave for St Helena on the 31st. In Cape Town, however, she received a confidential telegram from Hely-Hutchinson containing the extraordinary information that the British government had in fact planned to return Dinuzulu early in February. However, as a result of a minute from the Natal ministers received on 17 January in which they expressed their opinion that Zululand must be incorporated into Natal before Dinuzulu was returned, the Secretary of State had on the next day decided to postpone the return. It was felt that Harriette Colenso should know this before she went to St Helena; however, she was instructed to treat this information confidentially.[11]

It was all impossibly complicated and confused, particularly when one realises that none of the parties involved had a complete view of what was happening. While the Colonial Office as the initiators of the plan did have an overview, it could not be sure what was being plotted amongst the Natal ministers. The imperial representatives in Natal and Zululand were in closer touch with the Natal ministry, but they had to defer to their superiors in London and were not privy to their deliberations. The Natal ministry, to its great annoyance, was not treated completely openly by either the imperial government or its local representatives. The chiefs, of course, were almost totally dependent on official sources for information, or information which had been officially vetted. However, they were in contact with the people of St Helena, and the latter with newspapers and passers-by from England, and they watched the movement of the ships and drew their own conclusions.

Harriette Colenso was deprived of information by both Natal and London. She still had no idea even of what Clarke's official report had recommended. She found the whole situation utterly 'bewildering' and held the imperial government responsible. It arose out of a totally unnecessary demand for secrecy, which deprived the officials of the chance to draw into their confidence the very people upon whose active support the plan depended. As a result the return of the exiles, for which she had been fighting for so long, had been postponed. But more than this, it seemed as if she was directly, but nonetheless inadvertently, involved in the process which had led to the postponement, although she still could not see how and why. She sailed from Cape Town determined to discover what was going on.

With her 'faithful attendant, Mubi Nondenisa' she arrived at St Helena on 15 February. Her pleasure at greeting the men she had last seen in the Eshowe gaol during those dreadful and exciting days of the trial was mixed with her anxiety and confusion at the still inexplicable news she had received at Cape Town that there had been an attempt to return the princes to Zululand, but that this had been delayed, and that somehow she was a party to the decision for the postponement.

Dear Mr Escombe

In some ways the very idea that Harriette Colenso, daughter of the Bishop of Natal, who had for twenty years fought against Natal's native policy and practices, and publicly exposed and condemned the manner in which Natal had brought devastation to the Zulu people, should support any move to link Zululand with Natal was preposterous. It was a policy which, on the surface at least, would seem to contradict the fundamental principles of her, and her father's, deeply held political objectives – objectives to which they had devoted their lives. How then could Harriette Colenso have come to support the idea of the incorporation of Zululand with Natal? Why did she do so?

The most immediate explanation would be that her emotional commitment to the exiled Usuthu, and her faith in Harry Escombe, were so intense that they clouded her political judgement. But this is just too obvious, and a touch sexist

– a middle-aged, single woman unable to resist the different pressures put on her by the men, black and white, who had come to mean so much to her. To understand the shift in her thinking in something of its complexity and its tragedy, one needs to look at the situation in which she had been placed in more detail, with a closer awareness of the context and the process by which she made the decision. This in turn requires a longer look at the man who was now Natal's Attorney-General.

We have seen how, during his defence of Dinuzulu before the Court of Special Commissioners in 1889, Harry Escombe had relieved her of some of the responsibility which she had been taking in Eshowe, and had earned her gratitude for the time and money he gave to the defence of the Usuthu. He had touched her deeply, creating in this dedicated, energetic, but quiet and composed woman an emotional bond which evoked the memory of the man she loved above all others, her father. In the years that followed, it was important and comforting to have a friend and supporter in the uppermost reaches of Natal colonial society. After the trials Harry Escombe and his wife had become Harriette Colenso's friends. From London, Harriette directed acquaintances, allies and people of significance visiting Natal to the Escombe house overlooking Durban Bay.[12] It was here, at the Escombes' invitation, that Sarah Frances and her daughters rested for a few days on their own return from London in 1893.

Harry Escombe was born in London in 1838 and emigrated in 1860 to Natal where he became a businessman, politician and Natal's leading lawyer. And yet we know little of Natal's second Prime Minister. There is no large collection of letters available, and the privately printed biography is uncritical.[13] Speeches were collected and published after his death; but although he had the reputation of being Natal's finest orator, in print the speeches are long, conventional, and deal largely with matters of contemporary significance only, with a concentration on the issue for which he is best remembered – the development of Durban's harbour. History books give little depth to his character – the *Dictionary of South African Biography* notes his strengths as a swimmer, angler, yachtsman and chess-player, and *A History of Natal*, although it suggests some interesting inconsistencies in his attitudes to race, is content to write that 'Harry Escombe's advanced principles suffered some diminution as he grew older and held high office'.[14]

Certainly his admission to John X. Merriman that he had defended the Zulu chiefs because of a promise made to savages in an unguarded moment is at odds with the impression of his moral commitment to a stable and peaceful Zululand with which he left Harriette at Eshowe in 1889 – but even this could be explained in terms of the requirements of conventional colonial, male bravado. For Harriette Colenso, Harry Escombe remained the man who had helped her organise the defence of the Usuthu, who had defended Dinuzulu with such legal skill and oratorical panache. The compromises that a politician had to make notwithstanding, Escombe was a friend to Bishopstowe, the Usuthu and therefore to Harriette.

It was to Escombe that she turned in December 1894 after Clarke and Hely-Hutchinson had refused to confirm or deny that plans were being made for the chiefs' return. Her position was an invidious one, she told him. She had been waiting a year for news at least of Clarke's report on Zululand. She was committed to visiting the exiles on St Helena, and yet there was little point in going unless she could give them some sort of idea of what their future might be. Escombe replied that he had also been thinking seriously about the situation: 'that he considered the next step to be taken, and one absolutely necessary, was the annexation of Zululand to Natal, that the Natal Ministry was already proposing this, and that if the matter were carried out without undue delay he should hope that arrangements for the exiles' return might be completed by the end of the year.'[15]

From this account, Harriette's it is true, it was Escombe who raised the possibility of incorporation before restoration. It must be accepted: she had no reason to mislead, and she did not know that Hely-Hutchinson and John Robinson had attempted to persuade Ripon that it was she who had forced Escombe's hand in this. The reasons she gives for reaching the decision must be valid, as far as they go. As she continued: 'A whole twelve-month more to linger, and then to an uncertain hope! Still, it seemed better to take this to St Helena than to further delay the little comfort a friend's visit might give.'[16]

But there was much more to Harriette's response than this. It was not just a question of impatience. It would seem that in their meetings, first in December 1894 and then in January 1895, Harry Escombe and Harriette Colenso talked at length about the chiefs, Natal and Zululand, and their futures. Much of it was politically and personally sensitive, and only emerged out of the shadow of confidentiality in the years to come. But the consequence was that, under the influence of Escombe's persuasive conversation, Harriette's ideas on Natal, Zululand and their future underwent a substantial change.

Escombe presented her with some of the problems associated with Dinuzulu's return. His argument was a subtly pragmatic one. He had no idea, he said, if the imperial government was going to return the chiefs or not. But if they did, the response in colonial Natal would be predictable. The Natal ministry would believe it had once again been slighted by the imperial government, its opinions disregarded and its interests ignored. The Natal electorate, its Zulu inheritance removed again from its grasp, might well turn against their ministers and charge

375

them, if not with complicity, then certainly with being naïve and compliant. The settlers would then obstruct the arrangements for the return and make them impossible to implement. Harriette did not have to be reminded of the ghastly consequences of Natal's opposition to the restoration of Dinuzulu's father. To return Dinuzulu and his uncles to Zululand in the face of Natal opposition could well have similar results. However, Escombe argued, to return them with the support of the Natal government, to a territory now under its control, would demonstrate a confidence in the colony which could well bring out the best in its leadership and the white population. Since the granting of responsible government there were indeed some indications of a better attitude towards Africans in Natal. There were signs of a break with the old jingoistic attitudes, dominated by officialdom, represented by the Shepstones and their cronies. It was hardly substantial but nonetheless discernible, and had to be encouraged. A 'New Natal' was emerging and had to be supported. Yet another slight from London would work against it. An expression of imperial confidence, however, could work in the other direction. It was time to think of the incorporation of Zululand in order to create and encourage this new mood in Natal. This in turn might assist in the creation of a better policy towards, not only the Zulu royal house, but all who lived in Natal and Zululand.

Harriette Colenso thought hard. His argument had weight. It would certainly be difficult for the reforms that she hoped Clarke was advocating for Zululand to be successful if Natal were resentful and determined to undermine them. There were other factors as well. There could be little doubt that Harry Escombe's role in Natal politics was going to be an important and, perhaps soon, the dominant one. And Escombe was a man she trusted. She had seen him at work. They had shared the experience of Eshowe in 1889. She had heard his ringing denunciations of injustice made in Dinuzulu's defence before the Court of Special Commissioners. With Escombe as Prime Minister, not only would the situation improve but, she dared to hope, Bishopstowe might gain some political influence.

Furthermore, she believed that the senior official in Zululand itself, Sir Marshal Clarke, was also determined to break with the past and work towards a new order. Consequently, if he were retained in his post as Resident Commissioner in Zululand, there would be in key positions two men of integrity, both of whom were prepared to judge the Usuthu fairly and treat them with justice. Never in its history had Bishopstowe had the ear of two such officials in key positions in government. Working together with the Usuthu chiefs they could bring out the best in the people of a new colony which united Zululand with Natal. Escombe assured her that if the two colonies were incorporated, the

Natal ministry would agree to support the idea that Clarke should retain his position in Zululand.

We can see some of the effects that these discussions with Escombe had on Harriette as January progressed. On the 11th she wrote to Fox Bourne, still secretary of the APS.[17] It was the first letter she had sent him since her return to South Africa. She remembered she had received a kind letter from him on the death of her mother a year previously but she had not replied to it – a not insignificant omission by a woman so scrupulous in her correspondence, to a man who, whatever their differences, had supported her with energy and treated her with consideration. It was a rather vague letter but its intention is clear – to reopen communication with the APS without seeming to be too abrupt, and to prepare Fox Bourne for changes in her thinking which, even then perhaps, she could hardly admit to herself.

But the changes were taking place, and by 16 January Escombe was sufficiently confident to thus inform his Prime Minister – who, as we have seen, passed it on to the Governor with the information that, as a result of Harriette Colenso's new attitude, Escombe was now forced to agree with his ministerial colleagues that the exiles should not return before incorporation.

The next English mail took the subsequent letter, written on 18 January, from Harriette Colenso to Fox Bourne. In it she was more explicit: although it seemed that London doubted that the return of the chiefs could ever take place if Zululand was under the authority of Natal, 'I do not share that doubt, on the contrary, under the present Natal Ministry, (which is likely to remain in office for a long time to come) I believe the exiles would be soon returned, and happily.'[18]

It is essential to understand that Harriette Colenso was completely ignorant of the crisis which was breaking just then between the administrations in Pietermaritzburg and London, and which culminated in Ripon's decision to postpone Dinuzulu's return. As far as she was concerned, an opportunity was being offered to her by a man she trusted implicitly to intervene politically in an impossible situation – to advocate incorporation as a means to effect a safer return for the Usuthu to a more positive political environment in Zululand.

It was now possible for her to travel to St Helena to make good her promises to the Usuthu exiles, and discuss with them her strategies for the future. On 23 January she had her final discussion with Escombe. By this time he knew that the attempt to force the Secretary of State's hand had failed. Escombe now made what can only be seen as a final bid to put pressure on the British government, using Harriette Colenso as a front, and also covering himself by providing evidence for what up to now had been his verbal assertion – that *she* supported incorporation before restoration.[19] He asked her to telegraph an appeal to the APS for the incorporation of Natal and Zululand before the return of the Usuthu leaders, and request that this be passed to the Secretary of State for the Colonies. He gave Harriette to understand that the Governor of Natal himself had suggested this. On 24 January she sent her telegram to the APS asking the society to urge her friends and the Secretary of State to support such a move. Her telegram was immediately intercepted by the Natal authorities, who passed it on to the Colonial Office as independent proof of the position she had now adopted.

The next day, from the Marine Hotel in Durban, Harriette wrote to Clarke in Zululand and informed him of what she had done, and gave some of her reasons:

> I have done so (1) because I am impressed with the danger of letting the adverse feeling in Natal in this matter get the start, get any handle against or advantage over the right feeling as represented by – say – Mr. Escombe; (2) because I venture to believe, from what little either of you have let fall, that you and he can work together in the matter, and (3) because I believe that it will need the whole influence of you both to bring about the results that I – may I not here say that we all three – hope for.[20]

She then boarded the ship for Cape Town – where she received the news that the chiefs' return had been about to take place but was now postponed because of the Natal ministry's demand that Zululand be first incorporated into Natal.

'Sharp practice'

Harriette Colenso was to return to January 1895 many times in the years to come, going through the arguments which Escombe had used to persuade her to urge her allies in England to support the incorporation before restoration of the Usuthu exiles. In a sense, with hindsight it is so easy to see her decision as a disastrous failure of judgement – the action of an isolated and vulnerable woman, in a moment of weakness, seduced into abandoning the ideals by which she stood for so long, capitulating to the arguments of a powerful man in search of more power.

But this point of view should be resisted, at least as a total explanation. First, the context has to be considered. The choices facing Harriette Colenso were so limited. If she were to move forward she needed allies, and where could she find them? The people of Zululand were cowed by the experiences of the 1880s and her Natal African supporters were only a tiny handful. By contrast, she felt that she had the confidence of the most powerful politician in Natal – Harry Escombe.

But it was not just Escombe – there was also Sir Marshal Clarke. He, she believed, had proved himself in Lesotho by working with African political authority rather than against it. In Zululand he had had the confidence to break with Shepstonian traditions of native administration and its wicked policy of divide, destroy and rule. In Escombe and Clarke she had two men, in key positions of authority, whom she could count as personal friends and political allies. It was potentially a powerful alliance. And when Escombe told her that the plan had the support of the Governor as well, she capitulated. Given the absence of other options it made good sense. It signalled a new direction, a new political alliance, the healing of old wounds and antagonisms. For Harriette Colenso it was no longer just a matter of the reincorporation of Zululand with Natal, but their reconciliation.

However, there was one possibility that did not occur to her – that Harry Escombe was a liar and a cheat. We don't know how much the other members of the Natal ministry, or even Sir Walter Hely-Hutchinson, connived in the plan to get Harriette Colenso to support the idea of the prior incorporation of Zululand, and thereby provide a weapon for the ministers and cover for Harry Escombe against the charge of inconsistency. It might have been a ministerial conspiracy – or it might have been conceived and carried out by Escombe on his own, or perhaps with a nod and wink to his colleagues. But the official in the Colonial Office was undoubtedly correct when he wrote: 'I suppose no one doubts now that this whole business was an attempted piece of sharp practice on the part of the Natal Government, who thought they had got Her Majesty's Government in a corner and could make their own terms.'[21]

We don't even need the historian's position of advantage – hindsight – to know that Harriette Colenso was tricked and manipulated. Even without direct evidence, the timing of events suggests strongly that one or more members of the Natal ministry had got to hear of the proposed return – perhaps leaked when the documents announcing the terms to Dinuzulu were sent from London for translation into Zulu. The fact that the return became a pressing issue at the precise moment to make the return impossible – not so early as to allow evasive action, or so late that they had already left the island – does suggest, despite the official denials, that Escombe discovered the Usuthu leaders were about to be repatriated, and he decided to use this, and Harriette Colenso, first to force incorporation – and then to provide an explanation and excuse for his apparent change of mind towards the conditions of their return.

It left Harriette Colenso in an impossible situation. Another about-face would make her appear to be totally unreliable. As a result, even when evidence of betrayal began to grow, it was difficult for her to admit what had been so obvious to so many – that she had made a mistake – without being charged with inconsistency not only by her enemies but by her allies. In the end, unable to go forward or back, she was left stranded. In a sense, given her gender, her commitments and the times in which she was living, it was her inevitable predicament – but not because she had acted out of stupidity, carelessness or simple naïveté, or merely because her judgement had been clouded by the attention of a strong man she believed was on her side and who reminded her of her father. It was a predicament into which she had been forced by her isolation, an isolation rooted in her being a woman supporting African autonomy in the age of imperialism.

Many years were to pass before she was able to see more of the context in which she had been working and admit openly what had happened. But, at the immediate, personal level, the recognition that she had been betrayed and cheated – and with her, the Usuthu cause as well – was only reached by Harriette Colenso slowly, step by painful step.

VII

BREAKING DOWN

CHAPTER 27

ST HELENA AND LONDON
(FEBRUARY–JUNE 1895)

❦

'Unspoilt'

Harriette Colenso arrived at St Helena on 15 February 1895. She had last seen the Usuthu exiles in the Eshowe gaol at the end of 1890. They had now been on St Helena for four years, and she knew that the experience had affected them profoundly. But their communications with her and with their followers and family in Zululand had had to pass through the hands of the authorities, and this limited the range of topics they could discuss. Moreover, the events of the past few weeks – the promise of return only to be followed by its countermand delivered by gunboat – made it even more imperative that they should meet. On all sides the visit was anticipated with eagerness and excitement.

The exiles' guardian, previously a storekeeper in Zululand, came aboard to welcome Harriette while the boat which had brought her from the Cape was still at anchor off Jamestown. Dinuzulu was left 'fuming' on the quayside, but they were able to walk together to the Castle where Shingana was waiting to greet her. Here she was introduced to the Governor, Grey-Wilson, who invited her to dine and stay at his residence, Plantation. Dinuzulu had hired a small carriage, and he and Harriette drove to where the Zulu stayed and Ndabuko was waiting.

Jamestown, on the great rocky outcrop in the Atlantic known as the island of St Helena, is wedged in a narrow gorge running down to the harbour. The chiefs lived at the far end of the town in a house called Maldivia. They had moved here, under protest, from their original residence, Rosemary Hall, built on the high ground, because it was thought that exposure to the rain and the wind off the ocean was the cause of the bronchial complaints from which many of the Zulu party were suffering. They were not closely confined, and their presence was the object of interest, and concern, to a range of the island's residents, from the Governor, the Bishop and those Harriette Colenso called 'fashion and rank' on the top of the hill, to the residents of Jamestown and the storekeepers, who appreciated the extra income brought to the island by the exiles.

383

The original party had numbered nine. Ndabuko and Shingana were each accompanied by a wife and a male attendant. Dinuzulu had a male and two female attendants. Paul Mthimkhulu had travelled with the party to attend to their spiritual and medical needs. In addition there was a white guardian and an African assistant guardian who served as interpreter. There were now five children as well (Dinuzulu's eldest boy had died). Shingana's wife had the eldest, a son, Bunya, and a daughter, Nozinhlanzi. Zihlazile, daughter of Qethuka of the Magwaza, had given birth on 24 March 1892 to a boy, David Nyawana, and in 1894 to Mphaphu, who was given the English name of Victoria Helena. On 8 January 1894 Umkasilomo, daughter of Ntuzwa of the Mdlalose, gave birth to Nkayishana Maphumuzana.[1] In the next century he was to succeed his father, Dinuzulu, and was known also as Solomon.

It was generally agreed by outsiders that it was Ndabuko who found it most difficult to adapt to the new situation. He was seen as reclusive, taciturn and unhappy. Shingana remained the opposite, sociable and talkative. Dinuzulu was considered to be an attractive young man, free and open, most concerned to present himself well, and determined to learn to read and write in English and Zulu. The uncles found this difficult although Shingana was able to plough through a Zulu text – but when Harriette asked them to sign a document they asked for a day in which to practise. Dinuzulu was different; his letters in Zulu were written in what Harriette called a fine, strong hand.

The chiefs had by now adapted to local social conventions, and dressed in a manner acceptable to the population amongst whom they now lived. They participated in local functions, including gatherings at the Governor's residence. Ndabuko offered the most resistance to this while Dinuzulu accepted and enjoyed it. By 1892 the guardian was able to write that visitors expecting to see 'a half naked Zulu savage' found instead 'an intelligent-looking negro gentleman'.[2]

Reports like this infuriated Natal's settlers – even more so when they heard that the chiefs were invited to dance and to dine at the Governor's residence. It was what they might have expected – upstart natives spoiled by the liberality of the Governor and the naïveté of the St Helenian islanders, who were completely unaware of the distance that should have been kept between themselves and the exiles. But Natal had minimal control over the Zulu on St Helena, and hospitality and entertainment were important to Dinuzulu, who spent a considerable amount of money providing for his guests in a manner that he believed befitted them. Magema Fuze was to write how

On occasions a dinner would be given by the Prince, and he would invite Mr Solomon and Mr Yon, wealthy residents, and I may mention the St. Helenian girls. There would be dancing in European fashion, the two royal uncles sitting as on-lookers, together with their brides (*abalobokazi* new wives). The girls who danced were Miss Cummings and Miss Cressy and her sister, who were brown in colour, their fathers having been captured as children whilst bathing in the Congo river, and Martha Williams.[3]

Such occasions were costly. Dinuzulu's account for luxury goods at Mr Thorpe's store was paid for by money raised amongst his supporters in South Africa, brought down by Mjwaphuna to Pietermaritzburg where Magema Fuze handed it over to the officials for transmission to St Helena. On one occasion Dinuzulu wrote a letter demanding that 'Everyone who still remembers my father will contribute a small amount. The man who refuses is no longer on our side; he is no longer one of us', but the Colonial Office intervened:

> I think Dinuzulu might be told that the Queen's Indunas have seen his letter and are vexed with him for having written it – that as long as he is maintained in comfort at public expense, and is living in a quiet place like S. Helena he can have no legitimate occasion for such large sums as he asked for in that letter, and that it is moreover an unbecoming thing for a man of high ancestry to beg money from common people. That will make him think twice before writing such a letter again.[4]

On her arrival at St Helena, Harriette Colenso found herself torn between the need to keep on the right side of the Governor and accept his offer of hospitality at Plantation, and the chiefs who wanted her to stay with them at Maldivia. The two residences were separated by an hour's tough scramble up the cliffs from Jamestown, and she divided her time as best she could between St Helena's dignitaries on the top of the cliffs and her friends down below.

Dinuzulu did everything he could to welcome her. She dined with him in his rooms at Maldivia at a table laid with table napkins, wineglasses and a wide range of dishes, including fish for her although it was taboo for him. They were waited on by two St Helenian girls, and Dinuzulu offered Harriette champagne, 'but I was cruel enough to decline it, but am now plied with sherry (he does not take more than one glass at a meal I notice) ginger-beer, lemonade, and tea and coffee'.

Was she critical? After all, she, her mother and sister had sacrificed much of their material security for the Usuthu cause and these three men. They had spent their capital on lawyers, were living in a rundown cottage, and their financial prospects, upon which their personal freedom depended, were grim. This

young man, for whom they hoped so much, spent his allowance from the imperial government and collected money from the Zulu poor, to dress and dine in style. Yet it was clear that he felt that she expected him to entertain in this fashion. And he was a prince – who, if things went as they hoped and planned, would have to live as one, in a changing world. If she did disapprove she could not bring herself to admit it. 'They are not spoilt at all,' she reported to her sister, 'or nothing to matter.'[5]

The Zulu party had their photograph taken on the steps of the veranda, one assumes, of Maldivia. It has been reproduced in books before, it would seem because of the apparent incongruities and contrasts between the conventional portrayals of Zulu warriors and their women and their depiction here in Victorian suits and satin. Yet no one has bothered to identify who is depicted, and certainly no one has read the picture. On the left and right Ndabuko and Shingana, the former in particular, still seem uncomfortable in chairs and suits – Harriette described the likeness as 'mere libels'– while Dinuzulu, in his mid-twenties now, wears his clothes with ease and confidence. The mothers, carefully dressed in the fashion of the times, pose their children for the camera. Mbhodiya,

Photo 35 (opposite page). The Usuthu and their friends on St Helena. This photograph is one of a number taken in February 1895. Dinuzulu stands on the right of the photograph, clearly the modernising prince. Ndabuko is seated on the left and Shingana on the right holding his son Bunya, whose mother, Nozinyoni, sits with her daughter, Nozinhlanzi, on the left next to Dr Welby. Next to her, behind Harriette Colenso, is Mbhodiya, nurse and midwife, and between her and Paul Mthimkhulu is Nozingwe, wife of Ndabuko. The women in the front of the picture are the mothers of Dinuzulu's children. On the left is Zihlazile okaQethuka holding Victoria Helena (born 25 May 1894). David (24 March 1892) sits next to her in boots and cap, and Solomon Nkayishana Maphumuzana (8 January 1894) is held by his mother, Umkasilomo okaNtuzwa. The man standing on the steps with the cap is Mubi Nondenisa. The contrast between the three young women on the veranda and the dedicated determination of Harriette Colenso in the centre is immediate.

Photo 36 (below). Dinuzulu kaCetshwayo, Paul Mthimkhulu and Ndabuko kaMpande on St Helena. There were many photographs taken of the exiles on St Helena. Harriette Colenso had them copied and sent to friends and possible supporters, and also made them into slides, which she used when she lectured. Dinuzulu soon became used to the camera, although he resented the friendly familiarity suggested by the guardian's hands in this picture, which he felt was ingratiating and hypocritical. Paul Mthimkhulu, their doctor, is seated on the right and Ndabuko on the left.

brought to St Helena for her skills in Zulu midwifery, sits near Harriette at the centre. And at the back a head-ringed attendant to the princes; Anthony Daniels, the interpreter; and, wearing a cap, Mubi Nondenisa, Harriette's confidant, attendant and friend.

The central figure of Harriette Colenso dominates. She projects an image of a far more stern and determined person than the Bible-holding crusader of London in the early 1890s, and very far from the compliant daughter in Grahamstown in 1882. This is no longer the world of protest and appeals to English sense of justice. She was now working in the context of imperialism, of Cecil John Rhodes and the British South Africa Company, and the political pragmatism which had persuaded her to pursue realistic goals, and thus advocate the incorporation of Zululand with Natal before the return of Dinuzulu. It was a difficult policy to follow, and she had to go to London to make the best of it – and to do this she needed the full support of her Zulu allies. They had to present themselves as men capable of taking up this challenge, of accepting change. Dinuzulu in particular had to be shown as a young man who was able to play a responsible role in the new Zululand of Sir Marshal Clarke, be strong enough to take on old Natal, and show the ability to gain the respect and support of the new Natal of Harry Escombe.

As in so many photographs, the figures on the margins, who were included inadvertently, have their significance. Thus the stiffness, the rectitude and the determination of Harriette Colenso is offset by the three laughing St Helenian girls behind them on the veranda. There could be no greater contrast with Harriette than their attitudes, dress and expressions. They also had an interest in the Zulu cause – but a very different one. In time Harriette had to confront this as well.

Despite the concerns of the present and the worries for the future, there was much that Harriette and the Usuthu enjoyed about her visit. Dinuzulu and she rode together to the highest point on St Helena, Diana's Peak. She got to know the Zulu children and their mothers. She shared in the uncles' excitement as they studied the plates in Angas's *Kafirs Illustrated* with its paintings of Mpande's kingdom, in which they had grown up. They watched the archery competition with the military, and visited Longwood where Napoleon had lived, like them, in exile. Dinuzulu and she dined together at the Governor's residence.

But they could not escape the reality of exile. Ndabuko felt it most severely. She saw this when she went with him to visit Father Daine, the Catholic priest who had befriended him. They attended mass together, a novel experience for the leading member of the Church of England in South Africa, and her heart went out to Ndabuko:

I thought I knew before how lonely he was! but I realized it when we sat together, the whole congregation save one small boy, while bowing and wavings and murmurings went on in front of us in Latin which I could no more follow than he could the English. Father Daine is just the one person here who has found Ndabuko, and he responds, goes and sits there for sympathy and with genuine reverence, but not as a convert by any means.

Shingana had more resources to fall back on, including his son upon whom he doted. But it was a tense and unhappy existence, and the answer lay in devising a political strategy not only to get off the island, but to return to a Zululand amenable to the needs and ambitions of the Zulu royal house and its followers.

A cruel practical joke?

Harriette Colenso and the Usuthu spent many hours trying to understand what had happened in January. It all seemed inexplicable. The exiles went over the events as they had experienced them. On 23 January they had been called by the Governor and told that in a fortnight a boat would arrive to return them to Zululand. He had given them a letter in Zulu which seemed to have indicated that Dinuzulu was to be chief of the Usuthu, and induna to the Zululand government, with a house at Eshowe and a salary of £500 a year. But they were suspicious and confused. They had examined the document closely. The si*Zulu* was ungrammatical and it was not signed or dated. This had increased their suspicions: it was 'as though the sender himself did not like to own it'.[6] From their correspondence with Harriette they also knew that she was shortly to visit them on St Helena. Was this document in fact part of a plot to move them off the island before she arrived? They could not believe that she and Escombe would be ignorant of any attempt to return them to Zululand.

Still they had their instructions and they began to sell and pack their possessions. Then, just a few days before they were due to leave, a gunboat had come from the Cape with the news that the return was to be postponed. The *Umkuzi*, which had been supposed to take them back home, seemed to them a 'small and dirty ship, far inferior to the ordinary passenger vessels which they were accustomed to see'. Perhaps, they had speculated, Harry Escombe had discovered a plan to spirit them away from St Helena and sent the Royal Navy with the message to postpone their departure.

Even after discussions with Harriette much of what had happened remained inexplicable. She felt that she had to get to London before she could reconstruct events. But there was one piece of information which she believed she could decipher, and it gave her hope. It was contained in the document given to Dinuzulu informing him of his (now postponed) return. Although most scornful of the *siZulu* and the translation, Harriette believed the essence of its message was clear: it had been recommended that Dinuzulu should return to a central position in the government of Zululand – as first suggested by Escombe in 1890, and repeated in her 1893 pamphlet *The Present Position among the Zulus*.[7] Thus, although the cause of the delay remained a mystery, the secret dispatch did indicate that their plans and proposals had met with some success – that Clarke had recommended that Dinuzulu be appointed to an important consultative position in the Zululand administrative structure, and this had been accepted by the Queen's ministers of state. Harriette's task now was to discover why the return had been postponed, and to remove that obstacle.

At the end of March she left St Helena for London to do just this. What she did not realise was that it was felt in official circles that the obstacle which now obstructed the exiles' return had been placed in the way by a naïve and interfering woman – one Harriette Colenso.

London

When he received Harriette Colenso's telegram of 24 January requesting him to inform not only her friends, but also the Secretary of State for the Colonies, that the annexation of Zululand to Natal should precede the chiefs' return, Fox Bourne of the APS was shocked. It made no sense at all, and he asked immediately for an appointment with Sydney Buxton at the Colonial Office. He then wrote to Harriette. As far as he could discover, the chiefs were to return to Zululand within a fortnight. On the admittedly limited information available to him, he totally disagreed with the strategy indicated by her telegram. There should be no postponement of the return. Everything indicated that the present Liberal government would soon have to leave office. With the Conservatives in power, Salisbury as Prime Minister, and her old antagonist Baron de Worms as Under-Secretary in the House, what chance would there be of the exiles returning? Immediate advantage had to be taken of the offer to return the chiefs – it was unlikely that it would be repeated in the near future. 'Half a loaf is better than no bread. I am convinced that there is no present prospect of Zululand being absorbed in Natal, and that to press for that as a preliminary to the exiles' return would only be prejudicial to them.'[8]

News of Harriette Colenso's about-turn began to leak out. A friend wrote to Frank Colenso of a conversation he had had with Sydney Buxton, who 'greatly surprised' him by telling that Harriette now objected to the return of the chiefs and 'this has put the Colonial Office in a difficulty – and he spoke as if it might be impossible to send back the exiles at all'.[9] On 11 February 1895 Fox Bourne had his interview with Buxton. He wrote to Harriette about it.

> He tells me that all had been arranged for the return of the chiefs to Zululand at once, under conditions which he understood from Sir W. Hely Hutchinson and Sir Marshal Clarke, would be satisfactory to you and the Zulus – but that the objections raised by you and others (who the 'others' are he would not say) have rendered this impossible, for some time to come at any rate ... The upshot ... seems to me most unsatisfactory. From what I can learn there is no immediate prospect of Zululand being handed over to Natal, or of Sir M. Clarke remaining much longer in Zululand ... As there is great likelihood of Lord Rosebery's government being at an end some time this year, perhaps within the next few weeks – before the Natal–Zululand question is settled ... it appears to me very desirable that Dinuzulu and his uncles should be restored while the present regime lasts. I have urged as strongly as I could on Mr Buxton that this should be done – appealing to him to let them be reinstated on a generous and equitable footing, while Sir M. Clarke is on the spot to plant them honestly and firmly. 'That' says Mr. Buxton (I summarise his actual words, but you must not quote the words as his) 'is what we wanted and hoped for. But Miss Colenso and her friends are preventing it ...'[10]

She arrived in London on 6 April and went as soon as she could to the Colonial Office for an interview with Buxton and to arrange one with Ripon. They could hardly help her. They had tried to do their best to adopt a policy which they thought would be satisfactory to the chiefs and to herself. But the matter was now confused with the question of the future relations between Natal and Zululand, and there would be a delay while this was sorted out. And, Buxton told Harriette, they resented being 'squeezed'.[11]

Harriette refused to be swayed. She still felt, or so she said to the world, that everything was on the right track. Nonetheless, there was already a suggestion that she had made at least one serious miscalculation, embarrassing in its naïveté. This was her assumption that Marshal Clarke would stay on in Zululand after its incorporation with Natal. In this she had failed to realise what was apparently patently obvious to everyone else: that it would have been an extraordinary step for an *imperial* officer to agree to remain in a post under a *colonial* government. It would be in effect a demotion, and she had in effect recommended Clarke's removal from Zululand.

Then she heard from Clarke himself. He chose to present her action as a personal betrayal. By

> advocating a course which would naturally terminate my connection with
> Zululand, you rather took my breath away – the chunk of old red sandstone
> was delivered by the fair hand of one I had regarded as a fellow worker and
> 'the subsequent proceedings interested me no more'.[12]
>   I don't think it is a breach of confidence for me to tell you that Mr
> Escombe informed the Governor that you had promised not only to move
> your friends to make the return of Dinuzulu dependent on the immediate
> incorporation of Zululand with Natal, but also to persuade the exiles to refuse
> repatriation unless such a measure was adopted.[13]

He could not have discussed the whole matter with her sooner – for example when they had met in Natal in December, for 'it is a point of honour for us officials not to divulge communications marked confidential and I had no choice in the matter'.

If her telegram had taken Clarke's breath away, then his reply must have done the same to Harriette Colenso. His scrupulous emphasis on confidentiality she could accept, even if she disagreed to its being applied to her in this particular case. But her decision had been based on the fact that Zulu interests would be secured by her allies in high places: Escombe in Natal and Clarke in Zululand. Her one condition to Escombe was that on incorporation Natal should recommend that Clarke be retained as supreme authority in Zululand. She had never thought that Clarke would find the idea impossible, let alone interpret it as an act of betrayal on her part.[14]

On 1 May she managed to secure another interview with Buxton, this time at the House of Commons. She liked the Under-Secretary, finding him 'open to reason', but their differences remained considerable and his guarded references to what had happened filled her with concern. Why, she asked him, did he always speak of Mr Escombe and not of the Natal ministry? She was told that 'the Colonial Office had been depending on Mr Escombe's support in this matter, and now he had turned round entirely – if he had stood by them they might possibly have been able to disregard Natal opposition'.[15] As we have seen, Escombe's explanation for turning round entirely was that he had been forced to because Harriette Colenso had done so. She of course did not know this – one wonders whether Buxton did.

Buxton's line was that it mattered little now what she or he thought should happen to Zululand and Natal. Politically the idea of incorporation was a nonstarter. The colony had only just been awarded responsible government, but instead of proceeding in a cautious manner they had become involved in the brawl around the Indian Franchise Bill. The House of Commons would not accept a proposal that Natal and Zululand be united. There was no point in even putting the proposal to the Cabinet.

Even her Liberal sympathisers in England disagreed with what she had done. As E. Marion Bryce told her, 'My husband thinks that it is very likely indeed that there might be opposition from some of our party on the annexation of Zululand to Natal, on the ground that the whites of Natal would ill-treat the natives. The idea that Natal is trying to squeeze the British government will also act with hostile effect on this proposal.'[16] Again the obvious inference was that she had miscalculated – and it was not just that she had misread the political situation in England – she had not bothered to read it at all. But Harriette was not to be moved. 'It seems to me that we have very fair chances. I wish that the rest of the Colonial Office were as open to reason as Mr. Buxton, who really does mean and try aright as far as I can judge – but then it would not be the Colonial Office at all.'[17]

For Harriette this was not the time to falter. There were elements in the Natal ministry which had to be supported if they were to succeed. Clarke, Escombe, Colenso would be a formidable political team once it was able to clear up the confusion being sown by its enemies. She still trusted Escombe. But as the months passed, it became more clear that he had some explaining to do. How was it that Sir Marshal Clarke had apparently only heard of her support for the incorporation of Zululand with Natal from her? She had been led to believe that he had been in consultation with the Natal ministry about it. Then there was Clarke's extraordinary story that Escombe had said that she intended to instruct Dinuzulu not to accept any offer of return before incorporation. There had to be some mistake, and she asked Clarke to tell Escombe what was being said about him. We now get the first hints of her concern; but it was only concern, not blame.

> Will you please, next time you can see Mr. Escombe, tell him what I say of the words attributed to him, because, for one thing, I must try to be clear as to my own responsibility in the matter, and for another – I know that it was not you who put out the lights – but one result of all this secrecy is to cause us – you and I and Mr Escombe – to jostle one another in the dark, and we must try to keep in touch.[18]

But these were private matters; publicly she had to be confident. On 12 June she sent to the Colonial Office a 25-page confidential pamphlet on the history of the attempt to secure their return from the point of view of the exiles, and a plea that they be returned, together with her reasons for requesting the annexation of Zululand to Natal.[19] It stood no chance. Buxton was courteous in his dismissal: 'I shall be glad to see you again, if you wish it, but I have nothing further to say, and I do not think it will be advantageous to go over the same ground again.'[20]

She wrote to Ripon privately, asking what she could tell Dinuzulu about his future. A week later she received a private letter in return:

> Dear Miss Colenso
>
> Your question is not very easy to answer. From the day when the return of Dinuzulu and his uncles became, as I think unfortunately, mixed up with the question of the annexation of Zululand to Natal the date of that return was rendered uncertain.
>
> It is impossible to deal hastily with such a question as the handing over of Zululand to Colonial administration.
>
> It is a matter which will not be lost sight of but which must be settled on its own merits.
>
> It is therefore impossible for me at present to fix any date for Dinuzulu's return.
>
> I sincerely regret his disappointment but I am not responsible for it.
> Yours very faithfully
> Ripon[21]

Ripon, we know, had refused to adopt the Natal Governor's suggestion that Harriette Colenso be held responsible for the postponement. But in that self-justifying, impatient last sentence, he made sure that Harriette knew that he was not to blame for the collapse of the arrangement to return the chiefs for which she had agitated so persistently for so long.

On the same day that Ripon wrote this letter, the Liberals were defeated in the House of Commons and resigned. They were substantially defeated in the election which followed. The Conservative government which followed them into power was that of the Marquis of Salisbury. The new Secretary of State for the Colonies was confident, aggressive, determined to utilise the enormous power in his hands to advance British interests in the era of high imperialism. Harriette Colenso now had to deal with Joseph Chamberlain.

CHAPTER 28

FIVE MEN AND A LOST CAUSE

An imperial vision

Chamberlain came to the Colonial Office determined to consolidate and build British power overseas and his own reputation in pursuit of an imperial vision. In South Africa this was challenged by the fact that it now appeared that the most extensive deposits of gold in the world lay within the Transvaal – an Afrikaner republic which, a little over a decade before, had been given its independence by a Liberal government of which Chamberlain himself had been a member. The new wealth had shifted the location of power within southern Africa, politically and geographically, towards the Boer republic. It had also created powerful individuals in South Africa, some pursuing a new political order and others determined to conserve the old. Rhodes had extended the control of the Chartered Company to the region north of the Transvaal, over the land of the Ndebele and the Shona. While his high ambitions and ruthless methods raised eyebrows, this was more than offset by the brash confidence and the economy with which he extended British interests, and he was rewarded with official support from London. It was risky, nonetheless, as Chamberlain was soon to discover: six months after taking office Rhodes's plot to overthrow the government of the Transvaal failed, exposing the Prime Minister of the Cape as a conspirator far too close to the officials in the Colonial Office.

As the aftermath of the Jameson Raid demonstrated in 1896, disturbances in South Africa could cause unease in the chancelleries of the powerful industrialising, militaristic national states which were now rival imperial powers. And in a world increasingly affected by international power politics being played at the edge, African rights and injustices in Africa were of little concern. In this context, the fate of three exiled African rebels had little bearing on British policy – especially when it became known that, at the very moment when the Colonial Office had attempted to return them to Zululand, their foremost supporter had, with all the perverse unpredictability of a woman who had involved herself in matters lying outside her proper sphere, sabotaged the plan.

As we have seen, Fox Bourne had without hesitation rejected Harriette Colenso's defence of her support for Natal's annexation of Zululand. He feared that she had turned down an opportunity that might never come again. And he was right. The political context was one in which a vision of imperial glory had gained a hold on the thinking of a widening range of people in Britain – including many of Harriette Colenso's liberal allies.

Harry Escombe

As 1895 progressed, so more and more evidence emerged, first of differences between Escombe and the Colenso sisters, then of the possibility that the latter had been treated dishonestly, and finally that Escombe had exploited his friendship with them in order to put pressure on Whitehall. Outwardly, however, they remained on friendly terms. Communication between Natal's Attorney-General and Bishopstowe, although not secret, was treated by both parties with discretion. Harriette Colenso was aware that potentially the relationship was politically embarrassing for him. She tended not to refer to him by name in their correspondence, using such terms as 'our friend'. Escombe and Agnes were in personal communication in Natal. Agnes visited him in Pietermaritzburg, and enjoyed their talks over a cup of tea in the evening as he smoked his pipe and reminisced about his friendship with her father. She handed over to him Harriette's accounts of her interviews at the Colonial Office, reported messages received at Bishopstowe from Zululand, and talked politics. This shy, awkward woman was touched and pleased at the confidence he showed in her. On his side he found in her and her sister an important source of information on subjects which ranged from the thoughts on South Africa of senior officials in Whitehall, to the attitudes of the Zulu leadership, to recent developments in Natal.

But it became more and more difficult for him to hide the double role he was playing. Thus, when in mid-1895 Agnes sent Escombe Harriette's pamphlet *Zululand, the Exiled Chiefs, Natal and the Colonial Office 1893–5*, he found a number of embarrassing and objectionable passages in it. The Governor, Hely-Hutchinson, was most annoyed when he discovered that Harriette had printed the fact that she had been made to believe that he, the Governor, supported Escombe in persuading her to advocate incorporation before the return. Whether the Governor was annoyed with Escombe for telling her this, or just because Harriette had alleged that Escombe had done so, is not clear.

Escombe was annoyed by the pamphlet as well, not only because it hinted at the double role he had played in the postponement, but because it contained an extract from a letter in which Mubi Nondenisa wrote of Natal's responsibility for Zululand's miseries. Harry Escombe did not see it this way and protested, and in so doing gave Harriette the chance to give voice to her concern about his attitudes. It sprang from a story Agnes had told her about a leader in John Robinson's newspaper, *The Natal Mercury*, which had been rankling for months. She circled a moment before the attack:

> take the Mercury of nowadays. Take the leader in the issue of April 16 1895, on 'The Future of Zululand.' What is a native to think of that? There are philosophical heights from which it is possible to treat that article as a praiseworthy example of 'climbing down'.
> 'The exiles must never return' used to be the cry.
> Now it is as follows. 'Having satisfied justice they have, of course, as perfect a right to be returned to their country as any old Botany Bay convict had to return to England.'
> I confess that my philosophy has a struggle with resentment and disgust every time I read that sentence. You have brought these remarks on yourself by 'looking very grave', over that paper and telling Agnes that the natives ought to be very grateful, and never writing a word to me about it.[1]

That the man, who as their defence counsel in 1889 had extolled with such eloquence the heroism and loyalty of the Usuthu chiefs, should now in 1895 fail to protest when they were characterised as criminals, was deeply disturbing to Harriette. She was worried and angry – but there was no question yet of a break between them: 'it remains true that the Zulu cause would never have arrived without Mr Escombe's help'. There were differences, but they were differences amongst allies: discussion and debate was still the way forward. It had to be.

Joseph Chamberlain

Harriette Colenso was now based in London, staying with her brothers. She was desperate for a hint of what policy was to be adopted towards Zululand and the chiefs, and her movements were determined largely by the Colonial Office. But the officials were greatly taken up with other far more significant matters and events. Consequently Harriette had to sit patiently in the ante-chambers off the corridors of power, waiting for a chance to tentatively and respectfully remind the great and the good of her presence.

The permanent officials knew her well by now – or should have. When she wrote to Edward Fairfield asking for an appointment he agreed, but denied that they had had any previous correspondence. She addressed a mock reply to him in a letter to Agnes.

> Not a bit of it young man [they were virtually the same age]. You answered the very last despatch I addressed to Lord Knutsford – and you were not half as rude as Mr. Sydney Webb. I shall have much pleasure in explaining this to you on Monday at 3.
> You are also the person who said to a lady friend the other day that 'Miss Colenso had succeeded in her mission.'[2]

Buxton, now out of office, remained friendly but frustratingly reticent. But she was still able to draw on the advice of the insightful and informed Leonard Courtney, who felt that Chamberlain might well be sympathetic to her cause. But the new Secretary of State was far too taken up with the duties of his new office and listening to the many other voices which felt they should be heard. The most insistent of these belonged to the emissaries of the British South Africa Company, spurred on from Cape Town by Cecil John Rhodes, who was making preparations to seize control of the Transvaal. For this it was necessary to deploy the Company's armed forces on the land of the Tswana on the Transvaal's western border. The cryptic coded telegrams giving the plotters' view of the situation moved back and forth from London and Cape Town, eventually providing the evidence to fix responsibility and apportion blame for Jameson's débâcle at the end of the year.

On 20 August Harriette asked for an interview with the Secretary of State, enclosing in her letter, as she habitually did, photographs of Dinuzulu, together with the pamphlet she had written for Ripon, *Zululand, the Exiled Chiefs, Natal, and the Colonial Office 1893–5*.[3] The reply came on 7 September – Chamberlain should be able to see her in November.[4] She scrutinised the letter, trying to reach beyond the formal wording to discover any indication of Chamberlain's personal feelings towards the exiles. There was nothing beyond the fact that Dinuzulu's name was at last spelt correctly, and 'there seems to be trace of something which is not red tape about the "yours very truly," but this is poor sustenance for two months!'[5]

During these two months the Colonial Office had little time to think of Zululand. First there was a crisis when Kruger closed the drifts on the Transvaal's borders to colonial traffic. He backed down under pressure. Meanwhile a party of other southern African chiefs – from Bechuanaland – came to Britain to petition against the handing over of their territory to the British South Africa Company. Sebele of the Kwena and Bathoen of the Ngwaketse

were led by Khama of the Ngwato.[6] Supported by two missionaries they succeeded in bringing their case before the British public. Chamberlain was sympathetic to the chiefs, and, in spite of Rhodes's demands, was only prepared to
grant the Chartered Company a strip of territory sufficient for a railway line to
the north. Harriette Colenso was pleased at their success – she also hoped that
the Zulu chiefs would be allowed to put their case in England – and she knew
Khama's secretary and interpreter, Simeon Seisa, whom she had once helped at
Bishopstowe. She called upon Khama and found him in his rooms in South Place
Hotel near Finsbury Square sitting at the window staring out at the traffic. They
had a brief conversation and he wished her well in her struggle – but she was all
too aware that her presence might be an embarrassment. The missionaries
accompanying Khama did not come from their rooms to greet her.

Harriette, of course, could only guess at the tense negotiations going on at the
Colonial Office as she waited. But on the last day of 31 October she reminded
Fairfield, as calmly as she could, that Chamberlain had 'promised to see me too
"in November." I suppose that we Zulus must wait until he has got through
some of the more prominent ones but you won't let him forget us? and that we
have been waiting a long time.'[7] The meeting was eventually held on 6
December but she gained little from it: 'Mr Chamberlain, as I hoped, is personally friendly *to us*, *Zulus*, but the Colonial Office is – as bad as I have ever
thought it.'[8] But she did find out, to her consternation, that she had misunderstood the attitude of the Natal government to the return of the chiefs.
Throughout 1895 she had been allowed to believe that the Natal ministers supported the idea that Dinuzulu should return to Zululand, whether it was to be
united with Natal or not. At the Colonial Office she discovered otherwise. As
soon as the interview was over, she wrote to Escombe, insisting that the Natal
ministry request the return of the chiefs with or without the incorporation of
Zululand into Natal.[9]

Thus, at the end of the 1895, she was still in pursuit of the reconciliation of the
Zulu people with the government of Natal. However, we see signs of her private
despair. Perhaps she already realised that in her desperation to liberate her
friends she had allowed herself to be persuaded to commit an irreversible political error. The missionaries attending the Tswana party had not responded when
she visited Khama and had left her card: they probably thought that it was not
'desirable now that he should be very friendly with a heretic like me, and a lost
cause like the Zulus'.[10] The irony notwithstanding, these were not the sort of
words that Harriette had ever used to describe the cause to which she and her
family had committed their lives. 'A lost cause'! – there had been a profound
change.

Cecil John Rhodes

On the very day that Chamberlain met Harriette Colenso at the Colonial Office, he had cabled a warning to the High Commissioner's private secretary in South Africa. It was on the subject of the prospect of an uprising against the Transvaal government, and in it he stated his eminently cynical assumption that 'I take for granted that no movement will take place unless success is certain, a fiasco would be most disastrous'.[11] By the end of the month the fiasco had taken place when Rhodes's man, Leander Starr Jameson, at the head of a mounted troop drawn from the British South Africa Company, invaded the Transvaal in support of a non-existent uprising in Johannesburg. They were quickly put out of action by the Transvalers. Rhodes, Prime Minister of the Cape, had to resign, and Joseph Chamberlain and his officials were widely suspected of complicity in the planning of the Jameson Raid. For months to come, business at the Colonial Office was taken up with devising a defence against this charge and finding a way out of the very disaster against which Chamberlain had warned. Harriette Colenso's appeals were buried almost out of sight.

But not her anger or her determination. Forced to wait for a decision on Zulu matters, desperately concerned about her own responsibility for the chiefs' continued exile, she kept up her work publicising their cause and protesting against the policies and attitudes now prevalent in Britain towards Africa. She followed imperial affairs and debates in the press and in the periodical literature. The intellectual climate of the times, with its increasing racism and the glorification of national power, brute force and militarism, was abhorrent to her, and she spoke and wrote against them.

Events in 1896 confirmed the warnings she had made to the APS about the dangers of not opposing without qualification the British South Africa Company and Cecil John Rhodes. First came the Jameson Raid and its consequences. Then in March the Ndebele rose up against the British South Africa Company settlers, who had usurped their sovereignty and seized their land and cattle. By May, Company reinforcements had arrived and the process of re-establishing Company rule began, with all the vicious cruelty of which a frightened settler community with modern arms is capable. The next month the Shona rose up against the Company, and the horrible process of reimposing Company rule began again.

It was from reports received from Rhodesia through 1896 that Olive Schreiner wrote *Trooper Peter Halket of Mashonaland* – a founding classic of South African protest literature. But while Olive Schreiner's attacks on Rhodes and the Company are part of the history of imperialism, the public critique that Harriette

Colenso developed of imperialism, out of her knowledge of recent Zulu history, is hardly known. She had already been watching Schreiner's progress eagerly.

So Olive Schreiner has entered the lists against Mr Rhodes! Well done! It is quite refreshing to see how respectfully the *Cape Times* thinks it necessary to handle her. For I should mention that the criticism is all I have yet seen of her paper, (I've ordered it though) the news boards advertize 'Olive Schreiner v. Cecil Rhodes' and 'That villain Rhodes'.[12]

For Harriette Colenso it remained Rhodes who embodied the worst of the spirit of the age. His preference for 'land over niggers' was referred to repeatedly in her lectures, interviews and articles. But a further evil lay in the way his ideas were accepted by men and women whose histories and political allegiances suggested that they should have known better – like her old parliamentary adviser, James Bryce, who returned from a visit to South Africa sounding, Harriette wrote, a 'Chartery, anti Boer tone': 'Mr. Rhodes' services to his country deserve that we should suspend judgment, and stuff of that sort. What services forsooth! He and his party have preferred land (or diamonds or gold) to niggers, right through, and have so disserved her.'[13]

Her lectures began increasingly to link what had happened to the Zulu with what was happening to the Ndebele and the Shona. Alice Werner supported her in the press and on the platform, and she thought long and hard about the nature of African rights at this time, turning to her friend John Westlake's dictum that 'the rights of uncivilized peoples are left to the conscience of the civilized state within whose recognised territorial dominions they lie'. The 'present trouble in S. Africa', Harriette wrote, 'is because the rights of the Matabele and Mashona people have been "left to the conscience" of a nation which has handed them over to a chartered Company'.[14]

There had to be a stop to this process by which African independence was crushed and African people dominated by invading powers. Existing African political authority had to be recognised and worked with; instead, every attempt was made to destroy it, creating not leaders but martyrs. She traced through newspapers the 'heartbreaking, and most humiliating' process whereby the Ndebele leaders asked for a fair hearing, and were shot down. She had seen it all before, she felt. She protested at the hypocrisy of the English liberal establishment, so ready to condemn the atrocities of others and incapable of seeing its own.

At last, as 1896 progressed, she had to admit that she had been wrong as well. 'I told *them* [the Zulu chiefs] to trust to English justice to protect them. I can never urge that again on anyone.'[15] This was indeed a change. Faith, ultimately, in English justice was one of the principles that had given meaning to her father's life and works, and therefore hers. This was no longer so.

Sir John Robinson

But although she could no longer accept that Britain would in the end act for the right, there was no way in which she could drop the cause in which she was fighting. Harriette Colenso now had to await the arrival of Natal's Prime Minister, Sir John Robinson, in London, and hope that this would precipitate some action on the future of Zululand.

A major item on Robinson's agenda was the incorporation of Zululand with Natal. But the Colonial Office, although not hostile to the project in itself, still objected to being squeezed by a bunch of colonial politicians. London's interests were much wider than those of Natal. Incorporation needed a thoroughgoing investigation and proper consideration of the implications for the imperial government and South Africa as a whole. As far as the Conservative government was concerned, its predecessor's statement of April 1895 still stood: that the matter would not be attended to at the moment, but when it was, Natal's 'prior claims' would be recognised.

Meanwhile, it remained an issue between the Natal ministry and the British government, over which they conducted an almost formalistic conflict. In careful diplomatic language they exchanged the courtesies which tried to hide their considerable mutual antagonism – the colonials towards the interfering imperial officials who assumed a high moral position without having to suffer the consequences, the officials in London towards the settlers who disguised greed as progress and a concern for the general good. At the same time Natal had to have London's support if it was going to get hold of Zululand, and London had to be sure of Natal as the tension between the British government and Natal's neighbour the Transvaal increased. Both sides were fully aware that an understanding would have to be reached. Until then the cycle continued: the Natal government asked for Zululand; the British government asked that the return of the chiefs be considered; Natal brought up incorporation; London, repatriation.

But while diplomatic relations were characterised by stalemate, radical changes were taking place in Zululand. We have seen how, in the opening years of the 1890s, a major argument in support of the continued exile of the Usuthu and against Harriette Colenso's petitions for their return was the report that, since the exile of the chiefs, stability had returned to Zululand and its economy was thriving. But from 1894 this changed: huge swarms of locusts devouring both crops and grazing were followed by drought. As hunger turned to starvation, the income from the hut tax fell and the colony's budget went into deficit. And an even greater catastrophe was looming. The cattle plague, rinderpest, was moving steadily southwards and would soon threaten Zululand's richest resource – its cattle-holdings. British Zululand, which only two years before had a surplus on its books, was now running into debt and perhaps economic catastrophe. It was not a propitious moment for the colony of Natal to ask for its incorporation.

Chamberlain felt that the Natal ministers 'will without doubt agree with me in thinking that this is not a favourable moment for making immediately any change in relations of Zululand and Natal'.[16] The ministers in turn felt the shortage of food and the threat of rinderpest made the return of Dinuzulu impossible, for 'loss and suffering may dispose natives to disorder owing to despair ... [and] he might possibly become a rallying point of the Bantu race'.[17]

Harriette Colenso disagreed with both sides: she argued in a letter to Chamberlain that the return of the Usuthu chiefs would improve the situation by raising Zulu spirits in these terrible times of drought and famine – an argument which reflects perhaps her own desperation. Chamberlain certainly disagreed with it. He told Harriette so in his reply, although he did express his hope that they could be returned 'at no distant date'. But, he continued, he did not want to have an interview with her about it, and he asked her 'to regard this letter as written in confidence'. She could do nothing. 'So I waited,' she wrote, 'resisting the temptation to retort that I would keep sacred this mighty confidence when I could discover it.'[18]

Prime Minister John Robinson, now a very ill man, was coming to England for health as much as for official reasons. On the way, the ship he was travelling on called at St Helena and he took the opportunity to have an interview with Dinuzulu. It was not a happy meeting. Robinson's prejudices were deep, and he exhibited them with unconcerned arrogance. As he waited for Dinuzulu, 'a small boy' informed him 'with a manifest sense of the importance of his announcement, "there's the King of the Zulus driving down the Signal Hill."'

If true, it was just what Robinson had suspected – 'the King of the Zulus'! He made a point of keeping Dinuzulu waiting till he had consulted with the Governor, from whom he heard that his predecessor, an 'old Indian official', had spoilt Dinuzulu by 'indiscreet indulgences'. This included shaking hands – and now it was difficult to withdraw this privilege.

An interview followed. Robinson observed Dinuzulu closely. He wore his flannel suit and tan shoes well but he 'seemed nervous and not quite at ease, and ... his bearing rather lacked the composure and dignity of the high-bred native chieftain'. Magema Fuze had recently arrived to assist in Dinuzulu's education, and he interpreted. 'My wife thought that he was the most dignified of the two.'

Robinson made a number of perfunctory announcements about the future of Natal and Zululand – and said nothing on the subject about which Dinuzulu obviously hoped to hear – his return. In a discussion with the guardian, Robinson discovered that the uncles were 'cantankerous and always complaining' and Dinuzulu was 'more and more exacting, and fond of arguing every point of detail'. There could be no question of a visit to England, 'owing to the imbecility of the British public in such cases'. Nothing he saw changed the Prime Minister's mind. Dinuzulu could not return to Zululand with any 'official status or authority … If he did not in his heart feel that he was, what the little St. Helena boy designated him, "the King of the Zulus," he would be more than human. He would certainly not be allowed to forget the claim.'

With one unpleasant interview completed, another awaited Natal's Prime Minister: that with Miss Harriette Colenso in London. At first he tried to put her off, but she wrote at intervals through October expressing her hope that his visit to London would enable the Natal ministry and the Colonial Office to work together to carry out the promise that had been made to the exiles two years before in the Queen's name. Robinson had no such intention. When Chamberlain asked for a response to the return of the chiefs, Robinson continued to procrastinate – this time saying that he would consult his ministers on his return to Natal.

But she persisted and on 30 November, just before he sailed, he agreed to a half-hour meeting. It was a grim encounter between two old antagonists – although Harriette could still write to Alice Werner that Robinson said 'that he was obliged to avoid excitements! (had been having interviews at Col. Off. so how formidable I must be!) … I did not excite him then, but went home and wrote at him.'[19] Yet behind her brave smile she was utterly serious – during the interview she had discovered proof at last for what she already must have known about Harry Escombe and his attitudes towards her and the Usuthu.

On 1 December, the day after the interview, Harriette posted her letter to Sir John Robinson. It began with a reference to a request he had made that she should use her influence to 'preach patience' to the Zulu exiles. How could she do so, she asked him, without knowing why they should be patient?

> To preach patience on this point usefully, I must first understand my text. I must – as I put it to you – know what to reply when Dinuzulu asks me why cannot he and his uncles be brought home at once?
>
> So far, I can only say that I have entirely failed to grasp any explanation which is not inadequate, and which does not fall to pieces on an attempt to formulate it. I am sure that you understand I must be convinced myself before I can hope to convince others, and before I can think it right to make an attempt.[20]

This was just what Robinson wished to avoid – being dragged into a correspondence with Harriette Colenso over the future of Zululand. He had no obligations towards her, her ideas were wrong just as her father's had been, and she had no right to assume that he was obliged to answer her on matters of policy. Nor should she assume that, by agreeing to an interview with her, he admitted that she had a right to participate in matters which concerned two governments, not private individuals, and certainly not a woman. The question of the return of the chiefs would be dealt with – when the officials saw fit.

But up to this point Harriette Colenso was only sparring. Her full, considered reply to their interview was being drafted. She completed it and sent it off on 3 December, although it missed the Prime Minister and was only to reach him when he was back in Natal. It revolved around one phrase that he had let slip.

> You must tell me 'frankly', you said, that your Ministry hold it to be out of the question to 'place Dinuzulu in a position of supreme authority;' and when I asked if you were aware of the position which had been proposed for him [in January 1895], you intimated that it was to this that you referred; that you had had this proposal before you, and that you object to it ...

This piece of information completely staggered Harriette. As far as she knew, there had never been such a proposal. It had never been thought that Dinuzulu should on his return be placed in a position of 'supreme authority'. No matter what Harriette might have wished would happen, she knew there could be no chance for the Zulu royal house to be restored to its position of *supreme authority*. What Escombe had proposed in his letter to her in 1890, and what she had suggested in her pamphlet and to Sir Marshal Clarke in 1893, and what she believed that Clarke had accepted and lay behind the proposals for the return of the exiles, was that Dinuzulu should return to a position of *central authority*, as a government induna and adviser to the Resident Commissioner.

But now here in London, she was informed, by the Prime Minister of Natal in whose administration Harry Escombe was himself a key minister, that he believed that the proposals of January 1895 were for Dinuzulu to return to supreme authority, not a central position. 'I have to say at once', she wrote to Robinson, 'that this statement by you is the first intimation I have received that such is the view taken by the Natal Ministry'. She had supported the call for incorporation before return, believing it would improve relations between black and white in Natal and Zululand. She had done so, it was now clear, on insufficient information.

The two years' delay has been a severe strain upon such confidence on the native side; the attitude you now disclose, *persisted in*, must shatter it. I give this warning very seriously, both to your Ministry and to the Colonial Office, in view of the grave troubles through famine which we have already to meet in Natal and Zululand, and throughout South Africa.

The attitude which you disclose completely nullifies my small support of the Natal Ministry in this matter, by sweeping away the very ground on which it was given. I desire to bring this point very plainly to your notice and to that of the Secretary of State for the Colonies, while you are still in England.

The break had been made. John Robinson's reaction meant little to Harriette Colenso. They were old enemies, and she had put her antagonism towards him to one side for the sake of reconciliation between Zululand and Natal. Now that this opportunity was gone, so had the need to work with Robinson. But Harry Escombe was a friend and ally. She had confidence in him. He had treated her with consideration; he had stood up for the Usuthu and given heart to a people crushed by a decade of official harassment. The question now for Harriette Colenso was, what was Escombe's role in this? Why had he not made sure that Robinson had been correctly informed about the basis of her support? How had Escombe let the Natal ministry proceed for two years on the totally incorrect, and politically impossible, assumption that the imperial government proposed to return Dinuzulu to a position of supreme authority in Zululand – a position that she knew Natal would reject?

The answer, it would seem, was that Escombe had not bothered. For Harriette the difference between 'supreme' and 'central' was crucial. Escombe understood this. But for the rest of the Natal ministry the distinction hardly mattered – Zulus were Zulus, the Colensos were sentimental do-gooders and trouble-makers, the return of Dinuzulu was a threat to white supremacy, and the Natal electorate wanted Zululand. But Harry Escombe was aware of what Harriette Colenso was doing and of the moral imperatives which drove her on. He acted towards Harriette not out of colonial ignorance and racism, but out of political ambition. In the very letter in which Escombe had made the suggestions upon which, ultimately, the proposals for the aborted return were based, he had told Harriette:

The success which has attended your resoluteness in the cause of right is an encouragement to all of us to persevere for conscience sake even when the fight seems hopeless. I thank you for the lesson.
Yours always,
Harry Escombe.[21]

Robinson dismissed Harriette Colenso; Harry Escombe exploited her.

Sir Marshal Clarke

One ally remained – Zululand's Resident Commissioner, Sir Marshal Clarke, and he, Harriette was informed, was about to visit London as well. Once again she began to hope. Perhaps some initiative was about to be taken. On 10 December she wrote to him, warmly and intimately, and told him of what had just happened between herself and John Robinson, sending him copies of their correspondence. 'This correspondence means, ~~of course~~, I presume, burning my ships with the Natal Government. I have *felt* it coming for some time, and in some ways it is a relief to have it over.'[22]

Harriette was now quite desperate and had almost, and quite uncharacteristically, to plead for a meeting. Sir Marshal agreed and, once again, Harriette discovered that a man she had treated as an ally was not so ready to be considered one. When she tried to see him again she wrote that 'I am inclined to think that you classed me with the Prince of Darkness' and 'We can go out "into the street" if you want to fight, I don't'. But she had to have information. She could not accept being excluded from political matters to which, it was public knowledge, she had committed herself and her family for so long and in which, she believed, she had acted with great responsibility. 'I can meet you', she wrote to Clarke, 'anywhere you like, and at anytime you like.'[23]

'Getting out'

January 1897 was a hard month in a hard winter for Harriette Colenso. It needed a supreme effort not to despair. Half-way through the month she was able to hint, in terse grim language, not only at the damage that had been done to her, but that she was coming to terms with it. 'I'm picking up the pieces that are left of me after the Sir J. Robinson skirmish.'[24] And in the advice she gave to Agnes who, in Natal, was defending the Church of England against the Church of the Province, she referred to her own very private battles with the past:

> Your fight with Bishop Baynes is very cheering. Fight it out. There is no compromise possible. And beware! I did not think that I was compromising in January 1895, and I am not sure yet of the division of responsibility then between Colonial Office, His Excellency, Harry Escombe and me. But I fear that Sir J Robinson has at last told me the truth as to Mr Escombe's position in the matter. *When* he changed is another point that I have not quite thrashed out.

I suppose his position is that his joining Sir J. Robinson's Government should have enlightened me. I think now that it ought, but that does not excuse (from a private friendship, and also from a Zulu point of view) his not telling me when he must have seen plainly over and over again, that I did not realize that fact.[25]

But she had made a error and must take responsibility for it:

In judging of what happened two years ago, I find it not easy to divest one's mind of information and impressions since received – and also of consequences. And excuses for oneself ~~appear so plain. It is so easy to put it~~ put themselves forward. 'I trusted Mr. Escombe.' But I ought not to have expected so much of him ... I think that I ought to have refused to act at all without the information which was denied me, and which it now appears would have reversed the opinion I then gave.

What the Zulus have got to forgive me is that I thought it possible under any circumstances to trust them to Natal ...[26]

Yet none of this was any reason to stop what she had begun. 'They are quite mistaken, all of them, if they think that I am going to sit down under this fresh betrayal of the Zulus, though I have been drawn into it myself.'[27] When Escombe protested to Agnes that her sister's letter to Robinson was an attempt to threaten the Natal ministry, Harriette wrote that 'it's nonsense to talk of my threatening – where is my power? except in being in the right – and if I am that I am bound to give warning – if I am wrong I am a cypher'.[28]

The power of being in the right – of justice giving meaning to action – this was a brave determined cry of defiance even as the forces generated by imperialism swept over her and her friends. It was time to find a way to move forward. She had already instructed Agnes to stop talking to Escombe about Zulu matters but not let Mjwaphuna, the Usuthu representative in Natal, know this: 'You must not tell Mr Escombe any more Zulu secrets ... Don't quarrel if you can help it, and don't "let on" to poor Mjwaphuna who would be in despair. I've been nearly there, but am now getting out, only it's twelve o'clock and I lecture at Leeds tomorrow night.'[29]

CHAPTER 29

THE WAGON BREAKS DOWN

'An undignified scramble'

By the beginning of 1897 it was clear that Harriette Colenso could do little
to penetrate the barriers that officialdom had raised against her. She was
completely excluded from the confidences of all the politicians and the
officials dealing with Zulu matters. They would contact her when they thought
fit – and she should be grateful when they chose to stoop in her direction.

But she could still protest. She travelled extensively in England giving lectures on Zulu and African affairs to interested church and discussion groups, and
women's organisations. Her starting point was predictable enough – Britain's
God-given duty towards all people under British rule. This was the pulse which
had driven Bishopstowe forward for half a century, providing the moral basis for
its protests and political interventions.

> The declaration that slavery under the British flag was at an end; that in future
> England would admit no distinction among her subjects on account of colour;
> was indeed a great event, for by it our country acknowledged the duty laid on
> her by the new insight which she had gained into the Moral Law, she recog-
> nized a fresh Revelation from on High. That England maintains these prin-
> ciples is indeed the very foundation of the position she still claims in Africa.[1]

From this standpoint she asked her audiences to consider this new imperialism,
not only as she had observed it in Zululand, but as it could be discerned in the
newspapers, the periodicals, and in the statements and actions of the heroes of
the age. Nowhere was its grabbing, squalid character seen more clearly than in
the actions and statements of Cecil John Rhodes.

> What then does it mean when one, at the time a highly placed Colonial
> Official, declares publickly that he 'prefers land to niggers,' or when a prom-

inent London journal, a partizan of the British South Africa Company, sets it forth deliberately that 'the black man' 'requires' 'firm and masterly handling', having explained a few lines before that this includes 'the use of the whip now and then'; and that 'In the Chartered Company's territories ... a little of the Dutch Africander firmness has been found a wholesome tonic' for the said black man, or 'native servant'.

And the same paper, in the same article, passes lightly over the extermination of Australian Blacks in Queensland, and of Bushmen at the Cape with the words 'in both cases the coloured man has been treated as vermin and exterminated. One cannot defend such acts,' says the London *Times* 'but in rough communities they will happen, even among men of our own blood.'

She turned to the Cronwright-Schreiners for evidence that Rhodes and his supporters, through the Glen Grey Act, were forcing labour and thereby creating a new slavery. She quoted the Revd John Mackenzie, who had said that in some ways '"slavery might, in practice, have been kinder; for the slave, like the horse, had always to be looked after; whereas under the Company, a sound man would always be had who would replace a man who had become incapable of work."' Imperialism caused not just suffering to the conquered but it degraded the conqueror.

To scramble is not dignified: yet the phrase ... is now widely and complacently accepted as describing the proceedings of the great civilised Power with regard to the continent of Africa. And the position of the native African in the scramble, the 'native question' as it is called, is treated as being on a different and inferior level from questions of like nature among Europeans.

There was no 'native question' – as a distinct set of problems and difficulties. White and black in Africa had to be considered as one social entity. The reality was that they were dependent upon one another, for labour, for education, for land, for access to the fruits of progress, for advancement. She spent much of her time educating her audience, arguing from her own experience and giving anecdotal contradictions to the racist stereotypes which were now so much part of popular culture. Growing up in Africa, speaking an African language, working in close proximity in education and politics with Africans, she contradicted statements on African laziness and incapacity for advancement. She gave evidence of the effectiveness of African political systems and African law, using Zulu examples. Too often, she argued, conclusions about Africa were drawn from ignorance or from the consequences of conquest. Always she came back to her own political cause, attacking the idea that the Zulu were a conquering minority, and emphasising the widespread identity of the people of Natal and Zululand with the Zulu royal house. African ability had to be recognised, African institutions had to be used not torn down, divisions healed not exploited, if there was to be progress.[2] She read or quoted extracts from Dinuzulu's letters as evidence that such capacity should be conserved and utilised, not wasted in exile. And she protested at the greed which dominated policy and action:

> What is the meaning – the spirit of this scramble for Africa? in what ever form it shows itself – as the lust for power domineering or the lust for gold in dividends – the Scylla of Chartered Companies, or the Charybdis of Imperialism – is the spirit of that scramble – is the spirit of that scramble anything but the spirit of unbelief – the worship of the lower self, of the only devil which is real?
>
> The taint is apparent everywhere – in the fever of speculation, in the hurried rush to waste the nation's store on engines of destruction – battle-ships; and further armaments, in the empty boast that brute force will in the last resort be relied upon to hold the British and this is the best that any European power now in Africa can hope for alas! they have all followed the example we have set, of handling ~~South Africa~~ that vast continent as though it existed for our private advantage without regard to the African.
>
> The scramble for Africa is a phrase we have all heard. But if we Europeans are to live down the past among the millions of Africans, the rights of the African partner in the business must be respected as scrupulously as those of any European. And we are far from beginning to respect them. ~~Witness our recent disgraceful acts in Ashanti. Witness the news of~~ Witness our tempting the Egyptians, who, we say, cannot govern themselves, to join us in raiding the Soudan. And thereby also tempting Italy, – who should appreciate a stand for liberty – tempting her to continue till it failed her invasion of the Abyssinian who has shown himself so moderate, so magnanimous in his victory.

Of course Harriette Colenso's critique of her times, of imperialism, still bore the marks of the evangelical liberalism with its origins earlier in the Victorian era. It was based on a notion of the shared responsibility for the less fortunate; of the dire consequences for all, both spiritual and material, for injuries to any of the human family; of the special part that the English played in the development and implementation of this high moral standpoint. It was universalistic in its fundamental precepts, chauvinistic in the role it awarded English humanitarianism, and evangelical in the beliefs which she derived from and shared with her father.

Thus she protested at one of the basic tenets of the imperial age:

> in the cynical assertion that everyman has his price, in the endowment of the
> church with the lands of tricked and slaughtered men – what indeed must be
> the deity whom such offerings could please! – and in the heartless sickening
> silence of the churches through it all, a silence the more marked for certain
> notable exceptions, while the ignorant natives perish, and our ~~English lads~~
> countrymen are led astray, and their lives wasted in an evil cause.
>
> Is it possible that there is One whom we have left out of the calculations –
> Even Him the Lord of the Spirits of all flesh, to whom the African belongs as
> well as the European.

In the structure and the content of these lectures – a biblical text to expose
the distance between Christian moral duty and their contemporary practice – we
see the powerful shade of her father stalking through the lecture halls of the ethical societies, socialist clubs and Unitarian chapels in which she spoke. At the
same time she spoke in a new context. Thus, she refused to support a petition
to protest against the supply of British arms to Turkey because

> this Memorial assumes to pass judgement on the bloodguiltiness of another
> nation on 'the horrors of Turkish rule,' of 'Turkish tyranny,' and I cannot
> before God, I dare not – join in such an utterance, while not even so much of
> protest is raised against the bloodguiltiness, the tyranny, in which our own
> country is at this moment engaged in parts of Africa ...
>
> Surely we, as a nation, by what we hypocritically call 'extending civiliza-
> tion' among the Africans, have forfeited for the time being the moral power by
> which alone such sacrifices are consummated, such victories are won.[3]

She challenged the ideological justifications for the new imperialism. For
example, she was able to turn the Social Darwinism of the times and allow it to
harmonise, rather than conflict, with her own religious thinking. 'I am here
tonight', she told an audience,

> only because I dare not miss an occasion offered me to say a word about
> Africa.
>
> So, with your permission, I will just touch on the main principles applic-
> able to our treatment of any races other than our own, and then give some
> examples of how we actually are treating certain African races, and so ask you
> to carry on the debate.

Our first principle is described in the terms of Modern Science as the Law of Mutual Help. A law which has recently been shown to obtain in the world of Nature, completing and explaining the previous revelation of the Law of the survival of the Fittest. For who are the Fittest? Science now answers, those who help one another. They survive being the fittest, even in this world, even amongst the insects.

Much more then must this be true of human beings, endowed with a moral nature, a sense of right and wrong, in modern phrase an 'ethical development' and further, the stronger a race of human beings is, the more bound to help.

'Believing in Miss Colenso'

However, although Harriette was able to respond to contemporary ideas, her background, her father's religious beliefs, her personality, the closeness of her family, her sense of individual responsibility, precluded a move to a more radical position. It is instructive to compare Harriette Colenso with two other women whom she knew, both only slightly younger, and both of whom had developed a radical public critique of their times: Olive Schreiner and Eleanor Marx.

Olive Schreiner was also from a South African mission background and, like Harriette Colenso, was outraged by what was happening to South Africa. For both women it was Rhodes who epitomised the degenerate spirit of the age. Nonetheless, the differences in their approaches are also most striking. In their letters, for example, the one is moved by deep personal and psychological distress to give voice to an intense creativity with which she explores her personal relationships, her sexuality, in a manner far ahead of the dominant spirit of her times. The other is as angry and distressed; but she is always calm, controlled and personally conservative, her psychic and physical life closed from view, presenting instead universal moral imperatives, the duties of the Christian, the responsibilities of the English, the memory of her father's example and ideals, and her personal obligations to the people of Africa, black and white.

Olive Schreiner's range was, of course, much greater. She not only attacked the political world of Rhodes and the violence of British imperialism against the Boers, but she also captured the imaginations of an enormous number of readers by her insights into their lives, those disaffected by the dominant ideas of the times, women especially. Harriette Colenso worked in a very different, African world. Her personal experiences in Natal and Zululand made her keenly aware of the effects of colonialism on the Africans of Natal and Zululand. Her skills enabled her to move between the conqueror and the conquered, giving her rare insights into the suffering and loss caused by imperialism, insights probably unique at the time. But her experiences and her teachings reached only a limited audience. Her energies were spent in a narrow political environment rather than a general literary one; her endeavours failed and have been largely forgotten. Libraries are lined with books about the men with whom she had to deal, directly or indirectly – Carnarvon, Wolseley, Frere, Shepstone, Gladstone, Kimberley, Knutsford, Buxton, Ripon, Escombe, Fairfield, Bryce, Bradlaugh, Chamberlain, Rhodes. Their journals, speeches and correspondence are still pored over; their lives, their insights, their shortcomings and reactions the continuing object of fascinated study. And yet which of them could have had the prescience to have written, as Harriette Colenso did at this time, 'I feel increasingly that the present state of things cannot last – perhaps in our lifetime. The native must before long have more to say in the management of the affairs on their own *continent*'?[4]

No memorial has been raised to her memory, and she is hardly remembered except as one of Bishop Colenso's eccentric daughters – not the one who fell in love with the British officer? – who was on the side of the Zulus.

Olive Schreiner's protest against Rhodes, the cruelty of the suppression of the Ndebele and the Shona risings, and the moral damage it inflicted on the oppressors, were given form in *Trooper Peter Halket of Mashonaland*. An advance copy reached Harriette Colenso and on 13 February she wrote to Olive Schreiner:

> My dear Madam,
>
> May we not meet, you and I, and shake hands over – South Africa? I should much like to do so, and believe too, that you may be able to help me in some information of which I am much in need.
>
> We may differ on some points of detail – I don't know what they are, or that we do, but admit the possibility – still we are certainly on the same side in the fight.[5]

A letter of solidarity, between South African women on matters of political principle, to consolidate their common protest at the racist violence by which modern southern Africa was built – but why the hesitation? They met at least twice in 1897, liked one another and exchanged friendly notes, but the relationship remained a formal, rather distant one. One has to suspect that part of the reason lay in Harriette Colenso's essential moral and social conservatism towards a woman known for her outspokenness and radicalism. Although unconventional in theological and church matters, Harriette was always the missionary in her general approach – broadminded in terms of the political conventions of the age but conventional in matters of self-discipline and personal morality. She was not opposed to the idea of the 'New Woman' of the 1890s – it was that they lived in different worlds. As she said of the editor of the *Women's Penny Paper*, which did so much to allow her to introduce herself to a sympathetic audience in Britain in 1889: 'The Mullers are funny people – Miss Temple invited me to dinner & inspected me. My private opinion is that I appeared too independent of woman's help, & too trustful of men.'[6]

Eleanor Marx, however, was an intimate friend of Olive Schreiner. She was the intelligent and spirited youngest daughter of Karl Marx, and had attended a meeting addressed by Harriette Colenso at the end of January 1897 and written it up for the socialist newspaper *Justice*.[7] She admitted that she had differences with the speaker.

> She believes in God who, in his good time, will make the crooked straight. I do not. I only believe in the straightening out of the crooked by the people working consciously and unconsciously along certain definite lines. But, although I may be unable to believe in an all-powerful and all-merciful deity, I do believe in Miss Colenso. Assuredly no one is more competent to speak upon certain phases of the South African question than this strong, brave, modest woman ... Miss Colenso told a story, the more impressive because so free from exaggeration and hysteria, of such hideous savagery, treachery, sordid baseness, on the part of the 'civilised' English, as made one ashamed to look up at one's neighbour ...
>
> It is an interesting and a curious fact that the only two persons who, from the very first, have dared to speak the truth with regard to South Africa are two women, the daughter of Bishop Colenso and Olive Schreiner.

A matter of great concern to radicals at the time was the famine gripping India, and a meeting to draw attention to it was being planned. 'Could not Miss Colenso and Olive Schreiner be induced to attend the St. James Hall meeting on the 10th? The story they have to tell of British capitalist misrule in South Africa could not but point the moral of the story Hyndman [the left-wing activist] will have to tell of British capitalist misrule in India.'

Eleanor Marx also said that Harriette Colenso pledged herself to address any meeting anywhere on the subject of imperialism in South Africa. Her promise was read by the secretary of the Wigan branch of the Social Democratic Federation, who invited her to lecture: 'You will do more good than can be known because we have been trying to make the question of India & Africa understood but you are better able to do so. Please replie early we whould like Sunday because that is the day we can get best meetings.'[8] Soon after her visit to Wigan one of the members died, and the branch felt sufficiently close to tell Harriette of how they were 'all sorrowing the loss of one of our most active comrades, one who considered no personal sacrifice too great to make for the principles which he believed to be true'.[9]

Eleanor Marx also responded to Harriette Colenso's warm-hearted commitment. In July 1897 she invited her to her house in south London to meet the friend and contemporary of Engels and her father, the German socialist, politician and journalist Wilhelm Liebknecht, known to the Marx family as 'Library',

> here on a short visit to recruit before going to prison for 4 months for lèse majesté – and he is very specially interested in the question of South Africa, & most anxious to learn something of the *real* facts of the case.
>
> He is here to visit – & he is an old man (72) so perhaps you will excuse his request that you might call here, & not he upon you.
>
> As Editor of the great daily paper 'Vorwarts' he would like to see you. As a man who for many years has followed South African affairs he would like to talk with you, who can speak with such authority on so many of the many South African problems … I know would give him pleasure, and, (however much you may differ on certain questions) I think you also would have pleasure in meeting this brave old fighter.

Harriette was asked to come early, so that they could talk in the garden before dinner. Liebknecht later assured Harriette that he would do whatever he could 'to assist you in your great work of justice and humanity. And if I can render you *any assistance*, however difficult, you have only to write to me – *to Berlin*. No other address is needed …'[10] The correspondence is especially poignant, not only because of the momentary proximity of Harriette Colenso to a great radical historical tradition, but also because of the personal agony, the 'fearful despair' that Eleanor Marx was hiding at the time. Within a year, just after welcoming her lifelong friend Liebknecht, 'dear, dear old Library', on his release from gaol, she was to poison herself under the most tragic of circumstances.[11]

Although Harriette Colenso continued to meet with radicals, and found much to sympathise with in their causes and learn from in their struggles, there were always limits to how far she could move towards them. She worked for them when she had the chance – yet in the end she did so to further her particular cause. And she was always the bishop's daughter – in the eyes of the public she had to be above suspicion. She still carried the moral burden passed on to her by the life of her father: to defend by her impeccable public behaviour a saintly man whom the world had condemned as a heretic and cast out as a publican and sinner.

At the same time there was a lightness in Harriette Colenso which allowed her at times to smile at the incongruities of her situation, even as she suffered under the ponderous weight of the men of position and power with whom she had to deal. On her fiftieth birthday she went to 'such a party' in the Strand thrown by a Catholic newspaper editor, and here she met Michael Davitt. There was an immediate accord between them – he had spent 'long years in an English prison as a rebel' and she spoke of the rebels she knew, now on St Helena, and told him of the affinity they felt for the Irish and their own struggles against the English.[12] The tea and strawberries were finished, but the talk went on and their host took them to a restaurant to continue the conversation, Harriette not getting home 'till after 10!' Such evenings were very few and can hardly be considered as a night on the tiles – nonetheless she was far more sociable, tolerant and free-thinking than her reclusive sister. 'Don't you be anxious about the Socialists,' she wrote to Agnes,

> they don't smoke when I come, as a rule, in fact that supper was the only occasion. They invite one another not to, and I say thank you. Even the 'Tobacco workers' Association Club and Institute, Whitechapel – and they have asked me to come again.
> It all helps, Darling.

The protection she gave Agnes was an essential feature of the relationship. It is a difficult one to assess – and its strangeness can be sensed in their letters. 'My darling child', Harriette wrote, and Agnes dutifully signed her letters 'your loving child', thus preserving the closeness of the Colenso family. The terms suggest the tenderness and comfort but also the isolation of their youth. Perhaps also they echo the kinship terminology of African society, which is extended into the realm of personal deference and political loyalty – after all, the princes of the kingdom were the *abantwana*, 'the children'. Whatever the case, the support they gave one another was essential to their well-being and their effectiveness.

This sisterly solidarity was a function of their isolation in colonial Natal. But were they lonely? Although their political struggles cut them off from the settler community, their religious thinking from white congregations, and monetary problems made it difficult to keep the social distance they were used to, one has to wonder whether the word 'lonely' applies to the Colenso sisters at all, at this time in their lives at least. There were their African comrades, at Bishopstowe and amongst the Usuthu, some of whom were close friends, and all of whose lives they shared. And they developed very close and supportive relationships with a number of women who were placed in social situations not dissimilar to their own.

Katie Giles was closest to Harriette, but a dear friend to Agnes as well. And it was during the 1890s that Harriette had made another intimate and supportive friend – Alice Werner. Alice stayed at Bishopstowe in the mid-1890s, and on her return to London she and Harriette worked together to protest against the atrocities committed during the Ndebele and Shona rising of 1896. Harriette went to listen to one of Alice's first attempts at public speaking and wrote to her about it:

> I must tell you with what satisfaction I listened to you yesterday, not only because you did so well, – and you had a mixed audience to please, containing some charter-worshippers, and several small 'guinea-pigs' – but also because I think that with a little practice you may set aside your paper, and just *speak* to them. That is what I should like to be able to do, but I can't. I think one should begin younger. But you may do it, and it's worth doing. Your voice carries well ... and after another lecture or two you would make the back seats in that room hear very well. Go on and prosper, Dear.
>
> Would it be possible for me to borrow the one slide of all Africa for Friday night?[13]

The winter of 1896–97 was particularly hard for Harriette Colenso in London. She had no speaking engagements to distract her, which meant that she dwelt on her interview with Sir John Robinson and the evidence he had provided that she had been used by Escombe. The day before Christmas she received flowers from Alice. 'They don't quite seem to belong to this foggy world', she wrote.[14]

Natal and Zululand

Harriette had found it hard to accept that it was Sir John Robinson's ill-health which made it so difficult for him to see her in London. Nonetheless he was genuinely ill, and for this reason he retired from office in February 1897. His successor as Prime Minister of Natal was Harry Escombe. His accession to the premiership should have vindicated the strategy that Harriette Colenso had adopted two years previously when she calculated that the Usuthu would soon have a powerful ally in the highest office in Natal. But she could no longer trust him. The women of Bishopstowe were now politically isolated, and the men in power were able to consider the future of Zululand at their own pace without being bothered by an interfering philanthropic pressure group – which had the annoying quality of being close to and well informed by African sources.

Thus, in London, decisions of the utmost importance to Zululand's future had been taken which would have greatly shocked Harriette Colenso had she known the details. In pursuit of imperial federation and the closer union of South Africa's colonial governments, Chamberlain felt he should now try to break the deadlock between Britain and Natal over the future of Zululand. On 4 May he sent a telegram to the Governor of Natal in which he stated that he was prepared to advise the Queen to authorise the annexation of Zululand to Natal – but under certain conditions. The most important of these was that there was to be no change in the existing system of land tenure in Zululand for five years. During this period a joint imperial and colonial commission would delimit land to be reserved for Africans as native reserves. The remaining territory could be disposed of by the Natal government as it thought fit – but the reserves would be inalienable without London's consent. The British territory to the north-east of Zululand, lying between Swaziland and the sea, would be incorporated at the same time. The Natal government was also reminded that Dinuzulu should be returned before too long.[15] None of this was public knowledge, of course, and Harriette remained ignorant of the content of these negotiations.

It had been an assumption for years that Zululand would eventually be absorbed by Natal, but it was clear Chamberlain was not going to risk a settler-driven scramble for the acquisition of land rights. Escombe, however, was fully aware of how important the opening up of Zululand was to Natal's colonists. A wait of five years would be of little help to the ministry in the coming elections in September, and the stipulated delay assumed, correctly but in Natal's eyes insultingly, that they were not to be trusted in native affairs. Escombe thus continued to procrastinate, a policy which delayed even longer the return of the chiefs but increased the chance, he felt, of extracting greater concessions from London. If the whole matter could be delayed until after the general election in September, then details of the 'future status' of Dinuzulu and land delimitation could be discussed in London when the new Prime Minister visited London in July 1897 for the Diamond Jubilee and the Colonial Ministers' Conference.

'Lest we forget!'

Just as the 1851 Great Exhibition is seen as the event which marks the culmination of Victorian material achievement and confidence, so Queen Victoria's Diamond Jubilee is considered to mark the high point of the British imperial ideal. On 22 June 1897 London experienced an extraordinary national exhibition of British wealth, power and dominance, celebrated at the very moment before being dragged off its imperial pinnacle by forces, some of the most important of which originated in South Africa itself.

Historians have been fascinated by the Jubilee and have found the celebra-

tions of 22 June full of meaning and significance.[16] There was the Queen's telegraphic message sent around the world in seconds: 'From my heart I thank my
people. May God bless them.' Detachments of troops had been gathered from
all parts of the Empire to parade through London: regular forces, colonial volunteers, and the outlandish Other – tamed, confined, and now safely marching
through the streets of the imperial capital in the company of their Queen. It was
a spectacle which is still relished:

> Chinese from Hong Kong – one of whom sported a pigtail that reached right
> to the ground – wore wide Coolie hats. The Zaptiehs, Turkish military from
> Cyprus wore fezzes. The Jamaicans wore white gaiters and gold-embroidered
> jackets. There were Dyaks from Borneo, and Sikhs, and Canadian Hussars,
> and Sierra Leone gunners, and Australian cavalrymen, and British Guiana
> police, and Maltese, and South Africans, and a troop of jangling Bengal
> Lancers led by a solitary English officer in a white spiked helmet. Some of
> the colonial coloured infantry seemed to be half-crippled by their unaccus-
> tomed boots. One of the Maori riflemen weighed 28 stone. One of the Dyaks
> had taken, 'in his former occupation', 13 human heads ...[17]

They were cheered by thousands, drawn from all classes. The Queen left
Buckingham Palace at 11.15 in an open carriage, passed through the West End
and down Fleet Street to halt at the steps of St Paul's Cathedral on which stood
churchmen and choristers, who sang 'All People that on Earth do Dwell'. To the
front and rear of her carriage were two Field Marshals. On the one side was the
Commander-in-Chief, Sir Garnet Wolseley, amongst whose imperial achievements was counted the conquest of the Zulu kingdom and the creation of the 13
chiefdoms which initiated the Zulu civil war. He was also the survivor of a sharp
confrontation over the Bishopstowe dinner table twenty years before, when he
had been 'attacked by the whole family about the native policy in very bad
taste'. But Wolseley was a man of the past. On the other side of the carriage was
Field Marshal Lord Roberts VC, a man of the future and soon also to play his
part in the further conquest of South Africa. The procession moved through the
City, across London Bridge and back past the Houses of Parliament to
Buckingham Palace. James Morris has written at the beginning of a large and
successful book which uses the Diamond Jubilee as the touchstone for his
evocation of British imperialism at its height,

> It is one of the happier imperial moments to describe, for all its brag, oppor-
> tunism and occasional brutality. The morality of imperialism as a principle was

not generally in question, and only a handful of radicals passionately opposed the right of any one people to impose its rule upon any other. The subject races had not yet developed that awareness of nationality which was later to make the colonial idea degrading both to rulers and to ruled: to most people, on both sides of the fence, British dominion seemed far more a blessing than a curse.[18]

Amongst the handful of radicals were some of the new generation of Labour leaders and Beatrice Webb, whose diary entry 'imperialism in the air, all classes drunk with the sightseeing and hysterical loyalty' is often quoted.[19] And stirring below the nationalist euphoria a brooding insecurity has been discerned, an awareness of the transience of power when viewed in the long historical perspective, and of the ephemeral loyalty of the cheering crowd, creating a deeper uncertainty which the celebration sought to obscure. Kipling's *Recessional*, published for the Jubilee, of course, captured something of this mood:

> The tumult and the shouting die;
> The Captains and the Kings depart;
> Still stands thine ancient sacrifice,
> An humble and a contrite heart.
> Lord God Hosts, be with us yet,
> Lest we forget – lest we forget!

Harriette Colenso, through Kipling's aunt Georgie Burne-Jones, tried to interest him in Zulu matters, but he refused to be drawn. Beyond agreeing that the British should be reminded of their moral duties and responsibilities, they would not have had much in common anyway. Harriette would, one feels, have found the poem pretentious and posturing. And she would certainly have objected to the expression of racial superiority which assumed the existence of 'lesser breeds without the Law' and gave the British privileged access to the 'Lord God of Hosts'. She hated the imperial euphoria all around her – it was a disease – she called it jubilitis.

Her brother Frank Colenso had been given a ticket to watch the procession. His new job as actuary with Eagle Life gave him access to the route. However, when he heard that the Rhodesian Horse were to be part of the procession he passed his ticket on to his sister-in-law, Emily. For Harriette the whole celebration was so awful that the presence of the Rhodesian Horse 'did not make it much worse, to my mind'.

Thus, this great demonstration of British might on 22 June 1897 took place without Harriette Colenso. She left London with her niece and 'had our jubilee in the country'.[20]

'My dear Mr Escombe'

As one of the Empire's colonial premiers attending the Jubilee, Natal's Prime Minister, Harry Escombe, had been in London since early June. He also intended to use the opportunity to negotiate the terms of the incorporation of Zululand with Natal. Natal had succeeded in delaying the return of the Zulu exiles for two and a half years now, and it was clear that this could not continue indefinitely. But he still hoped to get Chamberlain to agree to limit some of the promises made to Dinuzulu in January 1895 and to speed up the process whereby Zululand would be passed to Natal.

He stayed with the other premiers at the Hotel Cecil in the Strand and avoided Harriette Colenso. She had to watch the newspapers for information on his movements. As she tried to get an appointment to see him, she attempted a jocular tone in her letters, suitable for communicating with an old acquaintance, but one with whom she had differences:

> I went to the Hotel Cecil yesterday, to find you and Mrs Escombe, and was directed to the 'Inquiry Office', as though you had been lost property, and we did not find you after all. That was not wonderful, as no one is to be found in London without arrangement. Do you think I shall know you again when I do see you? At any rate you must give me a chance of doing so. I have heard of the '200 letters', but the 'two clerks' must be getting on with them by now, so please find half-an-hour, as soon as maybe, and tell me when and where to find you. With love to Mrs Escombe, and a welcome to England to you both if you care for it, I am,
> My dear Mr Escombe,
> Yours affectionately,
> H.E. Colenso, Natal Colonist and Zulu.[21]

She had to wait until 3 July for their first meeting. Escombe began by trying to ingratiate himself with her. As far as he was concerned, he told her, there was more to their relationship than 'business', and he asked her to tell him of anything he might be able to do for the Zulu. But at the same time he reminded her that she had to be realistic: while he was a friend he was also a politician with a cabinet and a constituency, whose demands he had to consider as well. The future arrangements were still under negotiation, but as they stood at the

THE WAGON BREAKS DOWN

moment the plan was to return Dinuzulu, as government induna with a salary of
£500 and a house in Eshowe. He was also to be chief of the Usuthu location. He
did not approve of Dinuzulu's appointment as government induna. As far as he
was concerned, Dinuzulu should be one chief amongst many, and nothing more.

Harriette waited and then told him that it seemed to her that for three years
they had been 'attempting to reconcile incompatibles, and that Natal is the
"breaking up" party breaking up the Zulus, I mean, as much as ever, and that
the Zulus would feel themselves betrayed'. She asked Escombe how he proposed to announce his policy to the Zulu, who had waited so long and so patiently for the return of the king's son. Escombe replied that he had no intention of
saying anything to the Zulu at all. The differences between them were now in
the open. For Harriette Colenso, effective government meant consultation; for
Escombe, the government of Africans was carried out by fiat.

But they were still fencing. Neither dared speak their whole mind – not
Harriette because she knew that to break finally with Escombe would leave the
Usuthu without even the semblance of a political strategy, and not Harry
Escombe because it would expose him to the charge that he had manipulated
their relationship for his political advantage and was holding the Usuthu chiefs
hostage for political gain. The meeting ended with them both promising to think
over their positions. Privately Harriette suspected that she had made a mark: 'I
don't know that I have not a bit shaken his cocksureness of being able to manage the Zulus – and me.'[22]

A week later she wrote to him. Even if he were not prepared to confront the
Zulu with the truth that they had been betrayed, surely, she asked, he would
admit that fact? If he did not, they could not go on at all:

> it seems to me essential, in order not to deprive your plan of any chance of
> success which it may otherwise possess, that you should admit – at any rate to
> yourself that this plan is a bitter, and cruel disappointment for the National
> party, including me; that after the pledges of January 1895, it is as much a
> mockery, as it is undeserved by the Zulus after their long and faithful waiting,
> and that your plan must start without any reserve of gratitude on their part to
> fall back upon.

She signed her letter

> I *am* My dear Mr Escombe
> Yours affectionately, but very sorrowfully,
> H.E. Colenso

Earlier in the week she had visited Sir Marshal Clarke, who was about to return to Zululand. She discovered a change here as well: as she told Agnes, 'I can't say I altogether enjoyed his attitude.'[23] Escombe had invited Harriette to ask him what he could do but insisted that it be done in writing, reminding her that she 'must always bear in mind that I have to think of colleagues who are responsible for all I may do or say'. She asked that the chiefs' request to visit England might be allowed. Escombe responded that such a decision was the responsibility of the Secretary of State for the Colonies.

The brush-off, the shifting of responsibility down and up the political scale, the recourse to proper political procedures, had been the treatment she had received for years now – but to receive it from Escombe was particularly distressing. Something important was happening in official circles as regards the future of Zululand, but Harriette Colenso was not going to get a hint of what it was until the officials thought proper. They were not going to encourage her assumption, and presumption, that she should be allowed to participate in the planning of policy towards the Zulu. And when the time came to make an announcement on the future of Zululand, the Usuthu, on St Helena and in Zululand, would hear about it from the voice of authority, not from the interfering Colenso women.

'Torn in three'

On Thursday 15 July 1897 Harriette wrote to Dinuzulu, Ndabuko and Shingana. There had been trouble on the island. Mubi Nondenisa, who had been left behind as a teacher, had already returned to Natal after a violent quarrel with Anthony Daniels. It was not easy for the African *kholwa* from Natal, very aware of their skills and who valued their independence, to satisfy the demands made on them by the members of the Zulu royal house. Magema Fuze had come from Bishopstowe to replace Mubi as teacher. Out walking one evening he had fallen over a cliff and broken his leg. It was suggested that he was drunk – Dinuzulu told Harriette that he was out visiting a woman. The *abantwana* were also upset by the fact that he had received a letter from her when they hadn't. Harriette protested: 'How could I turn away from one belonging to me who was in trouble?' But she had no news for them. She herself did not know what to do – she felt 'torn in three' by wanting to consult with the Usuthu in Natal and Zululand, visit St Helena, and stay to see what was developing in London. She spoke of her suspicions that something was happening but that she was not being told about it. 'Indeed sometimes even to me it seems as if we were just water, dashing ourselves on stones. However, even so, we know that as between water and stones it is the water which is likely to survive in the end, the stones breaking against one another. Let us stand firm, therefore, and be ready.'[24]

She posted the letter on Friday evening to catch the St Helena mailship. The same vessel carried a letter from Chamberlain to the Governor of St Helena asking him to inform the chiefs that 'I expect to be able to make arrangements for their return to Zululand by the end of the present year, and that it is probable that about the same time Zululand will come under the Government of Natal. They will be informed further as to details when the time for their repatriation has been definitely fixed.'[25]

In this manner Dinuzulu and his uncles were officially informed of their return and the annexation, in a letter which arrived by the same mail as one from Harriette Colenso informing them that there was no news of any decision on their future. The timing was deliberate. It had to be impressed upon the exiles that all initiative lay with the officials. Such attempts to diminish in Zulu eyes any role that Harriette Colenso might appear to have in the announcement of their return, infuriated her. But it saddened her more. It led to such confusion and created such mistrust. How would it be possible ever to work together constructively in such a situation?

'Grabbing'

Because she had been excluded so totally from official circles, Harriette knew that news of Zululand's future would be public knowledge in Natal long before anything she wrote about it would reach there. And with these official announcements would come the knowledge of her failure, and the failure of the Usuthu campaign, to return the exiled chiefs with any real authority, or to preserve Zululand for the Zulus. All she could do was to try to ameliorate the blow when it was received by the Usuthu. And, most difficult of all, without being able to suggest a practical strategy, she had to try to give them the courage to continue the struggle. The whole matter, she wrote to the Usuthu representative in Natal,

> is grievous because we know that there are certain people who desire it from the desire to grab, thinking that they will so get a chance to grab land in Zululand.
>
> You know that such grabbing is hateful to me, and that long since we of Sobantu's family devoted ourselves as a protest against it, and also that we continue to protest against it.

But it was all still so uncertain, and so few details had been announced. Her message should therefore be seen essentially as one of solidarity: 'This letter is merely a token that I give you, Mjwaphuna, my hand, knowing that your ears are now struck by painful reports, and saying to you "Yes, I too hear them, but nevertheless let us still be of good courage and stand together."'[26]

Everything depended upon the terms under which the exiles were going to be returned and the manner in which the two colonies were to be joined together. The final details were in fact being negotiated between Escombe and the Colonial Office at that moment. On 21 July Escombe wrote to Chamberlain from the Hotel Cecil. He agreed to the five-year period before there would be any change in land tenure, as long as the Secretary of State would consider exceptions within that period. He confirmed that Dinuzulu would return as an induna, and a chief of one district 'without authority over any other Chief'. The word 'confidant' or 'adviser' was not to be included in the terms under which Dinuzulu returned to Zululand. Chamberlain hedged rather over the exact role of Dinuzulu as induna, for it was clear that Ripon had intended more than this. Nonetheless, Chamberlain agreed on 30 July 1897.[27]

On the same day, Escombe visited Harriette to inform her of the final agreement and to bid her farewell. It must have taken some courage for him to do so. While all plans had of course to be confirmed by his ministry and the Legislative Assembly in Natal, Dinuzulu was to be returned before the end of the year. The Natal government would assume responsibility for him once he arrived at Durban. Once in Zululand he was to become local chief of the Usuthu in the north, and government induna, for which he would receive £500 a year and a house in Eshowe. There would be no change in existing land tenure for five years. After this period a commission would divide the land into native locations, with the remainder at the disposal of the government of Natal. The catastrophe against which she had worked and which she had so feared was upon them.

That evening she wrote two letters. The one was to Agnes and recounted the interview with Escombe. She had told him that she felt the Zulu had been betrayed. Escombe disagreed and regretted that she could not find a way for them to work together for the good of the Zulu. 'So the position is that I treat his plan as the least of all the evils before the Zulus.'[28]

The other letter was to Mjwaphuna, the Usuthu representative in Natal. She told him of Dinuzulu's appointment as government induna, which was in accord with the original decisions of Her Majesty's Government. But there was more than this. There was the terrible news that the land was to be demarcated between white and black. In informing the Usuthu of this, Harriette adopted different voices, using different names by which she was known by the Zulu. Mr Escombe had said that there will be a division of the land, and that a portion will be for sale, by the Governor.

The end of Mr Escombe's words:–

That last one is shameful for me since I too am a white-person.

Nevertheless (here speaks Inkanisi [the stubborn one], who is a Zulu) if this is done according to the laws of Natal, and not those of the Cape, we Zulus may ourselves buy the land, in the future.

What I have to say now is this. I, Matotoba [the slow, careful one], say: Yes, friends! through the length of the journey, and the ~~heat~~ greatness of the burden, our wagon has broken down. What we bring with us now is as much as we can carry, which we have taken from the wagon load. I mean the Princes themselves, and the position of Induna.

[When we all return] I shall wish for us to meet and agree how we shall manage to forge for ourselves again a wagon, and gather the National load.

For verily, Friends, while waiting here, listening to the affairs of many lands, and turning them over in my mind, I have perceived that in spite of the deadly ills which we are feeling, and of those which we have suffered in the past, this Zulu People may yet rise – indeed it *should* rise, to be admired, and to be great.

I am Matotoba, Mandiza [the one who flies], Daughter of Sobantu.[29]

She tried to find some cause for optimism; but what brightness there was, was only apparent in relation to the 'seething mass of Jingoism and slavery the rest of white South Africa presents'.[30] At least Robinson, a real enemy of the Zulu and champion of the land-grabbers, was out of office. Escombe was there instead,

so that even amidst this annexation there is what may be of help to us, there is what may ward off the evil that happened on the King's return.

Also, if I look at all Africa, and think of the dangers surrounding us natives, I come to be not far from thinking – supposing this annexation to take place – that things might be worse.

Because you cannot be made into nobodies, unless you make yourselves so.[31]

She was desperate to know when the return would take place. But she was told nothing: the Colonial Office was not going to allow her to interfere. She began to make plans to return to Natal. She would take a boat which called at St Helena and, if the exiles were still on the island, stay with them till their return. If they had gone already, then her people at Bishopstowe would have to organise their reception.

And as she tried to act with political responsibility towards her Zulu friends on St Helena, she was reminded of her private responsibilities to her women friends in Natal. Katie had developed lumps in her breast which they feared were cancerous. Harriette's advice was informed and her counsel sound as, amidst her disappointments and other worries, she thought of ways to change the plans for her return if her dear friend had to come suddenly to England for treatment.

'O my Agnes, we shall deserve to be together again some day, you and I', she wrote at the height of the crisis through which she passed in the late summer of 1897.[32] In a huge correspondence, it is one of the very few remarks which suggest the personal cost of her actions.

Dinuzulu

In September Harriette Colenso left England for the last time. Robert and Frank were at Waterloo Station to see her off on the boat train to Southampton. She travelled second class on the *Pembroke Castle* – a new experience for the bishop's daughter. The passengers were a 'very mixed lot' and included a Natal policeman, a British sergeant, teachers, new colonists and old, a Durban restaurant owner, a Free State 'Dutchman' and a 'circus lady', with their assorted families, friends, companions. She had to share a cabin with a 'mother (colonial)' and two children, and it was strange to be visited by the first-class passengers, like the daughter and son-in-law of the Governor of St Helena, rather than share their table. Nonetheless, she declared, at least to her sister, she didn't find second class all that different from first. But she did have to adjust to new perspectives on the British class system.

> When at table I asked for the wine card, the guardian angel observed with sad severity 'we do not have them *here*, Madam, I've always been accustomed to them, but *here* the custom is to pay when you ordered'. He brought me the card though, and continued to do so, and presently confided to two or three of us ... that 'he was accustomed to the 1st class, and "had had" the Duke and Duchess of – Orleans, I think, on one voyage'. – His manners were equal to it, and we humbly tried to live up to them at meal times.[33]

She gave a few brief lectures on the Zulu situation to the passengers, who were very interested in Dinuzulu when he came aboard to greet her on arrival off St Helena on 20 October. He was invited to lunch by the Dutchman, and even an 'old colonist' shook him by the hand.

The exiles were now living in different houses, Ndabuko and Shingana at

Maldivia on the outskirts of Jamestown, and Dinuzulu out of the valley, on the high ground, in a house called Frances Plain, not far from the Governor's residence. During her visit Harriette was scrupulous in her efforts not to give the impression that she favoured either one of the residences. The first night she spent at Maldivia where Shingana and Ndabuko had prepared a room for her and hired a maid – whom she 'dispensed with' as soon as she could. In their domestic arrangements the exiles kept to Zulu custom and segregated the living space of the women from that of the men. Shingana, however, dined with Harriette knowing, he said, that she was not used to eating on her own. She was worried about the extra expense that she was causing them, and the sherry and ginger-beer they bought for her, much preferring the *utshwala* when they were able to brew it. She did what she could to enter into the life of the household, paying particular attention to the children, and impressed their mothers with her attempts to assist them in grinding the maize.

She then moved to Frances Plain, which she reached exhausted by the climb out of the valley despite her guide's attempt to refresh her with a decanter of *utshwala*. The house was organised according to the same principles, with the two women and their children in their own rooms and the Zulu midwife and nurse, 'dear old Mbodiya', sharing her time between them. They also employed a St Helenian housemaid. Harriette renewed her acquaintance with Dinuzulu's children: David now five years old, Solomon nine months younger, Victoria Helena, and Mshiyeni born the day before she had left on her last visit.

Dinuzulu also dined with Harriette while she was there. His 'is the only European bedroom. This was appropriated to me, and he slept in the sitting room, on a sofa, and performed his toilet in his "office," just big enough to hold a chair bedside the writing table. My position towards him being that of a paternal Aunt the arrangement is strictly proper.' To live in this style cost a considerable amount of money. It was raised by the people of Zululand, indirectly by taxation and also by individual contribution. The amounts were large – one remittance alone at the end of 1895 amounted to over £800.[34] When it came time to leave St Helena and to settle Dinuzulu's debts, they were thought to total over that amount. The Governor believed it was the result of Dinuzulu's determination to entertain his guests royally, providing them with only the best food and drink. There is little evidence, in her letters to Agnes, that Harriette disapproved of this lifestyle, the maid servants, and the fact that alcohol played an important part in their entertainments. There can be no doubt that she was sensitive to all this – but she chose, it would seem, not to make them issues between herself and the Usuthu. Their exile, and the disappointments they had suffered, were severe enough without her admonishments.

She shared in their religious services, during which Dinuzulu played an American organ with some skill. She tried when she could to assist in some of their problems and disputes with the locals. Paul Mthimkhulu had his own household now, for he had married a St Helenian woman and had a child. Magema Fuze had become an embarrassment to the good name of the exiles by getting himself into trouble over a woman. Ndabuko had fallen out with his friend Father Daine over the payment for a shotgun. As much as she disliked it, she had to participate in the social life of St Helena and attended the wedding reception of the Governor's daughter in the company of Dinuzulu. Neither of them joined the dancing, however, and after advising Dinuzulu that it would not be good manners for him to stay too late, she left without him. Her fear had always been that he would be adversely affected by the demands made on him by St Helenian society. But in the end, her first impression was favourable: 'He is as nice and good as ever, I think. The St Helena isms are only outside and will wear off, and he will be a blessing to his Father's people yet.'[35]

But the deep and serious political question of the future of Zululand, and the role in it of Dinuzulu and the royal house, had to be attended to as well. On receiving the news of the coming annexation of Zululand to Natal and his return before the end of the year, Dinuzulu, with his uncles, had written a letter to Chamberlain. They expressed their hope that 'our country should not be taken away from us by getting it distributed into farms, because we shall have no place for grazing our cattle and for ploughing'. Further: 'We beg, though we may be governed by Natal, that we should be governed by England too.' The loss of land to the Boers was still a bitter memory. They appealed for British intervention for the return of the graves of their royal ancestors at Emakhosini, and protested, yet again, at the loss of land to the Boers.[36]

Chamberlain would have none of it. They were well aware of the boundary that Havelock had laid down in 1887, and he repeated the charge they had heard so often: 'the Zulus themselves were responsible for the arrangement by which the best of Zululand was made over to the Boers.'[37] They had been deeply disappointed. There had been a determined and, it would seem, successful attempt to annihilate any claim the Zulu royal house had to authority in Zululand, and they were fully aware that they were facing a severe political crisis. As Harriette wrote to Agnes: 'it is very sickening, and I only hope that the rest of us don't see through my cheerfulness quite so plainly as I do through theirs.'

They went over recent history again: Harriette Colenso's support for Mr Escombe, and the idea of incorporation before return, the events of January 1895 and the possible explanations for why the return had been aborted. The scoring out in her draft of her report of the discussions shows that she could not share all her thoughts with the Usuthu – and also something of her pain:

> I have told them that in 1895 when I was coming here, Mr Escombe ~~urged~~ ~~that~~ told me that his Government I cannot tell them was suggesting their return, and asked me to support annexation ~~as the best~~ means of checking, by responsibility the evil feeling against them, they have a proverb which ~~fits the~~ ~~case~~ tends that way insizwa itungiswa isilala, a young man (Natal) is steadied by the headring.
>
> to strengthen the hands of their friends in Natal, and as being the safest And that I had agreed, ~~though~~ They had spoken before then plainly enough against the annexation as a scheme of their enemies.
>
> ~~And~~ Now – at a crisis they leave the word to Ndabuko, he said very gently ~~yet softly~~ 'They ~~deceived~~ beguiled Mr Escombe there.' Nothing more, and only in that delicate way did they ~~let me understand~~ imply that I too had been wrong.[38]

Harriette Colenso still felt that she should not accuse Escombe directly or demean him in the eyes of the exiles. They might have to work with him yet, and he might still have something to offer. Anyway, there was no one else. Then came the news of the elections in Natal. Escombe had been voted out of office. For the Usuthu on St Helena, the reason for his defeat was that the colonists believed that he supported them: 'How Natal does hate us,' they said.

The advent of a new ministry in Natal provided an opportunity to try yet again to delay the return of the chiefs. But Chamberlain was not prepared to go along with this – he had promised that the chiefs would return in 1897. So through October and November the British and the Natal governments made the final demands and compromises for the 'Act "To provide for the Annexation to the Colony of Natal of the Territory of Zululand."'

CHAPTER 30

OUR GREATEST SAFETY

A modernising prince

On 29 October Chamberlain had instructed the Governor of St Helena to inform the chiefs that they would be leaving the island on the *Umbilo* on 19 December, which should then reach Natal on 30 December. Dinuzulu was to be told very clearly about his future status in Zululand. He would be government induna, with an annual salary of £500. However,

> He must clearly understand that he does not return to Zululand as Paramount Chief; he must respect, listen to, and obey those officers of the Government who are placed in authority over him ...
>
> He will be chief over those people residing in the location marked off for the Usutu. He will govern amongst them and will rule them by the same laws and form of Government as other chiefs of tribes in Zululand, and he will himself, like those chiefs, be under the laws of the Government of Zululand.[1]

It fell to Governor Sterndale to deliver these instructions, and he invited Miss Colenso to attend. Harriette had made a point of getting on with Sterndale and found him personally sympathetic to the chiefs. But it must have been a bitter experience for her to have to listen to the message which detailed the limitations imposed on Dinuzulu, and galling to hear the Governor patronise the men.[2]

Nonetheless, even Harriette Colenso's patience began to wear thin when packing began. They were, after all, a total of 18 people now and they were reluctant to leave anything behind including 'empty shoe boxes, which are too weak to be trusted to carry things but cannot be left behind – and then the top hats! and the empty paraffin tins – and the stone on which we have ground for 8 years!'

But it was not only material possessions that were difficult to leave behind. Two days before the party was due to sail, Dinuzulu informed Harriette Colenso that one of the young St Helenian women, Mary Johnstone, intended to travel back to Zululand with the party. The draft of Harriette's letter to her exists:

> I hear from Dinuzulu that you seriously mean to go to Zululand with the chiefs. As I wish to be a friend to you as well as to them, I must now tell you what I think about it.
>
> I see that here at St. Helena you are very useful to Dinuzulu and I see that when he gets to Zululand he will want very much some one to help him about English customs.
>
> But I do not see that you can help him in Zululand as you do now, because you know that it is not an English custom for a gentleman to be waited on and served by a young woman as you serve Dinuzulu. If you did that in Zululand it would injure you and injure Dinuzulu also with English people. 'Bansondo' as the Zulus say, I mean with people like Sir Marshal Clarke, and Bishop Carter, and if you do not mind injuring yourself, I think that you would be sorry to do harm to Dinuzulu.

She would be a stranger in Zululand, imposed on the Zulu, and not only would she be disliked for it, but her life might be in danger. Chiefs could bring changes to custom, but they had to do so slowly and carry their people with them.

> I say nothing about your going to Zululand at some future day. That is not my business.
>
> But it is my business to speak about your going now, though it is not I who take you, but it is my business because I am an older woman than you, because I am an Englishwoman, and a Missionary. It is my business because I believe that if you go now, unexpected, you will go to great misery, and perhaps you will get killed. Dinuzulu does not see this, he thinks perhaps that it is kind to take you – and unkind to leave you. I see that it is cruel to take you
> …
> Now I have told you what I think, and when I come up to Frances Plain this evening, you can give me your answer to this letter before I speak to your mother – for if you intend to go I must say the same to her.[3]

Fierce, uncompromising, intrusive and severe, unlike anything else in her extant correspondence: it was partly a response to the threat posed by a young woman to Harriette Colenso's place as Dinuzulu's guardian, guide, mentor and helpmate. And while it certainly is this – it is not just this. First we have to remind ourselves of the nature of the relationship between Harriette Colenso and

Dinuzulu kaCetshwayo. As she perceived it, it was based on the friendship forged between their fathers out of adversity: it was a relationship between families and between fathers, sons and daughters in the House of Sobantu and the House of Senzangakhona. It was a kinship bond created and confirmed by the struggle for justice and for African rights in South Africa, indeed in all Africa – a struggle which the naïve and irresponsible feelings of a St Helenian girl could not be allowed to jeopardise.

For Mary Johnstone had no idea of the depths of the prejudices that existed in South Africa and the eagerness with which Dinuzulu's return with a young female companion would be exploited. She also had no conception of the significance of Dinuzulu in the lives of the Zulu people and the role that he could play in their future. For Harriette, both the crime and the error of colonialism and imperialism were their determination to destroy the traditional leadership – their failure to use (not merely exploit) the real power the chiefs had over their people, for progress. And it was not just in Dinuzulu's role as a traditional leader, as the son of his father, who was the nephew of Shaka, that Harriette saw his strength. She was also convinced that Dinuzulu kaCetshwayo had the talents to be a great modernising African leader and an example to his people.

It had always been her great fear that life on St Helena, the boredom and the isolation, the depressed economy, its social limitations, the opportunities for lax behaviour, would damage the personalities of the exiles, men whom she had seen in Zululand as leaders of integrity and forceful character. She protested at the drunkenness of the guardians and the inadequacy of the interpreters. She had done all she could to give the exiles the chance to improve themselves on the island. She arranged for Mubi Nondenisa and then Magema Fuze to go to St Helena as teachers and tried to make sure that her own letters were as informative and stimulating as possible. Magema was asked to write down traditional poetry, songs and legends – some of which she had heard from the exiles herself, and which Ndabuko made a point of relating to her. She put Dinuzulu in contact with correspondents in England with a view to adding to his knowledge of the world. Thus, for example, in the depth of the winter of 1896–97 while she was still suffering in the aftermath of Sir John Robinson's visit, she wrote a long letter to St Helena which included information on the most recent scientific discoveries. She told them about 'pictures of a great wonder which has just appeared ... For the learned men have just discovered a new form of lightning, a light is made with this, when the pictures are taken, which causes the shadow of man's flesh, and of his garments to be light, but the shadow of his bones to be dark. Also the shadow of all metals is dark.'[4] If Dinuzulu were to become recognised as the leader of his people he had to be well informed. If only he had been allowed to come to England she would have shown him the real achievements of the modern world, not the poor echoes of it to be found on St Helena.

Dinuzulu's progress in writing pleased her greatly. She was fascinated by the intelligence with which he confronted literacy, his comments on the limitations of Zulu orthography, and his first attempts at scholarship. As she told Sir Marshal Clarke, Dinuzulu believed that 'the alphabet in Zulu required, he says, several additional letters; and a collection should be made of specimens of all the living creatures of Zululand and he has already prepared lists of them, from the elephant to the – mosquito, including over 200 different birds'. On the evening of 10 November she wrote to Agnes from Maldivia, enjoying the company as Shingana's children turned the pages of a school book, and worrying about the health and domestic problems she now shared with the exiles. Dinuzulu, dressed in respectable Western clothes, looking round his 'much adorned little sitting room', had spoken to her of how he would have to adapt to changed circumstances back at home – of how difficult it would be

> to keep up all the outward forms of civilisation – because there the *amadoda* [men] are accustomed to discuss affairs, sitting around in their huts, and he would be expected, and it would be his duty to join them – he could not refuse to go into people's huts, and the way one has to sit in a hut, together with the *amafuta* [fat] prevalent, is 'extremely antagonistic to trousers.' Now that is exactly the case, and I was glad to perceive that if one of the two must give way, it would be the trousers, and not the people.

In spite of the stories in the Natal press, of the rumours about his being spoilt, she was convinced that exile had not changed Dinuzulu or his uncles.

> They are as good at heart, and as united as ever, and Dinuzulu's 'civilisation' will not be a barrier between him and his father's people, which has been one thing I have feared. Not that he has not plenty of new ideas. He is anxious to plant, and get the people to plant a greater variety of crops and fruit, and to cultivate what they plant, to build granaries to store the grain in years of plenty, to feed the cattle in winter. 'There should be butter, fresh butter, in Zululand, all the year round,' he says. To import and breed donkeys, as hardier, and more useful to poor people than horses.[5]

Harriette Colenso is writing of a progressive modernising prince who, given the chance, would lead his people into the twentieth century. It was his duty, and hers, to ensure that he went on to take his place in African history. As she had said to the Usuthu, 'This Zulu People may yet rise – indeed it *should* rise, to be admired, and to be great.'⁶ So much depended on Dinuzulu himself: 'because he is his father's son is given by God power over the hearts of the ~~Natives~~ people which we white ~~people~~ folk cannot have, provided he is able to ~~rule~~ govern himself ~~to~~ as he has ~~as from~~ done hitherto to restrain himself that he ~~was~~ be not the slave of drink, nor of anger, nor of idleness. ~~Therein~~ In this lies the whole ~~question~~ affair.'⁷

The return

On 19 December the party sailed for Natal on the *Umbilo*. Harriette Colenso had received permission to travel with them – at her own expense. Once on board they discovered that the cabins had been organised so as to put the men and the children in the first-class cabins, and the women forward – an impossible division according to Zulu custom. The guardian, an ex-Natal policeman, retired to the chief officer's cabin, 'and as soon as the Captain realised – in ¼ hour or so – that if Madden was the official guardian, I was the working one, we got along famously'. The children were moved in with the women, the men left in the first class, and Harriette and Mbhodiya, the nurse and midwife, occupied the cabin set aside for the guardian. It solved the immediate problem, although Harriette wrote later with fine tact that 'It was a very interesting voyage, but one such may last a person for some time'.⁸

The ship arrived off Durban in the evening of 5 January 1898. In the tug that came out to meet it were Agnes Colenso, Mubi Nondenisa and Mjwaphuna. Also present was S.O. Samuelson, the new Under-Secretary for Native Affairs in Natal. His task was one of some historical significance – to supervise the assumption of colonial authority over the Zulu prince who had hitherto been in imperial charge. While Natal officials had involved themselves in Zulu affairs for over half a century, it had always been as agents of the imperial government. Zululand was now a province of Natal.

They met in the saloon of the *Umbilo* where, in the company of Agnes and Harriette Colenso, they were told that Natal and Zululand were now under one government located in Pietermaritzburg. The Chief Commissioner and Magistrate, a Natal official, Charles Saunders, would live at Eshowe. Samuelson then outlined the terms of their return. Dinuzulu took the papers from Samuelson, read them, remarked that they were the same as those he had been given at St Helena, and asked that Samuelson read them to his uncles.

The Zulu party had to be removed from Durban and pass through Natal as quickly as possible. Their request to shop in Durban was turned down, and their hope that they might be allowed to travel to Pietermaritzburg to see the Governor was ignored. A special train was to come to the quay early the next morning and take them directly to the railhead from where they would travel to Zululand by wagon.

It was soon discovered that neither the train nor the three wagons were of sufficient capacity to take all their possessions. Samuelson reported: 'Miss Colenso said there were about 40 tons of furniture and other things by sight measurement. There were also six donkeys, ten dogs, some rabbits, fowl pens, a canary, a parrot, and a monkey, belonging to Dinuzulu ...'[9] The train left Durban docks early the next morning carrying as much of the luggage as possible. It stopped briefly at the main station to allow Sir Marshal Clarke to greet them – and say farewell. It was a courtesy call only. Clarke no longer held an official position in Zululand. With his departure went another of the struts with which Harriette Colenso exactly three years previously had hoped to build a new Zululand.

The train moved off north, through Phoenix to Verulam. It was here nearly ten years before that Harriette and the Usuthu defence had changed to the horse-drawn carriage for their journey to Eshowe to appear before the Court of Special Commissioners. Since then the line had been extended and now reached Tongathi. Here the Zulu party changed to the wagons for the final leg of their journey. They had to leave most of their possessions and their animals for the Natal authorities to transport.

The remainder of the journey was a difficult one. It lasted four days, was dreadfully hot, and there was insufficient space in the wagons and the tents. But it could have been worse. Just as they arrived in Eshowe on 10 January, heavy rain turned the roads into swamps and the rivers flooded. Agnes had stayed behind in Natal to assist in the transport of the party's possessions. But these were caught in the floods and much damage was done. Dinuzulu's St Helenian donkeys, which he hoped would lighten the burdens of the poor in Zululand, had suffered but survived the rough weather of the voyage. But four of them, 'hardier, and more useful to poor people than horses', died on their way to Zululand.

Province of Zululand

So much had changed. Three deaths took place in the early 1890s which marked this. In July 1892 a great figure in Zulu history died, Mnyamana kaNgqengelele of the Buthelezi, chief minister to the last Zulu king, and the man who tried so desperately to stop the course of civil war in the 1880s, in which all sides lost. Finally, confirming the line in his praise poem, 'he who succeeds when there is no chance of success', he formally gave his allegiance to the authorities in 1889, thereby breaking the close relationship he had with the royal family with and for whom he had worked for so long, but allowing his immediate followers to escape further punishment and suffering. To follow the history of Mnyamana kaNgqengelele and the Buthelezi through the years of civil war is to understand the immensity of the tragedy of these years.

Sir Theophilus Shepstone died in Pietermaritzburg in June 1893. He had imposed his will on the people of the region by persuading some of its most powerful African figures to work with him and be rewarded for it. More than that of any other individual, it was his vision which subjugated Zululand to Natal. No Governor was confident enough to resist him, and by the time he died his ideas on segregation were being accepted, to serve a purpose which did not even exist when he developed them – the super-exploitation of the massive, unskilled labour force upon which modern South Africa was built, with the appalling social and economic consequences that democratic South Africa is still trying to contend with and cure.

Sarah Frances Colenso died at Christmas in 1893. She was a figure of no public importance but one of great significance for the events with which this book has been concerned. Not only did she leave an incomparable record, but she inspired in her children the attitudes of an age, the ideals of the mid-Victorian, liberal, evangelical intelligentsia, ideas of great significance for South African history and which so marked the African nationalism that grew out of the narrative of conquest and subjugation. The story told here is about the way in which these ideals – English justice, equality under the law, Protestantism and progress – were being smothered by the violence of imperialism. For in the last quarter of the nineteenth century there had been a major shift away from what is characterised as Gladstonian liberalism, with its aversion to the extension of political responsibilities overseas, towards aggressive expansion and control – towards, that is, the new imperialism. These were seismic shifts not only in policy but also in consciousness. Harriette Colenso came to London in 1890 charged with the spirit of an age fast disappearing – the high-minded evangelical humanism of the earlier nineteenth century – and was thus unable to counter the brutal, chauvinistic drive for national supremacy which was soon to dominate the new century.

In Zululand the conquest initiated by invasion twenty years before was now complete. Politically the members of the old order had been annihilated. The resistance of 1888 and 1889, the devastation and looting by British troops, Zulu loyals and African levies in putting it down, and the subsequent exile of the leadership put the final finish to the process. Central authority was now firmly in the hands of the Commissioner. Local authority was delegated to magistrates, who in turn depended upon a more amenable class of regional officers called chiefs, who were responsible for the day-to-day rule of the districts and the administration of justice.

The creation of a pliable chieftainship had been one of the objectives of Resident Commissioner Melmoth Osborn through the 1880s, and a major cause of the civil war. In this he was following the practice of his guide and mentor, Theophilus Shepstone. His successor, Marshal Clarke, had to try to break with this and take into account Zulu feeling by acting more generously towards the Zulu chiefs from Zululand, and reduce the power of policemen and indunas who had been rewarded for their services to the Shepstone family in Natal with chieftainships in Zululand. Clarke's reforms, however, had been very limited. Zululand, when Dinuzulu returned at the beginning of 1898, was a mosaic of chieftaincies, carefully bounded, often tense on the borders where population pressure and old rivalries were already causing 'faction fights'; with each chief assessed in terms of the number of huts under his control, for the amount of tax to be collected from his people annually.

It was the successful collection of this tax upon which the whole colonial edifice was constructed. For the first four years it was a remarkable success. The hut tax made up three-quarters of all the revenue that was collected. It covered the cost of the whole administrative establishment, the exiles on St Helena, and the Zululand Police, and still left a healthy balance. It was earned beyond Zululand's borders, on the farms and in the households of colonial Natal, and on the Natal Government Railways reaching desperately out to the gold mines of the Transvaal, or on the mines themselves.

For the officials in Eshowe, the Governor in Pietermaritzburg and the Colonial Office, it vindicated the policy which had been attempted since the invasion of 1879 but which the Zulu royal house and their white advisers had tried to subvert. The social and economic costs of migrant labour in Zululand – the loss of its young men, the abuses of the chiefs and the labour agents as they forced men out to work, the penalties imposed for failing to pay the hut tax, the deaths and injuries in the mining industry – were in official eyes completely outweighed by the benefits of wage labour. Echoes of the personal consequences of that labour reached as far as St Helena. Here Dinuzulu's attendant was told that her brother had returned from Johannesburg 'both his eyes blinded by dynamite'.[10] 'I also report the death of Nsungula's son ... named Mjatshi, who died at work at Johannesburg, and was killed by dynamite.'[11]

Harriette Colenso's was one of the minute number of voices to protest at the social consequences of migrant labour. In response the official spokesmen in the House of Commons pointed to the fact that Zululand's books were in bal-

439

ance. But by 1894 the brittle and ephemeral nature of Zululand's apparent economic prosperity was brutally exposed. In 1894–95 locusts destroyed the grain crop. An increased number of men left the colony to work for wages to meet the tax and to purchase food. Then the spring rains were late and the 1895–96 crop failed. In those areas where grain was available from traders and storekeepers it was sold at inflated prices which kept it from all but the most wealthy, and the wages earned outside the colony were insufficient to pay the shortfalls in the hut tax. Government attempts to stabilise the price of grain proved to be prohibitively expensive. At the end of 1896 the government of Zululand could not cover its current expenses and had to ask for a loan in advance of the next year's hut tax.[12]

Fragmented, controlled, taxed, dependent on wages earned outside its borders, its budget in deficit – this was the country Dinuzulu returned to, a country whose independence had gone. The official reports of the time speak of a Zululand unchanged: backward-looking, traditionalist, unproductive, ignorant of the market, a subsistence economy fettered by the chains of custom and tradition. It was not this, of course. Dinuzulu, now just another chief, returned to a Zululand revolutionised, with a compliant chieftainship, an administration dependent on hut tax and therefore on wage labour, a legal system based on a travesty of traditionalism called customary law, administered by colonial magistrates of variable but for the most part indifferent capacities. Its economy was devastated by the effects of war, pillage, drought, pestilence and plague – it had suffered the full impact of developing capitalism in an imperial age.

If one date had to be chosen to mark the final, the irretrievable end of Zululand independence, 2 August 1897 would not be inappropriate. It was on this day, in the Nquthu district – just at the same time the colonial dignitaries were making their way home from London after the magnificent celebrations of the Diamond Jubilee – that an event, long awaited, greatly feared, completely devastating and apparently inevitable, took place in Zululand: the first Zulu cattle died of rinderpest.

When Dinuzulu returned it was estimated that some 160,000 head had died and the disease was still moving amongst the Zulu herds, killing, and then turning back to mop up those pockets of animals which had escaped. By the middle of 1898 about 80 per cent of the cattle of Zululand had been lost. Cattle lay at the heart of the pre-conquest Zulu system. They were not only its means of subsistence as food, clothing and weaponry, but at the heart of production, the domestic order and of political power, and played a crucial role in religious belief. Literally, symbolically or metaphorically, the decimation of the herds of the Zulu can be taken to mark the end of Zulu independence.

'Our greatest safety'

Dinuzulu spent a month in Eshowe before moving north to Osuthu. It was a testing time. They lived in the new cottage and tents, although Harriette Colenso was once again offered hospitality from the officials, which she accepted as an indication of goodwill towards the Usuthu although she personally was excluded from official meetings. Hot weather alternated with heavy rain bringing most of the party down with fever, and the rivers down with floods, delaying the arrival of their luggage and their return to their homes in the north of the country. When it did arrive the problems of storing it safely, and then moving it on, were huge; and more of the animals died in the wet, tick-ridden grass.

Harriette Colenso felt she had to be with the returned exiles until they were safely settled in their homes: she had committed herself to them ten years before when she pledged the support of the House of Sobantu if they surrendered to the authorities. But her dream of 1889 was gone – the idea that she would appeal to the conscience of England, expose the evils and injustice of the existing system, and work towards bringing to Zululand a more enlightened system of government with the participation of the accepted leaders of the country, the Zulu royal house. This now seemed a wild miscalculation based on a fundamental misunderstanding of both the men and the politics of the times. But the idea of failure could not be openly admitted – it lay outside the world in which she felt she had to work – a world where justice had meaning and power. But as a political actor, a force in Zululand, she now had little relevance.

For the Usuthu, Eshowe remained a fearful place, filled with the evil wrought by the medicine of their enemies. They suffered feverish attacks. Ndabuko retreated to the forests of Eshowe to receive the attentions of traditional healers. Harriette fell heavily from a horse lent to her by the Zululand Police, just as Ndabuko had done after he had sat upon the chair offered him at his meeting with the Governor in 1887. Harriette admitted to the contradictory situation in which she was now placed when Mansel gave Dinuzulu a present: 'a delightful new Gun', 'with all the newest and most horrible improvements, – To think that I should be downright grateful for such a gift!! But I am ...'[13]

After a month they were ready for the next stage of the journey, from Eshowe to Osuthu in the north. According to *The Times of Natal*, 'The weary years at St Helena had certainly alienated Cetshwayo's son from his people.'[14] But in Harriette's view, it was a royal progress through his kingdom.

'Dinuzulu's journey from Eshowe to Nongoma was a triumphal march! His people – including the Government chiefs – from remote quarters, and in vast

441

numbers met him all along the route, giving him their allegiance and presenting him with money. One of the most striking facts in connection with this is
that the Kolwas, or so-called Christian Zulus, were as eager in their protesta-
tions and monetary gifts as the veriest heathen ... a purely spontaneous outburst of loyalty.'[15]

Ndabuko and Shingana went back to their homes to rebuild. Harriette Colenso
stayed with Dinuzulu's family in tents at Osuthu, as the people came to pay tribute and the young men to begin rebuilding the homestead. The lack of space,
the changeable weather, the leaking tents, made it difficult for them all.
Harriette Colenso shared their discomfort, and at the same time made friends
with the local storekeeper and the Magistrate, J.Y. Gibson, knowing that she
would help Dinuzulu and his family by so doing, but making it absolutely clear
whose side she was on. A decade earlier, when Harriette had eventually to leave
Eshowe, Dinuzulu had expressed his fear that they would be left without protection from the arbitrary violence of the officials, like grasshoppers for the birds
to peck. Now this situation seemed indeed to have come about: they were
exposed to the storms which flooded their tents, to the derisive reports of the
officials about Miss Colenso, whose 'boots are worn out and there (are no others
large enough to be had in Zululand)', to the informers who reported that
Harriette was claiming that it was she, not the government, who was responsible
for the return of Dinuzulu.

For although the local officials, Gibson and Saunders, were not unsympathetic, this was not the case with their superiors in Pietermaritzburg. The hostility
towards the Zulu royal house on the part of the new administration in Natal was
as deep and prejudiced as it had ever been, and whatever his intentions
Dinuzulu stood no chance of overcoming it. From the time he arrived at Osuthu
the Natal ministry, led by the SNA, James Liege Hulett, began to attack him.
The familiar complaint that young men were visiting the prince without the
authority of their chiefs began again. With the encouragement and assistance of
the Boers, Zulu were coming in from the Transvaal and gathering around him.
Dinuzulu was alleged to be building a military homestead.

From Zululand, Saunders and Gibson tried to suggest to the officials in Natal
that reports about Dinuzulu should be treated with more circumspection. But
Liege Hulett would have none of it. Dinuzulu wrote a letter to Saunders apologising for the presence of young men at Osuthu, and assured him that he had
ordered them to return home. However, he addressed Saunders as 'Umnumzana'. Dinuzulu's attempt at co-operation, and the historical significance of the
fact that Dinuzulu was corresponding with the colonial authorities in his own

hand, were lost on Hulett. He was furious. 'I specially draw your attention to the slighting manner in which Dinuzulu addressed his Magistrate', he minuted. *Umnumzana* is and was a term of respect; as far as Hulett was concerned, however, it meant 'Headman'. Officials had to be addressed as *Inkosi*, meaning chief.

The SNA was unaware that the judgment he was passing on political terminology was based on colonial misinterpretations of the Zulu language. Saunders wrote that Dinuzulu 'disclaims any intention to be disrespectful' and thought that the use of *umnumzana* was the equivalent of addressing the Magistrate as 'Sir'. But nothing could be done to assuage the SNA's hostility. Its roots lay too deep – the intensity of Natal's fear and hatred was too great. And there were more immediate material demands as well – after all, it was James Liege Hulett, landowner and planter, who was leading the move to build a railway into Zululand to exploit the coal deposits at Hlabisa, and who was soon to appropriate the land on which to found the sugar industry in Zululand. 'It seems to me', he wrote,

> that we are bound, at once, to put our foot down and not to allow the slightest act on the part of Dinuzulu to take place which tends to give him ground for claiming privileges appertaining to a paramount and independent chief, and which, if allowed, would, in the view of the native population of Zululand be tantamount to the Government recognising Dinuzulu as something more than an ordinary chief.[16]

Dinuzulu's position was an impossible one. He was without any real authority except in his own 'location'. His every move was watched and reported upon. His duties as government induna were always unclear, reflecting an imperial promise emptied of content by Natal's opposition. And that opposition was murderous. For example, soon after Dinuzulu's return, Charles Saunders, the new head of the Zululand administration, attempted to reconcile the Usuthu and the Mandlakazi. On 4 June 1898 the main protagonists, Dinuzulu and Zibhebhu, met in the Chief Magistrate's office in Eshowe. Dinuzulu, Zibhebhu asserted, had not been responsible for the civil war, and he wished for a reconciliation. Dinuzulu accepted this:

> Yes, father, as regards what you say about the origin of the quarrel, I admit your words are appropriate ... I know nothing about how the quarrel arose, for, as you state, I was but a child at the time. I only took up the quarrel. With regard to the blood that had been shed, as you argue, so do we argue, viz, that

we only defended ourselves. There is nothing uncommon in this, that people who have quarrelled and been at war with each other for a long time eventually become fast friends. I say let this be so; we are the last people who ought to quarrel and if you are in earnest, in the desire that we should become friends, let it be so. I bear no malice.

Saunders was highly gratified: 'On going outside they and their followers saluted each other and commingled in friendly intercourse. On departing from the precincts of the Office, they did so in a body – Dinuzulu and Zibhebhu riding up the main street of the township side by side.'[17]

For the Chief Magistrate this was an historic moment reflecting a considerable victory for the new administration in Zululand. The SNA in Pietermaritzburg saw it completely differently. 'I cannot but feel an intense anxiety as to the future result', James Liege Hulett wrote.

> Zibhebhu has now recognised Dinuzulu, and in that one act has removed his faith from the ruling power, which he considers has injured him, to that of the Royal House of his people.
>
> The jealousies between the native chiefs in Natal, have ever been our greatest safety, [and in Zululand as long as members of the royal house] are divided the chiefs and people remain divided, but when the union of interests centres in one principal head, tribal differences are for the time forgotten.

The wisdom of a policy of reconciliation amongst members of the Zulu royal house, Hulett felt, 'is open to very grave doubt'.[18]

'Flung broadcast'

And so Natal's long-standing policy of undermining all attempts at African unity, on whatever basis, continued. Meanwhile the general situation worsened for Dinuzulu. The year after his return war broke out between the British and the Boers, and he was greatly exercised by the consequences this had for northern Zululand. It also delayed the work of the Joint Imperial and Colonial Commission whose task was to divide the land of the Zulu. This was done between 1902 and 1904, and 40 per cent of what was left of Zululand, the major part of it the most commercially productive, was taken over. The remainder was to become Zulu native reserves.

The land crisis in Natal, the sale of Crown land, the need for more land, the inadequacies of the old locations set up in the early years of Shepstone's term of office: it was these, as we have seen, which lay behind the drive into Zululand in the last quarter of the nineteenth century. By the twentieth century, population increase had only made the situation more desperate. To this was added the disruptive consequences of wage and migrant labour, the undermining of African patriarchal authority, the inadequacy of the customary law, and resultant widespread dislocation and distress amongst the African population. The Natal authorities tried to cast the tax net further, and in 1905 announced that African men not paying hut tax would be liable to a poll tax. The news was received with desperate anger. Resistance began in the Natal Midlands, and spread to the valley of the mid-Thukela under a chief called Bhambatha who gave his name to this culminating tragedy of Natal native policy, an uprising in 1906 against settler greed and racist oppression which was put down with hideous cruelty.

Although now severely hampered by settler hostility and shortage of funds, Harriette and Agnes did what they could to support those whom Natal tried to punish through the courts – they could do little for those who suffered at the hands of the colonial militia. The legacy of recrimination and accusation continued after 1906 as settler Natal sought an explanation for the rising which would exclude its own culpability. It lit on Dinuzulu kaCetshwayo, a tribal chief with pretensions to being an African king, one with a troublesome history and a potential for agitation. For the Africans of Natal and Zululand he was the son of Cetshwayo, the descendant of Shaka, hated by the oppressor, invested with the glories of the past, who had attained many of the skills of the present, and who had to carry the burden of their suffering. One of the many stories of signs and wonders circulating in the colony before the uprising was one that Dinuzulu had travelled, alone and unseen, to Pietermaritzburg. There he had climbed the clock tower of the City Hall. The next day he was gone – but had left behind, for the astonished whites to see, writing, in his own hand.[19]

In 1907 he was arrested and charged on 23 counts including high treason, public violence, sedition, rebellion, and murder or accessory to murder. For Dinuzulu, the explanation for this persecution lay in Zulu history:

> My sole crime is that I am the son of Cetshwayo. My trouble is like that of no one else. It beset me when I was a child and my father was taken by the white people and it is still besetting me. I could not bury Cetshwayo, my Father; he died while I was being chased ... I did not bury my Mother, Okamsweli; she had died while I have been a prisoner. All our family die of harassing ... and now of all our house I am left alone ... My children are still small and have not got eyes. There is no one who can take care of them for

Photo 37. The Two Sisters. In 1903 Harriette and Agnes Colenso felt that their friends and supporters deserved a photograph in which 'we don't look so woeful as in some photos'. The nineteenth-century struggle was over. The new century's struggles were about to start.

me. Nkosi, what is grievous is to be killed and yet alive. To die outright is nothing, for then one rests and does not feel trouble …[20]

Harriette Colenso, now herself threatened with eviction from Bishopstowe by the Church of the Province, organised his defence. After a long trial at Greytown he was found guilty on some of the minor charges and sentenced to four years' imprisonment. In 1910 the first Prime Minister of South Africa, Louis Botha, who had known Dinuzulu from the time of the New Republic, arranged for him to move to a farm, but one beyond the borders of Natal. Here Dinuzulu died in 1913 at the age of 43.

The other men whose experiences make up the story told here were already dead. Ndabuko, Dinuzulu's father's full brother who had shared his exile, died as the new century opened, aged about 55. Shingana kaMpande had been pursued by Natal's SNA, Arthur Shepstone (years before, the first Magistrate of the Lower Mfolozi district), who in 1909 banished him to the Natal south coast. Harriette Colenso found him there, impoverished and ill, and tried to get help. She was with him 'when the poor old man was sinking, and just starting now and then to say "Come in inkosazana" as he used to do in gaol at Eshowe'.[21] They had met first in 1880 when he had 'jumped over the precipice' and come to Bishopstowe to tell of the loyalty amongst the Zulu for the exiled king; now she wrote 'of my dear old friend, Shingana, Dinuzulu's uncle. They have killed him at last ...'[22] Harry Escombe died, at the age of 61, at the beginning of the war with the Boers. Harriette Colenso believed he was 'heartbroken ... at the ruin/the disgrace of European South Africa'.[23]

Harriette and Agnes Colenso still had many years, struggles, some victories and many disappointments to endure. They were no longer able to do battle under the banner emblazoned 'English justice' as they had done for most of the nineteenth century. But one would need more space and time than is available here to examine their twentieth-century struggles in the prisons, hospitals and courts, if one were to get beyond cardboard characterisations of 'brave women ahead of their time'.

In June 1910 the Natal parliament passed the Church Properties Act. It was one of the last actions of the legislative body which for so long had provided a forum for settler opposition to the women and men of Bishopstowe. It gave the Anglican Church what it had desired for so long. The land on which Bishopstowe and Ekukhanyeni had been built was sold. The African tenants, teachers, printers and preachers, friends who lived and worked with Harriette and Agnes, and some of them with their father John Colenso, were dispersed.

'Both we and they intend to sprout vigorously where we have been flung broadcast', wrote Harriette to her old aunt Eliza Bunyon. But it was difficult. At the very moment that Bishopstowe was sold, the news reached them that their brother Frank had died in England. Their dear friend Katie Giles had died two weeks earlier, Harriette nursing her to the end. Slowly the sisters moved their possessions from the hillside outside Pietermaritzburg into the house in which Katie had lived in the town. From there they were to move again later to a cottage at Sweetwaters in the hills on the other side of Pietermaritzburg. Now marginal figures, they used to take a train into the city – two elderly women in long, home-made dresses and men's hats, with their African friends helping them carry the shopping back to the station; strange figures who, it was said, had been women of some importance when they were young. By the time they died, in 1932, within a few months of one another, little more was known of them than that.

Harriette Colenso's last major public (but highly confidential) intervention was to secure the succession to his father's inheritance of Solomon Nkayishana Maphumuzana,[24] in the photograph on page 386 the small boy in the large hat on the steps of the house on St Helena. He was never recognised officially as Zulu king, but during his lifetime there was a substantial shift in attitude on the part of elements within white Natal towards him and the Zulu royal house. As the impact of wage labour, capitalist production and rural impoverishment bit deeper, and radical ideas and movements began to influence African workers and peasants, so the structured patriarchies of Zulu traditionalism, with the Zulu kingship at its apex, seemed more attractive. Thus the 1920s saw the emergence of an alliance between conservative forces amongst certain whites and blacks in Natal, supporting the political recognition of the Zulu royal house. This trend was to continue with Solomon's successors, Cyprian and Goodwill Zwelithini, as forces coming from different parts of the political spectrum attempted to make use of the monarchism deep in the culture of the Africans of KwaZulu-Natal and indeed beyond. The contradictions and ambiguities in such processes have contributed to the complexities of modern South Africa. But what has been constant is the emotional hold of the Zulu royal house, its central position in African tradition and, of course, in African history. Far from being the 'rope of sand' of Natal's settler tradition, it has proved to be a social construct made up of strong and resilient historical memories, connecting the present with the past, and around which alliances continue to be made and battles fought.

It is a history which has been and will be used for purposes as varied as the society of which it was part. Traditionalists, modernisers, whites and blacks, wise men and women, the committed and the opportunistic, the charitable and the murderous, eccentrics and charlatans, historians popular and academic, have all found and continue to find in the Zulu royal house a past which fills a need in the present.

The story told here is a small part of the long history of the descendants of Senzangakhona. But it was during these years that its continuity hung by a thread, to be saved by the energetic interventions of men and women determined to protest, to argue, and to record events and act on their imperatives. I have concentrated on one group in this process – the people at Bishopstowe. Although they failed in their objectives, their contribution to our history was an important one. It is largely unknown for the same reasons that so much African history in South Africa has still to be told – sexism in the one case, racism in the other. Their leader was Harriette Colenso, a woman with few material resources but charged with a vision of justice in Africa shared across the racial and cultural divisions. It was a radical and a conservative vision – a contradictory one in which the past was invoked to facilitate and ease the pain of change.

Although she did find some allies, black and white, Harriette Colenso's vision was ignored, ridiculed or exploited by most of her contemporaries. A century later, we can see clearly the shortcomings of her detractors and antagonists, caught up in the prejudices of their times. Harriette Colenso's vision, however, with all its specificity and limitations, still has social pertinence and a moral validity. She was determined to give expression to what a man she once knew, John Ruskin, called 'the grand instincts of virtue', those defining features of humanity which were, to her, manifest in all people. This awareness of the good in others enabled her to escape the racist and religious prejudices which so dominated her times. And it gave her a moral confidence without which her struggle would have been impossible. With it, it was everything. She seldom spoke of her personal feelings, but we glimpse them in the answer she gave to her own question when, in 1897, she was charged with threatening those responsible for good government in Natal: 'it's nonsense to talk of my threatening –', she said, 'where is my power? except in being in the right ...'

GLOSSARY

amaBhunu Boers
ibandla council or congregation
indoda | amadoda a man
idlozi | amadlozi guardian spirit, ancestor
induna | izinduna official
ikhanda | amakhanda royal homestead
ikhohlo the people who make up the left-hand side of the homestead or lineage
ikholwa | amakholwa a Christian, literally a believer
khonza to pay allegiance
isikhulu | izikhulu the great ones of the kingdom, the hereditary chiefs
inkosi | amakhosi a person of the highest political authority; in the colonial context, a chief

impi an armed force
inceku | izinceku personal attendant and confidential adviser
inganekwane fairytale
insangu dagga, marijuana
umntwana | abantwana prince, the 'child' of the king
umnumzana | abanumzana homestead head
iziqu wooden beads worn to denote bravery
ubushokobezi white cow-tail, the Usuthu badge
utshwala beer
umuzi | imizi the homestead, the physical structure or its occupants; a lineage
isiZulu the Zulu language

451

LIST OF PHOTOGRAPHIC SOURCES

1. [page 4] Ndabuko kaMpande. I initially believed this to be a photograph of the redoubtable Dabulamanzi kaMpande, taken in Pietermaritzburg, where his presence, dressed in similar clothing, was recorded in the press. I now suspect that those who disagreed with this identification were correct and it is in fact a photograph of the king's full brother Ndabuko. (NA C873)

2. [page 4] Sitheku kaMpande. Note that the print in the Natal Archives is identified as a photograph of Dabulamanzi. (NA C874)

3. [page 4] Shingana kaMpande. (NA. C875)

4. [page 5] Melmoth Osborn. (J.Y Gibson, *The Story of the Zulus*. London: Longmans, Green, 1911)

5. [page 8] Cetshwayo kaMpande. Photographed in 1882 at Bassano's in London. This is photograph that Frances Colenso used as the frontispiece to the second volume of her book *The Ruin of Zululand*. (F.E. Colenso, *The Ruin of Zululand*. Vol. 2. London: William Ridgeway, 1884)

6. [page 9] Dinuzulu kaCetshwayo. From a photograph taken in November 1888 in the Pietermaritzburg Police barracks, which was widely pirated by photographers at the time. (KC A42.003)

7. [page 10] Zibhebhu kaMaphitha. (NA C740)

8. [page 11] Hamu kaNzibe of the Ngenetsheni of the Zulu. From the print reproduced in J.J.Guy, *The Destruction of the Zulu Kingdom*. London: Longman, 1979

9. [page 16] The Colenso family from a photocopy of a photograph in the library of Rhodes House, Oxford. There is also a copy in the Campbell collections of the University of Natal.

10. [page 17] Sarah Frances Colenso and her daughters. A detail from a larger photograph. The identification is my own and speculative. (NA C109/11)

11. [page 20] John William Colenso, in the 1850s. (NA C108/3)

12. [page 21] William Ngidi. There is a print of this photograph in the Museum of Mankind, the British Museum, AF B79 21. The copy in the Campbell collections in Album A50 from which this was taken seems to be the

---

453

one made by Harriette Colenso in the 1890s from the British Museum print.

13. [page 24] Bishop Colenso and his sons. (RH MSS Afr. s.1283(5))

14. [page 24] Sarah Frances with her daughters. (RH MSS s. 1285(17))

15. [page 24] Harriette Emily and Agnes Mary Colenso (RH MSS Afr. s. 1285 (17))

16. [page 30] Bishopstowe. (NA C835)

17. [page 35] Theophilus Shepstone. (NA C 418)

18. [page 54] Anthony Durnford. (J.P. Mackinnon and S. Shadbolt. *The South African Campaign*. London, 1880)

19. [page 55] Frances Colenso. (RH MSS Afr .s. 1285(17))

20. [page 62] Harriette Colenso and her father in Grahamstown in 1881. (KC HE:F)

21. [page 116] September 1884: Bishopstowe destroyed by fire. (NA C841)

22. [page 118] The Colenso family at Seven Oaks. (NA C843)

23. [page 119] Mother and daughters at Seven Oaks, c.1885. (NA C842, detail)

24. [page 228] The levies. (NA C554)

25. [page 232] British officers at Eshowe. (Private collection)

26. [page 235] The Nongqayi. (NA C5055)

27. [page 259] 'Rebels', Pietermaritzburg, 1888. (Private collection)

28. [page 263] Brunner's Store in Eshowe. (*Twentieth Century Impressions of Natal*. Natal: Lloyd's Greater Britain Publishing Co., 1906)

29. [page 266] The Eshowe gaol. (NA C759)

30. [page 267] Osuthu at Eshowe. (NA C837)

31. [page 317] Harriette Colenso, Birmingham.

32. [page 333] The Colenso family in the 1890s. (From a photocopy of a print in the Natal Diocesan Archives)

33. [page 359] Natal's first Cabinet. (NA)

34. [page 360] Sir Marshal Clarke. (Godfrey Lagden, *The Basutos*. Vol. 2. London: Hutchinson, 1909)

35. [page 386] The Usuthu and their friends on St Helena. (NA C760)

36. [page 387] Ndabuko kaMpande, Dinuzulu kaCetshwayo, Paul Mthimkhulu. (NA C668)

37. [page 446] The two sisters, 1903. (NA C774)

BIBLIOGRAPHY

I have tracked many of the official records covering the events related in this book as they moved through the different government offices in Zululand and Natal, and then to London. Although there have been lengthy interruptions I have been researching this material for more than thirty years, and during this time some of the archival collections I used have been reorganised and restructured. Thus the Colenso collection in the Pietermaritzburg Archives Repository (previously the Natal Archives Depot) has been resorted and reboxed. This raises problems for precise citation, but these are slight when compared with those raised by the reclassification and binding of the Natal Government House series which, in my opinion, has so dispersed related documents that the series has been rendered virtually unusable. Fortunately, at least for this book, the Zululand Government House series, although the folders were split as a first step towards binding, has not been reclassified and bound, and can therefore still be used.

As a consequence of such 'reorganisation', comprehensive citations would have to reflect the history of the archival collections. This is clearly impossible, but I have attempted to give sufficient information for subsequent researchers to track down the documents I have used. Where possible my references are to the most accessible versions of official documents – that is, the correspondence published in the British Parliamentary Papers. And it should be remembered that a major reason why the Parliamentary Papers are so comprehensive is that the authorities were forced to publish the official records as a result of the public controversy provoked by Bishopstowe and its allies.

I have made much use of the correspondence and papers of the Colenso family. The major collections are in the Pietermaritzburg Archives Repository (NA), in which incoming letters to Natal and personal papers predominate; Rhodes House (RH), which houses the correspondence of the Aborigines' Protection Society (Anti Slavery (AS) papers) and the incoming correspondence to members of the Colenso family living in England (MSS African); and the Campbell

---

455

Collections of the University of Natal (KC), in which sets of correspondence are housed largely as a result of the interest shown in them by Killie Campbell herself. In 1979 I pointed out that the very important papers printed at Bishopstowe had yet to be collated and classified by a bibliographer.[1] This has still to be done, and so I follow the classification I used then.

Over the years Brenda Nicholls published articles on aspects of the events recounted here, and in 1997 she completed her doctoral dissertation on the activities of the Colenso family in this period. I read it after I had completed the draft of this book but, although there are points of contact with my research, based as it is on so much of the same source material, her method, approach and conclusions appeared so different from mine that I decided not to engage with them here.

There are a number of names used in this book whose meaning and significance have changed over the century – 'natives' and 'tribes' are only the most obvious. I have not littered the text with quotation marks, however. Instead I rely on the context and what Mahmood Mamdani called in his comments on the same point 'the reader's continued vigilance and good sense'.[2]

Many of the quotations in this book are from the original letters. Generally I have not cited the accession numbers inserted by archivists on private letters: in too many cases there is confusion because this has been attempted more than once – and there will have to be still one more attempt by someone with a detailed knowledge of the history of the letters before such classification can be of genuine assistance to the researcher. I have edited these letters lightly, used the full word for most abbreviations, and in most cases made the Zulu spelling consistent with that used in the text, in which I have been guided by the spelling and orthography of *The James Stuart Archive* edited by Colin Webb and John Wright. However, this is not always possible; for example, certain spellings of a Zulu word or name are so much part of the writer's historical personality that to correct the spelling would be a distortion. I cannot bring myself to accept 'Somsewu' for the hybrid 'Somtsewu', and have retained 'Usuthu' for the royalist party.

The approach to publishing historical photographs from Natal and Zululand has been, generally speaking, to reproduce them as unproblematic representations of the past. Portraits of the leaders of society in the colony, street views of its towns, and transport systems – the railway in particular – dominate, together with stereotypical photographs of 'natives in tribal dress'. Mirroring the historiography of the region itself, inordinate interest has been shown in photographs of the British invasion of Zululand in 1879. Local photographers did what they could to exploit the fact that an event of world interest was taking place on their doorstep, and the fact that they were unable to create a corpus of work of any stature has been no obstacle to the repeated reproduction of their images as writers on the war and their publishers try to promote books weighed down by tired and repetitive texts. The photographs are often not sourced, or are incorrectly sourced, and frequently misidentified, the result usually of uncritically transcribing the errors and marginal speculations of archivists and researchers over the years. But identification, correct or incorrect, is not the major problem: it is the gratuitous reproduction of images whose connection with the text or the events which they are assumed to represent is left unexplored.

In this book I try to break with that tradition. It does not pretend to be a radical break: there is not a photograph which would not support an extended analysis in itself. But this commentary is different in that it does not assume that a photograph represents reality. It does, however, assume that a photograph represents realities, for the photographed, for the photographer and for the person who has selected the image and manipulated it visually and verbally, and for the observer of this image. I have located the image within a commentary which seeks to elucidate some of these realities. All comments, with or without qualifiers, should be seen as tentative and interpretative.

Most of these photographs are from prints in the Pietermaritzburg Archives Repository, the Killie Campbell Collection in Durban, or the Rhodes House Library in Oxford, and I have been as accurate as possible in acknowledging the source of these prints. However, it must be remembered that the proliferation of prints in different collections sometimes make this difficult, and in a few cases I have been unable to identify with certainty the location of the original print.

Books, articles and theses cited in the text

Bradlaugh, C. and Watts, J. [Iconoclast]. *Half-hours with the Freethinkers*. London, 1868.

Brookes, E.H. and Webb, C. de B. *A History of Natal*. Pietermaritzburg: University of Natal Press, 1965.

Burd, V.A. (ed.). *The Winnington Letters: John Ruskin's Correspondence with Margaret Alexis Bell and the Children at Winnington Hall*. Cambridge, Mass.: Harvard University Press, 1969.

Buthelezi, M.G. 'The Past and Future of the Zulu People', *Munger Africana Library Notes*, January 1972.

Caine, B. *Destined to be Wives: The Sisters of Beatrice Webb*. Oxford: Clarendon Press, 1986.

Campbell, W.Y. *With Cetywayo in the Inkandhla, and the Present State of the Zulu Question ...* Durban: P. Davis & Sons, 1883.

Cell, J. 'The Imperial Conscience', in P. Marsh (ed.), *The Conscience of the Victorian State*.

Syracuse: Syracuse University Press, 1979.

Colenso, F.E. [Zandile]. *Two Heroes*. Privately printed [1873].

Colenso, F.E. [Atherton Wylde]. *My Chief and I, or Six Months in Natal after the Langalibalele Outbreak*. London: Chapman & Hall, 1880.

[Colenso, F.E.]. 'A Royal Progress round Bishopstowe', *Macmillan's Magazine*, January 1881.

Colenso, F.E. *The Ruin of Zululand: An Account of British Doings in Zululand since the Invasion of 1879*. 2 vols. London, 1884–5.

Colenso, H.E. *Cases of Six Usutu Punished for Having Taken Part in the Disturbances of 1888*. London, 1893.

Colenso, H.E. *The Present Position among the Zulus (1893) with Some Suggestions for the Future*. London, 1893.

Colenso, H.E. *Zululand, the Exiled Chiefs, Natal and the Colonial Office 1893–1895*. London: Burt & Sons, n.d.

Colenso, H.E. 'The Problem of the Races in Africa', *The Imperial and Asiatic Quarterly Review*, 4, 7, July 1897.

Colenso, J.W. *First Steps of the Zulu Mission*, reprinted in R. Edgecombe (ed.), *John William Colenso: Bringing Forth Light – Five Tracts on Bishop Colenso's Zulu Mission*. Pietermaritzburg: University of Natal Press; Durban: Killie Campbell Africana Library, 1982.

Colenso, J.W. *Zulu–English Dictionary*. Fourth edition, edited and revised by H.E. Colenso. Natal: Vause, Slatter & Company, 1905.

Cope, N. *To Bind the Nation: Solomon kaDinuzulu and Zulu Nationalism 1913–1933*. Pietermaritzburg: University of Natal Press, 1993.

Cope, T. (ed.). *Izibongo: Zulu Praise-Poems*. Oxford: Clarendon Press, 1968.

Cope, R.L. 'Shepstone and Cetshwayo, 1873–1879'. MA thesis, University of Natal, 1967.

Cox, G.W. *The Life of John William Colenso, D.D., Bishop of Natal*. 2 vols. London: Ridgeway, 1888.

Darby, I. 'Anglican Worship in Victorian Natal'. MA thesis, University of Natal, 1977.

Duminy A.H. and Guest, W. (eds.). *Natal and Zululand from Earliest Times to 1910: A New History*. Pietermaritzburg: University of Natal Press and Shuter & Shooter, 1989.

Fuze, M.M. *The Black People and Whence They Came*. Pietermaritzburg: University of Natal Press; Durban: Killie Campbell Africana Library, 1979.

Guy, J. *The Destruction of the Zulu Kingdom: The Civil War in Zululand, 1879–1884*. London: Longman, 1979.

Guy, J. 'The Destruction and Reconstruction of Zulu Society', in S. Marks and R. Rathbone (eds.), *Industrialisation and Social Change in South Africa: African Class Formation, Culture and Consciousness 1870–1930*. Harlow: Longman, 1982.

Guy, J. *The Heretic: A Study of the Life of J.W. Colenso*. Johannesburg: Ravan Press; Pietermaritzburg: University of Natal Press, 1983.

Guy, J. 'Making Words Visible: Aspects of Orality, Literacy, Illiteracy and History in Southern Africa', *South African Historical Journal*, 31, November 1994.

Guy, J. 'Class, Imperialism and Literary Criticism: William Ngidi, John Colenso and Matthew Arnold', *Journal of Southern African Studies*, 23, 2, 1997.

Guy, J. 'Imperial Appropriations: The Dynamic History of *Iziqu*', *The Annals of the Natal Museum*, December 1999.

Hollis, P. *Ladies Elect: Women in English Government 1865–1914*. Oxford: Clarendon Press, 1987.

Hamilton, C. *Terrific Majesty: The Powers of Shaka Zulu and the Limits of Historical Invention*. Cape Town: David Philip, 1998.

James, R.R. *The British Revolution: British Politics 1880–1939. Vol. 1: From Gladstone to Asquith 1880–1914*. London: Hamish Hamilton, 1976.

Jeal, T. *Baden-Powell*. London: Hutchinson, 1989.

Judd, D. *Empire: The British Imperial Experience, from 1765 to the Present*. London: HarperCollins, 1996.

Kapp, Y. *Eleanor Marx: The Crowded Years 1884–1898*. London: Virago, 1976.

Kearney, B.T. 'A House for Harry: An Architect Looks at the Former Residence of Harry Escombe', *Natalia: Journal of the Natal Society*, 2, 1972.

Krueger, C.L. 'Clerical', in H.F. Tucker (ed.), *A Companion to Victorian Literature and Culture*. Oxford: Blackwell, 1999.

Laband, J. *Rope of Sand: The Rise and Fall of the Zulu Kingdom in the Nineteenth Century*. Johannesburg: Jonathan Ball, 1995.

Lago, M. (ed). *Burne-Jones Talking: His Conversations 1895–1898 Preserved by his Studio Assistant Thomas Rooke*. London: John Murray, 1982.

Levine, P. *Feminist Lives in Victorian England: Private Roles and Public Commitment*. Oxford: Basil Blackwell, 1990.

Mabin, A. and Conradie, B. (eds.). *The Confidence of the Whole Country: Standard Bank Reports on Economic Conditions in Southern Africa, 1865–1902*. Johannesburg: Standard Bank Investment Corporation, 1987.

Mamdani, M. *Citizen and Subject: Contemporary Africa and the Legacy of Late Colonialism*. Cape Town: David Philip, 1996.

Marks, S. 'Harriette Colenso and the Zulus 1874–1913', *Journal of African History*, 4, 3, 1963.

Marks, S. *Reluctant Rebellion: The 1906–8 Disturbances in Natal*. Oxford: Clarendon Press, 1970.

Marks, S. *The Ambiguities of Dependence in South Africa: Class, Nationalism, and the State in Twentieth-Century Natal*. Johannesburg: Ravan Press, 1986.

Martineau, J. *The Life and Correspondence of Sir Bartle Frere*. Vol. 2. London: John Murray, 1895.

Morris, J. *Pax Britannica: The Climax of an Empire*. London: Faber & Faber, 1968.

Nicholls, B.M. 'The Colenso Endeavour in Its Context 1887–1897'. Ph.D. thesis, University of Natal, 1997.

Packenham, E. *Jameson's Raid*. London: Weidenfeld & Nicolson, 1960.

Parsons, N. *King Khama, Emperor Joe and the Great White Queen: Victorian Britain through African Eyes*. Chicago and London: University of Chicago Press, 1998.

Preston, A. (ed.). *The South African Diaries of Sir Garnet Wolseley*. Cape Town: A.A. Balkema, 1971.

Rees, W. (ed.). *Colenso Letters from Natal*. Pietermaritzburg: Shuter & Shooter, 1958.

Rotberg, R.I. *The Founder: Cecil Rhodes and the Pursuit of Power*. Johannesburg: Southern Book Publishers, 1988.

Ruskin, J. *Sesame and Lilies*. Everyman's Library. London: J.W. Dent & Sons, 1970.

Samuelson, R.C.A. *Long, Long Ago*. Durban: Knox, 1929.

Schreuder, D.M. *Gladstone and Kruger*. London: Routledge & Kegan Paul, 1969.

Statham, F.R. *The Fiery Furnace*. London: Gibbings & Company, 1895.

Shepstone, T. 'The Native Question', *The Natal Mercury*, 29 January 1892, reprinted in *Natalia*, 2, 1972.

Smith, W.S. *The London Heretics 1870–1914*. London: Constable, 1967.

Stuart., J. *UKulumetule*. London: Longman, 1925.

Swan, M. *Gandhi: The South African Experience*. Johannesburg: Ravan Press, 1985.

Tower, C. *Harry Escombe and Natal*. Privately printed, 1990.

Vicinus, M. *Independent Women: Work and Community for Single Women 1850–1920*. London: Virago, 1985.

Walker, E.A. *W.P. Schreiner: A South African*. Johannesburg: Central News Agency, n.d.

Walker, L. 'Party Political Women: A Comparative Study of Liberal Women and the Primrose League 1890–1914', in J. Rendall (ed.), *Equal or Different: Women's Politics 1800–1914*. Oxford: Basil Blackwell, 1987.

Ware, V. *Beyond the Pale: White Women, Racism and History*. London and New York: Verso, 1992.

Webb, C. de B. and Wright, J.B. (eds.). *The James Stuart Archive*. Pietermaritzburg: University of Natal Press; Durban: Killie Campbell Africana Library. Vol. I, 1976; Vol. II, 1979; Vol. III, 1982; Vol. IV, 1986.

NOTES

Preface

1. S. Marks. 'Harriette Colenso and the Zulus, 1874–1913', *Journal of African History*, 4, 3, 1963. See especially her *Reluctant Rebellion: The 1906–8 Disturbances in Natal*. Oxford: Clarendon Press, 1970 and *The Ambiguities of Dependence in South Africa: Class, Nationalism, and the State in Twentieth-century Natal*. Johannesburg: Ravan Press, 1986.

Chapter 1

1. W.Y. Campbell, *With Cetywayo in the Inkandhla, and the Present State of the Zulu Question* ... Durban: P. Davis & Sons, 1883. 29.
2. NA. Sir Theophilus Shepstone collection. Osborn to T. Shepstone, 16 June 1883.
3. BPP. C4037. No. 44, Bulwer to Derby, 16 February 1884, enc. 1.
4. BPP. C4037. No. 16, Bulwer to Derby, 16 February 1884, enc. 1.
5. J.J. Guy, 'Making Words Visible: Aspects of Orality, Literacy, Illiteracy and History in Southern Africa', *South African Historical Journal*, 31 November 1994.
6. This section is based on BPP. C4037. No. 44, Bulwer to Derby, 16 February 1884.
7. Bulwer was wrong in this.
8. KC. Colenso collection. Harriette Colenso [hereafter HEC] to Frank Colenso, 10 February 1884.

Chapter 2

1. I have struggled to find suitable names to refer to both Sarah Frances Colenso and her second daughter, Frances Ellen. They were both known as Frances, but Frances Ellen was also known as Fanny to her friends, and later in her life to her intimate friends as Nelly. In this text I call the mother Sarah Frances – and her daughter Frances.
2. W. Rees (ed.), *Colenso Letters from Natal*. Pietermaritzburg: Shuter & Shooter, 1958. 201.
3. Rees (ed.), *Colenso Letters*. 120.
4. RH. MSS African. 1284. S.F. Colenso to Sophie Colenso, 19 August 1888.
5. Rees (ed.), *Colenso Letters*. 20.
6. Rees (ed.), *Colenso Letters*. 27.
7. J.J. Guy. *The Heretic: A study of the Life of J.W. Colenso*. Johannesburg: Ravan Press; Pietermaritzburg: University of Natal Press, 1983. 45.
8. Rees (ed.), *Colenso Letters*. 194.
9. Rees (ed.), *Colenso Letters*. 374.
10. Rees (ed.), *Colenso Letters*. 316.
11. Rees (ed.), *Colenso Letters*. 96.
12. J.J. Guy, 'Class, Imperialism and Literary Criticism: William Ngidi, John Colenso and Matthew Arnold', *Journal of Southern African Studies*, 23, 2, 1997.
13. KC. Colenso collection. J.W. Colenso to W.H.I. Bleek, 4 September 1861.
14. The notion that Colenso was a slight and comical figure remains so deeply embedded in the academic literature that nothing, it seems, will remove it. For a recent instance see C.L. Krueger, 'Clerical', in H.F. Tucker (ed.), *A Companion to Victorian Literature and Culture*. Oxford: Blackwell, 1999. 148.
15. Rees (ed.), *Colenso Letters*. 70, quoting

Georgiana Burne-Jones in E.T. Cook, *The Life of John Ruskin*, II. 101–2.

16. V.A. Burd (ed.), *The Winnington Letters: John Ruskin's Correspondence with Margaret Alexis Bell and the Children at Winnington Hall*. Cambridge, Mass.: Harvard University Press, 1969.

17. J. Ruskin, *Sesame and Lilies*. Everyman's Library. London: J.M. Dent & Sons, 1970. 67–8.

18. Burd, *Winnington Letters*. 414, John Ruskin to John James Ruskin, 8 August 1863, states that the conversation was with Frances but Ruskin gives Miss Colenso's age as 16 – Harriette's age at the time.

19. F.E. Colenso [Zandile], *Two Heroes*. Privately printed. Copy in the British Library inscribed 1873.

20. F.E. Colenso, *Two Heroes*. 25.

21. F.E. Colenso, *Two Heroes*. 145.

22. Rees (ed.), *Colenso Letters*. 99.

23. Rees (ed.), *Colenso Letters*. 131.

24. Rees (ed.), *Colenso Letters*. 207.

25. Rees (ed.), *Colenso Letters*. 248.

26. Rees (ed.), *Colenso Letters*. 130.

27. *New York Times*, 1 April 1883.

28. Rees (ed.), *Colenso Letters*. 107.

29. Rees (ed.), *Colenso Letters*. 192.

30. Rees (ed.), *Colenso Letters*. 193.

31. Rees (ed.), *Colenso Letters*. 218.

32. Rees (ed.), *Colenso Letters*. 220.

33. KC. Colenso collection. J.W. Colenso to Domville, 17 July 1869.

34. Rees (ed.), *Colenso Letters*. 227.

35. RH. MSS African. s. 1288. F.E. Colenso to Frank Colenso, August 1886.

36. Rees (ed.), *Colenso Letters*. 123.

Chapter 3

1. For two recent examples of this see M. Mamdani, *Citizen and Subject: Contemporary Africa and the Legacy of Late Colonialism*. Cape Town: David Philip; London: James Currey; Princeton: Princeton University Press, 1996; and C. Hamilton, *Terrific Majesty: The Powers of Shaka Zulu and the Limits of Historical Invention*. Cape Town: David Philip, 1998.

2. T. Cope (ed.), *Izibongo: Zulu Praise-Poems*. Oxford: Clarendon Press, 1968. 194–9.

3. This interpretation was originally suggested to me by the late Mosebi Damane, historian of nineteenth-century Lesotho.

4. J. Martineau, *The Life and Correspondence of Sir Bartle Frere*. London: John Murray, 1895. II, 304.

5. KC. Stuart papers. Miscellaneous notes collected by James Stuart for proposed life of Sir Theophilus Shepstone. Evidence of Lazarus Xaba.

6. BPP. C1141. Langalibalele and the Amahlubi Tribe ... Statement of Ndabezimbi, body-servant of Mahoyiza, when he went to Langalibalele. 107.

7. BPP. C1141. Langalibalele and the Amahlubi Tribe ... Note by Magema. 111.

8. BPP. C1141. Langalibalele and the Amahlubi Tribe ... Appendix V – The Appeal to the Lieutenant-Governor and the Executive Council. (iii) Examination of Ungwadhla and Umnyengeza.

9. BPP. C1141. Langalibalele and the Amahlubi Tribe .... J.W. Colenso to T. Shepstone, 10 March 1874.

10. Rees (ed.), *Colenso Letters*. 282.

11. Quoted in Guy, *The Heretic*. 218–19.

12. A. Preston (ed.), *The South African Diaries of Sir Garnet Wolseley, 1875*. Cape Town: A.A. Balkema, 1971. Entry for 6 May 1875. 176.

13. Rees (ed.), *Colenso Letters*. 314.

14. BPP. C1401 – I. No. 25, Bulwer to Carnarvon, 13 September 1875 and enclosures.

15. Rees (ed.), *Colenso Letters*. 315.

Chapter 4

1. Colenso, 'Extracts from the Blue Books'. 843. These printed documents from the Bishopstowe press have yet to be formally organised. I refer to the system I use in the Bibliography.

2. BPP. C2079. No. 39, T. Shepstone to Carnarvon, 5 January 1878.

3. M. Magwaza, 'A Visit to King Ketshwayo', *Macmillan's Magazine*, 1877–8.

4. Guy, *The Heretic*. 287–8.

5. F.E. Colenso [Atherton Wylde], *My Chief and I, or Six Months in Natal after the Langalibalele Outbreak*. London: Chapman & Hall, 1880.

6. M. Lago (ed.), *Burne-Jones Talking: His Conversations 1895–1898 Preserved by his Studio Assistant Thomas Rooke*. London: John Murray, 1982. 30–1.

7. RH. AS papers. 130/29. F.E. Colenso to Chesson, 11 July 1881.

8. NA. Sir Theopilus Shepstone collection. A.W. Durnford to T. Shepstone, 15 August 1877.

9. NA. Sir Theophilus Shepstone collection. T. Shepstone to A.W. Durnford, 17 September 1877.

10. KC. Colenso collection. HEC to Frank Colenso, 11 December [1877?].

11. KC. Colenso collection. HEC to Chesson, 2 September 1879.

12. KC. Colenso collection. HEC to Chesson, 6 September 1879.

13. KC. Colenso collection. HEC to Chesson, 31 August 1879.

14. KC. Colenso collection. HEC to Chesson, 26 October 1879.

15. G.W. Cox, *The Life of John William Colenso, D.D. Bishop of Natal*. London: Ridgeway, 1888. II, 538–9.

16. KC. Colenso collection. HEC to Chesson, 9 November 1879.

17. Colenso, 'Extracts from the Blue Books'. 607–8 and 690–6.

18. Colenso, 'Extracts from the Blue Books'. 739.

19. 'A Royal Zulu Progress over Bishopstowe', *Macmillan's Magazine*, January 1881.

20. Colenso, *First Steps of the Zulu Mission*, reprinted in R. Edgecombe (ed.), *John William Colenso: Bringing Forth Light – Five Tracts on Bishop Colenso's Zulu Mission*. Pietermaritzburg: University of Natal Press; Durban: Killie Campbell Africana Library, 1982. 76.

21. Colenso, 'Digest on Zulu Affairs'. 749–50.

22. J.J. Guy, *The Destruction of the Zulu Kingdom: The Civil War in Zululand, 1879–1884*. London: Longman, 1979. 127.

23. PRO. CO 179/138. 19985. Minute by Kimberley.

24. PRO. CO 179/140. 1848. Memorandum by T. Shepstone, December 1881.

25. BPP. C3466. No. 57, Cetshwayo to Kimberley, 18 August 1882.

26. KC. Colenso collection. HEC to Chesson, 6 March 1881.

27. KC. Colenso collection. HEC to Chesson, 28 January 1882.

28. KC. Colenso collection. HEC to Chesson, 9 July 1882.

29. Guy, *Destruction*. 164.

30. Colenso, 'Digest on Zulu Affairs'. 409.

31. Guy, *Destruction*. 185.

Chapter 5

1. Rees (ed.), *Colenso Letters*. 374.

2. KC. Colenso collection. F.E. Colenso to Chesson, 30 June 1883.

3. KC. Colenso collection. F.E. Colenso to Chesson, 23 September 1883.

4. KC. Colenso collection. F.E. Colenso to Chesson, 30 June 1883.

5. KC. Colenso collection. HEC to Chesson, 24 June 1883.

6. RH. MSS African. s. 1288. F.E. Colenso to Sophie Colenso, 9 July 1883.

7. RH. MSS African. s. 1285. (1) Frank Colenso (quoting his mother) to Sophie Frankland, 14 August 1876.

8. Colenso, 'Digest on Zulu Affairs'. 739–40.

9. Colenso, 'Digest on Zulu Affairs'. 740.

10. KC. Colenso collection. HEC to Chesson, 27 July 1883.

11. KC. Colenso collection. HEC to Chesson, 22 July 1883.

12. RH. MSS African. s. 1286. HEC to Chesson, 30 October 1883.

13. RH. AS papers. 130/80. HEC to Chesson, 12 August 1883.

14. Colenso, 'Digest on Zulu Affairs'. 837.

15. Thwayisa Mabaso, 'headman of the Bishop's chief Mission Station of Ekukhanyeni (Bishopstowe), with his attendant Letshe, and Mubi Nondenisa, of the Bishop's printers, who had been with him from a child, and was able to keep a

rough journal'. Colenso, 'Digest on Zulu Affairs'. 830. The translation of this journal can be found on 832–42. Magema in his book refers to Bubi Mthuli kaNondenisa and Thwayisa kaQambi Mabaso. I have followed Harriette Colenso and use Mubi and Thwayisa.

16. Or perhaps 5th, the diary is not very clear.

17. Colenso, 'Digest on Zulu Affairs'. 837.

18. PRO. CO 179/145. 614. Bulwer to Derby, 12 January 1883 (telegram).

19. NA. ZGH 844. Bulwer to Derby, 19 and 21 August 1883 (telegrams).

20. PRO. CO 179/146. 15114. Minute.

Chapter 6

1. BPP. C3864. No. 92, Bulwer to Derby, 1 October 1883, enc. 4 Osborn to Bulwer, 20 September 1883, Cetshwayo to Osborn, 20 September 1882.

2. NA. ZGH 690. Rudolph to Bulwer, 7 July 1884.

3. BPP. C3864. No. 80, Bulwer to Derby, 17 September 1883, enc. Osborn to Bulwer, 5 September 1883, Statement by Mfanawendlela, 3 September 1883.

4. BPP. C4037. No. 14, APS to Colonial Office, 14 February 1884, enc. 3, 8 January 1884.

5. PRO. CO 179/151. 2478. Bulwer to Derby, 15 January 1884 (confidential).

6. Quoted in D.M. Schreuder, *Gladstone and Kruger*. London: Routledge & Kegan Paul, 1969. 393.

7. BPP. C4191. No. 9, Bulwer to Derby, 6 May 1884, enc. Osborn to Bulwer, 25 April 1884.

8. An account of the difficulties in treating the documentation of the 'Boer movement' into Zululand would require an essay in itself. Reference to this visit was removed from the Governor's report when it was published in the Blue Book as BPP. C3864. No. 50, Bulwer to Derby, 14 September 1883. Part of the excised portion reads 'there is no doubt that Cetshwayo has been in negotiations with persons in the Transvaal state' and can be found in PRO. CO 179/147.

9. The early history of Dinuzulu, like the history of the man himself, is in dispute. The

paragraphs which follow draw on various sources. For his (uncertain) year of birth see NA. Colenso collection [Box 174], note in HEC's hand, where it is given as December 1869, although it might have been a year earlier. For the official report on his origins see BPP. C4587. No. 43, Bulwer to Derby, 3 March 1885, enc. Memorandum by Osborn, 6 February 1885.

10. C. de B. Webb and J.B. Wright (eds.), *The James Stuart Archive*. Pietermaritzburg: University of Natal Press; Durban: Killie Campbell Africana Library, 1982. III. Evidence of Mkebeni, 200ff.

11. Webb and Wright (eds.), *The James Stuart Archive*. IV. Evidence of Ndabazezwe, 191–2.

12. This section is based on the documents collected by Bulwer on the origins of the Boer movement. They were forwarded to Havelock. NA. GH 699. Herbert to Havelock, 11 March 1886, confidential. See also NA. ZGH 695, Mitchell to Stanley, 12 December 1885, confidential, Statement by Coenraad Frederick Meyer to St Vincent Erskine, 29 November 1885.

13. Nonetheless, in this book I continue to use 'Boer' without quotation marks. So long as one is aware of the shortcomings of the name, it covers the movement well enough for the level of generalisation required here – and what other name could be used? We cannot follow Harriette Colenso and call them 'filibusters'. At the same time the differences between these men must always be kept in mind. For while it might cover a majority of the people involved, on the borders, in search of land, and was used at the time, it does not cover them all and can become a misleadingly simple, racial epithet.

14. From *The Natal Mercantile Advertiser* written in mid-1883 and reprinted in Colenso, 'Digest on Zulu Affairs'. 680.

15. NA. Colenso collection. HEC to Dixie, 26 October 1885[?].

16. In his old age Maphelu left an account of these events now in the papers of the Zulu

Society in the Natal Archives. Although obviously an account from the perspective of a man living, working and fighting in a very particular part of Zululand, and place in its political structure, it is extraordinary in its details, which time and again confirm or explain passages in the contemporary documents. I have used and adapted translations done by a number of students at Roma, Lesotho, in the early 1970s.

17. Although it is quite possible that exaggerated prominence was given to Mnyamana's opposition to the alliance with the Boers, in order to provide a way out in the event of future disagreement, this does not mean that evidence of his opposition was fabricated after the event. Mnyamana's opposition is consistent in all the accounts, and even if this were not so, the question would remain why Maphelu should sustain this distortion over half a century later.

18. See p. 89. We don't know who did it – but we do know that a year later Mehlokazulu threatened a man with the messengers' fate. KC. Shepstone collection. Folder F. Magwaza to the SNA, 5 June 1885.

19. Colenso, series 3. Statement by Melakhanya, 13 January 1885. 5.

20. BPP. C4037. No. 65, Bulwer to Derby, 12 April 1884; C4191. No. 8, Bulwer to Derby, 28 April 1884, enc. Osborn to Bulwer, 22 April 1884, Statement by Zibhebhu's messengers.

21. BPP. C4191. No. 31, Bulwer to Derby, 20 May 1884, enc. Committee of Dinuzulu's Volunteers to Hamu, 1 May 1884; and No. 70, Bulwer to Derby, 17 June 1884. A. Committee of Dinuzulu's Volunteers to Zibhebhu, 1 May 1884.

22. Colenso, series 3. Statement by Melakhanya, 13 January 1885. 9.

23. NA. Maphelu, 48.

24. For information on the installation that reached the Natal authorities see BPP. C4191. No. 7a, Bulwer to Derby, 28 May 1884 (telegram); and No. 54, Bulwer to Derby, 31 May 1884, enc. Pretorius to Bulwer, 25 May 1884; C4214. No. 4,

Bulwer to Derby, 15 July 1884, enc. Schiel to Colonial Secretary, Natal, Proclamation, 21 May 1883.

25. There are many examples in BPP. C4191.

26. BPP. C4191. No. 66, Bulwer to Derby, 16 June 1884.

27. BPP. C4191. No. 82, Derby to Bulwer, 19 August 1884.

28. These figures are, of course, very rough estimates from sources which vary tremendously.

29. KC. Colenso collection. J.W. Colenso to Chesson, 12 March 1880.

30. KC. Colenso collection. HEC to Chesson, 30 September 1883.

31. Colenso, 'Digest on Zulu Affairs'. 715.

32. RH. AS papers. 136/12. Grant to Chesson, 24 June 1883.

33. KC. Colenso collection. HEC to Chesson, 8 July 1883.

34. KC. Colenso collection. HEC to Chesson, 24 August 1883.

35. RH. AS papers. 136/83. Grant to Chesson, 17 July 1884.

36. RH. AS papers. 136/84. Grant to Chesson, 1 August 1884.

37. Colenso, series 3. Grant to HEC, 26 August 1884. 24.

38. Colenso, series 3. Grant to HEC, 26 August 1884. 22.

39. BPP. C4214. No. 44, Bulwer to Derby, 26 August 1884, enc. *The Natal Mercantile Advertiser*, 26 August 1884.

40. BPP. C4913. No. 1, Memorandum by Bulwer, 14 January 1886. 8.

41. The wording in the proclamation.

42. Colenso, series 3. Grant to HEC, 26 August 1883. 24.

43. I. Darby, 'Anglican Worship in Victorian Natal'. MA thesis, University of Natal, 1977. Chapter 14.

44. Rees (ed.), *Colenso Letters*. 339.

45. RH. AS papers. 130/41. F.E. Colenso to Chesson, 30 September 1884.

46. RH. AS papers. 131/92. Grant to Chesson, 4 February 1885, although it is not quite clear whether this passage is from this letter or 131/92g.

Chapter 7

1. BPP. C4274. No. 44, Bulwer to Derby, 25 November 1884.
2. BPP. C4587. No. 74, Bulwer to Derby, 7 April 1885; and BPP. C4274. No. 36, Bulwer to Derby, 11 November 1884.
3. BPP. C4037. No. 59, Bulwer to Derby, 10 March 1884; and No. 75, Bulwer to Derby, 31 March 1884.
4. BPP. C4191. No. 11, Bulwer to Derby, 6 May 1884, enc. 3, Osborn to Bulwer, 28 April 1884.
5. The public reports on these events as published in BPP. C4191 do not reveal the full extent of the ferocious and undiscriminating nature of these attacks by the administration's allies, Hlubi Molife and John Dunn, which can be found in PRO. CO 179/152.
6. NA. ZA 2. 38, Bulwer to Osborn, 21 July 1884.
7. PRO. CO 179/153. Minute by Fairfield, 20 August 1884 on Bulwer to Derby, 15 July 1884.
8. BPP. C4214. No. 23, Bulwer to Derby, 22 July 1884, enc. 2, Bulwer to Osborn, 5 August 1884.
9. BPP. C4214. No. 18, Derby to Bulwer, 30 August 1884 (telegram).
10. BPP. C4214. No. 62, Bulwer to Derby, 9 September 1884, enc. Osborn to Bulwer, 4 September 1884, 'Message from the General to the Chiefs, Headmen, and People of the Nkandhla'.
11. BPP. C4274. No. 10, War Office to Colonial Office, 30 October 1884, enc. Smyth to Secretary of State for War, 19 September 1884.
12. 'The gloom has deepened'. Editorial comment in Alan Mabin and Barbara Conradie (eds.), *The Confidence of the Whole Country: Standard Bank Reports on Economic Conditions in Southern Africa, 1865–1902*. Johannesburg: Standard Bank Investment Corporation, 1987. 150.
13. Einwald's letters to Bulwer are in NA. ZGH 690 and 693 and were summarised in PRO. CO 179/154. 865. Bulwer to Derby,

16 December 1884, confidential.
14. PRO. CO 179/154. 22242. Bulwer to Derby, 1 December 1884, confidential, enc. A. Schiel to Bulwer, 19 November 1884 (translation).
15. Minute by Herbert on PRO. CO 179/153. 18948. Bulwer to Fairfield, 22 September 1884, confidential.
16. BPP. C4587. No. 13, Admiralty to Colonial Office, 24 January 1884, enclosure.
17. Reports on the surveying of Zululand make up a considerable part of BPP. C4587.
18. BPP. C4587. No. 31, Bulwer to Derby, 3 February 1885, enc. Topham to Private Secretary.

Chapter 8

1. RH. MSS African. s. 1284. S.F. Colenso to Frank Colenso, 21 October 1883.
2. RH. MSS African. s. 1284. S.F. Colenso to Frank Colenso, n.d.
3. RH. MSS African. s. 1286. HEC to Frank Colenso, 8 September 1884.
4. RH. MSS African. s. 1286. HEC to Frank Colenso, 8 September 1884, postscript by S.F. Colenso.
5. RH. MSS African. s. 1284, S.F. Colenso to Sophie Colenso, 19 October 1884.
6. NA. Colenso collection. HEC to Cox, 8 November 1885.
7. NA. Sir Theophilus Shepstone collection. File 21. T. Shepstone to Wheeler, 4 November 1885.
8. NA. Colenso collection [Box 158]. Undated fragment in Frances Colenso's hand.
9. RH. MSS African. s. 1284. S.F. Colenso to Sophie Colenso, 14 December 1884.
10. KC. Colenso collection. J.W. Colenso to Chesson, 28 April 1883.
11. KC. Colenso collection. HEC to Chesson, 22 July 1883.

Chapter 9

1. NA. Colenso collection. HEC to Chesson, 10 February 1885.
2. BPP. C4587. No. 46, Bulwer to Derby, 9 March 1885, enc. 1, Statement of Siziba and

Mkhosi.
3. BPP. C4587. No. 40, Bulwer to Derby, 23 February 1885.
4. BPP. C4587. No. 46, Bulwer to Derby, 9 March 1885, enc. 2, Reply to message, 7 March 1885.
5. KC. Shepstone papers. T. Shepstone to Bulwer, 15 June 1884.
6. BPP. C4645. No. 5, Bulwer to Derby, 30 June 1885, enc. 2, Reply to message from Mnyamana and other Zulu chiefs, 30 June 1885.
7. BPP. C4587. No. 106, Bulwer to Derby, 12 June 1885.
8. RH. MSS African. s. 1284. S.F. Colenso to Frank Colenso, 30 October 1885.
9. CO. Confidential Print. African No. 300. Memorandum on Zulu Affairs. See also PRO. CO 179/157. 11468. Minute by Fairfield, 13 July 1885 on Bulwer to Derby, 1 June 1885.
10. PRO. CO 179/157. 14037. Minute by Herbert, 12 August 1885, on Bulwer to Stanley, 11 August 1885 (telegram).
11. BPP. C4587. No. 94, Bulwer to Derby, 26 June 1885 (telegram); BPP. C4645. No. 7, Bulwer to Derby, 21 July 1885, and No. 13, Bulwer to Derby, 28 July 1885.
12. KC. Shepstone papers. Folder M. Meek to J.W. Shepstone, 4 August 1885.
13. RH. AS papers. 130/256. HEC to Chesson, 4 August 1885.
14. BPP. C4645. No. 52, Mitchell to Stanley, 15 December 1885, enclosures and map.
15. BPP. C4645, No. 49, Stanley to Mitchell, 4 January 1886.
16. RH. AS papers. 131/3. HEC to Chesson, 23 February 1886.
17. Accounts of Boer intimidation at this time can be found in R.C.A. Samuelson, *Long, Long Ago*. Durban: Knox, 1929. 127–8 and 129–36. NA. ZGH 696 contains numerous accounts from different sources. Many of these reached the Colonial Office and the Cabinet. See PRO. CO 179/163. 4070. Mitchell to Stanley, 8 February 1886, confidential; and 4071. Mitchell to Stanley, 11 February 1886, confidential; and PRO. CO

879/25/329. No. 135, Havelock to Stanley, 1 March 1886, confidential.
18. NA. ZGH 696. ZA 38. Osborn to Mitchell, 17 February 1886, Statement by messengers sent by Dinuzulu, Ndabuko, and Mnyamana to Resident Commissioner, 16 February 1886.
19. BPP. C4913. No. 1, Bulwer, 'Memorandum on the Situation in the Zulu Country', 6 January 1886.
20. BPP. C4913. No. 1, Bulwer, 'Memorandum'. 3.
21. BPP. C4913. No. 1, Bulwer, 'Memorandum'. 4.
22. BPP. C4913. No. 1, Bulwer, 'Memorandum'. 8.
23. BPP. C4913. No. 1, Bulwer, 'Memorandum'. 10.
24. BPP. C4913. No. 1, Bulwer, 'Memorandum'. 12.
25. BPP. C4913. No. 2, Bulwer, 'Further Memorandum on the Situation in Central Zululand ...', 14 January 1886.
26. PRO. CO 179/166. 298, 1500. Minutes on Bulwer's memorandums.
27. RH. AS papers. C131/3. HEC to Chesson, 23 February 1886.

Chapter 10
1. NA. Sir Theophilus Shepstone collection. Havelock to T. Shepstone, 7 March 1886.
2. RH. MSS African. s. 1284. S.F. Colenso to Frank Colenso, 3 April 1886.
3. BPP. C4913. No. 25, Havelock to Granville, 23 March 1886 (extract), enc. 1, Statement by Mfunzi and Martin Luthuli, 5 March 1886.
4. PRO. CO 879/25. 329. No. 24, Granville to Havelock, 12 March 1886 (telegram).
5. BPP. C4913. No. 25, Havelock to Granville, 23 March 1886 (extract), enc. 2, Reply by Havelock, 22 March 1886.
6. NA. ZGH 697. ZA 76. Cardew to Havelock, 18 March 1896. Statement by Ndabuko, Shingana and other chiefs, 17 March 1886.
7. BPP. C4913. No. 16, Granville to Havelock, 11 March 1886.
8. NA. Colenso collection. HEC to Jorrissen,

25 March 1886.
9. NA. ZGH 697. ZA 79. HEC to Havelock, 30 March 1886 and enclosures.
10. RH. AS papers. C131/7. HEC to Chesson, 6 April 1886.
11. RH. AS papers. C131/8. HEC to Chesson, 13 April 1886.
12. BPP. C4587. No. 106, Bulwer to Derby, 12 June 1885.
13. NA. Colenso collection. Grant to HEC, 13 April 1886.
14. RH. AS papers. C131/9. HEC to Chesson, 4 May 1886.
15. NA. Colenso collection. Grant to HEC, 3 May 1886.
16. NA. Colenso collection. HEC to Grant, 6 May 1886.
17. BPP. C4913. No. 50, Havelock to Granville, 23 May 1886, enc. 1, Zulu deputation interview, 7 May 1886.
18. BPP. C4913. No. 50, Havelock to Granville, 23 May 1886, enc. 2, Zulu deputation interview, 10 May 1886. 93.
19. RH. AS papers. C131/10. HEC to Chesson, 10 May 1886.
20. BPP. C4913. No. 54, Havelock to Granville, 31 May 1886, enc. 1, Statement by Ndabuko, Shingana and others, 18 May 1886. 99.
21. NA. ZGH 698. ZA 138. HEC to Havelock, 17 May 1886, 'Notes on letter'.
22. RH. AS papers. 131/14. HEC to Chesson, 30 May 1886.
23. RH. MSS African. s. 1284. S.F. Colenso to Frank, n.d., but internal evidence places it in mid-1886.
24. RH. AS papers. 131/21. HEC to Chesson, 20 July 1886.
25. BPP. C4980. No. 3, Havelock to Granville, 10 July 1886, enc. 3, Extract from *The Natal Mercantile Advertiser*, 6 July 1886.
26. BPP. C4980. No. 3, Havelock to Granville, 10 July 1886.
27. BPP. C4913. No. 55, Havelock to Granville, 8 June 1886 and enclosures.
28. BPP. C4980. No. 16, Havelock to Granville, 6 September 1886, enc. 1, Luthuli to Havelock, 4 August 1886.

29. BPP. C4980. No. 16, Havelock to Granville, 6 September 1886, enc. 4, Message from Havelock, 6 September 1886.
30. PRO. CO 179/164. 14420. Havelock to Granville, 10 July 1886, Minute by Herbert, 18 August 1886.
31. BPP. C4980. No. 8, Stanhope to Havelock, 9 September 1886.
32. BPP. C4980. No. 17, Havelock to Granville, 6 September 1886, enc. Havelock to Meyer, 6 September 1886.
33. BPP. C4980. No. 26, Havelock to Stanhope, 27 September 1886, enc. Cardew to Havelock, 24 September 1886, 'Umzingeli's statement', 23 September 1886. See also the documents collected in NA. ZGH 699, ZA 301 and ZA 302.
34. BPP. C4980. No. 42, Havelock to Stanhope, 24 October 1886.

Chapter 11
1. RH. MSS African. s. 1288. F.E. Colenso to Frank Colenso, 9 August 1886.
2. NA. Colenso collection. Burne-Jones to F.E. Colenso, 15 January 1886. Written on 17 January 1886.
3. NA. Colenso collection. Box 6, Burne-Jones to F.E. Colenso, 29 July 1886.
4. NA. Colenso collection. Burne-Jones to F.E. Colenso, 17 August 1886.
5. NA. Colenso collection. Luard to F.E. Colenso, 5 September 1886.
6. RH. AS papers. 130/59. F.E. Colenso to Chesson, 14 September 1886.
7. RH. AS papers. 130/70. F.E. Colenso to Chesson, 18 December 1886.
8. RH. MSS African. s. 1288. F.E. Colenso to Sophie Colenso, 19 November 1886.
9. NA. Colenso collection. Burne-Jones to HEC, 6 January 1887.
10. Colenso, series 5. HEC to Havelock, 1 November 1886.
11. BPP. C4980. No. 62, Havelock to Stanhope, 19 November 1866, enc. 6, Notes of interview between Havelock and Zulu deputation, 10 November 1886.
12. BPP. C4980. No. 62, Havelock to

Stanhope, 19 November 1866, enc. 7,
Second interview, 11 November 1886.
13. BPP. C4980. No. 62, Havelock to
Stanhope, 19 November 1866, enc. 10,
Martin Luthuli (for Shingana and others)
to Her Majesty the Queen, 11 November
1886.
14. BPP. C4980. No. 62, Havelock to
Stanhope, 19 November 1866, enc. 7,
Second interview, 11 November 1886.
15. RH. AS papers. 131/38. HEC to Chesson,
16 November 1886.
16. BPP. C4980. No. 62, Havelock to
Stanhope, 19 November 1886.
17. BPP. C4980. No. 63, Havelock to
Stanhope, 19 November 1886, enc. 1,
HEC to Havelock, 13 November 1886.
18. BPP. C4980. No. 63, Havelock to
Stanhope, 19 November 1886, enc. 2,
Minute by Osborn, 16 November 1886.
19. NA. Colenso collection. HEC to Professor
Kuenen, 7 November 1886.
20. RH. MSS African. s. 1288. F.E. Colenso to
Sophie Colenso, 3 December 1886.
21. RH. AS papers. 130/70. F.E. Colenso to
Chesson, 18 December 1886.
22. RH. MSS African. s. 1288. F.E. Colenso to
Sophie Colenso, 26 November 1886.
23. RH. AS papers. 130/73. F.E. Colenso to
Chesson, 15 January 1887.
24. RH. AS papers. 130/82. F.E. Colenso to
Chesson, 24 February 1887.
25. NA. Colenso collection. F.E. Colenso to
S.F. Colenso, 12 January 1887.
26. RH. AS papers. 131/71. HEC to Chesson,
8 June 1887.
27. RH. AS papers. 131/64. HEC to Chesson,
2 April 1887.
28. NA. Colenso collection. Chesson to F.E.
Colenso and HEC, 16 and 24 March 1887.
29. RH. AS papers. 130/84. F.E. Colenso to
Chesson, 18 March 1887.
30. RH. MSS African. s. 1288. F.E. Colenso to
Sophie Colenso, 26 November 1886.
31. NA. Colenso collection. F.E. Colenso to
S.F. Colenso, 12 April 1887.
32. RH. MSS African. s. 1288. S.F. Colenso to
F.E. Colenso, n.d.

33. RH. MSS African.s. 1286. HEC to F.E.
Colenso, 17 April 1887.
34. NA. Colenso collection. Durnford to F.E.
Colenso, 27 April 1887.
35. NA. Colenso collection. Chesson to S.F.
Colenso, 3 May 1887.
36. RH. MSS African. s. 1286. HEC to F.E.
Colenso, 11 May 1887.
37. RH. MSS African. s. 1284. S.F. Colenso to
Frank Colenso, 11 May 1887.
38. RH. AS papers. C130. F.E. Colenso to
Chesson, 9 February 1887.
39. *Pall Mall Gazette*, 8 February 1887.
40. RH. AS papers. C130. F.E. Colenso to
Chesson, 15 January 1887. I have replaced
'solely' in original with 'slowly'.

Chapter 12
1. RH. AS papers. 131/38. HEC to Chesson,
16 November 1886.
2. NA. Maphelu, 66.
3. NA. ZGH 701. ZA 412. Statement of
Swayimana to S.O. Samuelson, 8 December
1886.
4. BPP. C4980. No. 22, Havelock to Stanhope,
22 October 1886 (telegram).
5. PRO. CO 179/165. 19519. Stanhope to
Havelock, 2 November 1886 (draft
telegram).
6. PRO. CO 179/165. 22173. Havelock to
Stanhope, 9 November 1886, confidential.
7. We have different accounts of this important meeting. Osborn's account is in BPP.
C4980. No. 97, Havelock to Stanhope, 9
January 1887, enc. 1, Osborn to Havelock, 3
January 1887, but is significant mainly for
what it leaves out. BPP. C5143. No. 7, enc.
1, Osborn to Havelock, 17 January 1887. 20,
has a number of paragraphs which sum-
marise the protests, but they are buried
without comment in this long report and
diary of the Boundary Commission. NA.
ZGH 702. ZA 37. H.A. Warren to Private
Secretary to the Governor, 8 January 1887,
has an account from Mnyamana of the
meeting. Yamela, Osborn's chief induna,
gave an account of the meeting in his evidence at the trial before the Court of

Special Commissioners (CSC), evidence of Yamela, 333. NA. Maphelu, 66–9 has a full account which in essence is confirmed by the contemporary records.

8. CSC. Evidence of Yamela, 333.
9. NA. ZA 4. Osborn to Havelock, 13 January 1887, confidential.
10. BPP. C4980. No. 97, Havelock to Stanhope, 9 January 1887. 178.
11. BPP. C4980. No. 105, Havelock to Stanhope, 13 January 1887, enc. Havelock to Osborn, 13 January 1887.
12. BPP. C5143. No. 7, Havelock to Stanhope, 8 February 1887, enc. Osborn to Havelock, 17 January 1887.
13. NA. ZGH. ZA 4. Havelock to Osborn, 13 January 1887, confidential.
14. It is significant that there is very little official documentation on this crucial fortnight at the end of January and the beginning of February. Osborn's own account in BPP. C5143. No. 10, Havelock to Holland, 21 February 1887, enc. 1, Osborn to Havelock, 8 February 1887 is inadequate and that of his induna Yamela in CSC. 332ff is confused.
15. BPP. C5143. No. 10, Havelock to Holland, 21 February 1887, enc. 1, Osborn to Havelock, 8 February 1887.
16. NA. ZGH 702. ZA 50. Osborn to Havelock, 4 February 1887, confidential.
17. NA. ZGH 702. ZA 52. Osborn to Havelock, 8 February 1887, confidential.
18. BPP. C5143. No. 10, Havelock to Holland, 21 February 1887, enc. 1, Osborn to Havelock, 8 February 1887.
19. BPP. C5143. No. 10, Havelock to Stanhope, 9 February 1887, enc. 3, T. Shepstone, Memorandum on the Zulu situation, 17 February 1887.
20. BPP. C4980. No. 107, Havelock to Holland, 16 February 1887 (telegram).
21. BPP. C4980. No. 108, Holland to Havelock, 18 February 1887 (telegram).
22. PRO. CO 179/170. 4614. Minute by Holland, 11 March 1887, on HEC to Holland, 6 February 1887.
23. PRO. CO 179/170. 5550. Minute by

Fairfield, 22 March 1887, on Havelock to Holland, 21 February 1887.
24. PRO. CO 179/170. 8806. Confidential Print. 'The Annexation of Zululand'.
25. BPP. C5331. No. 2, Havelock to Holland, 26 June 1887, enc. 1, Zululand II, Laws and Regulations for the Government of Zululand.
26. BPP. C5331. No. 2, Havelock to Holland, 26 June 1887, enc. 3, Memorandum by T. Shepstone, 23 April 1887.
27. BPP. C5331. No. 1, Havelock to Holland, 26 June 1887 and enclosure.
28. NA. ZGH 704. ZA 157. Secretary of State to Havelock, 28 March 1887.
29. PRO. CO 179/161. Minutes on Mitchell to Stanley, 20 November 1885.
30. PRO. CO 427/1. 14884. Havelock to Holland, 28 June 1887.
31. BPP. C4153. No. 45, Havelock to Holland, 26 June 1887.
32. BPP. C4153. No. 45, Havelock to Holland, 26 June 1887, enc. Osborn to Havelock, 22 June 1887.
33. The one well-known chief known to be associated with the Usuthu who did attend was Siganada, who lived nearby and was also at the time in dispute with the Usuthu leadership over the possession of cattle seized at Etshaneni.
34. PRO. CO 427/1. 12617. Havelock to Holland, 30 May 1887, confidential.
35. CSC. Evidence of Vusindlu, 770–1.
36. CSC. Evidence of Yamela, 336.
37. BPP. C5331. No. 7, Havelock to Holland, 20 July 1887, enc. Osborn to Havelock, 16 July 1887.
38. NA. Maphelu, 74. Maphelu's account of this meeting is crucial. As a transcript of an oral account made many years after the event, the precise chronology and detail do not necessarily reflect those of the contemporary written sources. Nonetheless, its insights are invaluable. The most significant conflict lies in the fact that Maphelu assumes that it had already been officially announced before this meeting that Zibhebhu was to be allowed to return to

Mandlakazi. This assumption colours all the debates at the meeting, as remembered by Maphelu. Although the official announcement had not yet been made, I believe that it was widely suspected by the Usuthu that he would be allowed to return, and I have written the narrative accordingly.

39. CSC. Evidence of Tshanibezwe, 311.

Chpater 13

1. CSC. Evidence of Tshanibezwe, 315–16.
2. An agreement was reached between the South African Republic and the New Republic for formal union under the South African Republic in September 1887. This was ratified by Britain in June 1888. I use the informal, but I feel more realistic, 'Transvaal' when referring to the land on the other side of the new Zululand boundary.
3. NA. ZGH 706. ZA 178. Osborn to Havelock, 16 August 1887, enc. Knight to Osborn, 14 August 1887, confidential; and ZA 168. Osborn to Havelock, 12 August 1887, Addison to Osborn, 8 August 1887, confidential.
4. NA. ZGH 706. ZA 179. Osborn to Havelock, 17 August 1887, Addison to Osborn, 14 August 1887.
5. NA. ZGH 706. ZA 180. Osborn to Havelock, 17 August 1887.
6. BPP. C5331. No. 16, Havelock to Holland, 31 August 1887.
7. BPP. C5331. No. 18, Havelock to Holland, 14 September 1887.
8. NA. ZGH 720. Z 227. Dumat and Campbell to Havelock, 18 March 1889, containing Osborn to Havelock, 9 September 1887.
9. CSC. Evidence of Vusindlu, 773. This account is based on Vusindlu's evidence and that of William Stewart Lecky, 829–32.
10. NA. ZGH 720. Z 227. Dumat and Campbell to Havelock, 18 March 1889, and Osborn to Havelock, 12 September 1887.
11. BPP. C5331. No. 26, Havelock to Holland, 8 October 1887, enc. Osborn to Havelock,

21 September 1887.
12. BPP. C5331. No. 26, Havelock to Holland, 8 October 1887.
13. For Paul Mthimkhulu see NA. Colenso collection. Notes on quarto paper in HEC's hand [Box 87].
14. NA. ZGH 708. Z 294. Dinuzulu to the 'Great Minister living at the Umlazi', 7 October 1887.
15. BPP. C5331. No. 30, Havelock to Holland, 20 October 1887, enc. 1, Message to Havelock from Dinuzulu, Mnyamana, Ndabuko by Siziba and Pakade, taken by H.C. Shepstone, 11 October 1887.
16. BPP. C5331. No. 30, Havelock to Holland, 20 October 1887, enc. 2, Reply of Havelock to the message from the Zulu chiefs, 18 October 1887.
17. RH. AS papers. 130/73. F.E. Colenso to Chesson, 15 January 1887.
18. PRO. CO 179/165. 21853. Havelock to Stanhope, 1 December 1886 (telegram).
19. BPP. C5331. No. 9, Havelock to Holland, 3 August 1887, enc. 4, Memorandum by Sir T. Shepstone, 31 July 1887.
20. NA. Sir Theophilus Shepstone collection. Havelock to T. Shepstone, 3 August 1887.
21. PRO. CO 179/170. 6059. Minute by Fairfield, 31 March 1887, on Osborn to Havelock, 19 February 1887, in Havelock to Holland, 26 February 1887.
22. PRO. CO 427/1. 17487. Minute by Fairfield, 3 September 1887, on Havelock to Holland, 3 August 1887.
23. PRO. CO 427/1. 17487. Minutes by Bramston and Herbert, 3 September 1887, on Havelock to Holland, 3 August 1887.
24. PRO. CO 427/1. 17487. Minute by Holland, 8 September 1887, on Havelock to Holland, 3 August 1887.
25. See above, p. 188.
26. RH. AS papers. 131/194. HEC to Campbell, 24 October 1887, confidential.
27. RH. AS papers. 131/77. HEC to Chesson, 26 October 1887, confidential.
28. BPP. C5331. No. 37, Havelock to Holland, 22 November 1887, enc. 2, Memorandum read to Dinuzulu and Ndabuko, 14

November 1887.

29. Colenso, series 8. Note on HEC to Havelock, 12 May 1888. 4.

30. BPP. C5331. No. 37, Havelock to Holland, 22 November 1887, enc. 4, Memorandum read to Dinuzulu and Ndabuko, 15 November 1887.

31. BPP. C5331. No. 37, Havelock to Holland, 22 November 1887, enc. 6, Osborn to Havelock, 17 November 1887 (extract).

32. NA. Colenso collection. Dinuzulu's statement, 22 December 1888.

33. CSC. Evidence of Umyembe kaDidiza, 305.

34. M.G. Buthelezi, 'The Past and Future of the Zulu People', *Munger Africana Library Notes*, January 1972. For a contemporary version see CSC. Evidence of Yamela, 342.

Chapter 14

1. BPP. C5331. No. 9, Havelock to Holland, 3 August 1887, enc. 3, Report by Resident Commissioner, 22 July 1887.

2. The major published sources for this description of the distribution of Zulu in the north-eastern district are BPP. C5522. No. 6, Havelock to Knutsford, 30 March 1888, enc. 2, Havelock to Osborn, 22 March 1888. The untitled document on pages 16–19 is in fact an annotated account of an Usuthu message given to Harriette Colenso, which I refer to here as 'Statement by Usuthu messengers'. Also important is BPP. C5522. No. 49, Havelock to Lord Knutsford, 22 June 1888, enc. Osborn to Havelock, 11 May 1888, Knight to Osborn, 30 April 1888; and C6684. No. 1, Mitchell to Knutsford, 27 October 1891 (extract) and enclosures. These enclosures give a detailed account of the distribution of the population in this area, and of the five boundaries laid down between 1879 and 1891.

3. J. Stuart, *uKulumetule*. London: Longman, 1925. Chapter 1.

4. Details of this incident were suppressed but for the attempt to arrest the chiefs see NA. RM. Lower Mfolozi 5/1/1. 108/87. A.J.

Shepstone to Osborn, 23 December 1887; and for their sentencing NA. RM. Lower Mfolozi 2/7/1. Civil Record Book. Cases 9, 10, 11, 12, 13.

5. The contemporary account by Osborn in BPP. C5331. No. 46, Havelock to Holland, 27 December 1887, enc. 1, Osborn to Havelock, 18 December 1887, should be read with the documents made public by Dinuzulu's counsel later in BPP. C5892. See also BPP. C5522. No. 6, Havelock to Knutsford, 30 March 1888, Statement by Usuthu messengers.

6. BPP. C5892. No. 172, Havelock to Knutsford, 5 June 1889, enc. Galloway to Addison, 1 December 1887.

7. BPP. C5892. No. 172, Havelock to Knutsford, 5 June 1889, enc. Galloway to Addison, 3 December 1887.

8. CSC. Evidence of Hemulana, 532.

9. NA. RM. Nongoma. 2/9/2. Addison to Osborn, 3 January 1888 (telegram).

10. BPP. C5522. No. 7, Havelock to Knutsford, 8 April 1888, enc. Havelock to Osborn, 16 December 1887.

11. BPP. C5331. No. 53, Havelock to Holland, 18 January 1888, enc. 2, Havelock to Osborn, 12 January 1888.

12. CSC. Evidence of Vusindlu, 787.

13. CSC. Evidence of Mangqongoza, 818–19. Evidence of Umlungoza, 820. For an account of both these cases by Dinuzulu's defence counsel see BPP. C5892. No. 170, Havelock to Knutsford, 31 May 1889, enc. 2, Escombe and Dumat to Knutsford, 20 May 1889, The trials of the Zulu chiefs, 'Ziziba's Case', and 'The 22 Men'.

14. BPP. C5892. No. 199, Mitchell to Knutsford, 31 August 1889, enc. Addison to Resident Commissioner, 20 August 1889.

15. BPP. C5892. No. 203, Mitchell to Knutsford, 20 September 1889, enc. 1, Addison to Resident Commissioner, 10 September 1889.

16. The basic documentation was only published much later. See BPP. C6684. No. 1, Mitchell to Knutsford, 27 October 1891,

enc. 1, Addison to Osborn, 1 February 1888.

17. NA. Colenso collection. Box 93. Ndabuko's statement, Eshowe gaol.

18. BPP. C5522. No. 6, Havelock to Knutsford, 30 March 1888, enc. 1, Statement by Usuthu messengers to Osborn, 3 March 1888. Much of the important evidence on the situation at this time was not published. For Addison's views see NA. ZA 21. R486/88. Addison to Osborn, 15 March 1888.

19. BPP. C5522. No. 1, Havelock to Holland, 15 February 1888, enc. 1, Osborn to Havelock, 5 February 1888.

20. For these messages see BPP. C5522. No. 6, Havelock to Knutsford, 30 March 1888, enc. 1, Statement by Usuthu messengers to Osborn, 3 March 1888, and enc. 2, Havelock to Osborn, 22 March 1888.

21. NA. ZGH 710. Z 136. Osborn to Havelock, 5 March 1888.

22. BPP. C5522. No. 6, Havelock to Knutsford, 30 March 1888, enc. 1, Statement by Usuthu messengers.

23. BPP. C5522. No. 6, Havelock to Knutsford, 30 March 1888, enc. 2, Havelock to Osborn, 22 March 1888, Message from Dinuzulu delivered to the SNA, 14 March 1888.

24. BPP. C5522. No. 6, Havelock to Knutsford, 30 March 1888, enc. 2, Havelock to Osborn, 22 March 1888, Reply of Governor, 20 March 1888.

25. NA. Colenso collection. HEC to Chesson, 21 March 1888.

26. RH. MSS African. s. 1286. HEC to Frank Colenso, 14 March 1888.

27. NA. Colenso collection. [Box 126] Notebook III. HEC to Chesson, 21 March 1888.

28. And of William Morris. I have always hoped to find some connection between Morris and Colenso through Chesson. After all, Frances and Morris were both close friends of Georgie Burne-Jones. As yet I have not established a link.

29. RH. MSS African. s. 1286. HEC to Frank Colenso, 23 May 1888.

30. Colenso, series 8. 18. This is Harriette Colenso's version of the initial Usuthu response to the boundary and related events during April 1888. Another version, substantially the same, is BPP. C5892. No. 34, Havelock to Knutsford, enc. 1, Statement by Sifo and Soni, 9 July 1888.

31. BPP. C5522. No. 49, Havelock to Knutsford, 22 June 1888, enc. Osborn to Havelock, 11 May 1888, Knight to Osborn, 30 April 1888.

32. BPP. C58592. No. 34, Havelock to Knutsford, 10 September 1888, enc. 1, Statement of Sifo and Soni; and Colenso, series 8. 18–20.

33. Colenso, series 8. 20.

34. Later R.C.A. Samuelson estimated the number at 3000. Harriette Colenso's estimate was 800 higher than that, with 1200 going into the South African Republic, 1100 as internal refugees, and 1500 going to Osuthu. The official figure was 608 ordered to move and 208 leaving voluntarily, but this figure was calculated on crop claims by the end of February. See BPP. C5892. No. 122, Havelock to Knutsford, 26 January 1889, enc. Osborn to Havelock, 22 January 1889; and No. 172, Havelock to Knutsford, 5 June 1889, enc. Escombe to Knutsford, List of kraals removed on account of Zibhebhu.

35. BPP. C5522. No. 16, Havelock to Knutsford, 4 May 1888, enc. 1, Osborn to Havelock, 26 April 1888.

36. This account of the 26 April incident is informed by the long enclosures written by the Usuthu defence in BPP. C5892. No. 170, Havelock to Knutsford, 31 May 1889, and the transcripts of Ndabuko's and Dinuzulu's accounts of the events made to the defence in the Eshowe gaol in the closing months of 1888, which before sorting were in Box 93 of the NA. Colenso collection.

37. The official account of this incident is in the enclosures to BPP. C5522. No. 16, Havelock to Knutsford, 4 May 1888. See

also the evidence of the following Crown witnesses in CSC: C.C. Foxon, 154; W. Windham, 161; J. Osborn, 163; and Uzindlu, 777–8.

38. NA. Colenso collection. [Box 93] Statement by Ndabuko, Eshowe gaol. Somcuba's first statement reporting the message he took from Ndabuko to the police.

39. BPP. C5522. No. 16, Havelock to Knutsford, 4 May 1888, enc. 1, Osborn to Havelock, 26 April 1888.

40. CSC. Evidence of Hemulana. 533.

41. Havelock appointed a private investigator to gather information on this. See NA. ZGH 715. Z 700. Affidavit of Francis Brant, Inquiry Agent, confidential.

Chapter 15

1. Dinuzulu's own account of his stay with the emGazini can be found in NA. Colenso collection [Box 93]. Dinuzulu's statement, 22 December 1888, Eshowe gaol. 23ff. Dinuzulu says on p. 23 that he had been at emGazini three or four days when he heard the report. I suspect that 'days' should read 'weeks' and has been inserted erroneously. There was no reason why Dinuzulu should have tried to mislead his defence counsel on this point. This account of the move to Ceza is based on this statement, and that of Ndabuko in the same collection, together with BPP. C5522. No. 21, Havelock to Knutsford, 16 May 1888; and No. 23, Havelock to Knutsford, 21 May 1888.

2. CSC. Evidence of Tshanibezwe, 320.

3. CSC. Evidence of Umbube, 181ff; Mahlungulu, 198; Ndabayeke ka Zagucha, 199; Tshokovu ka Jipa, 202ff; Cobotshisa kaUmbanejelwa, 206ff; Nonkoza ka Gula, 209ff.

4. BPP. C5522. No. 27, Havelock to Knutsford, 28 May 1888.

5. NA. ZGH. ZA 7. Z 247. Havelock to Osborn, 24 August 1888.

6. See her letters to him printed in Colenso, series 8.

7. NA. Colenso collection. Havelock to HEC, 14 June 1888.

8. BPP. C5331. No. 13, Havelock to Holland, 20 August 1887, enc. Memorandum by Sir Theophilus Shepstone, 12 August 1887.

9. It can be found quoted opposite the title page in J. Laband, *Rope of Sand: The Rise and Fall of the Zulu Kingdom in the Nineteenth Century*. Johannesburg: Jonathan Ball, 1995.

10. RH. MSS African. s. 1286. HEC to Frank Colenso, 31 May 1888.

11. Colenso, series 8. HEC to Havelock, 25 June 1888. 13.

12. NA. Stabb collection. Vol. 4, 2/2. H.C. Shepstone to Stabb, 16 June 1888.

13. RH. MSS African. s. 1286. HEC to Frank Colenso, 31 May 1888.

14. Colenso, series 8. Message to the chiefs, 26 May 1888. 8.

15. BPP. C5522. No. 34, Havelock to Knutsford, 3 June 1888, and enclosures; BPP. C5892. No. 77, Havelock to Knutsford, 21 November 1888, enc. 2, Minute, Gallwey to Havelock, 6 November 1888.

16. For the official view see BPP. C5522. No. 15, Havelock to Knutsford (telegram n.d., received 4 June 1888); and No. 35, Havelock to Knutsford, 6 June 1888; and No. 38, Havelock to Knutsford, 10 June 1888 and enclosures. The Usuthu viewpoint is expressed by witnesses in the trials of Ndabuko and Dinuzulu and printed as evidence in CSC. But see also the relevant portions in Ndabuko's and Dinuzulu's statements made in Eshowe gaol, in NA. Colenso collection [Box 93]. See also the relevant enclosures in BPP. C5892. No. 170, Havelock to Knutsford, 31 May 1889.

17. BPP. C5522. No. 38, Havelock to Knutsford, 10 June 1888.

18. CSC. Evidence of Mansel, 192.

19. Mtokwane in NA. Colenso collection [Box 93], Ndabuko's statement.

20. CSC. Evidence of Mansel, 193–4.

21. NA. Colenso collection [Box 93], Dinuzulu's statement, 22 December 1888. 29–30.

22. Colenso, series 8. Mubi Nondenisa to HEC, 3 July 1888. 15.

Chapter 16

1. Adapted from the overused and clumsily translated version of Dinuzulu's praise poem in Samuelson, *Long, Long Ago*. 285.
2. BPP. C5522. No. 35, Havelock to Knutsford, 6 June 1888.
3. NA. ZGH 712. Z 338. Osborn to Havelock, 12 June 1888. A portion of this dispatch was published in BPP. C5522. No. 43, Havelock to Knutsford, 18 June 1888, enc. Osborn to Havelock, 12 June 1888 (extract).
4. PRO. CO 427/3. 264. Havelock to Knutsford, 30 November 1886, confidential, enc. 2, Saunders to Osborn, 22 June 1888, Dunn to Saunders, 21 June 1888.
5. PRO. CO 427/3. 264. Havelock to Knutsford, 30 November 1886, confidential, enc. 1, Report by Saunders, Resident Magistrate, Eshowe district, 4 November 1888.
6. NA. ZA 6. No. 17a, Havelock to Osborn, 27 June 1888.
7. NA. ZGH 712. Z 337. Osborn to Havelock, 17 June 1888.
8. NA. ZGH 712. Z 335. Osborn to Havelock, 7 June 1888.
9. See NA. Colenso collection [Box 87]. Notes in HEC's hand on quarto paper.
10. This section is based largely on evidence taken at the trials of the men involved. See CSC. Trial of Somkhele, Ndabayake, Mthatheni, Masekwana, Lugoloza, Dlemudlemu, 67–142. Uxibilili and three others, 545–75. Umpikwa and Usiyabi, 859–884; NA. ZA 104. *Regina v. Somopho* and *Bhejana*, 10 December 1890; ZA 103. *Regina v. Mafukwini*; BPP. C5522. No. 54, Havelock to Knutsford, 4 July 1888.
11. BPP. C5892. No. 66, Havelock to Knutsford, 5 November 1888, enc. Colonel on the Staff to Governor, 27 October 1888, Colonel on the Staff to Asst. Military Secretary, 19 October 1888. 98.
12. CSC. Evidence of Umtundulu, 89.
13. CSC. Evidence of W.F. White and E.W. Knight, 93ff.
14. BPP. C5522. No. 67, Havelock to Knutsford, 18 July 1888, enc. Osborn to Havelock, 6 July 1888.
15. This account is based on BPP. C5522. No. 66, Havelock to Knutsford, 16 July 1888 and enclosures; and No. 75, War Office to Colonial Office, 28 August 1888 and enclosures; and PRO. CO 427/2. 16001. Havelock to Knutsford, 2 July 1888, private, enc. 'An Account of Attack on Tshingana's Stronghold, Hlopekulu'; CSC. Evidence of Mansel, 438.
16. BPP. C5892. No. 1, War Office to Colonial Office, 3 September 1888, enc. 1, Smyth to Secretary of State for War, 17 July 1888.
17. BPP. C5892. No. 66, Havelock to Knutsford, 5 November 1888, enc. Colonel on the Staff to Governor, 27 October 1888, Colonel on the Staff to Asst. Military Secretary, 19 October 1888.
18. NA. ZGH 713. Z 523. Osborn to Havelock, 4 August 1888, enc. McKean to Osborn, 30 July 1888.
19. For this see NA. ZGH 712. Z 502. Browne, Secretary for Governor to Osborn, enc. *The Natal Mercury*, 28 July 1888; Report by Knight, 16 August 1888; Supplementary report by Knight, 7 September 1888; Minute by Havelock, 11 February 1889.
20. NA. ZGH 713. Z 547. Addison to Osborn, 9 August 1888, Report by a follower of Mnyamana.
21. The information here is taken from T. Jeal, *Baden-Powell*. London: Hutchinson, 1989. 134ff. I deal with this and other events associated with Baden-Powell's campaign in Zululand in 'Imperial Appropriations: The Dynamic History of *Iziqu*', *The Annals of the Natal Museum*, December 1999.

Chapter 17

1. See above, pp. 221–2.
2. For their account of the journey see Colenso, series 8. 'Statement of Twaisa Mabaso and Mubi Nondenisa ...'. 16–17.
3. The message can be found in Colenso, series 8. 'Statement of Sifo, assisted by Soni, made at Bishopstowe, July 1888 ...'. 18–20.
4. BPP. C5522. No. 47, Havelock to Knutsford,

20 July 1888 (telegram).
5. BPP. C5892. No. 34, Havelock to Knutsford, 10 September 1888.
6. RH. MSS African. s. 1286. HEC to Frank Colenso, 6 June 1888.
7. The section of the ordinance which established the powers of the 'Supreme Chief' in Natal.
8. NA. Colenso collection. HEC to Escombe, 12 July 1888, private and confidential.
9. RH. MSS African. s. 1286. HEC to Frank Colenso, 24 October 1888.
10. BPP. C5892. No. 3, Havelock to Knutsford, 6 August 1888, enc. 2, HEC to the Heads of the Zulu People, 31 July 1888.
11. NA. Colenso collection. HEC to Havelock, 17 July 1888.
12. NA. Colenso collection. Notebook III. HEC to Stabb, 30 July 1888.
13. NA. Colenso collection. HEC to Escombe, 23 September 1888.
14. NA. Colenso collection. HEC to Escombe, 27 September 1888.
15. NA. Colenso collection. Escombe to HEC, 29 September 1888.
16. NA. Colenso collection. HEC to Escombe, 22 October 1888.

Chapter 18

1. BPP. C5892. No. 24, Havelock to Knutsford, 29 August 1888 and enc. Report by Sir M.H. Gallwey, 27 August 1888.
2. See the correspondence between HEC and Havelock and the Attorney-General and Havelock in NA. ZGH 714.
3. BPP. C5892. No. 31, Knutsford to Havelock, 8 October 1888.
4. *The Natal Advertiser*, 15 November 1888.
5. NA. Colenso collection. HEC to S.F. Colenso, 12 November 1888.
6. NA. ZGH 714. Z 643. HEC to Havelock, 20 October 1888.
7. *The Natal Advertiser*, 15 November 1888, quoting the correspondent from *The Natal Witness*. For official documentation see NA. ZA 98 for the death warrants and a draft of Osborn to Havelock, 16 October 1888; ZA 103. High Court of Zululand. Notebook.

September 1888 – August 1889; ZGH. Z 297. Knutsford to Havelock, 11 March 1889.
8. NA. Colenso collection. 'The Zulu Trials'. 8.
9. BPP. C5892. No. 80, Havelock to Knutsford, 24 November 1888.

Chapter 19

1. The President's notes of evidence before the Court of Special Commissioners were printed and copies placed in the libraries of the Houses of Parliament in London. I refer to this vast, rich, unused and problematic body of evidence as CSC. In the cases of obscure witnesses I have tended to use their names as they appear in the CSC rather than attempt to regularise the spelling.
2. This example, taken from many, is in CSC, 6.
3. CSC. No. 1, Indictment and registrar's record, 6–9; President's notes of evidence, 10–49.
4. BPP. C5892. No. 59, Havelock to Knutsford, 30 October 1888, enc. 2, In the Court of the Special Commissioners for Zululand.
5. CSC. Evidence of Somhlolo, 48.
6. CSC. President's notes of evidence, 49.
7. CSC. Evidence of Unsurrswana, 21.
8. NA. Colenso collection. Mansel to HEC, 9 November 1888.
9. NA. Colenso collection. HEC to Agnes Colenso, 27 November 1888. HEC's letters to her during this period have been placed in Box 16.
10. NA. Colenso collection. HEC to S.F. Colenso, 27 November 1888.
11. NA. Colenso collection. HEC to S.F. Colenso, 20 November 1888.
12. CSC. No. 2, Indictment and registrar's record, 67–72; President's notes of evidence, 73–142.
13. See above, pp. 230 ff.
14. CSC. Evidence of Somkhele, 126.
15. NA. Colenso collection. HEC to S.F. Colenso, 25 November 1888.
16. CSC. No. 4, Indictment and registrar's record, 143–53; President's notes of evidence, 154–362.

17. See above, pp. 209 ff.
18. See above, pp. 223 ff.
19. See above, pp. 227 ff.
20. BPP. C5892. No. 59, Havelock to Knutsford, 30 October 1888, enc. 1, In the Court of the Special Commissioners for Zululand.
21. NA. Colenso collection. HEC to S.F. Colenso, 4 December 1888.
22. NA. Colenso collection. HEC to S.F. Colenso, 29 November 1888.
23. Rees (ed.), *Colenso Letters*. 423.
24. NA. Colenso collection. HEC to Agnes Colenso, 2 December 1888.
25. NA. Colenso collection. HEC to S.F. Colenso, 2 December 1888.
26. NA. Colenso collection. HEC to S.F. Colenso, 4 December 1888.
27. BPP. C5892. No. 69, Harry Escombe to Colonial Office, 6 December 1888, enc. 3, Letter to the editor of *The Times*.
28. These minutes were written between 7 and 10 December on 24094, Escombe to Colonial Office, 6 December 1888, in PRO. CO 427/3.
29. PRO. CO 427/3. 24582. Fairfield's minute on Havelock to Knutsford, telegram received 12 December 1888.

Chapter 20

1. NA. Colenso collection. HEC to S.F. Colenso, (Thursday) 23 January 1889.
2. PRO. CO 427/4. 3632. Minutes on Havelock to Knutsford, 17 January 1889, and enclosures; and NA. Colenso collection. HEC to Hancock, 6 January 1889.
3. PRO. CO 427/2. 1776. Minutes of 23 January 1889 on W.Y. Campbell to Havelock, 14 December 1888; and NA. ZGH 717. For the originals of BPP. C5892. No. 108, Havelock to Knutsford, 26 December 1888, enc. 2, Report by Attorney-General, 21 December 1888.
4. BPP. C5892. No. 110, Havelock to Knutsford, 7 January 1889, enc. 2, Havelock to Osborn, 6 January 1889.
5. PRO. CO 427/4. 184. Minutes of 4 and 5 January 1889 on Havelock to Knutsford, 3

January 1889 (telegram).
6. PRO. CO 427/4. 2533. Havelock to Knutsford, 7 January 1889, Minute of 6 February 1889.
7. RH. MSS African. s. 1284. S.F. Colenso to Sophie Colenso, 16 January 1888.
8. NA. Colenso collection. HEC to S.F. Colenso, 23 January 1889.
9. RH. MSS African. s. 1284. S.F. Colenso to Sophie Colenso, 11 December 1888.
10. NA. Colenso collection. HEC to S.F. Colenso, 18 December 1888.
11. NA. Colenso collection. HEC [to Hancock], Extracts, 30 December 1888.
12. NA. Colenso collection. HEC to S.F. Colenso, (Thursday) 28 December 1888.
13. RH. MSS African. s. 1284. S.F. Colenso to Sophie Colenso, 11 December 1888.
14. CSC. No. 4, Indictment and registrar's record, 143–53; President's notes of evidence, 154–362.
15. See above, p. 225.
16. CSC. Evidence of Ndabuko, 243.
17. CSC. Evidence of Ndabuko, 195–6.
18. CSC. No. 5, Indictment and registrar's record, 363–72; President's notes of evidence, 373–544.
19. CSC. No. 7, Indictment and registrar's record, 579–92; President's notes of evidence, 593–856.
20. RH. MSS Br. Emp. s. 22. G12/6. Vol. 3. Zululand Trials by a Reporter (George Burgess).
21. NA. Colenso collection. HEC to S.F. Colenso, 17 March 1889.

Chapter 21

1. RH. MSS African. s. 1286. HEC to Frank Colenso, 17 March 1889.
2. See, for example, her letter to Frank Colenso, 24 March 1889 in RH. MSS African. s. 1286.
3. RH. MSS African. s. 1286. HEC to Frank Colenso, 26 March 1889.
4. RH. MSS African. s. 1286. HEC to Frank Colenso, 17 March 1889.
5. NA. Colenso collection. HEC to S.F. Colenso, 24 March 1889.

6. NA. Colenso collection. HEC to S.F. Colenso, 8 April 1889.
7. NA. Colenso collection. HEC to S.F. Colenso, n.d.
8. Most notably M. Vicinus, *Independent Women: Work and Community for Single Women, 1850–1920*. London: Virago, 1985.
9. *South Africa*, 7 June 1890. 432.
10. NA. Colenso collection. HEC to S.F. Colenso, 2 March 1889.
11. CSC. Evidence of Nobafo, 802 with marginal comments by HEC in the copy in NA.
12. RH. MSS African. s. 1286. HEC to Frank Colenso, 1 April 1889.
13. For *iziqu* see Guy, 'Imperial Appropriations'.
14. The official point of view is in BPP. C5892. No. 126, Havelock to Knutsford, 8 February 1889 and its enclosures.
15. BPP. C5892. No. 148, Havelock to Knutsford, 1 May 1889, enc. Escombe to Secretary of State, 29 April 1889. Record of meeting, Usuthu chiefs and headmen, 22 April 1889.
16. There is a typescript of Escombe's speech in NA. Colenso collection.
17. NA. Colenso collection. HEC to S.F. Colenso, 28 April 1889.
18. NA. Colenso collection. Escombe to S.F. Colenso, 24 April 1889.
19. South African Library. Merriman papers. 211. Escombe to Merriman, 26 April 1889.
20. NA. Colenso collection. HEC to S.F. Colenso, 28 April 1899.
21. *Women's Penny Paper*, 29 June 1889. Miss Colenso and Zululand. Prayer said at Usutu service, 28 April 1889.
22. NA. ZGH. Z 735. Mitchell to Cardew, 12 January 1891.
23. RH. MSS African. s. 1286. HEC to Frank Colenso, 2 July 1889.
24. PRO. CO 427/14. 18470. Minutes on Mitchell to Knutsford, 18 August 1892.
25. I examined these consequences in an article 'The Destruction and Reconstruction of Zulu Society', in Shula Marks and Richard Rathbone (eds.), *Industrialisation*

and Social Change in South Africa: African Class Formation, Culture and Consciousness 1870–1930. Harlow: Longman, 1982.

Chapter 22

1. *Women's Penny Paper*, 16 February 1889.
2. RH. MSS African. s. 1286. HEC to Frank Colenso, 27 August 1889.
3. I refer in particular here to P. Hollis, *Ladies Elect: Women in English Government, 1865–1914*. Oxford: Clarendon Press, 1987.
4. RH. AS papers. C150/188. HEC to Fox Bourne, 16 April 1889.
5. NA. Colenso collection. Frank Colenso to HEC, 7 March 1889.
6. NA. Colenso collection. Chamberlain to Frank Colenso, 6 March 1889, transcribed in Frank Colenso to HEC, 7 March 1889.
7. RH. AS papers. C150/193. HEC to Fox Bourne, 24 June 1889.
8. BPP. C5892. No. 182, Crown Agents to Colonial Office, 1 August 1889, enc. 2, Sutton and Ommanney to Crown Agents, 31 July 1889.
9. NA. Colenso collection. Frank Colenso to HEC, 1 August 1889.
10. RH. MSS African. s. 1286. HEC to Frank Colenso, 27 August 1889.
11. H.E. Colenso, *Cases of Six Usutu Punished for Having Taken Part in the Disturbances of 1888*. London, 1893.
12. PRO. CO 427/17. 13345. Fairfield's minute on HEC to Colonial Office, 5 August 1893.
13. RH. MSS African. s. 1286. HEC to Frank Colenso, 27 May 1889.
14. NA. Colenso collection. HEC to S.F. Colenso, 12 May 1889.
15. NA. Colenso collection. HEC to Agnes Colenso, 21 June 1889.
16. NA. Colenso collection. HEC to S.F. Colenso, 12 November 1889.
17. NA. Colenso collection. HEC to S.F. Colenso, 11 June 1889.
18. NA. Colenso collection. HEC to Agnes Colenso, 2 May 1889.
19. NA. Colenso collection. HEC to S.F. Colenso, 7 July 1889.
20. NA. Colenso collection. HEC to S.F.

Colenso, 9 July 1889.

21. RH. MSS African. s. 1286. HEC to Frank Colenso, 27 July 1889.

22. RH. AS papers. C150/197. HEC to Fox Bourne, 2 October 1889.

23. Rees (ed.), *Colenso Letters*. 426.

24. NA. Colenso collection. HEC to S.F. Colenso, 22 November 1889.

25. RH. AS papers. C150/198. HEC to Fox Bourne, 11 December 1889.

26. NA. Colenso collection. HEC to Giles, Friday. For letters to Kate Giles see Box 73.

27. PRO. CO 427/5. 13106. Minute by Fairfield on dispatch published as BPP. C5892. No. 172.

28. BPP. C5892. No. 162, Havelock to Knutsford, 27 May 1889 (extract), enc. Osborn to Havelock, 15 May 1889.

29. PRO. CO 427/5. 12417. Minute on Havelock to Knutsford, 27 May 1889.

30. PRO. CO 427/5. 9017. Minute on Havelock to Knutsford, 3 May 1889 (telegram).

31. PRO. CO 427/10. 6016. Minutes on APS to Colonial Office, 28 March 1890.

32. PRO. CO 427/10. 1991. Minutes inserted after copy of Wragg to Colonial Office, 31 January 1890, published as BPP. C6070. No. 1.

33. PRO. CO 427/8. 3988. Minutes on Mitchell to Knutsford, 3 March 1890.

34. BPP. C6070. No. 11, APS to Colonial Office, 28 March 1890.

35. BPP. C6070. No. 16, Havelock to Colonial Offices, 14 April 1890, enc. Memorandum, 14 April 1890.

Chapter 23

1. 'The Expatriated Zulu Chiefs: An Interview with Miss Colenso', *South Africa*, 1 March 1890. 353.

2. NA. Colenso collection. F.E. Colenso to HEC, 29 February 1887.

3. NA. Colenso collection. Bunyon to HEC, 21 February 1890.

4. Hollis, *Ladies Elect*. 90.

5. NA. Colenso collection. Westlake to HEC,

1 March 1890.

6. NA. Colenso collection. Quilter to HEC, 14 April 1890.

7. For Kate Courtney, and a useful background to the women's liberal organisations see Barbara Caine, *Destined to be Wives: The Sisters of Beatrice Webb*. Oxford: Clarendon Press, 1986. 163ff.

8. NA. Colenso collection. HEC to Giles, 27 March 1890.

9. *Women's Penny Paper*, 22 February 1890.

10. NA. Colenso collection. HEC to Giles, 20 June 1890.

11. NA. Colenso collection. HEC to Giles, 7 May 1890.

12. C. Bradlaugh and J. Watts [Iconoclast], *Half-hours with the Freethinkers*. London, 1868. Copy in the South African Library.

13. NA. Colenso collection. HEC to Browne, 22 July 1890.

14. NA. Colenso collection. A.L. Browne to HEC, 24 July 1890.

15. *Parliamentary Debates*, Third series CCCXLVIII, 12 August 1890, column 791.

16. *Parliamentary Debates*, Third series CCCXLVIII, 12 August 1890, column 801.

17. See above, p. 295.

18. RH. MSS African. s. 1286. HEC to Frank Colenso, 2 July 1889.

19. Linda Walker, 'Party Political Women: A Comparative Study of Liberal Women and the Primrose League, 1890–1914', in Jane Rendall (ed.), *Equal or Different. Women's Politics 1800–1914*. Oxford: Basil Blackwell, 1987.

20. NA. Colenso collection. Ryley to HEC, 15 June 1890.

21. See W.S. Smith, *The London Heretics 1870–1914*. London: Constable, 1967.

22. For Isabella Ford and her family see P. Levine, *Feminist Lives in Victorian England: Private Roles and Public Commitment*. Oxford: Basil Blackwell, 1990.

23. NA. Colenso collection. HEC to Giles, 29 January 1891.

24. Her father's phrases in a letter to Chesson in KC. Colenso collection, 24 April 1880.

25. Quoted in R.R. James, *The British*

Revolution: British Politics, 1880–1939. Vol. 1. London: Hamish Hamilton, 1976. 170.

26. R.I. Rotberg, *The Founder: Cecil Rhodes and the Pursuit of Power*. Johannesburg: Southern Book Publishers, 1988.

27. *The Aborigines' Friend* Annual Meeting, No. V. Vol. IV. New series. June 1891.

28. RH. AS papers. C150/202. HEC to Fox Bourne, 25 May 1891.

29. HEC to the editor of *Anti-Caste* in a letter dated 6 June 1891 housed in the Natal Society Library, Pietermaritzburg. For *Anti-Caste* see V. Ware, *Beyond the Pale: White Women, Racism and History*. London and New York: Verso, 1992. 184ff. Catherine Impey, the editor, had visited Harriette in May.

30. RH. AS papers. C150/203. HEC to Fox Bourne, 1 June 1891. Interestingly it is just this speech of which a historian has written: 'If members of the audience disagreed, they did not say so.' John Cell, 'The Imperial Conscience', in P. Marsh (ed.), *The Conscience of the Victorian State*. Syracuse: Syracuse University Press, 1979. 207.

31. *Parliamentary Debates*, Third series CCCLV, 10 July 1891, column 937.

32. *Parliamentary Debates*, Third series CCCLV, 10 July 1891, column 954.

33. See above, p. 287.

34. *Parliamentary Debates*, Third series CCCLV, 13 July 1891, column 1063.

35. *Parliamentary Debates*, Third series CCCLV, 13 July 1891, columns 1068–9.

36. *Parliamentary Debates*, Third series CCCLV, 13 July 1891, column 1075.

37. NA. Colenso collection. HEC to Giles, 12 August 1891.

38. NA. Colenso collection. HEC to Giles, 12 August 1891.

39. NA. Colenso collection. HEC to Giles, 19 August 1891.

40. RH. MSS African. s. 1287. Agnes Colenso to Sophie Colenso, 6 January 1924.

41. NA. ZA 21. Notes of an interview at the Resident Commissioner's office, Eshowe, 19 January 1890.

42. NA. ZGH 727. Z 260. Dinuzulu to his mother, 21 March 1890.

43. NA. ZGH 740. Z 612. Paul B. Mthimkhulu to Elizabeth Mthimkhulu, 7 June 1891.

44. NA. ZGH 740. Z 612. Dinuzulu to okamSweli, n.d.

45. NA. ZGH 740. Z 612. Dinuzulu to Magema Magwaza Fuze, 6 June 1891.

46. Fuze's account of this period in M.M. Fuze, *The Black People and Whence They Came*. Pietermaritzburg: University of Natal Press; Durban: Killie Campbell Africana Library, 1979 is particularly useful.

47. NA. ZGH. Report by Dr Frederick Welby, 3 June 1890.

48. NA. ZGH 731. Grey-Wilson to Knutsford, 10 September 1890, confidential.

49. NA. ZGH 733. Bishop of St Helena to Grey-Wilson, 15 September 1890.

50. NA. ZGH 739. Dinuzulu to Governor of Zululand, 6 June 1891.

51. NA. ZGH 737. Report of the guardian of the Zulu chiefs for quarter ending 1891.

52. NA. ZGH. 741. Dinuzulu to HEC, 3 September 1891.

53. NA. Colenso collection. Dinuzulu to HEC, 13 December 1891.

Chapter 24

1. NA. Colenso collection. Ryland to HEC, 28 January 1892, and Chamberlain to HEC, 10 February 1892.

2. NA. Colenso collection. Morris to HEC, 21 February 1892.

3. *Parliamentary Debates*, Second Volume of 1892 Session, Fourth series, columns 1250–68.

4. NA. Colenso collection. Searle to HEC, 8 June 1892.

5. R.R. James, *The British Revolution*. I, 136.

6. PRO. CO 427/15. 16749. Minute by Fairfield, 28 September 1892, on APS to Ripon, 22 August 1892.

7. PRO. CO 427/14. 16322. Minute by Fairfield, 20 August 1892.

8. PRO. CO 427/14. 18470. Minute by Fairfield, 20 September 1892, on Mitchell

to Knutsford, 18 August 1892.

9. PRO. CO 427/15. 17595. Minute by Fairfield, 29 September 1892, on HEC to the Secretary of State, 5 September 1892.

10. NA. Colenso collection. HEC to Giles, 17 November 1895.

11. NA. Colenso collection. Box 73. HEC to Giles, 7 October 1895.

12. See above, p. 299.

13. NA. Colenso collection. Westlake to HEC, 8 December 1892.

14. PRO. CO 427/14. Minute on telegram by Mitchell, 26 August 1892.

15. PRO. CO 427/17. 3136. Osborn to Fairfield, 24 January 1893.

16. NA. Colenso collection. Copy of letter to Clarke, in HEC to Giles, 16 February 1893.

17. KC. Colenso collection. HEC to Werner, 2 January 1893.

18. KC. Colenso collection, HEC to Werner, 20 January 1893.

19. H.E. Colenso, *The Present Position Among the Zulus (1893) with Some Suggestions for the Future*. London, 1893. 29.

20. HEC, *The Present Position Among the Zulus*. 30.

21. PRO. CO 427/17. 3490. Minute, 2 March 1893, on HEC to Secretary of State, 1 March 1893.

22. PRO. CO 427/17. 3907. Minutes on HEC to Secretary of State, 7 March 1893.

23. PRO. CO 427/17. 13345. Minute by Buxton, 8 August 1893, on HEC to Colonial Office, 5 August 1893.

24. Natal Society Library. Colenso pamphlets. Printed four pages beginning 'At the Annual Meeting of the Aborigines' Protection Society, on May 17th, 1893'.

25. NA. Colenso collection. Fox Bourne to HEC, 18 July 1893.

26. RH. AS papers. C150/207. HEC to Fox Bourne, 18 July 1893.

27. NA. Colenso collection. Frank Colenso to HEC, 19 January 1894. Incoming letters to HEC for 1894–5 can be found in Box 30.

28. S.F. Colenso to Miss Brown [*sic*], 30 November 1893, in Rees (ed.), *Colenso*

Letters 427–8. The letter was never finished.

29. RH. MSS African. s. 1284. S.F. Colenso to Sophie Colenso, September 1893.

30. RH. Lagden papers. Clarke to Lagden, Box 22, November [1893] and placed apparently erroneously in the file for 1897.

31. NA. Colenso collection. 'To our dear Friends who are at St Helena, to Ndabuko, and to Tshingana, and to Dinuzulu'. January 1894.

32. Quoted in S.F. Colenso to Brown [*sic*], in Rees (ed.), *Colenso Letters*. 428.

33. S.F. Colenso to Lyell, 25 April 1879, in Rees (ed.), *Colenso Letters*. 343.

34. RH. MSS African. s. 1286. HEC to her brothers and sisters. Dated Christmas day 1893 but added to after that day.

35. NA. Colenso collection. 'To our dear Friends who are at St Helena, to Ndabuko, and to Tshingana, and to Dinuzulu'. January 1894.

Chapter 25

1. *The Natal Witness*, 29 June 1893.

2. T. Shepstone, 'The Native Question', *The Natal Mercury*, 29 January 1892, reprinted in *Natalia*, No. 2, 1972.

3. Examples are legion. For the nearest at hand at the time of writing see Sibani Mngadi, 'Dealing with the King in a New Way', *The Natal Witness*, 11 March 2000.

4. For a history of the movement for responsible government see E.H. Brookes and C. de B. Webb, *A History of Natal*. Pietermaritz-burg: University of Natal Press, 1965. Chap. XVIII; and A.H. Duminy and W. Guest, *Natal and Zululand from Earliest Times to 1910: A New History*. Pietermaritzburg: University of Natal Press and Shuter & Shooter, 1989. Chap. 9. See also BPP. C6487. *Natal. Correspondence relating to the Proposal to establish Responsible Government in Natal*.

5. NA. ZGH 751. Z 432. Ripon to Clarke, 2 June 1893, confidential.

6. PRO. CO 427/17. 417. Clarke to Hely-Hutchinson, 8 December 1893, confiden-

tial, in Hely-Hutchinson to Colonial Office, 16 December 1893, confidential; and 860. Clarke to Ripon, 16 December 1893, confidential; PRO. CO 427/18. 3035. Clarke to Ripon, 18 January 1894, in Hely-Hutchinson to Colonial Office, 24 January 1894, confidential.

7. See above, p. 352.

8. PRO. CO 427/17. 417. Minute by Fairfield on Clarke to Hely-Hutchinson, 8 December 1893, confidential, in Hely-Hutchinson to Colonial Office, 16 December 1893, confidential.

9. See above, pp. 347–8.

10. PRO. CO 427/18. 3035, Minute by Fiddes on Clarke to Ripon, 18 January 1894, in Hely-Hutchinson to Colonial Office, 24 January 1894.

11. M. Swan, *Gandhi. The South African Experience.* Johannesburg: Ravan Press, 1985. Chap. 2.

12. PRO. CO 427/18. 6911. Hely-Hutchinson to Colonial Office, 31 March 1894, confidential.

13. PRO. CO 427/18. 6911. Minute by Fiddes, 25 April 1894, on Hely-Hutchinson to Colonial Office, 31 March 1894, confidential.

14. PRO. CO 427/18. 7715. Hely-Hutchinson to Colonial Office, 3 May 1894 (telegram).

15. PRO. CO 427/18. 9639. Minute by Ripon, 23 August 1894.

16. CO. Confidential Prints African (South). No. 471: Zululand. J. Fairfield to Grey-Wilson, 30 October 1894.

Chapter 26

1. PRO. CO 427/19. 22549. Hely-Hutchinson to Buxton, 8 December 1894.

2. CO. Confidential Prints African (South). No. 471: Zululand. No. 43, Hely-Hutchinson to Ripon, 10 January 1895 (telegram).

3. Hely-Hutchinson's words when describing the minute to London. CO. Confidential Print African (South). No. 471: Zululand. No. 44, Hely-Hutchinson to Ripon, 23 January 1895.

4. CO. Confidential Print African (South). No. 471: Zululand. No. 44, Hely-Hutchinson to Ripon, 17 January 1895 (telegram).

5. CO. Confidential Prints African (South). No. 471: Zululand. No. 45, Hely-Hutchinson to Ripon, 18 January 1895 (telegram). For a longer retrospective report see No. 92 in the same volume.

6. CO. Confidential Prints African (South). No. 471: Zululand. No. 46, Ripon to Hely-Hutchinson, 18 January 1895 (telegram).

7. CO. Confidential Prints African (South). No. 471: Zululand. No. 52, Hely-Hutchinson to Ripon, 23 January 1895 (telegram).

8. CO. Confidential Prints African (South). No. 471: Zululand. No. 57, Ripon to Hely-Hutchinson, 17 January 1895 (telegram).

9. CO. Confidential Prints African (South). No. 471: Zululand. No. 64, Hely-Hutchinson to Ripon, 27 January 1895 (telegram).

10. CO. Confidential Prints African (South). No. 471: Zululand. No. 70, Ripon to Hely-Hutchinson, 29 January 1895 (telegram).

11. H.E. Colenso, *Zululand, the Exiled Chiefs, Natal and the Colonial Office, 1893–1895.* London: Burt & Sons, n.d. 13–15. The copy in the South African Library in the W.P. Schreiner papers, MSC 27, 7 (1282) was amended and annotated by HEC on 8 April 1897 in the light of subsequent events and is the version that I use here and below.

12. B.T. Kearney, 'A House for Harry: An Architect Looks at the Former Residence of Harry Escombe', *Natalia: Journal of the Natal Society,* No. 2, 1972.

13. C. Tower, *Harry Escombe and Natal.* Privately printed, 1990.

14. Brookes and Webb, *A History of Natal.* 173.

15. HEC, *Zululand, the Exiled Chiefs.* 9–10.

16. HEC, *Zululand, the Exiled Chiefs.* 10.

17. RH. AS papers. 150. HEC to Fox Bourne [11 January 1895].

18. RH. AS papers. 150/215. HEC to Fox Bourne, 18 January 1895.

19. This is a crucial point. I base my recon-

struction on subsequent letters and also
the following in HEC, *Zululand, the Exiled
Chiefs*. 12–13. 'He then proposed that she
should support the position taken by the
Natal Ministry on the Zulu question by
sending a message by cable to England ...
an intimation that the idea that she should
be asked to send such a message originated with the Governor himself, relieved the
anxiety which she felt at first lest such an
act might seem presumptuous, or might
even jar with some of those plans for the
Zulus of which it seemed she might not
know.'
20. NA. Colenso collection. Box 73. HEC to
Clarke, 25 January 1895.
21. PRO. CO 179/190. 3031. Minute on Hely-
Hutchinson to Ripon, 23 January 1895,
secret.

Chapter 27
1. The official record (ZGH 799) gives 1893.
But photographs suggest this was an error.
Spelling of his mother's name varies.
2. NA. ZGH 746. Z 433. Report of the
guardian of the Zulu chiefs for quarter ending June 1892.
3. Fuze, *The Black People*. 134.
4. PRO. CO 427/17. 15163. Haden to Colonial
Office, 12 August 1893; Minute by
Fairfield, 4 September 1893; and letter by
Dinuzulu, 28 June 1893.
5. NA. Colenso collection. HEC to Agnes
Colenso, 1 March 1895.
6. HEC, *Zululand, the Exiled Chiefs*. 16.
7. NA. Colenso collection. HEC to Agnes
Colenso, 1 March 1895; HEC, *Zululand, the
Exiled Chiefs*. 17.
8. NA. Colenso collection. Fox Bourne to
HEC, 25 January 1895.
9. NA. Colenso collection. Lyell to Frank
Colenso, 5 February 1895.
10. NA. Colenso collection. Fox Bourne to
HEC, 12 February 1895.
11. NA. Colenso collection. HEC to Agnes
Colenso, 3 May 1895.
12. Some of these references are obscure – but
they do suggest the level of intimacy that

existed between the correspondents.
13. NA. Colenso collection. Clarke to HEC, 25
April 1895.
14. NA. Colenso collection. HEC to Clarke,
May 1895.
15. NA. Colenso collection. HEC to Agnes
Colenso, 3 May 1895.
16. NA. Colenso collection. Bryce to HEC, 14
May 1895.
17. NA. Colenso collection. HEC to Escombe,
3 May 1895.
18. NA. Colenso collection. HEC to Clarke,
May 1895.
19. H.E. Colenso, *Zululand, the Exiled Chiefs*.
20. NA. Colenso collection. Copied in a letter
from HEC to Escombe, 21 June 1895.
21. NA. Colenso collection. HEC to Escombe,
21 June 1895; Ripon to HEC, 20 June
1895.

Chapter 28
1. NA. Colenso collection. HEC to Escombe,
28 August 1895. The editorial also congrat-
ulated the Natal ministry on the way it had
successfully aborted the attempt to return
the exiles.
2. NA. Colenso collection. HEC to Agnes
Colenso, 16 August 1895.
3. NA. Colenso collection. HEC to
Chamberlain, 20 August 1895.
4. NA. Colenso collection. Wilson to HEC, 7
September 1895.
5. NA. Colenso collection. HEC to Courtney,
10 September 1895.
6. N. Parsons, *King Khama, Emperor Joe and the
Great White Queen: Victorian Britain through
African Eyes*. Chicago and London:
University of Chicago Press, 1998.
7. NA. Colenso collection. HEC to Fairfield,
31 October 1895.
8. NA. Colenso collection. HEC to Agnes
Colenso, letter dated 4 December 1895 but
left open to report on the interview.
9. NA. Colenso collection. HEC to Escombe,
6 December 1895.
10. NA. Colenso collection. HEC to Lyell, 16
September 1895.
11. E. Packenham, *Jameson's Raid*. London:

483

Weidenfeld & Nicolson, 1960. 203.
12. KC. Colenso collection. HEC to Werner, 20 September 1895. Schreiner and her husband had read their paper 'The Political Situation' in Kimberley a month previously.
13. NA. Colenso collection. HEC to Agnes Colenso, 24 January 1896.
14. NA. Colenso collection. HEC to Cox, 19 April 1896.
15. NA. Colenso collection. Box 73. HEC to (copy unfinished). 13 September 1896.
16. CO. Confidential Prints. Chamberlain to Hely-Hutchinson, 27 May 1896, telegram.
17. CO. Confidential Prints. No. 24, Hely-Hutchinson to Chamberlain, 9 October 1896.
18. NA. Colenso collection. HEC to Clarke, 10 December 1896.
19. KC. Colenso collection. HEC to Werner, 13 December 1896.
20. NA. Colenso collection. HEC to Robinson, 1 December 1896.
21. Natal Diocesan Archives. Escombe to HEC, 10 September 1890, private.
22. NA. Colenso collection. HEC to Clarke, 10 December 1896. These are drafts of letters by Harriette Colenso. This fact should be kept in mind in assessing them. The corrections and emendations are often very suggestive of the state of HEC's mind, and I have reproduced them in the text when I think they might be significant.
23. NA. Colenso collection. HEC to Clarke, 10 January 1897.
24. KC. Colenso collection. HEC to Werner, 18 January 1897.
25. NA. Colenso collection. HEC to Agnes Colenso, 20 January 1897.
26. NA. Colenso collection. HEC to Clarke, 2 February 1897.
27. NA. Colenso collection. HEC to Agnes Colenso, 20 January 1897.
28. NA. Colenso collection. HEC to Agnes Colenso, 19 February 1897.
29. NA. Colenso collection. HEC to Agnes Colenso, 29 January 1897.

Chapter 29
1. There are a number of drafts of different speeches in NA. Colenso collection, Box 82 which need sorting and collating before adequate citations can be made to specific manuscripts. This section draws on a selection from these documents.
2. Many of the themes in these lectures can be found in H.E. Colenso, 'The Problem of the Races in Africa', *The Imperial and Asiatic Quarterly Review*, 4, 7, July 1897. V. Ware, in *Beyond the Pale*, provides important comparative material on HEC's contemporaries while probing questions of race, class and gender. It is HEC's close relations with the Usuthu and the royal house in particular which make her case so specific and, in a sense, difficult to compare with women with whom, at another level, she shares so much.
3. NA. Colenso collection. HEC to Wicksteed, March 1897.
4. NA. Colenso collection. HEC to Agnes Colenso, 9 July 1897.
5. NA. Colenso collection. HEC to O. Schreiner, 13 February 1897.
6. NA. Colenso collection. HEC to Giles, 7 December 1890.
7. *Justice: The Social Democrat*, 6 February 1897.
8. NA. Colenso collection. Hill to HEC, 15 February 1897.
9. NA. Colenso collection. Jones to HEC, 30 April 1897.
10. NA. Colenso collection. Liebknecht to HEC, 24 July 1897.
11. Yvonne Kapp, *Eleanor Marx: The Crowded Years, 1884–1898*. London: Virago, 1976. 694ff.
12. NA. Colenso collection. HEC to Davitt, 5 July 1897.
13. KC. Colenso collection. HEC to Werner, 26 October 1896.
14. KC. Colenso collection. HEC to Werner, 24 December 1896.
15. BPP. C8782. No. 19 and No. 20, Chamberlain to Hely-Hutchinson, 4 May 1897.
16. See J. Morris, *Pax Britannica: The Climax of*

an Empire. London: Faber & Faber, 1968; and also 'Queen Victoria's Diamond Jubilee, 1897', in D. Judd, *Empire: The British Imperial Experience, from 1765 to the Present.* London: HarperCollins, 1996.

17. J. Morris, 'High Noon of Empire', *The British Empire,* Vol. 4. 198. No publication details in the bound volumes.

18. Morris, *Pax Britannica.* 21.

19. Judd, *Empire.* 133.

20. NA. Colenso collection. HEC to Agnes Colenso, 25 June 1897.

21. NA. Colenso collection. HEC to Escombe, 16 June 1897.

22. My reconstruction of this meeting is based on the letter Harriette wrote to her sister on the day it took place, NA. Colenso collection. HEC to Agnes Colenso, 3 July 1897, and also her letter written to Escombe, after she had 'thought it over' on 9 July 1897.

23. NA. Colenso collection. HEC to Agnes Colenso, 9 July 1897.

24. NA. Colenso collection. HEC to 'To our dear Friends who are at St Helena', 15 July 1897.

25. BPP. C8782. No. 26, Chamberlain to Sterndale, 16 July 1897.

26. NA. Colenso collection. To Mjwaphuna son of Malungwana, 23 July 1897.

27. CO. Confidential Prints African (South). No. 535, No. 73, Graham to Escombe 17, July 1897; No. 74, Escombe to Colonial Office, 21 July 1897; No. 75, Chamberlain to Escombe, 30 July 1897.

28. NA. Colenso collection. HEC to Agnes Colenso, 30 July 1897.

29. NA. Colenso collection. HEC to Mjwaphuna, son of Malungwana, 30 July 1897.

30. NA. Colenso collection. HEC to Agnes Colenso, 30 July 1897.

31. NA. Colenso collection. HEC 'To our dear Friends, the Zulu Chiefs at St. Helena', 13 August 1897.

32. NA. Colenso collection. HEC to Agnes Colenso, 6 August 1897.

33. NA. Colenso collection. HEC to Agnes

Colenso, 17 October 1897.

34. NA. ZGH 767. Z 1145. 22 December 1895.

35. NA. Colenso collection. HEC to Agnes Colenso, 17 October 1897.

36. BPP. C8782. No. 27, Sterndale to Chamberlain, 4 September 1897, enc. Dinuzulu kaCetshwayo, Ndabuko kaMpande, Tshingana kaMpande to Secretary of State for the Colonies, 4 September 1897.

37. BPP. C8782. No. 32, Chamberlain to Sterndale, 29 October 1897.

38. NA. Colenso collection. HEC to Clarke, 12 November 1897.

Chapter 30

1. BPP. C8782. No. 33, Chamberlain to Sterndale, 29 October 1897, enc.

2. BPP. C8782. No. 46. Sterndale to Chamberlain, 23 November 1897.

3. NA. Colenso collection. HEC to Johnstone, 17 December 1897.

4. NA. Colenso collection. HEC to 'our dear Friends', 23 December 1896.

5. NA. Colenso collection. HEC to Clarke, 12 November 1897.

6. NA. Colenso collection. HEC to Mjwaphuna, son of Malungwana, 30 July 1897.

7. NA. Colenso collection. HEC 'To our dear Friends, the Zulu Chiefs at St. Helena', 13 August 1897.

8. KC. Colenso collection. HEC to Werner, 3 September 1898.

9. BPP. C8782. No. 56, Hely-Hutchinson to Chamberlain, 14 January 1878, enc. Report by the Under-Secretary for Native Affairs, 11 January 1898.

10. NA. ZGH 771. Z 678. Umkasilomo's letter from her father Ntuzwa, 23 June 1896.

11. NA. ZGH 765. Z 657. From the Usuthu to the Zulu chiefs, forwarded 20 August 1895.

12. This section draws on Guy, 'The Destruction and Reconstruction of Zulu Society'.

13. NA. Colenso collection. HEC to Agnes Colenso, 15 January 1898.

14. *The Times of Natal,* 12 February 1898.

15. Harriette Colenso used this passage in a letter saying it was from a Natal newspaper. I have, however, been unable to track it down.
16. NA. SNA 1/1/280. 742/1898. Minutes by Hulett, 19 April and 2 May 1898, and by Saunders, 1 June 1898.
17. NA. SNA 1/1/281. R920/98. Minutes of meeting, 4 June 1898.
18. NA. SNA 1/1/281. R920/98. Draft memo 1124a/1898.
19. Fuze, *The Black People*. 139.
20. E.A. Walker, *W.P. Schreiner: A South African*. Johannesburg: Central News Agency, n.d. 153.

21. RH. MSS African. s. 1286. HEC to Sophie Colenso, 23 April 1911.
22. NA. Colenso collection. HEC to W. Schreiner, 8 April 1911.
23. RH. MSS African. s. 1286. HEC to Sophie Colenso, 27 December 1899.
24. N. Cope, *To Bind the Nation: Solomon kaDinuzulu and Zulu Nationalism, 1913–1933*. Pietermaritzburg: University of Natal Press, 1993. 40.

Bibliography

1. Guy, *The Destruction of the Zulu Kingdom*. 253–4.
2. Mamdani, *Citizen and Subject*. 7.

INDEX